Handbook of

SMALL GROUP RESEARCH

HANDBOOK OF

Small Group

Research

By A. PAUL HARE

The Free Press of Glencoe

For information, address:

THE FREE PRESS OF GLENCOE
A DIVISION OF THE MACMILLAN COMPANY,
THE CROWELL-COLLIER PUBLISHING COMPANY
60 Fifth Avenue, New York 11

DESIGNED BY SIDNEY SOLOMON

THIRD PRINTING   DECEMBER 1963

Library of Congress Catalog Card Number: 60-13778

To Rachel T. Hare

Preface

*E*VERYWHERE I TURN the small group is being rediscovered. In the psychiatric hospital ward, a patient's relations with the other patients have been found to influence the course of his recovery. In the classroom, the extent to which the instructor is "teacher-centered" or "learner-centered" appears to affect the learning process. In industry, "brainstorming" in "group-think" sessions has been introduced as a creative problem-solving technique. Psychologists, who used to be content to describe the subject's response to the color wheel or the rat's response to the maze, now study the influence of group norms on individual judgment or the ways in which groups of animals influence the behavior of their fellows. Sociologists, who might once have studied whole societies or institutions, now record the behavior of small groups either in the laboratory or in the field.

The research results which pour in from the academic laboratories are being supplemented by applied research in the armed services, hospitals, industrial plants, court houses, and government bureaus. From all of these sources together have come more than one thousand books and articles relevant to the study of *social interaction in small groups*. Additional articles are being written at the rate of about two hundred a year. My own response to this rapid development has been to make a first excursion through the literature in order to make available to students, researchers, and practitioners a catalogue of the field together with some suggestions of principles by which it may be organized.

This book is intended as a reference work rather than as a college text. Since the goals of producing both a comprehensive reference work and a selective introductory text are basically incompatible, I found that I could not write *one* book to serve both needs. I chose to write the reference work at this time because it seemed to represent the next step along the path which has led from bibliography to readings and which may lead eventually to a unified theory of small group behavior.

In its largest sense, the study of the forms of social interaction is the subject matter of sociology. Although the present analysis is written from the point of view of the sociologist, I expect to limit my discussion to the forms of social interaction in small face-to-face groups. However, many of the findings of current research could undoubtedly be generalized to larger formal organizations or to larger elementary forms of collective behavior such as the acting crowd.

This analysis covers a field which is not as broad as social psychology, since subjects such as individual motivation, socialization, psycholinguistics, and mass phenomena, which are included in Lindzey's *Handbook of Social Psychology* (1954) are not treated in this volume.

In the late 1940's and early 1950's there were a number of references to the growing interest in small group research. For example:

There is a new focusing of interest on the small group in American empirical sociology (Shils, 1947, p. 27).
The small social group has become the focus of considerable interest on the part of social scientists (Argyle, 1952a, p. 269).
In the past few years the study of small groups as an area of experimentation has been attracting the interest of an increasing number of social scientists (Roseborough, 1953, p. 275).

Another index of the growth of the field is found in the dates which marked the introduction of terms referring specifically to small group research as categories for classification in the *Psychological Abstracts*.

The subheading "sociometry" was first used in the *Psychological Abstracts* in 1940 with references to research by Moreno, Jennings, and Sargent (1940), Dodd (1940), and Zeleny (1939b). Next, the subheading "group dynamics" was introduced in 1945 with a reference to the work of Lewin (1944). Finally, the subheading "small group" appeared in 1950 with references to Bales (1950b) and Deutsch (1949a).

So far as is known, the first seminar carrying the title "small groups" was taught by Bales at Harvard in 1946. At that time the two major developments in the field were the sociometric movement of Moreno and the theory and practice of group dynamics carried on by Lewin and his followers (Deutsch, 1954).

The growth of the field is also reflected in the increasing frequency with which articles relevant to the study of small groups were published between 1900 and 1954 (see Table 1) when the first comprehensive bibliography of small group research was published (Strodtbeck & Hare, 1954).

Table 1—Number of Separate Bibliographic References to Small Group Studies: 1890 through 1953

Period	Number of Years	Items	Items per Year
1890-99	10	5	.5
1900-09	10	15	1.5
1910-19	10	13	1.3
1920-29	10	112	11.2
1930-39	10	210	21.0
1940-44	5	156	31.2
1945-49	5	276	55.2
1950-53 *	4	610	152.5

* Note: Four-year period.

Since 1953, I have had a continuing interest in assembling and codifying the results of research on social interaction. This interest led first to the bibliography mentioned above, next to the book of readings, *Small Groups: Studies in Social Interaction* (Hare, Borgatta, & Bales, 1955), which included an annotated bibliography of some 584 references, and finally to the present volume.

The present canvass of the literature goes back to the 1954 bibliography for some early research and to some foreign publications which were not included in the 1955 bibliography, and extends the survey through February, 1959. In the course of this review of the literature, three sets of abstracts have been checked completely: the *Psychological Abstracts* from volume I (1927) through volume 32 (6), 1958; the

Sociological Abstracts from the first volume in 1953 through volume 7 (1), 1959; and the *Annual Review of Psychology* from volume 1, 1950, through volume 10, 1959. In addition, the following journals which most frequently publish articles on social interaction in small groups were examined issue-by-issue from 1950 through February, 1959: *American Journal of Sociology, American Psychologist, American Sociological Review, British Journal of Sociology, Current Sociology, Human Organization, Human Relations, Journal of Abnormal and Social Psychology, Journal of Applied Psychology, Journal of Consulting Psychology, Journal of Educational Psychology, Journal of Educational Sociology, Journal of Personality, Journal of Psychology, Journal of Social Psychology, Journal of Social Issues, Psychological Bulletin, Psychological Reports, Social Forces, Social Research, Sociology and Social Research,* and *Sociometry.*

Reviews which have been used as a guide are Cartwright and Zander's *Group Dynamics: Research and Theory* (1953), the chapters in Lindzey's *Handbook of Social Psychology* (1954) by Kelley and Thibaut on "Experimental Studies of Group Problem-solving and Process," and by Riecken and Homans on "Psychological Aspects of Social Structure," Roseborough's "Experimental Studies of Small Groups" (1953), and Eister's "Basic Continuities in the Study of Small Groups" (1957).

The present review will focus on the content of the research findings with only a brief outline of the methods of research given in the appendix. For summaries of current research techniques for the study of social interaction in small groups, the reader will find the following sources helpful: books on method such as Jahoda, Deutsch, and Cook, *Research Methods in Social Relations* (1951), and Festinger and Katz, *Research Methods in the Behavioral Sciences* (1953), and chapters in Lindzey's *Handbook of Social Psychology* (1954).

I have only begun the task of abstracting from this mass of research a single theoretical formulation. I have learned a great deal through this exercise of reviewing the literature and I am still learning at a rate which makes it impossible to feel that the present formulation is anywhere near final. However the task of rereading all the articles mentioned to drain from them the last full measure of evidence of their interconnectedness remains for some future time and perhaps some other author.

A. PAUL HARE

Haverford, Pa.
September, 1960

Acknowledgments

IN CONSIDERING the events which led directly to the present book, I am particularly indebted to Dr. Edgar F. Borgatta who worked long and hard with me in our survey of the literature, in preparing the annotated bibliography, and in selecting the articles for our previous volume; to Professor Robert F. Bales whose continued interest throughout the four years of writing has helped immeasurably to bring the final version of the manuscript into focus; and to Dr. William C. Schutz whose three-dimensional analysis of interpersonal relations has had a primary influence on the conceptual scheme developed here.

I am indebted to Dr. Gene C. Kassebaum for abstracting some of the small group studies which appear as illustrations; to Irving K. Zola who collected most of the data which are presented in the figures summarizing research relevant to specific generalizations and who checked the accuracy of references, and to Paul E. Breer and Winthrop D. Thies who helped with the editing. Carol Connell and Joan G. Blackett also helped with the typing and editing. Throughout the first two years of the project, facilities and encouragement were provided by Dr. Erich Lindemann and Dr. Gerald Caplan.

I wish to acknowledge the assistance of the authors and publishers who made it possible to include pictures, charts, and other materials from previously published sources. Specific credits are given in the text.

CONTENTS

ILLUSTRATIONS

Introduction

*I*N THE THREE PARTS of the book, essentially the same material is organized in three different ways: first, by considering the central tendencies of the interaction process and group structure; second, by emphasizing the deviations from typical patterns that may result from variations in such factors as members' personalities, group size, and leadership; and finally, by reviewing differences in productivity related to variations in group process and structure.

In Chapter One, the elements of social interaction are introduced. These concepts are elaborated in later chapters as parts of the conceptual scheme are discussed in detail. Since the basic problem in social psychology is *social control,* I include, in Chapter Two, a review of research on the process through which culture develops, persists, and changes. In Chapter Three, I consider the interaction process as group members solve problems through discussion. An analysis of some of the details of social perception is included here, since the observation of social objects is an important phase in the cycle of the social act. Part One of the text concludes with two chapters on aspects of group structure: the role system of the group and the network of interpersonal choice.

In Part Two, I review some of the factors which can be varied to produce changes in group norms, the interaction process, the role system, and the pattern of interpersonal choice. These factors are the personalities of members, social characteristics of members, group size, task, communication network, and leadership.

Part Three is a summary of the literature from the point of view of productivity. Here I consider questions such as: "When is a group more productive than an individual?" and "What are the characteristics of the most productive groups, given the central tendencies which are described in Part One and the variations which can be produced through manipulation of the factors described in Part Two?"

In bringing together in one volume references to all of the relevant research on small groups published between 1900 and February, 1959, two devices have been used to make the presentation of so much detail a little more palatable. First, when a number of studies seem to lead to substantially the same conclusion, only a general reference to the findings is given in the body of the text and the relevant details of each study are summarized in an exhibit. This does not reflect a judgment on the relative value of the studies but only their cumulative nature. Second, at least one relevant piece of research has been reported in some detail in each chapter to allow the reader to evaluate its results in the context of the complete research design. Whenever possible, "classic" pieces of small group research have been used for this purpose. In some cases excerpts from these classics are quoted directly with minor changes in wording. In others there has been considerable editing to shorten the article while maintaining many of the author's original phrases. In general, tables or original data have not been given except to illustrate the findings in these key pieces of research.

One of the major problems in reviewing the literature is that of finding the least number of generalizations under which to subsume results of research. It has therefore been necessary to develop a conceptual scheme to bring some order into previously nebulous aspects of behavior. The present scheme was suggested in part by Schutz's (1958) analysis of three dimensions of interpersonal behavior and by Bales's analysis of the basic elements in an interaction system (see for example Bales & Slater, 1955). The scheme is not a *theory* in any formal sense. Although some attempt is made to indicate what appear to be some of the basic elements in the interaction process and some of the relationships which exist between these elements, the whole set of elements and generalizations has not been tied to a single, integrated framework. In many instances terms are used as the authors originally defined them. As a result, a variety of meanings have been attached to the same term and a variety of terms appear with substantially the same meaning.

§ Other points of view

ALTHOUGH THE CONCEPTUAL SCHEME outlined in this text has some elements which are common to most theoretical analyses of the inter-action process, it does not represent a summary of existing points of view. A number of analyses and reviews of the literature are available, some with broad application (Bonner, 1959; Olmsted, 1959; Thibaut & Kelley, 1959; Stogdill, 1959); others with particular applications, such as industry (Argyle, 1957b), education (Benne & Muntyan, 1951; Benne & Levit, 1953; Horwitz, 1953), or group work (Coyle, 1930, 1937; Kozman, 1951).

A number of authors have suggested a set of theoretical categories very similar to that presented here in Figure 1 (Lasswell, 1939; Wirth, 1939; Znaniecki, 1939; Cattell, 1948, 1951a, 1951b; Loomis & Beegle, 1948; James, 1950; Carter, 1953; Horowitz & Perlmutter, 1953; Bogardus, 1954; Maas, 1954a; Dodd, 1955; Jackson, 1959a). The most compre-hensive scheme to have been presented however is that of Homans (1947, 1950, 1958; see also Brown & Brown, 1955). His work has been extended and elaborated by Klein (1956) and stated in mathematical terms by Simon (1952).

Collections of articles on small group behavior have been edited by Guetzkow (1951), Swanson, Newcomb, and Hartley (1952), Cart-wright and Zander (1953, 1960), Hare, Borgatta, and Bales (1955), and Maccoby, Newcomb, and Hartley (1958). Additional articles reviewing the literature commenting on the small group field have been published by Strodtbeck (1954b, 1956), Argyle (1955), Coser (1955), Stirn (1955), Israel (1956), Bales (1958), Marie Borgatta (1958), and Hare (1958a). The *Annual Review of Psychology* always includes some comprehensive articles on small groups in the chapter on "Social Psychology and Group Processes." [1]

---

1. Articles appearing in this review have been written by Bruner (1950), Katz (1951), Smith (1952), Newcomb (1953b), Crutchfield (1954), Festinger (1955), French (1956), Cartwright (1957), Heyns (1958), and Gilchrist (1959).

A bibliography of small group research from 1900 through 1953 has been published by Strodtbeck and Hare (1954), and related bibliographies are available for small group research in military settings (Criswell & Petrullo, 1957; McGrath, 1957), the family (Hill, 1951), and group therapy (Corsini & Putzey, 1957).

Part One

GROUP PROCESS AND STRUCTURE

1

ELEMENTS
OF SOCIAL
INTERACTION[1]

THE OBJECTIVE OF THE REVIEW of the literature on social interaction in small groups which led to the present volume has been to develop the broad outlines of a conceptual scheme for the analysis of human interaction. In reviewing the research over the past fifty years, it became apparent that each social scientist was reporting some part of the social act which seemed important to him and which should be included in an overall theory of human interaction. Many of these previous researchers seemed to be talking about the same thing. The only problem was that they talked about it from different points of

---

1. The article by Hare (1960) was based on this chapter.

view and with different vocabularies. In the present review, some of
the concepts are used in familiar ways, whereas others have been
broadened to include several more specific concepts. The generalizations
are made at a rather gross level, leaving the more subtle aspects of
social interaction to be specified by future research.

§ Elements in the
Interaction Process

THE MAJOR ELEMENTS appearing in most category systems for the
analysis of social interaction are given in Fig. 1. Although the present

Figure 1—Elements of Social Interaction

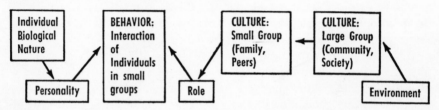

focus is on the prediction of the interactive behavior of individuals in
small groups, it is assumed that the same elements would appear in a
theory which attempted to describe interaction of individuals in
larger social units such as communities or nations. In the conceptual
scheme to be developed here, *social interaction* is seen as a compromise
between the inputs from man's *biological nature* and *personality*, on the
one hand, and *role, culture,* and *environment,* on the other. Here "environment" refers to the natural and man-made nonhuman elements
which form the situation in which the interaction occurs. To predict
some aspects of social interaction, we need know only how an individual's
biological nature typically responds to his environment. For some predictions, particularly with a clinical population, personality may be the
dominant element in the system. However, we can predict many of
the details of everyday life if we know only the patterns of behavior
which are typical of the group or groups to which a person belongs.

Man's *biological nature* and his *environment* represent a different
order of data than the other elements of the system since they can be

measured independently of the social behavior which one wishes to predict. However, the social nature of the individual and the social nature of the group are both abstractions from interactive behavior. Those tendencies to behave which are consistent for an individual as he moves from group to group are called *personality*. The expectations shared by group members about the behavior associated with some position in a group, no matter what individual fills the position, are called *role*.[2] The same individual usually plays roles in a number of groups at the same time; some of these groups are small and some large. For example, an individual who is a student may also be a son, a husband, a club man, and a citizen. Although there are many occasions when he acts in only one role, there are enough instances of conflicting expectations, particularly between small and large groups, to justify the designation of multiple group membership as a primary element in the conceptual scheme. The terms "small" and "large" are used here in a relative sense. Except for the group of two, a group may be broken down into subsystems. For groups of any size there is always some larger group to which an individual may also belong.

The sum of the expectations for the roles of all members of a group plus the expectations for behavior of members in general is the *culture* of a group. The culture includes patterns of behavior which are transmitted from one generation to the next. These patterns include ways of thinking, ways of acting, and ways of feeling.

§ The Small Group

THERE IS NO DEFINITE cutting point in the continuum between a collection of individuals, such as one might find waiting for a bus on a corner, and a fully organized "group." There is also no definite cutting point between the small, intimate, face-to-face group and the large, formal group. For a collection of individuals to be considered a group

2. Although a number of authors use the concept of *role* in a similar fashion, to refer to the "expectations" for behavior, others use it in a more general sense to refer to everything associated with a position in a group. When *role* is used in this general way the emphasis is on the *behavior* of the person playing the role rather than on the "expectations" for behavior. The term is actually used in both senses throughout the text. In the interest of having a conceptual scheme composed of nonoverlapping concepts, I have used *role* to mean "expectations," but in the interest of reviewing the literature without doing too much violence to the authors' original intentions, I have also used the term in the more general sense.

there must be some *interaction*. In addition to the *interaction* of the members, four features of group life typically emerge as the group develops (Znaniecki, 1939; Sherif, 1954a):

1. The members share one or more *motives* or *goals* which determine the direction in which the group will move.

2. The members develop a set of *norms*, which set the boundaries within which interpersonal relations may be established and activity carried on.

3. If interaction continues, a set of *roles* becomes stabilized and the new group becomes differentiated from other groups.

4. A *network of interpersonal attraction* develops on the basis of the "likes" and "dislikes" of members for one another.

There are then, in sum, five characteristics which differentiate the *group* from a *collection of individuals*. The members of the group are in *interaction* with one another. They share a common *goal* and set of *norms*, which give direction and limits to their activity. They also develop a set of *roles* and a *network of interpersonal attraction*, which serve to differentiate them from other groups.

Small groups include all those having from two up to about twenty members. However, even larger groups may be considered "small" if face-to-face interaction is possible, and collections of fewer than twenty individuals may actually include several smaller groups. The most commonly used definition of a small group is that given by Bales:

A small group is defined as any number of persons engaged in interaction with each other in a single face-to-face meeting or a series of meetings, in which each member receives some impression or perception of each other member distinct enough so that he can, either at the time or in later questioning, give some reaction to each of the others as an individual person, even though it be only to recall that the other person was present (1950b, p. 33).

§   Process, Structure,
and Change

THE RELATIONSHIP of the elements in social interaction may be examined from three points of view: process, structure, and change. When the focus is on *process*, we analyze the act-by-act sequence of events as it unfolds over time. This is a longitudinal approach. The same data may be used to describe the *structure* of the group where the focus is on the relations among elements in the system at a given time. This is the cross-sectional approach. The analysis of *social change* typically focuses on changes in the *structure* of a group over time.

These three themes of process, structure, and change appear at many points throughout the volume. In Part One, they form the basic framework around which the material is organized. Process is reviewed in Chapter Three, two aspects of structure (roles and interpersonal choice) in Chapters Four and Five, and change in Chapter Two.

§ The Form and Content
of Social Behavior

WITH THIS GENERAL OUTLINE of the elements in an interactional system and some notion of the characteristics of a small group, we can now look a little more closely at the *behavior* of individuals in interaction. Observers of social behavior tend to break behavior down into three different categories. In some cases the focus is on *inter*personal behavior, such as cooperative problem-solving. In other cases it is on *intra*personal behavior, as evidenced in tension or anxiety. In still other cases the focus is on aspects of *individual performance*, which may characterize an individual whether he is alone or in a group. In this text, intrapersonal behavior and individual performance will be combined, leaving two very general categories—*interpersonal behavior* and *personal behavior*.

Although many different category systems can be used in describing interpersonal behavior, the categories of interaction given in Fig. 2 appear to represent the major "dimensions" of observed behavior. The categories are given here in simplified form and will be elaborated at later points in the text, particularly in Chapter Six on personality.

Figure 2—A Paradigm for the Analysis of Interaction

Form	Communication network
	Interaction rate
Content	Task behavior a. observe b. hypothesize c. propose action
	Social-emotional behavior a. control b. affection

The form of interaction is less specific than content and is more easily recorded. As one approaches a group from the "outside," the first aspect of interaction which becomes apparent is the communication network (i.e., who speaks to whom), and next the amount of interaction carried by each of the communication channels. For a closer analysis of *what* is going on in the group, one needs some content categories. Here the most frequent division is between content directed primarily towards the solution of task problems *versus* content directed primarily towards the solution of social-emotional problems. Within the social-emotional area, the categories of control and affection represent the predominant types of behavior, whereas in the task area there is less consensus on the "typical" problem-solving categories. The minimum set of categories would probably parallel the steps in the scientific method, namely of observation, hypothesis formation, and the testing of hypotheses.

Each of the major categories in Figure 2 can be defined as follows:

FORM

Communication network—The channels of communication between group members.

Interaction rate—The frequency of interactions, sometimes represented by the number of contributions, sometimes by the relationship between the number and duration of contributions, i.e., action and silence, and sometimes by the number of contributions times the average duration of each, i.e., total talking time.

CONTENT

Task behavior—Interaction directed toward the completion of group or individual tasks. The minimum number of categories would include observing, hypothesizing, and formulating action.

Social-emotional behavior—Interaction directed primarily toward the relationships between group members that form the basis for problem-solving. The minimum number of categories would include control and affection.

Each of these categories can be used at the level of personality, behavior, and role. At the personality level they represent *tendencies to act,* and at the level of role they represent *expectations for behavior.*

§ Output and Input: Form

THE DESCRIPTION of the behavior of an individual from the interactional point of view includes not only how he acts towards others (output), but also how others respond to him (input). For this reason, the minimum number of actors involved is two, the minimum number of acts is two (one action and one reaction), and the minimum number of time periods in which interaction occurs is two (Bales & Slater, 1955).

The output and input characteristics for both form and content of interaction can be considered with varying degrees of complexity. For the communication network, one could record simply the total number of channels for outgoing messages and incoming messages. At the other extreme one could specify the extent to which each channel from a subject to every other member of the group is open for output or input. Similarly, the interaction rate can be described simply as the total number of acts an individual gives and the total number he receives, or the output and imput rate could be given for each channel in the communication network.

Although it is possible to differentiate output from input for the communication network, particularly in exepriments where the communication network is the major variable, the correlation between output and input for a given channel is very high. The person who speaks most often in a group is usually the one who is spoken to most often. In those cases where the correlation is high, specification of the input characteristics may add little to the description of the interaction process.

This type of reduction in the number of experimental "variables" occurs over and over again in those experiments which use comprehensive category systems for recording the interaction process. Since relatively few categories of behavior are appropriate in any given situation, most of the interaction tends to take place within two or three categories. As a result, the remaining categories are either correlated with these or appear too infrequently to yield reliable measures.

§ Output and Input:
Content

FOR THE ANALYSIS of behavior where one may wish to consider several categories of content simultaneously, the characteristics of an individual's interaction for either output or input may be described by a set of *interaction profiles* similar to those used by Bales (1951). If only one dimension or area of content is to be considered at a time, a graphic plot may be used to advantage, with one axis representing output and the other input (see Fig. 3). The explicit recognition of the distinction between input and output may help clarify some theoretical issues, especially in the construction of typologies.

Figure 3—Representation of Input and Output in a Two-dimensional Plot

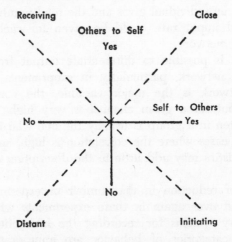

In the description of behavior tendencies in the area of control, for example, the vertical axis might represent the behavior desired from others ranging from *yes,* he wants to be controlled by others, to *no,* he does not want to be controlled by others. The horizontal axis could then represent the desired behavior toward others ranging from *yes,* he wants to control others, to *no,* he does not want to control others.

The individual who wants strongly to control or to be controlled has been called *authoritarian*. On the other hand, the individual who wants neither to control nor to be controlled may be said to desire a situation in which there is distance between group members. In the extreme, this kind of independence has been called *anarchism*.

On the opposite diagonal are individuals who vary from wanting to control but not be controlled, the *dominators*, to those who want to be controlled but do not want to control, the *submitters*. In the center are those individuals who want both to control and to be controlled in a moderate degree, a type of behavior which tends to be called *democratic*. All other combinations of tendencies to give or receive control can be represented as points in this two dimensional space.

In the description of *personality*, the two axes in Fig. 3 would represent the tendencies to give and receive, which the individual brings to the situation. In the description of *role*, the axes would represent expected behavior, the duties (output) and the rights (input) associated with each role. The expectations for behavior would vary along each axis from behavior which is required to that which is prohibited.

§ Personal Behavior

IN ADDITION to the interpersonal categories, there are dimensions of *personal* behavior, which also play a part in the activity of a group. The personal categories include those dimensions usually associated with personality such as intelligence, social sensitivity, and adjustment, as well as aspects of the individual's biological nature such as age, sex, and physical strength. These categories like the previously discussed interpersonal categories can also be used to describe "tendencies" within the individual and "expectations" for the role he is to perform.

Although the mean or average behavior in each category is stressed in the present formulation, this should not obscure the fact that the mean may not be as important for the prediction of behavior in a particular instance as some measure of the extent of variation and the conditions under which the variation occurs.

§ Predicting Behavior
from Personality
and Role

To PREDICT an individual's behavior in one of the form or content areas, one could first indicate on the plane a point representing the tendency in the personality (see Fig. 4) and also a point representing the expected behavior called for by the individual's role in the group.

Figure 4—The Relationship between Personality, Behavior, and Role in One Content Category

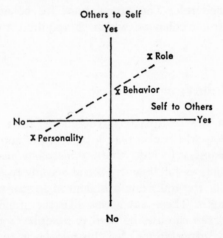

The actual behavior would then lie somewhere along the line between the personality and the role.

In a ceremony, such as a marriage, the actual behavior would be very close to the role. At the other extreme, when role is not well defined, for example, the role for a patient in a mental hospital ward, the behavior would be close to the tendencies in personality. Since in many personalities and in many roles one of the content areas may be more salient than the others, an individual's behavior may be predominantly in *one* of the content areas.

§ Variations in Interaction Rate

THE CHARACTERISTIC of an individual's interactive behavior most frequently reported in the literature is his interaction rate. An individual's interaction rate can vary while the content of interaction remains relatively stable. In most situations the interaction rate of a single group member is related to the rates of the other members of the group as well as to his own personality.

An increase in the interaction rate of an individual may be associated with activity in any one of the content areas. In some experiments, an increase in interaction has been found to be associated with attempts to control a deviant member (Schachter, 1951). In other research, a high interaction rate is correlated with task success (Strodtbeck, 1954). In still other studies, as for example in the observation of working girls doing piecework which does not require control, the interaction rate is highly correlated with affection (Homans, 1950).

§ Choice Behavior and Cohesiveness

THE CRITERIA which individuals use in making interpersonal choices may fall into any of the content areas. However, in social research, subjects are often asked to designate group members whom they would like to work with (a criterion which appears to combine task ability and control), and whom they would like to play with (a criterion which appears to be primarily affection). Since individuals who desire to be close to people will choose others who prefer closeness, it is generally true that "birds of a feather flock together." However, individuals who like to initiate tend to choose those who like to receive, so that it is also true that "opposites attract."

Groups containing a large number of mutual choices on either a "work" or "play" criterion are often said to be highly "cohesive" in that they will "stick together" longer than groups in which there are few mutual choices. Although groups are often referred to as being highly "cohesive" without specifying the basis on which the choices were made, the criterion is important. Subjects who have chosen each other because they like to work with each other should be more productive than those who have chosen each other because they like to play together, provided, of course, that the task calls for the type of control relationships which they prefer. A group composed of anarchists who had chosen each other could not be expected to do well on a task requiring authoritarian relationships.

The importance of the criterion on which choice is based is not always evident in the literature since many subjects will make the same choices regardless of the criterion which the experimenter suggests. In some cases, the multiple choice is justified since there are "great men" who are actually high on all criteria (Borgatta, Couch, & Bales, 1954), but in other cases it appears that the subject has his own preferred criterion for choice and will use the same one no matter what the experimenter suggests (French, E.G., 1956). That is, a subject with a salient need for affection would always choose others whom he expected to satisfy his affectional need whether the situation called for affection, or some other predominant category of behavior.

§ Formal and Informal Structure

SINCE EXPECTATIONS for behavior tend to vary in the extent to which they are "formally" defined by group members, it is often useful to differentiate the *formal* role structure of the group from the *informal* role structure. Of the two types of structure, the formal structure is usually more visible since it is often recorded in the group's table of organization. In the *informal* structure, such positions as "best-liked" or "scapegoat" can be identified through the use of "sociometric" tests on which group members indicate their choices or rejections of other group members. The direction of interpersonal choice may also be inferred from behavioral indices, such as frequency of association, or the content category which dominates the interaction with a given individual.

Within the role structure, the various positions may be ordered in a hierarchy according to their relative evaluation. Some investigators treat the role structure of the group (either formal or informal) as if it consisted of only a single *hierarchy* in which each role included expectations for behavior in all categories. Other investigators treat the structure as if it were composed of several *hierarchies*, each composed of roles which are represented by some predominant category of interaction; for example, "task ability" or "likeability." In the latter formulation, an individual could be seen as having a high status in one hierarchy and a low status in another.

§ Four Problems for Groups

ANOTHER WAY of looking at social behavior is to consider the goal to which the behavior is directed. The categories in Fig. 2 suggest the range of observable variation in the social behavior of two or more individuals working together on a common task, but they do not specify the types of tasks which groups may have as a central focus or the direction the interaction process may take. If one assumes that human behavior is directed primarily toward the solution of problems, particularly the problem of survival, then all human behavior in groups can be described in relation to the solution of four types of problems represented by the four cells in Fig. 5.

Figure 5—Four Problems for Groups

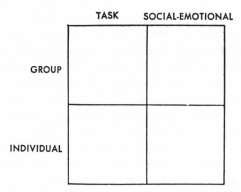

Two of these problems are at the group level, and two are at the individual level. At the group level, the first problem is that of the task, the solution of a publicly stated problem of the group. Second is the solution of group problems in the social-emotional area. These problems often take the form of a "hidden agenda" dealing with shared anxieties which are not explicitly stated and dealing with the establishment of the group structure. The third type of problem is the task for the individual, a publicly stated individual goal. The fourth type consists of the individual's social-emotional problems, his efforts to deal with his own problems of membership and self-integration.

Although these four types of problems are present in all groups, some groups emphasize one type rather than another. For example, a typical action group, such as an industrial team, sees problem-solving of the first type as its goal. Some seminars in group dynamics emphasize a goal of the second type, an awareness of the social-emotional problems of the group. A goal of type three is typically the goal of most educational enterprises, while the fourth goal of individual social adjustment is the concern of group therapy (Thelen, 1954). In some analyses of group problems, only those of types one, two, and four are emphasized (Harnack, 1953).

This table of four types of goals, two for the group and two for the individual, can be expanded to a table of eight if one considers each of these problems first in relation to the group being studied and then secondly in relation to other groups. That is, the success of the resolution of the publicly stated problem of the small group can be evaluated in its own terms or in terms which are relative to the solutions contributed by other groups. The structure of the group can be examined from a position internal to it, or one can relate the structure of the small group to that of the larger society.. The individual's goals can be evaluated from within the group or from the outside, and so on. For example, at the individual level, the task goal might be to gain good grades in a particular class, but in the larger social system, to earn a college degree. Or, at the individual social-emotional level, the individual may want to satisfy only some of his needs in one group, because other needs are satisfied in other groups to which he belongs.

These four types of problems for individuals and groups usually have a priority for the individual member in the reverse order in which they have been presented. That is, the individual views as most important a problem of type four, then three, two, and one. The individual must satisfy his own social-emotional needs before he has energy to devote to his individual task. In turn, sets of individuals or groups must solve the problems of group structure before they can work on the group task.

§ Norms and Social
Control

INDIVIDUALS AND GROUPS form and conform to norms to achieve goals. Since goal achievement for a group depends upon concerted action, some consensus on acceptable task and social-emotional behavior must be attained before the members of a group can act together. For this reason even competition requires a minimum of co-operation in establishing and maintaining the rules of the contest. The goal which is achieved through conformity may be at any one or any combination of the four levels of group task, group structure, individual task, and individual integration.

§ Summary

THE GOAL of the first chapter has been to develop the outlines of a conceptual scheme for the analysis of human interaction in small groups. The major elements in the scheme are man's biological nature and personality, which influence his interaction from the "inside" and his roles in the small and large group, and environment, which influence his interaction from the "outside." Interactive behavior is thus seen as a compromise between the needs of the individual and the demands of the situation.

Although there is no definite upper limit to the size of a "small" group, a group is usually defined as "small" if each member has the opportunity for face-to-face interaction with all others. The process by which a collection of individuals becomes a group includes the evolution of a set of goals and norms, the development of a role system, and the establishment of a network of affective ties. The relationship of the elements affecting the interaction of group members may be examined from the point of view of process, structure, or change.

Behavior, personality, and role each have both interpersonal and personal aspects. The interpersonal categories include, under form, communication network and interaction rate, and, under content, task behavior and social-emotional behavior. Both input and output characteristics in each category would be included in a complete description of the interaction process. Because of the limitations set by role expectations, the interaction rate of an individual may be correlated with behavior in one of the content areas.

Interpersonal choices, which represent a frequently studied aspect of social interaction, may be based on criteria which fall into any of the interpersonal categories. The criteria actually used by an individual will vary with his personality and the situation in which the choice is made.

In many groups, there is an informal structure which is indicated by the network of interpersonal choice as well as a formal structure which may be represented by an organizational chart. Within each structure, the roles tend to be ordered according to their relative evaluation into one or more hierarchies.

Group members have four types of problems to solve, two at the group level and two at the individual level. At each level there are both task problems and social integration problems. The individual must usually satisfy his own needs and reach his own goal before he is willing to give time to the organization of the group and the accomplishment of the group task. Conformity to norms is necessary to solve problems at all levels.

The approach to the analysis of interaction in small groups outlined in this chapter is suggested as a framework for organizing ideas. The elements included in the theory have been found to be important sources of variation in social behavior in a variety of situations. However, the prediction of behavior in any specific situation may require knowledge of only a few of these elements or, on the other hand, an elaboration and differentiation of these concepts well beyond the present level of analysis.

2

NORMS AND SOCIAL CONTROL

THE FRAMEWORK for the analysis of social interaction outlined in Chapter One indicated that the interaction process was the
result of a compromise between the needs of group members, (biological
nature and personality), and the demands of the situation, (role
expectations and environment). The present chapter analyzes the process
by which the group brings pressure to bear on its members to conform
to group norms. In laboratory experiments on conformity, the extent of
group influence on an individual's judgment is found to be a function
of the *object* to be judged, the *subject* who is making the judgment,
and the *situation* in which he finds himself. The study of the process
of *social control* is a basic problem for social psychology, since it is

only with some type of social control that individuals can carry out concerted action and thus become a group.

§ Formation of Norms

GROUP MEMBERS tend to form and conform to norms. Norms are rules of behavior, proper ways of acting, which have been accepted as legitimate by members of a group. Norms specify the kinds of behavior that are expected of group members. These rules or standards of behavior to which members are expected to conform are for the most part derived from the goals which a group has set for itself. Given a set of goals, norms define the kind of behavior which is necessary for or consistent with the realization of those goals (Bates & Cloyd, 1956). When the *norms* refer to the expectations for a single individual they constitute the individual's *role*. The norms are then, in effect, the expectations for the role of an "undifferentiated group member." Each person has within him a set of norms and goals which are a composite of his own idiosyncratic ideals, the expectations of the group in which he is participating at the moment, and the expectations of other groups of which he is also a member.

The shared expectations developed in the current group are added to the prior ones as group members go through the process of culture building. Especially in the early meetings of a group, much of the members' attention is taken up with decisions about rules for appropriate behavior. This process may not be recognized by the group members until the group bogs down on some simple issue, such as the length of time for a coffee break. It is only when they are faced with the problem of allotting time (a scarce commodity) for particular activities that the members discover that they have not reached a consensus of such basic issues as the relative importance of the needs of the task *versus* the needs of the individual members. The concern over *norms* and *goals* is the old problem of the *means* and the *ends*, and there is no basis for *organized* interaction in a group until some agreement is reached about each of these kinds of expectations.

When the individual's norms and goals are in accord with those of the group, his behavior will meet approval. However, if the individual finds that his behavior deviates from the group norms, he has four choices: *to conform, to change the norms, to remain a deviant,* or *to leave the group.* Of course, he may also be removed from the group without his consent. The literature on the formation of norms and social control in the small group deals with the first three types of behavior, *conformity, change,* and *pressures on the deviant.* Current research with leaderless groups has little to say about the choice to leave the group, since most of these experimental groups are disbanded after only a few meetings. The problem of withdrawal of a group member is a real one for the group therapist, however, since the antisocial person may be just the type that he is trying to reach through this kind of therapy.

§ Social Control

The process by which the individual manipulates the behavior of others or by which group members bring pressure on the individual is the process of *social control.* Through social control, behavior is confined to acceptable limits, limits which maximize the possibilities of survival for the individual in the group. Social control can be thought of as *formal,* the rules and regulations imposed by a large organization, or *informal,* the social pressure of the small intimate group. Although there are many instances in which social control is forcibly applied by others, in most cases social control is *self-control.* This is the self-control which takes place during the initial phase of the social act when the individual modifies his behavior as a result of his anticipation of the response of the other person. If the individual is at all effective in his social relationships, the process of social control will be over before his overt act. Since the absolute degree of conformity to a group norm is a function of the initial distance from the norm, individuals who show the greatest deviation can also show the greatest amount of change toward conformity (Goldberg, 1954).

This process of modification of behavior may range from an individual's conscious attempts to conform to norms to the unconscious acceptance of group or individual directives. The latter case is exemplified by the psychological experiments in "operant conditioning." In these experiments, subjects are "conditioned" to carry out sequences of behavior, such as taking the top off a fountain pen and putting it back, by continually "rewarding" bits of behavior, until the final sequence of behavior which the experimenter desires is produced (Verplanck, 1956).

§ The Autokinetic Effect and Group Norms

SHERIF (1935, 1936; Sherif & Sherif, 1956) uses the autokinetic effect to demonstrate the relation between individual and group norms. Each subject is placed in a dark room and asked to judge how far a dot of light moves. The light actually does not move but only appears to. Under these conditions, each subject develops a range in which he makes his estimates. When these same individuals are placed together in groups of two and three members, their judgments converge in a group standard or norm. If the subjects make their first judgments in a group, their judgments tend to converge even more rapidly. The group norm persists for the individual member when he faces the same stimulus alone at a later time.

The same experimental results have been obtained by others using slightly different experimental designs (e.g., in groups in which all responses other than that of the subject are tape-recorded) (Schonbar, 1945; Blake & Brehm, 1954; Linton, 1954; Rohrer, Baron, Hoffman, & Swander, 1954; Olmstead & Blake, 1955; Downing, 1958) and are predictable enough to be used as a classroom demonstration (Ray, 1951).

§ Effects of Group Opinion on Judging Line Lengths

A SECOND EXAMPLE of the experimental work which has been undertaken to operationalize certain pertinent concepts and problems regarding conformity to or independence from group standards of judgment will be described in more detail.[1] Solomon Asch, a psychologist of the Gestalt tradition, designed an ingenious study to yield objective

---

1. In each chapter one or two studies will be presented in enough detail to give the reader some feeling for the theory, the method, and the results of the research. Those parts of the study which are not relevant for the particular chapter in which the study is reported have generally been omitted. Most of these studies are the "classics" in the field, early pieces of research which provided the stimulus for rapid growth of the field. A list of books and articles in this category which were published from 1931 through 1953 appears in Strodtbeck and Hare (1954), pp. 111-112.

measures of conformity of an individual's psycho-physical judgments when confronted by an incorrect majority opinion (Asch, 1951, 1952, 1955, 1956).

In this experiment, a number of persons are instructed by the experimenter to unanimously give incorrect judgments in what is ostensibly an experiment in visual perception. The stimulus materials are two sets of white cards. One set consists of cards, each of which displays a single black line (the standard). Each card of the other set bears three lines, one being the same length as the standard, the other two being easily recognizable departures from this length. These cards are illustrated in Fig. 6. The task is to match the correct line

Figure 6—A Pair of Stimulus Cards

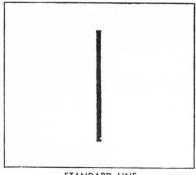
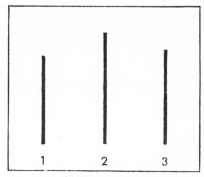

STANDARD LINE   COMPARISON LINES

of the three with the standard. All judgments are expressed orally. In the experiment proper, a single "naive" subject is placed in a group of "coached subjects," the total number varying in different experiments from seven to nine. The behavior of the "coached subjects" and the manner of assembling for the experiment give no indication of the collusion between group and experimenter. The naive subject is seated at the end (or in some cases next to the end) of the line of subjects. The experimenter shows a pair of cards and one by one the subjects state their opinions of the line which matches the standard. A series of eighteen trials consists of twelve critical trials, in which the coached members unanimously give incorrect responses, and six neutral trials, in which the coached members give correct responses. This performance in the experimental groups may be compared with a control series in which all members of the group are "naive" and uninstructed and merely write their judgments down on paper, trial by trial.

Using this basic experimental design, 123 college students were placed in the minority situation described above. When a subject was faced with an incorrect majority opinion, there was a significant increase in his errors, always in the direction of the majority. Nearly 37 per cent of the subjects' responses were in error, as compared with almost no error in the control groups. Thus, influence of group opinion on the individual was in many cases sufficient to dissuade him from responding in terms of his immediate sense impressions, which were clearly in contradiction to the group. However, in most instances a different judgment by the majority was not enough to make the individual conform.

The percentage of the 123 subjects who made correct judgments on each of the twelve critical trials is indicated in Fig. 7 by a solid line.

Figure 7—Percentage of Correct Estimates for Critical Trials

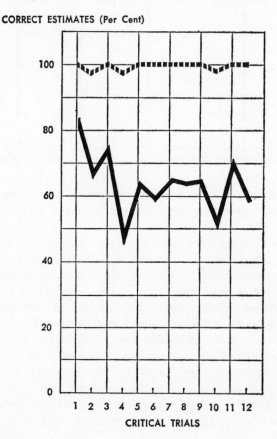

CORRECT ESTIMATES (Per Cent)

CRITICAL TRIALS

The accuracy of subjects who are not under group pressure is indicated by a dotted line. The largest percentage of correct judgments was made on the first critical trial (over eighty per cent), while the smallest percentage of correct judgments was made on the fourth trial (less than fifty per cent).

More information about the subjects who yielded and those who did not was obtained in the interviews which were conducted with the subjects immediately after the experiment. Asch interpreted his interviews as indicating three types of independent subjects and three types of yielding subjects. Among independent subjects he found independence accompanied by confidence. This type of individual was aware of majority opinion, but did not allow it to shake his reliance on the evidence of his eyes. A different type was the withdrawn individual, who seemed to be more oriented in terms of "explicit principles concerning the necessity of being an individual." His third type was described as independent, but felt anxious and uncomfortable over the public declaration of minority judgments. He would rather be with the majority but was unwilling to join them at the cost of discarding his sensory impressions, which were in this instance so clear.

The subjects who yielded on more than half of the critical trials were categorized by Asch into those who distorted their perception, those who distorted their judgment (decided they were inaccurate and the group was accurate) and those who distorted their action, yielding overtly only because of a great need not to appear deviant in the group.

It is evident that this experiment must be evaluated in terms of the restrictions under which it was performed. The discrepancy between majority opinion and immediately present sensory information was quite marked and the problem for judgment was clearly defined. The types of yielders derived from the interviews may, therefore, not obtain when individuals are judging psycho-physical or non-physical problems in which the discrepancy is not as marked and the problem not as clearly delimited. Another feature of the experiment is that interaction between members was not permitted. The process by which discrepancies are detected betwen majority and minority opinions, and the complexities of adjustment, accommodation, and conflict between such positions when they are detected, are not explored in this research design. Finally it may be noted that, in part, the classification of yielders is based on differences in personality, such as the need to join the majority. In order to investigate the relationship between personality structure and conformity, as studied in this experiment, some objective assessment of relevant aspects of personality would be necessary.

§ General Conditions Affecting Conformity

THE EXPERIMENTS by Sherif and Asch give evidence of the general tendency to conform to norms, but other types of experiments are needed to suggest the conditions which affect the extent to which a person may conform. Although all of the physical and social factors which affect any type of behavior also have a bearing on conformity, a few factors have received most of the attention in the literature. An individual is more likely to conform to group opinion in the following cases: when the *object to be judged is ambiguous,* if he must make his *opinion public,* if the *majority holding a contrary opinion is large,* and if the *group is especially friendly or close knit.* The influence of each of these factors is subject to the individual's awareness that his opinions are deviant (Mausner, 1955). If individuals make judgments and remain unaware of the judgments of others, no tendency towards conformity can be expected (Jenness, 1932b). In one experiment which provides an example of the effects of *not* applying social influence, individuals who were *not* members of groups, under no pressure to conform, told to use their own judgment, certain that they were correct and uncertain that others were correct, did not conform to norms (Deutsch & Gerard, 1955).

Homans (1958) has suggested that conformity can be seen as a case of the economic principle: that the individual tries to maximize his reward and minimize his cost in any transaction. Thus the individual will conform to group opinion if the cost of deviation is high and the rewards (e.g., liking) for conformity are high, or any other combination of reward and cost which yields some profit. The individual would be least likely to conform when the cost exceeds the reward.

Generalizations derived from research on conformity are organized in this chapter under three headings: the *object* about which a judgment is to be made, the *subject* who is making the judgment, and the *situation* in which the group has the primary influence.

§ Conformity
and the Object

INDIVIDUALS are called upon to make judgments about two general classes of objects: those which are unambiguous, such as the length of a line or the number of dots on a card, and those which are ambiguous, such as the merit of a painting. In addition to real ambiguity there are also objects for which there is actually an objective standard of judgment although they are perceived as ambiguous by the subjects. Generally, *the greater the ambiguity of the object, the greater will be the influence of other group members in determining the judgment of the subject.*

The relative influence of *perceived ambiguity* is illustrated by a series of studies in which pairs of individuals are asked to identify the objects in drawings which become progressively more or less ambiguous as the experiment progresses. When the drawing is complete in all its details the partner's opinion has no influence (Luchins, 1945, 1955; Luchins & Luchins, 1955b). The same effect has been noted with other kinds of ambiguous objects (Berenda, 1950; Crutchfield, 1955; Blake, Helson, & Mouton, 1957), although the effect is not always apparent (Wiener, Carpenter, & Carpenter, 1957). Even though the object is ambiguous or hard to judge, subjects who are correct when there is an objective standard are less likely to be influenced by others in the group (Thorndike, 1938b, Luchins, 1955).

When the phenomenon is actually *ambiguous*, the subject cannot be objectively "correct" in his judgment, but the extent to which he is *certain* of his judgment will have a similar effect on his conformity. The autokinetic situation can be used as an example, although not a pure one since the light objectively *does not move*, but only appears to move. There is no fixed standard for the length of the *apparent movement*. In one experiment individuals alone and in pairs were examined for fluctuation in judgments under three conditions of uncertainty. The greater the uncertainty, the greater was the individual's fluctuation in judgment and the more important was the group interaction (of the pairs) in reducing the range of fluctuation (Sherif & Harvey, 1952).

When the object is *unambiguous* group opinion has little impact on individual judgment. In one experiment sixty pairs of children of ages ten to twelve measured objects such as lines, parallelograms, and blocks with two different rulers. In each case the child using a linear ruler, who was told he was correct, announced his judgment first. Following this, the child using a metric ruler announced his judgment. There was little tendency for the second child to conform (Luchins & Luchins, 1956). If the subject is particularly suggestible however, or the situation is more coercive, as in the Asch experiment (1955), some conformity will take place even with an objective standard.

Since the *social value* of any object is always ambiguous in the sense that it varies from group to group and is a product of group interaction, the individual is forced to compare himself with a group on many issues. Although some have posited the existence of a *drive* to determine the correctness of opinion (Festinger, 1954, 1957), the present theory suggests that this *drive* may be accounted for by an action system in which an individual attempts to learn which response will follow from any given behavior, where the nature of the response is relative to the deviation of the behavior from the norm, so that he can predict the consequence of his act (Kelly, 1955, p. 49).

§ Conformity
and the Subject

THE INDIVIDUAL *brings with him into the judgment situation certain tendencies to conform or not conform which may be related to his personality* (Crutchfield, 1955), *his skill or previous success with the task, and prejudgments about the phenomena which are "anchored" in some other group.* An example of *personality* as a variable occurs in an experiment in which 64 subjects with all combinations of two personality traits, anxiety and neuroticism, were given social approval or disapproval of their opinions in a five-to-seven minute discussion with two role players. All of the subjects participated more when approved. The high-neurotic subjects were more rigid in holding their opinions when under disapproval, especially when they were also high-anxious (Cervin, 1955a, 1956). However, no differences in behavior between emotionally stable and unstable subjects were observed in a similar situation when the subjects were praised rather than subjected to disapproval (Cervin, 1955b).

A similar relationship between nonconformity and high neuroticism was found in a hospital study in which neurotic patients from a psychiatric ward conformed less in an experiment using autokinetic effect than patients from the medical wards (Levine, Laffal, Berkowitz, Lindemann, & Drevdahl, 1954).

Some studies report that subjects who receive high scores on the F Scale of "authoritarianism" conform more than low "F" subjects (Wells, Weinert, & Rubel, 1956; Berkowitz & Lundy, 1957). However, other research with the F scale suggests that a subject who receives a high score may simply be one who is willing to agree with a number of fairly extreme statements such as "Prison is too good for sex criminals, they should be publicly whipped or worse," rather than one who necessarily seeks situations in which he can both control and be controlled (Cronbach, 1946, 1950; Owens, 1947; Leavitt et al., 1955; Shelley, 1956; Chapman & Campbell, 1957b; Chapman & Bock, 1958; Couch & Keniston, 1960). Unfortunately for research, many subjects who answer "agree" to the F Scale items in the form in which they are usually given, also answer "agree" to similar items in which the meaning has been reversed. Thus a subject who scores as a high authoritarian on one test, scores as a low authoritarian on the next (Bass, 1955, 1957; Jackson & Messick, 1957; Jackson, Messick, & Solley, 1957; Messick & Jackson, 1957; Rabinowitz, 1957; Cristie, Havel, & Seidenberg, 1958; Kerlinger, 1958; Hare, 1961). The F Scale may then simply be another measure of submissiveness like the Ascendance-Submission scale, or a rating made from the content of stories told in response to pictures of the Thematic Apperception Test. Subjects who are rated as submissive or dependent in these tests or who describe themselves as submissive are found to submit more frequently to majority opinion (Barron, 1952; Helson et al., 1956; Kagan & Mussen, 1956; Gage, Leavitt, & Stone, 1957). Apparently, whatever the device for measuring conformity, whether it be a paper-and-pencil test as in the case of the F Scale, a measure of conventionality derived by comparison of a subject with the mean response of his group (Beloff, 1958), or a test of the Asch type (Rosner, 1957), subjects who conform in one situation will probably conform in another. (See also Block and Block, 1952.)

Other related characteristics of conforming individuals appear to be a high need to be approved by others, a low need to be outstanding as an individual (Moeller & Applezweig, 1957; Krebs, 1958; Schroder & Hunt, 1958), and a feeling that parental figures are harsh, punitive, restrictive, and rejecting (Mussen & Kagan, 1958). Sex also appears to be a factor, since women have been found to yield more to a bogus group norm than men (Tuddenham, 1958); however, this may be the result of a feeling that men are more skillful at the task (Tuddenham, MacBride, & Zahn, 1958).

The fact that self-confident subjects will resist pressures to conform (Hochbaum, 1954; Coleman, Blake, & Mouton, 1958) has already been indicated in the discussion of the effects of the ambiguity of the stimulus. This self-confidence can result from skills which the subject brings with him or it can be built up experimentally by allowing the subject to experience success in a series of individual trials before he is placed in a group (Kelman, 1950; Mausner, 1954b; Kelley & Lamb, 1957; Mausner & Bloch, 1957; Samelson, 1957; Goldberg & Lubin, 1958; Harvey & Rutherford, 1958). On the other hand, if the subject does not possess the necessary skills or characteristics which would make it possible for him to conform, he may fall behind, like the new recruit in a long infantry march, and remain a deviant (Levi, Torrance, & Pletts, 1954).

An individual may also be a nonconformist in one group if his opinions are well "anchored" in another group. The family, for example, is one of the principal reference groups for many subjects (Rosen, 1955b). The general tendency for individuals to have particular reference groups in mind is usually discussed in relation to large aggregates such as religious groups, political parties, or nations. In most of the experiments on face-to-face groups, the extent of "anchorage" of opinions is left as an unspecified part of the variance in conformity. In a study which exemplifies the "anchorage" of opinions in large aggregates, highschool and college students who were members of a church expressed attitudes which were farther from the norms of their church when they were influenced by contrary norms, an indication that influence was possible. But, in addition, the highschool students were less influenced if they were first reminded of their church affiliation, thus making the reference group more prominent in the mind at the time that they were asked to make a series of judgments (Hovland, Janis, & Kelley, 1953; Kelley, 1955).

In another study, opinions were first "anchored" in an *ad hoc* experimental group which served in later discussion as a reference group. When individuals' opinions on a fictitious labor-management dispute were discussed in three-man laboratory groups, subjects who were told that they would get along extremely well with each other made more attempts to influence each other than did subjects who were told that they would not do well together. When challenged by a role player about the opinion formed in the *ad hoc* "reference group" a week later, members of "high attraction" groups who were in initial agreement on their opinions were less likely to change than those who were in initial disagreement. Members of "low attraction" groups did not show the same trend, presumably because their opinions were not well "anchored" (Gerard, 1954).

A reference for an opinion need not be a whole group, it may be a single person whose opinion is highly valued. The presence of a highly valued person within a group may give the group members the appearance of consensus or agreement with each other, when in fact the members are similar only in that they agree with the central person. When his opinion shifts all other opinions will also shift.

§ Conformity and the Situation

THE RELEVANT ASPECTS of the situation are those which have to do with the subject's "commitment" to the group. *The subject is more apt to conform if his alternative is to go on record as a deviant in a group to which he is highly attracted and whose influential members disagree with him* (Festinger & Aronson, 1960).

Opinions given in public are often different from those expressed privately. Generally, the views expressed in public or with a possibility of being made public are more conforming (Schank, 1932; Festinger, 1947, 1950a, 1950b; Gorden, 1952; Kelley & Volkhart, 1952; Hovland et al., 1953; Mouton, Blake, & Olmstead, 1956; Argyle, 1957a), although this is not always the case (Bennett, 1955), since the first persons to vote publicly are often the ones who are the most confident of their opinions (Terman, 1904; Gurnee, 1937a; Thorndike, 1938b) (see Exhibit 1 [2]). Some of these early responders will influence later responses. In such a case, the opinions of the first to answer will turn out to represent majority opinion because they had a part in its formation. Other individuals, equally confident of their opinion, will turn out to be deviants. In either event, if a person expresses his opinion (or intended course of action) publicly, he is more likely to follow up the opinion with appropriate behavior than if the opinion is given privately, especially if the group restraints against giving an opinion are high (Schachter & Hall, 1952). In addition, if a group member is allowed to make his point in a group discussion, even if he does not win others over to his opinion, he will be more satisfied with the discussion and more likely to accept the final group judgment (Preston & Heintz, 1949; Bovard, 1951a; Hare, 1952).

Since deviant opinions are generally suppressed once the group norm is known, the *apparent conformity* of the members to the norms may be

---

2. When a number of articles appear to support the same generalization, the relevant details of each article are summarized in an exhibit rather than included in the text. Only those parts of the methodology and findings which are relevant to the generalization are noted in each abstract. Articles have been treated in this way so that the reader can form his own judgment about the cumulative nature of some of the research results.

increased (Wheeler & Jordan, 1929). This apparent conformity, which is based on public compliance without private acceptance, occurs when the individual is restrained from leaving the situation or when there is a threat of punishment for noncompliance. That is, where pressure is exerted on a person to express an opinion different from the one he privately affirms, there is a tendency for him to change his overt opinion (Janis & King, 1953; Kelman, 1950). Public compliance with private acceptance occurs if the individual desires to remain in the existing relationship with those who are attempting to influence him (cf. Festinger, 1953a).

In work groups or living groups, members who are highly attracted to the group either for its prestige, its productivity, or the friendship of its members will conform more to the standards of the group than will members who place a low value on these criteria (Festinger, Schachter, & Back, 1950; Back, 1951; Festinger, 1951b; Schachter, Ellerston, McBride, & Gregory, 1951; Moreno, 1953; Kelley & Shapiro, 1954; Rassmussen & Zander, 1954; Thrasher, 1954; Thibaut & Strickland, 1956; Berkowitz, 1957a; Brehm & Festinger, 1957; Siegel & Siegel, 1957; Kidd, 1958; Jackson & Saltzstein, 1958; Steiner & Peters, 1958). The attraction to the group may be increased if members first have to undergo a severe initiation (Aronson & Mills, 1959; Festinger & Aronson, 1960).

In a panel study of 2,500 ninth and tenth grade students from fifteen highschool grades, the students who were chosen as "liked" were more often conforming in their behavior than those who were disliked. The authors suggest that the high-status members may be surrounded by conformity-approving relationships (with those who like them) and deviance-disapproving relationships (with those who dislike them). These networks may be more effective for social control than the networks of low-status members which tend to be made up exclusively of deviance-disapproving relationships (Riley & Cohn, 1958). However, in some *ad hoc experimental groups,* the amount of convergence on a norm (such as the number of dots in a square) may not be correlated with the amount of liking of the members for the group (Bovard, 1953), or of the group for a particular member (Dittes & Kelley, 1956).

The relation between friendship and conformity is evident in the Relay Assembly Test Room study which was part of the Western Electric Researches (Mayo, 1933; Turner, 1933; Whitehead, 1938; Roethlisberger & Dickson, 1939). To study the effects of lighting, rest periods, and other situational factors on productivity, five female workers were placed in a special test room. Two pairs of girls had known each other before the study began. Over the five years of the experiment other friendships were formed. As time went on, high correlations between the fluctuations of the output rates of several of the girls began to appear in the data, especially between girls who were friends and sat next to each other. This happened in spite of the fact that the girls were making telephone assemblies so fast that their conformity could hardly have been the result of conscious effort. However, when the seating arrangement was changed so that friends no longer sat next to each other, the high correlations disappeared for a time, reappearing gradually as new friendships were formed.

Although this group had only five members, it does illustrate the point that behavior, in this case the output of relay assemblies, may be highly correlated with the norms of some *subgroup*, here the pair, whatever may be its relation to the norms of the group as a whole. This effect is also evident in boy gangs, which would be rated as highly cohesive subgroups of a larger society from whose norms they consciously deviate (Sherif & Cantril, 1947).

Friendship within the group increases conformity only if the norm or standard has been set by the group itself. If the standard is set by some agent outside the group such as an experimenter or other authority, then conformity to this standard may occur only when the members are not well known to each other, so that each member can assume that his opinion will not be recognized and recalled by other group members and that he will not be held accountable for his opinion (Festinger, Pepitone, & Newcomb, 1952).

The size of the majority whose opinions oppose those of the individual members is directly related to the amount of influence on his opinion (Thorndike, 1938b; Bennett, 1955; Luchins & Luchins, 1955a; Kelley & Woodruff, 1956). Subjects in some experiments are found to be more anxious as measured by their galvanic skin response when disagreeing with the majority (Smith, 1936; Hoffman, 1957; Lawson & Stagner, 1957). The influence is greatest when the subject perceives near-unanimity of opinion in the group. For example, in an experiment in which the major elements of the early Lewin experiment (1943) were combined in various ways, an attempt was made to influence groups of eight to sixteen college students to volunteer for social science experiments. Group discussion and lecture methods were each compared with control groups under different conditions of decision, public or private commitment, and degree of consensus. Neither did discussion, lecture, and control groups differ in number of volunteers, nor did public commitment increase the probability of executing the decision. However, if the *majority* of the subjects in a group decided to volunteer and *each subject perceived that the majority was in favor*, then the probability of actually acting on the decision was greater (Bennett, 1955).

A number of experiments which illustrate these phenomena have been performed by Asch (1952, 1955). In his original experiment described earlier in this chapter, the naive subject was confronted with a unanimous majority opinion which did not agree with his perceptual experience. Under this kind of group pressure one-third of the naive subjects distorted their judgments in the direction of that given by the majority.

In a variation of the same experiment the naive subject was given a "partner" who gave the true estimate of the line length. The effect of this alliance was to reduce the number of times that the subject would conform with the majority. However, if the partner changed over to the majority opinion in the middle of the experiment, the majority's influence was again felt with full force. On the other hand, if the partner began with the majority and joined the naive subject halfway through the experiment, the subject was encouraged to become independent of the majority.

In one series Asch varied the size of the opposition from one to fifteen persons. The results which are given in Fig. 8 showed a clear trend. When a subject was confronted by a single individual who contradicted his answers, he continued to answer independently and cor-

Figure 8—Percentage of Errors with Majorities of One to Fifteen Opponents (Asch, 1955)

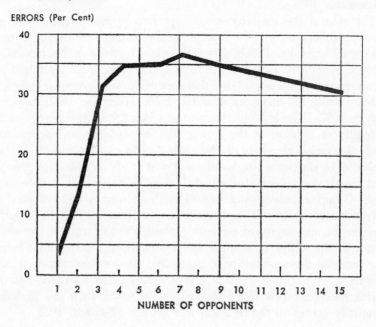

ERRORS (Per Cent)

NUMBER OF OPPONENTS

rectly on nearly all trials. When the opposition was increased to two, the pressure became substantial. Minority subjects now accepted the wrong answer 13.6 per cent of the time. Under the pressure of a majority of three, the subjects' errors jumped to 31.8 per cent. However, further increases in the size of the majority only increased the tendency to conform to majority opinion by a relatively small percentage. Asch concluded that when a naive subject was confronted with the contradictory opinion of only one or two persons he remained relatively independent. But when three persons were in opposition, the full effect of the majority was felt and no further significant differences appeared with majorities as large as fifteen.

Other experiments confirm the hypothesis that having even one person support the subject increases the number of times he will hold out against a majority (Mouton et al., 1956; Brodbeck, 1956; Hardy, 1957). The support will be especially effective if it comes from the leader or a high prestige person (Maier & Solem, 1952; Jones, Wells, & Torrey, 1958). As group size increases, there is an increase in the opportunities to form subgroup coalitions representing minority opinions (Hare, 1952).

It is the *relative* size of the majority rather than the *absolute* size which is important since in a group of two the "majority" influence may be exerted by only one person (Grosser, Polansky, & Lippitt, 1951; Fisher & Lubin, 1958). The amount of influence of this majority of one is in turn related to the characteristics of the two persons composing the group. In one experiment with groups of two the pressure to conform was higher if it came from a highly emotional partner, (i.e., one who received a high score on a test of emotional responsiveness), unless the subject himself was also highly emotional (Cervin, 1957).

Seeing one person comply with a suggestion is also enough to increase the probability of compliance (Rosenbaum & Blake, 1955; Rosenbaum, 1956). Some subjects were *asked* by an experimenter whether or not they wished to volunteer for an experiment after they had seen (1) someone asked who refused, (2) someone asked who complied, or (3) no one else asked. In the cases in which the subject had seen another person volunteer to participate in the experiment, the probability was greater that he would also volunteer. An important difference between this and other studies was that the subjects were *asked to conform*. A similar effect was observed in an experiment in which subjects tolerated a more intensive electric shock when they believed that a partner was receiving the same treatment (Seidman, Bensen, Miller, & Meeland, 1957).

The majority of the studies on the influence of group norms on indi-

vidual judgment deal only with the results of the subject's internal
struggle to reconcile his own opinion with the weight of the contrary
opinion. If one wishes to maximize conformity, then direct appeals to
change opinion and coercion must be added to the types of "pressures
toward uniformity" discussed up to this point. The influence of the direct
appeal will be discussed in a section on changing the norms, but the
effects of coercion are not treated in detail since everyday examples
of police and military action give evidence of its effectiveness.

The influence of "majority" opinion, of course, extends beyond the
small face-to-face group. In a number of early studies (Dashiell, 1935)
individuals were given information about the majority opinions of such
large groups as the student body of a high school or a college, or all
adults in general. In all of these studies there were shifts in the direction
of greater conformity with majority opinion even though the opinions
communicated to the subject were those of broad classes of people which
might not coincide with any to which the subject belonged.

The size of the majority is related to the amount of influence on a
subject only if the members of the majority have equal or higher status
than the subject. If a minority or a subgroup of equal size has high
status through power, popularity, or expert knowledge, then the minority
view will prevail. (See Exhibit 2.) Subjects who are aware of the opinions of a person with high power, such as a teacher in a classroom of
students, will limit the range of their opinions and conform more to the
opinions of the high-status person (Berenda, 1950; Ziller, 1955). A newcomer to a group may have relatively little power to influence group
opinion or activity (Philips, Shenker, & Revits, 1951), whereas the behavior of the popular child in camp is "contagious" in that it is copied
by other campers (Polansky, Lippitt, & Redl, 1950a; Lippitt, Polansky,
& Rosen, 1952).

A member who is an expert, either because he has demonstrated his
skill in the past or because he appears at the moment to have the ability
to make correct decisions, will have more influence than one who is not
as successful (Sherif, 1935; Mausner, 1953, 1954a; Luchins & Luchins,
1955b). The expert will tend to have more influence in the absence of
any apparent homogeneity of opinion in the group (Gerard, 1953) and
under conditions which allow him to defend his position with rational
arguments (Cole, 1954).

If the whole group is successful in the decision task then the whole
group becomes the "expert." In one experiment, some three-man groups
"succeeded" on a series of collaborative tasks and others "failed." When
the members of the successful groups were then asked to estimate the

number of flickers of a light during a five-second time interval, they conformed more to a fictitious "average judgment" for their group than did members of unsuccessful groups. Presumably their previous success "reinforced" their confidence in their group's opinion (Kidd & Campbell, 1955).

§ Leaders Also Conform

GROUP LEADERS who would be expected to have the greatest power to bring about a change in the group norms also find it difficult to resist their influence once the norms are established (Pellegrin, 1953). Sherif (1935) noted that, in cases where one person took the initiative in an initially leaderless group, the group norm which was then established would reflect his judgment. However, if the same member changed his individual norm after the group norm was established, he was no longer followed. Further evidence for this hypothesis is found in a study of nursery school children (Merei, 1949). Some of the children in the nursery school who were relatively docile and ineffectual in the open playroom were formed into separate groups and placed in a room by themselves with a new set of toys. In time, each new group developed its own set of rules, habits, and traditions of play. After the new set of norms had developed, a child was added to each group who had been unusually influential and powerful in the initial nursery-wide situation. The success of these old "leaders" in maintaining their dominant position in the new group varied; however, not even the most successful and adept leaders were able to abolish the new norms.

We see then that group leaders conform to the norms, but for different reasons than the followers. Where the follower may conform because he is coerced by majority opinion, the leader's opinion may be close to that of the group because he played a major part in the formation of group opinion (Jackson, 1944; Hare, 1952; Talland, 1954). Since his influence over the group is usually measured by the number of members who agree with his opinion, it is often difficult to tell whether he is the most "conforming" or the most "influential" (Simpson, 1938). On the other hand, the leader may be accorded more freedom to deviate from the norms than other members who are less secure of their status in the group (Hughes, 1946). Leaders, as well as others who appear to conform, are often the most popular members of the group (Newcomb, 1943; French, 1951). To be popular, the individual must be careful to conform only to the behavioral norms of the small group. If the individual conforms more to the norms of the larger organization, he may be classed as an over-conformist (e.g., teacher's pet) and thus be less popular than a person who is willing to deviate when it will serve the group's interest.

§ Norms of the Primary Group

SOME INDICATION of the relative influence of the norms of a small primary group, such as a family or peer group, and of a large secondary group, such as a religious or occupational group, has already been given in the discussion of the anchorage of opinions in reference groups. In general, the norms of the *primary group* are more important for the individual than those of the *secondary group*.

Disasters, such as floods and tornadoes, which affect a whole community bring out ordinarily latent conflicts between loyalties to primary and secondary groups. Under these conditions the loyalty to the primary group is usually the most demanding but, if a person is trained as a disaster worker or is responsible for the work of a large organization, he may stay by his post (Killian, 1952).

In another example, the food preferences of a sample of urban children were found to be closer to those of their small peer group than to the larger religious organization which specified certain food taboos (Rosen, 1955a).

Conflicts in group norms have been most apparent over the years in industry, where the systematic attempts on the part of management to overcome "soldiering" or "gold-bricking" among the workers go back at least to Taylor's first efforts at "Scientific Management," when he persuaded men in a steel mill to shovel coal from coal cars individually rather than in groups. Once freed from the influence of the group norm, his workers were able to earn 60 per cent more wages ($1.85 per day, rather than the prevailing $1.15) and were no more fatigued than when working under the old pace (Taylor, 1903, 1911). This same tendency for the informal group to depress the output rate has been noted in the Western Electric Researches (Mayo, 1933; Roethlisberger & Dickson, 1939; Whitehead, 1938; Homans, 1946) and in other industrial studies (Wyatt, Frost, & Stock, 1934).

Race relations is another area in which informal groups are able to enforce norms which are not in line with those leading to maximum efficiency of the larger organization. Hughes (1946) describes a plant in which three-man teams who worked closely together were nearly all members of the same ethnic group, as well as being related in other ways. When management attempted to introduce workers from a second ethnic group into these teams, the workers who were "old-timers" forced them to quit by obvious forms of pressure. However, a three-man team composed of members of the second ethnic group was able to stay on the job, although not fully accepted by the other workers. In another part of the same plant women from the second group were partially accepted by other women workers in a situation in which each worker could work independently. However, the workers in the second ethnic group did not conform to the informal production norms since they were not members of the informal cliques.

Similar findings have been duplicated in the laboratory where highly cohesive groups produce substantially less than those with lower cohesiveness when the group standard is for lower production (Schachter et al., 1951, Seashore, 1954), and over-achievers tend to modify their goals to conform to the group norm (Hilgard, Sait, & Margaret, 1940).

The norms of the primary group are not always in conflict with those of the secondary group. They may provide informal social control which is more effective than the formal control of the larger organization in fulfilling the goal of the organization (Gross, 1953). Several examples of this come from experiences in armies during World War II where soldiers in both the American Army and the German Wehrmacht derived their motivation to fight from their loyalty to their military primary group rather than from their acceptance of strategic or political goals (Dicks, 1944; Shils & Janowitz, 1948; Stouffer et al., 1949; Shils, 1950). The success in ending segregation in the American armed services during the same war has also been attributed to the fact that Negroes became co-members of primary groups with white soldiers and thus shared common loyalties (Mandelbaum, 1952).

As a follow-up of the war experience, one test of the hypothesis that primary group affiliation is related to institutional group morale was made with a sample of students from a large university. In this instance, the number and strength of the ties in a friendship group did not appear to be related to "institutional morale," as measured by the extent of the desire to remain in college if the subject was not doing well academically (Zenter, 1955).

§ Pressures on the Deviant

SINCE INDIVIDUALS GENERALLY perceive their opinions as being closer to group norms than they actually are (Travers, 1941; Wallen, 1943; Gorden, 1952), the deviant, who tends to be marginal to the group and less informed about group decisions, may not be aware of the norms or of the extent of his deviation (Newcomb, 1943; Festinger et al., 1950; Chowdhry & Newcomb, 1952). Under these conditions, his own attempts at *self-control* may not bring him close enough to the group standard to satisfy the other group members. Since the group members cannot tolerate deviation without being forced to re-examine their concept of reality (Festinger, 1954), they will make overt attempts to secure the conformity of the deviant.

Conformity can be expected to be greater when the limits of the group's tolerance and the penalties for deviation are clearly specified (Riecken, 1952). In groups which are of primary importance for the members, punishment may take violent forms. Present-day examples are found in industry where new workers are punished for rate-busting (Taylor, 1911; Hughes, 1946), or for holding unpopular ideologies.

Interaction with the deviant increases when the group first recognizes his deviancy, but falls off if he begins to conform or if other members feel that he is a lost cause (Festinger & Thibaut, 1951; Schachter, 1951; Festinger et al., 1952; Israel, 1956). (See Exhibit 3.) In one study of high-school students in clubs, the amount of pressure on the deviant was also related to the attractiveness of the club for the other members. The more highly the club was rated by its members, the greater was the pressure exerted towards the deviant (Emerson, 1954). Rejection of the deviant appears to be an almost universal phenomenon as experimental evidence from a number of different cultures has indicated (Schachter, Nuttin, De-Monchaux, Maucorps, & Osmer, 1954; Israel, 1956); however, an exception is found in a study which was made in England. There the presence of the deviate, persisting quietly and unaggressively with his own choice, seems to have reinforced the strength of other individual opinions. Other group members appeared to reason, "If he won't give up his choice, why should I?" (De Monchaux & Shimmin, 1955). In addition to punitive control of the deviant, the group exerts positive control by giving more support to the opinions of well liked members (Horowitz, Lyons, & Perlmutter, 1951).

An analysis of deviant behavior in a series of therapy groups provides a further example of some of the processes underlying deviance and conformity (Stock, Whitman, & Lieberman, 1958). In these groups, a person was seen as a deviant if he interfered with the group's solution to some focal conflict, causing the other members to re-experience the tensions and anxieties which were present before the solution was reached. When a deviant appeared, the other group members would either exert influence on the deviant to conform, reinterpret the deviant's behavior so that it no longer threatened the group's solution to the conflict, or modify the solution to include the deviant behavior. The individual who was most likely to become a deviant was the one who tried to force his habitual solutions to emotional problems on the group.

Small groups as well as large groups will reject deviant members if the group can survive more effectively without them than with them. However, members whose deviance in one area is counterbalanced by skills in another area which the group needs may be retained by the group at the expense of a change in group norms.[3]

§   Changing the Norms

SINCE NORMS ARE FORMED through group interaction, they can also be changed through group interaction (Lippitt, Watson, & Westley, 1958). Although some patterns of behavior, such as fads of dress, speech and mannerisms, change through contagion (Polansky, Lippitt, & Redl, 1950a), group discussion is generally found to result in more change than other forms of persuasion, such as lectures or directives. In one industrial plant twenty-nine supervisors were divided into three groups of nine, nine, and eleven members. The first group was given a one-and-one-half hour lecture on the technique and theory of "merit rating," and questions were answered. The second group held a discussion of the problem of rating the job rather than the man, and decided how it would solve the problem. The third group was a control group which was given no instruction. The purpose of the lecture and the discussion was to reduce the tendency of the supervisors to rate certain workers highly simply because they

---

3. Hollander (1958) suggests that each group member has a certain amount of "idiosyncrasy credit," and that a member will deviate from the group norm to the extent that he is allowed to do so.

held highly skilled jobs. A comparison of the average "before" and "after" merit ratings by individuals in each of the three groups indicated that there was some reduction of ratings in the lecture group, a greater reduction in the discussion group, and no change in the control group (Levine & Butler, 1952).

A second example of behavior change is found in the "action research" of Lewin and his colleagues during World War II. They were seeking the best way to convince housewives to buy low priority foods which they were not accustomed to eating (Lewin, 1943, 1947a, 1951; Willerman, 1943; Guthe, 1945; Radke & Klisurich, 1947). As in the industrial study mentioned above, Lewin brought together key persons or "gate-keepers" (Lewin, 1947b) who exert the major influence on some small group to which they belong. In the case of food habits, the housewife is the "gate-keeper" who exerts the major influence on the family diet. More housewives changed their behavior and attitudes about various types of foods after participating in a group discussion than after hearing a lecture on the value of eating these same new foods. Once the new group standard had been formed through group discussion, it was easier for the housewives to change their behavior to conform to the new standard.

In addition to these two examples, other studies report changes in pattern over a wide range of behavior (Cartwright, 1951): [4] community problems are solved (Williams, 1947; Jaques, 1948; Dean & Rosen, 1955), alcoholics cured (Bales, 1945), productivity raised (Kelly & Ware, 1947; Lewin, 1948, pp. 125-141; Coch & French, 1948; Jenkins, 1948; French, 1950; Lawrence & Smith, 1955), group skills improved (Bradford & French, 1948; Lippitt, 1949; Coffey, Freedman, Leary, & Ossorio, 1950), student attitudes changed (McKeachie, 1954a; Lawlor, 1955; Kipnis, 1958; Miller & Biggs, 1958; Mitnick & McGinnies, 1958), and personality patterns changed (Slavson, 1947; Burchard, Michaels, & Kotkov, 1948; Foulkes, 1950; Kotkov, 1950; Jones & Peters, 1952; Schneider, 1955; Corsini & Putzey, 1957; Kelman & Parloff, 1957; Briskin, 1958; see Exhibit 4).

When discussion groups are compared with each other in their effectiveness in bringing about change in opinion, the groups in which the opportunities for discussion are maximized are found to be the most effective. The amount of participation is usually controlled through some "democratic" leader who urges all members to take part in the discussion

---

4. In some of these cases where the small group discussion is used to change indirectly the norms of a larger group to which the members also belong, the members of the small group are only brought together for one discussion.

(Preston & Heintz, 1949; Maier & Solem, 1952; Hare, 1953). The discussion leader will tend to have more success in changing opinions if he is the "natural" group leader rather than a leader, such as an instructor, who has only joined the group for this purpose (Torrance & Mason, 1956).

There is evidence that the important element in change is not so much having a chance to discuss the problem as it is in providing an effective method for breaking down the old value system before adopting a new one (Alpert & Smith, 1949), an emotional as well as an intellectual process. As the process of change takes place, group members tend to show the greatest resistance to change just before they yield to the new set of values (Redl, 1948). An intensified version of this technique of breaking down old values was developed in China after the Korean War as part of the Chinese political re-education program (Lifton, 1956; Schein, 1956). On the other hand, if the change of "opinion" involves only learning new information without a change in commitment to a new norm, then information from an expert, teacher, or book may be as effective as group discussion (Robinson, 1941). If also the task of the group is simply to discuss the merits and demerits of an issue and not to form a new policy for handling the issue, no change in attitude may result (Timmons, 1939). Resistance to changes in norms is based on the strength of the initial patterns. The patterns are more easily maintained in the absence of all the *conditions for change* previously described.

§ Summary

GROUP MEMBERS tend to form and conform to norms. The *norms* are the group standards which set limits for present behavior, while *goals* are standards to be achieved. There is no basis for *organized* interaction until group members reach some agreement about each of these kinds of expectations. If a group member finds that his behavior deviates from the group norms, he has four choices: to conform, to change the norms, to remain a deviant, or to leave the group.

Both formal and informal social pressures are brought to bear on deviant members. The informal pressure to conform is illustrated by the experiments of Sherif and Asch which demonstrate that knowledge of the majority opinion on some issue is enough to lead some individuals to conform publicly to a judgment which differs from the one they privately hold.

The factors which influence the general tendency to conform to group opinion are found in the *object* about which the judgment is to be made, in the *subject* who is making the judgment, and in the *situation*. The subject will conform more to group opinion when the object to be judged is ambiguous, if he must make his opinion public, if the majority holding a contrary opinion is large, and if membership in the group is highly valued. A minority view will prevail if the minority has high status, through power, popularity, or expert knowledge. The group leader is an example of a high-status member whose opinions are influential in the formation of group opinion. Although he may be allowed more freedom to deviate than other group members, the leader must also conform to the norms once they are formed if he is to maintain his leadership.

Since the norms of the intimate primary group are usually more important to the individual than the norms of the larger secondary group, the norms of a large organization may be changed by first bringing about change in the smaller informal groups through group discussion.

Exhibit 1
Public Expression of Opinion

A.

Investigator: Schanck (1932).

Focus: A study of a community and its groups and institutions conceived of as behavior of individuals.

Sample: 23 inhabitants of "Elm Hollow."

Method: Attitudes expressed publicly were contrasted with private attitudes on a great number of issues.

Relevant Findings: There was a high degree of connection between the appearance of an institutional attitude (J-shaped curve in response to question) and the prevalence of a belief that other members universally hold the same attitude. There was also a high degree of connection between the appearance of the institutional attitude and a belief that other members of the community expected this institutional attitude. However, in the privacy of the subject's home, among his close friends, or at certain private gatherings, this institutional attitude was replaced by a personal one. The distribution of private opinions followed a normal curve. The responses were given more freely and were less conforming.

B.

Investigator: Gurnee (1937a).

Focus: A comparison of collective and individual judgments of facts.

Sample: Three groups ranging from eighteen to 66 in membership.

Method: Two votes were taken in each group, one privately and one publicly.

Relevant Findings: An increase of correct responses was apparent in the group vote. Doubtful subjects tended to delay their vocal or manual reactions just long enough to observe the majority opinion and then vote accordingly. It appeared that initially correct subjects would respond somewhat more quickly and vigorously than incorrect subjects. In the long run, the doubtful subjects were more often influenced in the right direction.

C.

Investigator: Thorndike (1938b).

Focus: The effect of discussion upon the correctness of group decisions where the factor of majority influences is allowed for.

Sample: Approximately 1200 students participating, 222 groups from classes in psychology, education, and sociology in several eastern colleges and universities; four to six in a group.

Method: Estimates of degree of confidence were obtained from the individuals for each of their individual judgments on a long series of problems.

Relevant Findings: Subjects holding the right answers were, on the average, slightly more sure of their judgments and had more influence on group decision. The tendency of group decisions to show a shift toward the right answer was, in part, a function of the greater confidence of subjects who originally held the right answers.

D.

Investigator: Gorden (1952).

Focus: Interaction between attitude and the definition of the situation in the expression of opinion.

Sample: A group of 24 who lived in a boarding house; age range from 21 to 37 years.

Method: Each subject first recorded his private opinion of a topic with emotional content on an attitude scale. He then answered the same type of question in a public situation where the other members of the group could easily hear him. Immediately after this response he was asked to rate the opinion of the group.

Relevant Findings: The subjects tended to conform to their conception of the group norms when giving their public opinion. The typical public opinion was a compromise between the subject's private opinion and his conception of the group opinion.

E.

Investigator: Kelley & Volkhart (1952).

Focus: The resistance to change of group-anchored attitudes.

Sample: Boy Scouts in a large New England industrial community; 145 subjects in twelve experimental groups.

Method: The subjects' attitudes about camping and woodcraft activities were studied both before and after hearing a speech which criticized the Scouts' emphasis upon these activities and recommended in their place various city activities. Half of the subjects were told that their attitude expressed in the second questionnaire would be kept absolutely confidential, while the other half were told that their attitudes would be made public and discussed.

Relevant Findings: Change of opinion was greater when there was a possibility that the opinion would be made public. When a subject thought that his opinion would remain private, the amount of change was inversely related to how highly the subject valued his membership in the group.

F.

Investigator: Bennett (1955).

Focus: Group discussion, decision, public commitment and perceived unanimity as factors in the effectiveness of "group decision."

Sample: 473 students of an introductory course in psychology assigned to 36 experimental groups ranging from three to sixteen members.

Method: Twelve groups carried on *group discussion* about their reactions to a request to volunteer as experimental subjects, twelve were given *lectures* whose content was equated with the subject matter raised by the discussion groups, and twelve *control groups* were exposed to no influence attempt. These three treatments were further subdivided into sets of three groups on the basis of their willingness to volunteer. Four sets were formed of groups in which there had been: (1) no decision, (2) anonymous decision, (3) partially anonymous decision, and (4) public decision to volunteer.

Relevant Findings: Neither did discussion, lecture, and control groups differ in the number of volunteers, nor did public commitment increase the probability of executing the decision. However, if the majority of the subjects in a group decided to volunteer and each subject perceived that the majority was in favor, then the probability of actually acting on the decision was greater.

G.

Investigator: Mouton, Blake, & Olmstead (1956).

Focus: The relationship between frequency of yielding and the disclosure of personal identity.

Sample: 48 subjects.

Method: In a variation of the Sherif and Asch experiments, a subject heard the answers of four other "subjects" (actually tape-recorded voices) through earphones prior to giving his own estimate of the number of clicks of a metronome. Half of the subjects gave their names before giving each of their judgments, while the other half maintained anonymity by responding with their report without reference to their personal identity.

Relevant Findings: When subjects identified themselves, fourteen subjects yielded three or more times, while only four subjects yielded when they remained anonymous.

H.

Investigator: Argyle (1957a).
Focus: Social pressure in public and private situations.
Sample: 27 school boys and 25 college students.
Method: Two subjects who were initially strangers were introduced and seated at opposite ends of a table with a screen between them. They were then asked to "discuss" a painting by passing notes. Each naive subject was led to believe that the other "subject" disagreed with his opinion.
Relevant Findings: When a subject was required to give his final opinion directly to the other "subject" he was more conforming than when he entered his final judgment privately on a questionnaire.

Exhibit 2
The Influence of a High-Status Minority

A.

Investigator: Polansky, Lippitt, & Redl (1950a).

Focus: An investigation of behavioral contagion in groups.

Sample: Eight boys' groups and eight girls' groups from two summer camps.

Method: Data were collected by observation, ratings of counselors, standard sociometric tests, and a special prestige and characteristic questionnaire.

Relevant Findings: The influence of a group member was related to his prestige and his perception of his position. Individuals with high-prestige ratings made more attempts at directly influencing others and also were initiators of contagion. They resisted attempts at direct influence but were more subject to contagion than persons with low prestige.

B.

Investigator: Lippitt, Polansky, & Rosen (1952).

Focus: The dynamics of power: a field study of social influence in groups of children.

Sample: Sixteen cabin groups of boys in two summer camps.

Method: A measure of attributed power was derived from scores on five variables as rated by fellow campers: (1) ability in athletics, (2) independence of adults, (3) having ideas for fun, (4) sex sophistication, (5) independence. In addition each child ranked every other child according to the latter's influence.

Relevant Findings: The average group member was more subject to the influence of a person with high power and tended to imitate him. The high-power person was usually approached by more nondirective techniques and with greater deference. He was more likely to initiate and be directive and successful in terms of influence, but personally to resist direct influence. High-power children were those with physical prowess who were liked. An individual's perception of his own power was related to rated power and to the associated pattern of behavior. The amount of a subject's social activity was related to his power; but nonsocial activity, experience in camp, and intelligence were not related to rated power.

C.

Investigator: Gerard (1953).

Focus: The effect of different dimensions of disagreement on the communication process in small groups.

Sample: 35 groups, nineteen composed entirely of women and sixteen of men. The groups ranged in size from eight to fourteen members. In all there were 393 subjects recruited from the various sections of an English class for university freshmen.

Method: Two variables were introduced by the experimeter. The degree of homogeneity of groups was varied by telling some groups that their members were alike in abilities and by advising others that there were experts in the group. The pressure toward uniformity was varied by telling half of the groups that it was necessary to agree because of the possibility of a later debate with another group. Thus four types of groups were formed: homogeneity—high pressure, homogeneity—low pressure, heterogeneity—high pressure, and heterogeneity—low pressure. Before and after the group discussion a vote was taken on several aspects of an issue which was discussed in the group.

Relevant Findings: Pressure toward uniformity was greater in homogeneous groups, whereas heterogeneous groups showed pressure to agree with experts. These pressures, in both cases, were greater under high pressure toward uniformity.

D.

Investigator: Cole (1954).

Focus: "Rational argument" and "prestige-suggestion" as factors influencing judgment.

Sample: Four groups of subjects were drawn from introductory psychology classes. There were no art majors, none had received special training in art, and none admitted to any unusual interest in the art area.

Method: Each subject twice ranked four paintings in order of artistic merit, once upon first exposure to the paintings and once after having been subjected to one of the four experimental conditions. The time interval between the two rankings was one week. A sociometric questionnaire was administered in order to facilitate the formation of the groups.

Relevant Findings: Group I: In a group with sociometric "stars" who differed from each other in their opinion of ranking of paintings there was no statistically significant change in the rankings of the paintings after a 30-minute discussion. *Group II:* The "stars" also differed in their rankings of the paintings, but they were provided by the experimenter with pseudo-rational arguments to be used in discussion in support of their position. In this group the overall significance of the changes in rankings exceeded the .01

level of confidence. *Group III*: An art professor gave her opinion of the paintings. The overall differences in reranking marking a shift to the position supported by the art professor were significant (P. < .01), but no more so than the shifts following the sessions in which peer leaders used "rational argument." *Group IV*: The experimenter led the discussion. During the last ten minutes he introduced the opinion of an art professor, but made no attempt to offer any justification for her opinion. The shifts in choice were not statistically significant.

E.

Investigator: Mausner (1954a).

Focus: The effect of one partner's success in a relevant task on the interaction of observer pairs.

Sample: 28 undergraduate students in college psychology classes.

Method: The subjects judged the lengths of one hundred lines first alone and then with a confederate of the experimenter. These confederates had demonstrated failure in a similar task with eleven of the subjects, and had demonstrated success with seventeen of them.

Relevant Findings: The subjects who worked with previously successful partners converged significantly more toward these partners in the group judgment than did the subjects who worked with previously unsuccessful partners.

F.

Investigator: Luchins & Luchins (1955b).

Focus: Previous experience with ambiguous and non-ambiguous perceptual stimuli under various social influences.

Sample: 144 college students.

Method: A series of pictures were shown in which a paid participant gave his opinion of the picture just prior to the opinion of a naïve subject. The variables were (1) degree of disparity with the right answer, and (2) support of the investigator.

Relevant Findings: A subject conformed more in the description of pictures when a single confederate gave true answers. The subject conformed to false answers when the pictures were ambiguous and when the confederate was declared right by the experimenter.

G.

Investigator: Ziller (1955).

Focus: Scales of judgment: a determinant of the accuracy of group decisions.

Sample: 36 crews of nine to thirteen members.

Method: The crews were asked to reach a group decision on the correct number of dots on a card which they were shown for fifteen seconds. Three experimental conditions were imposed: (1) preceding the group discussion a census of estimates was taken in which members were called upon according to their position in the power structure of the group; (2) preceding the group discussion a census of estimates was taken in which the voting order was counter to the power structure of the group; (3) no census preceded the group discussion.

Relevant Findings: When the census of opinions was taken in accordance with the group's power structure, rather than counter to the power structure, the scale of judgment was more uniform, mainly as a result of the contagion following the publicly stated estimates of the group leaders or power figures.

Exhibit 3
Pressures on the Deviant

A.

Investigator: Festinger & Thibaut (1951).
Focus: Interpersonal communication in small groups.
Sample: 61 groups, 24 composed entirely of women, 37 of men. The size of groups ranged from six to fourteen members.
Method: The perceived homogeneity and pressure to uniformity were varied by instructions to each group. Members were told they were or were not alike and that unanimous opinion, a plurality, or little agreement was desired, thus creating six experimental conditions. Each group discussed two problems during which the rate of communication to each member was recorded.
Relevant Findings: When there was a range of opinion in the group, communications tended to be directed towards those members whose opinions were at the extreme of the range. Under high pressure toward uniformity and a perception of homogeneous group composition, there was an increased tendency to communicate to these extreme opinions. High pressure toward uniformity and perception of the group as homogeneous were accompanied by greater change toward uniformity.

B.

Investigator: Schachter (1951).
Focus: Deviation, rejection, and communication.
Sample: 32 clubs of four types (eight of each) each with from five to seven members and three paid participants who were perceived as fellow clubmembers.
Method: Four types of clubs, high cohesive-high relevance, high cohesive-low relevance, low cohesive-high relevance, low cohesive-low relevance, were created. In order to create high cohesiveness, members were assigned to the clubs of their choice, and to create high relevance, members were given problems to discuss in line with the purpose of the club. On the issue to be discussed the paid participants took the role of modal, slider (first deviate then move toward norm), and deviate. The recipients of all communications were recorded.
Relevant Findings: Communications to the deviate increased continuously throughout the meeting with the exception of the high cohesive-high relevance clubs where a peak of communication was reached and a gradual decline

followed. In all conditions, communications to the slider decreased during the meeting as the slider shifted from a deviate to a modal position.

C.

Investigator: Festinger, Gerard, Hymovitch, Kelley, & Raven (1952).
Focus: The influence process in the presence of extreme deviates.
Sample: 443 college undergraduates in 64 experimental groups, forty male and 24 female.
Method: After giving their opinions on a human relations case, subjects were led to believe that their opinions in some cases conformed to and in other cases deviated from the modal group opinion. The subjects were then allowed to "discuss" the case by writing notes to each other.
Relevant Findings: The subjects who appeared to conform to the modal opinion directed an average of forty words to other subjects who appeared to be three steps removed from their opinion, eighteen words to those who appeared one step removed, and four words to those who appeared to hold opinions the same as their own.

D.

Investigator: Emerson (1954).
Focus: Deviation and rejection.
Sample: High school students who had volunteered to join nine "case-study" clubs and nine "editorial clubs."
Method: A replication of the Schachter (1951) experiment.
Relevant Findings: The deviant was rejected more in the highly cohesive groups. The number of communications addressed to the deviant increased throughout the experiment. (The authors suggest that length of communication should also be considered.)

E.

Investigator: Israel (1956).
Focus: Rejection of deviants.
Sample: 234 Swedish school boys in 29 groups.
Method: Boys who had joined model airplane "clubs" were asked to reach a group choice of a model plane to build. One subject was privately instructed to hold out for a deviant choice.
Relevant Findings: The deviant was less popular after the experiment on two sociometric criteria: "working-together" and "presidential ballot." However, only the "presidential ballot" gave statistically significant results.

Exhibit 4
Changing Group Behavior through Discussion

A.

Investigator: Bales (1945).
Focus: Social therapy for a social disorder—compulsive drinking.
Sample: Members of Alcoholics Anonymous.
Method: Observation at group meetings.
Relevant Findings: As a member of a concrete group with which an individual was closely identified and in which he had a particular role, the ideas and desired behavior patterns were thoroughly integrated with goals which could only be activated and satisfied in social context. Learning in this context was actively pursued, because the knowledge had an immediate relevance to the most pressing practical problems of the individual. The stability of learning was insured through constant reaffirmation in overt action with group sanction and approval. The principle of self-help through the helping of others was used to facilitate the final degree of identification with the new patterns.

B.

Investigator: Coch & French (1948).
Focus: Overcoming resistance to change.
Sample: Four groups of factory workers ranging in number from seven to fourteen, roughly equivalent with respect to (1) the efficiency ratings of the groups before transfer, (2) the degree of change involved in the transfer, and (3) the amount of "we-feeling" observed in the groups.
Method: Three procedures were used in notifying and acclimatizing the groups to proposed changes in their job. The first variation (Experimental Group I) involved the participation of representatives of the workers in designing the changes to be made in the jobs. The second variation consisted of total participation by all members of the group in designing the changes (Experimental Groups II and III). In a control group the members were merely informed of the change, and the new method was explained. Two and one-half months later the control group was reassembled and was also given the "total participation" treatment before transfer to a new job.
Relevant Findings: Experimental Group I showed an unusually good learning curve. At the end of fourteen days it had attained the set standard. During this period its members were generally co-operative and permissive among themselves and with their supervisors. No one quit the job. Experi-

mental Groups II and III recovered faster than Group I, attaining a level
14 per cent above the prescribed norm. Their members worked well with
their supervisors, no aggression was noted, and no one quit. The control
group improved little beyond its early efficiency ratings and did not attain
the prescribed standard. There was much resistance and aggression toward
the management standard and 17 per cent quit during the first forty days.
However, when the "total participation" technique was used with this same
group on a new transfer two and one-half months later, it rapidly achieved
and exceeded the standard of production.

C.

Investigator: McKeachie (1954a).
Focus: Individual conformity to attitudes of classroom groups.
Sample: Six sections of from 25 to 35 undergraduate students of a college
psychology course.
Method: To produce differences in cohesiveness between the groups the
instructors agreed that their techniques should differ in: (1) opportunity of
class members to know other members of the class, (2) amount of direct
interaction between class members, (3) number of decisions which the class
would be allowed to make about its own goals and procedures. Decisions were
made either by group discussion and vote or by a lecture by the instructor
giving both sides of the argument followed by a vote.
Relevant Findings: Attitude changes were correlated with changes of
group norms. Conformity between individuals' attitudes and their perception
of the group norm was less in group-centered classes, although members'
liking for the group was greater than in leader-centered classes. Group
decision produced more conformity between individuals' attitudes and the
group norm, but less between attitudes and the perceived group norm.

D.

Investigator: Lawrence & Smith (1955).
Focus: Group decision and employee participation.
Sample: Two pairs of five- and six-man groups working in a factory.
Method: Two groups engaged only in discussion over a five-week period,
while two others discussed and set their own group-production goals.
Relevant Findings: Although both groups showed an increase in average
individual production, it was found that those groups setting their own goals
showed significantly greater increases.

E.

Investigator: Kellman & Parloff (1957).

Focus: Interrelations among three criteria of improvement in group therapy.

Sample: Fifteen neurotic patients from three therapy groups.

Method: Several measures were used for each of three criteria of improvement: comfort, effectiveness, and self-awareness.

Relevant Findings: A significant change after group therapy was found on some measures but not on others. The authors suggest that both the criterion and the measure should be carefully specified.

F.

Investigator: Mitnick & McGinnies (1958).

Focus: Influencing ethnocentrism in small discussion groups through a film communication.

Sample: Eighteen nine-man groups of highschool students who were high, medium, and low on an ethnocentrism scale.

Method: Members of some groups saw a film intended to influence ethnocentrism, others saw the film and discussed it afterwards, while others did nothing. Members who had seen the film, or seen the film and discussed it were then tested on facts and attitude change. All subjects were tested on the ethnocentrism scale one month later. The information test was also readministered to the experimental groups.

Relevant Findings: Members of both types of experimental groups showed a significant reduction in ethnocentrism immediately after the experiment, however there was less regression one month later for the discussion groups. Subjects who were initially high on ethnocentrism learned less from the film. The most active participants in the discussions learned most.

3

INTERACTION
AND DECISION
PROCESS

To PROVIDE SOME BACKGROUND in the methodology of research on social interaction, some examples of category systems which are in current use will be discussed in this chapter. These category systems are used to analyze the process of interaction as it occurs in a small discussion group during a single meeting and as it changes from meeting to meeting. The major emphasis in research has been on the problem the group faces in establishing an equilibrium between the time spent on the task and the time spent on the social-emotional problems of maintaining the group structure. The other two types of problems which were referred to in Chapter One, namely, the progress toward each individual's private goal, and the solution of each individual's social-emotional problems have not been elaborated in the literature.

Although there has been some attempt to study the characteristic modes of interaction *between* small groups of persons, the primary focus in the social-psychological literature has been on *within-group* or *between-person* interaction. The term "interaction" refers to all words, symbols, and gestures with which persons respond to each other; however, in actual research only verbal behavior is usually recorded, or at the most, overt or easily identifiable attempts of one person to communicate with another. Communication is important for humans because it enables two or more persons to maintain simultaneous orientation towards each other and towards other objects (Newcomb, 1953a).

Every word or gesture carries with it at least two kinds of information: task and social-emotional. First, it has implications for the task of the group (or the individual), that is, it affects the decision-making process. Second, it has implications for the relative evaluation of members as well as the emotional attachments among members. Although these two types of implications of any individual act are always present, and it is difficult to talk about one without talking about the other, the *decision-making* aspect of interaction will be emphasized in this chapter, and interaction in relation to the development of a differentiated internal structure in Chapter Five.

In the final pages of this chapter, the first step in the problem-solving process, *observation*, will be considered in some detail. Here, however, the focus will only be on the observations made of the self and of others in the course of social interaction. This aspect of observation has been called *social perception*.

§ Category Systems

BEFORE ONE IS ABLE to indicate the implications of a particular act for the task and social-emotional life of the group, it is necessary to develop a category system or method of content analysis which allows one to break the interaction process into small units and to assign each unit to one of the categories. The number of different kinds of acts included in the category system depends on the theoretical orientation of the observer. Some category systems divide all interaction into two types, action and silence (Chapple, 1942), some use more than one hundred types (Ruesch & Prestwood, 1950). Some systems record only one type of verbal content, such as personal pronouns (Conrad & Conrad, 1956), others are used to rate words, gestures, and any other form of bodily activity which indicates the individual's mental state (Freedman, Leary, Ossorio, & Coffey, 1951).[1]

§ Reliability

A RECURRING PROBLEM in the use of category systems is that of interobserver reliability. Since most of the systems attempt to describe all behavior, an observer's decision to place an act in one of several categories is not an independent event. That is, if there are three categories in a system and one decides to call an act *category 1*, then it cannot also be *category 2* or *3*. Therefore, a *high* frequency of acts in *category 1* results automatically in *low* frequencies in the other two categories, making it difficult to apply statistical tests.[2]

Despite these difficulties, the reliability of trained observer judgments is usually sufficient to encourage the use of interaction categories. In one report on consistency, judgments of an individual's interpersonal behavior were made on the basis of interaction in three-man groups during a fifteen-minute discussion. The membership of the three-man groups was reconstituted between sessions, the observers were different, and the task was different. In this experiment the reliability in several categories was substantial (Blake, Mouton, & Fruchter, 1954).

§ Scoring the Unit Act

THE CATEGORY SYSTEM developed by Bales (1950) is an example of the most common method of coding interaction. Bales takes as his unit act a bit of behavior (usually verbal) which can provide enough of a stimulus to elicit a meaningful response from another person. In practice, this is usually a sentence. Each sentence or comparable act is given only one score to indicate the element of task behavior or social-emotional behavior which appears to the observer to dominate the act. For example, if a group member says "Let us all get back to work" and laughs as he finishes his remark, his statement would be scored as *giving a*

---

1. A more complete discussion of the varieties of category systems and of the problems involved in their use appears in the Appendix.

2. A method of analysis for estimating reliability has been developed by Schutz (1952a).

suggestion and the laughter which occurs after the statement is completed would be given a separate score as *showing tension* or *tension release*, depending upon the nature of the laugh. The fact that the subject may laugh while he is making the suggestion would not be scored, since the observer is trained to record only the dominant characteristics of the act.

In contrast to Bales' approach, the category system suggested by Bion (1948-1952) and developed by Thelen (Thelen, Stock, et al., 1954; Thelen, 1956; Stock & Thelen, 1958), is based on the assumption that every statement contains some element of work as well as some element of emotion. The observer's job is to score the amount of each in each act. In the Bion-Thelen formulation, work is scored at four levels ranging from very little help to remarks which integrate the present group activity with universal goals. The basic emotional states in a group are seen as fight or flight, pairing among group members, and dependency on the leader. Using the Bion-Thelen category system, the statement, "Let us all get back to work," accompanied by laughter, would be scored as *work at level three* and *flight*, if the laughter seemed to indicate that the subject was a bit hesitant about his suggestion and was laughing to indicate that it should not be taken too seriously or that he was about to withdraw it.

Both the Bion-Thelen and the Bales categories crosscut the set of content areas suggested in Chapter One in different ways. In the Bion-Thelen system the work category is equivalent to the task area, while dependency represents an aspect of control and pairing an aspect of affection. The fight or flight category is a mixture of hostility and withdrawal from the communication network. Within the Bales system of twelve categories the six categories representing asking for and giving suggestions, opinions, and information appear to be primarily in the task area, while showing solidarity and antagonism are in the social-emotional area. Agreeing and disagreeing appear to be on the border between tasks and social-emotional behavior. Showing tension and tension release seem to refer more to personal rather than interpersonal behavior.

§ Bales Categories for Interaction Process Analysis

SINCE THE CATEGORIES for interaction process analysis developed by Bales have been used by a number of investigators in research on behavior in small groups, his system will be treated in some detail at this point. In this system each act is scored in one of twelve categories. These categories are listed in Table 2 together with the interaction profiles for a sample of laboratory groups (Talland, 1955) and psychiatric interviews (Hare, Waxler, Saslow, & Matarazzo, 1960). The profiles represent average percentages of the total number of acts for a single group meeting which fall into each of the twelve categories.

Table 2—Interaction Profiles for Laboratory Groups and Psychiatric Interviews

	PERCENTAGE OF ACTS	
Category	Laboratory Groups	Standardized Psychiatric Interview
1. Shows Solidarity: jokes, raises other's status, gives help, reward	3.4	0.1
2. Shows Tension Release: laughs, shows satisfaction	6.0	0.5
3. Shows Agreement: passive acceptance, understands, concurs, complies	16.5	0.9
4. Gives Suggestion: direction, implying autonomy for other	8.0	0.5
5. Gives Opinion: evaluation, analysis, expresses feeling, wish	30.1	16.7
6. Gives Information: orientation repeats, clarifies, confirms	17.9	56.9
7. Asks for Information: orientation, repetition, confirmation	3.5	12.9
8. Asks for Opinion: evaluation, analysis, expression of feeling	2.4	2.8
9. Asks for Suggestion: direction, possible ways of action	1.1	0.0
10. Shows Disagreement: passive rejection, formality, witholds help	7.8	0.6
11. Shows Tension: asks for help, withdraws "out of field"	2.7	6.1
12. Shows Antagonism: deflates other's status; defends or asserts self	0.7	1.8

In Table 2 the first three categories, "shows solidarity," "shows tension release," and "shows agreement," are *positive reactions* which, coupled with the three *negative reactions*, "shows disagreement," "shows tension," and "shows antagonism," constitute *social-emotional* behavior. The six categories describing *task* behavior also are grouped in sets of three. "Gives suggestion," "gives opinion," and "gives information" are *problem-solving attempts*, and "asks for information," "asks for opinion," and "asks for suggestion" are *questions.*

The principal categories of activity in the laboratory discussion groups in this sample are giving opinion and giving information, which account for approximately 48 per cent of the acts. In the psychiatric interview these same two categories account for 74 per cent of the acts. These differences in interaction pattern reflect the difference in the group task. The laboratory groups must discuss a human-relations problem and reach a solution within forty minutes. This is a task which requires a wider range of behavior than the psychiatric interview in which the primary purpose is to encourage the patient to give personal information which can be evaluated by the psychiatrist.

§ Action and Reaction

So FAR, only the total interaction profile of a group has been considered. However, the central concern in the observation of interaction is more often the typical patterns of action and reaction which constitute the group process. These act-to-act sequences change over the period of a meeting and over a series of meetings. In generalizing from these patterns, the reader should keep in mind the fact that most of the observations of interaction are made on initially leaderless groups of college students, usually males, who do not know each other before the experiment begins and are brought together for the first time in the laboratory to solve a series of human-relations or construction problems. . . . Any generalizations emerging from these experiments would therefore be more applicable to *ad hoc* committees composed of persons of equal social rank than to groups, such as the family, which have been organized for a long period of time and contain a definite structure. In general, each of the factors discussed in Part Two of the book, such as personalities of members, group size, or task, may modify the central tendencies of interaction in some important respect. Unless otherwise noted, the setting for the interaction described is usually the small-task-oriented group without a formal leader.

An analysis of the typical actions and reactions in a small discussion group (Bales, 1950, 1954, 1955), as given in Fig. 9, shows that about half (56 per cent) of the acts during a group session are problem-solving attempts, whereas the remaining 44 per cent are distributed among positive reactions, negative reactions, and questions. In this two-sided process,

Figure 9—Interaction Profile for a Small Discussion Group
        [This profile is the same one that appeared in Table 2, this time presented in graphical form. The figure is taken from Bales (1955).]

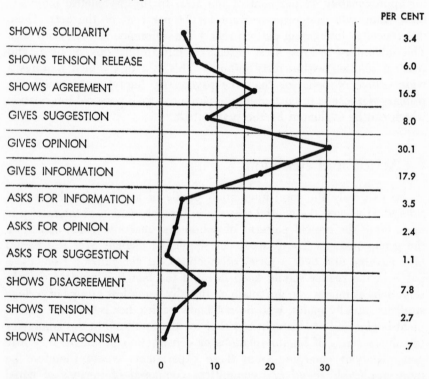

	PER CENT
SHOWS SOLIDARITY	3.4
SHOWS TENSION RELEASE	6.0
SHOWS AGREEMENT	16.5
GIVES SUGGESTION	8.0
GIVES OPINION	30.1
GIVES INFORMATION	17.9
ASKS FOR INFORMATION	3.5
ASKS FOR OPINION	2.4
ASKS FOR SUGGESTION	1.1
SHOWS DISAGREEMENT	7.8
SHOWS TENSION	2.7
SHOWS ANTAGONISM	.7

0   10   20   30

the reactions act as a constant feedback on the acceptability of the problem-solving attempts. A typical interchange between two group members is illustrated by the following example:

MEMBER 1: "I wonder if we have the same facts about the problem? (*Asks for opinion.*) Perhaps we should take some time at the beginning to find out." (*Gives suggestion.*)

MEMBER 2: "Yes. (*Shows agreement.*) We may be able to fill in some gaps in our information. (*Gives opinion.*) Let's go around the table and each tell what the report said in his case." (*Gives suggestion.*) (Bales, 1955.)

As in this example, a speaker's first remark is likely to be a reaction, and if he continues speaking, the probability is very high that his second act will be a problem-solving attempt. Figure 10 sums up this finding

Figure 10—A Comparison of a Speaker's First Act with His Following Act (Bales, 1955)

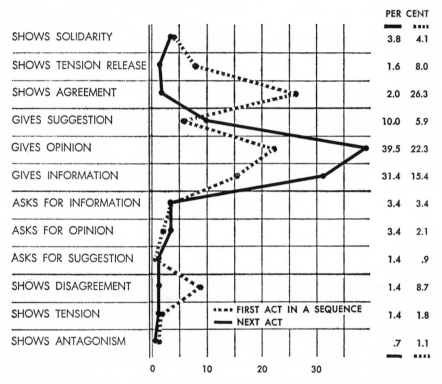

	PER CENT	
	▬▬	▸▪▪▪
SHOWS SOLIDARITY	3.8	4.1
SHOWS TENSION RELEASE	1.6	8.0
SHOWS AGREEMENT	2.0	26.3
GIVES SUGGESTION	10.0	5.9
GIVES OPINION	39.5	22.3
GIVES INFORMATION	31.4	15.4
ASKS FOR INFORMATION	3.4	3.4
ASKS FOR OPINION	3.4	2.1
ASKS FOR SUGGESTION	1.4	.9
SHOWS DISAGREEMENT	1.4	8.7
SHOWS TENSION	1.4	1.8
SHOWS ANTAGONISM	.7	1.1

▪▪▪▪ FIRST ACT IN A SEQUENCE
▬▬ NEXT ACT

0   10   20   30

statistically: about 50 per cent of the time a member's first remark in a series is a reaction; if he continues, about 80 per cent of the succeeding comments or other offerings are classed as attempts to solve the problem.

There are about twice as many positive as negative reactions. This indicates that the members share a common definition of the situation and can make problem-solving attempts which will be in line with the group's goals most of the time.

Although an action is usually followed immediately by the "appropriate" reaction, the reaction may be stored (remembered) and appear at a later time in its original or perhaps a disguised form. This delayed reaction would be especially evident if the interaction was interrupted either through outside forces or because the individual felt that his reaction would be inadvisable at that time. The effect of the interruption by an outside force is evident in a communication experiment in which, following an act of hostility on the part of a paid participant, some subjects were allowed to communicate back to him immediately whereas others were not. Subjects who were allowed to react immediately showed more postexperimental friendliness to the hostile paid participant than those who were forced to store their negative feelings until the opportunity for reaction arose (Thibaut & Coules, 1952).

§   Group Differences in
    Task and
    Social-emotional
    Activity

IN GROUPS of long standing, the leadership style, the social class or personalities of the members, or other factors, may produce characteristic differences between groups in their patterns of task and social-emotional activity. "Democratic" leaders who act positively toward their group members and set a standard for cooperative activity between members tend to receive positive reactions, while leaders who are "authoritarian" provoke negative reactions and intermember hostility (Lewin, Lippitt, & White, 1939).

An example of the influence of social class is found in a study of ten adolescent clubs, five with members from the lower class and five with members from the middle class. The lower class members were more aggressive with each other and collaborated more with the adult leader, whereas the middle class members directed more collaborative and aggressive acts to the club president who was a peer (Maas, 1954b).

Group differences which result from the personalities of members are best illustrated by studies which contrast groups of mental patients where extremes of activity in the task area (compulsiveness) and the social-emotional area (hysteria) as well as extremes of inactivity (withdrawal) have been observed (Rowland, 1938; Chapple & Lindemann, 1942; Roberts & Strodtbeck, 1953). Even with relatively "normal" college students, pairs of subjects whose common psycho-sexual disturbance has been aroused by reading materials, and who *project* as a defense mechanism, tend to perceive their interaction as more negative than pairs of subjects who utilize other defenses, are less aroused, or use differing defenses (Cohen, 1956).

It is also possible to alter the characteristic task or social-emotional activity by stimulating one category of act. For this purpose, less global methods than changing the leadership style or the group composition can be used. For example, subjects in paired interaction increased their rate of giving opinion when the experimenter reinforced their opinions by repetition or agreement (Verplanck, 1955).

In addition to differences in content of interaction between groups, norms are also established within groups which tend to regulate the frequency and duration of member interaction (Talland, 1957a) and the channels through which communications are allowed to travel.

The principal content category associated with a high interaction rate varies from group to group and over time within the same group depending upon the problem the group faces at the moment. In some types of groups a high interaction rate is associated with the expression of both positive and negative feeling in the area of affection (Blake, 1953; Festinger & Hutte, 1954; Homans, 1954), in other groups a high interaction rate is associated with control as members try to bring a deviant into line (Festinger et al., 1952), and in still other groups a high interaction rate is associated with leadership and task behavior (Stephan & Mishler, 1952).

Further differences between groups in task and social-emotional activity are described in Part Two, where these and other examples are given in more detail.

§ Individual Interaction Characteristics

PERHAPS THE MOST CONSISTENT FINDING in all of the research on social interaction is that *some people talk more than others*. The person who initiates the most action tends to receive more than anyone else and to address more of his remarks to the group as a whole than to specific individuals (Bales, 1951; Bales, Strodtbeck, Mills, & Roseborough, 1951; Keller, 1951; Stephan & Mishler, 1952). In one experiment, low ranking persons sent more messages up the line to high-status persons even when the high-status persons were not initiating most of the activity (Kelley, 1951).

Since relative rate and direction of interaction are such basic dimensions of individual and group activity, they are perhaps the first things to be affected by any changes in the group. As the size of the group is increased from three to twelve members, the differences between the relative interaction rates of members tend to disappear, while the difference between the leader and the average member becomes more apparent (Bales et al., 1951; Stephan, 1952; Stephan & Mishler, 1952). The rate of interaction for any one member is inversely related to the rates of the other members composing the group (Borgatta & Bales, 1953b) and directly related to the freedom to participate allowed by the communication net (Bavelas, 1950). An individual's communication rate can be increased by removing the high interactors from the group (Stephan & Mishler, 1952), by having the leader encourage equal participation (Bovard, 1951a), or by placing him in a favorable position in the communication net, which may mean simply having him sit at the head of the table (Strodtbeck & Hook, 1956).

Previous experience and training can also affect the participation rate of the group member. In a therapeutic setting, therapists who had been psychoanalyzed were found to be more active with their patients than therapists who had not been psychoanalyzed (Strupp, 1955c).

Not only the form of an individual's interaction pattern, but also the content is predetermined in part by his role and his personality. Again to take an example from the therapeutic interview, therapists who had been trained to be "nondirective" were found to "reflect" more of the patient's statements and to show less inclination to set therapeutic goals than analytically oriented therapists (Strupp, 1955a; Strupp, 1958). In a similar comparison of social workers with psychiatrists, the social workers were found to reassure the patients more whereas inexperienced psychiatrists explored more of the patient's problems but did not interpret as much. However, in both professions differences in content which were related to level of training were greater than differences between professions (Strupp, 1955b). The inexperienced therapists who were less certain of their role tended to be more limited in their range of behavior.

Some indication of the effect of personality type on interaction content is evident in a study in which 75 college students judged the amount of aggression in the "tone of voice" of a sample of thirty Air Corps officers who had either high or low blood pressure and related personality characteristics. The judges found that aggression was more apparent in the tone of voice of the officers with high blood pressure (Starkweather, 1956).

In another study of the content of a problem-solving discussion held by six pairs of men, the subjects judged to be "emotionally mature" made more statements which had mutual satisfaction as their aim, while the immature subjects made more statements for self-gratification (Lichtenberg, 1955). Further examples of differences in individual interaction characteristics which are associated with different group roles and different personality types are given in Chapters Four and Six.

§　Phase Movement

THE BALANCE between task and social-emotional activity appears over the course of a whole meeting. However, when problem-solving discussion meetings are divided into three time-periods, the predominant type of activity shifts from one phase to another in a manner which reflects the stages in the group's progress toward a decision (Bales & Strodtbeck, 1950; Plank, 1951; Bales, 1952; Landsberger, 1955b). These shifts are illustrated in Fig. 11. The rate of acts of information decreases

Figure 11—Phase Movements in Group Progress toward a Decision (Bales, 1955)

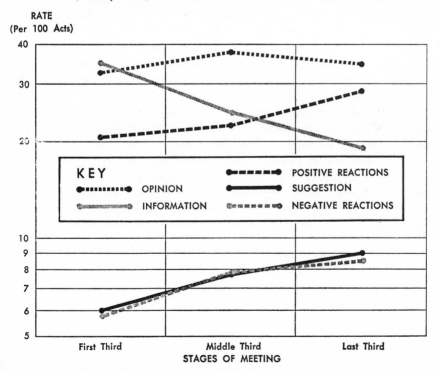

steadily from initial to final phase, while the rate of acts of suggestion rises. Acts of opinion increase in the middle phase and then fall off again. Both positive and negative reactions increase in rate from the initial to the final phase, with the positive reactions increasing more rapidly in the final phase. In phase one, the group members are collecting information, in phase two, evaluating the information, and in phase three, pressing for a decision with a concomitant increase in support of some members and rejection of others.

The increase in positive and negative reactions may be connected mainly with the social-emotional problems of the group process. Since the ratio of negative to positive reactions tends to be higher in response to suggestions than to factual statements, the *decision point* is the critical bottleneck in the process. Once the decision point has been passed, the rates of negative reaction usually fall off and the rates of positive reaction rise sharply. Joking and laughter, indicating solidarity and tension release, become more frequent. With the problems of the task settled for the time being by the decision, the group apparently turns its attention to the emotional states of the individuals and their social relationships.

The tendency of negative reactions to increase from phase to phase also appears when subjects react negatively to the attempts of leaders or counselors to control future action (Lippitt, 1940; Rogers, 1941). Evidence that the nature and duration of the phases which may appear are directly related to the task of the group is found in a study of therapy groups in which the Bales categories for interaction process analysis were used (Talland, 1955). In these groups, the phases described above did not appear, nor was there any tendency to establish equilibrium, since the group did not have to reach a decision and the therapist's job was to keep the level of emotional involvement sufficiently high so that the patients would talk about their problems.

In an initially leaderless group, the persons who play the roles of leaders and followers may change about as the group moves from one phase to another, since some persons have greater skill at one type of activity, or find the emotional climate which accompanies a particular phase more compatible with their personality.

§ Meeting to Meeting Trends

IN ADDITION to shifts or phase movements in activity within a single meeting, patterns of activity in groups also change from meeting to meeting.[3] In a series of four meetings, members of initially leaderless groups gradually spent less time in task behavior and more time in positive social-emotional behavior as the series progressed from the first to last meeting. Negative social-emotional behavior rose briefly in the second meeting during the "status struggle" in which the hierarchy was established (Heinicke & Bales, 1953). The tendency for groups to shift from task groups to friendship groups is so strong that some groups attempt to persist on a friendship basis long after the task which originally brought them together is completed. In Table 3, these tendencies in *ad hoc* groups with *high* status consensus over four meetings are indicated by decreasing rates of activity in the task-oriented categories (giving information, opinion, and suggestion) and rising rates in the social-emotional categories. Negative reactions are low in the first meeting, show a sharp rise during the second, and then drop off again.

There are two different trends within the area of positive reactions. Overt showing of agreement shows a steady downward trend, which is counteracted by a sharp rise in showing solidarity and tension release through joking and laughing, especially in the final session. In other words, there is a marked shift from the more neutral and tentative task-oriented agreement to the more emotional positive reactions as the meetings progress.

Although groups with *low* consensus on the relative status of members go through a similar period of social-emotional conflict, in general the trends within each of the categories are not as sharply focused as they are in the *high* status consensus groups. As a result of their continued attention to "social-emotional" problems, the low status consensus groups tend to be less efficient and less satisfied with their group and with their group's solution to the problem. Phase movements similar to those in the high status consensus groups have also been noted in discussion groups over a longer series of meetings (Theodorson, 1953).

If the members of the group have the experience of taking part in a series of meetings, each with a different set of group members, then the effect is the same as if the group is meeting for the first time. Although

3. A theory of group development is given by Bennis and Shepard (1956) and Shepard and Bennis (1956).

Table 3—Mean Percentage of Group Interaction in Various Categories and Combinations of Categories in Successive Sessions for Groups with High Status Consensus *

CATEGORIES	WEEKLY SESSIONS				LEVEL OF SIGNIFICANCE FOR TOTAL TREND
	1	2	3	4	
A. Positive Reactions					
1 + 2 Shows Solidarity & Tension Release	6.1	7.4	15.2	18.4	‡
3 Shows Agreement	17.7	16.4	14.7	12.6	
B. Attempted Answers					
4 Gives Suggestion	9.0	10.2	9.1	9.0	
5 Gives Opinion	27.2	27.4	23.7	23.3	
6 Gives Information	16.8	12.1	13.8	12.6	
C. Questions					
7 + 8 + 9 Asks for Information, Opinion, & Suggestion	4.2	3.4	2.9	3.5	
D. Negative Reactions					
10 Shows Disagreement	12.8	17.8	11.4	11.2	
11 Shows Tension	.18	.49	.45	.47	
12 Shows Antagonism	.06	.20	.01	.44	
Subtotals for Four Classes of Categories					
A. Positive Reactions	24.6	24.2 †	30.3	31.1	
B. Attempted Answers	53.9	50.2	47.6	45.4	
C. Questions	4.2	3.4	2.9	3.5	
D. Negative Reactions	13.3	18.7	11.9	12.6	
A — D (Positive reactions minus negative reactions)	10.5 †	2.7 ‡	16.2	17.5	†

* Heinicke & Bales, 1953. (Note: Volumes 1 through 18 of *Sociometry* were edited by J. L. Moreno and published by Beacon House, Inc.)
† .05 level of significance
‡ .01 level of significance
Note: A dagger placed between two numbers indicates that the difference is significant.

the task and other aspects of the situation remain the same, the individuals must take time to get to know the other group members at the beginning of each meeting. Group structure is not given a chance to develop and the status struggle usually reflected in the interaction pattern of the second meeting does not take place (Borgatta & Bales, 1953a).

§ Phase Movement and Trends in Psychotherapy

A MODIFICATION of the Bales categories was used in an analysis of communication between psychotherapists and their patients (Lennard, Bernstein, Hendin, & Palmore, 1960). This study provides another example of phase movement within a session and trends between sessions. Tape recordings were made of eight therapies (four therapists with two patients each) for a period of eight months. One hundred and twenty of the five hundred recorded sessions were then subjected to content analysis. Previous to and concurrent with the therapy each patient and therapist responded to eight questionnaires and interviews. For the content analysis, six sets of categories were used covering type of content, grammatical form, affective content, interaction process, and role-system reference.

A major theme throughout the study was the analysis of the process through which the patient learns his patient role with the possibility of later transferring what he has learned about role patterns in therapy to other significant role relationships. The "socialization" of the patient in his role appears to be more of a conscious effort at the beginning of the therapy. As therapy progresses the amount of discussion about therapy itself and about the reciprocal therapist-patient roles tends to decrease. There is a similar decrease within each session. At the same time, there is an increase in the amount of communication about affect as the patient learns to put his thoughts and feelings into words. The therapist and patient establish rather stable "norms" for their interaction rate with the patient talking most of the time. However, in a given hour, if the patient talks less, the therapist will talk more. When patient and therapist differ initially in their expectations about the activity of the therapist, the therapist spends more time in the socialization process.

§ The Equilibrium Problem

ONE WAY of looking at the status struggle in laboratory groups that takes place in the second session is to note that while group members are in this type of social-emotional activity they have less time and energy available for the task. In industry, for example, the most productive teams were found to spend less time on "within" team interaction (Horsfall & Arensberg, 1949). In another study, when carpenters and bricklayers who were accustomed to being assigned to work teams each day by their foremen were given a chance to choose the men they would prefer to work with, they showed marked differences in performance when compared with teams composed in the usual way (Van Zelst, 1952). In the groups of buddies, job satisfaction increased, labor and material costs dropped, and labor turnover decreased practically to zero. These effects presumably occurred because the "buddies" did not have to spend as much time in the solution of status problems.

This tendency of the group to swing back and forth between attempts to complete the task and attempts to maintain the group and to satisfy the needs of its members has been identified by Bales as the *equilibrium problem* (Bales, 1953). Pendulum-like swings in activity occur as members become more absorbed in the task and neglect individual member needs and then lose sight of the task as they turn their attention to group solidarity. In an extreme case, members of three-man groups who were drugged by an "anxiety-reducing medication" (a mixture of Seconal and Benzedrine) showed little anxiety, were elated, unassertive, and happy but carried out little task-related behavior (Lanzetta, Wendt, Langham, & Haefner, 1956).

As we have noted in the industrial studies, the time spent on the task can be increased by selecting members who have similar feelings concerning the criteria for establishing group structure and as a result spend less time on the "status struggle." Since persons will choose as friends others with a similar personality type or basic orientation (Hare & Hare, 1948), the sociometric test in which individuals are asked to choose others that they would like as teammates is in a sense an indirect way of selecting compatible personality types. If one knew enough about the types of personalities which would get along together, one could eliminate the question of liking and simply put persons of appropriate types in the same group with the expectation that productivity would increase. This has been done successfully with naval recruits and college students, at least on the personality dimension of *affection* or "personalness" (Schutz, 1958a). When subjects who preferred close intimate relations with others (as a personality characteristic) were placed in a group and given a series of tasks, they were more productive than mixed groups composed of some subjects who liked close intimate relations and some who wanted to keep others at a distance.

The problem of equilibrium between task and social-emotional categories is, however, one of many factors related to group productivity. A more detailed discussion of individual and group performance characteristics appears in Part Three.

§ The Initial Phase of
the Act

THE REMAINING PAGES of this chapter give a more detailed analysis of research on the initial phase of the social act. This includes a description of the individual's *perceptions* of himself and others, and the part these perceptions play in the imagined interaction between self and others through which the individual *pretests* his behavior. The pretest phase tends to occur between the steps of hypothesizing and proposing action.

Before the individual acts, he first imagines himself carrying out the act, then imagines the response of another person to his action. If the imagined response is favorable, he will proceed with the overt act, but if the imagined response is not favorable, he will modify his intended action before actually carrying it out (Cooley, 1909; Cottrell, 1942; Mead, 1950; Blumer, 1953; Turner, 1956). In either event, the actual behavior of the other person serves as a check on his perceptions. The perceptions of the "self" and "other person" are then modified to correspond to the new evidence presented by actual behavior. (Sullivan, 1938).

Group members are generally aware of their behavior and of the effect that it is having on other group members (Crowell, Katcher, & Miyamoto, 1955). Behavior is apt to be least selfconscious in a small group in which the individual is highly involved (Goffman, 1957) and most self-conscious in larger groups which provide some time for reflection between acts.

§ First Impressions

ALTHOUGH THE PERCEPTION of another person usually changes as new information is gathered about him, one's first impression of a person may color all subsequent information. In laboratory experiments and in classroom settings, the effect of the first impression has been demonstrated by presenting a list of adjectives which presumably describe a person with the word "warm" as the key adjective for half of the subjects and the word "cold" as the key adjective for the other half.

In one laboratory experiment, groups of students were given two lists of discrete qualities said to belong to a person. The first list was: *intelligent, skillful, industrious, warm, determined, practical,* and *cautious.* The second list was identical with the first, except that the word "warm" was replaced by the word "cold." The subjects were then instructed to write personality sketches of these two persons and to select from a checklist of pairs of opposite traits the terms that best fitted the impression they had formed. The reactions to the two lists of persons differed markedly. The "warm" person was perceived as wise, humorous, popular, and imaginative, whereas the "cold" person was perceived less favorably in some, but not all, of these traits (Asch, 1946).

In a classroom experiment, students in three sections of a college course in psychology were introduced to a new instructor who was to take over the class. They were told that research was being conducted to find out how they reacted to different teachers. Appended to the description of the research was a short "personality sketch" of the new instructor, allegedly obtained from a person who knew him well. The sketches given to each student were identical, except that on half of the sheets he was described as "rather cold," while on the other half the phrase "very warm" was substituted. After the class meeting, the students were asked to write a free description of the instructor and to rate him on fifteen rating scales. Differences in the briefing as to the warmth or coldness of the instructor were found to influence student judgment, since the instructor received more favorable ratings when he was expected to be warm than when he was expected to be cold. The "warm" instructor was described as more informal, sociable, popular, humorous, and humane (Kelley, 1950).

Another example of the influence of first impressions is found in the research on group "cohesiveness" (Schacter et al., 1951) in which subjects were told that they were either similar to each other in interests and personality, and would get along well together, or that they were mismatched, and would probably not do very well together. After a short period of interaction during which the subjects solved some problems together, the subjects who had been told that they *would* like each other reported that they *did* like each other better than those who had been told that they would not be attracted to each other.

§ The Group Basis of Perception

INDIVIDUALS ARE CONTINUALLY making observations, sometimes about things, sometimes about people. The *perceptions* which remain the same over a long period of time are here called *attitudes*. The concept of attitude has been used historically in a number of different ways, and the present definition is one of several current meanings (Allport, 1954). Put another way, the attitudes which are transmitted from one generation to the next play a major role in defining the categories in which persons will be socially perceived. The individual's perception, at any given time, is a function of the *attitudes* of the society transmitted in culture, the more transient *perceptions* of the small group involved in the action of the moment, and an idiosyncratic component which results from the personality of the perceiver and the perceived and other unique situational factors. The fundamental part of the individual's perceptual base is, however, to be found in his assessment of the perceptions of his group (Cartwright, 1952; Zander, 1958). Although the influence of the group on individual judgment has already been discussed in detail in Chapter Two, some further indication of the influence of the group upon judgments of the self and others will be given here.

The self concepts of men living in a dormitory in four-man living units have been found to be influenced by others' perceptions of them over a period of months of living together (Manis, 1955). In another study the ways in which individuals rated themselves on four personality traits in ten college classroom and fraternity groups of 8 to 48 persons were analyzed. The subjects' self-perceptions were compared with the actual feelings of others in the group about these traits, with their perceptions of others' attitudes, and with their perception of the attitudes of the *members of most groups* or a *generalized other*. The self-perceptions were found to be related to the actual attitudes of others in the group. However, the self-perceptions were even more related to the subjects' perceptions of others' attitudes, and most closely related to the subjects' estimates of the generalized attitude (Miyamoto & Dornbush, 1956).

The group's percepion of an individual will have more influence on his self-perception when he is highly attracted to the group and when the other group members place a high value on his participation (Festinger, Torrey, & Willerman, 1954; Stotland, Thorley, Thomas, Cohen,

& Zander, 1957). Under these conditions the individual will pay more attention to the opinions of the group, and the group members in turn will be more explicit in their valuation of the individual.

The group basis of the perception of others is also evident in the research on attitudes towards different classifications of people. The concept of *stereotype* is used to refer to the group prejudgment of a class of persons which so colors the "first impression" that the individual characteristics which do not fit the stereotype are suppressed (Cronbach, 1955).

§   Perceptual Accuracy

INDIVIDUALS DIFFER in their ability to perceive accurately the characteritics of others. Some of the factors relevant to this differential perception are found in the age, sex, and personality of the perceiver, in the characteristics of the perceived, and the content area in which the predictions are to be made (Bender & Hastorf, 1950; Bruner & Tagiuri, 1954; Taft, 1955; Tagiuri & Petrullo, 1958).

To measure the *ability* to perceive accurately, one must first rule out the accuracy which could be expected if only chance factors were operating (Tagiuri, Bruner, & Kogan, 1955) and then, since the subject may *project* his own values on the other person, (Murstein, 1957; Alfert, 1958), as is the case where students are found to project their own values on their chosen faculty members (Precker, 1953), one must rule out the apparent accuracy which is due only to the fact that the *subject* and the *object* are similar (Lindgren & Robinson, 1953; Gage & Cronbach, 1955; Halpern, 1955; Hastorf, Bender, & Weintraub, 1955; Gage, Leavitt, & Stone, 1956; Runkel, 1956; Suchman, 1956). In addition to these difficulties in dealing with data on social perception, there are a variety of technical problems which can occur in the collection and analysis of data which make this type of analysis "a breeding ground for artifacts" (Cronbach, 1958).

Perceptual accuracy apparently increases with age, at least among children, since eleven-year-olds show greater perceptive ability than seven-year-olds (Dymond, Hughes, & Raabe, 1952). Sex is also a factor, since the general notion in the folklore that women are more intuitive (perceptive) than men is borne out by some experimental results (Exline, 1957).

When the relationship between empathic ability and personality is explored through direct and projective tests, high-empathy persons appear to be outgoing, optimistic, warm, emotionally secure, and interested in others. Low empathy is associated with rigidity, introversion, emotionality, self-centeredness, and interpersonal incompetence (Dymond, 1949, 1950; Chance, 1958). Within a clinical population, mental patients who have "improved" as a result of hospitalization also appear to be more accurate in their descriptions of interpersonal relations than those who have not "improved" (Kalis & Bennett, 1957). In another study of patients in group therapy, the perceptions of eight patients regarding part of the interaction during a therapy session were compared with the perceptions of their therapist. The patients were found to vary widely in their perceptions of the same incident, each having his own point of view. The therapist tended to see the events in longer time perspective while the patients were more apt to use ego-defense responses or selective inattention to defend against some aspect of the situation (Stock & Whitman, 1957).

Further evidence of the relationship between personality and perception comes from a series of experiments with college-age subjects who were classified on the single personality dimension of authoritarianism. In one experiment, the individuals who were rated as high authoritarians on a personality test were paired with low authoritarians for a twenty-minute general discussion. In a second experiment, high authoritarians were paired with high, and low with low. After the discussion, the high authoritarians rated their partners as high on authoritarianism whether they were high or low, while the low authoritarians thought all their partners were either middle or high. Apparently the highs thought that everyone was just as high as they were, whereas the lows thought that no one could be as low as they (Scodel & Mussen, 1953; Crockett & Meidinger, 1956; Scodel & Freedman, 1956). High authoritarians were even found to rate the attitude of a "typical student" as also being high without any intervening interaction (Rabinowitz, 1956). This finding suggests that twenty minutes of interaction did little to alter the highs' original perception that most people were authoritarian.

Other types of distortions of perception which are related to personality factors are those which result from being overanxious to see others' behavior as related to a particular goal the individuals may have, or being unwilling to accept indications of hostility from another person who may be thwarting the goal (Pepitone, 1950). There are also general tendencies in individuals to either overestimate or underestimate the position of themselves or others in the hierarchies based on interpersonal choice (Schiff, 1954).

If individuals have similar feelings for each other their perceptions will tend to be more accurate because otherwise they may mask their feelings to avoid conflict (Tagiuri, Blake, & Bruner, 1953; Taylor, 1957; Tagiuri, Bruner, & Blake, 1958). An individual may also attempt to mask his feelings if he does not trust another group member. In one study 244 pairs drawn from a population of 330 professional scientists engaged in laboratory research were compared on their attitudes about the long-run consequences of a new research program, their attitudes of trust toward each other, their reports as to whether they had ever discussed the new program, and their estimate of each other's attitudes about the issue. If a scientist did not trust another scientist, he tended to conceal his own attitudes about an issue so that the accuracy of the other's perception was impaired (Mellinger, 1956).

The effect of training upon the accuracy and variability of inter-personal perception has been studied by Crow (1957). In his experiment, 72 senior medical students were divided into an experimental group who received training in physician-patient relationships and a control group who did not receive such training. At the beginning, during, and at the end of their senior year, the students estimated the real status and self-ratings of patients presented in sound-film interviews. Actual self-ratings and relevant personality test scores (MMPI) were available for these patients as criteria. As a result of the training, the experimental group became *less* accurate and increased their variability of estimates significantly more. A possible explanation offered is that training programs may decrease accuracy when they increase the trainees' responsiveness to individual differences. This hypothesis is in line with the results of a similar experiment with medical students in which a "response set" to "stereotype" others was found to be more stable than differential accuracy from test to retest. Here it appeared that consistency in perception was largely due to consistency in response set (Crow & Hammond, 1957).

Because of the tendency of individuals to predict that others will fit a "stereotype," some further refinement in data analysis must be introduced if one wishes to know when a subject has been accurate simply because the other person fits the "stereotype." One solution is to note the "accurately shifted items" and the "inaccurately shifted items" which are different from the responses one would expect on a test of social perception if only stereotyped responses were given. In this way measures of two kinds of accuracy in predicting another's responses would be derived: (1) a measure of how well the subjects could distinguish the characteristics of an individual from those of the average members of the group, and (2) how misled the subject was by individual cues (Stone, Gage, & Leavitt, 1957).

§ Perception of Friends

IN GENERAL, if one subject likes another, he tends to think that his liking is returned (Tagiuri, 1957), and if he likes two other subjects he will perceive them as liking each other (Kogan & Tagiuri, 1958a).

Group members who have many friends in the group are generally more accurate in their perception of the informal group structure and of the characteristics of others in the group than are individuals who are relatively isolated (Dymond et al., 1952; Gronlund, 1955a). Accuracy of perception of the informal hierarchies on the part of well liked members of the group may result from the fact that, when friendship choices are openly reciprocated, the place of the self in a hierarchy is more evident (Tagiuri, 1952; Taguiri, Kogan, & Bruner, 1955; Tagiuri & Kogan, 1957; Foa, 1958a; Kogan & Tagiuri, 1958b). The isolated person who may like others but is less sure of the extent to which his liking is returned may not be as accurate in his judgment.

Pairs of friends tend to be more accurate in the perception of each other's personalities than pairs of nonfriends, partly as a result of increased knowledge of the other person from continued social interaction (Bieri, 1953; Suchman, 1956; Taylor, 1957; Vernon & Stewart, 1957) and partly as a result of a tendency to project one's own values on a friend (Fiedler, Warrington, & Blaisdell, 1952; Davitz, 1955).

This tendency of subjects to describe others whom they like best as more similar to themselves than those they like least (Lundy, Katkovsky, Cromwell, & Shoemaker, 1955) presumably reflects some of the common interests which brought the pair together as friends in the first place. Marital happiness for twenty university student couples, for example, was found to be positively associated with similarity of self-perception of mates (Corsini, 1956). Further evidence of the relation between similarity of values and perception of friends is found in a study in which each of ninety college women classified one hundred self-referent statements in a "Q-Sort" for her self-concept, ideal self-concept, and her perception of her first- and second-best friend. The perception of each friend's personality was more similar to the ideal self-concept of the subject ($r = .42$) than to her self-concept ($r = .33$). Here the ideal self appeared to be a composite of traits valued both in the self and others (McKenna, Hoffstaetter, & O'Connor, 1956). Although it would be desirable to know the points of similarity and dissimilarity of friends' self-concepts and perceptions in each of the interpersonal and personal categories, it is not possible to carry the analysis much further from the published results of research, since few authors using a 50-to-100-item checklist give any indication of the items the list contains. More detailed evidence concerning the relationship between projection and perceptual accuracy is given in Exhibit 5.

§ Changing Perception through Interaction

EVIDENCE FOR BOTH the consistency and change of perception as a result of interaction between two individuals has been presented in the literature (Cronbach, 1955). On the one hand, research on the importance of "first impressions" indicates that judgments of persons once formed are slow to change and, on the other hand, research on friendship suggests that the longer two individuals know each other and the more intimate their interaction, the greater will be the accuracy of their interpersonal perceptions (Bieri, 1953). Since individuals may or may not increase their perceptual accuracy as a result of interaction, further evidence must be presented to enable one to predict the conditions under which increased accuracy of perception occurs. It might be expected, for example, that persons with high test-scores on insight or empathy would increase their accuracy more than those with low scores. However, in one study, after thirty minutes of interaction in twelve-man, leaderless discussion groups, subjects with high empathy scores were not able to estimate the way in which one member's personality traits would be viewed by the other members any more effectively than low scorers (Bell & Stolper, 1955).

Whether or not the subject focuses attention on himself or the other person does seem to make a difference, since in one experiment paired interaction increased the accuracy of a member's prediction of another's values, if he focused attention on the other person, but changed the prediction towards his own values and away from those of his partner when he focused attention on himself (Lundy, 1956a).

Apparently close contact on a work basis does not increase the accuracy of perception to the same extent as interaction on a basis of friendship. For example, a female psychologist was asked to describe, using a "Q-Sort," her typical interactive behavior with her professional associates at work and with some friends known in other situations. Her descriptions were then compared with the descriptions of the same interactions by each of the other persons involved. Her descriptions of interactions with friends known off the job were found to agree more with their own descriptions than did her descriptions of interactions with professional associates (Block & Bennett, 1955). In another example of the relation between intimacy and perception, married couples were found to make more accurate predictions of each other's responses than couples who were dating (Kirkpatrick & Hobart, 1954). When changes in accuracy of perception do occur as a result of increased communication or intimacy between the members of a pair, the changes can be expected to be more pronounced if the members initially have the same underlying attitudes (Runkel, 1956).

In addition to changing his perception as a result of increased knowledge of the typical behavior of the other person, the subject also changes his perceptions as a result of his own reactions to the other person. For example, in discussion groups, members who were seen as being influential were assigned desirable personality traits (Perlmutter, 1954), presumably because the group members wished to feel that they were being influenced by worthy persons.

In a similar fashion, a subject in a hypothetical interpersonal situation (i.e., one in which he was asked to give the most probable responses of an actor in a series of fictitious incidents in which the actor was criticized) was more likely to change his negative reaction to a positive one following a criticism if he were then told that the criticism was intended for his own good (Pepitone & Sherberg, 1957).

On the other hand, if one member fails to contribute to the group task or makes things more difficult for the other members, he may then be perceived as having less desirable personality traits (Harvey, Kelley, & Shapiro, 1957; Jones & de Charms, 1957; Steiner & Dodge, 1957). The perception of certain behavior as undesirable can, in turn, become more favorable, if the original behavior is compared with behavior which is even more undesirable (Cohen, E., 1957a).

Initial perceptions can also change as a result of the ways in which other members appear to be affected by the subject. Subjects who "won over" two role players to their point of view after a discussion thought that the role player who was presumed to have the higher status was probably convinced by the logic of their arguments, while a role player with lower status than the subject was presumed to have been coerced into changing his opinion (Thibaut & Riecken, 1955b).

Once an individual has established himself in a high-status position, his performance may be overvalued by other group members when his group is in competition with another group. In one experiment, college women who were members of sixteen campus cliques containing a total of 74 individuals were selected from a larger population because they represented four pairs of friendly and four pairs of antagonistic groups. Members of each group were first asked to list city names while listening to a distracting tape recording, and then to estimate the number of names written by each subject as her list was flashed on a screen. This task was performed once while only members of the same clique were present, and once in the presence of a friendly or antagonistic clique. In each case, subjects overestimated the performances of the members of their own clique. The performances of members with high leadership status were over-estimated more than those of members with low leadership status. This was especially true in the presence of an antagonistic out-group. Furthermore, the performance of the antagonistic outgroup was greatly underestimated (Harvey, 1956).

§   Perception and
    Adjustment

ALTHOUGH it might be supposed that the person with the greatest insight should be able to make the best adjustment to the group, the evidence to support this generalization is not clear. Some studies (see Exhibit 6) suggest a positive relationship between adjustment and the ability to estimate one's own position as seen by the group (Green, 1948), as well as the tendency to be more accurate in the perception of others (Gage, 1953; Baker & Sarbin, 1956). Other studies report no correlation between insight and effectiveness in interpersonal relations (Lemann & Solomon, 1952; Gage & Exline, 1953).

These conflicting findings may indicate that insight or accuracy of perception is a necessary but not sufficient condition for effectiveness, since some deviant members may be well aware of their position in the group and yet be unable to get along well with the other group members. Steiner (1955) has suggested that accurate social perception should promote "interpersonal competence" and group efficiency if (1) the group members are motivated to co-operate, (2) the accurately perceived qualities are relevant to the activities of the group, (3) members are free to alter their own behaviors in response to their perceptions of other members, (4) the behavioral changes which are a consequence of accurate social perception are the kinds which produce a more thoroughly integrated system. Whenever any one or more of these conditions is not met, accurate social perception will not affect adjustment to the group.

In cases in which perceptual accuracy and level of adjustment are related, changes in the individual's level of adjustment brought about by therapy can be expected to change his perceptions (and vice versa; Butler, 1952). For example, 21 patients who received counseling were given projective tests before and after therapy. In these tests the patients' own self-descriptions were found to be less loaded with feeling after therapy (Dymond, Seeman, & Grummon, 1956).

§   Leader's Perception

THE SAME FACTORS which affect the perceptions of the average group member also operate on the perceptions of the leader. In addition, since the leader is in the center of the communication net and is usually selected or arises because of his ability to put himself in the place of others (Mead, 1950; Bell & Hall, 1954), his perceptions of others tend to be more accurate than the average member (Trapp, 1955), although it has been suggested that some of this apparent superiority may be a statistical artifact (Campbell, 1955). As evidence of the superior per-ceptual accuracy of leaders, school teachers were found to perceive accurately the choice structure of their classes (Gronlund, 1956a), and teachers who were the most accurate in perceiving the structure of the classroom also perceived accurately the structure of their own peer group of teachers (Gronlund, 1956b). The leader, on the other hand, may be more favorable in his self-perceptions than he appears to other members of the group (Gebel, 1954).

As a result of his favored position, the leader is usually superior to nonleaders and isolates in his ability to judge group opinion on issues which are relevant to the group's activity (Chowdhry & Newcomb, 1952). However, if all members of the group actually share the same opinion on an issue and there is a high rate of interaction among group members, the difference in perception between leaders and nonleaders may not appear (Hites & Campbell, 1950).

The importance of being in the center of the communication net for accurate perception is further demonstrated by evidence from studies in which communication between all members is maximized either because the groups are small (Travers, 1941) or because the members have known each other longer. In these cases, all members may be able to predict group opinion or group structure more accurately than members of groups with less effective communication (Greer, Galanter, & Nordlie, 1954), although one study of high school students in discussion groups of fourteen to sixteen members revealed that estimates of group opinion on certain issues were no more accurate after discussion than they were without discussion (Stone & Kamiya, 1957).

In the previous discussion of perceptual accuracy and adjustment, the average individual's social adjustment was not found to be clearly related to his perceptual ability. Nevertheless, leaders who are more discriminating in their social perception are apparently better able to organize group activity. The most preferred co-worker chosen by members of winning high school basketball teams and highly rated college surveying teams was found to be the one who in turn perceived his preferred and rejected co-workers as differing and perceived little similarity between himself and his co-workers (Fiedler, Hartmann & Rudin, 1952; Fiedler, 1953a, 1954a). Since subjects tend to perceive those they like as similar to themselves, Fiedler concludes that the member who differentiates in his perceptions of other group members is also the one who maintains enough emotional distance from others and has enough task orientation to make him an effective team leader (Fiedler, 1953b, 1958). Similar findings have been reported with bomber crews and tank crews in the armed forces (Fiedler, 1954b, 1955, 1960).[4]

This positive association between the ability to influence and perceptual accuracy is also evident in the study of a seventeen-man training group. Members whose perceptions were accurate in that their judgments of the power of others agreed with the average group judgment were considered effective by observers and valuable and powerful by the other group members (Smith, Jaffe, & Livingston, 1955).

The results of any attempt to change the perceptions of leaders can be expected to vary with the personality of the leader and the situation in which he finds himself. In one experiment, 22 leaders of youth groups were given a course designed to increase their perceptions of causal

---

4. Steiner and McDiarmid (1957) suggest that Fiedler's Assumed Similarity Score can be broken into two components: (1) the perceived discrepancy between the overall "goodness" of the traits possessed by the two co-workers, and (2) the perceived dissimilarity between the patterns of traits possessed by the two co-workers. Foa (1958b) notes that variables such as assumed similarity, empathy, and conformity will be correlated if they are composed of similar "facets," e.g., actor, observer, level, and alias.

factors in behavior. By the end of the course, leaders who tended to project blame on others and who led informal groups, and leaders who tended to blame themselves and who led formal, clearly structured groups, showed changes in the expected direction by being more aware of causal factors in behavior. However, leaders with the opposite type of group placement (i.e., extra-punitive leaders in formal groups and intra-punitive leaders in informal groups) showed some undesirable changes in modes of perceiving members' behavior. These undesirable changes consisted of either an increase or no change in the number of perceptions distorted by judgments of blame and a decrease or no change in perceptions which were accompanied by questions about the cause of the behavior (Maas, 1950).

§ From Perception to
Action

AFTER THE INDIVIDUAL has *observed* the elements in the situation and perceived the similarities and differences in the other group members, he next formulates some *hypotheses* about behavior appropriate to the situation. After pretesting the hypotheses in imagined behavior, he *proposes action.* Since only the action which follows the final step in the social act is open to public observation, the existence of the other steps is generally inferred. Responses to a person who appears to deviate from the group norm differ from responses to those who appear to conform (Schachter, 1951). Forms of address and behavior which are used for social equals differ from those used with inferiors and superiors (Maas, 1954b; Zander & Cohen, 1955). Women talk to women about things different from those that men talk to men about (Landis & Burtt, 1924).

A further example of differences in the content of interaction which may follow from differences in the social characteristics of the members of the interacting pair is found in an analysis of the paired interaction of teachers and children, parents and teachers, and parents and children. Teachers were most interested in friendliness in all the relationships. Power and control were paramount in both the teacher-student and parent-child relations, while parents, teachers, and children all shared an interest in extra-curricular activities. However, these similarities and differences in interaction content were generally not perceived by the subjects (Jenkins & Lippitt, 1951).

Many more examples of this type appear in Chapters Six and Seven on *personality* and *social characteristics of members.*

Clear, organized perceptions seem to provide a basis for more assertive action. In an experimental study, discussion groups composed of five to eight subjects who perceived clear boundaries for objects on Rorschach cards were compared with groups composed of subjects who did not perceive clear boundaries. The subjects who were found to be high in boundary perception were also found to be more assertive, more self-initiating, and more achievement-oriented, and to talk more in the leaderless discussion groups. In the groups composed of subjects who saw fewer clearly defined objects, the interaction rate was slower. The members tended to sit back and wait for the emergence of a leader who would then organize things for them (Cleveland & Fisher, 1957).

On the basis of the initial definition of the situation the individual member may also posit a goal for interaction which influences his behavior for several acts. This initial goal will be held for a period of time even in the face of evidence that the goal is unobtainable. For example, one can infer that in the experiment performed by Asch (1952) the subject first organizes his behavior to conform to the goal set by the experimenter, to make correct visual judgments. The subject then finds that this goal is untenable if he is to maintain his perception of himself as an adequate (and conforming) group member and so posits a new goal of taking the group judgment into account.

The goal for interaction has the greatest effect when the subject is "self-conscious" and rehearses each act carefully before carrying it out. The goal changes more rapidly when he acts "off the top of his head" and responds more directly to present stimuli. The goal is much more likely to persist if it is shared with other group members and becomes a group norm.

The goal of behavior in a group can be primarily individual in response to some self-oriented need (Fouriezos et al., 1950), a goal for which members compete with each other, or a goal which can only be reached through mutual co-operation. In each case the individuals would be sensitive to different aspects of the behavior of the other group members, such as emotional rather than task response, if the goal is self-oriented, behavior that would block his efforts to reach the goal if he is in competition, or behavior that moves the whole group toward the goal if he is co-operating.

The relative importance of social goals and individual physical needs is illustrated by a study of frustration in adult subjects. The experimenters were more successful in frustrating the subjects by preventing them from fulfilling group expectations and goals, than by depriving them of food (Lindzey & Riecken, 1951).

§ Summary

THE OBSERVATION and analysis of the interaction process usually depends upon a category system which allows the observer to code each act in one of a limited set of content areas. Current usage of category systems is represented by the work of Thelen, who gives a double score to each unit act by noting the amount of task and social-emotional behavior it contains, and by Bales, who scores each act on its predominant content. The Bales system has twelve categories which are subdivisions of four general types of acts: positive reactions, negative reactions, problem-solving attempts, and questions.

In the typical interaction pattern of a small leaderless group, there is a balance between action and reaction. About half of the acts during a group session are problem-solving attempts, while the remaining half are distributed among positive reactions, negative reactions, and questions. This balance between task and social-emotional activity will vary with the nature of the task and the characteristics of the members. Although each individual has a characteristic rate of interaction, these same variables affect the average interaction rate for the group.

The dominant content of interaction changes within a single meeting as a group moves from phase to phase in the discussion, and between meetings over a series of meetings. In the first phase of a discussion, the group members are collecting information, in the second phase, evaluating the information, and in the final phase, pressing for a decision. Over a series of four meetings, members gradually spend less time in task behavior and more time in positive social-emotional behavior. Negative social-emotional behavior rises briefly in the second meeting during the "status struggle" in which members establish the hierarchy. In their attempts to solve problems in both task and social-emotional areas, groups face an *equilibrium problem*. If they become too absorbed in the task, they will neglect group of individual needs, and if they pay too much attention to group structure and member satisfaction, productivity will decline.

The "first impression" which one member forms of another is found to be an important factor in *observation* or *perception*, since it tends to color subsequent perceptions of behavior. However, the more intimate the interaction becomes, the more accurate will the perception of others be; e.g., friends are more accurate in their perceptions of each other than nonfriends.

Group leaders tend to be more accurate in their perceptions of other members and of the structure and norms of the group. The accuracy of other members is increased if they can share the leaders' central position in the communication net or if the group is very homogeneous in traits or opinions. The average member's perceptual accuracy is not clearly related to his adjustment in the group.

Exhibit 5
Projection of Values and Perceptual Accuracy

A.

Investigator: Fielder, Warrington, & Blaisdell (1952).
Focus: Unconscious attitudes as correlates of sociometric choice in social group.
Sample: 26 students who were members of one college fraternity.
Method: Each student sorted 76 statements descriptive of personality traits on a forced normal distribution (1, 5, 12, 20, 20, 12, 5, 1), placing the most characteristic statement at one extreme and the least applicable at the other extreme. He was asked to (1) describe himself, (2) describe how he would ideally like to be, (3) predict how his best liked fellow group member would describe himself, and (4) predict how his least liked fellow group member would describe himself.
Relevant Findings: Students perceived persons whom they liked best as more similar to themselves than others whom they liked less (significant at .01 level of confidence), and also as more similar to their ideal self than persons whom they liked least (P. < .05). However, no correlation was found between "ideal" self-description of pairs of friends.

B.

Investigator: Precker (1953).
Focus: The attribution of values.
Sample: 242 students and 42 faculty members at a small college.
Method: Students ranked 39 items according to their own preference and according to their perception of how their favorite faculty members would rank the same items. The items consisted of characteristics considered important in evaluating the college tutorial system.
Relevant Findings: The average agreement between the student's conception of his chosen advisor's ranking of the items and his own actual ranking ($\bar{x} = 22.68$) was found to be significantly higher (P. < .05) than the average agreement between the student's actual ranking and the advisor's actual ranking ($\bar{x} = 14.90$).

C.

Investigator: Davitz (1955).
Focus: Social perception and sociometric choice.
Sample: 39 children; 21 girls and 18 boys enrolled at a summer camp. The ages ranged from 6.5 to 12.9 years with a mean age of 9.8 and standard deviation of 1.8. The subjects lived in cabin groups of four to six members of approximately the same age.
Method: Each subject filled out a sociometric questionnaire. Social perception was determined by his answers to an activity questionnaire in which he (1) stated his own preferences, (2) predicted the preferences of his highest sociometric choice, and (3) predicted the preference of his lowest sociometric choice.
Relevant Findings: Highest sociometric choices tended to be perceived as more similar to self than were lowest sociometric choices (P. < .05). Highest sociometric choices also tended to be perceived as more similar to self than they actually were (P. < .02).

D.

Investigator: Lundy, Katkovsky, Cromwell, & Shoemaker (1955).
Focus: Self-acceptability and descriptions of sociometric choices.
Sample: 54 college undergraduates.
Method: Each student completed a multiple-choice personality description blank describing himself, his ideal self, and his best liked and least liked fellow student of the same sex. A self-acceptability score was obtained for each subject from the number of items on which the self- and ideal self-descriptions were the same, and a self-unacceptability score, from the number of items on which the self- and ideal self-descriptions differed.
Relevant Findings: Descriptions of positive sociometric choices tended to be more similar to the subjects' acceptable self-descriptions and negative sociometric choices more similar to the subjects' unacceptable self-descriptions. In general, subjects were found to describe persons they liked best as more similar to themselves than persons they liked least.

E.

Investigator: Suchman (1956).
Focus: Social sensitivity in the small task-oriented group.
Sample: Three groups of five persons each, one group male, one female, and one mixed. All subects were college undergraduates.
Method: At the end of a planning period for a skit, each individual filled

out a four-part questionnaire: (1) eight statements which represented feelings a subject might have had during the planning situation (each item had four degrees of intensity), (2) statements of feelings that a subject might have had toward other group members during the planning session, (3) estimations of the feelings of the other four subjects, and (4) estimates of how the subject thought each other subject felt toward him.

Relevant Findings: The level of accuracy between any two members was related positively to the degree to which the pair regarded each other favorably. A positive relationship was also found between a pair's similarity on other criterion ratings and their combined accuracy. However, the level of accuracy between any two members of a group did not show a significant positive relation to the similarity between them in their feelings about themselves and toward each other.

F.

Investigator: Alfert (1958).

Focus: Two components of assumed similarity.

Sample: 27 students in an adult extension course and thirteen undergraduates.

Method: Subjects were asked to guess the response of strangers to 20 pairs of self-descriptive traits. Each subject checked the list of traits first as he would rate himself and then as he would describe his ideal.

Relevant Findings: Traits checked for both the real and ideal self were attributed to others to a greater extent than traits which were checked for the real self but not the ideal self. Assumed similarity between a subject and a person he is predicting includes both traits in which ideal self and self coincide and those in which ideal and self differ.

Exhibit 6
Perception and Adjustment

A.

Investigator: Green (1948).

Focus: Insight and group adjustment.

Sample: 23 graduate students at the Alexandria Institute of Education, Egyptians of mixed tribes and religions, and 23 girls from an English girls' college at Alexandria, mixed nationalities.

Method: Each member was asked to rate himself and all other members of the group on a five-point scale of leadership. His choices were compared with the choices of the group as a whole. Observations by teachers and professors of each subject's individual adjustment were also compared with his choices.

Relevant Findings: In the graduate student sample, an individual's leadership rating was positively associated with a high correlation between individual and group choices (.73 to .94) and with a small disparity between his self-estimate and the estimate of his fellows. Neurotic tendencies appeared to be linked with lower rank correlations (.36 to .68) and high disparities of self-estimate. Similar results were obtained with the group of girls.

B.

Investigator: Lemann & Solomon (1952).

Focus: Group characteristics as revealed in sociometric patterns and personality ratings.

Sample: Three groups with approximately twenty members each, containing female students between the ages of 18 and 21 at an Eastern college, who had been living together for at least four months.

Method: Sociometric questionnaire asking (1) choice of a roommate, (2) choice of a double-dating companion, (3) choice of a person to take home for the weekend, (4) choice of a person for future contact. At the same time, the subjects were asked to rate themselves and their choices on a series of ten traits on a seven-point scale.

Relevant Findings: Insight—Using the consensus of her living associates as an approximation of a girl's true position on a trait scale, insight was defined operationally as the discrepancy between self-rating and mean rating received. The smaller this discrepancy was, the greater insight the subject showed. No significant relation was found between insight and group adjustment (i.e., group status), although there was a trend in the direction of greater insight with higher status. *Over chosen members*—Groups with very high status or with very low status exhibited a consistent tendency to give to or receive from each other a higher proportion of choices than would be expected by chance (P. < .01).

C.

Investigator: Gage & Exline (1953).

Focus: Social perceptions and effectiveness in discussion groups.

Sample: Four discussion groups, of from fifteen to 22 members, who were delegates at the National Training Laboratory for Group Development.

Method: Subjects were asked to estimate group opinion on fifty items, satisfaction of other members of the group with the meeting, and the five most productive members of the group as chosen by group vote. They were also asked with whom they would like to spend leisure time and which group members were most sensitive to feelings and attitudes of others.

Relevant Findings: Accuracy in predicting (1) the group's opinions, (2) satisfaction of individuals with the meeting, (3) the ratings of productivity, did not correlate highly or positively with perceived effectiveness in group work as measured by the individual's sociometric, sensitivity, and productivity ratings.

D.

Investigator: Baker & Sarbin (1956).

Focus: Differential mediation of social perception as a correlate of social adjustment.

Sample: 41 delinquent and 48 nondelinquent adolescent boys.

Method: A subject was shown two short films of other boys being interviewed and then asked to guess how the boy in each film answered a ten-item nonverbal preference test. The correct answer was given the subject after each of the ten predictions.

Relevant Findings: The delinquent and nondelinquent subjects did not differ in their accuracy. Both sets of subjects improved in their accuracy from the first half to the second half of the task. Delinquents, however, tended to use more nondifferentiating responses; that is, they tended to predict the same preferences for each of the dissimilar social objects as they gave for themselves.

E.

Investigator: Dymond, Seeman, & Grummon (1956).

Focus: Patterns of perceived interpersonal relations.

Sample: 21 patients who had received nondirective counseling.

Method: Cluster analysis of relationships revealed in TAT stories before and after therapy.

Relevant Findings: Three patterns were found in the follow up TAT's: (a) external description of relations, (b) affective release, and (c) comfortable adjustment. After therapy self-descriptions were less loaded with feeling, and less hostility was shown in relations with others.

4

ROLES

*A*s GROUPS GROW in size and complexity, individuals tend to specialize in some aspect of the interaction process. The expectations for behavior in these specialties are represented by the roles of the group members. The development of the informal structure and some of the problems which arise from conflicting role expectations are considered in more detail in this chapter.

§ Role: A Set of Expectations

THERE IS A ROLE which goes with the informal position of the best-liked person in a group just as there is a role which goes with the formal position of foreman of a shop crew. In each case the term "role" refers to the set of expectations which group members share concerning the behavior of a person who occupies a given position in the group (Bates, F. L., 1956; Bates & Cloyd, 1956; Gross, Mason, &

McEachern, 1958; Levinson, 1959; Southall, 1959).[1] The actual behavior of a person occupying a position in a group remains as something to be understood in terms of the expectations which are imposed from without and the tendencies of his personality which express themselves from within.

Some evidence that behavior in a role does not always agree with the expectations for that role is reported in two studies of the relationship between the ideologies of aircraft commanders and educational administrators and their actual behavior (Halpin, 1955a, 1955b). In these studies the "ideology" of the subject represents his perception of the expectations for his role since each subject had been asked to indicate how he believed he should behave as a leader. Ratings of the actual behavior of the aircraft commanders and administrators were made by their subordinates.

In one study, the behavior of commanders of ten- to eleven-man aircraft crews in the categories of "initiating group structure" and "consideration" as rated by members of their crews was found to be lower on the average than the "ideology" of the commanders. Thus it is apparent that the commanders did not live up to the expectations for their roles. In addition, the ideology of the commanders was not correlated with their rated performance, an indication that knowledge of expectations alone may not be enough to predict behavior. In the other study, the educational administrators showed greater "consideration" and less "initiating group structure" than aircraft commanders in both ideology and behavior, an indication of differences in the expectations for the two roles. As before, however, there was only a low correlation between real and ideal behavior.

The expectations for a role may be formalized in laws, such as those which outline the rights and duties of the President of the United States; they may be less formal but generally agreed on regulations, such as Robert's Rules of Order, which outline appropriate behavior for a good committee chairman; or, they may exist in a group without any overt awareness on the part of the members. However, moving down toward the informal end of the scale, one would eventually reach a point where the concept of role would not be useful. In a case where a person actually carried out the same type of behavior meeting after meeting, but where the other group members did not have any

---

1. Although some authors use the term "role" to refer to the behavior which an individual directs toward fulfilling expectations (Newcomb, 1950; Sarbin, 1954), in this text the term "role" is used to refer only to the expectations associated with a position in a group.

expectations about this person because of his regular behavior, the term *role* would not be applied.

Individuals vary in their ability to play a given role (Sarbin & Jones, 1955). The expectations for a role are met most easily by the individual whose personality fits the role (Rapoport & Rosow, 1957). The first person to occupy a new position in a group has the opportunity to create a role which is most compatible with his own personality. If his personality traits are somewhat unique, the group may never be able to fill the role satisfactorily again after he leaves the group.

Some of the consequences for a group if a member does not fulfill his role expectations are illustrated in a study of the effects of clear and unclear role expectations on group productivity and defensiveness. College students played the game of "Twenty Questions" in groups of five members. Each group contained two confederates who remained silent throughout the game. When the silence on the part of these two members was unanticipated, the productivity and satisfaction of the other participants decreased and their defensiveness increased. However, the groups did better if the silent subjects announced that they would remain silent before the experiment began, thus altering the expectations for their roles in the group (Smith, 1957).

§ A Paradigm for Role
   Analysis

THE CONTENT of role expectations can be visualized along the two axes in Fig. 12. The behavior expected from others to the self and by the

Figure 12—A Paradigm for Role Analysis in the Control Area

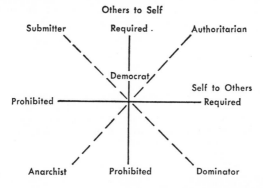

self to others can, in each case, extend from that which is *required* to that which is *prohibited*.[2] As indicated in Chapter One, these expectations include both the form and content of interaction. To some extent there are also expectations for the personal characteristics of the individual who will fill the role.

The central tendency of the expectations for a role in each area could be indicated by a point on a graph which has as its coordinates a measure of the extent to which behavior in that area is required or prohibited along each axis. Some typical roles in the control area would be those of the "authoritarian" who is required to control and be controlled, the "anarchist" who neither controls nor is controlled, the "dominator" who is required to control and cannot be controlled, and the "submitter" who is required to be controlled, but cannot control. The "democrat" would appear in the middle of the figure as one who is required to control or be controlled as the occasion demands.

In addition to these expectations for the content of interaction, a role can be seen as also including expectations for the frequency and duration (i.e., pattern) of interaction and the communication network involved for both output and input in each of the content areas. To continue the example in the control area, the expectations for the behavior of self to others would include a specified degree of control, carried out with a given frequency and duration, to specified group members. In the same way the control of the self by others would have a given interaction pattern, emanating from given members of the group.

Although this method of delineating the expectations for a role may prove too complex to be used in its complete form, it may prove relevant for some research problems. For example, one might wish to distinguish a role which required an individual to interact in a controlling way frequently but for a short duration, from one in which the individual was expected to act with the same degree of control infrequently but over a longer period of time. Or, in another case, two roles might be equal in power and similar in interaction pattern, and yet different in that an individual in one role might control only one other person, while in the other role he might control a dozen persons.

---

2. The *rights* and *duties* of the person occupying the position are often stressed in the literature (Sarbin, 1954). In the present formulation, the *rights* include those behaviors which others are expected to direct toward the individual and the *duties* include those behaviors which the individual is expected to direct toward others. Roles tend to be reciprocal, so that the "rights" of one role are the "duties" of another (Bates, F.L, 1957).

Similar variations might occur in the interaction patterns and communication networks which govern the control of the self by others.

The concept of role as it is used in the literature does not generally involve all of the aspects of behavior which have been suggested here. Rather, each author tends to limit his description of role to some aspects which are particularly relevant to his experiment. In some cases the subject's position in a communication network (e.g., central person, member, or isolate) is seen as the most important aspect of the role, in others his position in the typical interaction rate or pattern (e.g., the person who talks most), and in others his position in the content area (e.g., task leader *versus* social-emotional leader).

§ Development of the Informal Structure

PERHAPS THE CLEAREST distinction between a *collection* of individuals of the sort one might find sitting in the last seven seats on a commuter train and a bona fide group is that the group has a structure.[3] The collection of people on the train may have common activities, such as reading the paper or getting off at the same station, but this activity would be described as elementary collective behavior and not as evidence of a functioning group.

The studies which deal with the development of the informal structure in the group tend to focus on the network of positions, rather than on the roles or expectations for behavior which go with the positions. In many of these studies the researcher is concerned with development of the simplest type of network, the straight-line hierarchy, in which a subject's position is operationally defined by the sum of the ratings he receives on some criterion.

In laboratory experiments, when the experimenter leaves the members to their own devices in developing a structure, the group is referred to as an "initially leaderless group." In other cases the roles are assigned

---

3. Blau (1957) sees the "structure" of a group as the network of interpersonal choice. He defines the "structural dimension" as "a network of social relations between individuals which finds expression in their interaction." The expectations for behavior appear in what he refers to as the "organizational dimension" which includes "relationships between personnel, policies, supervisory practices, and interaction among workers."

by the experimenter before the group begins its task, or are developed in response to some style of leadership which has been planted in the group.

In most large organizations and in many types of small groups, there is a formal structure, a set of "official" positions which incorporate the accepted division of labor for the group's task. Other positions are "unofficial" and make up the informal structure.

All aspects of the work situation including the formal structure influence the development of the informal structure (Roesthlisberger & Dickson, 1939). In some groups the formal structure and informal structure may be the same. This would be especially true in clubs which developed first on an informal basis and were later formalized. In either case, the structure tends to develop around the leader (Freud, 1949), or some other type of central person, such as the tyrant, idol, or scapegoat (Redl, 1942). The relationship of the group structure to the type of central person will be discussed in Chapter Eleven.

The attempts of children to establish a hierarchy (Hanfmann, 1935) are perhaps more apparent than those of college-age students, who characteristically wait until the second meeting of a laboratory discussion group before launching their struggle for status.[4] The greater the agreement among members concerning the potential status of individuals in an initially leaderless group, the less time it will take to solve the status problem. Some groups never solve the problem, to everyone's satisfaction, i.e., never develop perfect consensus with respect to the ranking system. Groups with low status consensus go through repeated crises. After they have passed through such crises, the men who come out on top in the groups where their status is recognized spend less and less time in interaction in attempts to gain and maintain a position of high rank.

Over a series of meetings in five-man discussion groups where agreement on status was high, the top three men shifted positions, while the men who ranked fourth and fifth in status tended to maintain their positions. In other words, once a man found himself in fourth or fifth position, he was likely to stay there. However, in the five-man

---

4. Some authors use the term "status" to refer to the rank of a group member on some criterion. Although "status" has also been used as synonomous with "position" in everyday usage, the term seems to be associated with a less well-defined set of expectations than the term "position." When the original author used the term "status" in this way, his usage has been adopted in many instances in reporting the results of his research.

groups which were low in their initial status-consensus, there were more shifts in position over time and the shifts involved men at all levels in the hierarchy (Heinicke & Bales, 1953).

These shifts of position are most evident in experimental groups or in groups in which the informal structure is not reinforced by a formal structure. If the power differences between members are obvious and firmly fixed from the start, the positions of the top men are less likely to be challenged by those down the line (Crockett, 1955). However, poker players try to bluff and beat the strongest player (Riddle, 1925), and players in a three-man game in which members are given an initially unequal point advantage tend to break up into a coalition of the two low-point men trying to unseat the high-point man (Hoffman, Festinger, & Lawrence, 1954). This tendency for the two-man coalition to attack the high-power person or, in the opposite case, to withstand attack from below from a low-power person is seen as a basic structural type in the three-person group (Simmel, 1902, Mills, 1953).

In most discussion groups in which members have approximately equal amounts of information and no one holds more cards or points at the outset, the leadership rank is established by the relative amount of talking of each member. The person who talks the most generally wins most of the decisions and becomes the leader (Bales, 1953; Strodtbeck, 1954a; March, 1956; Shaw & Gilchrist, 1956; Bass, Pryer, Gaier, & Flint, 1958; Riecken, 1958; Kirscht, Lodahl, & Haire, 1959; see Exhibit 7).

§ Streetcorner Society

WHYTE'S STUDY of gangs of corner boys in an Italian urban area provides many examples of the development and maintenance of an informal structure in a group (1943). In the final chapter of his book, Whyte summarizes his impressions of the typical gang structure, with illustrations taken from his study of a gang called the "Nortons," led by "Doc":

The corner-gang structure arises out of the habitual association of the members over a long period of time. The nuclei of most gangs can be traced back to early boyhood, when living close together provided the first opportunities for social contacts. School years modified the original pattern somewhat, but I know of no corner gangs which arose through classroom or school-playground association. The gangs grew up on the corner and re-

mained there with remarkable persistence from early boyhood until the
members reached their late twenties or early thirties. In the course of years
some groups were broken up by the movement of families away from
Cornerville, and the remaining members merged with gangs on nearby corners; but frequently movement out of the district does not take the corner
boy away from his corner. On any evening on almost any corner one finds
corner boys who have come in from other parts of the city or from suburbs
to be with their old friends. The residence of the corner boy may also change
within the district, but nearly always he retains his allegiance to his original
corner.

Home plays a very small role in the group activities of the corner boy.
Except when he eats, sleeps, or is sick, he is rarely at home, and his friends
always go to his corner first when they want to find him. Even the corner
boy's name indicates the dominant importance of the gang in his activities. It
is possible to associate with a group of men for months and never discover
the family names of more than a few of them. Most are known by nicknames
attached to them by the group. Furthermore, it is easy to overlook the
distinction between married and single men. The married man regularly
sets aside one evening a week to take out his wife. There are other occasions
when they go out together and entertain together, and some corner boys
devote more attention to their wives than others, but, married or single, the
corner boy can be found on his corner almost every night of the week.

His social activities away from the corner are organized with similar
regularity. Many corner gangs set aside the same night each week for some
special activity, such as bowling. With the Nortons this habit was so strong
that it persisted for some of the members long after the original group had
broken up.

Most groups have a regular evening meeting-place aside from the corner.
Nearly every night at about the same time the gang gathers for "coffee-and"
in its favorite cafeteria or for beer in the corner tavern. When some other
activity occupies the evening, the boys meet at the cafeteria or tavern
before returning to the corner or going home. Positions at the tables are fixed
by custom. Night after night each group gathers around the same tables. The
right to these positions is recognized by other Cornerville groups. When
strangers are found at the accustomed places, the necessity of finding other
chairs is a matter of some annoyance, especially if no nearby location is
available. However, most groups gather after nine in the evening when few
are present except the regular customers who are familiar with the established
procedure.

The life of the corner boy proceeds along regular and narrowly circum-
scribed channels. As Doc said to me: "Fellows around here don't know
what to do except within a radius of about three hundred yards. That's the
truth, Bill. They come home from work, hang on the corner, go up to eat,
back on the corner, up a show, and they come back to hang on the corner. If
they're not on the corner, it's likely the boys there will know where you can
find them. Most of them stick to one corner. It's only rarely that a fellow
will change his corner."

The stable composition of the group and the lack of social assurance on the part of its members contribute toward producing a very high rate of social interaction within the group. The group structure is a product of these interactions [see Fig. 13].

Figure 13—The Nortons, Spring and Summer, 1937

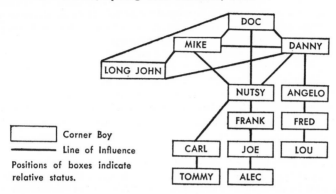

Out of such interaction there arises a system of mutual obligations which is fundamental to group cohesion. If the men are to carry on their activities as a unit, there are many occasions when they must do favors for one another. The code of the corner boy requires him to help his friends when he can and to refrain from doing anything to harm them. When life in the group runs smoothly, the obligations binding members to one another are not explicitly recognized. Once Doc asked me to do something for him, and I said that I welcomed the chance to reciprocate. He objected: "I don't want it that way. I want you to do this for me because you're my friend. That's all."

It is only when the relationship breaks down that the underlying obligations are brought to light. While Alec and Frank were friends, I never heard either one of them discuss the services he was performing for the other, but when they had a falling-out over the group activities with the Aphrodite Club, each man complained to Doc that the other was not acting as he should in view of the services that had been done him. In other words, actions which were performed explicitly for the sake of friendship were revealed as being part of a system of mutual obligations.

Not all the corner boys live up to their obligations equally well, and this factor partly accounts for the differentiation in status among them. The man with a low status may violate his obligations without much change in his position. His fellows know that he has failed to discharge certain obligations in the past, and his position reflects his past performances. On the other hand, the leader is depended upon by all the members to meet his personal obligations. He cannot fail to do so without causing confusion and endangering his position.

The relationship of status to the system of mutual obligations is most clearly revealed when one observes the use of money.

Doc did not hesitate to accept money from Danny, but he avoided taking any from the followers. The leader spends more money on his followers than they on him. The farther down in the structure one looks, the fewer are the financial relations which tend to obligate the leader to a follower. This does not mean that the leader has more money than others or even that he necessarily spends more—though he must always be a free spender. It means that the financial relations must be explained in social terms. Unconsciously, and in some cases consciously, the leader refrains from putting himself under obligations to those with low status in the group.

The leader does not deal with his followers as an undifferentiated group. Doc explained: "On any corner you would find not only a leader but probably a couple of lieutenants. They could be leaders themselves, but they let the man lead them. You would say, 'They let him lead because they like the way he does things.' Sure, but he leans upon them for his authority. Many times you find fellows on a corner that stay in the background until some situation comes up, and then they will take over and call the shots. Things like that can change fast sometimes."

The leader mobilizes the group by dealing first with his lieutenants.

The leadership is changed not through an uprising of the bottom men but by a shift in the relations between men at the top of the structure. When a gang breaks into two parts, the explanation is to be found in a conflict between the leader and one of his former lieutenants.

This discussion should not give the impression that the leader is the only man who proposes a course of action. Other men frequently have ideas, but their suggestions must go through the proper channels if they are to go into effect.

The actions of the leader can be characterized in terms of the origination of action in pair and set events. A pair event is one which takes place between two people. A set event is one in which one man originates action for two or more others. The leader frequently originates action for the group without waiting for the suggestions of his followers. A follower may originate action for the leader in a pair event, but he does not originate action for the leader and other followers at the same time—that is, he does not originate action in a set event which includes the leader. Of course, when the leader is not present, parts of the group are mobilized when men lower in the structure originate action in set events. It is through observation of such set events when the top men are not present that it is possible to determine the relative positions of the men who are neither leaders nor lieutenants.

Each member of the corner gang has his own position in the gang structure. Although the positions may remain unchanged over long periods of time, they should not be conceived in static terms. To have a position means that the individual has a customary way of interacting with other members of the group. When the pattern of interactions changes, the positions change. The positions of the members are interdependent, and one position cannot change without causing some adjustments in the other positions. Since the group is organized around the men with the top positions, some of the men with low standing may change positions or drop out without upsetting the balance of the group. For example, when Lou Danaro and Fred Mackey stopped participating in the activities of the Nortons, those activities continued to be organized in much the same manner as before, but when Doc and Danny dropped out, the Nortons disintegrated, and the patterns of interaction had to be reorganized along different lines (pp. 255-263).

§   Fluctuations in
    Organization

SINCE GROUPS which are well organized are usually the most productive (French, 1941; Darley, Gross, & Martin, 1952), any movement of members from one position to another within the role structure, or any discrepancies in the criteria for establishing status in the group, such as age and pay, result in more activity in the social-emotional area in an attempt to re-establish the structure or resolve the differences with a consequent decrease in productivity (Heinicke & Bales, 1953; Adams, 1953; Bales & Slater, 1955, 1957; Shepherd & Weschler, 1955; Wheeler, 1957).

§   Permanent and
    Temporary Groups

WHERE THE STATUS OF MEMBERS is fixed by the formal structure, as in the air corps, the authority of the formal leader will probably go unchallenged, even in groups composed only for the purpose of an experiment. In assessing the influence of a formal structure on the interaction process within a group, it is important to distinguish between status relations which are ascribed and status relations which have been developed through some considerable previous interaction. It is likely that the clarity with which a structure is perceived, as well as the degree of influence it can exert over the group's activity, will be related to the length of time during which the structure has developed. Torrance, in a study of some consequences of power differences on decision-making in "permanent" and "temporary" three-person groups (1954a), demonstrates differing effects of the same official position when groups whose members had been a unit for several months are compared with *ad hoc* groups formed for research purposes. The crews in both instances were B26 bomber crews consisting of a pilot, navigator, and gunner. Both pilot, who was also aircraft commander, and navigator were commisioned officers, while the gunner was an enlisted man. Each of 62 permanent and 32 temporary (composed for experiment) crews was given four problems which required a group decision.

The first problem was the Maier Horse-Trading Problem. "A man bought a horse for $60 and sold it for $70. Then he bought it back for $80 and sold it for $90. How much money does he make in the horse-trading business?" Each individual was asked to write on a slip of paper his solution without conferring with anyone. Crew members were then asked to confer to reach a crew decision.

The second problem required the subjects to estimate the number of dots on a 16″ x 21″ card with 3155 black dots scattered evenly but not geometrically over a white background. The card was exposed for fifteen seconds, and then each subject was asked to write his individual estimate on a slip of paper. They were then asked to confer to decide upon the best estimate. Finally, each man was asked to write on a slip of paper the number of dots he personally *really* thought were there.

The sketch of the conference group in the Michigan Group Projective Sketches was used in the third problem. Subjects were instructed to write within a five-minute limit a story about the picture. After the individual stories had been collected, the subjects were asked to agree upon and write, within a ten-minute limit, a crew story about the same sketch.

The fourth problem was a survival situation in which the crew had been downed in enemy territory. After two days, one of the members of the crew had been slowing down the attempts to reach safe territory, estimated to be about 40 miles away. He developed severe blisters on his feet and felt he was nearing exhaustion. He does not believe he can continue and urges the other two men to go ahead without him. The crew was instructed to designate one member to act as the man who insists on giving up, and to make its decision as it would be in an actual situation.

After the four decision-making problems, a very brief questionnaire regarding their reactions to the fourth decision-making problem was administered, along with a question concerning their attitude toward being transferred to another crew (pp. 483-484).

The resulting data may be examined for two sources of influence on final group decision:

(1) differences among the three positions in the group,

(2) differences between temporary and permanent groups. With respect to the Horse-Trading Problem, in the permanent groups 31 per cent of the pilots, 50 per cent of the navigators, and 29 per cent of the gunners had recorded correct answers individually. Pilots were most successful and gunners least successful in gettting the crew to accept their answers as the group decision. In temporary crews, any member who had the correct answer was likely to influence the group

regardless of his position, thus indicating a lessened effect of position on decision-making in groups where the positions had not been operative over a considerable period of time.

Results from the Dot Test display no differences which are significantly different from chance, though the tendency is in the direction of less influence from the gunner.

The Conference Group Story, possibly because of the difference in task (in the direction of more ambiguous criteria of performance), yields clearer results. Since individuals wrote their stories about the conference group sketch before the crew story, Torrance developed an index of influence for each person.

In each case, the five most salient aspects of each story were identified and then the individual stories checked for the presence of these same five aspects. If all five aspects were common to the crew and individual stories, a score of 5 was assigned; if four aspects were common, a score of 4 was given, etc. If four or five aspects were common, it was considered that the individual exerted a strong influence on the crew's decision. If three elements were common, the individual was considered to have exerted "some influence." Less than three common aspects was considered as evidence of little or no influence (p. 487).

The results of the conference group story task shown in Table 41 indicate that the members of permanent crews influenced the crew's decision according to the power structure (differences significant at better than the 5 per cent level of confidence.)

Table 4—Consequences of Power Differences on Influence on Decision Concerning Story about Conference Group

	PERCENTAGES		
Degree of Influence	Pilots	Navigators	Gunners
Strong influence	58.7	37.7	0
Some influence	23.4	26.9	23.2
Little or no influence	17.0	34.6	78.6

For various reasons the survival problem does not permit straightforward comparison with the other three problems. First, there is no record of individual positions held prior to group discussions. Second, the measure of influence is not direct. Third, member self-ratings which were not a feature of the other three tasks are employed.

In his report of the findings on a post-discussion questionnaire for the survival problem, Torrance concluded that, in permanent groups, according to self-reports, the pilots and gunners made less effort to influence the crew's decision (P. < .01) and did not feel that they influenced the decision greatly. None of the gunners felt that he greatly influenced the decision.

A comparison of permanent with temporary groups via content analysis of their discussions of the survival problem showed temporary groups more frequently made a series of decisions which required testing and modification, rather than single decisions which would be final. More of the permanent crews decided to retain the disabled member under any circumstances. Although the *esprit de corps* was higher in permanent crews (93.7 per cent of permanent crews were concerned with keeping the crew together, compared with 71.8 per cent of temporary crews), the temporay crews manifested less rigid, more pragmatically directed thinking in these problem sessions.

The evidence from each of the four problem-solving tasks supports the generalization that individuals with high formal rank in a group will have more influence on a group decision than those with low rank. This tendency was more evident in permanent three-man crews than it was in crews composed of members who had been brought together temporarily for the purpose of the experiment.

§   Structure in Therapy
    Groups

THE THERAPY GROUP is a good example of a simple group structure. The formal structure of the therapy group, like that of the classroom, is given in the simplest possible terms. There are only two formal positions, leader and follower. The members of the therapy group are brought together to discuss their common emotional problems under the guidance of a clinician. Members of groups with this simple structural type are related to each other primarily because they are all related in the same way to the leader. Little formal role differentiation is expected of the members.

During the first few meetings the therapy group passes through the phases of being an assemblage of patients waiting for the therapist to initiate action, a participating audience, and finally an interacting group (Luchins, 1947). Since the therapist's position as leader is secured by the formal structure, a member with inclinations for power can only hope to play the informal role of the "doctor's assistant" (Frank, Margolin, Nash, Stone, Varon, & Ascher, 1952; Margolin, 1952) or the role of leader of the subgroup which resists suggestions made by the therapist (Bion, 1951; Herbert & Trist, 1953).

In one study of therapy groups, each member's rank in the group on a task-effectiveness criterion was found to be almost identical with his rank based on a social-emotional criterion (Talland, 1957b). This overlap apparently occurred because the task of the group was to handle social-emotional problems of the members. As a result, the person who made the most contributions and was seen as the task leader was also the best liked person because his activity was instrumental in helping other members with their problems. A similar overlap in the task and social-emotional hierarchies has been observed in other types of discussion groups which also serve the purpose of meeting members' social-emotional needs (Theodorson, 1957).

§   Differentiation in
    Hierarchies

ALTHOUGH THE HIERARCHIES of task and social-emotional positions may at first appear undifferentiated, there is a tendency, particularly in large groups, for them to separate as the group grows older. In the initially leaderless group the most apparent differentiation of informal roles is the gradual development of a *task leader* and a best-liked person or *social-emotional leader* (Benne & Sheats, 1948; Norfleet, 1948; James, 1956; Grusky, 1957). In a series of four meetings of groups which met to discuss human relations problems (Bales, 1953), the member most chosen as "liked" was usually also chosen for "best ideas" and "guidance" in the first meeting; however, this coincidence of choice became less likely in later meetings. In fact, when observations for all four meetings were summarized, the member who ranked highest on "guidance" and "best ideas" and who inititiated most of the activity in the group was found to be the member who was *disliked* most (i.e., received the most negative votes) and ranked only third on *liked* choices. The second or third man on "guidance" and "best ideas" was usually best liked.

When the same person is capable of playing both the *task* and *social-emotional leader* roles, he usually favors being best liked and gives up the task leader role. In ten cases where the same person played both roles in the first meeting of an initially leaderless group, the "best ideas" role was dropped nine times in favor of the "liked" role. In the remaining case, the person dropped both roles (Bales, 1953). This same trend has been noted in groups over a longer series of meetings. In one case, a high correlation of .70 between choices on the criterion of productivity (task) and choices for spending leisure time (best liked) obtained at the end of the first day of a series of group meetings, declined to around .55 by the end of the third week (Lippitt, 1948).

Investigation of an established group will usually uncover similar differences between choices on a task and social-emotional basis (Jennings, 1947a, 1947b; Coffey, 1952), where the top man in either category may be regarded as a *leader* if he initiates most of the activity in his specialty. However, high rank in these two categories is not always correlated with all criteria for leadership (Gibb, 1950).

The tendency for role differentiation which involves sharing the leadership activity may be resisted by members of groups who expect to have a strong central leader. In high-level conferences in business, industry, and government, for example, leadership was shared only when the group had an urgent problem to solve and its leader was relatively weak (Berkowitz, 1953).

Since the roles which develop in a group do so in response to the requirements of the task and the particular constellation of individuals who compose the group, the specific content of any role may be expected to vary primarily with the group's task and secondarily with the characteristics of the members. In groups which have a life which is longer than any of the individual members, the task requirements would be less variable than the social-emotional requirements.

§   Culture and Role
    Differentiation

IN THE TYPICAL middle-class family in the United States and Great Britain the father is the task leader and the mother the social-emotional leader (Bott, 1955, 1956; Parsons, et al., 1955; Kenkel, 1957), but this is not always the case in other cultures or even within all subcultures to be found in the United States. Strodtbeck (1951) observed husband-wife interaction in three subcultures in the southwestern United States and found differences in the amount of activity and power of the husband

and wife in each of the cultures. Married pairs of Mormons, Texans, and Navahoes were asked to make independent evaluations of other families in their neighborhood and then to reconcile through discussion any differences in their evaluations. Among the Mormons, a patriarchial group, the husbands won most of the decisions, (Table 5) and among the Navahoes, a matriarchy, the wives won the most. The husbands and wives were about equal for the Texans who are the most equalitarian, although the husbands won slightly more decisions. No matter what the culture, the spouse who did most of the talking won most of the decisions (Table 6).

Table 5—Decisions Won, by Spouse and Culture

CULTURE	NUMBER OF COUPLES	DECISION WON BY:	
		Husband	Wife
Navaho	10	34	46
Texan	10	39	33
Mormon	10	42	29

Table 6—Decisions Won and Talking-time for 34 Married Couples

SPOUSE WHO TALKED MOST	SPOUSE WHO WON MOST	
	Husband	Wife
Husband	14	5
Wife	5	10

§ Cliques and Cabals

ANOTHER EXAMPLE of group structure which emphasizes the subgroups within the informal structure is taken from a factory study. Burns (1955) differentiates "cliques," which allow men who are partial failures some protection and a chance to withdraw from the institution, and "cabals," which offer the possibility of "illegitimate" control to members who wish to move up in the organization.

The "cliques" were formed by groups of older men whose conversation reflected a tendency to withdraw from the situation as far as they could. Their lack of acceptance of the changes in the engineering firm for which they worked, their position in the age-grade hierarchy, and their previous experience and qualifications led them into positions whose functions were well defined but were not the key production positions. Their positions were also out of the main line of career opportunities, so that they had, to this extent, resigned from the race. Their cliques had a specifically protective, reassuring purpose. They reassured themselves by being critical of certain features of the organization. They complained that the factory's chief product was scrap, that the place was full of youngsters from universities who knew nothing about industry and yet told experienced craftsmen what to do, and that the craftsmen who were made lab technicians were spoiled for good work thereafter. This older group thought of their jobs in contractual terms, as employees in a firm in which they were prepared to do certain specified work and to undertake specific duties in return for a salary, rather than in terms of responsibility shared with colleagues in a professional group for the discharge of a whole task that the whole firm set.

In contrast, the "cabals" were formed by younger men in the factory. These men were executives who were well satisfied with their positions, were well placed in the age-grade system, and had developed their careers during the years that they had been members of the firm. A member of a "cabal" identified himself and his interests much more with the firm but did not on this account accept the "ways of doing things" which were criticized by members of the older groups, but rather discussed them as features of policy emanating from this or that person and subject to improvement or change if sufficient pressure or persuasion were applied. Thus, the needs for reassurance about possible failure and the need to improve the chances of success by "illegitimate" means (i.e., means that were infractions of the rules and order prevailing in that particular milieu) were met through membership in "cliques," which appeared to offer compensation to the older workers, and "cabals," which provided improved chances of success to the younger generation.

§ Role Collision,
Incompatibility,
and Confusion

THERE IS USUALLY agreement among group members concerning some specific attributes of a member's role (especially in highly cohesive groups; Hall, 1955), but there are also areas in which the expectations for role behavior are contradictory or ill-defined. The clash of expectations concerning some aspects of a role have usually been called "role conflict." These conflicts can arise in a number of different ways. The term *role collision* will be used to indicate the type of conflict which may occur if two different individuals in a group hold roles which overlap in some respect. In a hospital, for example, two doctors are often called in to treat the same patient. Each is expected to prescribe treatment for the patient, but unless the doctors coordinate their behavior the patient's wounds may be bound up one day and left open the next, depending upon which of the doctors last visited the ward.

Another example of role collision may occur in the family, where the father and mother roles may collide in some areas but not in others. While the father may carry out the principal economic activities and the mother the household tasks, their roles may collide in the area of child-rearing, where both play a part. Tension in that area may be indicated by an increase in the number of disagreements on who is to perform an activity and who is the source of authority (Herbst, 1952).

A second type of role problem is that of *role incompatibility* in which an individual is forced to meet expectations for different roles which are incompatible (Simmel, 1955, p. 155; Gross et al., 1958). This phenomenon appeared in a small group of clothing salesmen where the expectations of "friend" were incompatible with those of "competitor" (Wispe, 1955).

Usually the problem of incompatibility is solved on a time basis: one role is allowed to "cool off" while the individual "warms up" to the next role (Yablonsky, 1953). The most common source of conflict for a man is between his roles at work and at home. This conflict may be solved by spending a limited number of hours in each place. During a busy season at the office, however, he may have to work late, making it impossible for him to fulfill all his obligations as a husband-father.

Since a doctor, for example, may be called away from his family at any time in an emergency, this conflict continually recurs. To solve the problem, the doctor's family may decide that when the conflict arises, the role of doctor has precedence over the role of father, but this does nothing to reduce the *number* of occasions of conflict.

The incidence of role incompatibility among married persons is related to their ratings of self-happiness. Women report fewer conflicts and rate themselves higher on happiness than men (Ort, 1950).

A third problem is that of *role confusion*. There are usually some inconsistent expectations concerning the behavior appropriate to any role. These incompatible expectations arise from three sources: (1) within the group there is agreement on the expected behavior, but there are expectations which are difficult to satisfy at the same time; (2) within the group there is disagreement regarding role definition; (3) other groups of which the individual is a member may disagree regarding the nature of his role (Seeman, 1953).

An example of the first subtype of *role confusion* is the problem of male cooks or countermen in the restaurant industry. These men have relatively high status within the industry and should be the ones to initiate activity, yet they must take orders from female waitresses who have low status in the hierarchy (Whyte, 1949). This situation produces interpersonal friction which is often avoided by various devices which make it unnecessary for a counterman to respond each time a waitress brings an order.

The second subtype of *role confusion* involves significant disagreement within the group regarding role definition. In a school study, teachers were asked ten forced-choice questions concerning the role of an "ideal superintendent." One question asked, "Should an ideal superintendent invite staff members to his home for social occasions?" and a second, "Should an ideal superintendent feel free to discuss his personal problems with the teachers?" Simple "yes and "no" answers were the forced-choice alternatives provided. In both cases, the split in opinion among the teachers was close to a 60-to-40 division, so that any move on the part of the superintendent to become intimate with the teachers would result in approval from some of his teachers and disapproval from others (Seeman, 1953).

Similar problems arise for children faced with conflicting suggestions from adults (Meyers, 1944) and shop stewards who can take an "active" part in promoting the interests of the workers only at the risk of antagonizing the foremen who expect them to be "passive" (Jacobson, Charters, & Lieberman, 1951).

In an office of a department store we find an example of the third subtype of *role confusion.* Here the informal group rated one office job as higher status than the other, while the management gave equal pay for both jobs. When an individual was shifted from the job which the informal group designated as high-status to the low-status job, he was dissatisfied, since the rights and privileges accorded to the two positions by management and the informal group were not the same (Homans, 1953).

This subtype of role confusion is also apparent where conflicting expectations are held by two family groups about "traditional" and "companionship" forms of marriage (Motz, 1952). The parents of one member of a newly married pair might expect the marriage to be formed on the "traditional" lines of the dominant male, while the other set of parents expect a "companionship" arrangement in which the husband and wife would share equally in decisions. In this case the confusion arises from conflicting definitions held by members outside the group in which conflict takes place.

Although role collision, incompatibility, or confusion may be found in the social structure at many points, not all individuals may experience stress in coping with the problems which arise in these situations. In the same way, not all persons will find stressful problems which may occur in *role transition,* when the individual gives up one role to take another, as is the case with a new job or marriage. There is some evidence that certain types of personalities find these "hazardous situations" especially stressful. In a study of the stresses involved in the conflict of officer and intructor roles in the air corps, a "conflict-prone personality" was identified, a man who tended to be feminine, nervous, introverted, depressed, cycloid, authoritarian, and extra-punitive (Getzels & Guba, 1955). Such a person found it especially difficult in his relations with enlisted men to reconcile the social distance required of the officer with the equalitarian behavior expected of the instructor.

Three similar types of role problems have been identified in the clinical analysis of family case-study material. In general, contradictions in the role expectations for a family member tend to make that individual more self-aware and on guard, forcing him constantly to make decisions about his role behavior. This type of family situation appears to foster more disturbed children (Spiegel, 1957).

§ Summary

THE TERM "role" refers primarily to the set of expectations which group members share concerning the behavior of a person who occupies a position in a group. The expectations for a given role are met most easily by the individual whose personality most nearly fits the role. The expectations for a role for any content category of behavior may be visualized as falling somewhere in a space defined by two axes. One axis represents the behavior which the individual is expected to direct towards others and the other axis represents the behavior which others are expected to direct towards him. In both cases this behavior ranges from that which is required to that which is prohibited. In addition to the specification of expected role content, the expected communication network and interaction rate may be viewed with various degrees of complexity.

Groups tend to have an informal structure, as well as a formal structure. The ease with which the informal structure is developed and maintained depends upon the relevant characteristics of the group members and the extent to which the formal structure is well defined. If individuals differ significantly in their characteristics, the *informal* structure will develop rapidly and remain relatively stable over time, since attempts of low-ranking members to displace those of higher ranks will fail. If fluctuations occur among the individuals who fill positions in the informal structure, members' energies may be diverted from productivity as they attempt to re-establish the structure. Whyte describes the development and maintainance of the informal structure of a group of "corner boys" in his account of "street corner society."

In newly formed leaderless groups without a formal structure, members tend to assume the same positions which they hold in other groups of long standing. Thus, the influence of air corps pilots, navigators, and gunners in "temporary" problem-solving groups is related to the relative power they hold in their own "permanent" crews.

The simplest type of formal structure is found in the therapy group where there are only two formal roles, leader and follower. Within the informal structure, however, there may be role specialization.

Although task and social-emotional hierarchies may at first be undifferentiated, there is a tendency for them to separate as a group develops or grows larger. The age, sex, and social characteristics required for the positions in each of the hierarchies may be determined by the culture of the society in which the group develops. In the family, for example, the role of task leader may be played by the father, by the mother, or shared, depending upon the culture.

In an industrial setting, two types of informal groups were identified: *cliques*, which had a social-emotional orientation allowing partial failures a chance to withdraw from the institution, and *cabals*, which had a task orientation offering the possibility of illegitimate control to members who wished to move up in the organization.

Three types of problems occur as a result of conflicting role expectations. In *role collision* two different individuals have roles which are in conflict in some respect; in *role incompatibility* the same individual plays roles which have contradictory expectations; and in *role confusion* there is a lack of agreement among group members about the expectations for a given role.

Exhibit 7
Interaction Rate and Leadership

A.

Investigator: Bales (1953).
Focus: The equilibrium problem in small groups.
Sample: Laboratory groups of college students.
Method: The interaction of the subjects as they discussed a human relations problem was recorded using the Bales categories. After the discussion the subjects rated each other on postmeeting reaction questionnaires.
Relevant Findings: The order produced by ranking individuals according to their "basic initiating rank" on total amounts of participation was fairly highly correlated with the order produced by their own ratings of each other as to "productivity," i.e., who had the best ideas, and who did most to guide the discussion effectively.

B.

Investigator: Strodtbeck (1954a).
Focus: The family as a three-person group.
Sample: 48 interaction records of families.
Method: After recording the answers of mother, father, and adolescent son to a set of questions, nine specific items were selected on which there was a difference of opinion. Each subject was at odds with the other two members of the group on three of the items and in coalition with another member (three with each) on the remaining six items. The family members were then instructed to try to achieve consensus. Their interaction was observed and recorded.
Relevant Findings: The most-speaking person was found to win the largest share of the decisions, and in all cases the least-speaking person won the least.

C.

Investigator: Shaw & Gilchrist (1956).
Focus: Intra-group communication and leader choice.
Sample: Ten groups of five subjects, each enrolled in psychology courses at a university.
Method: Four problems were used which required inter-member com-

munication for solution. Communication, however, was not face-to-face and was conducted by passing written notes which were identified by number rather than name.

Relevant Findings: Leaders emerged in the initially unorganized groups. These individuals received a higher rank on leadership from their peers, initiated more items attempting organization and giving information, and responded in an unexpected way less frequently than did other group members.

D.

Investigator: March (1956).

Focus: Influence measurement in experimental and semi-experimental groups.

Sample: Ten five-man groups of college students. In half of the groups the subjects were well acquainted, in the other half strangers.

Method: Subjects ranked and agreed on a group rank for five items in three sets (beautiful girls, communicative paragraphs, and ink-blot titles).

Relevant Findings: A subject's rating of another's influence was associated with high participation and a large number of influence attempts on the part of the other.

E.

Investigator: Kirscht, Lodahl, & Haire (1959).

Focus: Some factors in the selection of leaders by members of small groups.

Sample: 22 three-man groups of college students.

Method: Each group discussed a human relations problem and then chose a representative to talk to a representative from another group. The total talking time and the number of leadership acts for each participant was scored.

Relevant Findings: Subjects chosen as representatives talked more and gave a larger proportion of leadership acts. The prediction of leadership was better ($r = .63$) if both form and content were considered.

5

INTERPERSONAL CHOICE

INDIVIDUALS INDICATE their interpersonal choices in a variety of ways: through frequency of association, through formal elections, and through ratings of other group members elicited by observers and experimenters. Ratings of the last type, popularized by Moreno, have been called "sociometric" ratings. Sociometric ratings are based on a variety of criteria which may fall into any of the content areas described in Chapter One.

Although an analysis of "sociograms," which depict the patterns of interpersonal choice, is useful in identifying the position of an individual in the informal structure of a group, it does not reveal the behavior which is associated with the position. The ratings on several criteria are often combined; thus, individuals are identified as "over-chosen" or "under-chosen" in the informal structure without reference to the particular position which they hold. Although the "over-chosen" members tend to be those who prefer close relationships with others, they are not necessarily the informal leaders.

The sociometric test has been used widely in studies of children in school populations. Here the principal problem for research has often been to determine the basis of friendship between pairs of children. The friendship bonds between individuals tend to be influenced by the following factors: (1) proximity, and similarities in (2) individual social characteristics, (3) interests or values, and (4) personality.

Sociometric ratings are often used to derive measures of morale or cohesiveness since individuals who are highly attracted to a group trend to be the most productive if the norms of the group specify high productivity. A measure of cohesiveness may then be used to predict productivity.

§ The Sociogram

THE TERM "sociometric" is usually used to designate the interpersonal choices which group members have revealed to an observer or experimenter, although the term has also been used to include a variety of forms of social measurement (Bjerstedt, 1956a). Sociometry was introduced by Moreno (1953), who has suggested six rules to be followed in using the sociometric test:

1. The limits of the group in which the test is given should be indicated.

2. There should be unlimited choices of other persons.

3. Individuals should be asked to choose and reject other group members with a specific criterion or activity in mind.

4. The results of the sociometric tests should be used to restructure the group; that is, the group should be reorganized by placing people together who have chosen each other as liked.

5. The opinions should be given in private.

6. Questions should be phrased in ways that members can understand.

In practice, these six rules are followed in only about 25 per cent of all "sociometric" studies (Lindzey & Borgatta, 1954). The most frequent deviations from the rules are the limitation on choices, usually to about three, and the omission of the action step of actual reorganization of the group in line with the results of the test.

Although interpersonal liking is usually determined by asking group members "sociometric" questions which can be simple or complex

Group Process and Structure

(Tagiuri, 1952; Weschler, Tannenbaum, & Talbot, 1952; Eng, 1954; Barr, 1955), other behavioral indices may be used such as time spent together (Moreno, Jennings, & Sargent, 1940; Fischer, 1953), visiting patterns, or work exchange (Loomis, 1941). The interpersonal choice data are then analyzed visually by using "sociograms" in which individuals are represented as circles and their choices as arrows pointing from one to the other (Borgatta, 1951a), or mathematically through matrix algebra (Ross & Harary, 1952). Further details concerning the use of the test are given in the methodological note which appears as an appendix to this volume.

One of Moreno's sociometric diagrams or "sociograms" is reproduced in Figure 14 (1953). Here he has plotted the pattern of interpersonal

Figure 14—Pattern of Interpersonal Choice in a Cottage Family
(Moreno, 1953, p. 267)

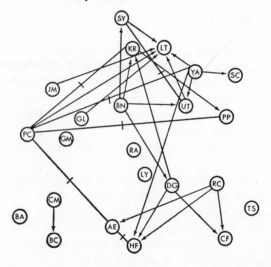

choice in one of the cottage families in a school for delinquent girls which provided the population for an early sociometric study made in collaboration with Jennings (1950a).

The circles in the diagram represent the girls in the cottage and the lines between them represent their choices of the five other girls from the cottage they most wanted to live with. Although it was not done for this group, the subjects are also often asked whom they would reject. The rejections may then be plotted on the same or a different sociogram. The arrowhead on a line indicates the direction of choice. If two persons choose each other, the arrows are joined in a straight line with a dash across the center.

After the choices of each girl in cottage C3 have been plotted, the resulting choice pattern indicates the following characteristics of the 23 girls:

Type	Number	Identification
Isolated	5	BA, GM, RA, LY, TS,
Unchosen	5	CM, JM, GL, RC, BN,
Mutual attractions (pairs)	6	AE-HF, AE-PC, PC-PP, PC-YA, PC-KR, UT-SY,
Chains	1	HF-AE-PC-KR-PP
Triangles	0	
Stars	1	LT (Note: LT is an "isolated star," as she chooses no one in return)

Moreno describes this group as one with an extroverted group organization. Its special features are a large number of nonparticipating individuals, low group cohesion, and low differentiation between underchosen and overchosen members.

§ Choice Criteria

THE CRITERION USED in Moreno's study of the cottage (i.e., choice of roommates), is similar to the criterion of "Whom would you choose as a friend?" which is used in many studies. Both criteria are rather general, but both would appear to lie primarily within the *social-emotional* area. A typical criterion in the task area is "Whom would you choose to work with?"

Subjects tend to make fewer choices on a friendship criterion than on a work criterion (Jennings, 1947b, Gibb, 1950). However, correlations are high between choices based on each of these criteria (Bjerstedt, 1956b; Hollander, 1956), since there are some "great men" (Borgatta, Couch, & Bales, 1954) who actually have desirable traits in all areas, and there are some subjects who will choose on a criterion which is important to them regardless of the experimenter's request.

An example of choice based on the subject's own criterion rather than that of the experimenter is found in an experiment by French (1956) using 137 air corps personnel in their seventh week of training.

The men were given a test designed to measure both achievement and affiliation motivation. They were then divided into groups of four to work on an "important concept formation test." The groups were so constructed that three of the subjects had previously rated each other as "liked" and the fourth member as "not liked." All subjects first worked individually on a sorting task in which the disliked member was made to succeed and the other members to fail. The subjects were then asked to make one or two choices for a work partner to repeat the same task in pairs. On this sociometric test the subjects who were high in achievement and low in affiliation motivation made significantly more single choices of the unliked members who appeared to be successful, while the subjects who were high in affiliation and low in achievement made significantly more choices of the two friends. Those who were high in both motivations made significantly more double choices involving both a friend and the successful person, while the subjects who were low in both motivations predominately chose a friend.

In this study the use of the sociometric test meets all the criteria suggested by Moreno, since a specific work criterion is used and the group is restructured on the basis of the choices; it is evident, however, that some subjects tend to disregard the criterion and choose on the basis of their predominant interpersonal need. An additional finding that the subjects in this experiment with high need for achievement differed from those with high need for affiliation in the extent to which they made "dislike" ratings in the first place suggests that the two types of individuals also have a different basis for choice on the more general criterion of "friend."

Different choice criteria also influence the form and content of interaction. In a study by Back (1951; see Chapter Seven for more detail), the "cohesiveness" of two-man groups was manipulated by telling some pairs that they would or would not like each other, others that they would or would not receive a prize for the best group performance, and still others that they would or would not serve as a model of a highly productive group. Back found that when cohesiveness was based on personal attraction, group members tended to make the discussion into a long pleasant conversation; when it was based on task performance, the members tried to finish quickly and efficiently; and when it was based on group prestige, the members acted cautiously so that they would not endanger their status.

Even though sociometric choices do vary to some extent with the criterion, the experimenter often pools the ratings made on several criteria so that the distinctions are lost (Jennings, 1943; Bassett, 1944).

Most of the literature on interpersonal choice is summarized in this chapter without regard to specific criteria, although it is possible, in some cases, to illustrate the variations in the behavior of a subject which are associated with his choices based on different criteria.

§ Reciprocal Choice

WHEN AN INVESTIGATOR asks the subjects to rate all other members of the group using some criterion of choice, the data include not only those choices which the individuals have consciously made before the experimenter arrives on the scene, but also those choices which have only been made for the purpose of the questionnaire, which played no major part in the development of the social structure. An individual who is ranked low by another individual may, therefore, be someone who is disliked, or someone who is relatively unknown to the first person. When group members are relative strangers mutual choices might occur simply by chance (Deutschberger, 1947). In general, however, choices are not random since in every group some persons are more chosen and some less than would be expected if only chance factors were operating. Some examples of research which support this generalization are given in Exhibit 8 (Moreno & Jennings, 1938; Barker, 1942; Bronfenbrenner, 1943, 1944). A number of mathematical models which may be used to determine the extent to which the choice pattern deviates from chance have also been reported in the literature (Leeman, 1952; Nehnevajsa, 1955a, 1955b). Reciprocation of choice will not appear, however, unless a sociometric question is asked which makes reciprocation of choice possible (Criswell, 1949; Katz & Powell, 1955). For example, mutual choices would not be expected if subjects were asked to nominate the best potential leaders in the group. Mutual choice would be expected with a criterion of "sit next to" or "room with."

§ Subgroups

THE PATTERN of interpersonal choices may reveal the presence of an *informal structure,* although sociometricians do not generally distinguish the choices which a person might receive because of his position in the *formal* structure from those choices which he might receive because of his position in the *informal* structure. In any case, the interpersonal choices indicate only the position which a person holds in the structure without describing the role which is associated with that position. Thus, an analysis of the sociometric data may reveal only the presence of *subgroups* within the larger group.

The tendency for the group to split into subgroups becomes marked as the group size increases (Homans, 1950; Hare, 1953). The typical sociometric chart of interpersonal choices shows a series of interlocking subgroups as the informal group structure. So characteristic is the tendency for members of groups to form subgroups on some choice basis (Roethlisberger & Dickson, 1939; Klein, 1956), that, even when the subgroups are imposed by some outside condition, the amount of friendly interaction within the subgroups increases and the number of social isolates in the group decreases (Moreno & Jennings, 1944; Thibaut, 1950). The straight-line hierarchy is perhaps only characteristic of the group of two, as is the case in the two-boy gangs where it has been observed that "Gerry is running Alfred now" (Thrasher, 1927).

The relative nature of positions in an informal structure is evidenced by the fact that if "over-chosen" or central members and "under-chosen" or fringe members are separated from each other into new groups, a new informal structure will form in each group in which some members will again be "over-chosen" and others "under-chosen" (Powell et al., 1956).

§   Groups in Harmony
and Tension

IN A SERIES of studies in a summer camp for boys, Sherif and his colleagues experimentally demonstrated that an *increase* in hostility toward some out-group is usually associated with an *increase* in affection for members of the in-group, (Sherif, 1956).[1] Sherif chose to study groups of the informal type, where group organization and attitudes would evolve naturally and spontaneously, without formal direction or external pressures. For this purpose eleven- and twelve-year-old boys were selected as subjects. These were normal boys of homogeneous background who were picked by a long and thorough procedure, which involved interviews with each boy's family, teachers, and school officials, an analy-

---

1. In a letter to the author, Sherif stressed the fact that this account is a composite picture of a series of three different experiments using different (but comparable) subjects. More detailed accounts of these experiments appear in Rohrer & Sherif, 1951; Sherif & Sherif, 1953, 1956; Sherif, White & Harvey, 1955; and Sherif, 1958.

sis of school and medical records and scores on personality tests, and observations of behavior in class and on the playground. By these means, the authors assured themselves that their sample included boys who were all healthy, socially well-adjusted, somewhat above average in intelligence, and from stable, white, Protestant, middle-class homes.

The boys thus selected spent three weeks in an isolated summer camp. Sherif continues:

> None of the boys was aware that he was part of an experiment on group relations. The investigators appeared as a regular camp staff—camp directors, counselors, and so on. The boys met one another for the first time in buses that took them to camp, and so far as they knew it was a normal summer of camping. To keep the situation as lifelike as possible we conducted all our experiments within the framework of regular camp activities and games. We set up projects which were so interesting and attractive that the boys plunged into them enthusiastically without suspecting that they might be test situations. Unobtrusively, we made records of their behavior, even using "candid" cameras and microphones when feasible (pp. 54-55).

§ Producing Intergroup Tensions

THE FIRST of the camps was conducted in the hills of northern Connecticut in the summer of 1949. Here Sherif and his staff began by observing how the boys became a coherent group. When the boys arrived, they were all housed at first in one large bunkhouse. As was to be expected, they quickly formed particular friendships and chose buddies. The boys had been deliberately put together for this reason, so that changes in their affectional relationships could be observed later when the boys were separated into different groups which were not formed on the basis of personal attraction. After a few days, the boys were divided into two groups, the Red Devils and the Bulldogs, each in its own cabin. Before doing this, each boy was informally asked who his best friends were, then "best friends" were placed in different groups as far as possible. The pain of separation was assuaged by allowing each group to go at once on a hike and camp-out.

Each of the two newly formed groups soon acquired an informal and spontaneous kind of organization as some members came to be looked upon as leaders, duties were divided among members, unwritten norms of behavior were adopted, and an *esprit de corps* developed (see Figs. 15, 16).

Figure 15—Percentage of Ingroup Friendship Choices of Bulldogs and Red Devils

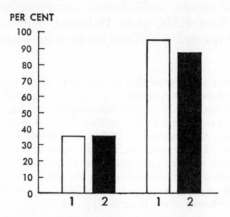

One boy excelled in cooking. Another led in athletics. Others, though not outstanding in any one skill, could be counted on to pitch in and do their level best in anything the group attempted. One or two seemed to disrupt activities, to start teasing at the wrong moment or offer useless suggestions. A few boys consistently had good suggestions and showed ability to coordinate the efforts

Figure 16—Friendship Choices of Bulldogs and Red Devils

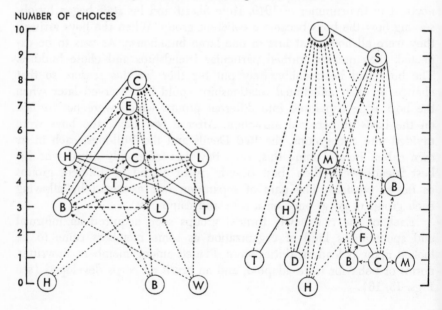

of others in carrying them through. Within a few days one person had proved himself more resourceful and skilful than the rest. Thus, rather quickly, a leader and lieutenants emerged. Some boys sifted toward the bottom of the heap, while others jockeyed for higher positions (pp. 55-56).

These developments were watched closely. Each boy's relative position in his group was rated not only on the basis of observations but also by informal sounding of the boys' opinions as to who got things started, who got things done, and who could be counted on to support group activities.

As the group became an organization, the boys coined nicknames. The big, blond, hardy leader of one group was dubbed "Baby Face" by his admiring followers. A boy with a rather long head became "Lemon Head." Each group developed its own jargon, special jokes, secrets and special ways of performing tasks. One group, after killing a snake near a place where it had gone to swim, named the place "Moccasin Creek" and thereafter preferred this swimming hole to any other, though there were better ones nearby.

Wayward members who failed to do things "right" or who did not contribute their bit to the common effort, found themselves receiving the "silent treatment," ridicule or even threats. Each group selected symbols and a name, and they had these put on their caps and T-shirts. The 1954 camp was conducted in Oklahoma, near a famous hideaway of Jesse James called Robber's Cave. The two groups of boys at this camp named themselves the Rattlers and the Eagles.

Our conclusions at every phase of the study were based on a variety of observations, rather than on any single method. For example, [in the 1953 experiment [2]] we devised a game to test the boys' evaluations of one another. Before an important baseball game, we set up a target board for the boys to throw at, on the pretense of making practice for the game more interesting. There were no marks on the front of the board for the boys to judge objectively how close the ball came to a bull's-eye, but, unknown to them, the board was wired to flashing lights behind so that an observer could see exactly where the ball hit. We found that the boys consistently overestimated the performances by the most highly regarded members of their group and underestimated the scores of those of low social standing.

The attitudes of group members were even more dramatically illustrated during a cook-out in the woods. The staff supplied the boys with unprepared food and let them cook it themselves. One boy promptly started to build a fire, asking for help in getting wood. Another attacked the raw hamburger to make patties. Others prepared a place to put buns, relishes and the like. Two mixed soft drinks from flavoring and sugar. One boy who stood around without helping was told by the others to "get to it." Shortly the fire was blazing and the cook had hamburgers sizzling. Two boys distributed them as rapidly as they became edible. Soon it was time for the watermelon. A low-ranking member of the group took a knife and started toward the melon.

---

2. Sherif, White, & Harvey, 1955.

Some of the boys protested. The most highly regarded boy in the group took over the knife, saying, "You guys who yell the loudest get yours last."

When the two groups in the camp had developed group organization and spirit, we proceeded to the experimental studies of intergroup relations. The groups had had no previous encounters; indeed, in the 1954 camp at Robber's Cave the two groups came in separate buses and were kept apart while each acquired a group feeling.

Our working hypothesis was that when two groups have conflicting aims— i.e., when one can achieve its ends only at the expense of the other—their members will become hostile to each other even though the groups are composed of normal, well-adjusted individuals. . . . To produce friction between the groups of boys we arranged a tournament of games: baseball, touch football, a tug-of-war, a treasure hunt, and so on. The tournament started in a spirit of good sportsmanship. But as it progressed good feeling soon evaporated. The members of each group began to call their rivals "stinkers," "sneaks" and "cheaters." They refused to have anything more to do with individuals in the opposing group. The boys in the 1949 camp turned against buddies whom they had chosen as "best friends" [on a sociometric test] when they first arrived at the camp. A large proportion of the boys in each group gave negative ratings to all the boys in the other. The rival groups made threatening posters and planned raids, collecting secret hoards of green apples for ammunition. In the Robber's Cave camp the Eagles, after a defeat in a tournament game, burned a banner left behind by the Rattlers; the next morning the Rattlers seized the Eagles' flag when they arrived on the athletic field. From that time on name-calling, scuffles, and raids were the rule of the day.

Within each group, of course, solidarity increased. There were changes: one group deposed its leader because he could not "take it" in the contests with the adversary; another group overnight made something of a hero of a big boy who had previously been regarded as a bully. But morale and cooperativeness within the group became stronger. It is noteworthy that this heightening of cooperativeness and generally democratic behavior did not carry over to the group's relations with other groups.

§ Restoring Intergroup
   Harmony

WE NOW TURNED to the other side of the problem: How can two groups in conflict be brought into harmony? We first undertook to test the theory that pleasant social contacts between members of conflicting groups would reduce friction between them. In the 1954 camp we brought the hostile Rattlers and Eagles together for social events: going to the movies, eating in the same dining room and so on. But far from reducing conflict, these situations only served as opportunities for the rival groups to berate and attack each other. In the dining-hall line they shoved each other aside, and the group that lost the contest for the head of the line shouted "Ladies first!"

at the winner. They threw paper, food and vile names at each other at the tables. An Eagle bumped by a Rattler was admonished by his fellow Eagles to brush "the dirt" off his clothes.

We then returned to the corollary of our assumption about the creation of conflict. Just as competition generates friction, working in a common endeavor should promote harmony. It seemed to us, . . . that where harmony between groups is established, the most decisive factor is the existence of "superordinate" goals which have a compelling appeal for both which neither could achieve without the other. To test this hypothesis experimentally, we created a series of urgent, and natural, situations which challenged the boys.

One was a breakdown in the water supply. Water came to the camp in pipes from a tank about a mile away. We arranged to interrupt it and then called the boys together to inform them of the crisis. Both groups promptly volunteered to search the water line for the trouble. They worked together harmoniously, and before the end of the afternoon they had located and corrected the difficulty.

A similar opportunity offered itself when the boys requested a movie. We told them that the camp could not afford to rent one. The two groups then got together, figured out how much each group would have to contribute, chose the film by a vote and enjoyed the showing together.

One day the two groups went on an outing at a lake some distance away. A large truck was to go to town for food. But when everyone was hungry and ready to eat, it developed that the truck would not start (we had taken care of that). The boys got a rope—the same rope they had used in their acrimonious tug-of-war—and all pulled together to start the truck.

These joint efforts did not immediately dispel hostility. At first the groups returned to the old bickering and name-calling as soon as the job in hand was finished. But gradually the series of cooperative acts reduced friction and conflict. The members of the two groups began to feel more friendly to each other. For example, a Rattler whom the Eagles disliked for his sharp tongue and skill in defeating them became a "good egg." The boys stopped shoving in the meal line. They no longer called each other names, and sat together at the table. New friendships developed between individuals in the two groups.

In the end the groups were actively seeking opportunities to mingle, to entertain and "treat" each other. They decided to hold a joint campfire. They took turns presenting skits and songs. Members of both groups requested that they go home together on the same bus, rather than on the separate buses in which they had come. On the way the bus stopped for refreshments. One group still had five dollars which they had won as a prize in a contest. They decided to spend this sum on refreshments. On their own initiative they invited their former rivals to be their guests for malted milks.

Our interviews with the boys confirmed this change. From choosing their "best friends" almost exclusively in their own group, many of them shifted to listing boys in the other group as best friends [see Fig. 17].

They were glad to have a second chance to rate boys in the other group, some of them remarking that they had changed their minds since the first rating made after the tournament. Indeed they had. The new ratings were largely favorable [pp. 56-58; see Fig. 18].

Figure 17—Intergroup Friendship Choices of Rattlers and Eagles

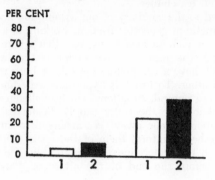

Figure 18—Negative Ratings of Opposing Group Members for Rattlers and Eagles

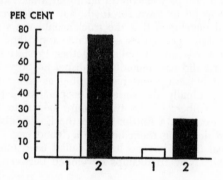

§ Consistency of the Informal Structure

SINCE THE FORMAL STRUCTURE of a group is usually instituted or altered in a way which is obvious to everyone, including the investigator, little attention has been given to the consistency of the formal structure in the literature. On the informal side, the persistence of the structure based on interpersonal choice is usually studied by administering sociometric tests at several points in a group's life. A number of investigators, whose work is summarized in Exhibit 9, find high correlaions between successive tests indicating that the informal structure persists or becomes more apparent over a period of time (Newstetter, Feldstein, & Newcomb, 1938; Criswell, 1939; Zeleny, 1939b; Jennings, 1937, 1942, 1950a; Williams & Leavitt, 1947; Byrd, 1951; Gronlund, 1955b; Klein, 1956; Davis & Warnath, 1957; Bjerstedt, 1958).

The reliabilities of sociometric tests used in 53 studies, including some of those in Exhibit 9, have been analyzed in detail by Mouton, Blake, and Fruchter (1955a). They conclude that there is enough evidence to justify the hypotheses that the consistency of sociometric choices between test and retest will be greater under the following conditions:

1. The time interval between test and retest is short.
2. The subjects are adults or near adults.
3. The subjects have known each other for a long time before the first test.
4. The criterion of choice by which judgments are made is relevant to the activity of the group.
5. A large number of discriminations is required by the technique of choosing.
6. The group from which the choices are made is large.

§ Bases of Friendship

MOST PEOPLE CHOOSE each other for a variety of reasons. The generalization that "birds of a feather flock together" is supported by most of the studies of friendship, although there is also evidence that "opposites attract."

The process by which persons are initially attracted to each other and finally become "reciprocal choices" or *friends* can be represented by a funnel with a series of filters in it. Each person has a funnel with filters designed to fit his particular criteria for a friend. In general, the filters are represented by: (1) *proximity,* (2) *similar individual characteristics,* (3) *common interests or values,* (4) *similar personality* (Newcomb, 1956, 1960). Anyone who successfully passes through these four filters becomes the true friend. *Proximity* is the first factor to operate, since persons who live near each other (Hunt & Solomon, 1942; Danielsson, 1949; Lundberg, Hertzler, & Dickson, 1949; Festinger et al., 1950; Festinger, 1951a; Willerman & Swanson, 1952; Blake, Rhead, Wedge, & Mouton, 1956), are near to each other on the job (James, 1951b; Kipnis, 1957), or in school (Maisonneuve, Palmade, & Fourment, 1952; Byrne & Buehler, 1955; Heber & Heber, 1957) become friends more often than persons who live or work farther apart. In the extreme case, persons who never meet never become friends. Once acquainted, persons who are attracted to each other seek each other out at lunch or other places of possible contact and so increase the "chance" of being together (Hughes, 1946). Friendship groups continue longest if the members have a work relationship with each other (Gross, 1956; see Exhibit 10).

Persons who choose each other tend to have *similar individual characteristics,* such as age, intelligence, sex, and athletic ability (Furfey, 1927; Parten, 1933b; Richardson, 1939; Smith, 1944; Faunce & Beegle, 1948; James, 1951b), although an occasional study reports no association between these variables and friendship formation (Bonney, 1946). Some examples of research on similar individual characteristics of friends are given in Exhibit 11.

Although individuals may be drawn together at first because of common attributes, their friendship is more likely to continue if they have *common interests* or *values* (Winslow, 1937; Richardson, 1940; Newcomb, 1943, 1960; Precker, 1952; Gross, 1954). For instance, in a study of the Supreme Court as a small group, three cliques were identified. The membership in these cliques appeared to be related to the ideology of the judges (Snyder, 1958). In student veteran families, the number of family friends increases with the length of residence in the community and the number of children in the family (Hare & Hare, 1948). Being an "old-timer" at camp or in the factory provides the type of common experience upon which friendship is based (Hunt & Solomon, 1942; Rich, 1952) and religion, ethnic group, and social class may provide a *common value orientation* (Hollingshead, 1949; Goodnow & Tagiuri, 1952; Dahlke, 1953; Oppenheim, 1955; Berkun & Meeland, 1958; Mann, 1958). In addition to providing a common value orientation, social class often serves the additional function of restricting the contacts of members of a given class to others within the same class (Rowland, 1939). The gross effects of class differences on behavior are seldom apparent in small group research, since the school populations which provide the subjects for most of the experiments present a sample of a very limited range of the total society.

Examples of research which indicate the relation between common values and friendship appear in Exhibit 12.

Finally, friendship is related to *personality,* in that individuals with the same personality type tend to choose each other (Maisonneuve, 1954) and marriage partners with similar personality traits are found to be more satisfied with their spouses (Burchinal, Hawkes, & Gardner, 1957).

Subjects are also found to choose others whose personalities they describe as being similar to their own positive traits (Thompson & Nishimura, 1952; Lundy, 1958) and to reject others whom they describe as being similar to their own negative traits (Lundy, 1956b; see Exhibit 13). However, as with the evidence on social characteristics and friendship, not all studies agree on the similarities in the personalities of friends, and some studies report no significant correlations (Pintner, Forlano, & Freedman, 1937; Zimmer, 1956; Hoffman, 1958). In one study of married couples, assertive persons were found to marry receptive persons. Other personality needs such as abasement, achievement, approach, and autonomy were found to be generally complementary (Winch, 1955, 1957; Winch, Ktsanes, & Ktsanes, 1954, 1955). In another study with a school population, friends were not found to be similar in neuroticism (Thorpe, 1955). This somewhat conflicting evidence may only mean that friends are similar on some but not all of their personality characteristics (Bowerman & Day, 1956; Rosow, 1957). Considering friendship in the light of the dimensions of personality which will be described in more detail in Chapter Six, friends might be expected to be similar on a given dimension in preferring to be either "close" or "distant" with others, but could differ in the extent to which they wished to "initiate" or "receive."

§ Overchosen and Underchosen Members

CERTAIN TYPES of personalities appear to be more "popular," since persons with these characteristics are chosen more often on sociometric tests. Specifically, girls in one college who were rated as generous, enthusiastic, and affectionate were chosen more often than those who were rated as stingy, apathetic, and cold (Lemann & Solomon, 1952), and girls with scores near the median on dominance, security, and femininity were the most chosen in another college (Lindzey & Urdan, 1954). These same personality characteristics (with the exception of femininity) have been found to be associated with popularity in a summer camp for boys (Hunt & Solomon, 1942). Popularity appears to be related to the extent to which a person exemplifies the group ideal (McCandless, 1942; French & Mensh, 1948; Bates, 1952; Stevens, 1953). If a person is popular, he may be receiving votes from some who are not like him in personality as well as some who are since friendship involves two-way or reciprocated choices, whereas popularity involves only one-way choices.

In many cases, the "popular" person may represent the "ideal" or "norm" of the group simply because the indications of what is "ideal" and who is "popular" are derived from the same source. That is, the observer asks group members on one occasion to indicate their preferred personality traits. The average rating on a trait then becomes a "norm." At another time the observer asks who is preferred for work or play. Since the majority of the group, who represent the norm, will tend to choose others like themselves, the result will be that the individuals receiving the most choices will also represent the norm. This may explain the finding that the attractiveness of certain personality types, as rated by members of the group, may be different than when rated by an outside judge or observer (Lippitt, Rosemary, 1941). The use of the same population to derive measures of "normal" and "popular" may also account for the "accuracy" of perception of popular members. When college subjects in a class of 48 were divided into five work-groups, the popular members were found to be more "accurate" than the task leaders in their "perception" of the popularity of others and certain group dimensions (those suggested by Hemphill, 1956). Here "accuracy" was measured by agreement with the group as a whole (Bugental & Lehner, 1958).

The individuals in the group who receive the most choices from all the group members also choose each other (Potashin, 1946; Weber, 1950; Lemann & Solomon, 1952; see Exhibits 14 and 6). These "overchosen" members also make more positive choices (French & Chadwick, 1956) have patterns of choice and rejection which differ from "isolates" (Jennings, 1941), and are highly chosen by members of other subgroups within the same social system (Festinger et al., 1950).

Part of the correlation between choices inside and outside of a given small group may be accounted for by the finding that status differences from large organizations carry over into *ad hoc* training groups so that individuals who have high "outside" status are chosen in the *ad hoc* group over those with low "outside" status (Horwitz, Exline, & Lee, 1953). In small discussion groups, these overchosen members also reveal a pattern of interaction which one would associate with leadership, especially if they rank high on both a control and an affection criterion (Borgatta & Bales, 1956).

Apparently, being well liked does not make a person especially friendly to those less popular, even though they may be friendly to him

(Newstetter, 1937). This is probably a reflection of the fact that high-status persons (upper social class or college class) are chosen in preference to those of lower rank and receive more communications because the low-ranking members would like to move up in the hierarchy (Dodd, 1935; Lundberg & Steele, 1938; Vreeland, 1942; Kelley, 1951). This same tendency to choose upward is also found when status differences are developed in the course of group interaction rather than ascribed to members before they join the group. For example, when a number of subjects were given intellectual tasks which appeared the same and some subjects were made to fail and some succeed, most of the subjects chose as a partner for a second similar task a person who had been successful on the first task. For the second part of the experiment pairs of subjects were composed of those who had chosen each other and those who had not. Again success was given to some, failure to others for both types of pairs. Finally, when each subject was asked to choose a partner for a second time, he again chose a person who had been initially successful or one with whom he had previously worked (Gilchrist, 1952). In a similar experiment, the successful partner was also chosen when the subject was allowed free choice (Shaw & Gilchrist, 1955).

When an opinion is presented in a group discussion, an individual tends to think that the group members he likes agree with his judgment and that those he dislikes disagree (Horowitz, Lyons, & Perlmutter, 1951). This effect, combined with the tendency of low-status persons to choose upward in the hierarchy, probably results in an overestimation by a low-status member of the backing he is receiving from the more "weighty" members of the group. For example, in a rural high school more of the lower-rank students (lower class and younger) tended to overestimate the number of their acquaintances, although the relationship was not statistically significant (Buck, 1952). Somewhat contradictory findings are reported in a study of therapy groups in England (Talland, 1958). There, men overestimated their rank received on leadership and popularity rankings, whereas women underestimated their rank.

Attempts at friendliness from low- to high-status persons will tend to subside if the low-status persons see no chance of improving their position. Friendliness of the high-status persons towards the lows will diminish if the high-status persons are worried about maintaining their positions at the top (Kelley, 1951).

In one study of school boys, the number of *negative* choices a boy received was found to be most predictive of his behavior. The largest number of negative choices was received by boys who tended to be the scapegoats. The boys who were rejected most often were either truants who had few friends or delinquents who had many enemies (Croft & Grygier, 1956). In general, individuals who are emotionally disturbed will initiate fewer positive relationships (McMillan & Silverberg, 1955), and therefore receive fewer positive choices in return. It is also possible to have central members who are poorly adjusted if they derive their "popularity" from a set of neurotic relationships with other group members (Scheidlinger, 1952).

§ Choices along the
   Close-distant and
   Initiate-receive Axes

THE STUDY by Lemann and Solomon (1952) is reported in sufficient detail to permit analysis of choices along the close-distant and initiate-receive axes of personality. In this study, six personality traits were compared for popular and unpopular members of three women's dormitories in an urban college. The scales which were all bi-polar were divided into two sets: "alpha" scales in which the ratings ran from good-to-bad (generous-stingy, affectionate-cold, enthusiastic-apathetic), and "beta" scales in which the ratings ran from bad-to-good-to-bad (dominating-submissive, shy-bold, stubborn-yielding). In general, Lemann and Solomon found that overchosen and underchosen members were different on the alpha scales but not on the beta scales.

When these scales are considered in the light of the output and input axes, the alpha scales appear to represent the close-distant diagonal while the beta scales represent the initiate-receive diagonal (see Fig. 19). As a result, the finding that choices are related to differences in alpha scale characteristics but not beta scale characteristics supports the hypothesis that individuals who want close relationships will not choose those who prefer distant relationships but that those who prefer to initiate may choose those who like to receive. This hypothesis receives further support from the fact that both high-status (close) individuals and low-status (distant) individuals chose those of similar status and rejected those at the opposite pole more often than could be expected by chance.

Figure 19—Lemann and Solomon's Alpha and Beta Scales and the Output and Input Axes

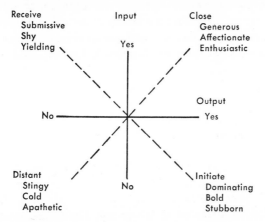

The finding that the girls who received the largest number of choices were generous, enthusiastic, and affectionate suggests that individuals who prefer close relationships tend to have more friends than those who prefer to keep their distance, since a close orientation encourages friendship.

Since there was no positive correlation between being dominating, bold, or stubborn and receiving many sociometric choices, there must have been passive as well as active members among the "sociometric stars." This confirms Gibb's (1950) observation that not all "stars" are leaders and not all active individuals are "stars." The amount of initiating behavior of a member was, however, related to her "noticeability." The noticeability score was computed by adding all choices and rejections for each subject. Girls who were high on noticeability were also more dominating, bold, and stubborn.

§ Popularity and Skill

HIGH-CHOICE STATUS has also been found to be positively related to skill in recreational groups, such as bowling teams (Whyte, 1943), and also to combat effectiveness, (Baier, 1947; Williams & Leavitt, 1947), individual productivity in work groups (Blau, 1954b; Jackson, 1959b), and influence in laboratory groups of children (Gard-

ner, 1956).[3] Popularity shows a negative correlation with accident-prone-
ness, sickness, and disciplinary offenses (Mouton, Blake, & Fruchter,
1955). However, the positive relation between skill and popularity in
industry may not be evident in cases in which choice status in the group
depends more upon the extent to which a person conforms to the production standards set by the informal group than to the overall production level of the whole industry (French & Zander, 1952).

§ Morale and
Cohesiveness

As WELL AS BEING an indication of the informal structure of a group,
interpersonal choices can also be used to form an index of morale or
cohesiveness. Groups are said to have high morale or to be cohesive if
members are highly attracted to the group. The terms "morale" and "cohesiveness" have generally been used interchangeably. Some authors
form an index of the ratio of ingroup to outgroup sociometric choices
which they call an "index of morale" (Zeleny, 1939), others call a similar
index an "index of cohesiveness" (Martin, Darley, & Gross, 1952), and
still others call it an "index of cohesiveness-morale" (Fessenden, 1953).

The term "cohesiveness" is generally favored by those whose work
follows the pattern set by Lewin (Schachter et al., 1951; Gross & Martin,
1952; Schachter, 1952; Cartwright & Zander, 1953; Libo, 1953; Keedy,
1956). They use an index of attractiveness to the group which is based
on any one or a combination of choices in the task or social-emotional
areas. One should be cautious, however, about combining the results
of studies which use different sociometric criteria for their indices. Attraction based on "likeability," for example, may lead to different forms
of interaction than attraction based on "task ability." If the group members come together with work as the primary goal, they will probably
spend little time on the social activity which would be characteristic of
a group formed on an affectional basis.

Where a distinction is made between cohesiveness and morale, cohesiveness is used more to represent the "desire to belong to a group,"

---

3. The individual's perception of his skill may not be accurate. In one study of
informal groups which were competing at dart throwing, the high-status members
tended to overestimate their own performance (Harvey, 1953). Other group members also tend to overestimate the skill of well liked members (Sherif, White, &
Harvey, 1955).

whereas morale includes an emphasis on a "disposition to act toward a goal" (Albert, 1953). In one methodological study of the concept of morale, for example, the concept was defined as "an average feeling of contentment or satisfaction about the major aspects of the work situation" (Campbell & Tyler, 1957).

An index of the attractiveness of the group for its members is often desired since the extent of the attractiveness is also found to be related to significance of the group as a reference group for judgments about the self and others, as indicated in Chapters Two and Three. Once an individual has dropped out of a group which has lost its attraction for him (Sagi, Olmsted, & Atelsek, 1955), the group will no longer be important as a positive reference group.

A group will tend to become cohesive if it is formally well organized, the members are individually motivated to do the task, and the group is successful (French, 1941; Deutscher & Deutscher, 1951; Pepitone & Kleiner, 1957). For example, some college rooming houses for girls contained girls who were very satisfied with their dormitory life. The houses with the largest number of satisfied girls (i.e., houses which were cohesive) were the ones which started with some core of members who had known each other before, lost fewest members over time, and whose members developed more new friends within the house than outside it (Darley, Gross, & Martin, 1951). At the other end of the continuum, in a school for delinquent girls, it was observed that cottages with a low percentage of choices made within the cottage were marked by a high degree of deviant behavior and low interest in controlling this behavior (Moreno, 1953). The relative number of within-group choices as an index of cohesiveness is less appropriate for children, since the number and strength of interpersonal relationships is correlated with age. Very young children make few choices either in or out of a group (Parten, 1932; Harrocks & Buker, 1951).

In industrial plants where the personal bonds are well established and newly recruited members are easily incorporated, there is less labor turnover than in plants which are similar in geographic location, technology, and labor force, but where the bonds between members are weak and no informal group standards are enforced (Fox & Scott, 1943; Mayo & Lombard, 1944). Absenteeism and turnover are especially high among the new workers in such plants. High ingroup choice is also related to effective performance on field problems by infantry rifle squads (Goodacre, 1951).

In an extensive study of group cohesiveness in industrial work-groups, data were drawn from 228 work-groups ranging in size from five to fifty members in a machine factory. The results indicated that members of high-cohesive work-groups exhibited less anxiety than members of low-cohesive work-groups. In the high-cohesive groups there was also less variation in productivity among the members, although the high-cohesive groups differed more frequently and in greater amounts from the plant norm of productivity than did the low-cohesive groups. The amount of cohesiveness in a group was positively related to the degree of prestige which the members of the group attributed to their own jobs, the opportunities for interaction as measured by the size of the group (i.e., the larger the group, the fewer opportunities for interaction), and the length of time members had been together on the job (Seashore, 1954).

§ Summary

EVIDENCE OF THE DIRECTION of interpersonal choice may be drawn from observations of behavior, from the results of formal elections, or from the group member's private expression of opinion on a sociometric test. The rules which govern a sociometric test, as it has been developed by Moreno, are that there shall be private expression of unlimited choices and rejections for a specific activity made with reference to a clearly defined group. As a result of the test, the group should be reorganized by allowing persons who have chosen each other to do such things as sit together, work together, or play together, depending upon the criterion of the test. The use of the test is illustrated by a sociogram of the pattern of interpersonal choice in a cottage family in a school for delinquent girls. Here "stars," "isolates," and other constellations of choice can be differentiated.

Correlations are often high between choices based on a variety of criteria. This result occurs because there are actually some individuals who, as "great men," actually have desirable traits in all areas, and there are some subjects who will choose others on the basis of their own preferred criterion regardless of the criterion the experimenter suggests. Because the correlations between choices based on different criteria tend to be significant, many experimenters pool the ratings made on several criteria so that the distinctions are lost.

There is a tendency for the group to split into subgroups as the group increases in size.

The stability of the informal structure, as revealed by a sociometric test, is greater in groups of adults who have known each other for a long time. The consistency of choice is also greater if the time between test and retest is short, if the criterion of choice is relevant to the group activity, if a large number of choice discriminations are required, and if the group from which choices are made is large.

Individuals vary in the intimacy of their interpersonal relations; interaction with an "acquaintance" is less intimate than that with a "friend." Four factors which influence the degree of intimacy in a friendship are: (1) proximity, (2) social characteristics, (3) interests or values, and (4) personality.

Popular individuals choose each other and are highly chosen by members of other groups. Although the popular person is usually one who desires to be close to people, he is not necessarily an active person. Not all sociometric "stars" are leaders and not all active persons are "stars."

If members are highly attracted to their group, their group is said to have high morale or to be cohesive. A cohesive group is usually more productive, unless the group members have agreed on a lower production rate in opposition to the norms of a larger organization.

Exhibit 8
Interpersonal Choice and Chance

A.

Investigator: Moreno & Jennings (1938).

Focus: Statistics of social configurations.

Sample: Seven groups of 25 individuals at the New York State Training School for Girls.

Method: The actual choice distribution (each individual had to choose three other individuals) of the members of these groups was compared with the expected frequency of choice which would occur by chance.

Relevant Findings: The actual frequency distribution compared with the chance frequency distribution showed the quantity of isolates to be 250 per cent greater. The quantity of overchosen individuals (receiving five or more choices) was 39 per cent greater, while the volume of their choices was 73 per cent greater. In the actual configurations the proportion of mutual choices was 213 per cent greater and the number of unreciprocated choices was 36 per cent less than the chance expectancy.

B.

Investigator: Bronfenbrenner (1943, 1944).

Focus: A constant frame of reference for sociometric research.

Sample: 127 children in six separate classes ranging in size from fourteen to 33. Average IQ's (Kuhlmann and Stanford-Binet) for each of the six classes ranged from 110 to 130 and average scores on achievement tests were, on the whole, well above national norms.

Method: A sociometric questionnaire on choices of companions for play, sit, and work with was filled out in the fall and the same questionnaire was repeated in the spring. The subjects were limited to a maximum of three responses.

Relevant Findings: A few persons received very few choices with chance expectancy and a few persons received a number of choices far in excess of chance expectancy, confirming the existence of social forces of acceptance and attraction. The frequency of mutual choices and the degree of cleavage along sex lines were far in excess of chance expectancy.

Exhibit 9
The Consistency of Informal Group Structure

A.

Investigator: Criswell (1939).
Focus: Social structure revealed in a sociometric retest.
Sample: 238 subjects in a New York public school 75 per cent of whom were Negroes.
Method: Two sociometric tests were administered six weeks apart. Each child was permitted to choose two classmates beside whom he would like to sit.
Relevant Findings: Of 216 children making two choices on both occasions, 38 per cent retained both choices, 42 per cent changed either first or second choice, and 20 per cent changed both choices. The change in first choice was 31 per cent, while that in second was 51 per cent (i.e., they did not appear as first or as second choice on retest). Reciprocated first choices only changed 20 per cent, while reciprocated second choices changed 40 per cent. There was, however, a constancy of choice: of the changed choices, 81 per cent were directed into the same sex group as before; of the changed inter-racial choices, 81 per cent were directed by Negro children into same race group as before, while 49 per cent were directed into the same race group by white children. In spite of fluctuation of choice, basic group structures remained the same. There was no alteration in percentage of isolated individuals or in reciprocated choices. Sex and race cleavage also remained the same.

B.

Investigator: Zeleny (1939).
Focus: Sociometry of morale.
Sample: 84 children.
Method: Sociometric questions.
Relevant Findings: The reliability of the choices made in this test is indicated in the following correlations between administrations to the same community of groups on successive days. The reliability of the "likes" or

Trial	N	R
1	15	.950
2	35	.938
3	34	.940

"acceptances" received is shown by similar correlations made between successive administrations. The meaning of these correlations must be discounted

Trial	N	R
1	15	.910
2	34	.916
3	33	.947

somewhat, because the expressions of "like" were not always consistent. It was possible for a person to receive on two administrations of the sociometric test the same number of likes but from different persons, in part. The degree of this inconsistency is shown as follows:

Trial	N	No. of "likes" received	Average No. of inconsistencies	Per cent of inconsistencies
1	15	14	1.4	10.0
2	34	33	5.7	17.3
3	35	34	4.9	14.4

Since the errors were not large, the authors concluded that this sociometric test was a relatively reliable measure.

C.

Investigator: Jennings (1942, 1950a).

Focus: Experimental evidence on the social atom at two time points.

Sample: The population of the New York State Training School for Girls.

Method: Two sociometric tests were given eight months apart. Choices given and received were combined for each subject in an "Inter-choice Ratio." If the number chosen by the individual exceeded the number choosing him, the ratio was less than 1.00, reflecting the degree of excess of the individual's choices compared with the choices of others for him. If the number chosen equaled the number choosing him, the ratio was 1.00, and if he was chosen by more individuals than he himself chose, his Inter-choice Ratio was greater than 1.00.

Relevant Findings: For the test population the median Inter-choice Ratio was .84 for test I and 1.27 for test II. On test II the number of subjects who had a ratio of less than .50 decreased from 37 to 26; the number with a ratio of 2.00 to 2.99 increased from five to 15; and the number having a ratio of 3.00 or over increased from four to 11. The mean Inter-choice Ratio showed an increase between the two tests from .99 to 1.29, which was statistically significant (C.R. = 2.47). The correlation between the individual's ratio on the two occasions eight months apart was .46 (P. < .01).

Thus the extent to which an individual reacted to other persons and the extent to which others reacted to him on a sociometric test remained relatively constant between different criteria, although the gross amount of reaction varied.

D.

Investigator: Williams & Leavitt (1947).
Focus: Group opinion as a predictor of military leadership.
Sample: One hundred marine corps officer candidates at a training camp.
Method: At the end of two weeks of training and at the end of five weeks, subjects were asked to rate other members of their platoon on five "traits" such as "desirability as a room-mate" and "all-round ability as a combat officer."
Relevant Findings: Ratings given at the end of two weeks were correlated .78 with the ratings given at the end of five weeks.

E.

Investigator: Byrd (1951).
Focus: A study of validity and constancy of choices in a sociometric test.
Sample: A fourth grade class of 27 children at a State University Demonstration School.
Method: After taking a sociometric test, the subjects were given an opportunity to exercise their choices four days later in a real-life situation. The sociometric test was readministered nine weeks later.
Relevant Findings: Of 155 choices expressed in the original sociometric test, 73 (47 per cent) were re-expressed for the same individuals in the life situation. Of 155 choices expressed in first sociometric test, 89 (57 per cent) were re-expressed for the same individuals on the readministration. Of 160 choices expressed in the life situation, 93 (58 per cent) were expressed for some individuals on the sociometric retest. Of 155 choices on the original sociometric test, 58 (37 per cent) were expressed for the same individuals in both the life situation and the sociometric retest. Thus as a group about half of the choices expressed are for the same individuals regardless of the situation. Using the Spearmen Rank-Difference correlation, the coefficients were as follows:

	R
Situation I and II	.76 ± .09
Situation II and III	.80 ± .08
Situation I and III	.89 ± .04

The correlation between sociometric test and retest is relatively high.

F.

Investigator: Klein (1956).

Focus: Relationships in three small groups.

Sample: Two groups of six and one group of seven English university students.

Method: The interaction of the groups was observed for ten meetings while the members discussed matters of common interest. After each meeting the subjects answered six sociometric questions.

Relevant Findings: Growing agreement in each group on the popularity status of each member was shown by the fact that the sum of the deviations from the mean of all members' rankings of each other diminished significantly as the series of meetings continued. The growing agreement was not specific to either likes or dislikes.

Exhibit 10
Friendship and Proximity

A.

Investigator: Danielsson (1949).
Focus: Some attraction and repulsion patterns among Jibaro Indians.
Sample: All male adults ($n = 65$) of Patuca, Yuruponza, and Yaupi.
Method: Interviews.
Relevant Findings: There was a positive correlation between the degree of hostility and geographical space.

B.

Investigator: Lundberg, Hertzler, & Dickson (1949).
Focus: Attraction patterns in a university.
Sample: 230 residents in four women's dorms of a large university.
Method: Sociometric choices of three most preferred future contacts after leaving college.
Relevant Findings: Women in residence made the following choices for future contacts: 391 or 61 per cent of their choices were to other women in their own house, 140 or 22 per cent to women outside their own house, and 113 or 17 per cent to men.

C.

Investigator: Festinger, Schachter, & Back (1950).
Focus: Social pressures in informal groups.
Sample: Two housing projects, Westgate and Westgate West, occupied by families of students of M. I. T.
Method: Observation and analysis of sociometric choices.
Relevant Findings: Data for two differently designed housing projects show a strong relationship between sociometric choice and physical distance. In both projects, the greatest number of choices were made to those living closest to the person choosing and the choices decreased continuously as distance from the home of the chooser increased, even though the actual measured distance was never larger than 180 feet.

D.

Investigator: Maisonneuve, Palmade, & Fourment (1952).
Focus: Selective choice and propinquity.
Sample: Two classes of a large educational institution. All students were boarders, average age, twenty years.
Method: Questionnaires on affinities (friendships) and interviews on how each student came to occupy his seat in the classroom were supplemented by observations of the order of successive arrivals (in the classroom), whether individual or collective.
Relevant Findings: An examination of seating arrangement and liking choices revealed that physical closeness was related to friendship choice even when the two subjects came from very different schools and backgrounds.

E.

Investigator: Heber & Heber (1957).
Focus: The effect of group failure and success on social status.
Sample: Second- and fourth-grade children in twelve four-man groups.
Method: Subjects were told that they would receive one grade for the whole group after each individual had completed an arithmetic test. Some groups were told they did well, others that they did poorly.
Relevant Findings: Subjects liked each other more after the experiment if they had worked in the same group, whether the group was successful or was told that the papers had not yet been corrected. However, if the group was unsuccessful the members lowered their "like" ratings of each other.

F.

Investigator: Kipnis (1957).
Focus: Interaction between members of bomber crews as a determinant of sociometric choice.
Sample: 705 airmen in eleven-man B-29 bomber crews.
Method: Crew members were given sociometric questionnaires and the choices on five questions pooled to obtain one score for liking.
Relevant Findings: Airmen liked each other more if they were near each other spatially and if their jobs required interaction.

Exhibit 11
Individual Characteristics of Friends

A.

Investigator: Furfey (1927).

Focus: Some factors influencing the selection of boys' chums.

Sample: 62 mutual choices in a sample of 35 boys from a university-directed recreational program.

Method: Pairs of friends were compared on the following items: (1) grade location, (2) neighborhood, (3) chronological age, (4) mental age, (5) developmental age or social maturity according to rating scale of author, (6) height, (7) weight.

Relevant Findings: Association either in school or in the neighborhood was the principal factor in the formation of these friendships. The other measures yielded low positive correlations with friendship which were not significant.

B.

Investigator: Parten (1933).

Focus: Social play among preschool children.

Sample: 34 children at a university nursery school.

Method: The children were observed daily during play hour.

Relevant Findings: Among the girls, 81 per cent of the five favorite playmates were other girls, and among the boys, 62 per cent were other boys. Every girl's favorite playmate was another girl and twelve of the nineteen boys had favorites of their own sex. All of the seven boys who preferred the companionship of a girl were under the median age of the nursery-school group. The IQ of favorite playmates showed little similarity. In age, the playmate pairs differed from zero to eighteen months, but the median age difference was less than three months.

C.

Investigator: Richardson (1939).

Focus: Studies of mental resemblance between husbands and wives and between friends.

Sample: Studies from 1928 to 1939.

Method: Review of the literature.

Relevant Findings: At all ages, with the possible exception of part or all of the preschool period, a tendency of friends to resemble each other in intelligence was found. Correlations between traits of temperament were lower, but still positive.

D.

Investigator: Smith (1944).

Focus: Some factors in the friendship selection of high school students.

Sample: 103 high school seniors (49 male, 54 female).

Method: On a questionnaire given at beginning of the second semester, subjects listed the names of three friends in addition to various items of collateral information including sex, place of residence, church preference, athletic school activities, non-athletic activities, non-religious community activities, mother's community activities, and father's occupation and community activities. Pairs of friends were compared on all items.

Relevant Findings: The sex factor was found to have the highest association with friendship, followed by church preference, father's credit rating, residence, and father's occupation.

E.

Investigator: Bonney (1946).

Focus: A sociometric study of the relationships of some factors to mutual friendships on the elementary, secondary, and college level.

Sample: About six hundred urban grade school children, high school students, and college students.

Method: Pairs of mutual friends identified by sociometric tests and observation were compared with pairs of children in which friendship was not reciprocated on data from a series of tests which included intelligence and preference tests.

Relevant Findings: Only a slight positive relation was found between friendship choice and academic achievement, intelligence, and general interests for subjects of all ages. However, a substantial correlation was obtained at the high school level with clerical interests and at the college level with social service and scientific interests. Although there was little relation between friendship and personality in the grade school and college sample, for the high school subjects there was a correlation between friendship and social and emotional adjustment.

F.

Investigator: Faunce & Beegle (1948).

Focus: Cleavages in a relatively homogeneous group of rural youth.

Sample: 189 rural adolescents in three separate summer camps; 102 boys and 87 girls. The sample was relatively homogeneous with respect to occupational interests and age.

Method: Shortly after arrival each subject filled out a questionnaire giving name, address, age, sex, marital status, hobbies, vocational plans, and a listing of the five persons (in order of preference) with whom he would most enjoy working during the summer session. At the end of the camp session, each participant was asked to list those with whom he would most like to work if the same group were to repeat the camp six months in the future. Work groups had been formed on the basis of the first set of choices.

Relevant Findings: While boys continued to choose boys on both occasions, girls shifted many of their choices to boys. Cleavages according to age remained constant, with the oldest group (over 21 years) remaining the most exclusive and strongly rejecting the younger age groups, especially those under eighteen. The youngest age group continued to select those in the same age group and rejected the oldest youth. The middle age group was least exclusive. At the beginning of camp there was a strong inclination for the youth to select persons from within their home county; at the end, however, the number of choices made outside the county increased greatly.

Exhibit 12
Values of Friends

A.

Investigator: Richardson (1940).

Focus: Community of values as a factor in friendships of college and adult women.

Sample: 46 pairs of mutual friends in a sample of 97 college women and 22 pairs of mutual friends in a sample of 42 adult women subjects.

Method: The Allport-Vernon "Study of Values" was administered to all subjects. A control group was obtained by chance pairings of the same population on a split-alphabet basis.

Relevant Findings: The average disparity in values for undergraduate friends was less but not reliably less than that for split-alphabet pairs. The adult friends, however, showed a reliably smaller disparity in values than any of the split-alphabet groups. While it appeared that community of values was a factor in friendships between women, it was more clearly demonstrated when the friends were mature women than when they were college students.

B.

Investigator: Hare & Hare (1948).

Focus: Family friendship within the community.

Sample: Seventy student veteran families from a veterans' housing community of one thousand units.

Method: Each family was interviewed to determine the relationship between the number of family friends and acquaintances and certain other variables in the family situation.

Relevant Findings: The median number of family friends (i.e., other couples who were friends of both husband and wife) was two with a range of zero to nine. The median number of acquaintances was nine with a range of 1 to 35. The number of friends and acquaintances increased with the length of residence in the community and with the number of children in the home.

C.

Investigator: Hollingshead (1949).
Focus: Elmtown's youth.
Sample: 369 boys and 366 girls of high school age.
Method: Data were derived from participant observation, schedules, interviews, official records, tests, autobiographies, newspaper articles, historical pamphlets, and visits with the adolescents, their parents, and other local people.
Relevant Findings: The detailed study of "who cliques with whom" disclosed that from 49 to 70 per cent of all clique ties were with class equals. It also revealed that the polar classes in the social structure were isolated from one another insofar as intimate, personal, time-consuming, ego-involving, and face-to-face relations were concerned. In every case the best friend listed by a subject was known to be a member of the clique of the person who listed him. Furthermore, 78 per cent of the girls and 71 per cent of the boys listed as their best friend a person who belonged to the same prestige class as they did.

D.

Investigator: Goodnow & Tagiuri (1952).
Focus: Religious ethnocentricism and its recognition among adolescent boys.
Sample: The subjects were Protestant, Roman Catholic, and Jewish students in a boys' preparatory school. Most of the boys came from homes in the upper-middle and upper social-economic levels. The living arrangements and school activities made it possible for each student to have almost the same opportunity for contact with every other student.
Method: Students were asked to indicate the names of students they would like to have as roommates for the next year.
Relevant Findings: Each religious group chose a larger percentage of its own members than would be expected by chance. Protestants chose proportionately fewer Jews than Catholics, Catholics chose fewer Jews than Protestants, and Jews chose fewer Protestants than Catholics.

E.

Investigator: Precker (1952).
Focus: Similarity of valuings as a factor in selection of peers and near-authority figures.
Sample: 242 subjects, the student body of a small college.

Method: After selecting three persons with whom he would like to have future contact, each student indicated on a questionnaire the criteria he felt were important for evaluating friends and rated each of his choices according to 39 criteria.

Relevant Findings: Students tended to select as friends those with similar values. The greatest similarity occurred in pairs of mutual friends.

F.

Investigator: Gross (1954).

Focus: Primary functions of the small group.

Sample: Informal groups of two to four enlisted men at a U. S. Air Force base.

Method: Three indices of cohesiveness were derived for informal groups: (a) integration—the degree of liking between men who took part in the same informal groups, (b) correspondence—the extent to which men would want to correspond with each other after leaving the air corps, and (c) frequency—a count of the frequency of association during 35 meals. The three types of cohesiveness scores were compared with the subjects' responses on five "morale" scales.

Relevant Findings: No single morale scale was significantly related to all measures of cohesiveness. However, some relationships, both positive and negative, were found between each of the three cohesiveness measures and the measures of satisfaction with the air force, site, job, personal commitment to group goals, and personal *esprit.*

Exhibit 13
Friendship and Personality

A.

Investigator: Thompson & Nishimura (1952).

Focus: Some determinants of friendship.

Sample: Eight pairs of best friends, three male and five female, chosen from a Japanese-American community group in Chicago.

Method: Each subject was asked to examine a list of traits and then to assign to each, one of the nine scale values, depending on how significant he thought the trait was with respect to (1) his own personality, (2) his ideal personality, (3) his friend's personality, and (4) the personality of an acquaintance who was not a close friend.

Relevant Findings: The two highest correlations were between each subject's ideal and his evaluation of his friend and between the ideals of pairs of friends.

B.

Investigator: Maisonneuve (1954).

Focus: A contribution to the sociometry of mutual choices.

Sample: Three groups (twelve to fourteen subjects), within a close age range (21 to 24 years), in the last year of college. Two of these groups were male, one female.

Method: Sociometric questionnaire and a rating scale which included thirty "polar" personality traits. Each subject was rated by all others on a five-point scale for each trait.

Relevant Findings: The number of pairs formed by subjects with similar profiles was higher than the number of "dissimilar" pairs, and was significant at the .05 level. The most highly significant correlations ($r \geq .70$) appeared more frequently for strong pairs than for weak pairs and more frequently for the latter than for chance pairs.

C.

Investigator: Winch (1955), Winch, Ktsanes, & Ktsanes (1954, 1955).

Focus: Complementary needs in mate selection.

Sample: 25 married couples.

Method: Each subject was studied by means of a structured interview to elicit evidence of his or her needs, a case-history interview, and an analysis of the responses to eight Thematic Apperception Test cards.

Relevant Findings: The need-interview data tended to support the hypothesis that mates choose each other to satisfy complementary needs. Assertive persons tend to marry receptive persons. The two other sources of data yielded correlations between needs which clustered around zero.

D.

Investigator: Bowerman & Day (1956).
Focus: Complementary needs of couples during courtship.
Sample: Sixty university couples who were dating.
Method: Responses of members to the Edwards behavioral preference check list were compared.
Relevant Findings: The authors found no evidence for need-complementarity in 225 correlations. They concluded that needs need not be all complementary nor all similar.

E.

Investigator: Lundy (1956b).
Focus: Self-perceptions and descriptions of opposite-sex sociometric choices.
Sample: 43 college subjects.
Method: Subjects indicated positive and negative choices of persons of the opposite sex with whom they would "most like to spend time," and checked their acceptable and unacceptable traits on personality inventories.
Relevant Findings: Subjects chose others whom they described as being similar to their own positive traits and rejected those whom they described as being similar to their own negative traits.

F.

Investigator: Zimmer (1956).
Focus: Motivational factors in dyadic interaction.
Sample: 73 airmen who were members of nine five- to ten-man air crews.
Method: Each subject chose members of his crew with whom he could "work together most easily" and those who "annoy and irritate most frequently." He then ranked himself and his crew members on eight personality traits. Pooled rankings were derived for each subject.
Relevant Findings: A factor analysis of the correlations between the rankings on the eight personality traits indicated three factors: ascendance-

submission, maturity-immaturity, and adjustment-maladjustment. Since only eight of the 64 correlations between various aspects of perception of self and others were significant at the .05 level, the author concludes that there is no relationship between the behavior tendencies or self-perceptions of subjects and objects, and no relationship between the deviation of a subject's perception of self from consensus of group and behavior tendencies of objects for either type of dyad.

Exhibit 14
Mutual Choice among Overchosen Members

A.

Investigator: Potashin (1946).
Focus: A sociometric study of children's friendships.
Sample: 124 upperclass children in fifth, sixth, and seventh grades.
Method: Analysis of sociometric choices.
Relevant Findings: Persons who had a mutual relationship were more often chosen by members of other pairs than were those in the one-sided relationships.

B.

Investigator: Weber (1950).
Focus: A study of peer acceptance among delinquent girls.
Sample: 110 students at a state training school for girls.
Method: Friendships were determined by a sociometric type questionnaire. Choices were weighted.
Relevant Findings: The highly chosen girls gave a greater portion of their positive choices to other girls who were high in peer acceptance.

Part Two

SIX VARIABLES THAT AFFECT

THE INTERACTION PROCESS

IN THE DESCRIPTION of the central tendencies of group process and structure in Part One, some of the variations which could be expected from groups of different member composition or different organizational characteristics were mentioned. In Part Two, the effects of six major "variables" on the interaction process are considered in more detail. Three of these variables are aspects of the composition of the group and three are aspects of the group organization.

Some of the chapters in this section, such as those on group size or communication network, deal with one fairly well defined variable. Other chapters, such as those on social characteristics and task, actually combine several more specific variables. Whether a variable has been treated by itself or in the company of others has been largely determined by the quantity of appropriate research in that area. Since leadership is the hardy perennial among research topics, it would be difficult to discuss it in less than a chapter. On the other hand, there has not been enough research to date on the effects of age and sex differences on decision-making to warrant a separate chapter.

The variable most directly related to the individual is *personality*.

To vary the personality composition of the group, the experimenter must have information about each individual member. The *social characteristics,* such as age and sex, are more easily varied since members can be selected from classes of individuals which are more easily identified than personality types. The third composition variable, *group size,* requires only adding or subtracting individuals without regard to personality or social characteristics.

The most inclusive way in which to specify the general outlines of group organization is to designate the *task* of the group. More specific restrictions are placed on the group organization by variations in the *communication network,* and the group's *leadership.*

6

PERSONALITY

THE FIRST OF SIX "factors" which can be "controlled" by the experimenter to create variations in the typical interaction patterns of groups is group composition according to variations in members' personalities. Research on the effects of variations of personality composition on group behavior provides a link between individual and group psychology. It is especially important since the categories which are used throughout this text to describe social interaction were derived in part from factor-analytic studies of personality traits.[1]

Although one may wish to summarize those individual behavior tendencies which remain constant, no matter what the situation, under the concept "personality," the basic tendencies of the individual are never seen in their raw form (Murphy & Murphy, 1935; Murphy, 1937). All intended behavior is modified to some extent before it becomes overt, so that the relative strength of the basic tendencies can only be

---

1. Some of the material in Chapters Six, Eight, Nine, and Ten was published in almost the same form in Bales, Hare, and Borgatta (see Gittler, 1957).

inferred by considering the force exerted in the situation to modify them. There are, however, individuals in clinical populations who are relatively insensitive to the pressures of the situation so that their own central tendencies in behavior are dominant. But, even in these cases, it would seem that an individual cannot remain a social being, a person, and stand wholly apart from social pressure.

§ Predicting Interaction
from Personality

ALTHOUGH PREDICTIONS from personality data to social interaction can take a number of forms (Bales, 1956), the most common method might be called the simple, unconditional prediction. Its logical form may be represented by the following statement:

1. Persons of type X (as measured by a personality test) tend to behave in way W in interpersonal relations.

An example would be the prediction that persons who have a high score on the "Manic" scale of a personality test will tend to talk a lot in an interpersonal situation. There is no attempt to predict differentially either according to the other characteristics of the subject or according to the characteristics of the other participants.

A second method which introduces more conditions takes the following form:

2. Persons of type X (as measured by a personality test) tend to behave in way W toward persons of type Y (as measured by a personality test) in interpersonal situations.

As an example, persons who like close personal relations with others would be expected to be incompatible with persons who wish to keep everyone at a distance, and therefore less productive when placed in a work-group.

A third type of approach takes still more complications into account. The predictions take the following form:

3. Persons of type X (as measured by a personality test) tend to behave in way W toward persons of type Y (as measured by a personality test), provided the person of type Y has a given social position within the group (as measured by the way persons Z behave toward Y).

An example would be the prediction that persons who tend toward values of equalitarianism, love, and integrity of subjective experience, tend to form alliances with rebellious, alienated persons and to protect them as long as they are in the position of underdogs and are under attack by group members.

Predictions of each of these three types have been made and tested in the experimental literature on behavior in small groups. Some studies deal with the central tendencies of certain personality types in different situations, some with the effect of one personality type on another in leaderless-group activity in which personality is the dominant variable, and some with the behavior of an individual in a specified role. The list of basic personality dimensions described in studies of each type is usually a long one which varies from experimenter to experimenter. However, factor-analytic studies of personality have indicated some of the independent dimensions which may be enough to account for the major variations in personality. The mathematical technique through which the dimensions are derived is described briefly in the appendix.

§ Factor-analytic Studies of Personality, Behavior, and Role

SOME OF THE STUDIES which involve factor analyses of ratings of personality, behavior, and role have been brought together in this chapter to indicate the basis for the category scheme described in Chapter One. Some of these same studies have been previously collected and analyzed by Carter (1954) and by Schutz (1958a), each of whom presents a three-dimensional view of behavior.[2] Since these two previous formulations did not differentiate *form* from *content* or *personal* from *interpersonal* categories, some of the studies which they cite as evidence are presented in a slightly different manner in the present scheme.

Although each of the factors derived in this series of studies was presumably "independent" of every other factor within the same study,

---

2. Schutz (1958a,b), who has developed a theoretical scheme based on the three dimensions of attention, control, and affection, gives further clinical examples to support his case for the three dimensions. These studies by Horney (1945), Fromm (1947), Bion (1949a, 1949b), and Freud (1930) are not included here since the developmental aspect of personality is not stressed in this text.

certain types of behavioral content which are related in one situation seem to be unrelated in another.[3]

In the following list which "matches" factors from a variety of studies to the present category scheme, the reader will be aware of a certain arbitrariness. It should also be apparent, however, that some categories and factors match quite well.

For each category the author, date, and factor designation are given below, with details of each study appearing in Exhibit 15. The abstracts include the items associated with each factor and in some cases the factor loadings. An item with a high factor loading is one which carries more "weight" in characterizing the factor. The category from the present scheme which has the best fit with a factor appears in parentheses.

§   Interpersonal
    Categories and
    Associated Factors

FORM

Communication network
   Sewell, Mussen, and Harris   Parent-child interaction
     (1955)
   Mitchell (1956)   Social isolation
Interaction rate
   Schutz (1958a)   I am a high participator in a group.

---

3. Like the height and weight of physical objects, personality factors can be measured independently, although for most populations the measures may show some positive correlation.

Although some of the personality factors given in Exhibit 15 seem to "fit" the category scheme rather well, most of the factors represent a combination of several categories. For this reason, each of the factors could be better represented as some rotation of the "dimensions" outlined below. However, a shift from a category-system point of view to a factor-analytic point of view of social behavior would go beyond the scope of the present text.

Couch (1960) provides an extensive analysis of behavior from the factor-analytic point of view. He suggests that the four factors of anxiety, emotionality, aggression, and conformity can be represented on the two-dimensional dominance-submission, positive-negative space. Anxiety is scored as lower left, i.e., submissive and negative; emotionality as upper right, i.e., dominant and positive; aggression as upper left, i.e., dominant and negative; and conformity as lower right, i.e., positive and negative. Using the factors scored in this way, Couch reports significant correlations of about .33 with behavior in small laboratory groups.

CONTENT

Task behavior
Sakoda (1952)   Intelligence
Couch and Carter (1952)   Group goal facilitation
Mitchell (1956)   Social acceptability

Social-emotional behavior
Control
Freedman et al. (1951)   Dominance-submission
Tyler (1951)   Social aggressiveness
Lorr and Jenkins (1953)   Dependence-encouraging
                                 Democracy of child training
                                 Organization and effectiveness
                                     of control
Couch and Carter (1954)   Individual prominence
Sewell, Mussen, and Harris   Nonpunitive treatment
    (1955)   Promotion of independence
Cattell (1956)   Unbroken success *versus* frustration
Mitchell (1956)   Aggressive maladjustment
Schutz (1958a)   I do things orderly and properly
Couch (1960)   Aggression
                                 Conformity

Affection
Freedman et al. (1951)   Affiliation-hostility
Couch and Carter (1952)   Group sociability
Sewell, Mussen, and Harris   Permissiveness in feeding
    (1955)
Schutz (1958a)   I want people to feel warmly
                                     toward me
                                 I am friendly toward people

§ Personal Categories

IN ADDITION to the factors in Exhibit 15 which fall into the *interpersonal* areas, some factors are reported which center on more *personal* behavior and others seem to cut across several categories. A list of the most frequently appearing factors which includes those of the *personal* type, is given by Mann (1959) in his review of research on the relation between personality and group behavior. Mann found that the seven personality factors which were reported most often in the literature were: intelligence, adjustment, extroversion-introversion, dominance, masculinity-femininity, radicalism-conservatism, and interpersonal sensitivity.

The first of these factors, *intelligence,* is typically measured by having an individual solve a variety of problems in a "test" situation as evidence of his ability to solve similar problems in "real life." Tests which have been developed to measure this factor tend to have greater validity than tests associated with any of the other factors, although even here a large part of the variance in behavior remains to be accounted for.

In the literature, the positive end of the factor of *adjustment* has been called good adjustment, ego strength, or normality, while the negative end has been called maladjustment, emotionality, neuroticism, or anxiety. The factor thus includes a variety of measures which are related to the effectiveness with which one can adapt his behavior to the situation and the strain he feels in either conforming or remaining deviant. The concept of neuroticism, for example, seems to include the idea that the individual tends to be motivated by personal concerns which may often be inappropriate for the role he is playing, and also the idea that he has trouble bringing his behavior into line with the expectations for the role. Anxiety appears to refer to the strain the individual feels when the tendencies of his personality and the expectations of his role are in conflict. As a rule, the individual whose personality traits represent the modal position in each of the content areas could be expected to be the best adjusted since he would have the least "distance" to move to adapt himself to a variety of group expectations.

Examples of factors related to adjustment are found in five of the studies in Exhibit 15. These are:

Tyler (1951)	General maladjustment
	Conflict
	Good social adjustment
Wheeler, Little, and	Concern with one's self
Lehner (1951)	Neurotic adjustment
Sakoda (1952)	Social adjustment
Cattell (1956)	Anxiety *versus* dynamic integration
	Cyclothyme *versus* schizothyme constitution
Schutz (1958)	I have anxiety

Kassebaum, Couch, and Slater   Ego-weakness *versus* ego-strength
  (1959)
Couch (1960)   Anxiety

The extroversion-introversion factor (see Cattell, 1956; Kassebaum et al., 1959; Couch, 1960; Exhibit 15), seems to refer to the active-passive axis within the interpersonal areas of control, and affection. These content differences appear to be combined with differences in interaction rate and preferred complexity of communication network. Sakoda's (1952) factor of physical energy and Giedt's (1956) factor of active *versus* passive role (see Exhibit 15) also have some of this quality of a general tendency to be either outgoing or self-contained.

Dominance and *radicalism-conservatism* also belong with the interpersonal categories since they both lie primarily in the area of control. The first appears to represent the active-passive axis and the second the close-distance axis.

The *masculinity-feminity* factor (see Tyler, 1951; Wheeler, Little, and Lehner, 1951; Exhibit 15) appears to represent a combination of traits. Some of these differences are described in more detail in the next chapter on social characteristics. In general, the masculine personality traits include more "instrumental" behavior, while the feminine traits include more "expressive" behavior (Parsons, Bales, et al., 1955).

Mann's factor of *interpersonal sensitivity* has been discussed at some length in Chapter Three. This factor represents the individual's potential for carrying out the first step in the problem-solving process, that of observation, where the problem requires some judgment about other persons. Although the research reviewed in Chapter Three does not conclusively demonstrate a positive relationship between accurate perception and good adjustment, analytic theory suggests that accurate perception is a prerequisite for realistic interaction.

The present category scheme has been presented as an indication of the underlying dimensions in observer ratings of personality, behavior, and norms. However, it seems likely that subjects' own reactions to each other involve the same or closely similar factors. Another way of looking at these categories is as a framework in which the content of social interaction is responded to by the perceiver. The framework is generalized to a highly consistent degree over a wide range of perceivers. At the manifest interaction behavioral level, at least, the number of different ways persons may respond can be seen as limited either in terms of how they actually respond, or in terms of how their responses may be perceived.

§   Personality Typologies
    Based on
    Interaction Rate

IN SOME RESEARCH on personality and interpersonal behavior, ratings
are made only of interaction rate without reference to content. Chapple
(1942; Chapple & Coon, 1942, pp. 47-50) and others who use his scheme
for the analysis of behavior are primarily interested in the *interaction
rate* of the individual (Matarazzo, Saslow, & Hare, 1958). During a
thirty-minute interview, a record is made of the duration of the subject's
actions, which are primarily verbal, and of the duration of his silences.

In the standard interview as Chapple has designed it, the half-hour
interview is divided into five periods. In periods 1, 3, and 5, the interviewer responds with a five-second utterance to each action of the subject
within one second after the subject has finished speaking. Periods 2
and 4 are periods of stress for the subject. In period 2, the interviewer
applies a silence stress by failing to respond to the subject for fifteen
seconds after the subject has finished speaking. If the subject speaks
again during the fifteen seconds, a new period of silence begins. In
period 4, the interviewer applies an interrupting stress by interrupting
the subject each time he speaks.

The interaction rate of a sample of hospital patients interviewed by
a doctor using this "standard" interview technique was found to be
consistent between a first and second interview by the same doctor and
between a first interview by one doctor and a second interview by
another doctor. Patients with low intelligence were found to have short
actions and long silences (Saslow, Matarazzo, & Guze, 1955; Matarazzo,
Saslow, & Guze, 1956; Matarazzo, Saslow, & Matarazzo, 1956; Saslow,
Goodrich, & Stein, 1956; Matarazzo, Saslow, Matarazzo, & Phillips,
1957; Saslow, Matarazzo, Phillips, & Matarazzo, 1957; Phillips, Matarazzo,
Matarazzo, & Saslow, 1957; Matarazzo, Ruth, Matarazzo, Saslow, &
Phillips, 1958; Hare, et al., 1960).

Using the same category system on a doctor-patient interview with
patients in a psychiatric ward, characteristic patterns were found for
varying diagnoses as well as specific differences between individuals
(Chapple & Lindemann, 1942).

In a series of conversations long silences (as compared with short
silences, short actions, and long actions) were found to be the most

characteristic indices of the individual's conversation activity (Goldman-Eisler, 1951).

Some studies in which a number of personality or behavioral ratings are made report frequencies of interaction initiated as the dominant variable because of its high correlation with such variables as the amount of action directed toward the individual in response to his activity (Bales et al., 1951; Stephan & Mishler, 1952) and the observer's rating of the desirability of the subject as a job candidate (Bass, 1951).

Each individual who is a prospective member of a group may usefully be regarded as having, in addition to his characteristic rate of interaction,[4] a characteristic upper bound (or relative limit on the variability of his performance), with a tendency to increase his rate of initiation in a given group in the direction of the upper bound as a function of the opportunity afforded by the rates and bounds of the other participants (Borgatta & Bales, 1953b). The rate actually achieved by a given person is an inverse function of the characteristic rates of his coparticipators. The total rate achieved by a given group is a positive function of the summed characteristic rates of the participants, but it is also a positive function of the differentiation of the characteristic rates. Why the latter should be the case is not immediately clear. For both individuals and groups, qualitative differences in interaction are associated with differences in gross interaction rates. For individual persons, specialization on the side of activities characteristic of task leadership is generally associated with high gross interaction rate. Persons with relatively lower rates tend to assume roles of supporting, modifying, qualifying, or rejecting. Persons with the lowest rates may be excluded or may withdraw; they tend to show high rates of tension, and may not contribute substantially either to the task or to the support of co-participators.

---

4. In experiments using the Bales categories, interaction *rate* usually refers to an individual's total number of acts. The total number of acts is equal to the number of *contributions* times the *duration*, measured in Bales acts, of each utterance. The interaction *rate* is usually highly correlated with the number of *contributions*. Contributions and duration, however, tend to be uncorrelated (Hare et al., 1960).

§   Personality Typologies
    Based on One
    Content Area

A SUBJECT'S RATING in the area of control was found to be related to his perception of others in an experiment in which subjects rated their partners on "authoritarianism" after a twenty-minute period of interaction. A high rating on "authoritarianism" was an indication that the subject liked to have a rigid set of rules, was uncritically submissive to those in power, was ready to punish anyone who deviated from the rules, and had a preoccupation with power (Adorno, Frenkel-Brunswik, Levinson, & Sanford, 1950). A subject who was himself high on authoritarianism thought that his partner was also high whether he was high or low, while a subject who was low on authoritarianism thought that all of his partners were middle or high (Scodel & Freedman, 1956).

Subjects who desire a controlling authority structure were found to be the most suggestible in the experimental situation in which groups of subjects make estimates of the distance a dot of light appears to move (Kelman, 1950), as well as in other experimental situations (Block & Block, 1952). An authoritarian attitude among naval recruits was also found to be negatively related to popularity, although differences in military rank were much more of a determining factor in sociometric choices received. High ranking members of military units received the most choices (Masling, Greer, & Gilmore, 1955).

One of the difficulties in using personality tests to measure "authoritarianism" has been referred to in Chapter One. Most of the studies of authoritarianism as a personality trait use the F Scale developed by Adorno et al. (1950) as their principal personality test. The number of items used in the scale varies from study to study, but the content of the items remains fairly close to those developed in the original study of the authoritarian personality (Titus & Hollander, 1957; Christie & Cook, 1958). The following four items are typical:

Obedience and respect for authority are the most important virtues children should learn.

What the youth needs most is strict discipline, rugged determination, and the will to work and fight for family and country.

Sex crimes, such as rape and attacks on children, deserve more than mere imprisonment; such criminals ought to be publicly whipped, or worse.

People can be divided into two distinct classes: the weak and the strong.

Subjects are usually asked to indicate the extent of their agreement with each item, from "strongly agree" to "strongly disagree." Unfortunately, for the use of this particular type of test, there are some subjects who are so "agreeable" that they will also answer "agree" to a reversed F Scale in which similar items with meaning reversed are presented (Bass, 1955; Jackson & Messick, 1957; Jackson, Messick, & Solley, 1957; Rabinowitz, 1957; Chapman & Bock, 1958; Couch & Keniston, 1960; Hare, 1961). Because of this tendency which some subjects have to agree with opinions presented on a personality questionnaire, many currently used personality scales may also be measures of a tendency to conform to an opinion which they assume to be that of the majority.

In therapy groups *affection* is found to be the most important personality dimension. Individuals who are affectionate or hostile to the group think that they arouse the same feelings in others and assume that the feelings are reciprocated (Taylor, 1954, 1955). Another study with a laboratory population provides more evidence of the results of the projection of feelings in the affection area. In small groups of four to six members, subjects who were high on affiliation motivation but who *feared rejection* by group members tended to "compete" with them in anticipation of the feared rejection. As a result, the high-affiliation subjects were found to be more productive in competitive tasks and less productive in co-operative tasks (deCharms, 1957).

§ The Consistency of Individual Behavior

FOR ANY given personality type, the simplest prediction is that the person will act in the same way in all situations. The extent to which the subject exhibits the same tendencies to act in a variety of groups, or in standardized settings, such as a paper-and-pencil test or role-playing, is a measure of the *stability* or *consistency* of personality.

There are significant tendencies toward stability or consistency in both quality and quantity of interaction initiated and received by the individual in both "actual" and role-playing situations, although certain qualities are more stable than others (Borgatta & Bales, 1953b). In general, the stability for all qualities of interaction over a series of sessions is dependably greater when the individual participates with the same individuals than when the individual participates with different ones, although consistency is shown in either event. Using an index based on interaction rate, sociometric popularity, leadership rating, and intelligence, "great men" can be identified in the first session who have simultaneously high scores on all four of these variables (Borgatta, Couch, & Bales, 1954). These "great men" often maintain their status in subsequent sessions in which they participate with different persons, and have, according to indirect measures, a significant influence on the satisfaction and effective functioning of the group.

Another study of the consistency of individual behavior which supports the hypothesis that the basic tendencies which make up the personality are derived from early experiences in the family was based on the direct observation of mother-child relationships. The child was left alone in a playroom for two half-hour play periods with the mother and for two additional half-hour sessions with a woman who was previously unknown to the child. Thirty-four mothers and their pre-school children (17 boys and 17 girls) served as subjects. Consistency in behavior was found for the mothers and for the children over the two sessions. By the second session with the neutral adult, each child would tend to stimulate his typical interaction pattern with his mother (Bishop, 1951).

A number of additional studies which report consistency of behavior between a test situation and observed behavior are summarized in Exhibit 16. Although it is evident that the variety of behaviors which have been predicted from paper-and-pencil or projective tests generally support the hypothesis of an underlying consistency in behavior, the evidence is not all positive. For example, one study reports that the expression in a discussion group of such "self-oriented needs" as dependency, status, dominance, aggression, and catharsis can be predicted from a battery of tests including the Rorschach (Fouriezos, Hutt, & Guetzkow, 1950), whereas another study reports little or no relation between Rorschach scores and behavior as scored by Bales' categories for interaction process analysis (Borgatta & Eschenbach, 1955).

§ Behavior Contingent
upon the Personalities
of Self and Others

A STUDY, which illustrates the increase in predictability obtained with premeasures of the personality and social characteristics of the subjects as well as the other group members, was made using twenty five-man groups of college students including both men and women (Breer, 1960). Before the experiment each subject was given the Leary Interpersonal Checklist, The Thurstone Test of Mental Alertness, the Bales-Couch Value Profile, and an information sheet asking for age, sex, and social-class background. Individuals were also rated on physical attractiveness.

Each group met for ninety minutes and was given the task of guessing an unnamed student's responses to the Bales-Couch Value Profile. The subjects were given the answers to five items from the Value Profile on which to base their initial guess. After each guess the true answer was revealed. An observer made an act-by-act recording of the meeting using the eight major categories of the Leary two-dimensional grid: ascendant-neutral, ascendant-affectionate, affectionate-neutral, submissive-affectionate, and so on around the grid. An index of how ascendantly man one behaved toward man two was computed by taking the absolute number of ascendant acts initiated, subtracting the number of submissive acts initiated, and dividing the difference by the total number of acts initiated. A similar procedure was used for the affection-hostility dimension.

For the prediction of how ascendantly a subject would behave toward some other particular person in the group, an index based on those attributes of the other person thought to correlate positively with his ascendance (intelligence, age, sex, social class, and pretested dominance) were subtracted from an ascendance index based on measures of the subject. This was done on the assumption that the more ascendantly the other person behaved toward the subject, the less ascendantly the subject would behave in return. For the prediction of affectionate behavior, the index also included the characteristics of the other three-group members.

A prediction based on pre-interaction measures of the subject and the other person was found to be superior to one based on attributes of the subject alone. The results were most striking in the case of ascendance-submission. Combining measures of both the subject and the other person, it proved possible to account for some 37 per cent of the variance in the subject's ascendance toward the other person ($r = .62$). With pre-interaction ascendance for subjects alone, the correlation was .51; with pre-interaction measures of others alone, the correlation was .46. Thus it was possible to account for approximately 21 per cent of the variance in the subjects' behavior toward others solely on the basis of what was known about the others.

The relationship between prediction and behavior for the affection-hostility dimension was not as marked. The correlation between affection predicted and affection observed was .33. The relative failure to predict differences along this dimension was attributed to the limited number of affectionate or hostile acts in a situation strongly oriented to logical problem-solving activity.

§ Personality and Compatibility

SOME PERSONALITY DIFFERENCES, such as those between individuals with high and low interaction rates, may still allow the individuals to work together productively in a group, since each type of person can select a role which fits his personality. This does not appear to be the case, however, with differences on the dimension of affection. Two experiments in this area have been carried out by the same author. In the first experiment with naval trainees as subjects, some five-man groups were composed of members who were "personal," that is, who preferred close, intimate relations with others. Other groups, matched for intelligence, were composed of men who were "personal" as well as men who were "counter-personal," that is, who preferred to keep others at a distance. Each group performed a number of tasks requiring co-operation under time pressure, and finally met groups of the opposite type in a series of "playoffs." The "compatible" groups whose members were either all "personal" or all "counter-personal" were judged to be more productive since they made the highest team scores and won more of the playoffs. Presumably the basic differences in orientation of the "incompatible" groups, whose members were a mixture of personal and counter-personal, prevented the members from reaching agreement on the basis for establishing intermember relations with a consequent loss in efficiency (Schutz, 1955). In a second experiment with male college students as subjects, similar findings were reported (Schutz, 1958a).[5]

Evidence that individuals with certain types of personalities tend to choose each other to form "compatible" pairs and friendship groups of larger sizes is presented in Chapter Five.

§ Personality and Role

MORE SPECIFIC PREDICTIONS can be made about the behavior of an individual with given personality types if something is known about the expectations for behavior in the particular situation in which he will find himself. Sometimes these expectations are indicated only in a general way, sometimes the role of the individual is specified, and sometimes the role of the person with whom the individual will interact is specified.

Since a role specified by the group may be composed of expectations for behavior which are modeled after the behavior of some former group member, there is probably someone in each society who is ideally suited to each role. A role could probably be found in which the behavior of the most extreme personality type would be appropriate. On the average, however, each individual has some range of role adaptability, such that a variety of roles can be learned even if they are not represented exactly by the particular combination of basic tendencies which the individual brings to the situation. Because of this adaptability or because of an underlying similarity in all personality types (since no one is ever so far out toward one pole of a dimension that he does not have some tendency to behave in the opposite way), some sets of expectations will elicit similar behavior regardless of personality type.

In addition to personality, the individual's previous experience in the role is a factor which influences his ability to play the role. Experience with the role can be introduced by either selecting an individual with prior experience or providing training in a test situation which will prepare him for the role. The effect of prior experience is evident in an experiment in which subjects were asked to play the role of a salesman while observers made judgments of their rigidity in the role. Two situations, one anxiety inducing and one neutral, were used. The role playing behavior was not correlated with the results of a paper-and-pencil test of rigidity under either condition. However,

5. This experiment is reported in more detail in Chapter Thirteen.

individuals with experience in selling showed less rigidity (Moldawsky, 1951). The effects of training are evident in a range of studies from those which introduce formal training for a specific role, such as that of a foreman in industry, to therapeutic methods with an individual alone or in a group which prepare him for a more general member role.[6]

In general the group's *expectations* for a given individual are revealed in the *behavior* of group members towards him. It is through the behavior of the other group members in response to an individual's act that the expectations of the group become known. Although the other group members may explicitly state their common expectations for the role of leader or follower, the individual's usual indication that he is still within the limits of the role comes from the approval or disapproval of the others. The problems which occur when role expectations are not uniform are discussed in Chapter Four in relation to role collision, incompatibility and confusion.

An example of the ways in which individuals with different personality traits react to approval and disapproval is found in an experiment in which 64 college-age subjects who represented the four combinations of two personality variables of anxiety neuroticism as measured by a paper-and-pencil test were given social approval or disapproval of their opinions in a five- to seven-minute discussion with two role players. All subjects participated more when approved of, an indication that when the subjects felt that the other group members valued their contributions they would respond in a uniform way. The same experiment, however, also provides evidence of the differential response of certain personality types to the same action on the part of other group members. The high-neurotic subjects were more rigid in holding their opinions when under disapproval, especially when they were also high-anxious (Cervin, 1956).

Thus far the individual's personality has been considered in relation to his own role. The way in which he responds to the personality of another member is also related to the role the other person is playing. High-authoritarian subjects were found to accept a high-status person who was hostile but to reject a low-status person with the same personality characteristic (Thibaut & Riecken, 1955). Another set of experiments involving the variables of high and low authoritarianism

---

6. See for example Chittenden (1942) in which ten experimental and ten control groups of preschool children were used as subjects. Highly dominating children were trained through doll play with an adult. The effect of the training was to reduce domination and increase co-operation. Maas, Varon, and Rosenthal (1951) studied the results of group therapy on schizophrenic patients from the wards of a mental hospital. After the therapy, patients made more purposeful acts and engaged in more verbal relationships.

and high and low status was carried out by Haythorn and his associates. These experiments will be treated in detail as an example of the relative influence of personality and role.

§ Authoritarian and
   Equalitarian
   Personalities in Groups

IN A COMPLEX RESEARCH DESIGN Haythorn, Couch, Haefner, Langham, and Carter investigated several aspects of leadership and membership behavior which are related to authoritarianism. Because of the complex design, not all of the details of their experiment will be described (Haythorn, Couch, Haefner, Langham, & Carter, 1956a, 1956b).

The first problem area under investigation concerned behavioral differences in groups whose members were all high or low on the Authoritarian Personality (F) Scale. Several hypotheses were advanced at the outset. It was expected that authoritarian (F+) persons would behave more aggressively, would be less effective in dealing with the group's problem, would be more concerned with the status hierarchy, would strive more for individual prominence, would be less concerned with asking for other people's opinions and more likely to support each other in discussions, than would be the more equalitarian (F—) subjects. It was also hypothesized that leaders emerging in the F+ groups would be more autocratic, less sensitive to others, and generally less effective than would equalitarian leaders.

To test these hypotheses, 32 high- and 32 low-F persons were selected from a sample of some 350 college men who had taken the F Scale and other screening tests; they were composed into four-man groups, each group being made up of uniformly high- and low-F persons. Their task was to construct a dramatic skit and tape-record their finished product.

While the group was at work at this, observers behind one-way glass categorized the behavior as it occurred, using a stenotype system of interaction recording devised by Carter (Carter, 1951). A scorer was relieved by a colleague every thirty minutes. Each observer rated the subjects on sixteen behavioral traits: individual prominence, friendliness, security, influence, equalitarianism, striving for group approval, submissiveness, striving for goal achievement, self-isolating behavior, effective intelligence, sensitivity to others, leadership, aggressiveness, autocratic behavior, social ability, and nonadaptability. These trait

ratings had an average interobserver reliability of .75 with a range of
.30 to .90. At the end of each session, all observers filled out reaction
sheets on which they made ratings of the group. There were 37 items,
such as "the atmosphere in the group was pleasant and cordial" and
"at least one member was sort of left out of things." Observers rated
the group on these items using a seven-point scale, and achieved
satisfactory reliability. In addition to these observer data, the subjects
also answered some standard sociometric questions about liking, disliking, and satisfaction. While they were making ratings, the observers
did not know the F type of group.

The various questions raised in the beginning of the study were
tested by *t*-tests for the significance of differences between mean values
for F+ and F— groups on each variable. The groups were found to
differ in general in the expected directions. Low-F subjects were rated
higher on effective intelligence and demonstrated more leadership behavior. In addition they had tendencies, although not statistically significant, for greater sensitivity to others, equalitarian behavior, more goal
striving, and greater security in the experimental situation. All differences
in trait-rated behavior between F+ and F— groups are given in
Table 7.

**Table 7—Differences in Rated Behavior between High F and Low
F Groups**

TRAIT NAMES	GROUP MEANS		*t*
	(N=8) F+ Groups	*(N=8)* F— Groups	
I. Individual prominence	3.58	3.56	0.08(F+)
II. Friendliness	3.68	3.79	0.51(F—)
III. Security	4.35	4.56	1.29(F—)
IV. Influence	4.33	4.33	0.00
V. Equalitarianism	3.35	3.87	1.26(F—)
VI. Striving for group approval	3.15	3.03	0.63(F+)
VII. Submissiveness	2.97	3.06	0.48(F—)
VIII. Striving for goal achievement	4.08	4.41	1.41(F—)
IX. Self-isolating	2.33	2.23	0.50(F+)
X. Effective intelligence	3.63	4.24	2.60(F—) †
XI. Sensitivity	3.16	3.70	1.38(F—)
XII. Leadership	3.39	3.77	2.02(F—) *
XIII. Aggressiveness	2.65	2.41	0.59(F+)
XIV. Autocratic	2.68	2.45	0.60(F+)
XV. Social ability	3.67	3.69	0.10(F—)
XVI. Nonadaptability	2.42	2.46	0.12(F—)

* Significant at .10 level.
† Significant at .05 level.

In examining the person with the highest average rank on leadership based on the rankings of the subjects within each group, the experimenters concluded that "persons who emerge as leaders in groups composed of equalitarian individuals behave differently from those who emerge in groups composed of authoritarian individuals. Leaders in F— groups were significantly more sensitive to others, showed more leadership, contributed more to moving their groups toward the group goal, showed greater effective intelligence, showed less concern with solidifying friendly attitudes from other group members, and were more submissive in their attitudes toward other group members." Only three significant mispredictions occurred in the recorded observations of the subjects' behavior, namely, in the findings that F— subjects supported their own proposals more, initiated more activities, and gave more opinions than did F+. In the predicted direction were the findings that F— subjects gave more acts of positive effect, asked for group evaluation more frequently, were less likely to engage in overtly directive acts, and were more often engaged in diagnosing and clarifying action.

In Table 8 are reproduced the results of postmeeting questionnaires. It will be noted that F+ subjects were more dissatisfied with their goal progress than were F— subjects and were more apt to rate their groups as lacking cooperation. F+ subjects also described their groups as having fewer differences of opinion and less competition among members. Both observers and subjects agreed on the direction of the differences for indexes in Table 8 which are significant.

After the groups were observed in the manner described above, the same subjects were observed with appointed leaders. Half of the new groups had leaders whose F scores were similar to those of their followers, and the other half of the groups had leaders whose F scores were different from those of their followers. This arrangement permitted comparisons of the following order: (1) F+ and F— leaders, (2) F+ and F— followers, (3) followers with F+ and F— leaders, (4) leaders with F+ and F— followers, and (5) followers with leaders whose F scores were similar and dissimilar to the followers. In other characteristics of observing and rating, these groups were conducted in the manner described for the first series.

The results of the trait ratings of the appointed leaders are summarized in Table 9.

Inspection of column g of this table reveals that leaders, irrespective of their F classifications, achieved greater individual prominence, acted more aggressively, and more autocratically with F+ followers. This the authors believe is due to the tendency for high-F followers to seek

Table 8—Differences between High F and Low F Groups on Subjects' Post-meeting Reaction Sheet Indices

	INDEX NAMES	GROUP MEANS		Ss PMRS
		(N=8) F+ Groups	(N=8) F— Groups	t
I.	Dissatisfaction with goal programs	3.29	2.69	1.93(F+) *
II.	Degree of equal participation	4.02	4.27	0.92(F—)
III.	Degree of personality conflict	2.34	2.56	0.93(F—)
IV.	Degree of informal friendliness	5.39	5.18	0.66(F+)
V.	Definiteness of leadership	4.26	4.04	0.80(F+)
VI.	Striving for equal participation	5.80	5.50	1.15(F+)
VII.	Satisfaction with leadership	5.56	5.38	0.81(F+)
VIII.	Degree of conflict within group	2.99	3.38	1.42(F—)
IX.	Competence of members	5.56	5.61	0.26(F—)
X.	Morale	5.80	5.76	0.12(F+)
XI.	Group productivity	6.62	6.41	0.55(F+)
XIV.	Motivation toward group goal	4.53	4.84	0.71(F—)
XV.	Formation of cliques	2.09	2.16	0.21(F—)
XXI.	Differences of opinion	3.73	4.59	3.633(F—) ‡
XXII.	Competition among members	2.31	2.78	3.524(F—) ‡
XXIII.	Lack of co-operation	2.84	2.12	2.175(F+) †

* Significant at .10 level
† Significant at .05 level
‡ Significant at .01 level

and accept more autocratic direction. F+ leaders, disregarding classification of followers (column *h*), were rated as striving less for group approval, being less equalitarian and more autocratic, demonstrating less effective intelligence, and less sensitivity to others. In the first experiment, F+ and F— leaders differed significantly on the rating of striving for group approval in the *emergent* session, with the F+ being rated higher. Yet, when appointed as leaders (in the second session), these same subjects differed significantly *in the opposite direction*, with the F— leaders showing more striving for group approval. Presumably the F+ leaders no longer felt it necessary to strive for group approval when they held the "official" leader's position.

Leaders of subjects with F scores similar to their own were seen as less submissive and more aggressive and autocratic as compared to leaders of subjects and dissimilar scores (Table 9, column *i*). Analysis of the observer's rating of followers on the same variables yields results similar to the analysis of ratings of leaders.

In the categorization of the interaction by the Stenotype system, there were no statistically significant differences in the acts of any of

Table 9—Trait Rating Results for Leaders in Appointed Leadership Session

Analysis of Variance TRAIT NAMES	Leader Mean					Effect on Leaders of:		
	F+ LEADERS	F— LEADERS	F— LEADERS	F— LEADERS		F+ vs. F— FOLLOWERS	LEADER'S PERSONALITY	GROUP'S COMPOSITION
Sessions	(F+ F)‡	(F— F)‡	(F+ F)	(F— F)	s²w	F	F	F
(a)	(b)	(c)	(d)	(e)	(f)	(g)	(h)	(i)
1. Individual prominence — II	4.76	3.19	4.08	4.13	0.16	14.574(F+)†	0.028(F—)	1.097(Homo)
III	4.51	3.08	4.28	3.52	0.77	6.298(F+)*	0.056(F—)	0.572(Homo)
5. Equalitarianism — II	3.56	4.76	5.29	4.82	0.70	0.747(F—)	4.569(F—)	3.954(Hetero)
III	3.27	4.04	4.89	5.48	1.00	1.837(F—)	9.350(F—)*	0.033(Hetero)
6. Striving for group approval — II	3.89	3.62	4.49	4.26	0.25	1.039(F+)	6.264(F—)*	0.008(Homo)
III	4.12	3.31	4.42	4.24	0.72	1.360(F+)	2.068(F—)	0.567(Homo)
7. Submissiveness — II	3.03	3.28	3.43	2.75	0.59	0.325(F+)	0.026(F+)	1.462(Hetero)
III	2.57	3.77	3.34	3.07	0.41	2.100(F—)	0.011(F—)	5.165(Hetero)*
9. Aggressiveness — II	2.98	1.78	1.92	2.49	0.39	1.013(F+)	0.329(F+)	8.037(Homo)*
III	2.95	1.63	1.96	1.34	0.51	7.441(F+)*	3.223(F+)	0.964(Homo)
10. Autocratic — II	3.64	1.99	2.21	2.61	0.56	2.773(F+)	1.150(F+)	7.459(Homo)*
III	3.56	1.98	2.20	1.64	0.43	10.821(F+)*	6.877(F+)*	2.471(Homo)
11. Effective intelligence — II	4.32	4.46	5.23	4.92	0.31	0.095(F+)*	5.963(F—)*	0.653(Hetero)
III	4.21	3.90	4.96	5.42	0.53	0.038(F—)	9.759(F—)†	1.099(Homo)
12. Sensitivity — II	3.27	4.26	4.89	4.47	0.77	0.423(F—)	4.361(F—)	2.607(Hetero)
III	3.28	3.85	4.80	5.39	0.83	1.616(F—)	11.304(F—)†	0.001(Homo)
15. Non-adaptability — II	2.01	1.38	1.31	1.70	0.14	0.407(F+)	1.055(F+)	7.469(Homo)*
III	1.45	1.75	1.45	1.08	0.60	0.008(F+)	0.759(F+)	0.759 Hetero

* P (.05) 4.75; df 1/12
† (.01) 9.33
‡ (F+ F), (F— F), refers to the personality of followers [(F+ Followers) (F— Followers)]
Note: In session II, three members who had been together during session I were placed together with an alien member who was appointed leader. In session III, two of the original session I members were reassembled with the member who had been withdrawn during session II. In addition, an alien member was introduced as the leader of that session.

the category indices between followers with F+ and F— leaders. For F— followers, disregarding the nature of their leaders, however, there were more requests for group evaluation, democratic behavior, and acts of a diagnosing or clarifying character, and less withdrawal, tension release, and out-of-field behavior.

Other findings of interest are that leaders with F+ followers were rated higher on autocratic behavior, that subjects and observers both rated groups with F+ followers as having more definite leadership, and that F+ followers rated their groups as being more dominated by the appointed leader. The hypothesis that followers are more secure in homogeneous groups was supported by the difference in rating of security by the observers. Followers in the homogeneous groups were also rated as striving for goal achievement more than in heterogeneous groups. A result not anticipated was that followers in the heterogeneous groups showed self-ratings higher on satisfaction with their appointed leaders. No satisfactory explanation was provided for this result.

In the summary, the authors are satisfied that most of their expectations were confirmed by the data reported, although not always to a statistically significant degree. Two of the five comparisons possible (concerning F+ and F— leaders and F+ and F— followers) were straightforward predictions from individual attitude and personality measurements. The other three, they point out, were concerned with combinatorial results which indicate the extent to which the inter-personal climate in a group affects the behavior of designated individuals, i.e., the degree to which the behavior of leaders is a function of the personality attributes of those who are led. The converse of this statement is also involved concerning follower behavior. This study is, then, further evidence that personality and group structure should be assessed in relational or combinatorial terms.[7]

---

7. Not all researchers have been as successful. Chapman and Campbell (1957a) found that they could not predict group performance on a guessing game and ball-and-spiral task from individual F Scale scores. In another study, a checklist designed to indicate the extent to which subjects were *superior-oriented* (i.e., sought control from an authority) did not predict their reactions to inadequate leadership (Campbell & Mehra, 1958).

§ Some Effects of Combinations of Personalities

IN THE INITIAL STAGES of group formation we may expect the characteristics of the group to be strongly conditioned by the personalities of the members. Some personality variables (as measured by Cattell's 16-Factor Personality Test) act in a more or less additive or subtractive way so that the group *mean* on the personality variable is the best predictive measure to externally defined characteristics of the group. Other variables seem to act on some kind of principle of compatibility (or incompatibility), so that the particular *combination* of values among the members is the best predictive measure (Cattell & Wispe, 1948; Cattell, Saunders, & Stice, 1953). Cases in which the combination of values is important include not only those in which high or low variance on a single variable predicts something about the performance of the group, but also those in which the combination of two or more different types of personality has some predictable effect.

High group *means* on personality characteristics of adventuresomeness, vigor, dominance, purposefulness, orderliness, willed application, and freedom from anxiety are associated with a congruent kind of group performance, i.e., high performance on tasks requiring vigorous coordinated action and a preference for such tasks over discussion.

High group *means* on personality characteristics of paranoid suspiciousness, nervous tension, emotional immaturity, worrying suspicious anxiety, and lack of self-sufficiency are associated with low observer ratings on degree of leadership, orderliness, we-feeling, level of motivation, degree of group organization and interdependence, and with high ratings on frustration. It is notable, however, that subject ratings do not coincide with those of observers, indicating that defense mechanisms must be taken into account in evaluating subjects' own estimates of the characteristics and performance of their group.

There is some evidence that high *variances* among members on personality traits of surgency (liking for carefree bustle and excitement), radicalism (liking for intellectual and "rational" examination of issues of convention and authority), and high variance on degree of internalization of social norms, along with high *mean* friendliness, intelligence, and general level of radicalism, are associated with a high level of accuracy on tasks requiring a judgment of facts from inferential grounds. The personality characteristic of surgency is related to a preference for this kind of verbal task, but observers report that groups with high means on this variable suffer from a lack of freedom in the group atmosphere (possibly as a reaction to a verbal free-for-all).

High variances on personality measures of tough- versus tender-mindedness, "Bohemian aggressiveness," and paranoid suspiciousness are associated with dislike for a task of resolving opinion and attitude differences, slowness in ranking attitude preferences, and a feeling by members that other members hinder group progress. Of these traits, two are similar to what are probably major factorial dimensions of the attitude universe (see Eysenck, 1954): tender- versus tough-mindedness and "Bohemian aggressiveness." Variance on these traits would be expected perhaps to lead to conflict of values. The other trait in this cluster is paranoid suspiciousness. Apparently what is involved here is an incompatibility of defensive mechanisms for dealing with threat induced by value conflict.

Finally, on the personality variable of emotional maturity (general freedom from defensive mechanisms), *low variance* or uniformity is found to be associated with a certain optimism and confidence in level of aspiration. This seems reasonable in cases where the mean level of emotional maturity is high, but its implications are not clear where the general level is low.

It is important to note that in the research of Cattell, et al. (1953) some characteristics of the groups are not significantly related to any of the personality measures included in their experiment. Some of these, such as performance on and preference for different tasks (card sorting, construction, planning, resolution of interests), may be more or less directly related to measures of personality characteristics not included in the tests. However, certain others may arise from small, accidental differences in group experience which have the peculiarity of exaggerating themselves by a feedback mechanism or which for some reason produce relatively large results. Here one could include a group elation factor, possibly as a success-failure consequence, and a factor related to high general evaluation of the integration of the group by the members (intrinsic group synergy). Factors might also be added which are related to observer ratings of a high degree of group organization and a concern with procedure, a pattern of low absolute but realistic level of aspiration, and a low general level of planning and verbal communication. All of these factors appear to be the result of a complicated synthesis of many small intangible causes, amplified into a general tangible effect through the interaction process. One might expect each of these factors to be found in the content of developing group norms and subject to normative control.

Using Cattell's personality test in a different way, results were obtained which generally confirm those reported above (Haythorn, 1953). In laboratory discussion groups, measured personality traits of members involving emotional maturity, friendly co-operativeness, trustfulness and adaptability, adventuresomeness, willed application, and freedom from anxiety were positively related to smooth and effective group functioning as judged by observers of the group. Conversely, the characteristics of paranoid suspiciousness, eccentricity, and coolness to others were found to be negatively related to smooth functioning as seen by the obserevers. In this study, observers also rated the behavior of individuals, and group members rated the characteristics of their group. Observer ratings on variables of individual behavior conceptualized as "facilitating the achievement of the group goal," such as co-operativeness, efficiency, and insight, tended to predict the ratings subjects gave their groups on such variables as morale, co-operativeness, productivity, motivation, and interest in job completion. Observer ratings of variables of individual behavior designated as "striving for individual prominence," such as aggressiveness, initiative, confidence, authoritarianism, interest in individual solution, and attempts at leadership, were negatively related to members' own ratings of the cohesiveness and friendliness of their group. Finally, observers' ratings of a third group of variables conceptualized as "social behavior" were related to members' own ratings of their group as noncompetitive, friendly, and talkative. In general, subjects chose as coworkers and nominated as best in leadership those members who seemed to "facilitate" group functioning, and rejected those who hindered smooth functioning.

§ Defense Mechanisms

AN EXPERIMENT by Cohen (1956) illustrates some aspects of the relation between defense mechanisms (i.e., unconscious ways of dealing with anxiety) and interpersonal behavior. Forty-four college students were given written tests to determine the area of their primary psychosexual disturbances and their preferred defense mechanisms. They were then paired in terms of defense, psychosexual dimension, and intensity of disturbance. No two subjects were paired if they had indicated one another as friends in a preliminary sociometric questionnaire. The basic pairs were of three kinds: pairs of projectors, pairs with similar defenses other than projection, and pairs where defenses were dissimilar. The members of each pair were then asked to read some short stories which would arouse their common area of disturbance, to make individual judgments about the motives of the actors in the stories, and to arrive at a common decision about the motives through group discussion.

The pairs of subjects who used *projection* (i.e., the tendency to attribute to someone else the impulses which the subject finds unacceptable to himself) as a defense perceived their own interaction as more hostile than pairs of subjects who utilized other defenses. These negative effects were obtained only when two projectors were paired. When projectors discussed the stories with persons using other defenses, they were no different in their perception of hostility from any other pairs having dissimilar defenses. The negative feeling was also less marked if only one of the partners was highly disturbed.

When pairs with similar defense preference were compared with other similar pairs on the extent to which they experienced their own interaction as negative, the rank order from most negative to most positive was: projection, regression, reaction formation, and avoidance. A similar ordering from negative to positive for the psychosexual conflicts was: sibling rivalry, castration anxiety, oral sadism, anal expulsiveness, and oedipal intensity.

§ Summary

PREDICTIONS ABOUT the interaction process which are based on the personality composition of a group can be simple in that they only consider the central tendencies of individuals of a given type no matter what situation they are in, or they can include estimates of the modifications of central tendencies which result from the presence of other personality types or of persons playing specific roles.

The factors of personality and interpersonal behavior which have been derived from a series of factor-analytic studies can be classified according to the scheme outlined in Chapter One. Personality contains both interpersonal and personal aspects. The major interpersonal categories which can be identified are:

1. Form
   a) Communication network
   b) Interaction rate
2. Content
   a) Social-emotional behavior
      1) control
      2) affection
   b) Task behavior

The personal categories which appear most frequently in the literature are intelligence, adjustment, and interpersonal sensitivity. Other categories which appear in the literature, such as extroversion-introversion and masculinity-femininity, cut across the present category system by emphasizing certain aspects of each category.

In some research, the effects of variations in only one of these categories have been studied. Some types of psychiatric patients, for example, can be distinguished by their interaction rate, persons who accept an authority structure are found to be more suggestible, and persons who reject others in therapy groups typically think that others reject them. The consistency of an individual's behavior increases with the similarity in the two situations in which he is being observed.

Groups composed of individuals who are compatible in that they all prefer close intimate relations are more productive than groups in which some individuals are "personal" and some are "counter-personal." Individuals will also be more effective when playing a role which is similar to their personality type.

In an experiment in which subjects who were high and low in authoritarianism were observed in separate groups as they worked on a task involving group discussion, the low authoritarian subjects were rated higher on effective intelligence and demonstrated more leadership behavior. The leaders who emerged in the leaderless group sessions differed according to the type of group. Leaders in the low-authoritarian groups were more equalitarian in their leadership behavior. The members in the high-authoritarian groups reported that their meetings showed little progress and were less co-operative. But they also reported fewer differences of opinion and less competition. In later sessions, the groups were assigned leaders who were either similar or dissimilar in their personality type. The leader's behavior varied with his own personality type and with the type of persons he was leading. The presence of an F+ leader or of F+ followers increased the amount of autocratic behavior.

Other research with leaderless groups indicates that the characteristic patterns of group interaction tend to be strongly influenced by the personalities of the members in the initial stages of group formation. As in the experiments with compatible groups, a high group mean on a personality trait usually results in a similar type of behavior for the group, while high variance on other traits may produce more effective groups if the task calls for variability in individual performance, or conflict if the task calls for similarity of individual performance.

Exhibit 15
Personality Factors

A.

Investigator: Freedman et al. (1951), Leary (1957).
Focus: The interpersonal dimension of personality.
Sample: Interview protocols, test records, group therapy meetings, and other material.
Method: Development of a classification scheme for interpersonal behavior which has two primary factors plus an intensity measure.
Factors:
1. *Dominance-submission* (Control): autocratic, bossy, dictatorial, leading, forceful, masterful, able to give orders; (*versus*) weak, submissive, spineless, obedient, meek, docile, deferent.
2. *Affiliation-hostility* (Affection): effusive, affectionate, friendly, warm, affiliative, praising, approving; (*versus*) unfriendly, hostile, irritable, critical, pugnacious, condemning.

B.

Investigator: Tyler (1951).
Focus: A factor analysis of fifteen MMPI Scales.
Sample: 107 female graduate students.
Method: Factor analysis.
Factors:

1. *General maladjustment* (Adjustment)

Loading	
.847	Social Introversion
.702	Prejudice
.698	Psychasthenia
.592	Depression
—.459	Dominance
—.538	Status

2. *Conflict* (Adjustment)

.489	Responsibility
.437	Psychasthenia
.411	Paranoia
.387	Hysteria

3. *Social aggressiveness**
    .843   Confident
    .602   Irresponsible
    .548   Apprehensive
    .501   Bashful
    —.482   Dependability
4. *Good social adjustment* (Adjustment)
    .544   Masculinity
    .482   Self-confidence
    .328   Optimism
5. *Femininity*
    .337   Concern over bodily functions
    —.525   Masculinity

C.

Investigator: Wheeler, Little, & Lehner (1951).
Focus: Internal structure of the MMPI.
Sample: 110 neuropsychiatric male patients in a veterans' hospital and 112 college students.
Method: Factor analysis of responses to MMPI.
Factors: †
1. *Concern with one's self* (Adjustment)
2. *Neurotic adjustment* (Adjustment)
3. *Masculinity-femininity*

D.

Investigator: Couch & Carter (1952), Carter (1954).
Focus: Performance of individuals as members of small groups.
Sample: College men in groups of four and eight members with three kinds of tasks: reasoning, mechanical assembly, and discussion.
Method: Factor analysis of nineteen observer ratings.
Factors.
1. *Individual prominence* (Control)
    Authoritarianism
    Confidence
    Aggressiveness
    Leadership
    Striving for recognition

---

* This factor is not close to any single category in the present scheme, although it seems to have some elements of control.
† There were some differences between patients and normal populations.

2. *Group goal facilitation* (Task behavior)
   Efficiency
   Co-operation
   Adaptability
   Pointed toward group solution
3. *Group sociability* (Affection)
   Sociability
   Adaptability
   Pointed toward group acceptance

E.

Investigator: Sakoda (1952).
Focus: Factor analysis of OSS situational tests.
Sample: Candidates for the OSS tested during World War II.
Method: Factor analysis of intercorrelations between ten observer ratings of candidate's behavior during situational tests.
Factors:

1. *Physical energy* (Extroversion-introversion)
   Energy and initiative
   Physical ability
   Leadership
2. *Intelligence* (Task behavior)
   Effective intelligence
   Observing and reporting
   Propaganda skills
3. *Social adjustment* (Adjustment)
   Social relations
   Emotional stability
   Security

F.

Investigator: Lorr & Jenkins (1953).
Focus: Factors in parent behavior.
Sample: Previously collected data similar to Champney (1941): same data as that of Baldwin, Kallhorn, & Breese (1945) and Roff (1949).
Method: Factor analysis of thirty scales describing parent-child behavior.
Factors:

1. *Dependence-encouraging* (Interaction rate)

Loading	
.65	Babying
.64	Child-centeredness of the home
.62	Solicitousness for child's welfare
.60	Protectiveness

.58   Intensity of contact
.56   Duration of contact
.44   Acceptance of child

2. *Democracy of child training* (Control)
.76   Democracy of policy
.74   Noncoerciveness of suggestion
.66   Nonrestrictiveness of regulations
.62   Nonemotionality toward the child
.62   Nonreadiness of criticism
.59   Readiness of explanation
.57   Favorableness of criticism
.49   Understanding of the child's problems
.46   Clarity of policy
.44   Absence of disciplinary friction

3. *Organization and effectiveness of control* (Control)
.59   Vigilance of enforcement
.47   Severity of actual penalties
.43   Accelerational attempt (pushing)
.41   Coordination of household

G.

Investigator: Sewell, Mussen, & Harris (1955).
Focus: Relationships among child training practices.
Sample: 162 five- and six-year-old rural children and their families from unbroken middle-class homes.
Method: A factor analysis (some factors were oblique) of 38 child-training practices derived from interview ratings.
Factors:

1. *Parent-child interaction* (Communication network and interaction rate)
Loading
.607   Much activity with father
.504   Much activity with mother
.500   Much activity with parents
.222   Success in bowel training rewarded
—.329   Short duration confined to playpen

2. *Nonpunitive treatment* (Control)
.628   Ignore child's neglect of jobs
.564   Spanked few times
.355   Ignore masturbation
.255   Ignore child's disobedience of mother

3. *Promotion of independence* (Control)
.427   Take child on picnics
.374   Child has own spending money
.324   Non-evasion of child's questions about sex
.290   Ignore child's fighting
—.404   Infant fed on demand

—.352   Night feeding stopped at late age
—.327   Infant slept with mother

4. *Permissiveness in feeding* (Affection)

.796   Short duration of bottle feeding
.755   Long duration of breast feeding
.475   Infant usually held when bottle fed
.298   Infant fed on demand
.233   Infant slept with mother

H.

Investigator: Cattell (1956), replication by Karson & Pool (1958).
Focus: Second-order personality factors in the questionnaire realm.
Sample: 408 subjects (181 college undergraduates and 227 air force trainees).
Method: Factor analysis of Cattell's 16-factor personality test.
Factors:

1. *Anxiety*-versus-*dynamic integration* (Adjustment)
   Loading
   .66   Lack of will control
   .62   Insecurity or free-floating anxiety
   .62   Nervous tension
   .54   Paranoid trend
   .53   Lack of ego strength

2. *Extroversion* versus *introversion*
   .51   Practical concern *vs.* bohemianism
   .48   Surgency
   .45   Cyclothymia
   .42   Conservatism
   .38   Lack of self-sufficiency
   .33   Adventurous cyclothymia

3. *Cyclothyme* versus *schizothyme constitution* (Adjustment)
   .56   Cyclothymia
   .53   Emotional sensitivity
   .48   Lack of sophistication
   .29   Lack of will control
   .25   Lack of ego strength

4. *Unbroken success* versus *frustration* (Control)
   .55   Radicalism
   .50   Dominance
   .34   Sophistication
   .23   Low superego strength

I.

Investigator: Giedt (1956).
Focus: Roles of patients in therapy groups.
Sample: 41 therapy patients.
Method: Cluster and factor analysis of 100-item checklist.
Factor: Active role in therapy (Extroversion-introversion)
High

    Starts group off on lively discussions
    Clarifies group's activity or feelings
    Aggressive actor and talker
    Expresses hostility
    Dominates

Low

    Discusses only unemotional and impersonal matters
    Attends group but says little
    Fidgets
    Goes to sleep
    Considers self at mercy and direction of others

J.

Investigator: Mitchell (1956).
Focus: Behavior patterns of children.
Sample: 98 pupils from three fourth-grade classrooms.
Method: Factor analysis of a "guess-who" questionnaire.
Factors:

1. *Social acceptability* (Task behavior)

Loading	
.92	Who are smart at games?
.90	Who understand things easily?
.89	Who are the most popular?
.89	Who have ideas for games?
.88	Who are good leaders?
.87	Who work for the good of the class?
.82	Who make good plans?
.78	Who would you like for best friends?

2. *Aggressive maladjustment* (Control)

.92	Who complain?
.76	Who are mean and cruel?
.74	Who break rules?
.68	Who quarrel and get mad?
.61	Who lie and steal?
.57	Who would you not like for friends?
.47	Who do you not notice?

3. *Social isolation* (Communication network)

.64	Who would you not like for friends?
.62	Who do you not notice?
.56	Who lie and steal?
.51	Who get bothered and upset when called on?
.49	Who are shy?
.36	Who stay out of games?
.35	Who are timid and afraid?
.31	Who break rules?

K.

Investigator: Schutz (1958a).
Focus: Fundamental interpersonal relations.
Sample: Sixty college freshmen.
Method: Cluster analysis of a test battery of seventy separate measures
Factors: One of the six clusters revealed by the analysis was made up entirely of scales from the Blacky Projective Test and is interpreted by the author as an artifact. Each cluster is listed together with the scales which constitute it.*

1. *I am a high participator in a group* (Interaction rate)
   Ratio

3.52	I'm a high group participator.
3.27	I participate in group discussions.
2.70	I participate in informal discussions.
2.24	I make suggestons in a group.
1.70	I talk about myself in a group.
1.35	I am a dominant (initiating) person.

2. *I do things orderly and properly* (Control)

3.44	I am dependent on rules and authority.
3.40	I think groups that follow rules are more efficient.
2.34	I feel better in a group that follows rules.
2.11	I am not intraceptive.
1.60	I use the defense of projection
1.44	I have a need for orderliness (order).
1.27	I value the acceptance of authority.
1.15	I have anxiety about anal retention.

3. *I want people to take good care of me* (Affection)

3.31	I like to get credit for a good idea.

---

* In order to give an estimate of how well each scale fits in the cluster, a ratio is given which is the ratio of the mean correlation between the scale and all other scales in the cluster, to the mean correlation between the scale and all scales not in the cluster. A ratio of 1.15 was established as the cutting point for exclusion of items from a cluster.

3.13	It's important for me to be liked.
2.36	I like people to help me (Succorance).
2.31	I don't like to do things by myself (Autonomy).

4. *I am friendly toward people* (Affection)

3.30	I like to talk about myself in a group.
3.27	I like groups where people get personal.
3.27	I am personal.
2.02	I initiate personal discussion.
1.41	I don't have anxiety over sibling rivalry.
1.30	I do not value individualism.
1.28	I like to have many friends (Affiliation).
1.26	I'm not aggressive.

5. *I have anxiety*

1.98	My father was a strong disciplinarian.
1.92	I have anxieties over oral eroticism.
1.92	I have high anxiety generally.
1.88	I have anxiety about castration.
1.36	I differentiate between people.

Investigator: Kassebaum, Couch, & Slater (1959).
Focus: The factorial dimensions of the MMPI.
Sample: 160 college freshmen.
Method: Factor analysis of thirteen clinical and validity scales and nineteen nonclinical scales from the MMPI.
Factors:

1. *Ego-weakness* vs. *ego-strength* (Adjustment)

Loading	
.91	Psychasthenia
.89	Schizophrenia
.88	Anxiety
—.85	Leadership
—.80	Tolerance
—.73	Ego-strength
—.72	Intellectual efficiency

2. *Introversion* vs. *extroversion*

.69	Repression
.46	Social responsibility
.58	Social introversion
—.63	Hypomania
—.55	Sociability

M.

Investigator: Couch (1960).
Focus: Psychological determinants of interpersonal behavior.
Sample: 58 college sophomores.
Method: Factor analysis of 222 variables including scales from MMPI, Cattell 16 P. F., Thurstone Temperaments, Value Profile, Parental Role Perceptions, and other unpublished tests.
Factors: °

1. *Anxiety: Manifested* vs. *controlled* (Adjustment)

Loading	
.86	Anxiety (MMPI)
.88	Dependency (MMPI)
.76	Insecure (CATTELL)
—.73	Ego-strength (MMPI)

2. *Emotionality: Extroversion* vs. *introversion*

.49	Warm, sociable *vs.* cold (CATTELL)
.49	Extrovertive (CATTELL)
—.36	Independent (CATTELL)
—.51	Repression-denial (MMPI)

3. *Aggression: Manifested* vs. *controlled* (Control)

.59	Psychopathic deviate (MMPI)
.54	Hypomania (MMPI)
.62	Validity scale (MMPI)
.47	Active (THURSTONE)

4. *Conformity: Authoritarian* vs. *non-authoritarian* (Control)

.37	Sophistication (CATTELL)
.63	Authoritarianism (VALUE PROFILE)
—.39	Emotional sensitivity (CATTELL)
—.42	Eccentric *vs.* conventional (CATTELL)

° Since Couch used from sixteen to 23 scales to measure each of the factors only four are given here to suggest the content of the factor. Scales from published tests were chosen; they are not necessarily the ones with the highest loadings.

Exhibit 16

Consistency Between Test Situations and Observed Behavior

Author	Sample	Test Situation	Observed Behavior	Consistency in Observed behavior
Washburn (1932)	Children	Old situation	New situation	Observed behavior
Fouriezos, Hutt, & Guetzkow (1950)	Fifteen college students	Rorschach, TAT, sentence completion, interviews	Group discussion	Expression of "self-oriented needs"
Swanson (1951)	Two adult discussion groups of twenty members median age 47	Blacky Test (projective)	Group discussion	Participation, being liked, influence
Borgatta (1955)	125 air corps enlisted men in three-man groups	Projective test, role playing	Group discussion	Task ability, supportiveness, & assertiveness if one considers written symbolic gymnastics
Borgatta & Eschenbach (1955)	125 air corps enlisted men	Rorschach	Group discussion	Not apparent between Rorschach and the Bales Categories
Lipsitt & Vallance (1955)	Fourteen college women in three-person groups	Questionnaire responses of their acquaintances	Group discussion and private opinion	Position on moral issues
Tear & Guthrie (1955)	156 college fraternity members, eight groups of 13 to 38 members	Peer estimates of co-operativeness	Visual estimation in a group of differences in size of squares	Co-operation

7

SOCIAL

CHARACTERISTICS

IT IS POSSIBLE to control the pattern and outcome of interaction by selecting members with certain combinations of social characteristics. Some of these characteristics, such as age and sex, are easily
identified, and others, such as social class, ethnicity, or friendship
group, can be discovered with relatively little investigation. Since these
characteristics of group members are so easily controlled, they have
usually been "held constant" in experimental studies of interaction by
selecting groups of persons who are of college age, male, middle class,
and unacquainted prior to the experiment. For this reason, the data
on the effects of some social characteristics of members on interaction
in small groups reported here are drawn largely from the child-study
literature which is based more on field than experimental studies.

As children grow older they play less by themselves and more with
others so that their group skills increase. By adulthood the children
have learned roles which are appropriate for their sex in their own

206

ilture. These roles vary by social class and ethnic group. Whether
iildren or adults, popular persons tend to have similar behavioral
iaracteristics and groups of friends behave differently from groups of
infriends.

Age

AGE AS A VARIABLE appears almost entirely in the child-study literature
hich describes the number and intensity of social relationships charac-
ristic of children in different age groups. The major generalization
garding the relation between age and social interaction is represented
y the work of Piaget (1932b), who observed that very young children
.ove through phases of isolated or egocentric play, parallel play, and
)-operative or competitive play as they mature from the ages of about
vo to seven years. The size of the group in which the children play
icreases with age (Green, 1933b; Parten, 1933b).

In experiments where children of different ages were observed
laying in pairs, quantitative scores for friendliness were higher than
iose for unfriendliness (Mengert, 1931). Competition and rivalry
eveloped gradually and began to dominate the interaction at age four
r five, although this was not true for all children of a given age
Greenberg, 1932; Leuba, 1933). Preschool children, ages two through
)ur, showed an increase in the number of social contacts with increasing
ge (Beaver, 1932). The number of individual children with whom
iey had contact decreased as they grew older, although there was an
icrease in the intimacy of the contacts which remained (Green, 1933a;
iernhart, Millichamp, Charles, & McFarland, 1937; Harrocks & Thomp-
on, 1946). The older children can form more intimate relationships
iecause of maturation and also because they have known the other
hildren in the group over a longer period of time (Salusky, 1930; Hag-
nan, 1933; Clampitt & Charles, 1956).

Jersild and Fite (1939) used the method of direct observation
upplemented by other data to study group trends and individual
iatterns of adjustment in the behavior of eighteen two-and-a-half to
iour-year-old nursery school children at the beginning of the school year
ind again (sixteen cases) in the spring. Children who had previously
ittended nursery school showed about twice as much social participation
is did "new" children during the first weeks of school, but the "new"
:hildren began to make rapid gains at once, and by spring the two
groups were equal. The higher "social contact" scores of the "old"

children in the fall were in a large measure due to special companion ships carried over from the previous year.

In one study of some consequences of age heterogeneity in adult decision-making groups, the effect of age on participation was found to be related to the sex of the group members. Twelve male and twelve female three-person groups were composed of teachers whose ages ranged from 21 to 63 years. Half of the groups in each set were heterogeneous with respect to age, containing three members who were approximately 20, 30, and 40 years of age. Each group had two tasks: one the discussion of the number of dots on a card and the other a judgment problem. All groups were observed using the Bales category system. In both male and female groups, the amount of participation was found to be related to age. However, in the male groups the older teachers talked the most, while in the female group the younger teachers talked the most. No differences were found in the Bales profiles (Ziller & Exline, 1958).

§   Sex

In ADDITION to differences in physical ability which are primarily biological in origin, males and females also differ, as a result of socialization, in typical ways of solving problems and in their efficiency in different types of tasks (Mukerji, 1940; de Montmollin, 1955b). In their earliest school years, girls assume adult female roles as they "play house" in the doll corner, while boys build machines with their blocks (Hartley, Frank, & Goldenson, 1952). In later years, in free discussion the content of their discussion differs. In one study of five hundred conversations overheard on the college campus, in street cars, hotel lobbies, barbershops, churches, and other public places, men were found to talk most of business and money, while women talked mostly of men and clothes (Landis & Burtt, 1924). In committee work, females are quicker and more accurate with personal interesting tasks (e.g., interpreting photographs portraying emotions) while males are superior on more abstract multiple-choice problems (South, 1927). Women tend to recognize this difference (Carey, 1958). In mixed committees, men tend to initiate activity and women tend to react to it (Strodtbeck & Mann, 1956; Strodtbeck, James, & Hawkins, 1957). A one-sex committee is usually more efficient than a mixed one, since less time is spent in social-emotional activity (South, 1927).

Further evidence of the importance of knowing the sex composition of the group in order to predict behavior comes from a study of kindergarten children in an experimental play situation. The boys were more dominating with other boys than the girls were with other girls, and the teachers were generally more dominating with the children than the children were with each other (Anderson, 1939). In another study boys tended to receive more disapproval from the teacher than girls (Meyer & Thompson, 1956).

The fact that the typical sex role is determined to a large extent by culture is evident in Strodtbeck's study (1951) described in Chapter Four, in which revealed differences in judgments between husband and wives in three cultures indicated that the amount of activity and power as defined by the culture was related to the way differences were settled. Husband-wife differences similar to those reported by Strodt-beck were also found among undergraduate married couples (Kenkel, 1957). The husbands did most of the talking and had the most influence on decisions while the wives tended to play a more social-emotional role.

Another experimenter recorded husband-wife interaction as they discussed the "revealed differences" in their opinions on a series of political questions. The questions involved labor, foreign, and local issues. In this sample of eight couples, the wives were all members of a women's ncnpartisan political organization. In addition to doing most of the talking (55 per cent), the husbands differed from their wives in the proportion of their acts which were scored as giving information, opinions, and suggestions. The proportion of the husbands' activity in these categories was highest for the labor issues, next highest for the foreign-affairs issues, and lowest for the local issues. When asked to rank the issues in the order in which they were appropriate for discussion by women's political groups, the husbands and wives generally agreed that the local issues were most appropriate, foreign next, and labor least (March, 1953).

In addition to differences between males and females in their own roles, differences are also found in the ability of each of the sexes to take the role of the other sex. In a study in which sixteen college students were tested in groups of four for the quality of performance in role-playing of four situations, each subject was asked to perform the roles of the other group members. The men were better in their performance of the roles of other men than they were of women in the group, and the same was true for the women. However, the men appeared to be more perceptive of the roles of the women than women of men (Brown, 1952).[1]

§ Sex Roles in Jury Deliberations

IN THE STUDY conducted by Strodtbeck and Mann (1956) the data employed arise from mock jury deliberations conducted in connection with the Law and Behavioral Science research of the Law School, University of Chicago. The participants in these deliberations are jurors drawn by lot from the regular jury pools of the Chicago and St. Louis courts. The jurors listen to a recorded trial, deliberate, and return their verdict—all under the customary discipline of bailiffs of the court. The deliberations are recorded with two microphones to facilitate binaural identification of the individual participants. The recordings are fully transcribed and these protocols are in turn scored in terms of interaction process categories. The scoring is done by an assistant who listens again to the recording and has available the indications of non-verbal gestures made by the original observer. The level of inter-scorer reliability is checked before the scoring begins and rechecked periodically while scoring is in process.

In Table 10, percentage profiles for 127 jurors split into inactive and active males, inactive and active females are presented. The data in this form show women to exceed men in the three Positive Reactions categories and to be exceeded by men in the three Attempted Answers categories. This finding strongly confirms the hypothesis that there is a continuance in jury deliberations of sex role specialization observed in adult family behavior.

Analysis of all the data of the experiment

suggests that men *pro-act*, that is, they initiate relatively long bursts of action directed at the solution of the task problem, and women tend more to *react* to the contributions of others. These important differences, which may be read from the interaction profiles, coexist with similarities arising from the information-exchanging, consensus-seeking nature of the deliberation problem. By and large, the jurors' interaction profiles are quite similar. In the face of this similarity the direction of attention of the differences associated with sex roles should not be permitted to obscure the determinative influences of the problem situation.

---

1. In an analysis of some of the determinants of role-taking accuracy, Powell and LaFave (1958) suggest that accuracy depends on such situational factors as: (a) type and circumstance of interaction, (b) motivational relevance of the situation, (c) acting ability of the other subject, and (d) attitudinal consistency of the other subject.

Table 10—Interaction Profile by Sex and Activity

Categories	MALE		FEMALE	
	Inactive	Active	Inactive	Active
A. *Positive reactions*				
1. Shows solidarity	1.14	1.03	1.39	1.45
2. Shows tension release	1.75	1.50	8.49	2.91
3. Shows agreement	10.50	8.26	16.98	20.59
B. *Attempted answers*				
4. Gives suggestions	3.50	3.54	2.31	1.52
5. Gives opinion	25.44	19.42	22.07	18.07
6. Gives information	41.59	48.49	35.96	34.95
C. *Questions*				
7. Asks for information	4.85	5.09	6.33	6.76
8. Asks for opinion	1.08	2.65	.77	1.26
9. Asks for suggestion	.00	.08	.00	.03
D. *Negative reactions*				
10. Shows disagreement	6.46	4.99	3.70	9.31
11. Shows tension	1.82	2.61	1.54	2.36
12. Shows antagonism	1.88	2.36	.46	.77
Total	100.01	100.02	100.00	99.98
Base frequencies	1486	12413	648	3093
Jurors	41	45	23	18

It should perhaps be stressed that the acts involved in the task and social-emotional distinctions are included in the repertoire of all persons. When taken in isolation, these acts do not suggest male or female behavior; it is only in the statistical analysis of aggregates of acts that the sex-typed connotation emerges. Among the various subjects, there are many individual instances in which men are more social-emotional than women, and vice versa. The twelve juries reported upon contained from one to six women, however, in the aggregate profiles there were no discernible trends associated with the increased number of women in the group [pp. 4-10].

§ Sex of Audience and Recall

An experiment by Grace (1951) indicates that even the order of recall of a set of objects is related to the anticipated sex of the future audience, and provides some evidence for the hypothesis stated in Chapter Two that the social act typically involves some modification of behavior to fit the expectations of the other group members. Grace varied the extent to which subjects would anticipate that a future audience would be a woman by asking a number of undergraduates, both men and women, to look at some objects on a table and then to report what they had seen to a person in the next room. Some subjects were told nothing about the person, some were told that they would report to a woman, and some were reminded several times that they would report to a woman. In each case the person actually was a woman who asked the subjects to name all of the objects on the table. Some of the objects were masculine, e.g., a supporter; some were feminine, e.g., a brassiere; and the remainder were neutral, e.g., sunglasses. Anticipation of the type of audience had no effect on the frequency with which the various items were recalled but it did effect the order of recall. Subjects who were reminded that the audience would be a woman recalled the female items earlier than they did when they were told only once or not at all. Since the actual audience was the same for all subjects, the difference is probably not due to restraints operating in the face-to-face situation, but to the effect of the anticipated audience on learning and recalling the items so that certain ones were more readily recalled than others.

Later experiments by Grace (1952a, 1952b) did not wholly confirm these results. In fact, in one experiment the males recalled male items earlier when reporting to a female audience. Grace concludes that "the strongest effect on the content of communication is achieved when the communicator and the audience are of the same background, and the communicator is definitely and deliberately briefed about the audience" (1952b, p. 95).

§ Social Class

DIFFERENCES in interaction pattern which are related to social class are found in membership roles of lower-class and middle-class adolescent clubs (Maas, 1954b). The lower-class member directed more collaborative interaction to the adult leader than did the middle-class member to his leader, the middle-class member directed more collaborative and aggressive interactions to the club president (who was his peer), and the lower-class member was more aggressive with other members.

Within adult discussion groups the members with higher social-economic status tend to participate more. In jury deliberations the jurors who were higher in social-economic status were found to talk more, have more influence on other members, and were perceived by fellow jurors as more competent for the jury task (Strodtbeck, James, & Hawkins,

1957). In community groups in which members discussed a mental health film, the members who participated more often were of higher social class, had high status within the group, and were familiar with the topic (Vaughan & McGinnies, 1957).

§ Ethnic Group

THE INFLUENCE of ethnic group in determining the typical interaction pattern of a group member is evident in Strodtbeck's study of husband-wife interaction in three cultures which is referred to above (1951). Marked cultural differences in the interaction of members of discussion groups are also reported in an analysis of committee-member behavior in four cultures (Gyr, 1951).[2]

Ethnic group affiliation is important in determining the lines along which subgroups will form, since members of the same ethnic group will tend to interact more with each other than with other group members. In a study of the role of group belongingness when voting for a leader (Festinger, 1947), girls from two religious groups tended to vote for members of their own group when the religion of the nominees for the leader position was identified. The trend was more apparent in a large group of 48 subjects than in a smaller group.

In another study four-man groups were composed of college students representing two different ethnic groups. The groups met for a total of over twelve hours, performing a variety of tasks. In each group the two members of the ethnic group with higher status tended to talk more to each other than to the two members from the group with lower status. The lower-status members also talked more to the high-status members than they did to each other (Katz, Goldston, & Benjamin, 1958).

§ Friendship

SINCE FRIENDSHIP is based upon common social characteristics, values, and personality, persons who choose each other for friends may well be of the same age, sex, social class, and ethnic group. For this reason friend-

---

2. A more detailed analysis of cultural differences in group behavior is found in Roberts' (1951) survey of 38 categories of behavior (e.g. technology, food, living routines) in three Navaho households. He finds a substantial array of differences that serve to distinguish the households as individual small group cultures.

ship is not as "independent" a variable as the other characteristics. The association between the number of friends and age, for example, has already been noted. In general, friends tend to be more homogeneous in their behavior patterns than nonfriends, they communicate to each other more (Philp, 1940), and are more productive, unless they spend too much time in social-emotional activity or conspire to slow down on the job. They also conform more to self-originated norms and show more resistance to change from the outside.

Friendship is used as an experimental variable in two ways. First, one may select the popular individuals from several groups and place them together in a new group. Second, one can select from a larger group a small group of mutual friends.

§ Similarities among
    Friends and Popular
    Members

FRIENDS ARE GENERALLY found to be similar in intelligence and temperament (Richardson, 1939), although no relationship between these two variables and friendship is reported in at least one study (Bonney, 1946). If the individuals studied are friends and are also among the *most chosen* members of the group, then the differences between friends and nonfriends are more apparent. Overchosen children are more apt to be high interactors, more co-operative, least hostile to members of competing groups, superior in emotional and physical adjustment, and more representative of the group norms (Hardy, 1937; Hunt & Solomon, 1942; Sherif, 1951; Bates, 1952; Bonney, Hoblit, & Dreyer, 1953; Bonney & Powell, 1953; Dahlke, 1953; see Exhibit 17).

Similar differences between popular and unpopular members have also been observed for adult groups. In industry, for example, overchosen members may be more satisfied with their jobs (Speroff, 1955). If a sample population for an industrial study is limited to friends, a further bias will be introduced in that pairs of friends are usually individuals who are near each other functionally, spatially, and are of the same sex (James, J., 1951b).

The effects of selecting popular individuals have been summarized in a review of 43 sociometric studies (Mouton, et al., 1955b). A positive relation has been found between sociometric choices received by an individual and productivity, combat effectiveness, training ability, and leadership, and a negative relation between popularity and accident proneness, sickness, and disciplinary offenses.

Some of the differences between the behavior of well liked or "over-chosen" individuals and that of other group members are illustrated by a study of a peer group of sixteen government agents (Blau, 1954b). Although the men in this group were supposed to work as individual inspectors and to consult only with the supervisor if they needed help with a case, in practice they formed an informal hierarchy based on a member's willingness to co-operate and skill in handling cases. Men at the top of the hierarchy were well liked because they would give advice to those farther down who were less skilled and needed help with their cases. In this way the men with less skill could avoid having their deficiencies come to the attention of the supervisor. In addition to the differences in skill and willingness to co-operate, high-status members received more contacts from within the group, made more contacts with outsiders, and were less concerned about the opinions of their secretaries than the low-status members.

Members who are "overchosen" and "underchosen" in a large group, when separated into two new groups will form new hierarchies so that in the group of former "overchosen" individuals some are now relatively "underchosen," and in the group of formerly "underchosen" individuals some are now relatively "overchosen" (Powell, 1956).

It is evident that the extent to which popular or "overchosen" members differ from the average of the population as a whole depends upon the characteristics of the subgroup of the total population from which they are drawn. To draw on an example from college life, the least active and least popular of the campus leaders in extracurricular activities may still be more active and more popular than the average undergraduate.

§   Friendship and
    Productivity

PAIRS OF CLOSE FRIENDS were found to be more efficient in the solution of problems than pairs of strangers (Husband, 1940). This effect also occurs in larger groups. Ratings of proficiency for twelve six-man reconnaissance units from the same army regiment were highly correlated (+.77) with the proportion of intra-unit friendship choices (Goodacre, 1951). Part of this effect may be due to higher "morale" or "attractiveness" of the groups containing the most friends, but it is also probably due to the increased ease of *communication*, since several studies on circulation of rumors support the assumption that friendship acts to reduce barriers in communication (Festinger, Cartwright, Barber, Fleischl, Gottsdanker, Keysen, & Leavitt, 1948; Festinger et al., 1950).

If too much time is spent by the friends in social-emotional activity, the productivity of the group will go down (Bos, 1937; Horsfall & Arensberg, 1949). A slowdown may also occur if the group members conspire to lower the output. The efforts of the group to impose a slowdown will be more effective if the group members are highly congenial (Schacter et al., 1951).

Having a friendly person to work with also appears to increase individual productivity. In an experiment with three-year-old children, intelligence tests were administered by a teacher who had previously acted friendly with some and distant with others. The children to whom she had been friendly performed better on the tests (Sacks, 1952).

§ Influence of Friends

In ADDITION to increasing the quantity of interaction, friendship also influences the quality of interaction. Children who were paired with friends in a frustrating situation showed more co-operation and, incidentally, more aggression toward the experimenter than pairs of acquaintances (Wright, 1943). A similar effect was observed with previously unacquainted pairs of college students who had been insulted by the experimenter. Pairs of students who had been told they would get along well with each other reacted with more hostility to the experimenter and the experiment and were less restrained in their interaction than pairs of equally unacquainted students who were told they would probably *not* get along well together (Pepitone & Reichling, 1955). The tendency for friends to be more co-operative has also been observed in adult groups in which an inverse relation was found between the degree to which a person strove for individual prominence and the amount of friendliness displayed in the groups of which he was a member (Haythorn, 1953).

Persons who are attracted to each other have more influence on each other, since individuals are more willing to agree with the opinions of others whom they like (Festinger et al., 1950). In a study made at a summer workshop, the friendship pattern of a group of twenty persons was first determined by sociometric methods. Then, after each group discussion, the investigators presented to the group three statements made during the discussion together with the name of the person who had made each statement. Each group member indicated on a questionnaire his perception of which other members agreed or disagreed with each of the assertions and his own agreement or disagreement. The data indicated that members agreed with a statement more if they liked the person who made it, and that they perceived other persons whom they liked agreeing more with statements they made (Horowitz, Lyons, & Perlmutter, 1951). The tendency for members to talk most to those they like best or like least and least to those to whom they are indifferent was also reported in a study carried out in two different cultures (Festinger & Hutte, 1954).

Friendship, unlike age and sex, is a variable which may be affected by experimental manipulation when some other factor is actually the focus of the investigation. For example, in one experiment teams were composed of ten- to twelve-year-old boys in such a way that at the outset of the experiment each group member found approximately half of his sociometric choices in his own group and the remaining half on the opposing team. When these groups were observed under frustration, the number of friendship choices within the groups at least persisted or improved for unsuccessful low-status and consistently high-status groups (Thibaut, 1950). (Here group status was manipulated by the experimenter who assigned different values to the tasks the groups performed.)

§ Influence through
Social Communication

BACK (1951) demonstrates some of the effects of "cohesiveness" on influence and productivity. He also provides evidence for the assumption, discussed in Chapter Six, that the criterion used to determine "cohesiveness" will affect the form and content of the interaction process. The main purpose of the experiment was to measure the effects of strength of cohesiveness on pressure toward uniformity within pairs of subjects and the consequences of this effect. *Cohesiveness*, which was defined as "the resultant of forces which are acting on the members to stay in the group," was varied in three ways by telling the members that they would or would not: (1) like each other, (2) receive a prize for the best group performance, or (3) serve as a model of a highly productive group. These three types of cohesiveness based on personal attraction, group goal, and group prestige were compared with a control group which received a negative treatment in which all forces to belong to the group were minimized.

Seventy pairs of college students who had not known each other previously and were of the same sex took part in the experiment. The pairs were divided by type of "treatment" into seven sets. After the subjects in each pair were introduced to each other, they were taken to separate rooms where each was instructed to write a preliminary story about a set of three pictures. They were then brought together and asked to discuss the story. Each was then asked to write a final story. Although the subjects thought that the sets of pictures were identical, there were actually slight differences which led to different interpretations. The subjects were also given the special instructions appropriate to their experimental conditions.

The amount of influence of one partner on another was measured by the number of changes in a subject's story which tended toward the position the partner had shown in either his first or final story. The actual discussion was recorded by two observers who used a set of twenty categories to identify influence attempts, reactions to attempted influence, and other types of behavior. After the discussion, each observer characterized the pair as "active" or "withdrawing" and each subject indicated the extent to which he was attracted to his partner.

The results of the experiment showed that, within this setting, certain effects could be expected to follow an increase of cohesiveness, independent of the basis of the cohesiveness. "In the high cohesive groups the members made more attempts to reach an agreement. Both the ratings of the total discussion and direct observation showed more serious effort to enter the discussion in highly cohesive groups. The subjects' own statements also confirmed the high pressures in these groups" (p. 22).

Attempted influence appeared to be more a question of personal preference in the low cohesive groups, while it was almost a necessary result of the pressures toward uniformity in the high cohesive groups. In the high cohesive groups, acceptance of the experimental situation, interest in the problem itself, and a desire to help the experimenter combined to motivate the subjects to make something of the discussion.

In the highly cohesive groups the discussion was more effective in that it produced influence, that is, group members changed more toward the partners' positions than they did in the less cohesive groups [see Table 11]. In

Table 11—Changes Influenced by the Partner

Group	Personal attraction	Task direction	Group prestige	Negative
Low cohesive	7.9	8.9	6.7	8.5
High cohesive	10.5	11.0	8.3	

$$F = \frac{\text{Var.: strength}}{\text{Var.: within cells}} = 3.13; \; df = 1 \text{ and } 54; \; p < .11$$

the highly cohesive groups the change was quite unevenly distributed between the members, while in the less cohesive groups the change was more evenly distributed. On the average, one member of the highly cohesive groups changed more than either member of the less cohesive groups; and the other member of the highly cohesive group was nearly the same as one member of the less cohesive group (pp. 22-23).

The differences among the ways in which cohesiveness was produced also led to differences in patterns of communication and influence.

If cohesiveness was based on personal attraction, group members wanted to transform the discussion into a longish, pleasant conversation. The discussion was taken as a personal effort, and rejection of persuasion tended to be resented.

If cohesiveness was based on the performance of a task, group members wanted to complete the activity quickly and efficiently; they spent just the time necessary for performance of the task [see Table 12] and they tried to use this time for the performance of the task only. They tended to participate in the discussion only as much as they thought it valuable to achieve their purposes.

Table 12—Time of Discussion (Seconds)

Group	Personal attraction	Task direction	Group prestige	Negative
Low cohesive	412.5	415.5	307.0	330.0
High cohesive	449.0	321.5	362.5	

t not significant $\quad t = 2.91 \qquad t = 3.65$
$\qquad\qquad\qquad\quad p < .01 \qquad\quad p < .01$

If cohesiveness was based on group prestige [the assumption that the group would serve as a model for other groups], group members tried to risk as little as possible to endanger their status: they acted cautiously, concentrated on their own actions, and adjusted to their partners as the social environment. One partner would easily assume a dominant role, and the submissive member was influenced more, without their actually trying to establish this relationship.

Finally, with cohesiveness at a minimum, the members of the pair acted independently and with little consideration for each other. As the subject did not try to adjust to the other member of the pair; each member was concerned only with his own discussion. Influence, accordingly, did not depend on the action of the partner but on the interest of the member himself in entering the group activity (p. 23).

§   Summary

CHARACTERISTICS SUCH AS AGE, sex, social class, ethnicity, and friendship, have the advantage of being more easily identified than personality. The effects of age on interaction patterns are evident as children develop through preschool age. During these years they pass through phases of egocentric play, parallel play, and group play. When they reach the third stage, they first make many social contacts and then, in latency and adolescence, restrict their contacts to a more intimate few. By adulthood boys and girls have assumed typical sex roles which usually require more activity in the social-emotional area for the women and more activity in the task area for the men.

This sex role differentiation is evident in mock jury deliberations where men tend to initiate relatively long bursts of activity directed at the solution of task problems, and women tend to react to the contributions of others. The sex of an anticipated audience is found to influence the order in which certain sex-linked objects are recalled.

Adolescents from different social classes are found to differ in their patterns of relationship to authority. Upper class adults tend to participate more and have more influence in discussion groups.

Members of the same ethnic group can be expected to have similar patterns of behavior and to choose each other as subgroups from within the larger group. Friendship, whatever its basis, produces marked differences in interaction. Groups of friends usually have higher morale, exert more influence on each other, and are more productive. Popular individuals, whether grouped with their friends or considered as individuals, are found to be more productive, better students, and less subject to accidents, illness, and disciplinary offenses.

Differences in interaction also appear between groups of "friends" if members in each group are attracted to each other for different reasons. In an experiment in which the basis for "cohesiveness" between members of a pair was varied, it was found that the members tried to turn the task into a social occasion if they were told that they would "like each other," that they completed the activity quickly and efficiently if they were working for a prize, and that they acted more cautiously when their group was to serve as a model.

Exhibit 17
Characteristics of Overchosen Members

A.

Investigator: Hardy (1937).
Focus: Social recognition at the elementary school age.
Sample: 215 boys and 194 girls observed in twelve different schools.
Method: Sociometric traits were judged by tests and teacher observation.
Relevant Findings: The most popular children had more desirable social and emotional traits of industry, conduct, intelligence, physical ability, and health. They also had more attractive and superior home conditions.

B.

Investigator: Hunt & Solomon (1942).
Focus: The stability and some correlates of group status in a summer-camp group of young boys.
Sample: 23 boys tested during the first two weeks of camp and 22 boys tested during the last six weeks. Ages ranged from five to eight years. All boys were upper middle class. The camp was divided into four cabin groups with two counselors in charge of each cabin.
Method: The question "Whom do you like best?" was asked on arrival and repeated every week until departure. Each of the counselors rated his campers on (1) generosity *vs.* stinginess, (2) physical attractiveness *vs.* ugliness, (3) ordered activity *vs.* restlessness, (4) obedience *vs.* disobedience, and (5) lack of egocentricity *vs.* egocentricity.
Relevant Findings: By the end of the camping period obedience to counselors was the only trait not correlated with popularity.

C.

Investigator: Bonney, Hoblit, & Dreyer (1953).
Focus: A study of some factors related to sociometric status in a men's dormitory.
Sample: 75 men in one dormitory unit of a state college.
Method: Sociometric questionnaire and observations.
Relevant Findings: High-choice men had a more sincere and objective interest in others, considerable self-respect and self-confidence, active participation in the more mature and socially approved forms of group activities, and were good conversationalists.

D.

Investigator: Bonney & Powell (1953).

Focus: Differences in social behavior between sociometrically high and sociometrically low children.

Sample: Ten sociometrically high children and ten sociometrically low children in a first-grade class.

Method: Behavior was sampled through observation over a period of several months. The children were also given the California Test of Mental Maturity and the California Test of Personality.

Revelant Findings: Of the 25 categories of observed behavior, only five showed a statistically reliable difference between the two extreme groups under consideration (P. < .02). The highly acceptable children were more conforming, smiling, and co-operative, and less likely to play alone.

E.

Investigator: Dahlke (1953).

Focus: Determinants of sociometric relations among children.

Sample: 163 children in a small-town elementary school.

Method: The children were given a personality test (California Test of Personality, Elementary Series) and a near sociometric test based on seating arrangement and clubbing questions. Observation and structure interviews were also used.

Relevant Findings: Children who received many sociometric choices had higher scores on the test of personality adjustment. More girls than boys were "overchosen."

8

GROUP SIZE

THERE IS NO EXACT specification of how large a group may be before one no longer feels it appropriate to call it a small group. An attempt to name some exact number would actually be misleading. The usefulness of the designation presumably rests on the fact that size is a limiting condition on the amount and quality of communication that can take place among members as individual persons, and hence tends to affect the character of interpersonal orientations that members develop toward each other (Krech & Crutchfield, 1948, p. 371). But other conditions may also be limiting in the same way. For example, the characteristics of the members and the time available may have a similar limiting effect. Consequently, the effects of size should be considered in conjunction with other relevant variables.

Some of the effects of increasing size will be considered as they relate to the form and content of interaction. Since the number of potential relationships between group members increases rapidly as a group grows larger, the larger group tends to break into subgroups with a more rigid hierarchy of positions. When the time for discussion is limited, the average member has fewer chances to speak and intermember communication becomes difficult. Morale declines, since the former intimate contact between members is no longer possible. Although the larger group has in its membership a greater variety of resources for problem-solving, the average contribution of each member diminishes and it becomes more difficult to reach consensus on a group solution. The pair and the three-person group have special characteristics of intimacy and of power structure which give each group some unique aspects. Although the optimum size for a group varies with the task of the group, a five-man group is found to have some advantages for problems which can be solved by group discussion.

§ Natural Groups

In terms of effective participation in group activity, it may be that certain group sizes are more "natural" and occur more frequently than others under particular conditions. Age seems to be a variable which is related to size in this way. It appears that the increasing maturity associated with age permits effective participation in larger groups. Preschool children tend to play first individually, although in parallel, then in pairs, then in larger groups. (Piaget, 1932b; Parten, 1933b; Green, 1933b).

Another variable which appears to be associated with "natural" sizes is the rural-urban continuum. Rural high school youth form cliques of about three persons, while town youth are more likely to form cliques of four to five persons (Hollingshead, 1949). The smaller size of the rural cliques seems to result primarily from the fact that the rural youth live farther apart.

Frequency and duration of contact between members is to some extent conditioned by size, as well as the converse. Among college students, as the size of the group increased, frequency, duration, and intimacy of contact decreased (Fischer, 1953). In two studies of the frequency of occurrence of small groups of different sizes, data were collected by observation and from records of the sizes of groups formed by pedestrians, shoppers, play groups, work groups, and congressional committees. The frequency of occurrence of groups of different sizes was found to be a negative function of size. The function described appears smooth, and the mean size for both counts was close to 2.4 (James, J., 1951a, 1953). There seems to be a tendency for face-to-face groups to gravitate to the smallest size, two. In another study of boys' gangs, the two- or three-boy relationship was often found to be more important to the individual boy than the relationship to the larger gang (Thrasher, 1927).

§   The Size of the Gang

THRASHER (1927) found in his study of adolescent gangs that the necessities of maintaining face-to-face relationships set definite limits to the magnitude to which the gang could grow. The size of one group, for example, was determined by the number of boys readily able to meet together on the street or within the limited space of their hangout. The gang did not usually grow to such proportions as to be unwieldy in collective enterprises or to make intimate contacts and controls difficult. Ordinarily, if all members were present, what was said by one of the group could be heard by all. Otherwise, common experience became more difficult and the group tended to split and form more than one gang. The number of "fringers" and hangers-on upon whom the gang could count for backing, however, might be larger, especially if it had developed a good athletic team.

Greater growth was accomplished only through modifications of structure, such as those resulting from conventionalization. When a gang became conventionalized, assuming, for example, the form of a club, it might possibly grow to large proportions. The original gang, however, now became an "inner circle," remaining the active nucleus in such cases. The additional members might develop their own cliques within the larger whole or maintain merely a more or less formal relationship to the organization. In many cases such a club was the result of the combination of two or more gangs.

Table 13—Approximate Number of Members in 895 Gangs

No. of Members	No. of Gangs	Percentage of Total
From 3 to 5 (inclusive)	37	4.1
From 6 to 10	198	22.1
From 11 to 15	191	21.5
From 16 to 20	149	16.7
From 21 to 25	79	8.8
From 26 to 30	46	5.1
From 31 to 40	55	6.1
From 41 to 50	51	5.7
From 51 to 75	26	2.9
From 76 to 100	25	2.8
From 101 to 200	25	2.8
From 201 to 500	11	1.2
From 501 to 2,000	2	.2
Total gangs	895	100.0

Table 13 includes only some of the gang clubs; these varied in number of members ordinarily from 20 or 25 to 75 or 100; only a few of the more prosperous clubs exceeded 100 members. It will be seen that 806 of these gangs had memberships of 50 or under; these were largely of the unconventionalized type. Most of the remaining 89 had membership ranging from 51 to 2,000 though not all of them had been conventionalized.

§ Size and Satisfaction

THE IMPORTANCE of the individual's relationship with a small group as a factor contributing to his satisfaction with the task is further indicated by evidence that infantry men in the American army who were sent into the front lines as replacements in a group of four buddies who had mutually chosen each other as well liked had higher "morale" than men sent as individual replacements (Chesler, Van Steenberg, & Brueckel, 1955). When coal miners in Great Britain, who were accustomed to working in three-man teams, were shifted to groups of 40 to 50 men (the "longwall" method of coal mining), they became highly dissatisfied with the work (Trist & Bamforth, 1951).

In general, as the size of the group decreases, the strength of the affectional ties between members increases (Coyle, 1930; Kinney, 1953) with the dyad allowing the possibilities for the greatest degree of intimacy (Wolff, 1950).

§ The Emergence of Leadership

As SIZE INCREASES, it presumably becomes more difficult for each member to keep each other group member in mind as a separate, differentiated person. Experiments on estimating the number of dots in a visual field with very short time exposures indicate individual subjects can report the exact number up to and including seven with great confidence and practically no error, but above that number confidence and accuracy drop (Taves, 1941). When report time is allowed to vary, time required increases as a function of number of dots on the card, up to six or seven dots and then flattens abruptly and remains about flat, suggesting that the estimation is being done by a different psychological procedure that somehow does not involve a separate discrimination of each dot (Kaufman, Lord, Reese, & Volkmann, 1949; Jensen, Reese, & Reese, 1950). Observers rating group members face a problem not unlike that of the dot estimators in the sense that they can pay attention to only a limited number of persons at a given time. Observers reach maximum agreement on leadership assessment at size six, as compared with sizes two, four, eight, and twelve (Bass & Norton, 1951). It may be that leadership tends not to emerge so clearly in the even sizes below six, and that above that size the observer may begin to run into cognitive difficulties. The coincidence of these findings suggests that the ability of the observing individual to perceive, keep track of, and judge each member separately in a social interaction situation may not extend much beyond the size of six or seven. If this is true, one would expect members of groups larger than that size to tend to think of other members in terms of subgroups, or "classes" of some kind, and to deal with members of subgroups other than their own by more stereotyped methods of response.

§ The Increasing Number of Relationships

Possibly a more relevant way of viewing size as a variable is to consider the number of possible relationships in the group by pairs and larger subgroups rather than the number of persons. As the number of individuals increases, the number of possible relationships increases much more rapidly than size.

The number of potential symmetrical relationships between individuals is given by the formula:

$$x = \frac{n^2 - n}{2}$$

where $x=$ the number of symmetrical relationships, $n=$ the number of individuals. For example, if there are three members in the group, there are $(9 - 3)/2$, or three potential symmterical relationships with the group. If the group is increased to six members, there are $(36 - 6)/2$, or fifteen relationships (Bossard, 1945). However, since the relationships between subgroups, as well as those between individuals, are usually important in the analysis of a group, a better approximation of the number of potential relationships between individuals, between subgroups, and between an individual and a subgroup is given by the formula:

$$x = \frac{3^n - 2^{n+1} + 1}{2}$$

Using the family as an illustration, the relationship between two brothers would be an example of a relationship at the individual level, between parents and children an example of the subgroup level, and between grandfather and grandchildren an example of the individual and subgroup level. The rapid increase in the potential number of relationships is indicated in Table 14.

Table 14—Increase in Potential Relationships (x) with an Increase in Group Size (n)

Size of Group	Number of Relationships
2	1
3	6
4	25
5	90
6	301
7	966

The addition of an in-law to a household of five members which includes mother, father, and three children means that 211 potential relationships have been added (Kephart, 1950).

The word "symmetrical" has been used to qualify the type of relationships referred to in these formulas, since the formulas are based on a global use of the term relationship to refer to the sum of all forms of mutual association which might take place between two persons. The bond between two persons can be thought of as the sum of a number of relationships which are usually neither totally present nor fully absent but present in some degree. If one takes as an example a relationship like *love*, and assumes that the relationship can either be present or absent for each pair of individuals (or a pair of subgroups, or an individual and a subgroup), then there are two ways to fill each of the symmetrical relationships represented by the second formula. The number of different *sets* of potential relationships would actually be 2^x, where x is given by the second formula. For the group of five the number is 2 to the 90th power which is already a very large number (Davis, 1954).

It may be expected, then, that when there is a desire for intimate and highly developed relationships or need for fine coordination, there will also be a tendency toward the restriction of size. It is worth noting in this connection that the appearance of a leader can permit a reduction of the psychological complication of the group to a series of pair relationships of each member with the leader for certain purposes of coordination. The development of leadership is possibly in part an alternative to an actual reduction in size.

A number of investigators associate the emergence of leadership with increasing size of the group. In the restaurant industry, increasing size of the organization is related to increasing difficulty in coordinating activities (Whyte, 1949). On the basis of a large questionnaire study, leader behavior in many different types of groups was found to differ as size increased (especially above size 31). The demands upon the leader role, moreover, became more numerous and exacting, and member tolerance for leader-centered direction of group activities became greater (Hemphill, 1950). In initially leaderless groups, correlations between observer ratings of members on "initiative," "insight," "leadership behavior," and also "authoritarianism" are greater in groups of size eight than those of size four (Carter, Haythorn, Meirowitz, & Lanzetta, 1951b). A similar increase in correlation between prediction of leadership skill made from TAT analysis and the amount of change toward consensus in group discussion is found when size five is compared with size twelve (Hare, 1952), since the larger groups "demand more skill from the leader." In a study of adjustment over time in a group of machine shop workers, a fluctuation in the underlying emotional tone was observed from an initial period of aggression and withdrawal to a period of dependency on the leader and then back to aggression and withdrawal, as size was increased (Rice, 1951). Members of larger groups tend to form subgroups with spokesmen for their opinions (Homans, 1950; Hare, 1952).

§ Time for
   Communication

THE TIME AVAILABLE per member for overt communication during a meeting of any given length decreases as the group size increases. Thus, each member has a more complicated set of social relationships to maintain and more restricted resources with which to do it. Members of discussion groups are aware of this, and report that they have fewer chances to speak in groups of size twelve as compared with size five (Hare, 1952). In addition, an increased proportion of the members report feelings of threat and inhibition of impulses to participate as size is increased (Gibb, J. R., 1951). As the size of kindergarten groups is increased from 14 to 46, not only does the average number of remarks per child and the percentage of the total number of children who participate decrease, but also the total amount of discussion decreases (Dawe, 1934). Thus, the effect of increasing size appears to involve not only a mechanical constriction of time per member, but also a feeling of threat or inhibition. In experiments with three-and-a-half-year-old children, the combination of one adult observer and two children results in a higher rate of talking and more "friendly intercourse" than the combination of observer with either one or three children (Williams & Mattson, 1942). Here size is interpreted as a factor of significance in the development of language skills. Such an interpretation may be derivatively correct if size is, as it appears to be, a factor which limits the character of performance of members of the group.

Not only does the average amount of participation per member diminish as group size is increased, but the distribution of participation also varies (Bales et al., 1951; see Fig. 20). Generally, in discussion groups of sizes three to eight, all members address some remarks to the group as a whole, but typically only one member, the top participator, addresses more to the group as a whole than to specific other members. As group size increases, a larger and larger proportion of the participators have total amounts of participation under their "equal" share, that is, under the mean for the group. At the same time, at least where a participating leader is appointed, the gap between the top participator and the others tends to grow proportionately greater as size increases. When the designated leader of a group is excluded, the gradient of total acts initiated by the remainder of the members tend to follow a simple curve that flattens as the size of the group increases (Stephan & Mishler, 1952). In one experiment involving a group of four males, each individual had sufficient latitude or space for interaction and thus the basic abilities of each individual could be expressed; in a group of eight, however, only the more forceful individuals were able to express their abilities and ideas, since the amount of freedom in the situation was not sufficient to accommodate all the group members (Carter et al., 1951b).

Figure 20—Rank-Ordered Series of Total Acts Initiated, Compared with Harmonic Distribution, for Groups of Sizes Three to Eight
(n = Persons in Group, s = Sessions, N = Hundreds of Acts)

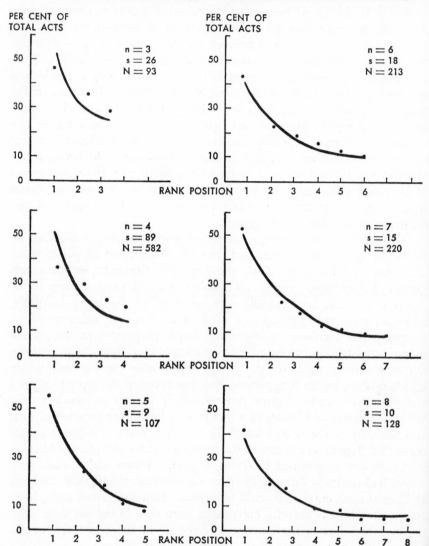

§ Increased Resources
versus
Diminishing Returns

WHILE SIZE MAY BE VIEWED as a limiting condition in certain respects, increasing size is obviously not in every respect a constricting factor. Many abilities or resources needed in task performance tend to have an additive character. They may include such things as the number of items of information which can be absorbed and recalled, the number of critical judgments available to correct errors of information and inference, the number of ideas or suggestions available for solution of problems, the range of values that are likely to be brought to bear, as well as the range of technical skills, abilities, and amount of muscular power that is available to implement decisions. For example, in a word-building task, the number of words built in a given time increased as the group size was increased from three to ten (Watson, 1928).

However, the familiar phenomenon of "diminishing returns" tends to set in at some point. The addition of a person to a group of a given size may not represent a unit addition to task ability. The tendency for difficulty of coordination to increase with size is one factor that may lead to diminishing net returns, but there are other factors also. In audience-like groups of eight sizes ranging from one to 96 persons (Gibb, J. R., 1951), the absolute number of volunteered ideas for the solution of a problem produced within a set time follows a negatively accelerated increasing function. The negative acceleration might possibly be due to some limit to the number of solutions available and reluctance to repeat, or to the increasing difficulty faced by the experimenter in recording all suggestions as they occur. However, the proportion of subjects who report feelings of threat or inhibition of their impulses to participate increases with size. In the same experiment, the design includes a situation which increases feelings of threat by creating a more formal procedure. This situation also leads to a reduction in the number of ideas proposed. One infers then that increased feeling of threat may reduce participation as size increases, and thus create an obstacle to the completion of the task.

On a task requiring physical pulling power, a four-man group was the most efficient (Moede, 1927). Above that size the pulling power per member decreased by ten percent with each additional member. One would suppose that difficulty of coordination may be an interfering factor in this case. Since an inverse relation between output per man and size of work group was also found in motor-car factories, it is possible that the formation of norms restricting output and the strength of the group sanctions may be additional factors which produce interference (Marriott, 1949).

On a concept formation task (Twenty Questions), groups of two persons obtained the answer in shorter time, used fewer questions, and failed less often at the task than did individuals (Taylor & Faust, 1952). Groups of four failed least often, but were not otherwise superior to groups of two. Here we see, apparently, a gain from having available a larger pool of questions to ask, and a gain from the exercise of critical judgment in eliminating poor ideas or testing closure on the solution, but both sources of gain are subject to diminishing returns. The number of man-minutes required per problem increases with size. This, of course, is typically the case. However, for many practical purposes, where the task is one in which some absolute level of effectiveness must be obtained in a set time to avoid complete failure, the lowered efficiency per unit of time per man may be a secondary consideration.

A number of early experiments include the finding that groups have a lower probability of failure or a greater probability of accuracy in problem-solving than individuals, since the groups have greater resources for ideas and error-checking (South, 1927; Shaw, 1932; Dashiell, 1935; Ziller, 1957b). However, the only clearly demonstrated gain so far is essentially of a statistical sort: "four judgments are better than one for the same nonsocial reason that four thermometers are better than one." The group effect is essentially a trend toward homogeneity or reduction of variance. "In a secondary way this usually increases the accuracy of individual judgments, or the size of the majority vote, but it does not by itself increase the accuracy of group judgment" (Johnson, 1955, p. 471). If the true value of the variable being judged is bracketed by the range of individual judgments, and if the errors are only of a random kind, the tendency to converge toward a group norm of judgments will increase the accuracy of the average individual judgment. If the true value is outside the range of judgments, the average error of the judgments will not be changed by the convergence effect.

The greater variety of opinion available as size increases may give some advantage of critical power, but has its price in the greater difficulty of reaching consensus. The difficulty is apparently most marked when the task is primarily one of modifying opinion, in the absence of any clear objective criteria for judgment. For example, groups of six took longer on tasks of this sort than groups of three (South, 1927), and groups of twelve took longer on a group decision than groups of five (Hare, 1952). On the other hand, if the task is a technical one with clear criteria of correct performance and requires some absolute level of intelligence, speed, or the like, the larger group may have a higher probability of containing some member who can obtain an answer easily acceptable to the others once it is presented. On "abstract" tasks, groups of six were faster than groups of three, possibly for this reason (South, 1927).

§ Interaction and Consensus in Different Sized Groups

IN THE EXPERIMENT designed by Hare (1952) which illustrates some of the difficulties in reaching consensus in larger discussion groups, some one hundred fifty Boy Scouts took part in small discussion groups. In a summer camp, nine groups of five boys and nine groups of twelve boys played a "camping game." First, the boys were told a story about a camping trip which ended in misfortune so that it was necessary for each boy to find his way back to civilization alone. Then the boys individually ranked ten pieces of camping equipment in the order of their importance for such a trip. The items of camping equipment were: pack, cook kit, sleeping bag, flashlight, waterproof match box, axe, compass, first aid kit, scout knife, and canteen. Each group was then asked to rank the pieces of equipment in the order of their importance. After the discussion, the boys as individuals again ranked the ten pieces of equipment. This was followed by a short questionnaire to record observations about the discussion. Some time after the game, the leader was interviewed and given a Thematic Apperception Test.

§ Measurement of Consensus

THE AMOUNT OF CONSENSUS in the group was measured by having each individual rank the ten pieces of camping equipment before discussion, the group rank the equipment during discussion, and the individual again rank them after discussion. The rank orders of equipment before discussion for each of the followers in a group were combined by using the statistic r_{av}, average correlation of all rank orders. The $\bar{r}_{av}$ was also computed for each group after discussion. The mean correlation ($\bar{r}_{av}$) before discussion for all groups of the same size represented the average amount of agreement among Boy Scouts about the importance of camping equipment, and the $\bar{r}_{av}$ after discussion represented the point to which consensus was increased as a result of the discussion.

Because an increase in consensus could not be made without some change in individual opinions, another statistic (the rank order correlation, r') was used to describe the amount of consistency in each individual as well as his change of opinion in the direction of the group decision. Three rank order correlations were computed for each individual: the individual's first ranking of the ten items of equipment was correlated with the ranking arrived at by the whole group after discussion (r'_{12}), the group ranking was correlated with the final individual ranking (r'_{23}), and the first individual ranking was correlated with the final ranking (r'_{13}).

A high correlation for r'_{12} indicated that the group discussion was close to that which the individual selected at first, and that he may have influenced the group. A low correlation for r'_{12} combined with a high r'_{23} indicated that, although the individual originally had ideas which were different, he had been won over to the group decision. Finally, a high correlation for r'_{13} indicated that the individual had not changed his opinion as a result of the discussion.

§   The Questionnaire

THE QUESTIONNAIRE was designed to reveal some characteristics of the nature of interaction during discussion. Among the factors about which information was sought were the role of persons other than the leader, the importance of enough time for discussion, the amount of participation of the members and their feelings of satisfaction or dissatisfaction, and the breaking of the groups into smaller factions with individual spokesmen.

§ Leader Skill

AN ATTEMPT WAS MADE to control and measure leadership by the use of specific directions for the leader during the game, and a projective test later to indicate his potential leadership skill.

The leaders were chosen, on the basis of recommendations by their camp counselors, as boys who had had leadership experience, held positions of responsibility in their troop, or were recognized as leaders by their peers. Before the group discussion, they were taken aside and given instructions as participatory leaders. These instructions emphasized that the leader was to participate himself, to see that every member had a chance to speak, to keep the discussion moving so that a ranking could be obtained in twenty minutes. Thus the leader was thought of as an agent who helped to facilitate the interaction of group members. To check this, he was observed during the game and questioned on his methods in a postexperiment interview.

On the basis of a Thematic Apperception Test administered to all leaders, the leaders were classified in three groups, representing a rough differentiation between their leadership potentials. These classifications of skill were:

1. Type A (good leaders)—above average leaders; boys who seemed to be able to handle others of their age reasonably well and who desired the status of leader.

2. Type B (average leaders)—boys not very different from other Boy Scouts who were able to exercise authority in well-structured situations where there was no great opposition from the followers.

3. Type C (poor leaders)—boys who were either so maladjusted or so constricted and passive that they could be expected to have trouble even in a well-structured and supervised situation.

§ Results

THREE OF THE HYPOTHESES which found support in this research are restated below, together with the data which are related to them.

As the size of a discussion group is increased from five to twelve members, the amount of consensus resulting from group discussion will decrease.

Table 15—Means of the Average Correlation of All Rank Orders before and after Discussion of the Followers in Groups of 5 and 12

Group size	Number of groups	$\bar{r}_{av}$ before	$\bar{r}_{av}$ after	Difference
5	9	.38	.88	.50
12	9	.37	.67	.30

This major hypothesis was substantiated by the $\bar{r}_{av}$'s for each set of groups before and after discussion. The average amount of agreement before discussion was almost the same for both groups, about .37 (Table 15), since the followers in the different-sized groups came from the same population with regard to their initial opinions about camping equipment. The average amount of agreement after discussion increased to .88 for the groups of five and .67 for the groups of twelve, a significant increase (Prob. $< .05$) in both cases. Furthermore, the average amount of change in consensus for the small groups (.50) was significantly larger than the average amount of change in the large groups (.30).

This relationship is also evident in the r' data (Table 16) where the followers showed less agreement with the group decision (r'_{23}) in the large groups.

Table 16—Average Rank Order Correlation Coefficients for Leaders and Followers in Groups of 5 and 12

	Number of groups	r'_{12}	r'_{23}	r'_{13}
Leaders				
Groups of 5	9	.85	.98	.91
Groups of 12	9	.64	.91	.78
Followers				
Groups of 5	36	.59	.97	.60
Groups of 12	99	.56	.88	.70

Within groups of the same size, the amount of change in consensus will be related to the leader's skill.

A second hypothesis was only partially verified since the measure of the leader's skill derived from the TAT stories had no predictive value in estimating the amount of change in consensus in the small groups; in fact, there was a negative relationship which approached but did not reach significance (Table 17). When the twelve-man groups

vere considered separately, however, there was a significant positive
correlation between the measure of leader skill and the amount of change
in consensus.

Table 17—Average Change in r_av by Leader Skill

Leader Skill	Number of Groups	Average Change in r_{av}
Groups of 5		
Good	3	.39
Average	4	.52
Poor	2	.62
Groups of 12		
Good	4	.41
Average	3	.24
Poor	2	.14

*The leader in the group of five will have more influence on the group
decision than the leader in the group of twelve.*

The data confirmed the hypothesis that the leaders in the small groups
will have more influence. The three rank order correlations for the leaders
in the groups of five were all significantly higher than the corresponding
correlations for the leaders in the groups of twelve (Table 16), indicating
that the average leader in the group of five agreed with the group more
before and after discussion and was more consistent with himself than
was the average leader in the group of twelve. These higher correlations
indicate that the group ranking was close to the leader's original ideas
in the smaller groups.

The postmeeting questionnaire provided evidence that the followers
in the large groups felt that they had too little time for discussion and
that the lack of opportunity to participate led to dissatisfaction with the
discussion. The followers in the large group also tended to feel that
their opinions were not important.

In this experiment a change in group size resulted in a change in
the *control* area, since the larger groups apparently placed more demands
on the skill of the leader, and a change in *interaction rate* since the
amount of time available for participation was restricted in the larger
groups.

§ Changes in the
Content of Interaction

THE FREQUENCY with which certain categories of acts appear tends to vary with group size. In groups of sizes two to seven engaged in a group decision problem, where the criteria of the goodness of the solution depended upon the values of the members (Bales & Borgatta, 1955), the rate of giving information and suggestion increased as size increased, while the rate of asking for opinion, giving opinion, and showing agreement decreased. These changes are consistent with the hypothesis that, as size increases, there is a tendency toward a more mechanical method of introducing information (by round-robin procedure, for example), a less sensitive exploration of the point of view of the other, and a more direct attempt to control others and reach solution whether or not all group members indicate agreement. All these effects are reasonably associated with the increasing constriction of time available per person. Rates of showing tension tended to decrease, but joking and laughter increased, which may indicate a tendency for less direct involvement of members in task success and for tension to be displaced into humor, rather than to be reduced directly through serious attempts to resolve opinion differences. In this sense, it is suggested that unresolved differences appear to be more tolerable in larger groups, and they may be handled by compartmentalization and other similar devices rather than by resolution.

§ The Dyad

IN ADDITION to these effects of size which show an increasing or decreasing trend, groups of two appear to show unique characteristics (Becker & Useem, 1942). They tend to have high rates of showing tension, consistently avoid disagreement and antagonism, have high rates of asking for opinion, but avoid giving opinion, and concentrate rather on exchange of information and agreement (or acknowledgment) (Bales & Borgatta, 1955). This pattern of rates is consistent with an interpretation that in groups of two a delicate balance of power exists when, as in *ad hoc* experimental groups, there are few group norms regarded as binding except those to which both members currently assent. In such a case there is no "public opinion," no majority to which either can appeal. Either member can prevent task completion by disagreement or withdrawal. Both members have to proceed within certain limits to avoid this reaction on the part of the other. The task of building a common set of norms in this situation is apparently an anxiety-provoking prospect, and tends to be avoided or in part glossed over by agreement on more specific and superficial matters. In a loose interpretation, the two-man group may be viewed as having built into it an implicit agreement that the two members will stay within spheres on which they can agree. In spite of the delicate balance of power, however, there is a strong tendency for two asymmetric roles to develop, that is, for the members to specialize in different types of overt behavior. The differences appear in practically all categories of behavior. Apparently, there is a tendency for one member to gravitate toward a more active role and exercise the power of initiative, while the other tends toward a more passive role and holds the power of veto. In this context, it is difficult to ascribe power or leadership to either role, for the passive person may be construed as defining the permissive range of the active person. In the sense that the group operates toward the achievement of a given task, leadership associated with proper completion of the group task certainly may be associated with both the initiating and control functions.

In a study of husband-wife pairs in three cultures, the norms in each culture defining the expected power of wife *versus* husband enable prediction of the tendency of one spouse or the other to take the more active role, and the tendency to win more decisions (Strodtbeck, 1951). A direct relation exists between the amount of participation and number of decisions won. The more influential spouse tends more frequently to ask questions, give opinions, and make rewarding remarks, while the less influential takes a more reactive role with more acts of agreement, disagreement, and antagonism.

Above size two there are significant differences between groups with an even or odd number of members (Bales & Borgatta, 1955). Groups of even size (four and six) have higher rates of showing disagreement and antagonism, and lower rates of asking for suggestion and possibly in showing agreement, than groups of odd size (three, five, and seven). These effects are attributed to the fact that in even sizes, a division of the group into two subparts of equal size is possible. Thus, in cases of disagreement in even-size groups, the probability of a majority and a minority is lower than in odd sizes, and this in turn may increase the probability that disagreements will remain deadlocked between two subgroups.

§ The Triad

THE POWER OF MAJORITY over minority is especially marked in groups of size three, since in this size any minority must be that of a single person, who is thus left isolated without the support of any other group member, at least with respect to the immediate discussion.

On the other hand, the three-person situation is the one in which an individual (or nation) has the opportunity to control through the technique of "divide and conquer" [Von Wiese & Becker, 1932; Simmel (in Wolff, 1950)]. If the power distribution in the group is unequal, these observations may not hold since the most powerful member may prevail (Caplow, 1956), or, as in one experiment, the weakest person may initiate a coalition with the strongest (Vinacke & Arkoff, 1957).

In laboratory discussion groups of three persons (Mills, 1953, 1956), a relationship in which the two top participators disagreed with each other and sought the support of the third low member was unstable through time within a meeting and tended to change toward the end of the meeting to a supporting coalition between the two higher participators with the low man excluded. In laboratory groups such as these, any pattern, once clearly formed, tends to be preserved with minimal alteration when a fourth member (a newcomer) is added to the group (Mills et al., 1957).

In more permanent groups of three (father, mother, and son), no one person was singled out for exclusion in a series of decisions (Strodtbeck, 1954a). It may be inferred that the power of a coalition of two in a three-person group to force a decision is considerable and is so employed with reference to particular disagreements. Indeed it may be so powerful that members tend to switch coalitions from one disagreement to another simply to maintain solidarity and avoid the permanent exclusion of one member. The overt interaction activity should, however, be considered as only one possible indicator of the existence of coalitions. If the coalition pattern in interaction is defined only by the amount of support that is overtly demonstrated between pairs, one may overlook the fact that where a coalition exists there may be no need for the supporters to demonstate to each other their agreement. In another study on coalitions, a third member was forced to change his behavior pattern completely by two role players who first allowed him to form a coalition with one of them, and then combined against him. He changed his opinion less often than his behavior, and he tended to retain his liking for the original partner in spite of the overt desertion (Mills, 1954). Another complicating consideration is the fact that, as one disagrees, one must also support, or the situation may deteriorate. In terms of interaction scoring, responses in the active support categories vary directly with those in the negative categories.

In general, these data suggest that the problem of deadlock is most severe in the two-person group, but in this case, each person is also without support in a deadlock, and if the group is to remain in existence, each person must respond to the emergency signs of the other. The level of tension may be high but the hostility must be controlled, since each person *must* face the other. In the four-person group, on the other hand, in a deadlock situation each person may have a supporter, and the deadlock may continue with each person still having available a source of support and gratification. In the three-person group the problem of the overpowerful majority is emphasized. At least some of the idiosyncracies of two-, three-, and four-man groups may thus be viewed as special cases of the odd and even effects, and these in turn, may be seen as results of the power of perceived consensus among a majority in persuading the minority (or single person) to change its views, or at least not to oppose outwardly the resolution of the disagreement.

§ The Optimum Size

A FINAL COMMENT may be made on the relation of size to member satisfaction. In one study, members of smaller (five-man) groups were more satisfied with the discussion than members of twelve-man groups (Hare, 1952), and in another sample of discussion groups the optimal size appeared to be five (Bales, 1954; Slater, 1958). Below this size, members complain that the group is too small, although amount of talking time available to each increases. This may be a reflection of the strains associated with the face-to-face relationship which have been noted above in the description of the two-, three-, and four-man groups, and the odd and even effects. Above the size of five, members complain that the group is too large, and this may be due to the restriction on the amount of participation. Size five combines the characteristics that: (1) a strict deadlock is not possible with an odd number of members; (2) the group tends to split into a majority of three and a minority of two, so that being in a minority does not isolate the individual but allows him sources of gratification; and (3) the group appears to be large enough for the members to shift roles easily and for any individual to withdraw from an awkward position without necessarily having the issue resolved.

§ Summary

ALTHOUGH THE SIZE of the "natural" group varies with the age and other social characteristics of the population, casual work or play groups most often have only two or three members, while the modal size for an adolescent gang is about ten members. Members are generally less satisfied with the group if the size is increased. Observers find it easier to identify leaders in discussion groups of about six members than either smaller or larger groups.

As each additional member joins a group, the number of potential relationships between individuals and subgroups increases rapidly, thus placing more demands on the leader in coordinating group activity. The time available to each member for communication decreases, an increased proportion of the members feel threatened and inhibited, and the gap between the top participator and the others tends to grow proportionately greater as size increases.

With the addition of members, the resources of the group are increased so that a variety of problems may be solved more efficiently, although after some point, depending upon the task, the addition of new members brings diminishing returns. The time for task completion is reduced at the expense of lowered efficiency per unit of time per man, and the range of ideas available is increased at the expense of greater difficulty in reaching consensus in the absence of any clear-cut criteria for judgment.

The quality of the interaction process for a group decision problem changes with increasing group size as groups use more mechanical methods of introducing information, are less sensitive in their exploration of differing points of view, and make more direct attempts to reach a solution whether or not all members agree. The interaction pattern in a group of two has unique characteristics which suggest a delicate balance of power in making decisions. Above size two, there are differences between groups with even and odd numbers of members. Probably as a result of a split into two opposing subgroups of equal size, there is more disagreement and antagonism in the even-sized groups. Laboratory groups of size three characteristically form a coalition of two, leaving one member isolated; however, the same tendency is not observed in family groups of mother, father, and son.

The optimum size for a small discussion group may be five members since members are generally less satisfied with smaller or larger groups. In smaller groups members may be forced to be too prominent and in larger groups they may not have the opportunity to speak. In the group of five, strict deadlocks can be avoided and members can shift roles swiftly.

9

TASK

THE TASK OF A GROUP or of an individual can be described in terms of six variables, each of which partially determines the way in which the task will be accomplished. The specification of each of these six variables is implicit in the directions for any task, although it is not always made explicit (Schutz, 1952b):

1. The kind of task (goal).
2. The criteria for task completion.
3. The rules (or roles) which must be followed.
4. The method of imposing the rules.
5. The amount of stress on the members.
6. The consequences of failure or success.

Although the "task" of the group is usually thought of as the stated objective of the group's activity, all but the most casual groups usually deal with tasks or problems at four levels simultaneously (see Chapter One). Two of these types of problems are at the group level and two at the individual level. At the group level, the first problem is the publicly stated problem of the group. At the second level, members deal with the establishment and maintenance of a group structure which is appropriate for the group task. At the third level is the publicly stated goal for each individual, and at the fourth level, the problems of individual social-emotional adjustment.

In Chapter One it was also suggested that generally problems of individual adjustment had to be solved before energy was available to solve problems at a higher level. In addition, the four types of tasks can be expanded to eight types if problems of relating the small group to the larger society are added at each level.

Since an adequate solution for the publicly stated objective of the group or individual is often reached only at the expense of the social-emotional goals of the group or particular individuals, the interaction pattern in groups which focus on one set of problems usually differs from the pattern of a group which focuses on the other set. This "equilibrium problem" was discussed in Chapter Three. These differences are evident in groups which have been instructed to concentrate on either "task" or "social-emotional" problems (Olmsted, 1954) and in groups which have been selected because they are task-oriented (socio-groups) *versus* those which are social-emotional-oriented (psyche-groups) (Jennings, 1947a, 1947b; Coffey, 1952). However, most of the laboratory research on "task" deals primarily with the level of the publicly state problem of the group.

Once a group has been formed to deal with problems at one of the four levels, the members will resist a change to activity at another level. For example, in small therapy groups, when members were asked to rate the value of the topics discussed, those topics which caused disturbance and those which could be discussed only in the permissive therapeutic group were judged to be of greatest importance (Talland & Clark, 1954).

The typical steps in task solution are described in Chapter Twelve, where various types of groups are compared in their effectiveness in carrying out these steps and in their productivity on each of the four levels of group problems.

The group task, as compared with the communication net (Chapter Ten) and leadership (Chapter Eleven), is the most global way of specifying the situation in which interaction will take place. The *communication net* emphasizes the form of interaction, *leadership* emphasizes the roles of members and the method of social control, while the *task* emphasizes the *goal* of interaction as well as the other five variables.

The task, in a sense, requires the minimum amount of intervention by an outside agent, since once the group has accepted a task it can complete the task outside the range of the continuing influence of an experimenter or observer. When a particular commuciation net is introduced, however, the group must accept a set of restrictions on the form that their interaction may take, and when a leader is introduced the group must accept a new member or a new set of behaviors from an old member.

§ The Kind of Task

THE KIND OF TASK a group is given is broadly defined by the goal to be reached and the outlines of the path the group should follow in reaching the goal. Some of the effects of differences in the clarity of the group path and the group goal upon the individual and his relationship to the group are illustrated by an experiment in which each subject was given the task of cutting out geometrical figures, presumably to be used by the other members of his group in constructing some three-dimensional objects. While the subject was involved in his paper-cutting he was permitted to hear, over a loudspeaker, a tape-recording of what the "others" were doing with the pieces he had provided. One half of the subjects were given, through the recorded discussion, a clear picture of the goal the others were working toward and what they were doing to achieve it. The recording heard by the other half of the subjects presented the group task as quite vague and ambiguous. As a result of the manipulation, the subject in the clearly defined situation became more group-oriented in his behavior and feelings, and experienced less hostility. He also tended to be more inducible by the "others." That is, he responded more readily and favorably to their requests (in the form of fictitious notes delivered by a messenger) (Raven & Rietsema, 1957).

Since the task is, in the most pertinent sense, what the group members subjectively define it to be as they respond to the *situation* in which they find themselves, all of the internal features of the social system are likely sooner or later to become relevant to task specification. The task should not be narrowly viewed in terms of what the experimenter intends, or what some objective sense of the situation apparently demands.

In its broadest sense, then, the definition of the task is the definition of the situation, and differences in behavior which appear between "situations" are the most general indication of differences in tasks.[1] Several studies of children provide evidence of situational differences in behavior.

Children from a public nursery school, when paired in an experimental play situation, had a higher rate of interaction, were more accepting and less dominating in their behavior than children from an orphanage nursery school (Anderson, 1937b). Although the differences in domination could be the result of differences in home background of the children in the two situations, they appear to be the result of the situation, since within the orphanage population, children attending nursery school were more dominating than those not attending school (Anderson, 1937a).

In another study of children, two year old children watched each other more and accepted suggestions more when playing with clay than when playing with blocks. Clay seemed to elicit more imitation and sociable co-operative behavior (Updegraff & Herbst, 1933). Dramatic play appeared to release tensions in children more than other types of play (Hartley et al., 1952).

§ Situational Differences
in Leader Behavior

IN A STUDY of situational differences in behavior, public grade school boys were found to be more aggressive on the school playground than in the neighborhood (Hare, 1957). Twelve nine-year-old boys who were leaders on the school playground were selected from the third grades of four New England public schools. During the winter and spring of the school year, the boys were observed on the playground during a free play period and in the neighborhood after school using the set of categories for interaction process analysis developed by Bales (1950b).

In field observation, interaction was scored rather than taken down verbatim and individual activity apart from the group was not scored. An observer scored only one boy at a time, recording all of his acts directed to others and all acts directed to him by other group members. The average observation period on the school playground was 4 sessions

---

1. Suggestions for a more detailed analysis from this point of view are given by Roby and Lanzetta (1958). Watson (1958) suggests three types of situations: work-oriented, familial, and sociable.

for a total of 47 minutes (204 acts), and in the neighborhood was 4 sessions for a total of 75 minutes (360 acts). Interaction with teachers, parents, or observers was not recorded.

Several significant differences (Prob. < .05) in the percentages of activity in the twelve behavior categories appeared between the two situations (see Table 18). Giving and asking for information were both greater in the neighborhood and showing antagonism was greater on the playground. Differences in giving suggestion, showing disagreement, and showing tension approached significance (Prob. < .10) with more suggestions and tensions on the playground and more disagreement in the neighborhood.

Table 18—Mean Percentage Interaction Output and Input of 12 Boy Leaders for Playground and Neighborhood *

	OUTPUT		INPUT	
	Playground	Neighborhood	Playground	Neighborhood
1. Shows solidarity	5.0 †	3.5	8.4	4.6
2. Shows tension release	7.4	7.4	1.4	4.5
3. Shows agreement	2.9	4.0	7.8	4.7
4. Gives suggestion	19.5	15.7	11.2	15.1
5. Gives opinion	7.2	7.3	8.0	7.2
6. Gives information	18.2	31.8	11.5	32.3
7. Asks for information	1.4	8.8	2.4	9.6
8. Asks for opinion	0	.2	0	.5
9. Asks for suggestion	0	.1	0	.1
10. Shows disagreement	2.2	4.1	4.4	4.6
11. Shows tension	7.1	3.7	.9	.9
12. Shows antagonism	19.8	8.2	24.1	8.6

* Average number of acts per boy is 149 on the playground and 218 in the neighborhood for output, and 55 on the playground and 142 in the neighborhood for input.

† The raw percentage was converted by the arc sine transformation for calculation and reconverted for the table. For this reason the sum of the percentages for each coulmn does not equal exactly 100.

Differences in input (acts by group members directed toward the leaders) were in the same direction. Significantly more information was given and asked for by members in the neighborhood and more antagonism was shown on the playground.

The higher amount of information in the neighborhood probably resulted from the fact that the children spent more time in making up games, while the increase in suggestion, tension, and antagonism on the playground reflected a more competitive situation in which the individual had to assert himself to maintain his status in a large group composed of children his own age playing games with established rules.

§ Intellectual and
Manual Tasks

WHEN VARIATIONS IN TASKS which had been given some experimental groups were analyzed by Carter, Haythorn, Shriver, and Lanzetta (1951), two principal types of tasks were evident. Some required intellectual skills and some required manual skills. In one study differences between intellectual tasks, clerical tasks, and mechanical assembly tasks were shown to affect leadership behavior. In general, the subjects who took the lead in the intellectual task also influenced their partners in the clerical tasks. The mechanical assembly task gave only low correlations with the other two problem-solving situations (Carter & Nixon, 1949a). In a similar study a factor analysis of the leadership ratings received by subjects in six types of tasks (reasoning, intellectual, construction, clerical, discussion, motor co-operation, and mechanical assembly) indicated two major factors which have been called "intellectual leadership" and "doing-things-with-one's-hands leadership" (Carter, Haythorn, & Howell, 1950). In another factor analysis of ratings of performance made in the OSS assessment program, two similar factors were attributed to situations or tasks that called for verbal intelligence *versus* those that called for active intelligence. It seems likely that, from the point of view of abilities required, the same abilities that can be differentiated from each other by individual testing will also be useful in the description of group tasks.

The sequence of events required to reach the goal in problem-solving groups varies between problems which range in substance from stories told about group projection sketches (Henry & Guetzkow, 1951) and chess, to group decision and planning problems with various degrees of reality (Bales & Strodtbeck, 1951).

§ Consistency of Behavior for Different Tasks

THE CONSISTENCY of some aspects of individual behavior has already been indicated in Chapter Six on personality. Since the central tendencies of the group members are modified by the expectations for the task, consistent behavior from one task to another could be anticipated under two conditions:

1. The tasks, such as projective tests, require little modification of individual central tendencies.

2. The tasks, such as group discussions, require standard behavioral responses, but differ only slightly in discussion content. Examples of the second type of consistency are found in the stability of leadership which exist when the task of holding a leaderless group discussion is varied by changing the discussion topic and the composition of group members (Bass & Wurster, 1953b; Blake, et al., 1954), and when the problem for group solution remains the same but the method of problem presentation is varied (Lorge, Tuckman, Aikman, Spiegel, & Moss, 1955a, 1955b).

§ The Criteria for Task Completion

THE CRITERION for task completion may be either an "objectively correct" answer or an answer which is simply a matter of group consensus. A considerable body of theory centering around motivations to compare oneself with others and to communicate with those more deviant in an effort to achieve uniformity has been developed (Festinger, 1954). These motivations are strongest in situations where the main criterion of correctness is agreement with "social reality"—that is, consensus. In general, it is more difficult to achieve consensus when the problem strongly involves values members are likely to hold individually in advance that are different, or believed to be different (South, 1927; Festinger & Thibaut, 1951). Although a variety of group tasks is used for the diagnosis of interaction, the type of task on which a number of the current observations of interaction process are made is a case-discussion problem with instructions that require assembly of information initially distributed among members, interpretation and evaluation of the information, and eventual group decision on a concrete and detailed plan of action (Bales, 1955). Several phases of a typical planning-execution cycle are thus included, but not the actual execution of a plan and re-evaluation of results. This task lies somewhere between a highly projective and highly realistic one.

§ Rules and Roles

THE RULES for the task can vary in their explicitness from those which allow no freedom for individual choice to those in which the roles which the members are to follow are left unstated and the members are free to make up their own rules. The most common tasks used in the experimental laboratories leave all of these aspects unspecified. Some tasks may not require interaction but may be best performed by an individual working alone. When rules are made a major part of the task, the most common contrast is between *co-operation* and *competition.*

Most of the "together and apart" experiments in which individuals work on the same types of tasks, both as individuals and in groups, are designed to reveal which tasks are completed more efficiently by individuals and which by co-operating with other members of a group. Many examples of this type of research appear in Chapter Twelve on group productivity. In one typical experiment, forty subjects worked alone and eighty subjects worked in pairs on three types of tasks: a word puzzle, a jig-saw puzzle, and five arithmetic problems. The time taken to complete each task was the measure of performance. Paired subjects were significantly faster than individual subjects, except on the arithmetic problems where no differences were observed (Husband, 1940). The differences in performance between tasks are presumably due to the fact that a division of labor was not efficient for the solution of the arithmetic problems. When a division of labor is required and the life of the group is relatively long, subgroups will tend to form among the members who play similar roles (Horsfall & Arensberg, 1949; Homans, 1950).

The rules should be appropriate for the goal if the group is to perform efficiently (Steiner & Dodge, 1956). Experiments which introduce a variety of task goals with a fixed communication net provide examples of some inefficient rules. Controlled communication channels in three-man groups were used with three kinds of tasks: (1) a simple reassembling of a list of standard words, (2) construction of a sentence, the words of which had been distributed among the group members, and (3) anagram formation. The relative efficiency of a given communication network depended upon the kind of problem the group was trying to solve. While the communication network was an important variable in the reassembly and construction problems, it had little effect on anagram formation. The reassembly task was the most efficiently solved in groups where all members could talk and listen to all other members. The sentence construction problem, however, was solved most efficiently in a group which had a man in a central coordinating position (Heise & Miller, 1951).

The rules for attaining the goal can be seen as including specifications or expectations for the average behavior and acceptable variations of behavior in each of the categories of form and content outlined in Chapter One. When viewed in this manner, certain variations in the major "factors" described in Part Two appear to produce the same results. Groups composed of individuals who are competing in their tasks, large groups, groups in which all communications are channeled through one person in the center of the net, and groups with an authoritarian leader tend to be similar. In all of these groups, the expected amount of interaction between members is low, the amount of interaction received by the leader or central person is high, the expected differentiation in authority is high (in competition each individual attempts to exert the most control), and the expected amount of affection between members is low. This particular combination of characteristics tends to result in high productivity with low member satisfaction.

§ Co-operation versus Competition

IN GROUPS which are motivated to co-operate, the members all work toward a group goal which depends on interdependent activity on the part of the members, while in competition an individual's reward depends upon his own achievement which can usually be maximized only at the expense of other group members (May & Doob, 1937).

In general, group members who have been motiviated to co-operate show more positive responses to each other, are more favorable in their perceptions, are more involved in the task, and have greater satisfaction with the task (Stendler, Damrin, & Haines, 1951; Grossack, 1954; Gottheil, 1955; Harnack, 1955; Phillips & D'Amico, 1956; Thomas, 1957; Mann & Mann, 1959). As a result of their co-operative effort, the members are less likely to work at cross purposes (Mintz, 1951), are more efficient and productive (Deutsch, 1949b; Smith, Madden, & Sobol, 1957; Shaw, 1958b), and are better able to recall meaningful material (Yuker, 1955) and their own contributions (Smith, Madden, & Sobol, 1957). While competition makes the average group less productive, it may spur an individual on to more productivity (Blau, 1954). The effects of co-operation may be minimized if the group members are not highly attracted to the group or to its goals (Dashiell, 1935). In one study of school children, co-operation of individuals who had volunteered to be members of a team resulted in greater efficiency than work in competition, while co-operation within an arbitrary group, chosen by the experimenter, resulted in lower efficiency· (Maller, 1929).

The effects of cooperation will also be minimal if the task does not lend itself to a division of labor, or if the rewards for the individual for co-operating are less than those for competing. With a task like reading or substituting items in a text, individual motivation to do better than one's self on the next trial and also to surpass a paired competitor actually resulted in more improvement than motivation for the group (pair) to surpass another group. The motivation to have a winning team, presumably implying some co-operation, resulted in only slightly better performance than asking the subject to "try to improve" when he was working alone (Sims, 1928). In another study of "co-operation" with children, the tasks of carrying marbles and buckets of sand were primarily individual tasks. Also, the instructions to work for a group reward would actually have resulted in less reward per member than work for an individual reward. "Collective or group remuneration" in this case meant that the toys which were given as prizes were not allowed to be taken home (as they could be in the competitive groups), but everyone would have to enjoy them as a collective possession. As a result "individual remuneration" stimulated greater efficiency than "group remuneration" (Sorokin, Tanquist, Partin, & Zimmerman, 1930).

§ Effects of Co-operation
and Competition upon
Group Process

DEUTSCH's (1949b) experimental study of the effects of co-operation
and competition upon group process illustrates the differences between
co-operative and competitive groups which can be expected, if other
variables like group organization and motivation are controlled. In his
study, ten experimental groups were established, Each group was composed of five students in an introductory psychology class who were
participating in the experiment as a substitute for their regular class
sections. Each group met once a week for a three-hour session for five
consecutive weeks. During the first week the ten groups were observed
and rated as they discussed a human-relations problem. The ratings of
the discussion productivity were then used to pair off equated groups.
For the five pairs, one group was assigned by a random procedure to
the co-operative treatment, while the other was given the competitive
treatment.

The "co-operative situation" was produced by instructions that the
group as a whole would be rated in comparison with the efforts of four
other similarly constituted groups; the grade or reward that each member received would be the same and would be determined by the relative
position of his group in contrast with the four other similar groups. The
"competitive" situation was produced by instructions which stated that
each member would be rated in comparison with the efforts of the other
four members composing his group and that the grade or reward that
each would receive would be different and would be determined by the
relative contributions of each to the solution of the problem.

Apart from the differences in instructions, all groups were exposed
to similar routines during their three-hour meetings. The first part of the
meeting was spent solving a Sunday-supplement type puzzle, the second
part of the meeting was spent discussing and writing some recommendations for a human-relations problem, and in the third part of the meeting
the instructor-experimenter informally lectured on psychology.

Three or four observers were present during the first two parts of
any meeting. Each observer filled out an overall rating sheet at the end
of the meeting as well as collecting other data. Information was also

collected from subjects who filled out a questionnaire every meeting after the human-relations problem and supplied additional data at the end of the experiment.

§ Instruments Used by the Observers

Two MAJOR TASKS, among others, were assigned to the different observers. The first job of the observer was to categorize each participation of the members on a Functions Observation Sheet in terms of the following: (1) who spoke (or gestured), (2) to whom the remark was addressed, (3) the intent of the participant, and (4) the length of the participation. Deutsch used the *utterance* to define a unit of participation, with the exception that, if more than one function distinctly occurred in any utterance, two or more categorizations would be made. To provide the possibility of cross-analysis with other instruments, a new *functions sheet* was used for each five-minute period. To facilitate the tabulation, no attempt was made to retain the sequence of utterances or to record who spoke to whom.

The categories used in the Functions Observation Sheet were divided into three broad groupings:

1. *Task functions* which included participations which were directed toward the task with which the group was confronted. These functions had as their immediate purpose the facilitation of problem solution. Included in this grouping were such functions as initiator-contributor, information-giver, position-stater, elaborator, coordinator, orientor, evaluator-critic, energizer, and information-seeker.

2. *Group functions* which included participations which were directed toward the functioning of the group. They had for their immediate purpose the maintenance, strengthening, regulation, or perpetuation of the group. Included here were such functions as encourager-rewarder, harmonizer-mediator, good group member, gate-keeper, standard-setter, follower, and group-observer.

3. *Individual functions* which included participations which were directed toward the satisfaction of the participant's individual needs. They had as their immediate objective an individual goal which was neither task nor group relevant. The goal was individual in the sense that the satisfaction aimed at by the participant could not be participated

in by the others, either at all or in the same way. Such functions included playboy, sympathy-seeker, aggressor, dominator, blocker, recognition-seeker, self-defender, and self-observer.

An observer, using this instrument, was trained for approximately thirty hours before observing the experimental group meetings.

The observers also used a series of nine-point rating scales covering such things as group-discussion productivity, group orientation, self-centeredness, involvement, communication difficulties, attentiveness, and acceptance-rejection.

In considering the various ratings, Deutsch noted that it was impossible to maintain any absolute standards. The ratings more or less presumed a standard of judgment based on experience with groups of introductory psychology students. Thus the emphasis throughout the analysis of the results is primarily on the direction of the obtained differences rather than on size of differences between the two types of groups.

§ Instruments Used by the Subjects

THE SUBJECTS filled out two types of questionnaires:

1. *The Weekly Questionnaire* which was used at each meeting after the discussion of the human-relations problems. The items on the questionnaire consisted for the most part of rating scales which roughly paralleled those in the observers' overall rating scales. In addition, the questionnaire included scales such as attentiveness, communcation difficulties, and acceptance-rejection; the subjects also rated interest, group feeling, amount of group co-operation, group productivity, individual productivity, and anticipated reactions of the others to their own contributions.

2. *The Postexperimental Questionnaire* which was given one week after the last experimental group meeting. The questionnaire attempted to get at such things as (a) when first and last names were learned, (b) amount and kinds of social activities mutually engaged in by group members outside of the class hours, (c) reactions to the small group meetings, the instructor, and the course, (d) the importance of different factors in motivating the subject to achieve during the solution of the problems, (e) reactions to the grading system, and (f) reactions to being observed.

The data collected from observers and subjects in the experimental groups allowed Deutsch to test a number of hypotheses derived from a theory of co-operation and competition which he had presented in an earlier article (1949a). As an example of his work the data relevant to four of his major hypotheses are presented here. All of his findings are summarized at the end of this excerpt from his research.

§ Perceived Interdependence

DEUTSCH HAD HYPOTHESIZED that members of the groups in the co-operative situation would perceive themselves to be more co-operative than would members of the groups in the competitive situation. Data relevant to this hypothesis are given in Table 19.

Table 19—Differences between Co-operative and Competitive Groups in Perceived Co-operation and Competition

VARIABLE	PROBLEM TYPE	TOTAL	
		M diff	P
Group-centeredness (A)	H. R.	+2.98	.001
Group-centeredness (A)	P	+2.54	.001
Group-feeling (C)	H. R.	+1.20	.01
Competitiveness (C)	H. R.	— .37	*
Desire to excel others (D)	H. R.	—2.30	.03
Desire to excel others (D)	P	—2.20	.01

* The differences for three of the pairs are in the same direction as the total difference; these differences have p values of .01, .01, and .13 respectively. The differences for the other pairs are in an opposite direction; these differences have p values of .14 and .23.
Key: P = Puzzles; H. R. = Human Relations problems; (A), (B), (C), or (D) = the measuring instrument. (A) refers to the Overall Rating Scales, (B) to the Functions Observations Sheet, (C) to the Weekly Questionnaire filled out by subjects, and (D) to the Postexperimental Questionnaire. Total M diff = average of the differences (co-operative minus competitive) between each of the five paired groups for each of the five experimental weeks. A plus sign indicates that the co-operative groups had more of the variable than did the competitive groups. Total p = the p value obtained by combining the p values for each of the five pairs. A combined value is given only when the direction of the differences for all five pairs is the same as the total mean difference.

Group-centeredness (we-feeling) was rated by the observers to be considerably higher in the co-operative groups for both the puzzles and the human-relations problems. The subjects' ratings in the weekly questionnaire pertaining to the human-relations problems, gave the same results. Co-operating members gave themselves credit for more "group feeling" than did competing members. These differencs with respect to group-centeredness and group-feeling were significant at the 1 per cent level for both the puzzles and human-relations problems.

A related hypothesis that competing members will see themselves to be more competitive than will co-operating members is partly supported by the same evidence. The competitive group members were rated to be more self-centered by the observers. Likewise, competing members rated themselves as being more self-oriented than did co-operating members. Perceived competition, however, seemed to Deutsch to include, in addition to "self-centeredness," the notion of "I" versus "the others." To measure this component, the subjects were asked in reference to the human-relations problem, "How competitive with the other members of your group did you feel you were during the discussion?"

The results obtained in response to this question were not so conclusive, although they tended to support the hypothesis (see Table 19, competitiveness). Deutsch suggested that the lack of cleancut resulis might be a reflection of the differing interpretations placed on the word *competitiveness* by co-operating members. This interpretation was supported by the fact that when the question was phrased, "How much did you desire to excel others?" on the Postexperimental Questionnaire, significant differences were obtained in the predicted direction (i.e., the members of competitive groups reported more desire to excel others).

In sum, the data tended to support the prediction that perceived co-operation would be greater among members in the co-operating situation and that perceived competition would be greater among members in the competitive situation.

§   Coordination of Efforts

ANOTHER HYPOTHESIS asserted that there would be a greater degree of coordination of efforts and that coordination would occur more frequently among co-operative members than among competitive members. Table 20 presents the relevant evidence.

The observers rated the co-operative group as working together more frequently (A) and as more highly coordinated (A) than the competitive groups. In answer to the question (C), "How co-operatively did the group work together on this problem?" the ratings of co-operating members indicated more working together than did the ratings of competing members.

Table 20—Differences between Co-operative and Competitive Groups in Coordination of Effort

VARIABLE	PROBLEM TYPE	TOTAL	
		M diff *	p *
Working-together (A) *	H. R. *	+2.42 *	.001
Working-together (A)	P *	+2.68	.001
Degree of coordination (A)	H. R.	+2.62	.001
Degree of coordination (A)	P	+2.57	.001
Group co-operation (C) *	H. R.	+1.18	.001

* See Table 19 for Key.

§ Communication

THE OBSERVERS NOTED significantly fewer communication difficulties among the co-operating members than among the competing members, for both the human-relations problems and the puzzles (see Table 21). In answer to the question, "Did you find that you had difficulty in getting

Table 21—Differences in Participation Volume, Attentiveness, and Communication Difficulties between Co-operative and Competitive Groups

VARIABLE	PROBLEM TYPE	TOTAL	
		M diff §	p §
Participation volume * (B) §	H. R.§	−22.8 §	†
Participation volume (B)	P §	+118 §	.001
Attentiveness (A) §	H. R.	+1.04	.01
Attentiveness (A)	P	+1.50	.001
Attentiveness (C) §	H. R.	+ .42	‡
Communication difficulties (A)	H. R.	−1.94	.001
Communication difficulties (A)	P	−1.39	.01
Difficulty in communicating to others (C)	H. R.	− .81	.001
Difficulty in understanding others (C)	H. R.	− .67	.001

* Participation Volume has the meaning of "total number of participations per 45 minutes." Thus, all participation volumes are equalled in terms of a constant time unit.
† The differences for three pairs are in the same direction as the total mean difference; these differences have p values of .007, .06, and .20. The other two pairs go in the opposite direction; these differences have p values of .12 and .73.
‡ The differences for three pairs are in the same direction as the total mean difference; these differences have p values of .03, .04, and .72. The other two pairs, in the opposite direction, both have p values of .83.
§ See Table 19 for Key.

your ideas across to others?" the ratings of co-operating members expressed significantly less difficulty than did the ratings of the competing members. The same results were obtained in answers to the following question (C): "Did you find that you had difficulty in trying to follow or get the point of what the others were saying?" Thus the competitive subjects experienced more difficulty with respect to the spread of common ideas, both in the roles of communicators and communicatees.

§ Productivity

QUANTITATIVE PRODUCTIVITY per unit of time was expected to be greater in the co-operative groups. The evidence given in Table 22 indicates that the co-operative groups solved the puzzle problem more rapidly than did the competitive groups and they also produced more on the human-relations problems (number of words written in the recommendations were taken as a crude measure of quantity of productivity).

The hypothesis that qualitative productivity would be higher for the co-operative groups was also supported by the observers' ratings of discussion productivity. According to observer ratings, the discussions

Table 22—Differences between Co-operative and Competitive Groups in Productivity

VARIABLE	PROBLEM TYPE	TOTAL	
		M diff *	p *
Discussion productivity (A) *	H. R. *	+1.86 *	.001
Discussion productivity (A)	P *	+1.90	.01
Discussion insight (A)	H. R.	+1.25	.001
Discussion insight (A)	P	+1.72	.02
Time per solution	P	−7.35 *	.01
		minutes	
Number of words written in product	H. R	+299	.001
		words	
Average individual productivity (A)	H. R.	+ .15	not sig.
Average individual productivity (A)	P	+ .58	.07

* See Table 19 for Key.

of the co-operative groups not only came out with more fruitful ideas for handling the problem presented to them, but also their group discussions showed more insight and understanding of the nature of the problem being posed to them. These differences with respect to group productivity and group insight were significant for both kinds of tasks.

Deutsch warned that average individual productivity should not be confused with group productivity. Group productivity ratings referred to the ideas that were agreed upon and accepted as a basis for action by the group. The ratings of average individual productivity showed no significant differences for the co-operative and competitive groups on the human-relations problems. For the puzzles, there was a difference approaching significance favoring co-operative individuals.

Further evidence that the differences in group productivity were not carried over to individual productivity appeared in the members' ratings of their own learning in the discussions and their grades on term papers. The co-operative group members in only three of the five pairs rated themselves as learning more from the discussion of the human-relations problem. Difference in term grades, although in the predicted direction, were not statistically significant.

In summary Deutsch found that, compared with the competitively organized groups, the co-operative groups had the following characteristics:

(1) *Stronger individual motivation* to complete the group task and stronger feelings of obligation toward the other members.

(2) Greater *division of labor* both in content and frequency of interaction among members and greater coordination of effort.

(3) More *effective inter-member communication*. More ideas were verbalized, members were more attentive to one another, and more accepting of and affected by each other's ideas. Members also rated themselves as having fewer difficulties in communicating and understanding others.

(4) More *friendliness* was expressed in the discussion and members rated themselves higher on strength of desire to win the respect of one another. Members were also more satisfied with the group and its products.

(5) More *group productivity*. Puzzles were solved faster and the recommendations produced for the human-relations problems were longer and qualitatively better. However, there were no significant differences in the average individual productivity as a result of the two types of group experience nor were there any clear differences in the amounts of individual learning which occurred during the discussions.

§ Co-operation versus Self-Oriented Needs

WHEN GROUP MEMBERS are expected to co-operate in a task, any behavior which stems from "self-oriented" needs is in effect competitive behavior since members compete with each other in their efforts to use the group to satisfy their own ends. In an industrial study, for example, 72 decision-making conferences, averaging ten members each, were observed and rated on the extent to which member behavior was directed primarily toward the satisfaction of ego-related or "self-oriented" needs without regard to the effect of this behavior on the attainment of the group goal or to the solution of the group's problem. The amount of self-oriented need expressed in the conference was found to be negatively related to satisfaction of members with the meeting, with the decision, and with the chairmanship. Groups exhibiting high frequencies of "self-oriented" behavior were also high in conflict and tended to perceive themselves as less unified. Although conferences of this type met for longer periods of time, they completed fewer of their agenda items than did groups rated low on self-oriented needs (Fouriezos, Hutt, & Guetzkow, 1950; Marquis, Guetzkow, & Heyns, 1951). The differences between these two types of conferences are similar to those found between groups in which co-operation and competition are experimentally controlled.

§ The Method of Imposing the Rules

THE RULES may be imposed upon the group by any of the means described in Chapter Two. Like other sets of social norms, however, those for co-operation need not be made explicit in order to introduce them to a group. Co-operation may be achieved simply by reinforcing co-operative behavior in the interaction of a group which is already formed. This has been done with pairs of children seven to twelve years of age where co-operation was developed and extinguished by the positive reinforcement of giving them a jelly bean each time they co-operated in a game (Azrin & Lindsley, 1956).

§ Stress

AN IMPORTANT ASPECT of the task is the amount of *stress* under which the task must be performed. Groups tend to respond to continuously increasing stress, like *all* living systems, first by a lag in response, then by an overcompensatory response, and finally by a catastrophic collapse of the system (Miller, 1955, p. 528). A representative curve based on animal studies of the effectiveness of individual performance as stress is increased over a period of time is presented in Fig. 21. After the

Figure 21—Performance under Increasing Stress

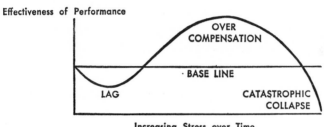

stress is applied to the individual, there is an initial dip in the curve in the direction of the final collapse which is the alarm reaction. This is followed by a rise of the curve above the level normally maintained by the organism, which constitutes a peak of activity of overcompensation or overdefensiveness. As the stress is increased, more and more defenses are called into play until finally no additional ones are available and the system collapses sudenly into death. There is some evidence that the activity of a family in a crisis brought about by the illness or death of one of its members follows a curve of this sort.

It is also probable that groups may react as individuals do under acute and prolonged stress. In military combat, for example, an acute, intense stress would be disorganizing for individuals with personality problems which made them particularly susceptible, while the same stress would produce reactions of a more temporary nature in a well adjusted individual. Under prolonged stress, however, even the well adjusted individuals would begin to feel the strain (Grinker & Spiegel, 1945).

The most common form of stress for a group is a time limit for the completion of the task. In many experiments, like that of Deutsch described above, the time it takes to solve the problem is one of the major dimensions of the task. Often the differences in productivity between groups organized in different ways are only apparent if the groups are under pressure to complete the task in limited time (Schutz, 1956).

Too much time can also be used as stress. Members who are incompatible may be able to ignore their differences in the short run but be forced to reveal their underlying differences if they must work together over a long period of time (Schutz, 1956). The effects of long association are evident in groups of men in arctic weather stations and other isolated outposts.

In a study of leadership and crisis, stress was applied by giving some groups a problem without any solution (Hamblin, 1958b). The behavior of leaders in twelve three-man groups with no solution to the problem was compared with that of leaders in a similar set of groups with a solution. All groups were playing a shuffleboard game. Leaders had more influence in the groups in "crisis," but the leader was replaced if he did not appear to have a good solution to the problem.

Stress can also be applied through challenges or threats or punishment if the members do not perform well. Under these conditions, the hostility generated towards the locus of the threat makes it difficult for the group to utilize the resources of its members and the effectiveness of the group falls off (Frank, 1944; Lanzetta, Haefner, Langham, & Axelrod, 1954). Threats are, however, often used in an attempt to increase productivity. In a controlled study of mother-child interaction, mothers who were motivated to have their child perform "well" demonstrated more directing, interfering, criticizing, and "structuring-a-change-in-activity" behavior than did mothers who had no aspirations for their child in the same play situation (Merrill, 1946).

For optimal performance the amount of stress should neither be so great as to result in collapse of the system or cause the group members to give up the task if they are frustrated in reaching the goal (Barker, Dembo, & Lewin, 1941; Hamblin, 1958), nor so small that the group members are not motivated to perform (Lanzetta & Roby, 1956). A mild stress appears to produce optimal performance (Lanzetta, 1955; Lanzetta & Roby, 1957).

The contrast between the effects of high and low stress is evident in two group experiments in which drugs were used to produce or reduce stress. Groups whose members were given lysergic acid diethylamide become much slower and inefficient in their interpersonal communications (Lennard, Jarvik, & Abramson, 1956). In contrast, members of three-man groups under threat who were given an "anxiety-reducing" medication (Seconal and Benzedrine) showed little anxiety, were elated, unassertive, and happy, but did little with the task (Lanzetta et al., 1956).

§ Group Behavior under Stress

IN THE EXPERIMENT by Lanzetta (1955):

Twelve groups, each composed of four naval reserve officer trainees, were exposed to three experimental conditions varying along a "stress" dimension. The twelve groups were randomly divided into two classes of six groups each, one class, termed "high motivation," being rewarded with a group prize for the best performing group, the other class, termed "low motivation," being offered no reward. Within each of these classes, each group was exposed to the three experimental stress conditions in a different order, there being six possible orderings. The three experimental conditions were:

non-stress—subjects were given no special instructions; they were given the task materials and told only that we were interested in how groups go about solving problems.

mild stress—a time limit was imposed, and reinforced by the announcement, at intervals, of time remaining.

high stress—a time limit was imposed, the subjects were badgered and belittled by the experimenter and there was a restriction of work space.

At each session the groups worked on a reasoning and mechanical assembly task. An attempt was made to collect extensive data on the social-emotional and problem-solving behavior of the group members. Techniques used were: (a) a continuous on-going recording of behavior, by two observers, in terms of 58 categories, (b) ratings, made by the two observers, of each individual, after each task, for each session, on twelve characteristics, (c) ratings of eleven group characteristics by both observers and participants.

All three independent variables, stress, motivation, and task, affected behavior, but there appeared to be little interaction between them. Quantitative comparisons between them indicated that changes in behavior under stress could be classified into three categories: (a) changes in behavior which would tend to increase interpersonal tension and friction within the groups, (b) changes in behavior which would tend to decrease interpersonal tension and increase integration, (c) changes in problem-solving behavior. There was a decrease in negative social-emotional behavior, in aggression, deflation, dissatisfaction, competition, etc., and in self-oriented behavior, under increased stress. There was an increase in positive group-oriented behaviors such as co-operativeness, friendliness, group discussion, and integrating acts under increased stress. These were interpreted as indicating that participants perceived the group as a source of security in the face of the external threat, and thus behavior which would lead to acceptance by the group was facilitated, while behavior which might lead to rejection was depressed.

Analysis of characteristics and behaviors related to performance indicated that the performance of the group was best under mild stress conditions, the relations of performance to stress being curvilinear. Participants did not perceive performance improving, although a similar curvilinear relationship obtained between their ratings of activity, motivation, morale, and interest in job completion. The inconsistency between observers' and participants' ratings could be explained by assuming a linear increase in level of aspiration as stress increased.

There were quite striking behavior differences associated with the two tasks. For the mechanical assembly task there were almost twice as many nonproductive behaviors, over five times as many equalitarian, group-oriented behaviors, and more group discussion regarding the task, than for the reasoning task. The reasoning task showed a greater number of negative social-emotional behaviors, more solidarity-oriented behaviors, and more initiating and insightful behaviors.

These results support the previously reported findings by Carter et al. (1951), that the reasoning task includes more initiating activity with emphasis on making diagnosis, while the mechanical assembly task involves much less behavior devoted to initiating action, but much more to action by the "followers" or "workers" (pp. 49-50).

In conclusion Lanzetta noted that the results of this exploratory study were limited in generality, since the experiment was performed on a selected sample of college males, working in co-operative groups on a limited sample of tasks.

§   Consequences of
    Failure or Success
    and Feedback

ONE FEATURE that is particularly dependent upon the definition given to it by the members is the degree and kind of "reality" of the task. This, in turn, is partly a matter of the *kind of consequences that are expected to result from action,* and also the amount of feedback that actually comes back from the environment. It is suggested that the less or the slower the feedback, the lower the degree of reality. In turn, the lower the degree of reality, the more the response is determined by internal features and tensions of the individual or group. This, in fact, is what happens in a "projective" test, where stories constructed by a group to describe ambiguous pictures are used to produce diagnostic information about the group (Horwitz & Cartwright, 1953).

A comparison of individual behavior through a range of degrees of "reality" from paper-and-pencil tests, to role playing, to actual behavior incidents (Moldowsky, 1951), indicates only slight correlation among performances in the different situations.

Holding the scoring categories constant, prediction is not found to be justified across the levels. For air corps subjects, a significant increasing trend in profanity was noted from actual behavior, to role playing, to paper-and-pencil test. Using a general measure of distance, role playing was found to be closer to actual behavior than was performance on a paper-and-pencil test (Borgatta, 1951b). However, role playing was still not as involving a task as actual discussion (Borgatta & Bales, 1953a).

Some of the consequences of success are evident in several studies. During the break after the task, members of (air corps) groups who were successful talked more about the task than those who were not successful (Berkowitz & Levy, 1956). The successful groups also tended to raise their level of aspiration for the next problem, while unsuccessful groups lowered their level of aspiration.

Members of groups which continued to experience success had a more favorable attitude toward their group and tended to accept the group's solution to a problem (estimating dots on a card), rather than their own solution (Shelley, 1954). Similar changes in level of aspiration were observed in individual subjects when a simulated "reference group" (tape-recorded responses of four other members) was more or less successful than they were on a task of estimating the number of sounds in a set (Kaiser & Blake, 1955).

Individuals who are successful in a task in a well defined situation are able to predict their future success in a similar situation (Gerard, 1956). Task success or failure also appears to affect the cohesiveness of the group (Stotland, 1959). In one experiment with groups which were either constantly rewarded or not rewarded, the proportion of ingroup choices increased while groups in which reward was varied did not show a similar trend (Thibaut, 1950). In a similar experiment, subjects who were motivated to succeed liked others who appeared to be doing well. However, highly motivated subjects who did poorly as a group also rated other members as highly attractive, presumably a reflection of greater integration in the face of threat (Berkowitz, Levy, & Harvey, 1957).

§ Task Completion and Recall

WHEN INDIVIDUAL SUBJECTS or members of a group perform a number of tasks, some of which are interrupted by the experimenter before the subject (or group) has a chance to complete them, the subjects usually recall more of the interrupted tasks (Horowitz, 1954; Horowitz & Lee, 1954). This happens presumably because when the subject begins the task a tension is set up which is not reduced unless the task is completed. As a result, the unresolved tension makes the uncompleted tasks easier to recall. However, if the subject works with a partner and the partner completes the interrupted task, the frequency of recall is no greater than it is for tasks which the subject completes himself. This suggests that the subject has identified himself with the group, so that whatever the group does is seen as an extension of himself (Lewis, 1944). This effect varies with the orientation of the subject. Subjects who were told that they were simply helping the experimenter try out some tasks but were not being tested themselves tended to recall the interrupted (partner-completed) tasks. In contrast, subjects who were given less pointed instructions, which seems to imply that they were being tested, tended to recall the tasks which they completed themselves (Lewis & Franklin, 1944).

§ Summary

THE TASK CAN BE DESCRIBED in terms of six variables:

1. The kind of task (goal).
2. The criteria for task completion.
3. The rules (or roles) which must be followed.
4. The method of imposing the rules,
5. The amount of stress on the members.
6. The consequences of failure or success.

The task is the most general way of specifying the expectations for group behavior; the task of the group in the broadest sense is to deal with the situation in which it finds itself.

Situational differences in interaction patterns are evident in studies of children's groups where orphanage nursery-school children are found to be more dominating than public nursery-school children, and children in the third grade at public school are found to be more aggressive on the school playground than in their neighborhoods after school. Intellectual tasks and manual tasks also appear to differ in the types of problem-solving behavior required. The consistency of behavior for different tasks is greater if the tasks require little modification of an individual's central tendencies or require standard behavioral responses which differ only slightly in content.

A solution to the task is more difficult to obtain if the criterion for completion is ambiguous. It is also more difficult if group consensus is required.

Contrasting sets of rules and roles have been imposed on groups by requiring competition vs. co-operation, facilitating or interfering with the development of a division of labor, and specifying the channels of communication which can be used. The most efficient groups are those in which the rules are appropriate for the task, although, in general, co-operation results in more individual motivation, division of labor, effective inter-member communication, friendliness, and group productivity. When group members expect to co-operate, any behavior which reflects individual "self-oriented" needs tends to disrupt the group.

When increasing stress is applied, groups, like individuals, tend to respond by a lag, then overcompensation, and finally collapse. A mild stress results in higher productivity than no stress or extreme stress. Motivation to perform is also higher when the task has a high degree of "reality." Members tend to recall tasks that are incomplete more often than those completed by themselves or a partner.

10

COMMUNICATION

NETWORK

IN LARGE MILITARY and industrial organizations, a subsegment of the organization often serves as an information-processing center. There the information is collated, displayed, evaluated, and decisions are made which affect the entire operating organization. Frequently some of the members involved are separated physically from each other and communicate by telephone and other devices in restricted networks. The frequency of concern with problems of communication in restricted networks has led to experimentive exploration of the properties of different sorts of networks.

The communication network is a factor in the situation which can be varied independently of the task or of the style of leadership in the group, although it is usually closely associated with it. When a task requires a particular type of communication network for optimum performance, the leader's style tends to place limits on the frequency duration, and direction of member communications. However, all three variables, task, communication network, and leadership, are similar in that they are ways of manipulating the situation for the group by setting norms for the form and content of interaction.

In addition to its implications for the more general categories of interaction, other aspects of the communication network are discussed in this chapter. These other aspects include the effects of varying amounts of "feedback" and "noise" in the network, the effects of the amount of participation on changing individual attitudes, and the relationship between leader style and the limitations on the amount and distribution of communication.

§ Relative Rates of
  Communication

MECHANICAL CONSTRICTIONS on communication, of course, constitute an extreme and obvious case of conditions that prevent the full and free interaction of each member with every other member. At one end of the continuum, subjects who are not allowed to communicate cannot be expected to have much effect on each other (Vinacke, 1957). But even in discussion groups where physical conditions of intercommunication are optimized, spatial location still plays some part. For example, members tend to address more communication to persons seated opposite to them at a table than to those next to them, presumably because of easier eye contact (Steinzor, 1950; Hearn, 1957). However, when the leaderless group is used as a technique for leader selection, seating position has little effect on final leadership ratings received by members (Bass & Klubeck, 1953). Presumably the difficulties of spatial location and interactive contact decrease as the size of the group decreases in a discussion situation. In a situation of this kind, the communication network is probably derived more from the expectations of the members than by other more mechanical considerations.

In free communication situations a gradient of activity-rates among members is the usual thing rather than equal participation (Bales et al., 1951; Stephan & Mishler, 1952). Members who talk most generally also receive the most interaction. This is probably a result, in part, of the tendency for a remark made by one person to be answered by some other, who may then continue to address the person who just spoke. In *ad hoc* problem-solving groups about half the remarks are addressed to the group as a whole, and about half to particular other members, that is, in pair relationships (Bales et al., 1951). About half the total content is devoted to substantive contributions while the other half is devoted to positive reactions, negative reactions, and questions. Both of these balances suggest that freely communicating groups devote about as much of their time to feedback (i.e., indications to the sender that the message has been received) as to specific problem-solving attempts. Low participators do not talk to each other as much as high participators talk to each other. The network of communication is thus in effect restricted more or less spontaneously by the members, so that links between low participators tend to drop out as size increases, especially above size seven. It appears to be generally true that status distinctions show a high positive correlation with amount of participation, although status based on popularity is not so highly related as status based on task criteria in task-oriented groups (Bales, 1953; Hurwitz, Zander, & Hymovitch, 1953; Bales & Slater, 1955). In free discussion groups the communication network and the network of interpersonal choice are interdependent, but also each is in some degree independently variable so that the congruence is seldom perfect.

§ Centrality and Control

IN A SERIES OF REPORTS which systematically examine some features of the communication network, Shaw (1954a) found that a measure of centrality proposed by Bavelas did not permit measurement of quantitative differences among individuals in the group. For Bavelas the most central person in the group was the one who needed the least number of communication links to interact with all other group members. Instead of this measure, Shaw proposed a measure which takes into account the number of communication channels available to the individual and to the group, and the number of individuals for which a person is a relayer of information. Independence was found to account reasonably for experimental measures of morale (general satisfaction), number of messages used, and recognition of leadership. In another experiment with four-man groups in three controlled communication conditions, the wheel, the slash, and the circle (Shaw, 1954c; Gilchrist, Shaw, & Walker, 1954; see Fig. 22) centrality varied inversely with the time required to complete an activity and directly with individual morale, the number of items transmitted, and the probability that a person would be chosen as the leader. The problems used in these experiments are essentially individual problems, such as mathematical problems. The group is said

**Figure 22—Communication Networks Used in Experiments with
Three- and Four-Man Groups**

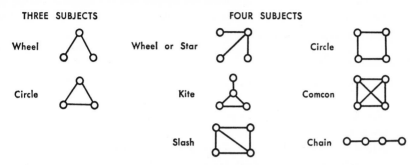

to have completed the problem when each person in the network knows the answer. In general leadership is more apt to emerge when there are large differences in the degree of centrality (Goldberg, 1955).

Similar results were obtained using four-man groups in star, slash, and "comcon" (all channels open) nets, with the additional finding that when the groups met once a day for ten days all groups solved problems faster, sent fewer messages, and were better satisfied as time passed (Shaw & Rothschild, 1956).

Increasing the amounts of information given to a person has an effect similar to increasing his centrality index. Using a systematic rather than random distribution of information in a net has the effect of allowing the members to reach faster solutions, with fewer errors, and greater satisfaction since they can group the data in their messages (Shaw, 1956). However, in group tasks which require each man to perform a separate function, the most efficient distribution of information is one which permits each individual the most autonomy in reaching his own decision and putting it into effect (Lanzetta & Roby, 1956).

It is also necessary for the central person in the network to reach a *decision* when the task calls for group participation. If the central person simply collects or transmits information and leaves the decision to some other member, his group will not be as effective (Mulder, 1959).

The relationship between leader style and communication network is evident in a controlled communication experiment using the wheel, kite, and comcon nets, in which authoritarian (appointed) leadership resulted in better group performance than nonauthoritarian leadership (Shaw, 1955). In the authoritarian situation, morale was lower but evidence in terms of errors indicated that the quality of performance was better. Morale was related to the independence of action permitted, while saturation, or the input and output requirements placed upon a position, was related to performance.

§ Personality versus
   Position in the
   Communication Network

ALTHOUGH *behavior* was conceptualized in Chapter One as a compromise between the tendencies of *personality* and the expectations of *role,* relatively few pieces of evidence have been presented to indicate the results which may be expected from the interaction of personality and role. Some evidence is provided by two studies of communication networks which deal primarily with the area of control.

In the first study ten four-man groups of college subjects solved three problems in a star communication network. Each group contained one subject who had been previously rated as highly ascendant, one who had been rated as being low on ascendance, and two who were moderately ascendant. The subjects had been previously screened from a larger population by the Guilford-Zimmerman Ascendance Scale; a high scoring person would be expected to dominate the interaction. In some groups the highly ascendant person occupied the central position and in other groups the central position was given to the person who was rated lowest on ascendance. In this case, the position in the network appeared to be the dominating factor since, after the first trial, the low ascendants in the center behaved like the highs and the highs in peripheral positions became more passive. In each case, the subject in the center was more satisfied (Berkowitz, 1956b).

In the second experiment, 44 previously unacquainted college subjects in three-man groups each received notes which created variations in his centrality and autonomy. Autonomy in the network was measured by the subject's access to task-relevant information. Each of the subjects had high or low autonomy needs as measured by a paper-and-pencil test. After the experiment, the subjects who had been given positions of high autonomy were the most satisfied, especially when they had high autonomy needs. No differences in satisfaction appeared to accompany differences in centrality. However, a subject perceived another's performance as more valuable if the other person held a position more central than his own. Differences in the relative autonomy of positions seemed to have no effect on the perception of value (Trow, 1957). Here differences in the value of performance were measured by having each subject answer the question, "If this were a commercial enterprise, how much do you think X should be paid in comparison with the person filling the position you had?" The subjects holding the more central positions were judged to be those who should receive more pay.

§ Communication
between High and
Low Status Members

THE STUDIES just mentioned show that positions in the communication network, especially those with one-way and limited connection restrictions, are related to frustration and antagonism on the part of the disadvantaged members and to satisfaction and leadership status for the central members. When member perceptions of status and possibilities for upward or downward mobility are experimentally established in a restricted network, the amount and kind of written communication initiated differs (Kelley, 1951). Persons who are led to believe that their job status is low are less well satisfied with their job and initiate more conjectures about the nature of the jobs at the high-status level. This is interpreted as the result of "phantasy" about upward mobility (Thibaut, 1950). They also initiate more communication with content irrelevant to the task, which is interpreted as a desire to escape from the position. The members who are led to believe they are in a higher status show evidence of constraint in addressing criticism of their job to lower status members, and constraint in expressing confusion about the job to anyone. Members of control groups where no impression of status differences is established are more free in criticism of other members than are subjects in either of the two status-conscious conditions. The perception of possibility of upward mobility for the lower status group increases the attractiveness of the job, and the perception of possible downward mobility for the higher status group decreases the attractiveness. Low status with no possibility of rising or high status with the threat of falling are the variations which are most destructive of interlevel cohesion (Kelley, 1951; Cohen, 1958).

§ Proximity and
Affection

THE COMMUNICATION NETWORK as it is defined here refers to the
channels of communication among members and subgroups of the group.
These channels of communication are evident in residential groups where
spatial location of members relative to each other and probability of
contact in the course of daily activity limit in a very tangible way who
is likely to interact with whom.

The spatial arrangement of members with respect to each other and
the probability of contact is in turn related to members' liking for each
other (Festinger et al., 1950; Wilner, Walkley, & Cook, 1952; Byrne &
Buehler, 1955). In general, the attraction of persons to each other tends
to be greater among those who are in spatial locations that promote
interaction, and liking tends to decrease, sometimes turning to hostility,
as physical distance increases (Merton, 1948; Danielsson, 1949; Lundberg, Hertzler, & Dickson, 1949; Homans, 1950; Sherif, 1951; Maisonneuve, Palmade, & Fourment, 1952; Simon, 1952).

On the other hand, once a subgroup has formed among those persons who are near each other there is some tendency to symbolize and
maintain social separation from other subgroups by maintenance of physical separation (Hughes, 1946). Liking, however, has complex determinants, as does the amount of interactive contact. Neither is a simple
function of the other. Particularly in periods of conflict, the two may be
"out of joint," since the amount of interaction with deviant members
tends to increase in an attempt to influence them, and then to fall off if
and when they are given up or rejected (Schachter, 1951). It would
appear that some contact is a prerequisite to the rejection or acceptance
of a person into another person's sphere of involvement.

The empirical connection between the amount of liking and amount
of interaction found in larger groups also appears to some extent in
small discussion groups. Pairs of friends spent more time in spontaneous
interactions in a pair discussion situation than did pairs of nonfriends,
and the members of friendship pairs were more nearly alike in the
amounts of interaction initiated to each other (Potashin, 1946). In another study, groups set up to encourage inter-member interaction (group-
centered) showed a higher average level of liking for each other than

der-centered groups where member-to-member interaction was lower
ovard, 1951b).

Feedback in Restricted
Networks

IN A SITUATION where there is one-way communication and the re-
ver of the information is given no opportunity to "feed back" ac-
owledgments, questions, or negative reactions to the sender, accuracy
d confidence are reduced for both sender and receiver (Leavitt &
ueller, 1951). An initial reaction of hostility on the part of the receiver
ward the sender tends to appear. Accuracy can improve with time,
t not as rapidly as with feedback, and depends more on the sender
an the receiver. An initial period with free feedback appreciably im-
oves subsequent communication without feedback. More time is re-
ired with the feedback condition, but with experience the amount of
ne decreases. Receivers who are permitted to communicate back to
person who has sent them an act of hostility show more postexperi-
ental friendliness to the instigator than those not permitted to com-
unicate (Thibaut & Coules, 1952). Apparently one-way communication
events not only expressive catharsis, but also the opportunity for build-
g new understanding and norms by which the members manage their
cial relationships and their process of communication. From this basic
apairment other problems may develop.

Some Effects
of Certain
Communication
Networks on Group
Performance

AN EXPERIMENT by Leavitt (1951; Bavelas, 1950, 1952) provides an
xample of some of the effects which certain communication networks
an have on group performance.

This approach, stemming from the imaginative work of Bavelas

(1948), begins by considering persons as self-contained, acting entities, each in a cell, like a phone booth. They can communicate with others according to the manner in which the booths are hooked up to one another. Any one of the possible patterns of linkage of a given number of such units can be selected as a communication network. The experimenter then examines the effects of a given network on task performance and the social-emotional relations of the members occupying each position.

In this specific investigation, one hundred male undergraduates serving as subjects were divided into twenty groups of five men each. Each group was composed in one of four types of network, making a total of five groups for each network. These networks are shown in Fig. 23

Figure 23—Experimental Communication Networks

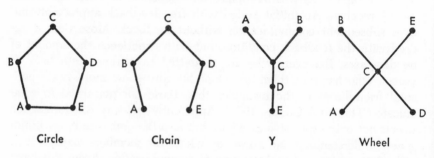

Circle   Chain   Y   Wheel

with the lines indicating two-way linkages in all cases. The nature of the network for any group was unknown to the subjects at the beginning of the experiment. All a specific individual knew was to whom he could send messages and from whom he could receive them. The idea of the overall network was gradually discovered in the experience of the task. It may be seen that positions differed with respect to how many lines of communication fed in to them, and how far (in terms of number of links) they were from other positions. This notion may be termed *centrality* of position. The most central position is the one closest to all other positions. The researchers hypothesized that if a group were working on a problem which required the collection, pooling, processing, and redistribution of information held by all members, both network efficiency (in making rapid, correct decisions) and behavioral differences for various positions would be related to centrality.

Centrality is a measure of one's closeness to all other group members and hence is a measure of the availability of the information necessary for solving

Figure 24—Symbol Distribution by Trial (Leavitt, 1951, p. 40)

Six Symbols Used:. O △ ◇ □ + ✻

Trial No.	Symbol Missing From:					Common Symbol
	White	Red	Brown	Yellow	Blue	
1	△	◇	✻	O	□	+
2	◇	O	□	△	+	✻
3	+	✻	□	△	◇	O
4	□	◇	△	✻	+	O
5	O	✻	+	△	□	◇
6	△	O	□	✻	◇	+
7	□	+	O	◇	△	✻
8	◇	✻	□	+	O	△
9	✻	◇	□	△	O	+
10	+	O	□	✻	◇	△
11	O	+	△	◇	✻	□
12	✻	O	□	△	+	◇
13	△	O	◇	□	+	✻
14	□	◇	+	✻	△	O
15	+	O	□	◇	✻	△

the problem. Availability of information should affect behavior in turn by determining one's role in the group. An individual who can rapidly collect information should see himself and be seen by others in a different way from an individual to whom vital information is not accessible. Such roles should be different in the extent to which they permit independence of action, in the responsibility they entail, and in the monotony they impose. Finally, differences in independence, in responsibility, and in monotony should affect the speed, the accuracy, the aggressiveness, and the flexibility of behavior (Leavitt, 1951, pp. 40-41).

The problem to be solved by the group members consisted of discovering which of six possible symbols they held in common. For a single trial each member held a card bearing five symbols. The missing (sixth) symbol which was different for each member and the common symbol are indicated in Fig. 24. Communication was restricted to the passing of notes through mail chutes in an arrangement of partitions corresponding to the apparatus in Fig. 25. There was no other communication between

Figure 25—Apparatus for Communication Network Experiment (Leavitt, 1951, p. 41)

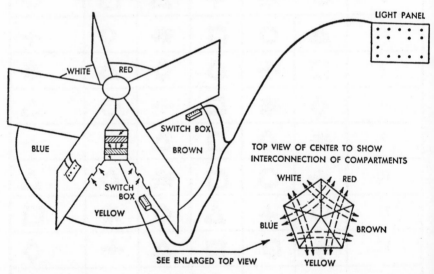

members. When a subject thought he knew the common symbol, he pressed one of six buttons in his cell, lighting a corresponding light in the experimental booth. When all five members had depressed their buttons, the trial was ended.

Information was gathered by recording the number and paths of messages sent, the time required for solution, the number of errors, the answers to postmeeting questionnaires, and the content of the messages themselves.

In general, the wheel network operated in the same manner in each of the five groups which employed it. Men on the periphery sent information to the center, a decision was made and sent back out. The "Y" also gave the man in the most central position the most decision-making authority. The chain sent information in from both ends to the center, the decision being sent out in both directions. This mode of operation was slower in establishing itself than the "Y" or wheel, but was consistent when once it was hit upon.

A measure of the fastest single trial of each group indicates that the wheel network at its peak was faster than the circle (see Table 23). The number of messages sent by each group during a correct trial was greater for the circle than for other networks. Although more errors were made in the circle than any other network, a greater percentage of these errors were detected and corrected by the group before the trial ended.

Table 23—Fastest Single Correct Trial for Each Communication Network

FASTEST SINGLE CORRECT TRIAL (IN SECONDS)	Circle	Chain	Y	Wheel	Diff.	p
Mean	50.4	53.2	35.4	32.0	Ci-W	$<.01$
Median	55.0	57.0	32.0	36.0	Ch-W	$<.10$
Range	44-59	19-87	22-53	20-41	Ci-Y	$<.05$
					Ch-Y	$<.20$

On the questionnaires which were administered after the group had completed the full series of fifteen trials, subjects were asked if the group had a leader and, if so, in which position. For all networks, the frequency of affirmative responses increased in the order, circle, chain, Y, and wheel. The amount of agreement as to the position held by the leader was in the same order. Some networks were more readily perceived by their members than others. Sixteen subjects in the wheel groups reproduced the correct network, while only one circle member recognized the circle network. Satisfaction with the "job in the group" decreased in the order, circle, chain, Y, and wheel, with circle members being more satisfied than wheel members. From the analysis of messages sent, it appeared that circle members sent more informational messages and more answers than did members of other networks. They also recognized more of their errors.

The data indicate that persons in the most central positions in the Y, wheel, and chain were more satisfied than anyone in a circle position. Persons in peripheral positions in these networks enjoyed their job less than those in any circle position.

Leavitt grossly characterizes the kinds of differences in this way: "the circle, one extreme, is active, leaderless, unorganized, erratic and yet is enjoyed by its members. The wheel at the other extreme, is less active, has a distinct leader, is well and stably organized, is less erratic, and yet is unsatisfying to most of its members" (1951, p. 46).

In drawing conclusions from such an experiment, it is necessary to bear in mind the limitations clearly outlined by the author in terms of task and group size. In a task of this sort, self-conception in role and status differentiation are perceptibly related to the amount of information and distributive power a position has relative to another position. Since the task required pooling information from all positions, successful action depended on subordinating individual contributions in the interest of the group goal. In another task, e.g., one emphasizing other types of contribution, or maximizing opposition, the observed correlation of satisfaction with centrality might not be found. It is clear, however, that differences in accuracy, total activity, leader emergence, and satisfaction are markedly affected by the arrangement of communication channels in the group.

In one repetition of this experiment, the central person became the leader, but other differences were not significant (Hirota, 1953). In another repetition of the experiment with three-man groups, the members in the wheel network used less time to solve the problem of the common symbol than did members in a circle network although the difference was not statistically significant. However, members in the wheel took longer to solve more complex problems which required simple arithmetical computations (Shaw, 1954b). For an even more complex task, that of the discussion of a human-relations problem, a star network required more time than a slash network, and a slash more than a comcon network (all channels open). No differences in satisfaction or number of messages were found (Shaw, Rothschild, & Strickland, 1957). It is possible that in solving problems requiring some skill the wheel network is only more efficient when the person in the center of the net is the most skillful member of the group.

In a similar experiment (Smith, 1951), the circle network permitted members to adapt more readily to a change requiring the breaking and relearning of a previously established set. The greater amount of interaction and feedback which characterizes the decentralized network seems to increase the probability of checking gross unanimous errors, to increase adaptability in the face of new demands for relearning, and to increase average member satisfaction, but at some cost in quantity of messages, duplication of effort, and general confusion.

Another experiment demonstrates the results of extreme conditions of lack of communication and feedback. Members of thirty six-man groups were given a problem which required closing their eyes and then raising a number of fingers so that the total would equal a number (e.g., six, five, or some smaller number) which the experimenter had previously announced. The subjects were placed in "communication networks" by being seated in a circle, seated at a table with a pair of members on two opposite sides and one member at each of the other sides, or seated in three rows of three, two, and one. To solve a problem requiring a total of five or fewer fingers, the subjects either would have had to have individually decided upon the same method of "co-operating" by having members in certain positions in the "network" raise one finger while others raised no fingers or would have had to reach the solution by chance. Twice as many subjects used a chance type of solution as did those who used a solution based on seating position. Few were able to actually solve the problem using either method (Berg, 1955).

§ Developing a Task
Hierarchy

THE LEAVITT EXPERIMENT was repeated (Guetzkow & Simon, 1955; Guetzkow & Dill, 1957; Guetzkow, 1960) with a modification of the design which made it possible to study the development of the task hierarchy within each type of communication network. Using the same problem of discovering the common symbol on a set of cards, five-man groups were tested in wheel, circle, and all-channel networks. Between each trial the group members were allowed a two-minute period in which to organize the group. In the wheel, the activity during this two-minute period was centered on discovering the organization which was already present, while in the all-channel and circle networks the members sought to develop an efficient hierarchy. In the circle the members tended to select a three-level hierarchy, and in the all-channel group the members formed either a two- or three-level hierarchy (see Fig. 26). As soon as the members of a group had worked out a hier-

Figure 26—Task Hierarchies in Wheel, Circle, and All-Channel Networks

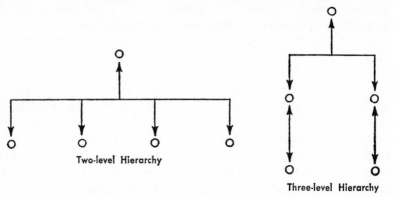

Two-level Hierarchy

Three-level Hierarchy

archy, they were able to do better in the task. Fewer task messages and more social-emotional messages were sent after the hierarchy was established. On the first few trials more messages were sent to those subjects who gave good information or who provided the right answer. As these channels began to be used more than others, they were gradually incorporated into the developing communication network. The all-channel networks were the slowest to establish hierarchies because the members had to make a selection from so many channels.

§ Noise

THE DIFFERENCES BETWEEN networks become more pronounced as "noise" is introduced into the communication channels. Here "noise" is used to refer to anything which interrupts the messages sent (Heise & Miller, 1951) or makes it difficult to understand and solve the problem, such as the introduction of irrelevant information (Shaw, 1958a).

In one experiment random noise was introduced into one- and two-way telephone circuits connecting three members as a shishing sound that had all frequencies of vibration present at equal intensities. This type of noise in the communication network served to heighten the differences between networks which were related to differences in group task. The group members in each network were given three kinds of problems to solve: (1) a comparatively stereotyped and unimaginative exchange of isolated words, (2) the formation of anagrams from a given word, and (3) sentence construction.

Performance on a task calling for individual mental activity where the products were not highly interdependent but simply additive (making the largest possible number of anagrams out of a given word) was little affected by the type of network or amount of noise (Heise & Miller, 1951). An information-collection task (completing a list of words, each subject having part of the list) was performed most rapidly in a network where each member was connected to each other with two-way communication. However, a task requiring assembly plus coordination (completing a sentence in proper order, each subject having part of the words) was performed most rapidly in a centralized network where a central person was furnished two-way communication with each of the two others, but no connection was provided between the two peripheral members. A one-way closed chain (no feedback, no centralization) was, in general, prone to error, inefficient in terms of time and number of messages, and suffered most with the introduction of noise. Members were most satisfied in the central position and felt "left out and unsure of themselves" when in an isolated position with no feedback facilities.

To counteract the effects of "noise" in the information theory sense, groups repeat the same information several times as a means of reducing error (Christie, Luce, & Macy, 1952; Macy, Christie, & Luce, 1953). Error is further reduced when members' comments are audible and understandable (Marquis et al., 1951).

§ Participation and Attitude Change

IN A LECTURE as opposed to a free discussion, two-way interaction is more or less drastically limited. Although the limitation is accepted by the audience, the results are in some ways similar to forced one-way communication. A whole series of studies shows that if one wishes to change attitudes and the subsequent behavior of a group, discussion and decision where all members participate as directly as possible tend to be more effective than "enlightenment" or "persuasion" by the lecture method, or by an unqualified order from above (see Chapter Two).

Job and rate changes in a factory setting are accomplished with less quitting of workers, less aggression toward supervisors, less drop in production, faster recovery, and higher final rate of production, if the workers are allowed to participate in the changeover decision

(Coch & French, 1948). The group decision method was also found to be effective in raising the production rate of a group of sewing-machine operators on individual piecework, whereas attention and encouragement from the plant psychologist proved to be ineffective (Bavelas, reported in Maier, 1946). Among college students and housewives, group decision resulted in substantial changes in the consumption of unfamiliar foods, whereas lectures had little or no effect (Klisurich, reported in Lewin, 1947c, and Willerman, 1953). In all of these cases, a change is made to a mode of behavior or performance that presumably is already within the available repertoire of the group members and does not require learning. The mode of behavior can be made the chosen response simply by the development of new group norms to supersede the currently dominant ones. Where learning of new technical content rather than performance or attitude change is required, the results are not so clear. Early studies of the lecture *versus* discussion in college courses display contradictory reports (Roseborough, 1953). Students participate more in permissive class sections and find them more interesting and enjoyable, but prefer directive classes for exam preparation (Wispe, 1951), although neither method may result in better exam grades (Zeleny, 1940a). Apparently the purposes and values of the members govern to some degree the reactions they will have to a more or less constricted participation procedure (McCurdy & Eber, 1953). Some students seem to learn better under one method, others under the other method (Wispe, 1953).

Constrictions adopted freely by the members in order to accomplish a purpose they value are probably less frustrating than those imposed without choice. Nevertheless, an effective change of norms probably requires knowledge of a new consensus which can best be achieved by full participation with free feedback.

§   The Leader's Influence

THE ATTITUDES and behavior of the leader apparently can influence the communication network appreciably, even though there are no mechanical constrictions. Indeed, this is one way of looking at the experiments on authoritarian and democratic leadership (Lewin & Lippitt, 1938). A "permissive" sort of leadership which consists mainly in management of the discussion process, without interjection of the leader's opinion (as compared to the nonparticipating "observing" leader), operates to protect minorities from social influence, and increases the probability that the single member with the correct answer to the problem will be able to convince the majority (Maier & Solem, 1952). As a result, the minority members who are wrong tend to stay wrong, but the average effect over all groups is definitely to increase the number of right answers through what amounts to a greater error-checking ability.

In a comparison of a "supervisory" type of leader, where the leader is instructed to stay out of the discussion, and a "participatory" type, where the leader injects his opinion as well as tries to insure equal participtaion for all members, participatory leadership resulted in more group agreement, greater and more permanent influence of the leader on the members, and more interest and enjoyment in the task for both leaders and followers (Preston & Heintz, 1949; Hare, 1953). It appears that members are more satisfied when the leader keeps the communication network balanced and also participates himself. Indeed, in some, if not most situations, the leader who expresses no opinions creates an anomalous and frustrating state of affairs. Lack of leadership is used as a therapeutically intended disturbance in some types of group therapy (Bion, 1948a). In business, industry, and government, too, there appears to be a general expectation that the socially designated leader, the conference chairman, should be the sole major behavior leader (Berkowitz, 1953). Leadership-sharing by members other than the designated leader tends to result in a decrease in group cohesiveness and satisfaction, except when problems are urgent. This holds when leaders are more or less permissive and even when the secondary leadership is supportive. It seems definitely indicated that the communication network and the gradient of participation set limits on the degree to which new norms can be formed and the degree to which sensitive regulation of the process can take place. The effects of constriction of communication within a given period are in turn dependent upon the values and expectations of the members.

§ Summary

ALTHOUGH MECHANICAL RESTRICTIONS on communication and seating position will prevent the free interaction between all members of a discussion group, a gradient of activity rates among members is typical even where "free" communication is allowed. A few individuals receive communications from almost every one in the group since low participators do not talk to each other as much as they do to high participators.

When communication is restricted, the person in the center of the network tends to become the leader and the most satisfied member. Once status differences are perceived by the members, differences in communication content up and down the status hierarchy may result.

Proximity in the communication network tends to increase inter-member attraction. However, if there is no opportunity for "feedback" between members who are close to each other, hostility may appear and efficiency in problem-solving declines. In a comparison of five-man groups in circle, chain, Y, and wheel networks, Leavitt found that the circle, at one extreme, was active, leaderless, unorganized, erratic, and yet enjoyed by its members. The wheel, at the other extreme, was less active, had a distinct leader, was organized, less erratic, and yet unsatisfying to most of its members.

The introduction of "noise" in the communication network is most disruptive when the task requires co-operation and the accurate exchange of information. To counteract the effects of noise, groups use redundant coding as a means of reducing error.

When an individual lectures to a group, the effects may be similar to forced one-way communication. As a result, discussion and decision in a group with full participation and free feedback tends to be more effective in changing attitudes or behavior than the lecture method. In a similar way, the contrast in "authoritarian" and "democratic" leadership styles may be seen as different ways of controlling the communication net. However, the satisfaction of the followers in either situation depends upon their prior expectations for the leader's role.

11

LEADERSHIP

THE LEADERSHIP in a small group can be varied by selecting an individual with a given set of personality characteristics or by
training an individual to perform a given set of behaviors. Variations in
leader style will produce the greatest effect on interaction if selection and
training are combined. In this chapter the general *traits* of leaders as
well as the *functions* of leadership for which an individual might be
trained will be summarized. Since leader selection is of particular
importance to the armed forces, many of the studies of small group
leadership have been made with military personnel. A leaderless group
discussion has been used to predict leader potential for a variety of
tasks. However, differences in the skills required for leadership in
manual and intellectual task have led to the development of a number
of situational tests and assessment techniques. Many of the effects of
differences in the structure, size, and communication network of a group
which also place differing demands on the leader have been discussed in
some detail in previous chapters and will only be reviewed briefly.

Although in most groups a single individual has the most power
and authority and is recognized as the formal leader, the leadership
functions may be divided formally or informally among several group

members. A common division of labor is that of having a *task leader* who is primarily concerned with task performance and a *social-emotional leader* or best-liked man who is primarily concerned with affectional relationships and member satisfaction.

§ Leadership Traits

THE VARIETY OF TRAITS which a leader may have is the same as that of any other group member, except that the leader is usually found to have a higher rating on each "good" trait. While correlations between "good" personality traits and leadership are generally positive, they are rarely large. As a result, only a little of the variance in leader behavior can be accounted for in this way (Gibb, 1954). There are indications that certain traits such as intelligence, enthusiasm, dominance, self-confidence, social participation, and equalitarianism are frequently found to characterize leaders (Chevaleva-Ianouskaia & Sylla, 1929; Goodenough, 1930; Partridge, 1934; Zeleny, 1939; Gibb, 1947; Green, 1948; Stogdill, 1948; Van Dusen, 1948; Martin, Gross, & Darley, 1952; Bass, McGehee, Hawkins, Young, & Gebel, 1953; Borgatta, 1954; Cattell & Stice, 1954; Hollander, 1954; Olmsted, 1957; Titus & Hollander, 1957; Gold, 1958; Beer, Buckhout, Horowitz, & Levy, 1959). Some examples of research on leader traits are given in Exhibit 18. Usually, however, the relation of the trait to the leadership role is more meaningful if consideration is given to the detailed nature of the role and the characteristics of the followers, as was the case in the experiment in which high or low authoritarian leaders were placed in groups with high or low authoritarian followers (see Chapter Six).

Although potential leaders tend to have more of all positive attributes than any of the members in their group, they cannot be so extreme that they become deviates. In one college, for example, the well-rounded man and campus leader was usually a "B" student. The "straight-A" man who excelled in nothing else was considered a "grind," who might even be branded as an outcast if he was suspected of being a "curve-wrecker," one who does so well that all the other members of the class receive poor grades by comparison (Davie & Hare, 1956). Or, to take an example which occurs over and over again in research on groups, the person who does most of the talking wins most of the decisions and becomes the leader (Terman, 1904; Belyaeff, 1930; Bass, 1949; Strodtbeck, 1951; Bales, 1953; Borgatta, 1954; March, 1956), *unless* he talks so much that he antagonizes the other group members.

Considering total personality as a cluster of traits, a common finding in research, particularly with children's groups, is that there are two basic personality types among leaders. Some are *self-oriented* (authoritarian), rather hostile persons with a driving need to be in the center of the group's activities, while others are *group-oriented* (equalitarian), persons who are able to reduce tension in a group, work toward a group goal, and take a follower role when it is appropriate (Parten, 1933a; Pigors, 1935; Anderson, 1939; Hare, 1957). However, leaders who emerge in leaderless group discussions tend to be more authoritarian in their behavior than leaders who are appointed (Carter et al., 1951). Presumably this occurs because more dominating behavior is required to establish a position of leadership in a group than to maintain one (Hare, 1957). In laboratory groups, leaders who are "elected" gain more acceptance from their followers than those who appear to "take over" (Raven & French, 1958a, 1958b; French & Raven, 1960).

A further indication of the behavior of authoritarian leaders in adult groups is reported in a study of 39 three-man air crews in training (Ziller, 1959). Each crew-leader was given a chance to throw dice to evade part of the crew's training. Only nine threw the dice, i.e., assumed responsibility for group action. These leaders were less concerned about differing with the opinions of their group members, had higher F Scale scores, and were more highly motivated. Additional references to the personality characteristics of leaders are given in Chapters Two, Three, and Six.

Since the *traits* of the effective leader are so closely related to the *functions* he will perform in the group, the most general rule for leader selection would seem to be to select those individuals who have the necessary skills plus a willingness to use them to satisfy the group's needs (Wolman, 1956). The leader should be most effective when the group's needs are clearly defined (Bouricaud, 1955).

§ Leadership Functions

AN INDICATION of the functions which are common to the leader role regardless of the group situation is obtained from Hemphill's (1949) extensive questionnaire study of leadership qualities. In this study each respondent to the questionnaire gave a description of the different groups to which he belonged and also reported his observations of the leaders' behavior. Five functions were identified which were common to leaders of all groups: (1) advance the purpose of the group, (2) administrate,

(3) inspire greater activity or set the pace for the group, (4) make the individual member feel secure of his place in the group, (5) act without regard to his own self-interest. Leader functions which are similar to some or all of those on Hemphill's list also appear in a number of other studies (Stogdill, 1950; Peterson, 1955; Warriner, 1955; Wilson, High, & Comrey, 1955; Stogdill & Coons, 1957).

In terms of the interpersonal categories of task and social-emotional behavior, the leader's function can be seen as that of facilitating behavior in each area which will maximize productivity on the group's task. Whether or not he fulfills these functions, the leader, through his activity in the group, is a major determinant in establishing the point at which the group will reach equilibrium along each dimension of interaction (Back, 1948).

Since the problem of role confusion is present for the leader role as well as for the other roles in the group (see Chapter Four), the answer to the question about leader functions will depend upon who is asked. In the armed forces where status differences are clearcut, the military rank of the individual determines both his own conception of leadership, and the types of leadership others expect of him (Roff, 1950; Campbell, 1953; Davis, 1954; Halpin, 1954). In the air corps, ratings by the superior officers of airplane commanders were found to have a negative correlation with the commander "consideration" score which was based on his friendship and mutual trust with crew members, and a positive correlation with his "initiating structure" score which was based on maintaining a formal organization within the crew. In contrast, crew members were most satisfied when their commander was high on "consideration" and low on "initiating structure."

Many military organizations have customs which require social distance between leaders and followers and which place a low value on the "consideration" of commanders for their troops. These customs may have the effect of increasing group effectiveness, not so much because the men will not follow a leader with whom they are too familiar, but rather because a leader who is too close to his men may find it more difficult to reach decisions when he is influenced by his feelings about his men (Fiedler, 1957).

Individuals who differ in personality dimensions also have divergent expectations for the leader. When subjects are ranked on an Authoritarian-Equalitarian Scale, two distinct sets of expectations for leadership are found. Authoritarians accept status-ladened, strongly directive leadership, demand that others adhere to ingroup values, and interact with the leader as a person rather than as a role (Sanford, 1950; Medalia,

1955). A similar dependent state may characterize the emotional atmosphere of a group during the early phases of group formation (Bion, 1949b). Some examples of research on leadership functions are given in Exhibit 19.

§ The Central Person

THE "LEADER," in the usual sense, is only one type of central person who may have the power to control the activity of a group. In a family, for example, a sick child may have more influence on family activity than the father or mother who usually takes the leader role. The variety of emotional relationships which a central person may have with the members of a group is illustrated by Redl's (1952) list of ten types of persons who provide a basis for group formation. Redl based his work on that of Freud (1922).

§ Ten Types of Central Person

THE CENTRAL PERSON as an object of identification
    On the basis of love
        Incorporation into conscience—*Partriarchal sovereign*
        Incorporation into the ego ideal—*Leader*
    On the basis of fear
        Identification with the aggressor—*Tyrant*
The central person as the object of drives
    As an object of love drives—[*Idol*][1]
    As an object of aggressive drives—[*Scapegoat*]
The central person as an ego support
    Providing means for drive satisfaction—*Organizer*
    Dissolving conflict situations through guilt-
    anxiety assuagement
        Through the technique of the initiatory
        act in the service of drive satisfaction—*Seducer*
        and in the service of drive defense—*Hero*
        Through the "infectiousness of the unconflicted
        personality constellation over the conflicted
        one" in the service of drive satisfaction—*Bad influence*
        and in the service of drive defense—*Good example*

---

1. Since Redl did not name the object of love or aggressive drives, the names "idol" and "scapegoat" have been added.

Descriptions of the patriarchal sovereign, idol, and organizer in classroom groups are quoted from Redl's article as illustrations of the three major types of central persons, as objects of identification, objects of drives, and ego supports.

§ The Patriarchal Sovereign

Illustrative example: This group is composed of approximately ten-year-old children, most of whom are just at that point in their development where they most fully represent the end states of "childhood" immediately before the outbreak of preadolescent symptoms. In charge of them is a teacher who fits the following description: "He is an elderly gentleman of stern but not unfriendly exterior, decided but fundamentally mild in his manner. He stands for 'order and discipline' but they are values so deeply ingrained in him that he hardly thinks of them explicitly, nor does it occur to anyone to doubt them in his presence. He believes in good and thorough work, knows very clearly what he expects and leaves no doubt about it in the minds of his students." The atmosphere of the classroom may be easily described. The children accept his values without question. Their emotions about him are a mixture of love and adoration, with an element of anxiety in all those instances in which they are not quite sure of his approval. As long as they behave according to his code they feel happily secure—sheltered. Thoughts and imaginations which do not comply with his code are suppressed in his presence. The jokes he makes, or acknowledges, are funny. If one youngster is not quite so ready as the others to concentrate his filial adoration upon this type of a teacher, makes unfitting remarks, unruly gestures, or shows lack of submission, the others will experience a deep feeling of moral indignation— even though they may have enjoyed this youngster's jokes a few minutes previously during the recreation period. They all love their teacher and trust him infinitely, but certain thoughts must never enter their minds in his presence. When questioned or doubted by this teacher, tears come more easily than words; behind the happy security felt in his presence there is a nagging fear of its loss which streams into awareness every once in awhile without apparent cause.

Explanation: These youngsters love their teacher, but that is not all that occurs. Their love is of a type which leads to "identification." It would be absurd to say that they want to be like their teacher, but they want to behave so that their teacher will approve of them.

Formula: These children become a group because they incorporate the "super-ego"—conscience—of the central person, into their own. On the basis of this similarity between them, they develop group emotions toward each other (pp. 576-77).

§ The Idol

IMAGINE A NUMBER OF WOMEN who are in love with a singer or pianist and crowd around him after his performance. Certainly each of them would prefer to be jealous of all others. However, considering their large number and how impossible it is for them to reach the aim of their infatuation, they resign and instead of pulling each other's hair, they act like a uniform group. They bring ovations to their idol in common actions and would be glad to divide his locks among themselves.

The life in the school class furnishes two similar examples for illustration.

Illustrative example, 1: There is a group of sixteen-year-old girls in a class of a girls' high school. In charge of them is a male teacher—young, attractive, but narcissistic enough so that they are not too greatly frightened sexually from the outset. It is known that in some such cases "the whole class falls in love with him." From that moment on, they will act like a group in many ways along the line of Freud's example. Despite their infatuation for him, it would not be surprising if the teacher complained that he had trouble with discipline—that these girls did not obey him or follow his wishes without pressure. It seems that this kind of "being in love" with the central person does not make for "identification" described in *Type 2*.

Illustrative example, 2: In a coeducational class of approximately sixteen-year-old children, there is one especially pretty girl, rather narcissistic. In similar situations one frequently finds a whole cluster of boys loving and adoring her in various ways, but equally unsuccessful insofar as their wish for exclusive possession goes. The girl is equipped with special skills for keeping them all equidistant and yet equally near. Symptoms of dense group formation may sometimes be observed among these boys. They seem very close to each other, and yet their relationship is not genuine friendship. It is on a group emotional basis. This becomes evident when the girl ultimately decides in favor of one of her suitors. The other boys then begin to hate him as their rival, with the exception perhaps of the one or two who may move even closer to the successful colleague and, thus, enjoy some of the satisfactions denied to them *via* the mechanism of *altruistic concession*.

Explanation: There is no doubt that the group emotional symptoms are genuine and that the teacher in *Example 1* and the girl in *Example 2* are playing the role of the central person without whose presence this type of group formative process would not have been evoked. However, it is also evident that these central persons could not be called "leaders" by any interpretation of the term—that the other children do not "identify" with them. Nor do they incorporate their central person's standards. The central person remains "outside" but does call out a display of group emotional symptoms in these children.

Formula: The children choose one and the same person as an object of their love, and on the basis of this similarity they develop group emotions between each other (pp. 578-79).

§ The Organizer

Illustrative example: In a class of approximately thirteen-year-old boys there are five who find clandestine enjoyment of the cigarette as a symbol of adulthood. And yet, all five are of the type who have decided worries about how they can obtain cigarettes. They have neither the money to buy them, the courage to do so, nor the impudence to steal them from their fathers. Preadolescent revolt against adult concepts of what a good child should be has not progressed far enough. A new boy, for whom smoking is no great problem, enters the class. He neither invites, instigates nor encourages the others in this enterprise. They all know that he can get the desired cigarettes for them if they but ask. In some cases hardly any other factor is involved. The boys neither love nor admire this youngster; on the contrary, he is rather looked down upon as socially inferior. They do not fear him nor does he use any direct or indirect pressure upon them. Yet, by the mere fact that he gets them the cigarettes, they suddenly become a regular "group," held together on the basis of their participation in the same forbidden pleasure.

Explanation: Perhaps this example seems more complicated—less credible —than the others. . . . Usually, it is coupled with other roles which the central person assumes for the potential group members. Although there are not many clear examples of this type, they cannot be reduced to any of the other types because neither love, hatred, nor identification is involved.

Formula: The central person renders an important service to the ego of the potential group members. He does so by providing the means for the satisfaction of common undesirable drives and thus prevents guilt feelings, anxieties, and conflicts which otherwise would be involved in that process for them. On the basis of this service, the latent undesirable drives of these youngsters can manifest openly. Through this common conflict-solution, group emotions develop in the interpersonal situation (pp. 579-80).

Some of these types of central persons, like the patriarchal sovereign, leader, or tyrant, are found most often among persons who hold the formal "leadership" positions in the group, whereas others like seducer, hero, or bad influence, are more apt to appear as informal leaders.

§ Power and Influence

ALL OF THE TYPES of central persons have in common the fact that they have influence over other group members. The "dynamics" of power are illustrated by a series of studies conducted in boys' camps (Polansky et al., 1950a; Lippitt et al., 1952). Boys who were rated by their peers as having the most power were the ones who were imitated more often by the others. The high power boy was actually approached nondirectively and with greater deference, while he was more likely to direct others and to resist the direction of others. The more powerful child was better liked by his associates and more frequently mentioned as a person the others would most want to be like.

The influence of a member in the informal structure will be enhanced if he is placed in a formal position of leadership. In one experiment, five- and six-man groups were given mathematical problems to solve. In some of the groups, a person was chosen by the group members to play a leader role and in other groups a person was selected to be an observer. In neither case did the elected person give his own opinions about the solution of the problem. The subjects recorded their answers to the problem privately both before and after the discussion. In both cases the discussion increased the number of correct answers, but the groups with leaders showed the most improvement. The effectiveness of the leader was especially marked when he made use of the opinion of minority members who were initially correct (Maier & Solem, 1952).

Another experiment indicates that an individual will *try* to exert more influence if he is placed in the leader role. One hundred forty-two airmen were placed in four-man "groups" in which each thought that he was coordinating the activities of the other three men in assembling a jigsaw puzzle. Each subject wrote notes to the other "members" and received fictitious notes in return. Before beginning the task, some of the subjects were told that they were bosses while others were told that they were clerks. In addition, specific functions of their role and the goal of the group were either made clear or left unspecified. An examination of the notes written by each subject during the experiment indicated that a subject *tried* to exert more control over the other members if he were told that he were "the boss," or if he were given specific directions to do so even though he were only a clerk. The bosses enjoyed the experience more (Gerard, 1957).

§ Selection Procedures

IN ADDITION to personality and performance tests (Carter & Nixon, 1949b), a frequently used technique for the selection of leaders is the leaderless group discussion. First developed by the German army during the first World War (Ansbacher, 1941, 1951) this technique was taken over by the British and American armies and is now used by other organizations. In a series of researches on this subject, Bass and his associates observed college students, officer candidates, and business executives in four- to ten-man groups (Bass, 1949, 1951, 1954a, 1954b; Bass & Norton, 1951; Bass & Coates, 1952; Bass & Klubeck, 1952; Bass, Klubeck, & Wurster, 1953; Bass et al., 1953; Bass & Wurster, 1953b; Gleason, 1957). As the candidates discussed a series of problems in a group in which no leader had been appointed, obervers recorded the amount of time each member talked and rated each member's behavior on a series of scales which had been found to be valid for identifying leadership potential. A high rating on leadership in an initially leaderless group of this type was found to have a positive correlation with leadership in training performance of army personnel, status of supervisors in an oil company, and extracurricular participation of college students (Bass & White, 1951; Bass & Coates, 1952; Bass & Wurster, 1953b; Wurster & Bass, 1953; Borgatta, 1954; Ames, 1955). Bass concluded, however, that in the case of the oil company supervisors the estimate of leader potential in the "leaderless" groups was not valid since the rank of each member in the oil company was known to the members and appeared to have a direct influence upon their participation (Bass & Wurster, 1953a).

In a similar study, nominations for the position of leader and "effectiveness" ratings were both made by the same leaderless groups of officer candidates. For this reason the low (.28, .18) but statistically significant correlations between nomination as a leader and effectiveness may have been only a reflection of the consistency of officer candidates' ratings of desirable characteristics (Berkowitz, 1956).

The possibility that one observer may be able to select the leader in an initially leaderless group simply by judging his appearance has also been investigated. In one study 24 college students were asked to judge leadership ability from individual pictures of police officers who had previously participated in four-to-six man problem-solving groups. Although the judges agreed among themselves on what a leader should look like (correlation .80), the average correlation between a judge's ratings and actual leadership performance was less than .18 (Mason, 1957).

Role playing has also been used as an assessment procedure (Tupes, Carp, & Borg, 1958). In a study of 221 army officer candidates, ratings of behavior were made in six role-playing situations. Low but significant correlations were found between role-playing ability and achievement in military academic subjects, military efficiency, and estimated officer effectiveness. Role-playing ability was also correlated with performance in leaderless group discussions and situational tests. Men with high scores were seen by their peers as better adjusted and "all-around" persons.

Leaderless group discussions as well as other group situational tests were combined with life histories, stress interviews, role playing (Symonds, 1947; Bronfenbrenner & Newcomb, 1948), intelligence tests, and personality tests in a week-long assessment program developed by the American OSS (Office of Strategic Services) for the assessment of men who could be used for special missions during World War II. Some indication of the kind of social stress placed on a candidate as part of the selection program is given in the following excerpt from the book *Assessment of Men* which describes the use of role players in a construction task (OSS, 1948, pp. 102-111).

§ OSS Construction Test

SOMETIME DURING THE MORNING of the first day each candidate had an appointment behind the barn. If hearing of the location made the men recall, sometimes with amusement, events in their boyhood when they had kept similiar appointments with their fathers, it is safe to assume that even such recollections failed to prepare them for what they would experience on this occasion.

Ostensibly this was a test of the candidate's ability to direct two helpers in building with him a frame structure out of simple wooden materials. Actually the situation was not so benign as it first appeared. To be sure, it was a test of *Leadership*, but more truly it was a test of *Emotional Stability* and frustration tolerance. *Energy* and *Initiative* in carrying out the work and the *Social Relations* of the candidate in relation to his helpers were also rated.

The building materials for this test were wooden poles of two lengths (five and seven feet), wooden blocks with sockets into which the poles could be fitted, and small pegs to hold the poles and blocks together. The blocks were of two sorts, full blocks and half blocks. The full blocks were of octagonal shape with sockets cut into each of the eight sides. Running through the center of each block was a circular hole of the same diameter as that of the poles. The half blocks had sockets in only three sides but attached to and protruding from the opposite long side was a dowel the thickness of a pole which could be inserted through the center hole of a full block. This equipment was a great magnification of the "tinker toy" sets of childhood. With this, each candidate was directed to build a five-foot cube with seven-foot diagonals on the four sides.

When the candidate came to the area where the test was to be conducted the staff member said to him:

"We have a construction problem for you now. We want you to build a structure using the equipment lying around here. Let's see. (*The staff member appears to ponder which of two or three models of different design to use.*) I guess we'll give you this model to copy. (*Staff member picks up the*

model which is always used from among the others and shows it to the student.)
You see there are short five-foot and long seven-foot poles lying on the ground.
(*Staff member points out one of each size.*) The sides of the frame which you
are to build are made of five-foot poles, and the diagonals of seven-foot poles.
(*Staff member demonstrates this on the model.*) Do you understand?

"Now (*staff member picks up the corner and points to the peg*) you will
notice there are holes for pegs like this at each socket, and similar holes in
the end of each pole. Be sure, whenever you put a pole into a socket, to
cinch it with a peg, because unless that is done all over the structure it will
not be stable. (*Staff member then throws the sample corner to the ground.*)

"This is a construction problem, but even more important than that it
is a test of leadership. I say that because it is impossible for one man working
alone to complete this task in the ten minutes allotted to do it. Therefore we
are going to give you two helpers who work here on the estate. You are going
to be the supervisor, their boss. You are going to guide them in their work,
but as foreman, you will follow more or less a hands-off policy. Let them do
the manual labor. You can assume that they have never done such work
before and know nothing about it. Any questions? (*Final pause to amplify
any details not understood by the candidate.*)

"All right. It is now ten o'clock. You have just ten minutes in which
to do the job. I'll call your two helpers."

At this the two assistants, who had been working in the barn, were asked
to come out and help the candidate. They complied, but waited for him to
take the initiative. These two members of the junior staff traditionally assumed
the pseudonyms of Kippy and Buster. Whoever played the part of Kippy
acted in a passive sluggish manner. He did nothing at all unless specifically
ordered to, but stood around, often getting in the way, either idling with his
hands in his pockets or concerned with some insignificant project of his own,
such as a minute examination of the small-scale model. Buster, on the other
hand, played a different role. He was aggressive, forward in offering imprac-
tical suggestions, ready to express dissatisfaction, and quick to criticize what
he suspected were the candidate's weakest points.

The two assistants were not permitted, by their secret instructions, to
disobey orders, and they were supposed to carry out whatever directions were
given to them explicitly. Within the bounds of this ruling, though, it was their
function to present the candidate with as many obstructions and annoyances
as possible in ten minutes. As it turned out, they succeeded in frustrating the
candidates so thoroughly that the construction was never, in the history of
S [the OSS testing unit], completed in the allotted time.

At first the assistants appeared cooperative, but if the candidate did not
introduce himself and ask their names, Buster would observe that a boss
interested in getting along with his men would at least find out their names.
If the candidate did not explain in detail what they were to do, referring to
the model, Buster would complain that they were receiving inadequate directions and remark that the candidate must be inexperienced. If he were either
peremptory or passive, he would be criticized for this. Buster might say that
that was a poor trait in a leader, and add that he found it hard to understand
how anyone could ever have thought the candidate was worthy of holding an

important position in the organization. If the candidate became so incensed at their unmanageableness that he laid a hand on them with the intention of getting them to work faster, the helper who was touched would take great offense. After the work had begun, Buster, or occasionally Kippy, might criticize the candidate's plan of operation and suggest other, often incorrect ways to proceed in order to test the forcefulness of the man's leadership. Kippy, for instance, might attempt to involve the boss in a debate about the relative advantages of the two plans. Or he might get into an argument with the other assistant over alternative methods of building a corner. Again, he might say that the octagonal edges of the corner blocks were the "rolling edges" and that they would not rest firmly enough on the ground to hold the structure. (Actually they would and that was the correct way to build the cube.) The assistants might try to get the leader to lay the blocks down flat, which was incorrect. They might even point to four holes in the ground, suggesting that those must be the places where previous worekrs had laid the corners flat. Or, in another attempt to divert the candidate from his plan, they might point out to him that the model was mounted on cardboard, and suggest that he search the area for cardboard with which to make the base for the structure so that it would be exactly like the model. If the candidate acceded to their suggestion, he wasted time, because he was not directed to build such a base.

Frequently the candidate began to construct the cube incorrectly. When this happened the assistants would follow his orders for a while and then point out the errors, at the same time tearing down the structure if the leader did not stop them. From time to time, if Buster discovered a pole that was not pegged into its socket, he would kick the two pieces apart, saying sharply that no sensible person would expect such a framework to hold together unless it was pegged. It was discouraging to any man to see his cube collapsing before his eyes, but the reactions differed. Some candidates became bitter; others gave up and refused to continue. On the other hand, good leaders would patiently begin again or direct the helpers to stop tearing the pieces apart until they had decided whether the mistakes could be more easily rectified.

Another stratagem used by the two assistants when the work was well under way was to distract the candidate's attention from the job. They asked questions about him—where he came from, what his real name was, how long he had been in the Army, where he got his accent, and so on. They made an effort to break through his cover story if he answered these questions, and often their attempts were successful. If he refused to reply to their queries because of concentration on the job, they accused him of being unsociable. If they noticed anything particularly distinctive about him—for example, a peculiar accent, baldness, a reserved attitude—they burlesqued this trait in order to irritate him further. If he mentioned any special interest, they encouraged him to discuss it. If he became distracted, they continued on that line for a while, and then Buster might suddenly tell the candidate he was neglecting the job. He might accuse him of being "the poorest leader I ever saw around here," and suggest, since he was so obviously inept, that he give up the assignment entirely. If, after a few minutes of such frustrations, the candidate stopped directing the others and began to do the work by himself, or showed any evidence of emotion, Buster would immediately note this reaction and make some caustic comment designed to heighten it.

While Buster was needling the candidate in this way, Kippy was moping about, doing little. If he was given a direction, he complied slowly and clumsily, showing no initiative, stopping as soon as he had completed the specific task. He sometimes went up to the candidate to request permission to leave for a minute "to go get a drink." In general he followed the policy of passive resistance, doing everything possible to sabotage the construction by his inertia.

To illustrate how the helpers turned the conversation in Construction into banter which could be exploited for purposes of personality assessment, a typical protocol is reproduced here.

Staff Member (calling toward the barn): Can you come out here and help this man for a few minutes?

Buster and Kippy: Sure, we'll be right out.

Staff Member: O.K., Slim, these are your men. They will be your helpers. You have ten minutes.

Slim: Do you men know anything about building this thing?

Buster: Well, I dunno, I've seen people working here. What is it you want done?

Slim: Well, we have got to build a cube like this and we only have a short time in which to do it, so I'll ask you men to pay attention to what I have to say. I'll tell you what to do and you will do it. O.K.?

Buster: Sure, sure, anything you say, Boss.

Slim: Fine. Now we are going to build a cube like this with five-foot poles for the uprights and seven-foot poles for the diagonals, and use the blocks for the corners. So first we must build the corners by putting a half block and a whole block together like this and cinching them with a peg. Do you see how it is done?

Buster: Sure, sure.

Slim: Well, let's get going.

Buster: Well, what is it you want done, exactly: What do I do first?

Slim: Well, first put some corners together—let's see, we need four on the bottom and four topside—yes, we need eight corners. You make eight of these corners and be sure that you pin them like this one.

Buster: You mean we both make eight corners or just one of us?

Slim: You each make four of them.

Buster: Well, if we do that, we will have more than eight because you already have one made there. Do you want eight altogether or nine altogether?

Slim: Well, it doesn't matter. You each make four of these, and hurry.

Buster: O.K., O.K.

Kippy: What cha in, the Navy? You look like one of them curly-headed Navy boys all the girls are after. What cha in, the Navy?

Slim: Er—no. I am not in the Navy. I'm not in anything.

Kippy: Well, you were just talking about "topside" so I thought maybe you were in the Navy. What's the matter with you—you look healthy enough. Are you a draft dodger?

Slim: No, I was deferred for essential work—but that makes no difference. Let's get the work done. Now we have the corners done, let's put them together with the poles.

Kippy: The more I think of it, the more I think you are in the Army. You run this job just like the Army—you know, the right way, the wrong way, and the Army way. I'll bet you are some second lieutenant from Fort Benning.

Slim: That has nothing to do with this job. Let's have less talk and more work.

Kippy: Well, I just thought we could talk while we work—it's more pleasant.

Slim: Well, we can work first and talk afterwards. Now connect those two corners with a five-foot pole.

Buster: Don't you think we ought to clear a place where we can work?

Slim: That's a good idea. Sure, go ahead.

Buster: What kind of work did you do before you came here? Never did any building, I bet. Jeez, I've seen a lot of guys, but no one as dumb as you.

Slim: Well, that may be, but you don't seem to be doing much to help me.

Buster: What—what's that? Who are you talking to, me? Me not being helpful—why, I've done everything you have asked me, haven't I? Now, haven't I? Everything you asked me. Why, I've been about as helpful as anyone could be around here.

Slim: Well, you haven't killed yourself working and we haven't much time, so let's get going.

Buster: Well, I like that. I come out here and do everything you ask me to do. You don't give very good directions. I don't think you know what you are doing anyway. No one else ever complained about me not working. Now I want an apology for what you said about me.

Slim: O.K., O.K., let's forget it. I'll apologize. Let's get going. We haven't much time. You build a square here and you build one over there.

Buster: Who you talking to—him or me?

Kippy: That's right—how do you expect us to know which one you mean? Why don't you give us a number or something—call one of us "number one" and the other "number two"?

Slim: O.K. You are "one" and he is "two."

Buster: Now, wait a minute—just a minute. How do you expect to get along with people if you treat them like that? First we come out here and you don't ask us our names—you call us "you." Then we tell you about it, you give us numbers. How would you like that? How would you like to be called a number? You treat us just like another five-foot pole and then you expect us to break our necks working for you. I can see you never worked much with people.

Slim: I'm sorry, but we do not have much time and I thought—

Kippy: Yes, you thought. Jeez, it doesn't seem to me that you ever did much thinking about anything. First you don't ask our names as any stupid guy would who was courteous. Then you don't know what you did before you came here or whether you are in the Army, Navy, or not, and it's darn sure you don't know anything about building this thing or directing workers. Cripes, man, you stand around her like a ninny arguing when we should be working. What the hell is the matter with you, anyway?

Slim: I'm sorry—what are your names?
Buster: I'm Buster.
Kippy: Mine's Kippy. What is yours?
Slim: You can call me Slim.
Buster: Well, is that your name or isn't it?
Slim: Yes, that is my name.
Kippy: It's not a very good name—Dumbhead would be better.

Slim: Well, I'd like to do as much of this as possible. Will you help me?
Buster: Sure, sure, we'll help you, but it doesn't seem to be much use. What do you want us to do now?
Slim: Well, one of you build a square over there just like this one while the other one puts in the uprights and diagonals on this one.
Kippy: May I ask a question?
Slim: Sure, go ahead.
Kippy: Why build one over there? What are you going to do with it then?
Slim: Well, we'll put it on top—the top of this cube is like the bottom.
Kippy: Well, if that isn't the most stupid thing I ever heard of. Since when do you build the roof of a house and lift it to the top? Why not build it right on the top. Listen, when you build a house you build the foundation, then the walls, and then the roof. Isn't that right?
Slim: Well, that is usually the way it's done, but I think we can do this job this way. In fact, I don't think it matters much which way we do it. Either way is O.K., I guess.
Buster: You guess, you guess. What kind of a man are you anyway? Why in hell don't you make up your mind and stick to it? Be decisive—didn't they tell you that in OCS?—be decisive—even if you are wrong, be decisive, give an order. What are you—man or mouse?
Kippy: Oh, it's no use talking, Buster, when he doesn't have a bar on his shoulder he doesn't know what to do. Listen, Mac, you're not on Company Street now. You haven't a sergeant to do your work for you. You're all alone and you look pretty silly. Why, you can't even put together a child's toy.
Slim: Now listen to me, you guys, are you going to work for me or aren't you?
Buster: Sure, we want to work for you. We really don't care. We'd as soon work for you as for anyone else. We get paid all the same. The trouble is we can't find out what you want done. What exactly do you want?
Slim: Just let's get this thing finished. We haven't much more time. Hey there, you, be careful, you knocked that pole out deliberately.
Kippy: Who, me? Now listen to me, you good-for-nothing, you squirt. If this darned thing had been built right from the beginning the poles wouldn't come out. Weren't you told that you had to pin these things? Why none of it is pinned; look at that, and that, and that! (*Kicks the poles which were not pinned out of position and part of the structure collapses.*)
Slim: Hey—you don't have to knock it all down!
Buster: Well, it wasn't built right. What good was it without pins?
Slim: I told you guys to pin it.
Kippy: I pinned every one you told me about. How did I know you wanted the others pinned? Jeez, they send a boy out here to do a man's job

and when he can't do it he starts blaming his helpers. Who is responsible for this—you or me? Cripes, they must really be scraping the bottom of the barrel now.

Staff Member: (*Walking in from sidelines*): All right, Slim. That is all the time we have. The men will take this down.

Buster: Take what down? There's nothing to take down. Never saw anyone get so little done.

It is difficult to say what is the most desirable behavior for a candidate under such trying circumstances. Certainly disparate sorts of solutions were attempted. Some candidates, after they had seen that they were being hindered rather than helped by the assistants, either neglected them or actually discharged them, trying to do as much as they could by themselves. However, this certainly was not the correct procedure according to the directions, because one man could not complete the task in the allotted time, and moreover he had been told he must act as a leader. Others became authoritative or military, attempting to discipline the assistants, but this tended to anger such "sensitive workers" and made them work even more poorly. Still others simply relinquished their authority and followed the directions of the assistants. Some lost their temper or became frustrated easily, and more than one candidate struck an assistant with his fist out of anger.

The best solution, presumably, was one in which the leader first explained what he wished to have done, then delegated specific tasks to each assistant, keeping his eye on both of them, directing them, and keeping them working. At the same time he had to maintain good social relations, treating his helpers like equals, answering their suggestions, justifying his decisions to them, and taking their criticisms lightheartedly. He did well to reply to them with responses calculated not to offend overmuch their delicate sensibililities. It was, of course, hard for the candidate to decide whether he could get more done in the ten-minute period by acting entirely alone or by relying on the dubious cooperation of the helpers. At any rate, the problem was never completed in the allotted time, and usually it was scarcely begun.

An adequate follow-up of the candidates who were selected by this battery of tests was not possible during World War II, so that the validity of all of the measures is not fully substantiated. In situations in which the criteria for effective leadership are well defined, prediction can be accomplished with far fewer measures. A single half hour stress interview, for example, may be as valid as a number of more intricate assessment techniques.

§ Consistency of
Leadership Behavior

THE ASSUMPTION of individual consistency in leadership behavior lies behind all leader assessment techniques. Individuals who receive a high rating on leadership behavior in one situation are generally expected to take the leader role in other situations. The consistency is especially high if the social characteristics of the members, group size, and task remain the same even though specific group members may be changed (Terman, 1904; Bell & French, 1950; Jackson, 1953; Blake et al., 1954; Hollander, 1957). Conversely, consistency will be low if these or other factors are varied (Hemphill et al., 1956). A change in the personalities of the followers from high authoritarian to low authoritarian results in less authoritarian behavior on the part of the leader regardless of his authoritarian rating (Haythorn et al., 1956a, 1956b) and a change in the communication network may result in an entirely different person assuming leadership (Bavelas, 1950).

Once an individual has established himself as the leader in an initially leaderless group situation, it may be difficult to unseat him even if another leader is appointed. In one experiment, 41 six-man teams of unacquainted subjects from an air corps officer candidate school were tested in twelve situational problems requiring team co-operation. After the first six problems, the teams were divided into three groups: seventeen teams in which a leader had clearly emerged, fourteen with no clear leader, and ten with two competing leaders. During the final six problems, the effectiveness of the emergent leader was reduced when another subject was *appointed* leader, but the emergent leader still exhibited more leader behavior than the other team members. The performance of the appointed leader was not significantly different from his performance as a follower (Borg, 1957). On the other hand, subjects who have had difficulty establishing themselves as the leader in a leaderless group may lose their leader position if the experimenter imposes a task which they did not favor (Katz, Blau, Brown, & Strodtbeck, 1957). Additional evidence of the consistency of leadership behavior is given in Chapter Six.

§ Leadership Training

THE EFFECTIVENESS of the leader can generally be improved by giving him training which fits him specifically for the type of group he has to lead. In experimental training programs, youth leaders have become more democratic, foremen have gained more acceptance from employees in introducing work changes, and college students have improved their discussion leadership techniques (Bavelas, 1942; Maas, 1950; Maier, 1953; Klubeck & Bass, 1954; Barnlund, 1955; Maier & Maier, 1957). However, not all training programs are as successful. In one study in which foremen were trained in "consideration," a comparison of tests taken before and after the school session showed more consideration, while in actual practice the same foremen were less considerate (Fleishman, 1952). A second program of the same type produced no differences in the foremen's test scores (Harris & Fleishman, 1955). Some examples of research on leadership training are given in Exhibit 20.

A number of books have been written over the past thirty years with the aim of helping the individual improve his leadership technique. Only a sample of these appear in the bibliography (Elliott, 1928; Sheffield, 1929; Coyle, 1937; Slavson, 1938; McBurney & Hance, 1939; Lasker, 1949; Gouldner, 1950; Cunningham et al., 1951; Haiman, 1951; Sheffield & Sheffield, 1951; Strauss & Strauss, 1951; Johannot, 1953; Whyte, 1953; Andrews, 1955; Laird & Laird, 1956).

§ Authoritarian versus Democratic Leadership

AUTHORITARIAN AND DEMOCRATIC LEADERSHIP STYLES are the two most common types of leadership which have been imposed upon experimental groups. As in any situation, the group will be more effective when the members' expectations about the behavior appropriate for that situation are met. Where group members anticipate a democratic organization, as they do in educational settings, such as children's clubs, discussion groups, or classrooms, the democratic style is usually found to produce the most effective group. In industry or the army, however, where members anticipate forceful leadership from their superiors, a more authoritarian form of leadership results in a more effective group.

The classic experiments in this area by Lewin, Lippitt, and White in 1939-40, resulted in an increased interest in the scientific study of group dynamics. The first experiment compared the group atmospheres created by authoritarian and democratic leaders and the second experiment added a laissez-faire leader (Lewin & Lippitt, 1938; Lewin et al., 1939; Lippitt, 1939, 1940; Lippitt & White, 1952). In the second experiment, which corroborated the findings of the first, four clubs of eleven-year-old boys were formed in such a way that they were equated with respect to certain of the personal and sociometric characteristics of their members and degree of interest in the task. All clubs met in the same clubroom setting, two at a time in adjacent meeting spaces, with a common equipment box. Four adults played the roles of "authoritarian," "democratic," and "laissez-faire" leaders in rotation so that, with minor exceptions, each adult played each leader role in each of the groups. The same activities were used in each club by the device of letting the democratic clubs select an activity and then imposing the activity on the authoritarian clubs. In the laissez-faire situation there were a number of potential activities of the same types as those selected by the democratic clubs.

The authoritarian leader determined all policies, techniques, and activities, maintaining his autonomy by remaining aloof from the group except when demonstrating the next step in the activity. In the democratically-led groups all policies were determined by group discussion with the leader taking an active role. In the laissez-faire groups the leader did not take an active part, but left the group members free to reach individual or group decisions. During the period of 21 weekly meetings, the leadership style of each club was changed at least once.

Fig. 27 illustrates some of the major differences in the patterns of observed behavior of the leaders. The comparison of average percentage of acts in each category is based on four democratic, four authoritarian, and two laissez-faire roles. About 60 per cent of all behavior of the authoritarian leaders consisted of orders, disruptive commands, and nonconstructive criticism compared with only 5 per cent for the democratic and laissez-faire leaders.

Some of the major differences between the democratic and laissez-faire leadership roles are found in the next three behavior classifications: guiding suggestions, extending knowledge, and stimulating self-guidance. The democratic leader made more suggestions and stimulated self-guidance while the laissez-faire leader spent more of his time giving out information when it was asked for. In the last three categories, the

Figure 27—Comparison of Behavior of Average Authoritarian, Democratic, and Laissez-faire Leaders

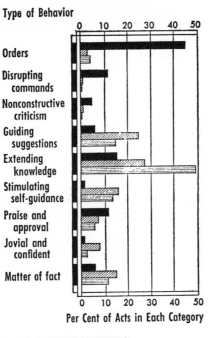

Type of Behavior

KEY TO CATEGORIES OF BEHAVIOR:
███ AUTHORITARIAN   ▨▨ DEMOCRATIC
▤▤ LAISSEZ-FAIRE

authoritarian gave more social recognition through social approval, the democratic leader was more jovial, and the laissez-faire leader more matter of fact.

During each experimental session four observers made a quantitative running account of social interaction, a minute-by-minute record of group structure, an interpretive running account of significant member interactions, and a continuous stenographic record of all conversation. These data were synchronized at minute intervals so that, when placed side by side, they furnished a continuous picture of the life of the group. In addition, interviews were held with club members, parents, and teachers.

The experimenters also postulated that a fruitful way to discover some of the major differences between the three types of group atmosphere would be to arrange comparable "test episodes" in each club. So at regular intervals the following events took place:

1. Leader arrived late.
2. Leader called away for an indeterminate time.
3. Stranger ("janitor" or "electrician") arrived while the leader was out and critically attacked work of an individual group member and then of the group as a whole.

§ Four Group Atmospheres

SOME OF THE MAJOR FINDINGS, summarized from stenographic records and other case material . . . are as follows: Two distinct types of reaction were shown to the same pattern of authoritarian leadership. All of the data, including the documentary films, indicated that three of the clubs responded with a dependent leaning on the adult leader, relatively low levels of frustration tension, and practically no capacity for initiating group action, while the fourth club demonstrated considerable frustration and some degree of channelized aggression toward the authoritarian leader. [This latter pattern is much more comparable to the behavior of the club under authoritarian leadership in a previous experimental study of two clubs (Lippitt, 1940)].

Fig. 28 indicates the major differences in the relations which developed between the group members and the adult leaders in the four resultant social atmospheres. In both types of authoritarian atmosphere, the members were markedly more dependent upon the leader than in either the democratic or laissez-faire situations, dependence being somewhat greater in the more passive clubs. All other clubs showed a somewhat greater feeling of discontent in their relations with the adult leader than did the members of the democratic clubs, members of the "aggressive autocracy" being outstanding in their expression of rebellious feelings. There is evidence from other sources that the actual "felt discontent" in the "apathetic autocracies" was somewhat higher than indicated by the conversation which was considerably more restricted than was that of the democratic and laissez-faire club members.

In both types of authoritarian situations the demands for attention from the adult were greater than in the other atmospheres. It seemed clear that getting the attention of the adult represented one of the few paths to more satisfactory social status in the authoritarian situation where all of the "central functions" of group life were in the hands of the dominator.

The category "friendly, confiding" indicates that the members of the democratic and laissez-faire clubs initiated more "personal" and friendly approaches to their adult leaders, and the data on "out-of-club-field conversation" further indicate the more spontaneous exchanging of confidences about other parts of one's life experience in the democratic club atmosphere.

Figure 28—Types of Group Reaction to Four Social Atmospheres

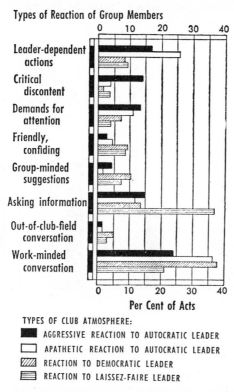

Types of Reaction of Group Members

TYPES OF CLUB ATMOSPHERE:
- ■ AGGRESSIVE REACTION TO AUTOCRATIC LEADER
- ☐ APATHETIC REACTION TO AUTOCRATIC LEADER
- ▨ REACTION TO DEMOCRATIC LEADER
- ☰ REACTION TO LAISSEZ-FAIRE LEADER

The data on "group-minded suggestions" to the leader show that the members in the democratic atmosphere felt much freer and more inclined to make suggestions on matters of group policy than in the other three group atmospheres. It is clear from other data that the lower level of suggestions in the laissez-faire situation is not because of any feeling of restricted freedom but because of a lack of a cooperative working relationship between the adult and the other group members.

The much greater responsibility of the members of the laissez-faire clubs to get their own information is shown by the fact that about 37 per cent of their behavior toward their leader consisted of asking for information, as compared to about 15 per cent in the other three club situations.

The final category in [Fig. 28] "work-minded conversation," indicates that a considerably larger proportion of the initiated approaches of the club members to their leaders were related to on-going club activity in the democratic and in the apathetic authoritarian situations than in the other two types of social climate (Lippitt & White, 1952, pp. 346-347).

Figure 29—Time Spent in High Activity Involvement by Groups of Four Leadership-Atmosphere Types According to Whether Leader Was In or Out

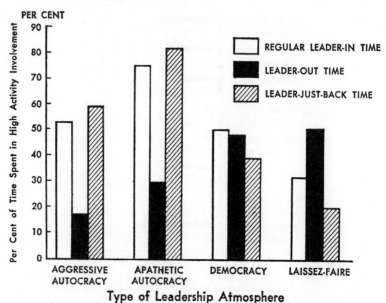

Type of Leadership Atmosphere

In Fig. 29 a comparison is made between the four types of groups in the amount of productivity when the leader was in the room, when he had left the room, and just after he had returned. While the leader was out, both types of authoritarian groups did very little, the democratic groups remained about as productive as they were, while the laissez-faire groups became more productive. Similar results were obtained when the leader was late. The authors suggest that the high rate of productivity for the laissez-faire group may have resulted from the fact that one of the boys who was a good leader was able to take over the group.

When groups which had previously been led by authoritarian leaders were shifted to a freer democratic or laissez-faire group atmosphere (Fig. 30) they showed a great burst of horseplay on the first day, an indication of unexpressed group tension. This need to "blow off" disappeared with more meetings in the freer atmosphere.

When the groups were subject to the hostile criticism of a strange adult (e.g., "janitor"), differences in reaction were also noted.

Figure 30—Amount of Horseplay by Group Members under Change in Leadership Type

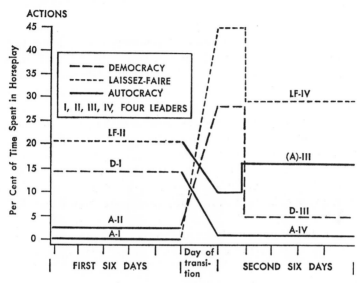

Period of Time Under Two Leadership Types

Members of the apathetic authoritarian clubs tended to accept individually and to internalize the unjust criticism or, in one or two cases, they "blew off steam" in aggressive advances toward an out-group [the other club meeting in the adjacent clubroom]. In the aggressive authoritarian situation, the frustration was typically channeled in aggression toward the out-group, although in several cases there was some direct reaction to the source of frustration, the hostile stranger. In the democratic atmospheres there was evidence of a greater readiness to unite in rejection of the real sourc of frustration, the stranger, and to resist out-group aggression (Lippitt & White, 1952, pp. 349-350).

When the overall productivity ratings of the three types of groups were compared, the authoritarian groups were highest in *quantity*, while the democratic groups were judged to be better in *quality*. This same tendency for authoritarian leadership to result in greater quantitative productivity and democratic leadership to result in higher morale has been noted in other studies (Gibb, 1951; Adams, 1954).

§ Other Similar
Leader Styles

OTHER VARIATIONS on the authoritarian-democratic theme use somewhat similar leader roles with discussion groups rather than activity groups (Fox, 1957; Ziller, 1957a, 1958; Bevan, Albert, Loiseaux, Mayfield, & Wright, 1958). In general, when leaders who have an active and positive relationship with their discussion groups are contrasted with those who hold negative attitudes, a greater incidence of supportive acts among members is reported for the positively led groups and a greater incidence of opposing acts in the negatively led groups. In addition, there tends to be a greater acceptance on the part of the members of opposing behavior in the negatively led groups, so that opposers receive high popularity ratings and are more highly satisfied with the group decision.

Some of these same effects were observed in a study of the relationship between the behavior of B-29 commanders in the air corps and the attitudes of their crew members. When the leader was considerate, the friendship, willingness, and confidence of the members increased (Christner & Hemphill, 1955).

Experiments have also been performed with discussion groups comparing "participatory" leaders who take part in the discussion and try to insure an equal chance for participation to all group members, and "supervisory" leaders who do not take part but whose job it is to make sure the group finishes the discussion on time. The data indicate that participatory leadership is more effective as a technique for changing opinion. The participatory leader has more influence on the group decision and the followers are better satisfied with the result of the group decision, apparently because each has had an opportunity to express his opinion even though it may not have been accepted by the group (Preston & Heintz, 1949; Hare, 1953).

It can be assumed that the leader who facilitates free discussion among the members will be more effective when the group task requires free discussion among peers. Many tasks, however, require for their successful completion more frequent participation by the more skillful members and a hierarchy of power and influence (Horowitz & Perlmutter, 1955).

§ Teacher-Centered
versus
Learner-Centered Classes

In learning situations two contrasting styles have been called "teacher-centered" and "learner-centered." In the examples given in Exhibit 21, the task-centered, demanding teachers were found to elicit from students hostility, apathy, and other signs of withdrawal, whereas accepting student-supportive teachers decreased anxiety and produced greater interaction and positive feeling among members both in class and outside the classroom (Thelen & Withall, 1949; Perkins, 1950, 1951; Bovard, 1951a, 1951b, 1952, 1956a, 1956b; Flanders, 1951; Di Vesta, 1954; Singer & Goldman, 1954; Gordon, 1955; Wischmeier, 1955; Zimet & Fine, 1955). Women appeared to be more affected by these changes in the classroom situation than men (McKeachie, 1958).

Some observers report more learning in the "learner-centered" classes, although some students prefer the more directive classes for examination preparation. Little difference has been found when students from both types of classes are given the same examination (Zeleny, 1940a; Wispe, 1951, 1953; Watson, 1953; Haigh & Schmidt, 1956; Maloney, 1956; Rasmussen, 1956). In addition, permissive instruction may increase the ambiguity of the teaching situation unless group members have the skills to set and achieve goals (McKeachie, 1954b). Dull children may do better under "teacher-centered" instruction (Calvin et al., 1957).

Differences similar to those between "teacher-centered" and "learner-centered" classes have been found between large lecture groups and small discussion groups. In both the "teacher-centered" discussion and the large lecture, a learning situation is created in which one person talks most of the time and has a superior position in the hierarchy of control, while the possibilities for close, intimate relations between members are limited. In contrast, in the "learner-centered" groups and the small discussion groups, all members receive their share of talking time, control is relatively equal, and intimacy prevails.

§ Democratic Leaders in Autocracies

In INDUSTRIAL ORGANIZATIONS and the armed services where members expect the leader to play an autocratic role, attempts to introduce more democratic procedures usually result in member dissatisfaction and low productivity which is similar to that usually associated with autocratic leadership in a democratic culture. In a study of 72 conferences in industry and government, leadership sharing was found to be negatively related to the attractiveness of the group and satisfaction with the conference (Berkowitz, 1953). In this population, the chairman was expected to exert a strong central control over the meetings and attempts of other members to make frequent proposals for the solution of problems were discouraged. However, if the group had an urgent problem, sharing leadership had no relation to satisfaction, apparently because members were free to deviate from the norms in times of crisis. In other industrial studies high productivity in a shop has been found to be associated with a well differentiated and authoritative style of leadership (Gekoski, 1952; Kahn & Katz, 1953).

In an air corps study, bomber-crew critiques of training problems were held with different types of leadership (Torrance, 1953b). Crews with critiques which were structured by having a well defined leader and procedure, more frequently showed improvement in a subsequent problem-solving situation than those with less structured critiques. In addition crews with an unstructured, nonauthoritarian leader and those who had no leader assigned but held a "self-critique" did no better than crews receiving no critique.

Similar findings are reported in studies of the smallest autocracies, the doctor and patient in a therapeutic interview. Here progress is found to be associated with high frequencies of directive, interpretive remarks on the part of the therapist (Keet, 1948; Dittman, 1952; Wiener, 1955).

Persons who make a successful adjustment to one regime may find that they lose some of their power when the leadership style is changed. In a training school for adolescent boys, two cottages were studied over an eight-month period while the government of one of the cottages was changed from the usual form of an adult-dominated quasi-autocracy to greater self-government. Before the change took place, independent measures of popularity and dominance were obtained for the boys in both cottages. A high positive correlation between rated dominance and sociometric popularity was found in both groups before the period of "democratization," supporting the hypothesis that the openly dominant boy in an autocratic society will be admired because he dares to react in the fashion that others would imitate if it were not for the fear of punishment. When the same measures of popularity and dominance were repeated eight months later, the correlation had dropped until it was not significantly different from zero in the group which had been democratized, while in the control group the correlation had increased. The increase in popularity among the originally least popular boys in the experimental group was more marked than the decrease in popularity among the six most dominant boys (McCandless, 1942). This is perhaps an indication that a change in a group's culture may make originally deviant individuals more popular, but may have less influence on the popularity of leaders since they will tend to adapt their leader style to fit the new customs.

§ Situational Factors

LEADERS CAN BE CREATED in the group by increasing the distance between members in the areas of control or affection, so that more initiating and controlling activity is required to maintain a productive group. When the communication network is arranged so that one person is in the center of the net and receives the greatest number of messages, the central members will tend to become the leader (Leavitt, 1951). Similar effects are obtained by reducing the number of messages which can be sent by the average group member through an increase in group size (Hemphill, 1950). Leaders can also be created by distributing power, prestige, or skill unequally in the group, or by giving the group a task which requires a division of labor. In such a situation, the person who provides the control or who has the greatest skill will tend to become the leader. Even in a group in which differences in ability are not a major factor, subjects who appear to be accepted by others will make more attempts to lead (Pepinsky, Hemphill, & Shevitz, 1958).

§ Distributed Leadership

STUDIES OF initially leaderless groups often report that the leadership functions are distributed between a task leader and a social-emotional leader (Bales & Slater, 1955; Slater, 1955; Bales, 1958; Parker, 1958), or that the individual who receives the most nominations for leadership is not necessarily the one who is best liked (Hollander & Webb, 1955). Similar differences appear in organized groups. In the air corps, for example, both in behavior and ideology the educational administrators showed greater consideration for the enlisted men and less organizing activity than did aircraft commanders (Halpin, 1955a, 1955b).

An exception to this tendency to distribute leader functions has been observed in labor mediations which involve only three persons: the mediator, a representative of management, and a representative of labor. It is the function of the labor mediator to guide the parties toward a settlement by his suggestions and powers of persuasion and thus to provide task leadership. Yet, because of the dispute separating and often alienating the parties, none of them is in a position to serve as the social-emotional leader. As a result the labor mediator must also perform this second type of leadership (Landsberger, 1955a).

§ Summary

THE GENERAL FUNCTIONS of the leader role and the traits of the persons who typically become leaders are related to the needs of the small task group. Since the needs of the group depend in turn upon the culture in which the group operates and the personalities of the members, the actual characteristics of the leader role are not the same for all groups.

Different leader styles may be imposed upon groups to create differences in the interaction process. To specify the leader style is, in effect, to give rather explicit directions to *one* group member about the nature of the task and the type of communication network which will be permitted, as well as setting the emotional tone which will pervade the interaction.

Potential leaders usually receive higher ratings than other group members on *traits* such as intelligence, enthusiasm, dominance, self-confidence, and social participation. These traits tend to be found in clusters which have been described as "authoritarian" and "equalitarian." The leaders who emerge in leaderless group discussions tend to be more authoritarian, presumably because more authoritarian behavior is required to establish a position than to maintain one.

Some leaders serve the *functions* of pace setter and coordinator for both task and social-emotional behavior. However, there may be role confusion for the leader, if superiors and inferiors or other reference groups have conflicting expectations for his behavior.

Although a single "leader" may be the controlling member in a group, other types of central persons also appear as objects of identification, objects of drives, and as ego-supports. Redl has described ten of these types: patriarchal sovereign, leader, tyrant, idol, scapegoat, organizer, seducer, hero, bad influence, and good example. Each of these central persons has power over other group members which will be enhanced if he is placed in a position of formal leadership.

The leaderless group discussion and other forms of situational tests were developed principally in the armed services to select potential leaders. A high leadership rating for a candidate in a situational test has been found to have a positive correlation with performance in organizational activity. Consistency of leadership behavior is especially high between situations which are similar in the social characteristics of members, group size, and task, even if the membership of the group is changed. The effectiveness of the individual possessing the traits of leadership can generally be improved if he is given training for his role.

In the experiments by Lewin, Lippitt, and White contrasting three group atmospheres, members of the authoritarian groups showed more dependency on the leader and more hostile and apathetic behavior between members. In the laissez-faire groups there was little dependency on the leader but greater irritability and aggressiveness among members and dissatisfaction with the task. The democratic group showed less dependency on the leader, more friendliness, and satisfaction with the activities of the club. The autocratic groups surpassed the others in quantity of output, but the products of the democratic groups were judged to be of the best quality.

This same tendency for autocratic leadership to result in greater quantitative productivity and democratic leadership to result in higher morale has been reported in other studies which contrast supervisory and participatory leadership and teacher-centered and learner-centered teachers.

Autocratic leaders are most effective in situations such as industry or the armed forces in which the task requires strong, centralized control. Similar leader roles can be created in the laboratory by increasing group size and channeling all communication through a central member. Leadership functions may be distributed between a task leader who deals primarily with productivity and a social-emotional leader who deals with interpersonal relationships.

Exhibit 18
Traits of Leaders

A.

Investigator: Chevaleva-Ianouskaia & Sylla (1929).
Focus: A study of leaders among children.
Sample: Four hundred groups of children.
Method: After determining the child who was the leader in one group, they placed him in a new group situation and rated the changes in the group and changes in leadership under diverse social conditions.
Relevant Findings: The leader was distinguished by a higher rating on duration of verbal excitation, rapidity in formation of associative reactions, predominance of processes of excitation over those of inhibition, facility in positive induction, difficulty in negative induction, adequacy of reaction, and degree of differentiation of reactions.

B.

Investigator: Goodenough (1930).
Focus: Inter-relationships in the behavior of young children.
Sample: 33 nursery-school children, seventeen boys and sixteen girls, age range two to five years.
Method: Each observer secured a total of 25 one-minute observations of each subject. Each observation was made on a different day and no two persons observed a child at the same time. During a training period observers reached at least 95 per cent reliability on the variables rated.
Relevant Findings: Leadership behavior was correlated (approximately .60) with physical activity, talkativeness, laughter, and social participation.

C.

Investigator: Partridge (1934).
Focus: Leadership among adolescent boys.
Sample: 143 boys in a summer camp and 226 boys in six urban Boy Scout troops.
Method: In summer camp, boys chose leaders who were compared with the other boys in camp on a number of characteristics.
Relevant Findings: The ten most popular leaders were on the average

more than twenty months older than the mean for the entire population in camp. Intelligence test scores were associated with popularity as a leader.

Method: In the Scout troops, the boys were asked to rate each other on five different traits: intelligence, dependability, athletic ability, appearance, and leadership.

Relevant Findings: The boys associated the four traits with leadership in the following order of importance: (1) intelligence, (2) dependability, (3) appearance, (4) athletic ability. A comparison among the various groups and between the camp studies and the troop studies showed a relationship between the length of time the group had been together and the intelligence of those they recognized as leaders. There was evidence that constant social interaction brought the intelligent individuals to the front as leaders.

D.

Investigator: Zeleny (1939).

Focus: Characteristics of group leaders.

Sample: Two studies of 56 students in classroom discussion groups of five or six students with student leaders.

Method: Observations of interaction were correlated with leadership and sociometric rankings of the students.

Relevant Findings: Participation, self-confidence, and prestige were the traits which distinguished leaders from nonleaders most clearly on a rating scale of leadership traits scored by participants.

E.

Investigator: Stogdill (1948).

Focus: Personal factors associated with leadership: a survey of the literature.

Sample: Only those factors which were studied by three or more investigators.

Method: A review of the literature.

Relevant Findings: The factors which are associated with leadership can be classified under the following headings:

1. *Capacity*—appearance, fluency of speech, intelligence, soundness of judgment and thought, insight, and originality.
2. *Achievement*—better students, specialized knowledge, and ability to get things done.
3. *Responsibility*—dependability, integrity and strength of convictions, and self-confidence.
4. *Participation*—adaptability, social and physical activity and mobility, sociability, co-operativeness, and ability to enlist co-operation.
5. *Status*—popularity.

Leadership is not a passive status or a combination of traits but a working relationship among members of a group. The leader acquires status through active participation and demonstration of his capacity for carrying co-operative tasks through to completion.

F.

Investigator: Van Dusen (1948).
Focus: Measuring leadership ability.
Sample: 245 Boys Scouts in groups of six to eight boys.
Method: Each boy was asked to choose the three boys who he thought would make the best patrol leaders, to choose the three who would be the poorest leaders, and to give reasons for each choice.
Relevant Findings: The dimensions of leadership in the order in which they were most often mentioned are: (a) interest and knowledge of the main group activity, (2) co-operativeness, (3) adaptability, and (4) honesty.

G.

Investigator: Martin, Gross, & Darley (1952).
Focus: Studies of group behavior: leaders, followers, and isolates in small organized groups.
Sample: The total population of a midwestern university co-operative girls' village consisting of thirteen residence units was divided into three groups: leaders, followers, and isolates. In this way 37 leaders were identified on the basis of the frequency with which they were chosen on several sociometric criteria as well as the fact of official recognition by election to office.
Method: Analyses and comparison of over one hundred variables from Minnesota Personality Scale, indices of socio-economic status, self-estimates, and peer ratings.
Relevant Findings: Leaders, followers, and isolates, sociometrically defined, were compared. Leaders were found superior in identification with middle class attitudes and self-appraisal of motor skills. Informal leadership was associated with lower socio-economic status; being both a formal and informal leader was associated with confidence. Few distinguishing features of leaders were found by the trait approach.

H.

Investigator: Cattell & Stice (1954).
Focus: Four formulae for selecting leaders on the basis of personality.
Sample: 34 groups of ten men; fourteen groups were candidates who had just arrived for officer candidate school in the air force and twenty of the groups were subjects who had just arrived to begin boot training.

Method: Each group performed for three sessions of three hours each in a wide variety of small group performances. Four leadership categories were designated: (1) persistent momentary problem solvers, picked for frequency of brief acts as leaders, (2) salient leaders who were observed to have a powerful influence on the group, (3) sociometric leaders as perceived by group members, (4) elected leaders chosen by voluntary election after experience in the group. These types of leaders were compared with each other and with nonleaders on 16 variables measured by personality tests and observation.

Relevant Findings: Leaders were higher than nonleaders on character integration or superego strength, absence of worrying "anxiousness," adventurous cyclothymia, deliberate will control, emotional maturity, dominance, polished fastidiousness, and absence of nervous tension (P. < .05). Problem-solving leaders were higher in general intelligence and elected leaders higher in surgency.

Exhibit 19
Leadership Functions

A.

Investigator: Roff (1950).

Focus: A study of combat leadership in the air force by means of a rating scale.

Sample: 350 bomber pilots rating subordinates, 204 fighter pilots rating subordinates, 474 bomber pilots rating superiors, and 275 fighter pilots rating superiors.

Method: A rating scale of characteristics relating to effectiveness in combat leadership was administered to flying officers to obtain information concerning the importance of different types of behavior in the command situation.

Relevant Findings: In a comparison of ratings made of officers considered very successful leaders with those made of officers considered very poor, the single characteristic found to discriminate most was ease of maintaining discipline on the ground. Characteristics such as severity, impartiality, and lack of concern for personal advantage were as effective in discriminating the upper from the lower groups as items relating to combat flying proficiency. Age and amount of formal education did not discriminate between these two groups.

B.

Investigator: Stogdill (1950).

Focus: Leadership, membership, and organization.

Method: Review of the literature.

Relevant Findings: Leadership is a process of influencing the activities of an organized group in its task of goal setting and goal achievement. A leader has authority. "Authority is an interactional process by means of which the organization defines for each individual the scope for action he has in making decisions, carrying out responsibilities, and enlisting the cooperation of others.

C.

Investigator: Halpin (1954).

Focus: The leadership behavior and combat performance of airplane commanders.

Sample: 52 B-29 crews.

Method: A factor analysis of the responses obtained from three hundred questionnaires.

Relevant Findings: Two major dimensions of leadership were identified: Consideration and Initiating Structure-in-Interaction. The correlation between these dimension scores was .45. The first factor was associated with behavior indicative of mutual trust, respect, and a certain warmth between commander and his crew. The second factor implied the organization and definition by the commander of the roles and expectations of each member of the crew.

D.

Investigator: Wilson, High, & Comrey (1955).

Focus: An iterative analysis of supervisor and group dimensions.

Sample: Questionnaires of one hundred shipyard workers.

Method: Iterative analysis of questionnaire responses.

Relevant Findings: Four supervisory dimensions were derived: lack of arbitrariness, communication, safety enforcement, and social nearness.

E.

Investigator: Stogdill & Coons (1957).

Focus: Description and measurement of leader behavior.

Sample: A collection of the Ohio State University leadership studies.

Method: A factor analysis of Hemphill's leader behavior description questionnaire.

Relevant Findings: Four factors were derived with the first and second factors accounting for 83 per cent of the factor variance: consideration, initiating structure, production emphasis, and sensitivity.

Exhibit 20
Leadership Training

A.

Investigator: Bavelas (1942).

Focus: Morale and the training of leaders.

Sample: Six "mediocre" WPA project playground leaders of children. Three experimental leaders were paired with three control leaders who were similar in age, sex, length of time on WPA, length of time on present WPA project, rating of technical skill, rating of leadership ability, and as far as possible on the relevant factors in their life history.

Method: All six leaders were tested by observing and quantitatively recording their actual behavior with the children "on the job." The three experimental leaders were then trained for three weeks by "sensitizing," broadening and restructuring the goal region and developing new techniques. The leaders continued working with their groups of children during the training period. At the fourth week, both the trained and nontrained leaders were tested again "on the job" by the same methods used at the beginning of the experiment.

Relevant Findings: After the experiment leader B, who had not been trained, still used authoritarian methods of direct control in over 80 per cent of his actions, while leader A (with similar characteristics) who had been trained and who formerly used authoritarian control 77 per cent of the time had dropped to 4 per cent and his democratic behavior increased from less than 5 per cent to 73 per cent. Similar changes were observed in the other two trained leaders. After the training period the average size of sub groups in which children worked was 2.5 for the trained leaders and 1.7 for untrained compared with a pre-experiment average of 1.2 for both types of groups. The shift of trained leaders from "classroom techniques" to "group methods" was evident in: (1) an increase in the number of children attracted to participate, (2) the enthusiasm and persistence of the group, (3) the "holding power" of the group for individuals, (4) the efficiency of the work organization, (5) the high degree of self-discipline, and (6) the quality and output of work.

B.

Investigator: Maier (1953).

Focus: An experimental test on the effect of training on discussion leadership.

Sample: 44 four-man groups in which the leader received eight hours of training in group discussion (the leader was chosen at random) and 36 other groups who were given no training except a lecture introducing them to the problem. All participants were industrial personnel, either first-line supervisors or intermediate managers.

Method: All groups were given a role-playing problem in which one member played a foreman and the other three his employees on a sub-assembly job. They were to discuss a problem of improving the work situation. The degree of success was measured by the type of decision, if any, they achieved.

Relevant Findings: 50 per cent of the control groups accepted the change in work methods suggested by the foreman, whereas 50 per cent rejected his recommendations. In the trained group, 59 per cent accepted the above mentioned change, 5 per cent refused to make any changes, while 36 per cent arrived at compromise decision. Only 11 per cent of the employees were regarded by trained foremen as problems, while the untrained foremen said that 25 per cent of their group members were problems. Employee satisfaction was also greater in groups with trained leaders.

C.

Investigator: Klubeck & Bass (1954).

Focus: Differential effects of training on persons of different leadership status.

Subjects: Twenty girls selected from each of seven different sororities at a state university. The 140 subjects were then divided into twenty groups, each of which contained a subject from each of the seven sororities so that the majority of the girls in each group were not well acquainted.

Method: The twenty groups of seven girls held leaderless group discussions before and after training. Member's behavior during discussion was ranked on a five-point scale on seven variables: effectiveness, good solution, initiative, giving orientation, motivating others to participate, influencing others, and leading the group. Observer reliability was .83. The training consisted of a discussion of some of the necessary qualities of leadership. The forty girls who ranked third and sixth in leadership status in their group (as obtained through behavior scores) were given training, the others were not.

Relevant Findings: There was a significant gain on a leaderless group discussion score (a combination of the seven variables) for the members who received training (Prob. < .01). However, the girls who had ranked third in their groups prior to training had the greatest increase in score while those who had ranked sixth were relatively unaffected by the training.

D.

Investigator: Barnlund (1955).

Focus: Experiments in leadership training for decision-making groups.

Sample: Sixteen experimental and ten control subjects. All were rated least effective by their classmates.

Method: An entire class was divided into small discussion groups. The average leadership ability of the members as measured by their classmates was the same for all groups. The experimental subjects were given a two-week leadership training course. They were rated by observers both before and after the training period.

Relevant Findings: Trained leaders showed an increase in initiating discussion, regulating the amount of participation, and resolving conflict.

E.

Investigator: Harris & Fleishman (1955).

Focus: Human relations training and the stability of leadership patterns.

Sample: Two groups of 31 foremen each of whom had been to the Central School in Chicago.

Method: Training was given to 31 of 72 foremen. Questionnaires were administered before and after training on worker's opinion of foreman and foreman's own leadership attitudes.

Relevant Findings: Although the trained foremen showed somewhat more change in attitude, their mean scores on questionnaire items were not significantly different from the entire group.

Exhibit 21
Teacher-centered vs. Learner-centered Classes

A.

Investigator: Thelen & Withall (1949).
Focus: Three frames of reference: the description of climate.
Sample: Two groups of students in a college laboratory classroom.
Method: Teacher-centered and learner-centered emotional climates, created by experimental teachers, were measured by observers' ratings, self-involved observers using two sets of illustrative behavior as norms, and pupils' reactions registered by push-buttons on an audience-reaction machine. Gross agreement was found between the three methods, although they differed in the depth and number of aspects presented.
Relevant Findings: The teacher-centered approach produced and maintained a higher degree of interpersonal conflict.

B.

Investigator: Perkins (1950).
Focus: The effects of climate and curriculum on group learning.
Sample: Six groups of in-service teachers representing two kinds of climate, group-centered and leader-centered, and three curriculum levels, first-, second-, and third-year child study.
Method: An instrument for categorizing the reported verbal statements of the subjects was developed and used in analyzing the data. The final form of the instrument contained categories for evaluating four kinds of learning: expressed child development concepts, quality of attitudes toward children, quality of statement substantiation, and quality of insight or overall mental process revealed.
Relevant Findings: Group-centered groups revealed a significantly higher ratio of expressed child-development concepts to total statements, an indication that they had learned more. In addition more of their expressed attitudes toward children were objective and warm. A greater proportion of the members supported their statements by quoting scientific or personal evidence and made statements which indicated real insight and sound quality of overall mental process.

C.

Investigator: Bovard (1951a).

Focus: Group structure and perception.

Sample: 119 students in four sections from an elementary course (leader-centered) and 119 students in six sections from an interpersonal relations course (group-centered).

Method: The members of each group under test were asked to estimate anonymously the length of a rectangle, they were then informed of the individual estimates and the average for the group and finally they were asked to re-estimate the length. The announced purpose of the experiment was to determine the effect of passage of time on accuracy of perception.

Relevant Findings: Group-centered classes showed more initial dispersion and greater shift toward a norm in judging the length of the rectangle than did the leader-centered classes.

D.

Investigator: Bovard (1951b).

Focus: The experimental production of interpersonal affect.

Sample: Six "stable" groups whose members had met together voluntarily for an average of 231 hours and were extremely likely to continue meeting together. Total membership 55. Seven "temporary" groups whose members had met together for an average of 2.47 hours and were not likely to continue meeting voluntarily. Total membership was 53.

Method: The groups were divided into leader-centered and group-centered. The verbal interaction was observed. Each individual was asked to indicate his liking for other group members on a five-point scale and to rate himself at the point on the scale where he would best like the group as a whole to put him.

Relevant Findings: More member-to-member verbal interaction took place in the group-centered groups and members rated each other higher on liking.

E.

Investigator: Flanders (1951).

Focus: Personal-social anxiety as a factor in experimental learning situations.

Sample: Seven subjects.

Method: Two adults were trained as "learner-centered" and "teacher-centered" teachers. All verbal statements made by each student were recorded. Each student was taught to use a lever, hidden from the teacher's view, to indicate positive and negative feelings as they were associated with working on the achievement task. The student pulse (heart beat) and skin resistance were recorded during all evaluation and learning periods.

Relevant Findings: Teacher-centered behavior elicited student behavior of hostility toward self or the teacher, withdrawal, apathy, aggressiveness, and emotional disintegration. Learner-centered behavior elicited student behavior of problem orientation, decreased interpersonal anxiety, integration, and emotional readjustment. In all cases the student's ability to name, elaborate, use, and recall the principles in question was greater for learner-centered periods.

F.

Investigator: Bovard (1952).

Focus: Clinical insight as a function of group process.

Sample: One leader-centered discussion group (sixteen members) and one group-centered discussion group (22 members) of an elementary psychology course.

Method: The major procedural difference between the two group processes was amount of member-to-member interaction, maximized in group-centered and held to a minimum in leader-centered. Wire recordings were made of a discussion of the film "The Feeling of Rejection." By this time each section had already met for a total of 39 hours. The two typescripts of the discussion were coded to determine relative orientation toward feelings, and relative amount of identification with the girl patient in the film evidenced in each. Two clinical psychologists then made blind analyses of both typescripts, independently of one another to determine the relative amount of clinical insight shown by each group into the problem.

Relevant Findings: Group-centered process leads to greater communication of feeling, more identification with another person and greater clinical insight into personality dynamics than the leader-centered process.

G.

Investigator: DiVesta (1954).

Focus: Instructor-centered and student-centered approaches in teaching a human relations course.

Sample: 94 airmen in sixteen six-man groups.

Method: Half of the groups were instructor-centered in which the instructor evaluated suggestions, techniques, and activities, and was the focus of attention. In the student-centered groups, the instructor encouraged suggestions from the class; techniques and activities emerged from class discussion, and the instructor was the focus of attention only when his advice was directly sought. The groups were given four tests on human relations problems, followed by a twenty-hour block of instruction, and a posttest.

Relevant Findings: The use of the student-centered discussion method appeared to have a slight advantage over the instructor-centered approach in improving leadership ability but no apparent difference on knowledge gained or attitude changed.

H.

Investigator: McKeachie (1954b).
Focus: Student-centered *vs.* instructor-centered instruction.
Method: Review of literature.
Relevant Findings: The effect of instructor permissiveness may well depend upon whether or not the group possesses the skills necessary to achieve their goals. In a new group the effect of instructor permissiveness may depend upon the presence or absence of individuals in the group who have had previous experience in working with democratic groups. If the instructor retains control of rewards, permissiveness with respect to means to the goal (such as assignments and classroom activities) may simply increase the ambiguity of the situation for the student and reduce student learning.

I.

Investigator: Singer & Goldman (1954).
Focus: Experimentally contrasted social atmospheres in group psychotherapy with chronic schizophrenics.
Sample: Two groups of ten patients each.
Method: Groups met weekly for therapeutic sessions over a five-month period. The "authoritarian" group was conducted in classroom atmosphere with lectures. The "democratic" group was conducted by therapists encouraging free expression and group participation in decisions and interpretations. Ratings were made for group cohesiveness, the amount of relevant material discussed, and direction of interpersonal communication.
Relevant Findings: Despite an initially greater proportion of relevant comments by patients, the authoritarian group declined rapidly in later sessions, while the democratic, less organized group in time surpassed it in this respect. In both actions and verbalization, the democratic group was rated higher on morale and cohesiveness.

J.

Investigator: Wischmeier (1955).
Focus: Group-centered and leader-centered leadership: an experimental study.

Sample: College students observed in a discussion group, divided into eight groups of approximately equal discussion ability.

Method: Sociometric questionnaires, rating scales for group member feelings, and ratings of four observers were compared for two discussion sessions of each group. In one session the designated leader played a leader-centered role and in the other a group-centered role.

Relevant Findings: Little difference was found between sessions in the subject's attitude toward the leader. On the sociometric questionnaire, all groups ranked the leader-centered leader significantly higher in terms of the value of his contributions to the discussion. Group-centered discussions showed more involvement, a warmer and friendlier atmosphere, greater ease in making contributions, and more co-operation.

K.

Investigator: Zimet & Fine (1955).

Focus: Personality changes with a group therapeutic experience in a human relations seminar.

Sample: Fifteen school administrators. Average experience thirteen years.

Method: The group met for sixteen weekly sessions of five hours each (two-hour periods separated by an hour for dinner). In the predinner meeting the group was given a lecture while the postdinner meeting was more oriented toward group discussion. Attitude and participation scales were used to measure the behavioral and perceptual effects.

Relevant Findings: While initially more defensive, the group-centered climate contributed more to a rapid and sustained positive gain than the lecture group. The lecture group did not show statistically significant gains in member interaction until it was changed to group-centered. After this change in orientation members of both groups were found to have had positive changes in attitude toward self, other adults, and children. Members also became more democratic with individuals, showing less need to be in command and to gain respect, but more concern about understanding, respecting, and aiding others.

L.

Investigator: Maloney (1956).

Focus: Group learning through group discussion: a group discussion implementation analysis.

Sample: Two groups of fifteen college students matched on academic ability measured by the Ohio State Psychological Examination, grades, and social-emotional adjustment by the Washburne Social Adjustment Inventory.

Method: Both groups met for period of twelve days. In the experimental class, the instructor sought to implement rather than lead the discussion. In the control group, no precise method was followed and often the instructor led the discussion. An observer was present in each group to record verbal and behavioral indices.

Relevant Findings: In the group in which discussion was "implemented" members learned neither more nor less, participated more in the discussion, sat closer together, liked each other more, and had no more problems.

Part Three

PERFORMANCE CHARACTERISTICS

*I*N THIS, the third and final section of the book, the literature on social interaction in small groups is reviewed again with emphasis upon the comparative performance characteristics of individuals and groups. In Part One some of the central tendencies in groups were considered in the chapters on the formation of norms and social control, the interaction process, roles, and interpersonal choice. Then in Part Two some of the variations from these central tendencies were described: variations which resulted from changes in the composition of the group or in the task, communication network, or leadership. Now in the third part of the book these central tendencies and variations in group behavior will be judged against a criterion of productivity.

Chapter Twelve, in which the productivity of the individual and the small group are compared, is based primarily upon the "together" and "apart" experiments and the child-study literature of the early 1900's. Chapter Thirteen serves as a summary of the whole book in a comparison of the productivity of groups with different characteristics.

PRODUCTIVITY:

Individual

versus Group

S OME OF THE EARLIEST EXPERIMENTS in social psychology compared the behavior of the individual when working alone with his behavior in the presence of others. Much of this early work was done by educators who were interested in finding out if schoolwork or homework could be better performed by the student when working alone or when others in the room were working on the same task (Mayer, 1903; Meuman, 1904; Schmidt, 1904; Burnham, 1905; Moede, 1914). This interest was revived by Floyd Allport in the 1920's (1920, 1924) and has survived to the present day as a focus of social-psychological research. The studies of group problem-solving and the comparisons of individuals and groups in the solution of problems which followed the work of Munsterberg (1914) were an offshoot of this main stem. These early "together" and "apart" studies and other researches appearing between 1898 and 1930 are listed in Fig. 31. Some of these

Figure 31

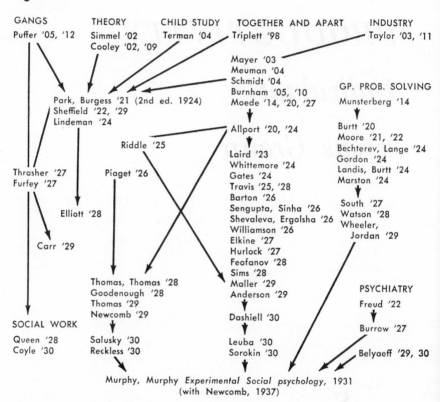

GANGS
Puffer '05, '12

THEORY
Simmel '02
Cooley '02, '09

CHILD STUDY
Terman '04

TOGETHER AND APART
Triplett '98

INDUSTRY
Taylor '03, '11

Mayer '03
Meuman '04
Schmidt '04
Burnham '05, '10
Moede '14, '20, '27

GP. PROB. SOLVING
Munsterberg '14

Park, Burgess '21 (2nd ed. 1924)
Sheffield '22, '29
Lindeman '24

Allport '20, '24

Burtt '20
Moore '21, '22
Bechterev, Lange '24
Gordon '24
Landis, Burtt '24
Marston '24

Riddle '25

Laird '23
Whittemore '24
Gates '24
Travis '25, '28
Barton '26
Sengupta, Sinha '26
Shevaleva, Ergolsha '26
Williamson '26
Elkine '27
Hurlock '27
Feofanov '28
Sims '28
Maller '29
Anderson '29

Thrasher '27
Furfey '27

Piaget '26

South '27
Watson '28
Wheeler,
Jordan '29

Elliott '28

Carr '29

PSYCHIATRY
Freud '22

Thomas, Thomas '28
Goodenough '28
Thomas '29
Newcomb '29

Dashiell '30

Burrow '27

SOCIAL WORK
Queen '28
Coyle '30

Salusky '30
Reckless '30

Leuba '30
Sorokin '30

Belyaeff '29, 30

Murphy, Murphy *Experimental Social psychology,* 1931
(with Newcomb, 1937)

studies are given in more detail in the present chapter and others have been included in previous chapters in the text.

This outline includes the major contributions to small group research from about 1900 to 1930. The influence of early contributions on later work is indicated by the arrows. The criterion for influence most frequently used is that the earlier author is cited by the later author in text or footnote. Only the major connections are indicated, so that with a few exceptions the authors who are listed in the same column may be assumed to be familiar with the work of those above them. Although Taylor (1903) studied the influence of group norms on productivity, his followers in "scientific management" focused only on the individual, so that industrial studies do not appear again until the mid 1930's. Since the Murphys summarized most of the major contributions in their 1931 text (revised with Newcomb, 1937), the year 1930 was selected as a cutting point for a detailed analysis of influence.

Some indication of the place of small group research in the general development of research in social psychology and sociology is given in several published reviews (Cottrell & Gallagher, 1941; Wilson, 1945; Shils, 1948, 1951; Ansbacher, 1951; Faris, 1953).

The presence of others working on the same task has been found to stimulate some individuals to greater productivity, distract others, and leave others unaffected. Usually one skilled individual is as efficient as a group in problem-solving, unless the problem calls for a variety of skills or a division of labor which can only be provided by a group (Cohen, 1953). The group also excels when the problem requires a judgment about an ambiguous stimulus. Some of the increased accuracy of the group, however, is due only to the fact that a mathematical average is obtained, a process which can take place without group discussion. Since the individual can learn from others or will be influenced to accept the group norm in judging an ambiguous object, the accuracy of the individual is often improved as a by-product of group discussion.

§ The Four Problem Areas

As INDICATED IN Chapter One, all groups have problems to solve in four areas. Two of these areas, achieving the group's purpose and arranging a satisfying social structure for the members, have received the most attention in research (Barnard, 1938). The other two areas of achieving individual task goals and individual social-emotional goals will not be considered in this chapter. Problems in the first two areas, the group task area and the group social-emotional area, are related to each other in a state of "dynamic balance" so that too much activity in the task area will leave unsolved problems in the social-emotional area. In its attempts to solve the social-emotional problems the group (or the individual) often swings too far in that direction and the task is left undone. The group then swings back and forth in its activity, tending toward a state of equilibrium (Bales, 1953).

A typical group problem-solving sequence requires both emotional and intellectual participation in the three stages of definition (observation), discussion (hypothesizing), and working-through (proposing action) (Alpert & Smith, 1949). Each member must re-examine his view of the problem in the light of the views of the group, a process involving tension and requiring opportunity for interaction followed by release of tension. The process may be obstructed by formalistic participation where tension is concealed through rules of procedure (i.e., much intellect, little emotion), and by anarchic participation where discussion seems to fail to bring new light on the problem and release tension because of lack of verbal skill (i.e., much emotion, little intellect).

In this chapter, those effects on productivity which result from the simultaneous presence of a number of workers will be distinguished from those effects which result from group effort. Some of these effects have only been measured at the end of the decision process, others have been described at various stages of the process. To show the relative importance of these effects, the steps in an "ideal" decision are presented.

§   Steps in the Decision Process

THE STEPS in the group decision process consist of observing an object or event, comparing it with several possible identifications, considering the associated facts, and, once the nature of the problem is understood, taking appropriate action. This is the same process which has been described earlier as the process by which an individual defines the situation and arrives at an appropriate social act. The process is described by Bales in a more logical framework in the seven steps shown in the accompanying chart (Bales, 1955):

To these seven steps an eighth step of ACTION can be added to make the social act complete.

These steps in the decision process are given here in more detail than they are usually given in research on productivity. For this reason the process has been collapsed to three stages for the purpose of analysis: (1) observing, (2) formulating hypotheses, (3) proposing action.

1 STATES PRIMARY OBSERVATION:

I OBSERVE A PARTICULAR EVENT, X.

---

2 MAKES TENTATIVE INDUCTION:

THIS PARTICULAR EVENT, X, MAY BELONG TO THE GENERAL
CLASS OF OBJECTS, O.

---

3 DEDUCES CONDITIONAL PREDICTION:

IF THIS PARTICULAR EVENT, X, DOES BELONG TO THE GENERAL
CLASS, O, THEN IT SHOULD BE FOUND ASSOCIATED WITH
ANOTHER PARTICULAR EVENT, Y

---

4 STATES OBSERVATION OF CHECK FACT:

I OBSERVE THE PREDICTED PARTICULAR EVENT, Y.

---

5 IDENTIFIES OBJECT AS MEMBER OF A CLASS:

I THEREFORE IDENTIFY X-Y AS AN OBJECT WHICH IS A MEMBER
OF THE PREDICTED GENERAL CLASS OF OBJECTS, O.

---

6 STATES MAJOR PREMISE RELATING CLASSES OF OBJECTS:

ALL MEMBERS OF THE GENERAL CLASS OF OBJECTS, O, SHOULD
BE TREATED BY WAYS OF THE GENERAL CLASS, W.

---

7 PROPOSES SPECIFIC ACTION:

THIS PARTICULAR OBJECT, X-Y, SHOULD THEREFORE BE TREATED
IN A PARTICULAR WAY, W.

§   Individuals—
Together and Apart

SINCE TRIPLETT's early study of children winding string with fishing reels in 1898, the "together" and "apart" design has been used again and again to determine the influence of the presence of other persons on individuals who are performing a variety of tasks. The apparatus used by Triplett for his study consisted of two fishing reels whose cranks turned in a circle of one and three-fourths inches diameter. These were arranged on a Y shaped framework clamped to the top of a heavy table as shown in Fig. 32.

Figure 32—Triplett's Competition Machine (Triplett, 1898, p. 519)

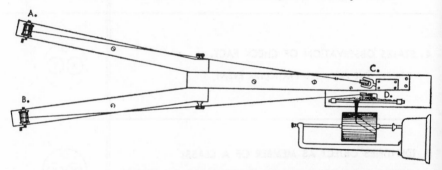

The sides of this framework were spread sufficiently far apart to permit two persons to turn the reels side by side. Bands of twisted silk cord ran over the well lacquered axes of the reels and were supported at C and D, two meters distant, by two small pulleys. The records were taken from the course AD, the other course BC being used merely for pacing or competition purposes. The wheel on the side from which the records were taken communicated the movement made to a recorder, the stylus of which traced a curve on the drum of a kymograph. The direction of this curve corresponded to the rate of turning, as the greater the speed the shorter and straighter the resulting line.

The subject taking the experiment was required to practice turning the reel until he had become accustomed to the machine. After a short period of rest the different trials were made with five-minute intervals between to obviate the possible effects of fatigue.

A trial consisted in turning the reel at the highest rate of speed until a small flag sewed to the silk band had made four circuits of the four-meter course. The time of the trial was taken by means of a stopwatch. The direction of the curves made on the drum likewise furnished graphic indications of the difference in time made between trials.

Triplett presented results based upon the records of forty children who had been tested in two sets of twenty. After the usual preliminaries of practice, six trials were made by each of the twenty subjects in the first set in the following order: first a trial alone, followed by a trial in competition, then another alone, and thus alternating through six efforts, giving three trials alone and three in competition. The second set of twenty children who were about the same age were given the six trials in the following order: alone, alone, competition, alone, competition, alone.

By this scheme, a trial of either sort, after the first one, by either of the two sets always corresponded to a different type of trial in the second set. Further, when the subjects in the two sets came to their fourth and sixth trials an equal amount of practice had been gained by an equal number of trials of the same kind. In his observations of the trials and examination of the results, Triplett found that all the subjects could be divided into three classes. Some were stimulated to work faster in the competition trials, some were stimulated in such a way that their performance was inhibited, and some appeared to be little affected by the race. As an example of Triplett's results, Table 24 gives the data for twenty subjects who were, on the whole, stimulated positively by the trials in competition.

Table 24—Time in Seconds for Subjects Stimulated Positively for Trials Alone and in Competition

		TRIAL					
	Age	1 Alone	2 Competition	3 Alone	4 Competition	5 Alone	6 Competition
Violet F.	10	54.4	42.6	45.2	41.0	42.0	46.0
Anna P.	9	67.0	57.0	55.4	50.4	49.0	44.8
Willie H.	12	37.8	38.8	43.0	39.0	37.2	33.4
Bessie V.	11	46.2	41.0	39.0	30.2	33.6	32.4
Howard C.	11	42.0	36.4	39.0	41.0	37.8	34.0
Mary M.	11	48.0	44.8	52.0	44.6	43.8	40.0
Lois P.	11	53.0	45.6	44.0	40.0	40.6	35.8
Inez K.	13	37.0	35.0	35.8	34.0	34.0	32.6
Harvey L.	9	49.0	42.6	39.6	37.6	36.0	35.0
Lora F.	11	40.4	35.0	33.0	35.0	30.2	29.0
Average	11	47.48	41.88	42.60	39.28	38.42	36.30
Probable Error		6.18	4.45	4.68	3.83	3.74	3.74
Gains			5.60	.72	3.32	.86	2.12

Triplett performed his experiment about seven years before the statistician, Gauss, introduced the "t" test which could be used to test the differences between means for small samples. The differences between the trials alone and in competition are generally not statistically significant.

Later researches tend to confirm Triplett's results: some children are stimulated positively by the presence of others while some are not (Shevaleva & Ergolska, 1926). In general, children seem to find the together situation more stimulating than do adults (Feofanov, 1928). Subjects with low intelligence are less stimulated (Abel, 1938). Under social influence subjects were observed to be more active but less accurate at the beginning of a task such as printing or putting pegs in a board (Sengupta & Sinha, 1926; Anderson, 1929; Leuba, 1933; Dashiell, 1930, 1935). A similar effect was observed when a second subject was added after the first subject was satiated with the task (Burton, 1941). Subjects were less likely to become bored if others were working at the same task (Taylor, Thompson, & Spassoff, 1937).

§ The Test Room Studies

FROM 1927 through the early 1930's, the Western Electric Company carried out a series of researches in a special test room and in other observation rooms in an attempt to measure the effects of certain physical, biological, and social factors upon the productivity of individual workers (Homans, 1941; Haire, 1954).

These Western Electric Studies have led to a number of research reports by Turner (1933) who, as a Public Health consultant, set up the original test room by Mayo (1933) who was called in as a psychologist to interview the employees when it was discovered that social factors were more important than physical factors, and by Roethlisberger and Dickson (1939) who made the most extensive report of the research results. Turner's account (1933) of the initial series of test room studies, which took place over a period of four years, provides a detailed illustration of the relative importance of social stimulation in increasing individual productivity.

In April, 1927, six experienced female operators, chosen at random, were removed from the department in which they were working to a small test room in the corner of a regular shop. Their work was the assembly of telephone relays and involved putting together a coil, an armature, contact springs and insulators in a fixture, and securing the parts in position by means of four machine screws. The girls were invited to the office of the Superintendent in charge where the plan and objectives of the study were explained to them. Although shy at this first meeting, they readily consented to take part in the study. They were expressly cautioned to work at a comfortable pace and not to make a race out of the test.

The working equipment in the test room was like that in the regular department except that there was a hole in the bench at the right of each girl's position into which completed relays were dropped. The relay falls through a chute actuating a flapper gate. The opening of the gate closes an electrical circuit which controls a perforating device which in turn records the completion of the relay by punching a hole in a moving tape. This tape moves at the rate of $\frac{1}{4}''$ per minute and has space for a separate row of holes for each operator. The punched tape furnishes a complete output record for each girl for each instant of the day. The tape mechanism also carries a bank of five message registers giving a numerical record of the total number of relays completed by each operator.

As we began the test, our objectives were stated in the form of six questions:

1. Do employees actually get tired out?
2. Are rest pauses desirable?
3. Is a shorter working day desirable?
4 What is the attitude of employees toward their work and toward the company?
5. What is the effect of changing the type of working equipment?
6. Why does production fall off in the afternoon?

Disregarding the problems of placement and working equipment, it has been our assumption that the effectiveness of an individual will vary with (a) his bodily status or physiological efficiency (health, skill, endurance); (b) his mental state (contentment and freedom from worry, fear, anger, hate, shame, or other morbid preoccupations); (c) his zest for work (determined by the enjoyment in performing the work, the feeling of justice in his treatment, and the desire for securing reward) (pp. 577-79).

To test these assumptions, certain specific changes having to do with the length of the working day or week, with the introduction of rest periods, and with the sitting position of the operators were made. These are described in Table 25.

At the beginning of the study, output records were kept for each girl in her regular department for two weeks without her knowledge. The girls were then moved to the test room where they worked for five weeks before any changes in working conditions were introduced. The intentional changes subsequently introduced have not by any means been the only ones studied.

Table 25—Changes in Test Room Conditions

Period Number	Period Name	Duration in Weeks
1.	In regular department	2
2.	Introduction to test room	5
3.	Special group rate	8
4.	Two 5-minute rests	5
5.	Two 10-minute rests	4
6.	Six 5-minute rests	4
7.	15-minute A.M. lunch; 10-minute P.M. rest°	11
8.	Same as No. 7, but 4:30 stop	7
9.	Same as No. 7, but 4:00 stop	4
10.	Same as No. 7, (check)	12
11.	Same as No. 7, but Saturday A.M. off	9
12.	Same as No. 3, (no lunch or rests)	12
13.	Same as No. 7, but operators furnish own lunch; company furnishes beverage	31
14.	Same as No. 11	9
15.	Same as No. 13	31
16.	Same as No. 13, except operators changed positions	4
17.	Same as No. 16, except 4:15 stop and Saturday A.M. off	25
18.	Same as No. 17, except Friday P.M. off	15

° Beginning with Period 7, rest periods were begun at 9:30 in the morning and 2:30 in the afternoon.

§ Differences between Test Room and Shop

IN THE TEST ROOM, the group piecework basis of payment paid each girl more nearly in proportion to her individual effort, since she was paid with a group of six instead of 100 or more. The girls in the test room assembled fewer different types of relays. The operators could read their exact output at anytime from the recorder. The test room was not quieter; if anything, it was somewhat noisier than the regular department. New conditions of work provided an element of novelty. The girls realized that the experiment was receiving the attention of company officials, which meant that they were being noticed as individuals.

There has been a fundamental change in supervision. There was no group chief in the test room, but instead a "friendly observer" of the experiment. Discipline was secured through leadership and understanding. The girls were allowed to talk and to leave the bench whenever they liked; they were not compelled to pick up parts from the floor at the time they were dropped. An *esprit de corps* grew up within the group.

The girls were given physical examinations every six weeks. They objected to this at first but later each trip to the hospital became a "party."

Three types of records were kept in the test room in order that changes might be measured in output, the individual, and conditions of work.

§ Test Room Results

THE FIRST SPECIFIC PROBLEM which the test room sought to study was the effect of rest pauses which were introduced in Period 4. We did learn much concerning rest pauses, but soon found that there was a continually rising output in the test room which was in large measure at least independent of rest pauses. At the end of four years, the individual operators had increased their output from 40 to 62 per cent. The relationship of this increase to rest pauses is shown in Fig. 33. It will be seen that output rose appreciably in Period 3 before rest periods were introduced. In Period 12, rest periods were entirely eliminated and during 12 weeks, output reached a new height. . . . With the reintroduction of rest pauses in Period 13, total output rose still further.

We inevitably became more and more concerned with the task of finding the explanations for the remarkably increased output. Was it because of better health or at the expense of health of the worker? Was it due to lessened fatigue? Was it due to changed pay incentive? Was it due to an improved mental state on the part of the worker, to the elimination of unhappy preoccupations, or a greater zest for work (p. 579-80)?

Although factors such as these *were* shown to be related to productivity, in the judgment of the girls themselves, the elements considered to be important in the test room situation were listed in the following order: the small group, the type of supervision, earnings, novelty, interest of the girls in the experiment, the attention given in the test room by officials and investigators.

As a result of his experience with the test room, Turner concluded:

We came to realize that neuromuscular fatigue is not of great importance in light industrial processes and that the mental attitudes of employees are of tremendous importance (p. 584).

Without intention, Turner and his colleagues had provided a classic demonstration of the positive influence on productivity which results

Figure 33—Average Daily Output for Operators, 3, 4, and 5 Relay Group

RELAYS

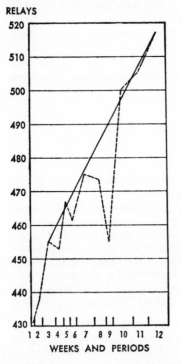

Solid line shows daily output increase from one full-day period to the next full-day period. Dotted line shows the actual average daily output. The work periods indicated at the bottom of the chart are as follows: (1) regular department (2 weeks), (2) test room (5 weeks), (3) special gang rate (8 weeks), (4) two 5-minute rests (5 weeks), (5) two 10-minute rests (4 weeks), (6) six 5-minute rests (4 weeks), (7) lunch rest (11 weeks), (8) lunch rest and 4:30 stop (7 weeks), (9) lunch rest and 4:00 stop (4 weeks), (10) same as period 7 (12 weeks), (11) lunch rest and Sat. a.m. off (9 weeks), (12) same as No. 3 (12 weeks), (Turner, 1933, p. 580).

from work in a "together" situation where the subjects are given special attention.

§   Social-Emotional
Distractions

THE QUANTITY AND QUALITY of an individual's activity in an intellectual task may be less in the "together" situation (Dashiell, 1935) if some attention of the subject is diverted from the task to social-emotional concerns (Allport, 1920, 1924; Anderson, 1929). On a reasoning task, for example, the presence of a group stimulates more conversational, expansive expression, while the individual alone is more logical (Allport, 1920). This effect may be observed even if the other persons working on the task are not physically present in the room with the subject (Dashiell, 1935). Of course, as Triplett's experiment demonstrated, the negative effects of social distraction may be overcome by greater motivation to perform in the social situation (Mukerji, 1940), provided that the other persons in the room are having more success. If the others are doing less well, the subject may lower his goals (Hilgard et al., 1940).

The negative effects of social distraction are heightened if the other persons present are not doing the same task, but serve as an audience to razz or threaten the subject (Laird, 1923; Coombs & Taylor, 1952). The most intelligent subjects find observation by an audience the most disruptive (Gates, 1924; Anderson, 1929). The details of some of these "together" and "apart" experiments are given in Exhibit 22.

In one study on the effects of an audience (Wapner & Alper, 1952), three different kinds of audience were used. A sample of 120 undergraduates of both sexes were asked to select one of two words which more closely fitted a given phrase. Each subject made his choices in a room with a one-way mirror under three variations of audience: (1) no audience other than the experimenter who was also in the room— the curtain was drawn before the one-way mirror; (2) unseen audience— the mirror was exposed and the subject was told that there were people behind it who could hear and see what was going on in the room, (3) seen audience—lights were turned on behind the mirror so that the subject could see the audience which consisted of a faculty member and three or four students. For the first half of the twenty-minute experimental session, the time that the subject required to select each word was least when there was no audience other than the experimenter, intermediate for the seen audience, and longest for the unseen audience. The unseen condition produced significantly longer decision times than either of the other two conditions. In the second half of the experimental session, no differences appeared and for all subjects there was a general decrease in decision time from the first to the second half. Presumably the unseen audience was the most threatening to the subject because he was unable to estimate either its expectations for his behavior or its penalty for deviation.

The social-emotional distractions created by the presence of others who are working at the same task are not always as subtle. Other members may actively coerce the subject to lower his output to conform to a group norm (Taylor, F. W., 1903).

§   Observations and
Hypotheses

UP TO THIS POINT in the chapter, individuals have been compared in "together" and "apart" situations primarily with regard to the final outcome of the problem-solving process. However, some studies suggest differences which may occur in the steps of *observation* and *hypothesizing*.

Observation, as we have seen in the discussion of norms and social control, is influenced by the presence of other individuals. Subjects tend to give up their individual standards of judgment in favor of group norms in judgments of phenomena such as line length, line movement, and weight (Allport, 1924; Farnsworth & Behner, 1931; Sherif, 1935; Asch, 1952; Sherif & Sherif, 1956). As a result, it is difficult to predict what an individual will report as his perception in a group knowing only his perceptual performance when no others are present (de Montmollin, 1955a).

If association and memory may be assumed to be related to the formation of *hypotheses*, then studies in these two areas will provide some information about the second step in the problem-solving process. In studies of word association, the subject in a social situation feels inhibited and restrained (Dashiell, 1935) and as a result makes fewer personal associations and more popular associations (Allport, 1920). However, the frequency of word associations is increased in the presence of others, especially for slow workers.

When a subject uses his memory as a source of hypotheses to apply to a current problem, it might be presumed that the same social distractions which may decrease productivity for an individual would inhibit his memory. As in the other steps of the process, however, the evidence is mixed. The presence of others does interfere with the ability to remember nonsense syllables (Pessin, 1933; Dashiell, 1935), but has no effect on maze-learning (Pessin & Husband, 1933). Information which is learned under adverse conditions may be retained longer than information learned under less stressful conditions (Elkine, 1927; Pessin, 1933).

Although the emphasis here has been on the effect of social stimulation on an individual's efficiency, there are of course more common ways to increase efficiency by providing incentives (Leuba, 1930), training (Marston, 1924), or therapy (Peters & Jones, 1951).

In summary, the presence of other persons may change the content of an individual's activity from personal to group-oriented, it may increase his activity if he is spurred on by the implied competition, or it may depress his activity through distraction, conformity to norms, or group resistance to the task.

§ A Paradigm for the Analysis of Productivity

UP TO THIS POINT the problem-solving behavior of individuals has been compared when the individuals were "alone" and when they were "together," but always with an *individual* task. These two situations are represented by cells C and D in Fig. 34.

Figure 34—A Paradigm for the Analysis of Productivity

	THE PROBLEM TO BE SOLVED:	
The Relationship of the Individuals:	TOGETHER	APART
Together	A	C
Apart	B	D

The next set of studies deals with cells A and D, the group working as a group *versus* the individual working as an individual. There is also research on co-operation *versus* competition in which the individuals are together but with either group or individual goals, cells A and C. Although persons with a common problem often try to solve it without face-to-face contact, by mail or telephone, there are few studies which explicitly deal with cell B, although some communication experiments are relevant here. A comparison of different types of groups in cell A is the subject matter of Chapter Thirteen.

§ Efficiency of the Group
versus the Individual

WHEN PAIRS or larger groups are compared in the solution of the same types of problems, the groups are found to be more efficient when a division of labor is possible. For problems similar to those used by the OSS in their assessment of men, such as crossing a mined road or building a bridge, five-man teams were found to ask more questions and produce better written and field solutions than individuals, regardless of the method of presenting the problem (e.g., verbal, photograph, or scale model) (Lorge et al., 1955a, 1955b). The group will be especially efficient if the members are friends (Husband, 1940). On the other hand, if a task does not lend itself to a division of labor (e.g., a mathematical problem), pairs take longer to solve each problem but have more correct answers, presumably because of the error-checking feature of interaction (Barton, 1926; Watson, 1928; Shaw, 1932; Klugman, 1944). In another study with a similar type of task three-man groups were no more effective than individuals in solving problems in symbolic logic (Moore & Anderson, 1954).

The individual will also be more efficient if the task requires a kind of coordination of the group which some of its members cannot supply because of low motivation, personality conflict, poor communication, or other reasons (Thorndike, 1938a; McCurdy & Lambert, 1952). In one experiment college subjects chose individual problem-solving over paired (Lichtenberg, 1956). On the other hand, the difficulties in co-operating co-operative effort when co-operation was seen as taking too much time may have unexpected "positive" effects. For example, failure on a non-creative task (finding combinations to locks) caused more persons working alone than working co-operatively to lower their estimate of the probability of successfully completing a second task. This occurred presumably because the subjects working co-operatively could attribute their difficulty to the possibility that they were not getting along together, rather than that they did not have the ability (Lichtenberg, 1957). More details of these experiments are given in Exhibit 23.

The differences between groups and individuals on the more manual tasks (jigsaw puzzles) and the more intellectual tasks (arithmetic problems) are in the same direction as those reported for individuals solving problems together and apart; that is, greater efficiency on manual problems and less on intellectual problems.

Although the group is usually better than the average individual, it is seldom better than the best individual (Marquart, 1955; Lorge, Fox, Davitz, & Brenner, 1958). It is therefore probable that in many cases the apparent superiority of the group results from the presence of *one* superior individual (Taylor & McNemar, 1955). The group effects in any case should be greater if the groups are composed of subjects who have made high scores as individuals (Comrey & Saats, 1955). However, in one series of studies, less than half of the variance of paired performance on a pegboard could be predicted from individual scores for college subjects (Comrey, 1953; Comrey & Deskin, 1954a, 1954b). Some of the effects of group interaction can also be attributed to the fact that individual subjects are working in the presence of others rather than *with* them on a common task. In terms of man-hours required, the groups are more expensive since the time for a group solution must be multiplied by the number of members in computing the cost of the product. For this reason the group method would seem to require more accuracy, member satisfaction, or some other result in addition to efficiency in terms of units per hour to justify its use.

§ Twenty Questions

THE EXPERIMENT by Taylor & Faust (1952) using the game "Twenty Questions" provides a more detailed example of the relative efficiency of the group and the individual. Here, too, groups were found to be more accurate but more costly in terms of man hours.

To start the game of "Twenty Questions," the participants were told only whether the object they were to attempt to identify was animal, vegetable, or mineral. In searching for the object which was the solution to the problem, they asked a series of questions, each of which could be answered "yes" or "no." To find the solution most economically, the subjects had to use a high order of conceptualization, gradually increasing the specificity of the concepts employed until they arrived at the particular object.

A total of 105 students from the elementary course in psychology served as subjects. The subjects were assigned by chance to work in solving the problems either alone, in pairs, or as a member of a group of four. There were 15 individual subjects, 15 groups of two and 15 groups of four. Each individual or group was given four problems a day for four successive days. On the fifth day, all subjects worked alone, each being given four problems.

From a longer list of objects originally constructed, 60 were selected for use as problem topics. Included were 20 animal, 20 vegetable, and 20 mineral objects. Excluded were objects which did not clearly fit in only one of the three categories; e.g., hammer was not included because, with a handle of wood and a head of metal, it would be classed as both vegetable and mineral. Also excluded were objects which could not be expected to be familiar to almost every college student. Examples of objects included are: newspaper, Bob Hope, scissors, camel, dime, rubber band.

With four problems a day for five days, a total of only 20 problems was needed for presentation to any particular subject or group. However, to minimize the possibility that a subject would have any knowledge of what problem object to expect, it was decided to use a total of 60 different objects (p. 361).

Since the nature of the learning curve was of interest, the order of presentation of the problems was controlled. The problems given on any one day were matched for difficulty with those given on any other day.

All subjects were told that both the number of questions and the time required to reach solution would be recorded, but it was emphasized that the number of questions was the more important score. In presenting each problem, the experimenter stated simply whether the object sought was animal, vegetable, or mineral. Time was measured by means of a stopwatch. A special data sheet was used for groups of two or four to record which subject asked each question. To each question, the experimenter replied "Yes," "No," "Partly," "Sometimes," or "Not in the usual sense of the word." If the question could not be answered in one of these ways or was unclear, the subject was asked to restate it.

The instructions given to groups of two or of four made clear that they might talk freely to each other, reviewing answers to previous questions or suggesting possible questions to ask. It was emphasized that they were not to compete against each other, but were to cooperate as a group to get the answer; they were told that the efficiency of their group would be compared with that of the other groups.

As the name of the game indicates, subjects are traditionally allowed 20 questions in which to obtain the solution. Pretesting showed, however, that with naive subjects this limit results in a rather large proportion of failures. Accordingly, to simplify the analysis of the data to be obtained, the number of questions permitted was increased to 30 (pp. 361-362).

§ The Rate of Learning

WHEN THE RATES of learning for the subjects in the three experimental conditions are compared the data in Fig. 35 shows that there is rapid improvement in the performance of both individuals and groups. By the fourth day the curves appear already to be flattening out. The score for an individual or single group for one day was the median of the number of questions required to solve each of the four problems on that day. The median was used instead of the mean because there were some failures. Each point plotted in Fig. 35 is the mean of these median scores on one day for 15 individuals, or for 15 groups of two or of four. In those few cases when an individual or group failed two

Figure 35—Number of Questions per Problem as a Function of Days of Practice and of Size of Group

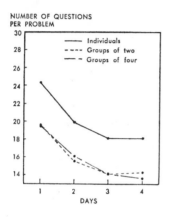

NUMBER OF QUESTIONS
PER PROBLEM

——— Individuals
– – – – Groups of two
— – Groups of four

DAYS

or more problems on a single day, the median was obtained by treating the failures as though solution had been reached in 31 questions; the number of such cases was too small to affect the results appreciably; after the first day there were no such cases except among individual subjects and even there they were rare.

The mean number of failures per problem on each day by individuals or groups is shown in Fig. 36. Thus, for example, on the first day the mean number of failures per problem among the 15 groups of four was .08; in other words, about one-twelfth of the problems were failed. The improvement in performance over four days in terms of number of failures per problem is consistent with that shown in Fig. 35 in terms of number of questions per problem solved.

Fig. 37 shows the decrease over four days in the amount of time required per problem. The time required, of course, is somewhat dependent on the number of questions asked, although not entirely so. The score for an individual or single group for one day was the median time required for solution of the four problems. In those few cases where there were two or more failures in one day, the median of the four times was taken simply as obtained; this procedure underestimates somewhat the median time that would have been required to solve all four problems, but as before, the number of such cases was too small to affect the general results appreciably.

Figure 36—Number of Failures per Problem as a Function of Days of Practice and of Size of Group

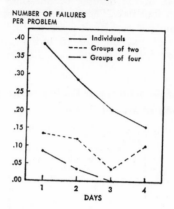

Figure 37—Time per Problem as a Function of Days of Practice and of Size of Group

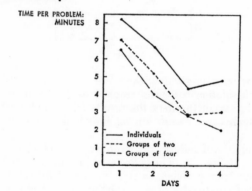

§ Size of Group

THE SECOND and major question with which the experiment was concerned involved the relation between efficiency in problem solving and size of group. As is evident in Fig. 35, there was no significant difference between groups of two and groups of four in terms of the number of questions required to reach solution. The performance of individuals working alone, however, was consistently inferior to that of either size group (pp. 362-363).

This same tendency holds for the number of failures per problem (Fig. 36) and the time per problem (Fig. 37). The individuals were less efficient than the groups but the groups did not differ in efficiency from each other.

However, if instead of counting the total time elapsed before the solution of the problem, an analysis is made in terms of the number of man-minutes required for solution, the nature of the results obtained changes sharply. The number of man-minutes for a problem will, of course, be equal to the elapsed time multiplied by the number of persons in the group. In terms of man-minutes, the mean of the scores for all four days was 5.06 for individuals, 7.40 for groups of two, and 12.60 for groups of four (p. 364).

The differences between these means are statistically significant indicating that the performance of individuals was superior to that of groups of two or of four and the performance of groups of two was superior to that of groups of four.

§ Individual Versus
Group Practice

THE THIRD QUESTION which the experiment was intended to answer was whether improvement in individual performance occurs more rapidly with individual practice or with practice as a member of a group. To answer this question, all subjects worked alone on the fifth day. As before, the score for each individual was the median number of questions required to solve the four problems. The mean of these scores for the 15 subjects who had previously worked alone was 20.8; for the 30 who had worked in pairs, 19.3; and for the 60 who had been members of groups of four, 19.1. None of the differences among these means is significant. Nor were any of the differences significant among the corresponding means on the fifth day for number of failures or for time scores. Learning went on as well in groups of two or of four as in individual practice (p. 365).

In summary the authors conclude that

group performances were superior to individual performance in terms of number of questions, number of failures, and elapsed time per problem; but the performance of groups of four was not superior to that of groups of two, except in terms of the number of failures to reach solution. The performance of individuals was superior to that of either size group in terms of number of man-minutes required for solution (p. 365).

§ Observation: Group
versus Individual

SINCE THE GROUP sees only through the eyes of its members who must reach agreement on what they see if they are to present a single group report, the tendency for the members to converge on a standard or norm is even more marked than it is for the individual in the presence of others. Initially the group members have a larger range of observations or opinions available from which to select the most relevant facts for the solution of the problem. Some of the observations can be eliminated through discussion because they are mutually contradictory (Marston, 1924; Shaw, 1932), while other observations are suppressed by the members if they are uncertain of their own opinions (Gurnee, 1937a). Opinions which are given in the group are generally more carefully and cautiously thought out before they are presented (Bos, 1937). However, because of difficulties in communication or because the opinion is given by a low-status or deviant member, correct ideas are sometimes not accepted (Bos, 1937). For reasons of this sort the *actual* intelligence of a group member may differ from his *effective* intelligence. Some groups can only use the contributions of an intelligent but low-status member after his suggestion has first been rejected and then restated by another member with higher status.

As a result of the factors which enter a group's decision, the group will tend to report fewer but more accurate facts than an individual (Dashiell, 1935), although a single trained judge may be better than a group of untrained subjects (Marston, 1924).

Similar results have been reported when groups and individuals submit written reports on their problem-solving process. Groups were found to under-report and individuals to over-report their thinking and their problem-solution (Lorge, Tuckman, Aikman, Spiegel, & Moss, 1956).

§   Statistical Pooling

FURTHER EVIDENCE of the fact that part of the increased accuracy of a group is due to convergence on a norm is found in studies which compare the mathematical mean of a set of individual judgments with the judgment of a single subject. If the subjects are asked to estimate the number of objects in a bottle or the opinions of a group, the mean judgment will be more reliable than individuals' judgments if the objects or the group members are familiar to them. The mean judgment will be less accurate in those cases where the group judgment is biased because the objects are not familiar or because of some optical illusion (Gordon, 1924; Stroop, 1932; Farnsworth & Williams, 1936; Preston, 1938; Travers, 1941, 1943a, 1943b; Klugman, 1945). The details of some of these studies appear in Exhibit 24.

Not only does statistical pooling of opinions tend to increase the accuracy and reliability of the estimate, but it also appears to produce judgments as accurate as those made by the same individuals when they actually arrive at a group judgment (Bevan et al., 1958). In a study of the prediction of social and technological events (Kaplan, Skogstad, & Girshick, 1950), 26 subjects made thirteen weekly sets of predictions about the outcome of a variety of political, economic, and scientific events to occur within a twenty-week period. The predictions were then compared with the actual outcomes. The panel members were all of a high educational level, 24 having college degrees, and thirteen of these with two or more years of graduate training. Nineteen of the subjects were mathematicians, statisticians, or engineers. Half of the panel members were placed in rotation in three kinds of quartets: *independent*—in which the subjects worked alone without discussion; *co-operative*—in which the subjects discussed the questions and then answered individually; *joint*—in which discussion was followed by a collective decision on a single answer for the entire group. The results indicate that predictions by groups are more apt to be correct than predictions by the same persons working separately, but also that the *mean* predictions of the four subjects comprising the independent quartets were virtually as accurate as either those made by the members of the co-operative quartets or those made as group decisions by the joint quartets.

In addition to "pooling," two other "group effects" of an essentially statistical nature should be considered in the comparison of the individual alone and in co-operation with other group members (Ekman, 1955). The first of these is the *summation effect* where the group productivity is simply the sum of the individual productivities. The second is the *probability effect* where a group may be more effective in a guessing problem because it has more chances to make a correct guess.

§ Accuracy of the
Individual after Group
Discussion

SINCE THE INDIVIDUAL tends to shift his opinion in group discussion in the direction of the group norm (Gurnee, 1937a; Jenness, 1932a), his opinion taken after discussion will be a more accurate estimate of the "correct" answer, provided that the group decision was close to the true answer (Munsterberg, 1914; Burtt, 1920; Jenness, 1932b; Dashiell, 1935;

Thorndike, 1938b; Timmons, 1939, 1942). Actually, the individuals need only be aware of the others' opinions to be able to modify their judgments (Bekhterev & Lange, 1924; Jenness, 1932b; Dashiell, 1935; see Exhibit 25).

The shift in individual opinion, as it is considered here, is only a by-product of group decision and not the main object of discussion, as it is in the experiments which seek to bring about a change in group norms. If improving the accuracy of judgment is the goal, then instruction by an expert may do as well as group discussion by relative novices (Wispe, 1951).

§ Group Learning

GROUPS OF THREE PERSONS recall more nonsense words than individuals working separately but in the presence of others, but no differences are reported in the recall of meaningful material between groups of three and two individuals. Presumably here the greater storage capacity of the group gives the group an advantage for recall of disconnected bits of information (Perlmutter & de Montmollin, 1952; Perlmutter, 1953).

In the experiment with nonsense words, 23 three-man groups were asked to learn a list of two-syllable nonsense words. Another equivalent list was memorized by the same sets of individuals working separately but in the same room. In the group the members were required to agree on each word before it was adopted to represent the group and they were not permitted to assign specific parts of the list to specific individuals. On a series of five trials, the average group recalled more words than the average individual, with the group scores in general equal to or better than the best individual scores. The experiment was arranged so that some subjects worked first as a group and others as individuals. Those who worked in a group first were able to do better as individuals on the second trial, possibly by using techniques learned in the group session.

Another interpretation can also be made of the fact that for the individuals who first had experience in the group the best individual score was as high as the group, but that the initial individual learning experience did not seem to effect the subsequent performance as groups. It is possible that both types of initial learning experience improved individual performance (as it does on judging tasks), but that the averaging effect of group discussion tended to reduce the effectiveness of the best individuals. The differences between individual and group performance would probably have been greater if the individuals had been tested alone, rather than with the social stimulation of other workers.

§ Summary

THE COMPARISON of individual productivity alone, in the presence of others, and in co-operation with others in a group has been a major research interest in social psychology from Triplett's experiment in 1898 to the present. Although it is theoretically possible to break the problem-solving process down into separate steps such as observation, hypothesizing, and proposing action, most researchers have concentrated on a comparison of the end-products of the process rather than the process itself.

Following Triplett, later experiments have generally confirmed the generalization that some subjects are stimulated positively by the presence of others, some are stimulated negatively, and some are unaffected. As a result, productivity is almost always related to some social factors as the Western Electric Researches have shown.

In the observation and hypothesizing steps of the problem-solving process, subjects tend to be less idiosyncratic when other subjects are working on the same task.

The superiority of the group over the individual with respect to productivity is usually greater on manual problems than on intellectual tasks. The group will lose its superiority in accuracy and efficiency if (1) no division of labor is required, (2) problems of control are too great, or (3) the group develops a standard of productivity which is lower than that of a separate individual. In terms of man-hours an individual is usually more productive.

Because of a tendency to converge on a norm, groups will report fewer but more accurate facts than individuals. However, some increase in accuracy can be obtained by eliminating group discussion and simply pooling the judgments of one individual or of several individuals. As a by-product of group discussion, the individual tends to be more accurate in his own judgment after he has heard the judgments of others.

Groups tend to recall more information than individuals, presumably because of their greater capacity to store information.

Exhibit 22
Individual Performance Alone and in the Presence of Others

A.

Investigator: Allport (1920).
Focus: The influence of the group upon association and thought.
Sample: 26 subjects.
Method: Subjects alternated between working in the presence of four others and working alone. "Free chain association" was tested by presenting the subject with sheets, each of which carried one stimulus word at the top, and requiring him to start from this stimulus and write as many words as he could in a given time.
Relevant Findings: When other persons were in the room, the subjects worked faster. The social increment was greatest in the first minute, less in the second, and least in the third. The effect of the group seemed to be at first stimulating, then steadying. More personal associations were written down alone than together; words suggested by the immediate surroundings were more numerous in the group.

B.

Investigator: Laird (1923).
Focus: Changes in motor control and individual variations under the influence of "razzing."
Sample: Eight college fraternity pledges.
Method: Scores for tapping speed, three-hole test, steadiness sitting, and steadiness standing were recorded in a "normal" test situation, and a situation in which each subject was "razzed" by future fraternity brothers.
Relevant Findings: "Razzing" depressed performance for all eight subjects in steadiness standing and for seven in steadiness sitting. However, all subjects improved in tapping and three subjects improved in the three-hole test.

C.

Investigator: Gates (1924).
Focus: The effect of an audience upon performance.
Sample: 25 college girls as control subjects and 37 as experimental subjects.
Method: Each of the control subjects took a series of tests (e.g., pegs in

holes, color naming, analogies) while alone with the experimenter. 26 of the experimental subjects took the first half of the test with the experimenter and the second half in the presence of from four to six observers. Eleven subjects took the second half in the presence of from 27 to 37 observers, who merely watched, saying nothing.

Relevant Findings: The audience had no clear influence on the total performance, although the audience was somewhat more disruptive for the better performers.

D.

Investigator: Anderson (1929).

Focus: An experimental study of social facilitation as affected by intelligence.

Sample: Ten high school boys, five with IQ's from 125 to 130; and five with IQ's from 100 to 105.

Method: Each subject was given three series of tasks: mathematical problems, cancelling *a*'s on a sheet of pied small-type letters, and sorting marbles into five different cells. Each series consisted of eight tests of five minutes' duration. For the first two types of tasks, the subjects were seated about four feet apart in chairs with desk-arms. In the marble-sorting task they sat at long laboratory desks with no two boys facing each other and with the experimenter absent from the room. The "alone" and "together" situations were alternated.

Relevant Findings: The boys with average IQ's were more responsive to the influence of the "together" situation than the brighter boys who were often inhibited under these conditions. Work done in the presence of others tended to be slightly more accurate and more variable, especially for the brighter boys.

E.

Investigator: Abel (1938).

Focus: The influence of social facilitation on motor performance at different levels of intelligence.

Sample: Two sets of subjects with subnormal intelligence: 38 girls with IQ's of 50 to 59, and 36 girls with IQ's of 70 to 79.

Method: Paper-and-pencil maze tests were administered to the subjects during four experimental periods. They were given twenty trials per period. The two sets of girls were further divided into four approximately equal subgroups. Subjects in subgroup A worked alone for three periods and in pairs in period 4, subjects in subgroup B worked in pairs for three periods and alone in period 4, and subjects in subgroups C and D worked alternately alone and in pairs.

Relevant Findings: As a whole both sets of girls did better on the paper-and-pencil maze when working in pairs, and showed greater improvement after social stimulation than after working alone. The girls with the higher IQ scores did relatively better under social stimulation.

F.

Investigator: Burton (1941).

Focus: The influence of social factors upon the persistence of satiation in preschool children.

Sample: 24 preschool children, ten boys and fourteen girls from a superior socio-economic environment.

Method: Each subject was motivated by instructions to do a simple, uniform, and repetitive task (peg insertions). The criterion for satiation was the rejection and nonresumption (for at least ten minutes) of this task when this rejection was not due to extraneous needs, i.e., hunger, toilet, and sleep. Following satiation and complete unwillingness of the subject to continue the task, a second motivated child was brought in to help the subject finish his "game."

Relevant Findings: The mean time to become satiated was 34 minutes, 4 seconds. After the partner was introduced the average child inserted 34 per cent of the number of pegs he inserted during an equivalent period of modal motivation, and was active for an amount of time equal to 43 per cent of an equivalent period of highest motivation.

Exhibit 23
Efficiency of the Group vs. the Individual

A.

Investigator: Watson (1928).
Focus: Do groups think more efficiently than individuals?
Sample: 68 graduate students.
Method: Three comparable forms of ten intellectual tasks varying greatly in complexity were given first to isolated individuals, then to committees of three to ten members, and then again to isolated individuals.
Relevant Findings: On tests involving the decoding of a cipher and tests involving the listing of steps necessary in solving a problem, the groups were superior to the average individual in quality and speed.

B.

Investigator: Shaw (1932).
Focus: A comparison of individuals and small groups in the rational solution of complex problems.
Sample: Five groups of four women, five groups of four men, nineteen individual men, and nineteen individual women, all college students.
Method: Groups and individuals were given complex problems involving a number of steps, all of which had to be correct before the right answer was obtained. The groups were roughly equated so that no one group was composed of four superior individuals.
Relevant Findings: Groups reached a larger proportion of correct solutions apparently because they rejected incorrect suggestions and checked errors. When reaching an erroneous solution, groups did not err as frequently as individuals.

C.

Investigator: Husband (1940).
Focus: Co-operative *versus* solitary problem solution.
Sample: 120 college students, forty working alone and forty in pairs.
Method: Three tests were used: word puzzle, jigsaw puzzle, and a series of five arithmetic problems. Time was recorded by a stopwatch. The subjects

were required to complete each problem before going on to the next, even if they became discouraged and felt like giving up.

Relevant Findings: Pairs were superior in the code and jigsaw tests, but in the arithmetic problems there were practically no differences between groups and single individuals. In terms of man-minutes required for a solution, the individuals were more efficient.

D.

Investigator: McCurdy & Lambert (1952).

Focus: The efficiency of small human groups in the solution of problems requiring genuine co-operation.

Sample: 23 individuals and 35 groups of three college students in two experiments.

Method: Subjects were given a learning problem which required throwing six switches in a combination which would close an electric circuit. In the group of three, each subject had two switches.

Relevant Findings: Individuals made fewer errors than groups of three. No difference in efficiency was found between groups in which free communication was allowed and those in which an appointed leader made all the decisions.

E.

Investigator: Lichtenberg (1956).

Focus: Time perspective and the initiation of co-operation.

Sample: College students.

Method: Each subject had the task of opening a set of boxes in a limited time. Some boxes had padlocks, others combination locks. The subject could either do the task by himself or choose one of two partners who differed in the accuracy of their memory.

Relevant Findings: Subjects performed the problem alone when it would have taken more time to choose a reliable partner.

Exhibit 24
Statistical Pooling of Individual Judgments

A.

Investigator: Gordon (1924).
Focus: Group judgments in the field of lifted weights.
Sample: Two hundred female college students.
Method: Each subject ranked ten bottles from heaviest to lightest.
Relevant Findings: Range of the correlations of individual judgments with the true order was + .95 to − .81 with a mean of + .41, and S. D. of 32.9. The judgments of forty mutually exclusive groups of five subjects were pooled and the composite order for each group was correlated with the true order. This mean correlation for the forty pooled coefficients was + .68 with a S. D. of 19.2. The subjects were then combined into twenty mutually exclusive groups with ten in a group. The mean correlation rose to + .79, S. D. 16.5. For the next grouping, ten groups of twenty, the mean correlation was + .86. Finally the judgments were pooled in four groups of fifty yielding correlations of + .92, + .92, + .94, + .95.

B.

Investigator: Stroop (1932).
Focus: Is the judgment of the group better than that of the average member of the group?
Sample: One hundred subjects from a college psychology class.
Method: Following Gordon's (1924) general procedure, forty subjects ranked the weights five times each, twenty subjects ten times each, ten subjects twenty times each, and four subjects fifty times each. Five rankings were made per sitting, never more than two sittings a day. Three sets of weights were employed and shifted so that no subject used the same set twice in succession during the same sitting.
Relevant Findings: When a large number of judgments or rankings of a series of weights (by the same subject or by different subjects) are grouped, correlated with the true order and averaged after Gordon's plan, the result will be an increase in validity. This increase in validity is not due to the fact that the judgments were made by different people but to the mathematical principle involved in this method of combining data.

C.

Investigator: Farnsworth & Williams (1936).
Focus: The accuracy of the median and mean of a group of judgments.
Sample: One hundred students in social psychology.
Method: A subject was asked to estimate the weight of two objects after he had been told the weight of a first object. He was not allowed to lift the objects simultaneously. Box A, the original box, had a designated weight of 3.5 from which the weights of Boxes B and C were to be estimated.
Relevant Findings: Both boxes B and C although different in size, had the same weight, so that the judgment would test the "illusion effect." The median of the weight estimates of the large Box C was found to be 2.6 and that of small Box B, 3.5. The means practically coincided with the medians (2.60 and 3.57). The estimates of 14 per cent of the subjects fell on the median for Box C; 4 per cent gave better than median estimates. Of the estimates for the weight of the Box B, 37 per cent were identical with the median and 20 per cent were better than the median.

D.

Investigator: Travers (1941).
Focus: A study in judging the opinions of groups.
Sample: Two hundred students taking postgraduate courses in a teachers' college.
Method: Subjects were asked to give "yes" or "no" answers to 33 questions, and then to estimate the percentage of the class that would be in favor of each of these propositions on the first 25 items and the percentage of the national population in favor of the last eight. Subjects' judgments of national opinion were compared with Gallup Poll results.
Relevant Findings: Although the errors of individual judgments of peer group and national opinion were on the average large, the mean was a fairly good estimate of group opinion.

E.

Investigator: Klugman (1945).
Focus: Group judgments for familiar and unfamiliar objects.
Sample: Sixty sixth-grade children.
Method: Subjects estimated the contents of five four-ounce jars filled with familiar and unfamiliar objects.
Relevant Findings: The pooled group estimate was generally better than the majority of the individual judgments, especially in the judgment of unfamiliar objects.

Exhibit 25
Accuracy of the Individual after Discussion

A.

Investigator: Munsterberg (1914).
Focus: Fundamentals of psychotechnics.
Sample: Four hundred students.
Method: Six pairs of black cards upon which there were white dots were presented to the entire class of four hundred. Each individual had to decide whether the upper or lower card had the larger number of dots. The number of dots was kept so nearly equal that the right judgments were only 60 per cent of the total. Each person in the classroom then indicated his decision by raising his hand. After twenty seconds, the experiment was repeated.

Relevant Findings: Awareness of the majority vote increased the correct judgments from 1443 to 1556 out of a total of 2400 judgments. Only about one-third of the students actually adapted themselves to the group judgment, a result due, according to Munsterberg, to a pronounced effect on the minority and little or no effect on the majority.

B.

Investigator: Burtt (1920).
Focus: Sex differences in the effect of discussion.
Sample: Twelve groups of college subjects, 88 women, 156 men.
Method: In an experiment in which the subject lied or told the truth about an imaginary crime, a group of persons judged his veracity by his observable reactions during examination. After five minutes of open discussion, a second judgment was made.

Relevant Findings: There was a considerable tendency to change one's decision as a result of discussion, but the change was in the wrong direction about as often as in the right. There were no appreciable sex differences in the ability to profit by discussion.

C.

Investigator: Bechterev & Lange (1924).
Focus: The results of the experiments in the field of collective reflexology.
Sample: Three audiences in Russian colleges.

Method: An object was shown for fifteen seconds without any instructions. As soon as the object was removed, each individual wrote down details which had been noticed, the descriptions were collected, and the group discussed the items noticed and recorded a decision. Each individual then indicated the differences between his opinion and that of the group.

Relevant Findings: After a picture of a locomotive was shown to 66 subjects, 284 details were noted in all, 29 of which were erroneously reported. After the group discussion, 118 correct details were added, together with seventeen mistaken ones. Thus while group did increase the number of mistaken observations, the percentage of correct observations after discussion was 86.1, compared with 80.9 before discussion. After observing two series of pictures of animals, thirteen subjects were asked to write down the differences which appeared between the representations of the same animals in the first and second series. Group discussion followed the individual reports. Thirty-three of the original observations were correct and nine incorrect before discussion and forty correct and only two incorrect after discussion. After observing pictures of a grown woman and a girl, 14, subjects noted shared characteristics of the two figures. The number of observed similarities more than doubled after the group discussion.

D.

Investigator: Jenness (1932b).

Focus: The role of discussion in changing opinion regarding a matter of fact.

Sample: Three groups of 26, 24, and 23 college students and a control group of 28 individuals.

Method: The experimental subjects estimated the number of beans in a bottle, discussed their estimates wtih one to three other subjects, and made a second estimate. Control subjects made two estimates without discussion.

Relevant Findings: Most of the subjects who took part in the discussions changed their opinions when they learned that others held different opinions. However, the same number of subjects changed their opinions when they made two estimates of the number of beans in the bottle without an intervening group discussion. Discussion reduced the range of judgment without improving its accuracy. Subjects who took part in discussions with others who held similar opinions did not change their initial opinions.

E.

Investigator: Thorndike (1938).

Focus: The effect of discussion upon the correctness of group decisions, when the factor of majority influence is allowed for.

Sample: 1200 college students in groups of four, five, and six.

Method: The subjects first recorded their individual votes on a variety of problems and then discussed the problems in small groups, working toward a unanimous group verdict. Problems were used for which some determination of the right answer was possible.

Relevant Findings: Majority vote was slightly more correct than that of the average member and discussion slightly increased the percentage of correct decisions. Individuals who were right held their positions more tenaciously than those who were wrong. A greater shift of opinion occurred in discussing matters of fact than matters of value.

F.

Investigator: Timmons (1942).

Focus: Can the superiority of discussion be attributed to averaging or majority influences?

Sample: 67 experimental four-man groups and 67 control four-man groups.

Method: After each experimental subject had read certain materials on the parole problem, he discussed the problem in a four-man group. The control subjects read the same materials and then restudied materials individually while the experimental groups were discussing. All subjects ranked five given solutions to the problem before reading, before discussion or restudy, and after discussion or restudy. On the basis of the rankings made by each individual after first reading, a control subject was paired with each experimental subject. In this way the 67 experimental groups were paired with the same number of artificially constructed control groups. From the ranks given the five solutions to the problem by the subjects in the "control" groups, three scores were computed: the average rank for each solution, the rank given by the majority for each solution, and a combined rank and majority score. For the combined score the average rank was used on each solution for which there was no majority agreement.

Relevant Findings: The discussants scored significantly higher than non-discussants when the influence of averaging and the majority factor were allowed for, either separately or in combination.

13

PRODUCTIVITY:

Group versus Group

*T*HIS FINAL CHAPTER is, in effect, a summary of the entire book. In Part One the central tendencies in group process were observed. Part Two described the deviations from these central tendencies which could be expected if certain individual or group factors were varied. Now at the end of Part Three we ask the question: Given these central tendencies and these expected deviations, what can be done to make some groups more productive than others?

A general answer is given first in a review of some of the characteristics of productive groups. This raises the question of the criteria for productivity since groups which are productive in the laboratory may not be productive in the field. Whatever the criteria, productivity in the task area is often achieved only at the expense of member satisfaction in the social-emotional area.

More specific variables related to group productivity are summarized in the last section of the chapter. Here the effects of variations in members' personalities and social characteristics, cohesiveness, group size, communication network, and leadership are reviewed. Task is omitted as a specific variable in this chapter since all of Part Three deals with variations in task performance.

§ General
Characteristics of
Productive Groups

THE MOST PRODUCTIVE GROUPS, like the most productive individuals, are found to be those which can best carry out the steps in the problem-solving process (Lippitt, 1948; Darley et al., 1952; Cattell, 1953; Gross, Martin & Darley, 1953; see Exhibit 26). Airplane crews, for example, which survive when they are forced to bail out of their plane over enemy territory are the ones which are most effective in clarifying an unstructured situation, resuming communication among members, and establishing a goal (Torrance, 1953a, 1954b, 1955a). In general, groups which are well organized and have high morale based on a large number of interteam friendships will be motivated to try harder and be the most productive (French, 1944; Goodacre, 1953; Horwitz & Cartwright, 1953; Horwitz et al., 1953). The motivation of the group is lowered if some members show an indifferent and neglectful attitude toward the task (Rosenthal & Cofer, 1948). This may be expected to occur less often among groups of friends. The organized groups are more productive not only because they have better procedures for solving task and social emotional problems, but also because the positions of members in the group are relatively stable and less time need be spent in a status struggle (Adams, 1953; Heinicke & Bales, 1953).

The self-perceptions of groups, as revealed in group projective tests, indicate that productive groups tend to be aware of characteristics which make them effective. In another study with airplane crews, crews rated good by instructors perceived in a series of projective sketches more satisfactory outcomes, less leaving the group, more orderly functioning and productivity, more interpersonal harmony, and fewer status differences (Torrance, 1953c).

To help a discussion group increase the accuracy of its self-perception, a nonparticipating observer has been used who supplies the necessary "feedback." He reports at the end of a discussion his observation on whether or not the group has stayed on the topic, the point reached in discussion, the rate of progress, and the amount of participation. Observations of this type are then used in group self-evaluation (Jenkins, 1948).

Groups which are initially low in productivity can be made more effective, either by increasing the task skill through training (Maier, 1953; Hall, 1957), by increasing their motivation by paying more attention to them (Mayo, 1933; Turner, 1933), or by providing other incentives (Berkowitz, 1957a).

§ The Criterion for
   Productivity

THE CRITERION used to predict group productivity may not always be the same for both the experimental and field situation. This is illustrated by a study of crew performance in a test situation as a predictor of field and combat performance. Seventy-one aircraft crews were classified according to combat experience and their actual success in missions, and rated on their effectiveness by their superiors. Although effective combat crews were not found to be different from less effective crews or crews which dropped out of training on some measures made in the test situation, they did differ on others. No differences were found in problem-solving scores, manner of team performance, or the members' perception of their group interaction, but the effective crews were better in use of manpower, completeness of participation, coordination, control, and flexibility. In their stories for the projective test, the successful crews described groups which were better organized, more friendly, and had a greater toleration for intermember conflict (Torrance, 1953a, 1955a).

In this case, attempts to predict from some criteria of *productivity* in the test situation (e.g., problem-solving score) to *productivity* in the field would have failed, since in the less stressful laboratory situation the crews which were later to do well in combat did no better on their problem score than those which would prove ineffective.

Although the problem of the criterion of productivity has been raised in the comparison of group with group, it also applies to the comparison of the individual and the group. The tendency of individuals to equal or surpass groups on certain *productivity* criteria in the laboratory, may disappear in other situations.

The problems of predicting productivity which result from different ways of measuring a criterion such as performance test, judges' rating, or group self-evaluation, have been discussed in Chapter Nine on group task.

§ Satisfaction versus Productivity

SINCE INDIVIDUALS TEND to join groups for three general reasons, either for the prestige of membership, to help the group reach a goal, or because they value the association with the group members (Festinger et al., 1950), their satisfaction with the group can be the result of success in any of these three areas. Their past experience which has prepared them for participation in the same or similar groups will in turn affect their ability to adjust to, and thereby be satisfied with, the present outcome (Burgess & Cottrell, 1939; Arsenian, 1943).

High productivity in the task area is not always associated with productive intermember relationships, since the former may sometimes be gained only at the expense of the latter. This is especially true in the comparison of various forms of competition with forms of co-operation. For example, in a case study of a group of clothing salesmen in a department store, competition among salesmen for the next customer resulted in morale lower than when a system of co-operative activity was initiated. However, more suits were sold when the salesmen were in competition (Babchuck & Goode, 1951).

In other studies of competition *versus* co-operation, individuals working together but with individual goals are contrasted with individuals working together with a single group goal (see Fig. 34, Chapter Twelve). The competitive groups are generally less efficient and less satisfying to the members (Deutsch, 1949; Mintz, 1951; Stendler et al., 1951; Grace, 1954), except in cases where members are asked to co-operate to receive a group score in a task in which it would be more appropriate to rate individual performance. For example, college students who were given group scores for discussion effectiveness rather than individual grades were dissatisfied with their group incentive system (Smith, 1955).

One element in competition which would appear to be related to member satisfaction is the fact that the members are competing for a high status in the group. Members of groups with a high consensus on status are in general more satisfied with the other members and also with the task performance than members of groups in which the status of the members is uncertain (Heinicke & Bales, 1953). When each member's status is apparent, the contributions of each will be given their appropriate "weight." Groups led by authoritarian leaders show results which are similar to competitive groups, since in these groups all members are in competition for status in the eyes of the leader. Productivity is higher and morale lower than for groups led by democratic leaders (Lewin et al., 1939; Adams, 1954), although in some research no differences are reported in variations of the two styles (McCurdy & Eber, 1953; see Chapter Eleven for a discussion of democratic and authoritarian leader styles). In each of these examples, the "productivity" refers to the quantity of the output, since the quality may be higher for the co-operative groups.

This trend only holds in groups in which there is an expectation that the leader will be democratic (Berkowitz, 1953). Also when most of the members of the group attempt to satisfy their "self-oriented needs" rather than work toward the group goal or the solution of the group's problems, the average member satisfaction with the meeting goes down. In the study of 72 decision-making conferences in governmental and industrial organizations, the degree to which these needs were expressed was related to various criteria of satisfaction and accomplishment. A high degree of self-oriented need expression was accompanied by a low level of satisfaction with the decisions reached, with the procedures used to reach the decision, with the chairman's handling of the meeting, and with the meeting as a whole. Members of groups high in self-oriented need expression also tended to perceive themselves as less unified, were rated as having more conflict by the observers, and completed fewer agenda items, although their meetings lasted longer (Fouriezos, Hutt, & Guetzkow, 1950; Marquis et al., 1951).

A second study was made by Guetzkow and Gyr (1954) of five- to twenty-man business and government conferences. In these groups, conflict over the task or interpersonal relations also resulted in less consensus. High consensus in all groups was associated with low expression of self-oriented needs, high need satisfaction during the meeting, pleasant atmosphere, and orderly activity. In those groups in which there was conflict over the task, higher consensus was achieved if the members used the facts, had an active chairman, and expressed warm interpersonal feelings. Higher consensus was also achieved in those groups in which there was interpersonal conflict if the members avoided some of the conflict by postponing difficult problems, showing little interest in the task, or withdrawing from interpersonal contact.

§ Members' Personalities

IN SELECTING MEMBERS with personality or social characteristics which will result in a productive group, the requirements of the task must be kept in mind. If the group has a purpose which tends to emphasize problems of control (or problems of affection), then it is best to select members who do not have so much internal conflict that they are unable to be effective in this area. This same generalization holds, of course, for the major steps in problem-solving. If the step of observation, hypothesizing, or proposing action is especially important for a particular group, then it would be wise to select members who have the required capacities (Green, 1950; Willerman, 1953). In addition, an individual can work best with others who are at least equal or better in skill (Rosenberg, Erlick, & Berkowitz, 1955).

Group members with given personality characteristics tend to have more influence upon the patterns of group interaction in newly formed groups than they may be expected to have in groups which have developed a stable culture pattern (Cattell et al., 1953). As groups move through the initial stages of development, members who have problems in one area may impede the progress of the group by forcing other members to continue to work in one problem area long after the problems in this area have been solved by the majority of the members. Thus, in one instance, the members who were absent most often from a therapy group formed a subgroup which challenged the formal leader and made it difficult for the group to move on to other problems (Herbert & Trist, 1953).

On the other hand, the effectiveness of the group can be increased if some members have personality characteristics which are considered particularly valuable by the group. Since the leader is a key person, the group will be more effective if he closely approximates the group's ideal of a leader (Greer, 1955).

§ Compatibility of Affectional Orientation

A GROUP'S ABILITY to handle feelings and emotions is especially important in tasks which require close, intimate relations with others or which arouse member feelings. If the group members have similar personality traits in the area of affection, they should be able to agree more readily on the extent to which they will permit close, intimate relationships within the group. If members differ in that some want close relationships while others prefer to keep at a distance, then the members will be basically incompatible, a condition which should decrease their productivity.

Compatible groups can be selected fully formed on the basis of past performance or they can be composed of members who have either chosen each other on an appropriate sociometric criterion or who possess the necessary qualifications as revealed by personality tests.

An experiment by Schutz (1958a, pp. 128-135) using composed groups of college students illustrates the relationship between compatibility and productivity. Schutz sent invitations to every tenth male student at a large university asking him to participate in an experiment to be conducted over a six-week period. When about 100 had accepted they were called together and given a personality test and other questionnaires. On the basis of the results of the personality test and a consideration of their mathematics and verbal scores on the Scholastic Achievement Test, twelve five-man groups were formed.

Four groups were composed according to Compatible Pattern A, four followed Compatible Pattern B, and four followed the Incompatible Pattern (see Table 26). Compatible Pattern A contained a member who was predicted to be a "focal person," a "main supporting member," and three subjects who were less intelligent and less assertive who would be members. All subjects in this pattern were personal in orientation with a liking for close, intimate relationships. The subjects in Compatible Pattern B were predicted to play similar roles except that they were all counter-personal in orientation, persons who liked to keep others at a distance. In the incompatible pattern there were two pairs of a "focal person" and a follower, one pair was personal and the other counter-personal. The incompatible pattern also contained one neutral person.

Each of these twelve groups was brought to the small group laboratory and run through fourteen meetings over a period of six weeks. There were four one-hour meetings a day at 4:00, 5:00, 7:30, and 8:30 P.M., Monday through Friday, and at 10:00 and 11:00 A.M. and at 1:00 and 2:00 P.M. on Saturday. Each group met twice a week at the same time (except Saturday), three days apart (e.g., Monday at 5:00 P.M. and Thursday at 5:00).

Each group was given the sequence of tasks listed in Table 26a.

Table 26—Composition Patterns for Compatible and Incompatible Groups of Personal and Counterpersonal Members

Compatible Group Members
(Type A)

	FP_p	MS_p	M_p	M_p	M_p
Personalness	H *	H	H	H	H
Dependence	L,M	L,M	L,M	L,M	L,M
Assertiveness	H	L,M	L,M	L,M	L,M
Intelligence	H	H	L,M	L,M	L,M

Compatible Group Members
(Type B)

	FP_c	MS_c	M_c	M_c	M_c
Personalness	L	L	L	L	L
Dependence	L,M	M,H	M,H	M,H	M,H
Assertiveness	H	L,M	L,M	L,M	L,M
Intelligence	H	H	L,M	L,M	L,M

Incompatible Group Members

	FP_p	S_p	FP_c	S_c	N
Personalness	H	H	L	L	M
Dependence	L,M	L,M	H	H	M
Assertiveness	H	L,M	H	L,M	L
Intelligence	H	L,M	H	L,M	L,M

Personal Subgroup	Counterpersonal Dependent Subgroup
Antagonistic Subgroups	

* Key:
H = roughly highest quarter
M = roughly second or third quarter
L = roughly lowest quarter
p = personal
c = counterpersonal

FP = Focal person
MS = Main Supporting member
M = Member
S = Supporting member
N = Neutral

Table 26a—Schedule of Activities of Groups

Meeting   Task

1. Indoctrination, discussion (choosing a group name), discussion (prison problem)
2. Building task (The Toy), discussion (cheating problem)
3. Intercept task (modified chess)
4. Intercept task, discussion (child rearing)
5. Free behavior, no task, standings announced, each group told that "all groups were close, they were among lower ones."
6. Discussion (how to improve groups), concept formation task
7. Building tasks
8. Intercept tasks, discussion (traffic problem)
9. Group projective, concept formation task
10. Building task, intercept task
11-14. Intercept contests (pairs of groups)

Productivity differences were measured by comparison of the scores received on the objective measures assigned to each task. The intercept contests in the eleventh to fourteenth meetings were games played between two teams of different compatibility types. Each team played approximately the same number of contests.

The discussion tasks were administered as follows. The experimenter would read aloud a short (three-paragraph) description of a situation involving a difficult decision, typically based on authority *versus* friendship, or something similarly related to the personality dimensions. Each subject would then write down what he would do in that situation and the reasons for his decision. Then the group would be allowed fifteen to thirty minutes to discuss the problem and come to a "group decision," a purposely ambiguous phrase not specifying unanimity, majority, or any other system of decision. Then the members were asked to appoint one member to be spokesman for the group and present the group's decision to the experimenter. The experimenter returned on signal and, before hearing the group's decision, first had the subjects write their own individual postdiscussion decisions.

A typical meeting proceeded as follows: The group would arrive about five minutes before the hour and would go right into the laboratory room. They had all been given a tour of the observation room at the first meeting, so they were fully aware of the observers. Recording apparatus would be turned on in the observation room. The experimenter would watch through the one-way mirror for several minutes, allowing the group time for free discussion. The group was under the impression they were simply waiting for the session to begin. Generally about five minutes was allowed unless there was some especially important interaction occurring.

The experimenter would then greet the group and present the day's activity. He would attempt to be distant friendly with all groups, trying not to encourage or discourage any single group. After he was assured the instructions were clear, the experimenter would leave the room to return only when summoned at the end of an activity. The experimenter attempted to be with the group only when necessary. After the group's activity was finished, he returned to the room and completed the hour's work. Usually he would then leave, allowing a few more minutes for free behavior, and then return and dismiss the group.

§ Conditions
of the Experiment

THE SUBJECTS were selected on the basis of personality tests from the college freshmen volunteers. They had a wide range of backgrounds, with the main differences from a random population probably being higher mean intelligence and higher mean social-economic status. All were from seventeen to 23 years old. An attempt was made to balance intelligence between groups. This was done successfully within the limits of scheduling.

All tasks used in the experiment were new to the subjects. There was no indication that any subject had special knowledge that would assist him in the solution of the tasks.

The previous acquaintance of the subjects with each other varied, but on the whole the members of any one of the five-man groups were not well acquainted and certainly no group had ever met as a group prior to the experiment.

There were virtually no restraints put on the groups as to seating arrangements or communication. With regard to leadership, the experimenter never designated a particular member as any type of leader. In some tasks the experimenter named certain roles which had to be filled by men chosen by the group itself. In all cases the group could remove the man they chose from his role at any time.

Motivation was engendered by (1) a talk to all subjects on the importance of the experiment to various industrial, governmental, military, and research activities, (2) a statement at the outset of the experiment that the experimenter wanted only participants who would appear promptly at every meeting and participate fully, (3) a reward of $25 to the "best" group, and several $10 prizes for the "best" individual performance, (4) payment of one dollar per hour of meeting for each subject, and (5) payment only if all members attended all meetings.

1. *Game* (Intercept). The non-discussion tasks given to the groups were: A modified chess-type game involving the whole group coming to a decision within thirty seconds. One man was chosen coordinator by the group who had complete authority and responsibility for making the decisions.

2. *Concept.* This is the task used by Bruner, Goodnow, and Austin (1956) for individual concept formation studies. It was adapted to the

group situation and administered similarly to the intercept task except, (1) there were two coordinators with equal authority, and (2) there was a penalty for total time rather than a time list for individual moves. This served to introduce a new type of decision, that between taking a chance and acting quickly, and being more deliberate.

3. *Toy.* This was a task in which the group was to build a specified structure as fast as possible. The materials used included heavy paper squares and triangles, reinforced with wooden dowels. This was a division-of-labor type task, requiring the coordination of several different jobs.

Data were collected by questionnaires, observation, and sociometric, tests. Throughout the course of the experiment, the following questionnaires were administered:

   a. Slater, *Parental Role Preference Questionnaire* (*PRP*).
   b. Blum, *Blacky Projective Test.*
   c. Blum, *Defense Preference Inventory* (*DPI*).
   d. Schutz, *Fundamental Interpersonal Relations Orientation* (*FIRO*).
   e. *California F-Scale* (Authoritarianism).
   f. Edwards, *Personal Preference Schedule.*
   g. La Forge and Suczek, *Interpersonal Checklist.*
   h. Guilford, *R.* (*Rhathmyia*) *and C* (*Cyclothmia*) *Scales.*
   i. Bales and Couch, *Value Profile.*

These questionnaires were administered over the entire fourteen meetings so as to spread the work required over a reasonable time period.

Each meeting was observed by two to five trained observers. No category system was used to record the act-by-act sequence behavior, except for a few meetings which involved special projects. The primary observational data were a series of ratings made once or twice a meeting. When there were two activities in one meeting, e.g., a discussion and a building task, one rating was made after each activity. If there were only one activity, only one rating was made per meeting. The ratings were made for a variety of roles commonly noted in group meetings, such as discussion guider, influencer, and promoter of personal feelings. The observer was first asked to decide whether or not any member or members of the group clearly fulfilled the description of the role, and then he was asked to rank all five group members with respect to this role. The weighted sum of all rankings for all meetings was computed for each role for each group member. These ratings were standardized and used as the behavioral data.

In order to obtain the most comparable data, the subjects were given a rating sheet almost identical to that used by the observers. A rating sheet was used at both the fifth and the tenth meetings. In addition the subjects filled out regular sociometric questions regarding "like," "work with," and "influences." These constituted additional sources of data.

§ Results of the Compatibility Experiment

SINCE ALL THE TASKS were of different types it was difficult to combine scores to get an overall productivity measure. It was therefore decided to rank all twelve groups on each task and use the sum of these ranks for the total productivity score.

There were four objective tasks: Toy, Concept, Game, and Game Contest. Where a task occurred more than once (as in Toy and Concept), the ranks were averaged to give a final rank for that task. Thus the final rank was based on one rank for each task (see Table 27).

Table 27—Ranks on Productivity for all Groups on all Tasks

Personal
Compatible Groups

	Toy	Concept	Game	Contest	Total	Final Rank
No. 1	3	8	7	10	28	9
No. 6	1	1	11	1	14	1
No. 9	7.5	4	2	4	17.5	2
No. 12	10	10	1	6.5	27.5	8
Total					87	20

Counterpersonal
Compatible Groups

No. 2	6	6	4	2	18	3
No. 7	2	7	10	3	22	4
No. 8	10	5	5	6.5	26.5	7
No. 11	7.5	2.5	2	11	23	5
Total					89.5	19

Incompatible Groups

No. 3	10	11.5	8	6.5	36	11
No. 4	12	11.5	9	9	41.5	12
No. 5	4.5	9	6	6.5	26	6
No. 10	4.5	2.5	12	12	31	10
Total					134.5	39

The difference in ranks between the combined "compatibles" and the "incompatibles" is significant beyond the .02 level (Mann-Whitney U-test).

There is virtually no difference in productivity between the Personal Compatibles (P-Com) and the Counterpersonal Compatibles (CP-Com). The CP-Coms have one "final rank" less while the P-Coms have two and a half total ranks less, neither difference is significant. The ideal result of the final ranking would have placed the "incompatibles" (Incom) in ranks 9, 10, 11, and 12, and seen the first eight ranks distributed among the compatible groups. Actually, this happened with the one exception of Incom group 5 and P-Com group 1 who ideally should have interchanged ranks six and nine.

However, the variations in the ranks makes it statistically tenuous to assume that the productivity rank for any group is highly stable. This may mean (1) the number of tests of productivity was inadequate to stabilize performance, (2) the tasks required different abilities of the groups; thus they performed differentially, or (3) groups are always erratic in their performance.

The results of the experiment with college subjects generally confirm the hypothesis that compatible groups are more productive than incompatible groups, although, contrary to the anticipated result, the groups composed of members who were counterpersonal performed as well as those composed of personal members.

Several predictions in the area of interpersonal choice which were supported by a previous experiment with naval recruits (Schutz, 1955) were not confirmed in the experiment with college subjects. In the incompatible group of college subjects, members of subgroups did not prefer to work with each other more, nor did the members of the personal subgroups like each other more as they did in groups composed of naval recruits. Although in the navy experiment a member of a personal subgroup tended to rank the man he liked best higher on competence than an objective measure would justify, the same tendency to overrate performance was not evident in the college groups.

In the college experiment the persons predicted to be focal and main supporting members in each group *did* rank each other highly as easy to work well with in the personal compatible groups, confirming the navy results. This was not true, however, in the college counterpersonal compatible groups. In the personal compatible groups, the person predicted to be focal *appeared* more central to the observers in both experiments.

§ Social Characteristics

IN THE SELECTION of productive members by their social characteristics, the major variables have been so apparent that they have received
little experimental substantiation: Adults are usually more efficient than
children, and older children more so than younger children (James,
1956). Single sex groups are often more efficient than mixed groups
because they spend less time on social-emotional activity (South, 1927;
Gurnee, 1937b), and men and women typically do better in the roles
for which their culture has trained them. Groups composed of friends
are more productive than groups of strangers (Husband, 1940; Zeleny,
1947; Goodacre, 1951; Van Zelst, 1952) unless, like the mixed committees, they spend all their time in social-emotional activity (Horsfall &
Arnsberg, 1949).

The relationship between productivity and duration of membership
in a group is illustrated by a study in which one member of a four-man
group was placed in another group as a "stranger" and later returned to
his own group. In each case, the task of the group was to list the objects
which could be seen in a series of Rorschach cards. The production of
ideas about the Rorschach card decreased for the experimental subject
when he was moved from his initial group to a second four-man group
as a stranger, and increased when he returned again. The subject presumably was inhibited in his productivity by the "strangeness" of the
social situation in the new group (Nash & Wolfe, 1957).

§ Cohesiveness

GROUPS WHICH ARE HIGHLY COHESIVE tend to work harder regardless of
outside supervision (Berkowitz, 1954a, 1954b; Cohen, 1957a). For example, when fifty six-man work units of five employees and their regular
plant supervisor were timed in the task of assembling two factory products, the group attributes of "character," "compactness," and "cohesiveness" were found to be correlated .76, .78, and .88 with a productivity
score. In this case, as in other industrial studies, member satisfaction was
not related to productivity (Danzig & Galanter, 1955).

Cohesive groups will be especially productive if they are also motivated to do the task well. In an air corps experiment, members of 81

eleven-man B-29 crews were asked to indicate how important they felt the B-29 was for defense as evidence of their own motivation and also to estimate the motivation of other crew members. Cohesiveness of each group was indicated by the extent to which they liked to spend time with other crew members and their feeling that the members respected each other. Effectiveness was measured by superiors' ratings and the percentage of missions failed. An analysis of the data indicated that in the crews with high cohesiveness, high motivation was related to effectiveness. However, in crews with low cohesiveness, effectiveness was negatively correlated with the discrepancy between actual and perceived motivation, regardless of whether the scores were both high or both low (Berkowitz, 1956a). That is, the crews who were not very friendly would still be effective if members had the same regard for the worth of their job in the air corps.

In some cases cohesiveness in a small ingroup may be generated primarily by antagonism toward some other outgroup (Sherif, 1951; Sherif & Sherif, 1953). This inter-group hostility may then make it difficult for members of both groups to join in a new group to arbitrate their differences. This apparently happens between groups of labor and management in some industries.

In a study of the interaction process in the mediation of labor-management disputes, it was found that ultimate success of the session could be partially predicted from the parties' states of mind when they embarked upon the session: the more hostile their expressed feelings, the less likelihood of success (Landsberger, 1955b).

§ Group Size

To SELECT the appropriate size group for a given problem, Thelen (1949) has suggested the "principle of the least group size." The group should be just large enough to include individuals with all the relevant skills for problem solution. Since larger groups provide fewer opportunities for each member to speak, require more control, and are generally less friendly, they tend to be less efficient (South, 1927; Hare, 1952). In addition to these problems, the average number of contributions made by each member decreases as more members are added to the group.

As a simple demonstration of the phenomenon of "diminishing returns," Moede (1927) found that, although a group of eight men could pull harder than a smaller group or a single individual, the decrease in average contribution shown in Table 28 became more and more marked as the group size increased. One person could pull 63 kilograms using 100 per cent of his capacity, but eight persons were able to use only 49 per cent of their average individual capacity in pulling 248 kilograms.

Table 28—Pulling Power of Different-sized Groups

	NUMBER OF PERSONS			
	1	2	3	8
Total pull in kilograms	63	118	160	248
Percentage of average individual capacity	100	93	85	49
Marginal pull in kilograms	63	55	42	

A similar effect with an intellectual task was noted in a study of groups of eight different sizes, ranging from single individuals to groups of 96 members (Gibb, J. R., 1951). As each group discussed one of three types of problems for a half hour, the members called out their contributions which were recorded on the blackboard. With the increase in the size of the group, the average number of ideas produced by each member decreased.

§ Communication Network

REGARDLESS of the characteristics of the individual members, a number of changes can be made in the communication network of a group which will increase productivity. Feedback from receiver to sender increases the accuracy of the messages transmitted through a communication network (Leavitt & Mueller, 1951), so that groups in which free communication is maximized are generally more accurate in their judgments, although they may take longer to reach a decision. A number of authors have suggested methods of measuring the effectiveness of discussion either by statistical indices or check lists (Findley, 1948; Brandenberg, 1953; Crowell, 1953). When there is role differentiation, groups which have the fewest communication links between the point at which information is received and the point at which a decision is made should be the most efficient (Roby & Lanzetta, 1956).

§   Leadership

STUDIES of organizational effectiveness typically report that good leadership is a primary criterion for efficiency (Gekoski, 1952). For example, questionnaires were given to 98 workers at a shipyard to isolate factors related to organizational effectiveness (Wilson, High, Beem, & Comrey, 1954). A factor-analysis of the data indicated four factors: supervisor-subordinate rapport, congenial work group, informal control, and group unity (i.e., the tendency to work for a common purpose). Four somewhat similar variables were reported in a review of industrial research: the supervisor's ability to play a differentiated role, the degree of delegation of authority or closeness of supervision, the quality of supportiveness by employees, and the amount of group cohesiveness (Kahn & Katz, 1953).

Although there is a tendency for groups led by autocratic leaders to produce more but of lower quality than groups led by democratic leaders, there is always higher productivity, when a skilled leader is playing the leader role (Maier, 1950; Rock & Hay, 1953; Borgatta et al., 1954; Ghiselli & Lodahl, 1958).

§   Summary

THE MOST PRODUCTIVE GROUPS are those which can carry out effectively the major steps in the process of solving task and social-emotional problems for the group and for the individual members. To accomplish this, the group must have a combination of members' personalities and skills, a type of group structure, and group problem-solving experience which is appropriate for the task. In an authoritarian setting the most productive group will tend to be authoritarian, whereas in a more democratic situation the equalitarian group will be more productive.

Predictions about group productivity should be more accurate when the test situation is similar to the field situation in all important respects. Since the amount of stress actually present in the field may be hard to duplicate in the laboratory, the factors which bring success in the laboratory may not be the same as those which lead to success in the field.

Members will be satisfied with the group if it has been able to solve the particular task or social-emotional problem in which they were most interested. However, high productivity in the task area is not always associated with satisfactory relationships in the social-emotional area. In authoritarian groups and competitive groups, high productivity is often gained at the expense of member satisfaction.

The influence of member personality traits on group productivity is illustrated in an experiment that compared five-man groups, in which all subjects either desired close relations with others or preferred to keep their distance, with groups in which some subjects desired close relations and some did not. In a series of group tasks and competitions between groups of opposing types, the "compatible" groups were found to be more productive, presumably because they were able to agree in the social-emotional area and thus free themselves to work on the task.

For the same reason groups tend to be more productive if they are composed of members of the same sex, are cohesive and small, have a communication network with maximum feedback, and have a skilled leader.

Exhibit 26
Organization, Morale, and Productivity

A.

Investigator: Rosenthal & Cofer (1948).

Focus: The effect on group performance of an indifferent and neglectful attitude shown by one group member.

Sample: Seven control and seven experimental groups of four subjects each, and five control and five experimental groups of five subjects each. All were male college students enrolled in an introductory psychology course.

Method: All subjects were told they were part of a large experiment to compare intellectual and motor processes (dart throwing) of college students with other groups of different academic, occupational, and social status. The fictitious score of the group to which the subjects were being compared was so high that no group reached it. Each subject made five successive dart throws in each of nine trials. The group score was the sum of all scores of subjects in that group. In each experimental group was one subject, who was in league with the experimenter, who after the first trial began to behave in a manner indicative of "indifference and neglect." Subjects were also given attitude tests.

Relevant Findings: There was a shift in attitudes in the experimental groups in the direction of disbelief in goal attainability and of disbelief that other group members would whole-heartedly participate to achieve the goal. The experimental groups also had more difficulty in setting a group level of aspiration.

B.

Investigator: Darley, Gross, & Martin (1952).

Focus: Studies of group behavior: factors associated with the productivity of groups.

Sample: Thirteen houses of a co-operative housing project.

Method: Each co-operative house produced a plan for improvement which was ranked for its excellence by five judges. The rank on the group plan was compared with the rank or each of eighteen other behavior variables as ranked by two participant observers.

Relevant Findings: The quality of the report produced was correlated .86 with the efficiency of the house organization, .64 with satisfaction with project life, and .59 with enthusiasm for the task. Low correlations with the other fifteen variables may in part be due to low inter-rate reliability.

C.

Investigator: Goodacre (1953).
Focus: Group characteristics of combat units with good and poor performance.
Sample: Thirteen highest ranking and thirteen lowest ranking rifle squads, 216 men in all.
Method: Thirteen questions were asked in interviews.
Relevant Findings: Men in good performance groups socialized together more after hours, took unauthorized initiative during the problem more often, reported fewer disagreements on how the leader ran the problem, more satisfaction with their status, and more pride in their squad.

D.

Investigator: Horwitz & Cartwright (1953).
Focus: A projective method for the diagnosis of group properties.
Sample: Five training groups of twelve to fifteen members.
Method: Groups were asked to make up stories about a TAT. picture. The ratio:

$$\frac{\text{Number of productivity choices made within own group}}{\text{Number of productivity choices made in total workshop}}$$

was computed for each member, and the mean of these ratios was computed for all members in a given group. Cohesiveness was measured by coding of statements of members regarding attractiveness of group, statements suggesting group disruption, and statements indicating that the individuals were leaving the group.
Relevant Findings: Correlating the rank orders of the groups on the measures of "cohesiveness" and "productivity," respectively, it was found that cohesiveness of voluntary training groups was directly related to perceptions of group productivity, Rho $= +1.00$.

E.

Investigator: Torrance (1953a, 1955a).
Focus: Perception of group functioning as a predictor of group performance.
Sample: 71 eleven-man B-29 crews.
Method: Crew members were shown two projective sketches. For the first,

individual crew members were asked to write stories; the crew then discussed which of the individual stories would be the crew's story. For the second sketch the procedure was revised, the crew composed a story first and individuals wrote private versions of a story later. Each crew was given a score on combat effectiveness based on ratings by superior officers and its percentage of successful missions.

Relevant Findings: Effective combat crews perceived more succesful outcomes, more remaining with the group, and productivity in the "task group" picture, and less harmony, and more discord, friendship, and pleasure in the "informal" picture than the ineffective or drop-out crews. Members of the effective crews tended to accept the crew stories as their own.

Appendix I

AN OUTLINE OF RESEARCH METHODS

SINCE THE PRINCIPAL emphasis in this text has been on the findings of research rather than the methods by which the results were obtained, only brief descriptions have been given of category systems (Chapter Three) and sociometric techniques (Chapter Five). As a guide to the literature on methodology, references which are especially relevant for the analysis of behavior in small groups are listed under the following general headings:

1. Research design and experimental method
2. Observation techniques
3. Sociometry
4. Questionnaires

The most comprehensive reviews of current methodology are found in three sources: Jahoda, Deutsch, and Cook (Eds.), *Research Methods in Social Relations* (1951),[1] Festinger and Katz (Eds.), *Research Methods in the Behavioral Sciences* (1953), and Lindzey (Ed.), *Handbook of Social Psychology* (1954). For some indication of the development of research methods in this area, the current texts can be compared with Lindeman's *Social Discovery* (1924) which reviews the methodology of the social sciences prior to 1924.

§ Research Design and Experimental Method

THE FOLLOWING ADDITIONAL REFERENCES describe some of the general problems in conducting experiments with small groups both in the laboratory and in the field: Miller, 1950; Swanson, 1951a; Whyte, 1951b; Argyle, 1952; Festinger, 1953b; French, 1953; Grossack, 1953; Rubenstein, 1953; Edwards, 1954; Sherif, 1954a, 1954b; Borgatta and Cottrell, 1957; Taylor and Mitzel, 1957. Typical tasks which have been used in research are described by Ray (1955). Some specific experimental designs are suggested by Crutchfield (1951).

§ Observation Techniques

THE CHAPTERS in the three major references mentioned above which describe observation techniques are by Whyte (1951), Zander (1951), Heyns and Zander (1953), Plak (1953), and Heyns and Lippitt (1954).

In the collection of data, the observer usually uses one of the following four general approaches:

1. *Recall*—the observer either recalls his own experiences in a group or asks others to do so. If he asks others to recall their observations of behavior, this method of data collection becomes the interview as it has been used with individuals (Puffer, 1905), or with groups (Hare & Davie, 1954, Davie & Hare, 1956). If other untrained observers are

---

1. A condensation of this same material appears in Sellitz, Jahoda, Deutsch, and Cook (1959).

asked to write down their impressions of a previous group meeting, the method becomes the questionnaire (Hemphill, 1949). In either event, the data, once recorded, can be processed by methods appropriate for other kinds of observation.

2. *Participant observer*—the observer takes an active part in the life of the group while making his observations. In some cases the other group members do not know that they are being observed. There is usually little time for note-taking unless the observer also plays the role of secretary for the group. The participant observer technique has been used with boys' gangs (Whyte, 1943), on psychiatric wards (Stanton & Schwartz, 1954; Banks, 1956), with discussion groups (Carr, 1929) and in studies of rumor transmission (Back, Festinger, Hymovitch, Kelley, Schachter & Thibaut, 1950). The observer may conduct a "field experiment" by behaving in some predetermined way to note the group's reaction.

3. *Nonparticipant observer*—most of the observations reported in the child-study literature have been made by nonparticipating adults who stood on the school playground or sat in the classroom (Piaget, 1926; Thomas & Thomas, 1928; Thomas, 1929; Reckless, 1930; Hare, 1957).

4. *Unseen observer*—in laboratory experiments the observer is frequently given some place to conceal himself. This may be a simple burlap screen (Lippitt, 1940) or an observation room with a one-way mirror (Bales, 1950). Some subjects are told that they are being observed, others are not (Cocherell, 1935). Bales and Flanders (1954) suggest a plan for the construction of a small group laboratory and observation room.

§ Quantity and Quality of Observations

HAVING DECIDED on his general approach to observation, the observer may attempt to record everything that goes on, he may use a category system, or he may make ratings.

1. *Complete transcript*—the most complete records of group behavior are not made by men but by machines: sound movies, time-lapse photography (Thelen, 1950; Withall, 1956), or sound-recording equipment. However, detailed transcripts can also be produced by stenographers or by trained observers who alternate with each other in observing a group or an individual over a long period of time (Barker & Wright, 1949; Barker, 1951). In the complete transcript the observer usually uses

the most complete category system he has—language. However, a complete language is not a very efficient category system since so many of the words mean almost the same thing and since there are too many categories to make quantitative analysis of the data possible. Complete transcripts are useful only as a basis for clinical insight or as illustrative material.

2. *Category system*—in a category system the number of words used to describe behavior is reduced and generality of the words is increased. The reduced set of concepts, seldom more than 100, is then used to describe the act-by-act sequence of events in group behavior. The problems of development and use of category systems are elaborated in the paragraphs below.

3. *Ratings*—summary ratings of certain aspects of group behavior are often made at the end of each session or at some specified intervals during the session. These judgments may be of individual behavior, they may compare or rank group members according to some criterion of behavior, or they may be judgments about the group as a whole (Wrightstone, 1934, 1951; Zander, 1948).

§ Category Systems

FIVE DECISIONS must be made by anyone using a category system. Each of these points is mentioned in Chapter Three and discussed in some detail in the general references on observation methods.

1. *Frame of reference*—behavior may be scored primarily by the intent of the actor or by his effect on others. The focus can be on the individual or on the group. Leary (1957) suggests the analysis of data at five levels (public, conscious, and private communication, the unexpressed, and values) through the use of different data collecting techniques.

2. *Unit act*—the unit of behavior to be scored may be a sentence, a paragraph, an interaction, or any bit of behavior to which another person may respond.

3. *Sample*—some observers score continuously (Bales, 1950b); others take short "time samples" at frequent intervals (Arrington, 1939, 1943).

4. *Single or multiple code*—if a given unit of behavior appears to have more than one implication (for example, it may contain both work and emotion), some observers score only the dominant characteristic of the act (Bales, 1950b), while others give it two scores (Thelen, 1954).

5. *Recording devices*—the ultimate objective with any recording device is to prepare the data for machine computation, since hand tabula-

tion is not feasible if any quantity of data is collected. The observer usually records the time that the act took place or the sequence in which it occurred, who initiated the act, who received it, and the content. The devices listed below are ordered from least to most efficient in preparing data for analysis.

a. FIXED FORM—the form can be simply a blank piece of paper on a clipboard, or a prepared form (Bales, 1950b). Acts are usually recorded in sequence. The stenotype machine (Carter, Haythorn, Meirowitz, & Lanzetta, 1951) and recording by voice into a portable recorder are in the same class since these methods preserve only the sequence of acts. Time must be written in if the record is to be compared with a sound transcript.

b. MOVING TAPE—when scoring is done on a moving tape, the actual time of the act is preserved. Bales and Gebrands (1948) have developed an Interaction Process Recorder which can be used with interchangeable category systems. Chapple has developed a portable recorder for use with his system. Polygraphs are used to combine categories with other types of behavioral or physiological measures (Boyd & DiMasio, 1954).

c. CHRONOGRAPH—Chapple's Interaction Chronograph (1940) (Matarazzo, 1956) is a device which partially processes the data while it is being recorded. A simpler version records action and silence but does not process the data (Kasl & Mahl, 1956).

d. DIRECT PUNCHING—the most direct method is to punch the interactions on IBM cards, one act per card, although this method has two disadvantages. It requires a large permanent installation and the ordinary punching machines may not operate fast enough to keep pace with a group discussion. The first disadvantage can be avoided by using "mark sense" cards in notebooks which can be carried into the field by observers and later fed to a machine to produce punched cards (Lippitt & Zander, 1943). The second disadvantage can be overcome by recording magnetically on a plastic tape which would then be used to produce punched cards.

Some experimenters have asked the group members to record their own reactions to a discussion on an audience reaction machine (Thelen & Withall, 1949; Thelen, 1950; Bass, Gaier, Farese, & Flint, 1957) or to recall their reactions when parts of the discussion were played back to them at a later time (Mills, Lichter, & Kassebaum, 1957).

§ Statistical Analysis of Observational Data

A NUMBER OF statistical indices of participation in discussion have been proposed (Findley, 1948; Pepinsky, Siegel, & Van Atta, 1952; Dickens, 1955). Other statistical problems are discussed by Bales (1950b, 1951)

§ Reliability and Validity

VARIOUS MEASURES have been used to test interobserver or self-reliability in the use of category systems. Usually the reliability for some categories is higher than others and varies with the topic of discussion (Borgatta & Bales, 1953c; Avery & Bachelis, 1956). A statistical test of reliability which could be applied to many systems has been proposed by Schutz (1952a) who actually developed his scheme for use with content analysis. In collecting and analyzing data, the observer using categories and the investigator who uses content analysis share many of the same problems (Berelson, 1952, 1954). The early workers in the child-study field made exhaustive studies of reliability (Thomas, 1932; Thomas, Loomis, & Arrington, 1933).

One of the problems in validity is that the observer, as any other measuring instrument, may affect the field of observation to some extent by his presence. Some of the effects of an observer upon a group are probably similar to the effects of an audience upon performance described in Chapter Twelve.

§ Early Category Systems

HISTORICALLY category systems received a great deal of attention between 1920 and 1930, primarily in the study of the social behavior of children. Dorothy Thomas and her associates (1929) had an intensive interest in the methodology of repeated samples of behavior which they called time sampling (Arrington, 1943). Other interesting early attempts were those of Moreno (1923, translated 1947), Piaget (1926), and Carr (1929).

Moreno's earliest category system first appeared in his book on *The Theatre of Spontaneity*, which was published anonymously in German in 1923. This book described a new kind of "spontaneous" theatre, which was the precursor of sociodrama and psychodrama introduced by Moreno in the 1930's to portray social and psychological problems. The following descriptions of "Notations for Spontaneity States" and an "Action Diagram" are taken from Moreno's translation of his original book on the spontaneity theatre (1947b, pp. 57-58, 98).

§ Notations for Spontaneity States

THE CONDITION of the player before beginning of action, the consciousness or zero state, is best expressed by the sign zero (0). The identification of consciousness with the zero state has a practical justification. The player, before he throws himself in a spontaneous creative act, is just conscious of himself and the life situation which contains, however, none of the creative-situational complex which he will be asked to produce any moment. It is a zero state from the point of view of the prospective creative state. If the player has—upon the instruction of the director—presented anxiety, and if he is given the task to pass from it into anger, he has really two tasks: one to produce a new state—anger—and another, to break away from the previous one—anxiety. The transition from anxiety into anger can take place directly by a jump, or indirectly over a zero level, by returning to it. Jumping from one state to another may cause impurities; a hangover from one state may influence and distort the next. As a sign for a spontaneity state, I suggest a vertically drawn pointed angle: ∧ . The upward line of the angle portrays the warming up from a zero level to the spontaneity state, the top part of the angle portrays its achievement, the downward line of the angle represents the loss of the stage, its cooling off and return to the zero level. Once this basic sign is accepted all other signs of the spontaneity alphabet develop logically. If one and the same state is repeated immediately after, the sign for it is a double angle with broken inner lines: ∧∧ . If the repetition is continuous, for instance five times, the sign accordingly is ∧∧∧ . In actuality the player does not return to the zero level, but remains midway, making short pauses. He may be given the task to produce a state of anger for a number of situations in a stretch. He would not produce it as a continuity, but in rhythmic time units. The separation of one unit from another may be hardly noticeable from without, but they are occurring just the same. If a state is not repeated but passes into a new one immediately followed by a jump without a pause, then the sign for it would be the inner lines of the vertically drawn pointed angle, connected by a horizontal line, before they return to a new plane: ⌐⌐⌐. However, if the player is to return from the state to zero and to climb from there anew, then the sign of the self is simply two connected vertical angles: *M* . For two types of opening states, the opening and the ending tempus at the beginning or at the end of a situation, the sign is an angle reduced in size ⋀ , starting and ending tempus amount together to the full duration of the state (½t plus ½t equals t) (see Fig. 38).

Figure 38—Moreno's Action Diagram

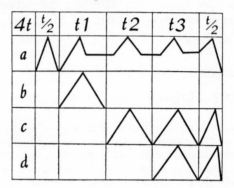

§ Piaget's Category System

To COLLECT QUANTITATIVE DATA for his study of *The Language and Thought of the Child* (1926), Piaget used a system of eight categories. Some of his hypotheses about the functions of language in young children and the typical interaction patterns between children were tested by comparing the frequencies of activity in each of the categories, others were tested by forming indices to represent the ratio of acts in two different categories. These two forms for data analysis have remained the basic ways of handling the data derived from the analysis of interaction. Piaget's eight categories were:

1. Repetition
2. Monologue
3. Collective monologue
4. Adapted information
5. Criticism and derision

6. Orders and threats
7. Question
8. Answer

His use of the categories is illustrated in an excerpt from his observation of Lev, a six-year-old boy in a French school (see Fig. 39).

Figure 39—Interaction of a Six-year-old Boy *

Number and Text	Category	Remarks
1. Lev puts his pencil down Geo's neck. Geo cries out, "Lev!" *It doesn't matter.* Lev begins to draw his hat again. He shows his work:	4	
2. *I look at things properly. What are you looking at?*	4	(This remark belongs to 4 because it is part of a dialogue. It calls forth an answer and then remark 3.)
3. *The hat.* Lev repeats some words which one of his companions is learning:	8	
4. *Luloid! celluloid!* Turning his drawing upside down and addressing himself to no one:	1	
5. *I want to see how it looks.* Ro brings some paper cigarettes. He distributees them. Lev asks for some:	2	
6. *How about me?* Lev goes back to his work. He points to the little ribs of straw on his hat and compares them with the drawing.	7	This is a request, but expressed in interrogative form; it therefore belongs to category 7.

* Piaget, 1926, p. 239.

§   Carr's Interaction
Diagram

THE LAST EXAMPLE of an early category system is taken from the work of Carr (1929), who was one of the first to describe the interaction of a small discussion group of college students. Similar small groups of students, unknown to each other until they are brought into the laboratory to solve some discussion problem, have become a standard research population for the social-psychologist. Carr formed three-man groups from members of his sociology class and asked them to solve some problem of an immediate practical character, such as how they were to spend some leisure time in the immediate future. One member of the group acted as note-taker to record the content of the remarks as they were made by each speaker so that the interaction process could be analyzed later. A segment of interaction diagram for one of these discussions is reproduced below, together with a key describing notations used and a table summarizing the number of *initiatives* and *contributions* for each member (see Fig. 40, Table 29).

Table 29—Initiatives and Solutions for a Laboratory Group

Persons	Total Initiatives	Possible Solutions Contributed
A	21	5
B	24	6
C	5	3
Total	50	14

§   Additional Examples of
Category Systems

EACH OF THE MANY category systems which have been developed is best suited for some particular type of group, type of subject, and

Figure 40—Carr's Interaction Diagram (Carr, 1929, p. 64)

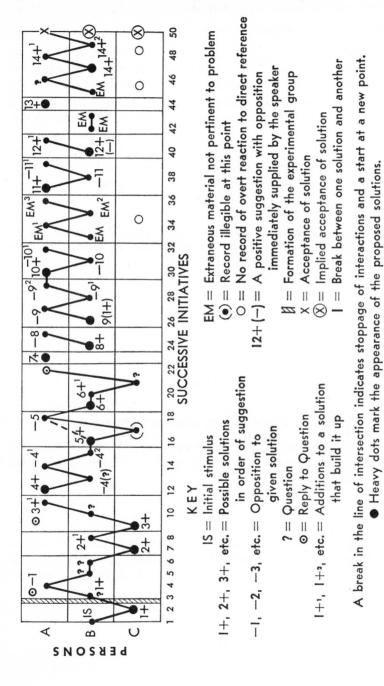

KEY

IS = Initial stimulus

1+, 2+, 3+, etc. = Possible solutions
in order of suggestion

−1, −2, −3, etc. = Opposition to
given solution

? = Question

⊙ = Reply to Question

1+¹, 1+², etc. = Additions to a solution
that build it up

EM = Extraneous material not pertinent to problem

(●) = Record illegible at this point

O = No record of overt reaction to direct reference

12+(−) = A positive suggestion with opposition
immediately supplied by the speaker

▨ = Formation of the experimental group

X = Acceptance of solution

⊗ = Implied acceptance of solution

I = Break between one solution and another

A break in the line of intersection indicates stoppage of interactions and a start at a new point.

● Heavy dots mark the appearance of the proposed solutions.

level of analysis. Four of these systems which have been used in several experiments are listed below with their major emphases by authors:

Author	Description of categories	Focus
Chapple (1940, 1942, 1953)	Two categories: action and silence. Both frequency and duration are recorded.	Activity rate of clients in a structured business or psychiatric interview.
Bales (1950b)	Twelve categories: six task and six social-emotional.	Problem-solving in small discussion groups. Widely used in other situations.
Carter et al. (1951a, 1951b)	Seven principal dimensions with subcategories; 53 in all, with special emphasis on leader and follower roles.	The identification of leaders in small leaderless discussion groups.
Freedman, et al. (1951), La Forge et al. (1954), Leary (1955, 1957), Leary and Coffey (1955), La Forge and Suczek (1955)	Sixteen categories in a circular continuum. Two basic dimensions: love-hate and dominance-submission.	The interpersonal dimension of personality in a clinical situation.

Additional category systems are listed by principal focus:

GROUP CLASSIFICATION AND DESCRIPTION

Sanderson, 1938; Lundberg, 1940; Hemphill and Westie, 1950; Jansen, 1952; Borgatta and Cottrell, 1955; Borgatta, Cottrell, and Meyer, 1956; Hemphill, 1956.

DISCUSSION GROUPS

Carr, 1929; Miller, 1939; Hardee and Bernauer, 1948; Alpert and Smith, 1949; Steinzor, 1949a, 1949b; Di Vesta, Roach, and Beasley, 1951; Brandenburg and Neal, 1953; Thelen, Stock et al., 1954; Kunsela, 1956; Stock and Thelen, 1958.

CLASSROOM TEACHING

Withall, 1949, 1951; Medley and Mitzel, 1958.

CHILD STUDY

Thomas and Thomas, 1928; Beaver, 1929; Hubbard, 1929; Thomas, 1929, 1932; Goodenough and Anderson, 1931; Bott, 1933; Thomas, Loomis, and Arrington, 1933; Smith, 1933; Cocherell, 1935; Anderson, 1937a, 1937b, 1939; Arrington, 1939, 1943; Buhler, 1939; Barker, Kouin, and Wright, 1943; Swanson, 1950; Biber, Murphy, Woodcock, and Black, 1952.

FAMILY

Merrill, 1946; Henry, 1951; Herbst, 1952; Chance, 1957.

COUNSELLING AND THERAPY

Queen, 1928; Porter, 1943; Curran, 1945; Snyder, 1945; Joel and Shapiro, 1949; Ruesch and Prestwood, 1950; Maas, Varon, and Rosenthal, 1951; Plank, 1951; Gorlow, Hoch, and Telschow, 1952.

§ Sociometry

GENERAL REFERENCES on the use and analysis of sociometric data are given in Proctor and Loomis, "Analysis of Sociometric data" (1951), and Lindzey and Borgatta, "Sociometric Measurement" (1954). Most of the references given in this appendix as well as many others will also be found in these two general references. No attempt has been made here to give a comprehensive review of sociometric techniques as they have been used; the aim, rather, is to suggest how sociometric techniques may be viewed in terms of the dimensions of behavior which have been described earlier in the text.

Sociometry was developed by Moreno, stemming from his work in Germany with the spontaneity theater. He early placed an emphasis on the importance of "liking" relationships and on development of informal structure. Moreno presented more than a technique, in effect, since his major work, *Who Shall Survive?*, first published in 1934 and revised in 1953, has the overtones of a religious tract as well as being a methodological work. From Moreno's work have also come two therapeutic techniques: (1) sociodrama, in which members from the audience participate in a spontaneous play to depict some social problems, and (2) psychodrama, in which a person with a problem acts as a central figure in a spontaneous play re-enacting some part of his life (see, for example, Toeman, 1944). Although some other investigators at the same time or earlier than Moreno used something like the sociometric technique in asking group members to reveal interpersonal choices (for example, Newstetter et al., 1938, asked for liking choices in a camp situation, and Terman, 1904, asked grade-school students to indicate persons they liked to be like best), Moreno provided the principal impetus for the introduction of sociometric techniques into the scientific literature. References which illustrate sociometric analysis and its relation to other research efforts are given in Moreno (1941, 1943, 1945, 1947a, 1951, 1953, 1954), Loomis and Pepinsky (1948), Gurvitch (1949), Jennings, (1948, 1950a, 1950b, 1953), Northway (1952), Nehnevajsa (1955c), and Bjerstedt (1956c).

§ Criteria for a Sociometric Test

MORENO's six criteria that define the proper sociometric test are given in Chapter Five.

A number of investigators ask group members to say whom they like, without specifying a specific criteria. These questions have been called "near-sociometric" (Polansky, Lippitt, & Redl, 1950b).

Gardner and Thompson (1956) have elaborated the sociometric technique by introducing an equal-interval scale which they hope will "permit an inter-comparison of different groups' potentialities for satisfying their members' psychological needs." Their work is based on analysis of four needs which are modifications of Murray's needs. The needs are: affiliation, play-mirth, succorance, and achievement recognition.

Sociometric ratings can also be made from data derived from direct observation (James, 1955) or using other behavioral indices, such as time spent together (Moreno, Jennings, & Sargent, 1940; Fischer, 1953), visiting patterns, or work exchange (Loomis, 1941). In children's groups, drawings of group activities may provide the basis for sociometric analysis (Hare & Hare, 1956). Ratings based on "group preference" rather than individual preference have also been suggested (Anikeeff, 1957).

Further evidence of the "sociometric status" of an individual may be gained if he is removed from the group and the group observed in his absence (Moreno, Florence, 1942).

§ Data Analysis

SOCIOMETRIC DATA can be analyzed in a number of ways (Proctor & Loomis, 1951):

1. *Sociogram*—a pictorial rendering of choices in which individuals are indicated by circles and their choices by arrows going from one individual to another. Suggestions for the analysis of sociograms are given by Criswell (1943), Borgatta (1951a), Clark and McGuire (1952), Bjerstedt (1952, 1957) and Moreno (1953).

2. *Index*—choices may be formed into indices of liking or disliking, the simplest of which are derived by adding the number of choices received for "like" and "dislike" from all members of the group. This index formation is facilitated if the choices are arrayed in a matrix (see, for example, Zeleny, 1940b, 1941, and Jones, 1959). However, if an index is all that is desired, sociometric questions may be less efficient than rankings. When group members know each other well, it is possible that they can rank each other in more than the two classes "accept" and "not accept" on a given criterion. Thus the sociometric type of question may reveal less information than is actually available (Borgatta, Cottrell, & Mann, 1958).

3. *Statistical analysis*—the data may be analyzed statistically by demonstrating that the choices given or received were more than those which might be received if only chance factors were operating (Leeman, 1952; Nehnevajsa, 1955a, 1955b, 1955d).

4. *Matrix algebra*—if the interpersonal choices are placed in a matrix which shows the number of times which choices between individuals are reciprocated, then matrix algebra may be used to derive the number of links which connect members in a group. For example, one may determine the number of members who are directly connected to each other through mutual choice, the number who are connected through one other person, etc. (Forsythe & Katz, 1946; Festinger, 1949; Luce & Perry, 1949; Beum & Brundage, 1950; Ross & Harary, 1952; Harary & Ross, 1954, 1957).

§ Reliability and Validity

THE RELIABILITY and validity of the sociometric tests are discussed in two articles by Mouton, Blake, and Fruchter (1955a, 1955b) which review a large number of sociometric studies. They suggest six conditions to increase the reliability of a sociometric test. These are given in Chapter Five.

The validity of the sociometric test has been illustrated by positive correlation between sociometric questions and such criteria as individual productivity and combat effectiveness, training ability, and leadership. A negative relationship has been found between popularity and criteria such as accident proneness, sickness, and disciplinary offenses. However, high interpersonal attractiveness in groups is not always associated with group productivity, an indication that persons are not always chosen on criteria which are related to task ability.

§ Problems in the Use of the Test

A NUMBER OF PROBLEMS occur in the use of the sociometric test which make the results difficult to interpret. There are too many relationships in large groups to be handled effectively in either a drawing or a matrix, since for groups much larger than a dozen the number of possible combinations and permutations of relationships is so large that the investigator has difficulty in knowing which of these groups are similar and which dissimilar. Formulas which suggest the potential number of relationships in a group have been given by Bossard (1945), Kephart (1950), and Davis, R. L. (1954).

The form of the test is so simple and the test is so easy to administer that it can be used indiscriminately; as a result it has been used in a wide variety of situations without a rigorous research design. Since the form is so simple, more attention must be given to the content of the criterion which is used. The extent to which sociometric choices correlate with any other behavioral criteria will depend primarily upon the original criterion of choice used. Lindzey and Borgatta (1954) have organized their review of the literature under a number of headings which suggest the importance of the criterion.

An index to measure the amount of agreement between the results of sociometric tests based on different criteria has been proposed by Katz and Powell (1953).

The sociometric test is essentially a way of selecting *compatible groups*. For this reason it makes a difference if the basis of compatibility is task or social-emotional. In selecting compatible subgroups from large populations such as a school, an industry, or an army, where individuals do not have the opportunity to know each other well enough to make reliable choices, it may be better to give direct tests of personality as a basis for group composition.

Several articles suggest further applications of the sociometric test in industrial, therapeutic, or military settings (Toeman, 1944; Jacobs, 1945; Smucker, 1949; VanZelst, 1952; Torrance, 1955b).

§ Questionnaires

ANOTHER DATA COLLECTION TECHNIQUE which is used in the analysis of small group behavior is the questionnaire. The questionnaire is usually given to subjects after each experimental session in the form of a "postmeeting reaction sheet." Several types of questionnaires have been adapted from the study of individual personality and the analysis of interaction process:

1. *Direct questions*—subjects describe their reactions to the group in their own words or on check lists (Riley et al., 1954; McGinnies, 1956; Stogdill & Coons, 1957).

2. *"Q" Sort*—subjects select statements which best describe their interaction patterns (Block, 1952; Ruesch, Block, & Bennett, 1953; Kalis & Bennett, 1957).

3. *Projective*—Subjects give their reactions to ambiguous pictures (Henry & Guetzkow, 1951), or to incomplete sentences (Klein & Keill, 1953).

§ Mathematical Models

MATHEMATICAL MODELS for interaction and group structure have been formulated for several current theoretical approaches. The model serves to extend theory by generating new hypotheses rather than by analyzing data (Guetzkow, 1958).

1. Rapaport (1947) has presented a mathematical theory which

assumes that two individuals each wish to maximize a satisfaction function which depends on remuneration and on effort extended.

2. Bavelas (1948) has suggested a model for group structures based on Lewin's topological concepts.

3. Simon (1952) has translated Homans' (1950) principal hypotheses into mathematical terms.

4. Hays & Bush (1954) have demonstrated the value of having a model for an "alternate" hypothesis as well as the null hypothesis. In most experiments without models, the null hypothesis is simply that the observed phenomenon could not have happened "by chance," a fairly weak conclusion.

5. Simon and Guetzkow (1955a, 1955b) have proposed models of the mechanisms involved in pressures toward uniformity in groups, based on Festinger's (1954) description of the communication process.

6. Cartwright and Harary (1956) have extended Heider's P-O-X system (referring to the relationships between a person, another person, and an impersonal entity) through graph theory. In this way the concept of balance in a relationship may be generally used for communication networks, power systems, and sociometric structures.

7. French (1956) has suggested a formal theory of social power following the "field theory" approach.

8. Cohen (1958) has presented a probability model for the Asch (1956) experiment in which one naive subject makes judgments of line length after hearing an incorrect majority opinion.

9. Hare (1961) has described an approach to computer simulation of interaction in small groups.

Appendix II

FACTOR
ANALYSIS

IN RECENT YEARS, the development of tests of abilities and personality, as well as research on group structure and behavior, has beeen facilitated by use of an empirical technique of considerable elegance and utility. This technique, multiple factor analysis, rests on a fairly involved mathematical basis, and in actual application requires rather detailed computing procedures which may include programming on large electronic computing machines. Neither of these aspects seem appropriate to discuss in the present context. (A full account of the method is given in Thurstone's *Multiple Factor Analysis* (1947), Cattell's *Factor Analysis for Social Science* (1952), and Fruchter's *Introduction to Factor Analysis* (1954). However, a short discussion of factor analysis will be presented here to acquaint the reader with the general approach and its attendant vocabulary.

There are various ways in which factory analysis can be construed, each reflecting, in part, the degree of intellectual commitment of the

413

investigator. The most direct perhaps is to regard factor analysis as a means of minimizing mental effort. Since all factor analyses begin with a matrix of correlation, let us assume that the problem and data are such that the computation of correlation coefficients is warranted. When the number of variables correlated becomes large, the matrix rapidly becomes difficult to grasp by eye, and except where specific hypotheses are made about specific variables, the problem becomes hard to manage. As a means of reducing detail without a corresponding loss of information, the extraction of factors permits one to compute the amount of variance of items (or the things which are correlated) which is common to other items. This means that instead of representing the degree of common variability in terms of "pairs of items" as in a matrix of correlations, one represents the variability of items in terms of one or more common sources of variance. Tables listing each item with its measure of association to these sources of common variability are called tables of factor loadings, or factor matrices. It is possible to reproduce the original matrix of correlations from such a factor matrix by a simple transformation formula. The number of linearly independent factors required to reproduce a correlation matrix is equal to the *rank* of that matrix. Factor analysis is essentially a method for testing the *rank* of a matrix; its complications result from a need to rely on estimation techniques and to minimize errors involved in complex problems yielding fallible data.

In addition to its use as a device for reducing data or detail, factor analysis can be used as a means to develop notions concerning the dimensions of a domain of values, attitudes, behavior or other class of variables. These notions will depend to a minimum degree on *a priori* ideas about the structure of that domain. In this sense, factor analysis differs from many other statistical techniques. Knowledge about the dimensionality of the domain under consideration markedly improves the possibilities of prediction to new situations, since it avoids the necessities of relying on scores which are an unknown combination of several distinct dimensions (such as some achievement score being a function both of, say, time in school and native intelligence). It also permits the design of new tests which will measure specific areas of the domain.

To summarize the technique of factor analysis: when a *factor* is extracted from a *matrix of correlations* by one of several extraction methods, each *item* or *test* (depending on which is the basis of the original correlations) is projected on this factor. This yields a numerical value called a *factor loading* and represents the percentage of the variance of that item which is accounted for by that factor. After the extraction of a factor, a *residual matrix* is computed by subtracting variance accounted for by the factor from the original correlations, leaving a matrix which shows the variance left in the matrix of items. The process of calculation of loadings, extraction of factors and calculation of residuals is continued until, according to one or several criteria, no significant variance is left. This is the stopping point since there is no rationale for factoring errors of measurement.

One more operation needs to be noted. This is *rotation*. In a sense, the specific placement of the original axes is arbitrary, since the correlated items can be projected on any pair of axes inserted anywhere in the plot. Thus the first loadings, usually called *zero order loadings*, are no "better" than other projections on axes inserted elsewhere in the plot. Changing the location of the axes by geometrical, trigonometric, or algebraic manipulation results in different rotated loadings, but the equivalence between the factor matrix and the correlation matrix remains unchanged. Thus rotation to certain criteria is usually performed on the extracted factors to achieve a simpler configuration, to remove weak factors, or to make possible measurement in desired areas.

What can be gained from an examination of the results of a factor analysis of a certain body of data? First, one can note the degree to which certain items "cluster" or co-vary by observing those items that load heavily on one factor and not on others. One can conceptualize the factors as underlying dimensions of the data by noting the content of their component items. One can estimate the *reliability* of the items by noting the *communality* (denoted h^2) listed in the tables, or computing same by summing the squared factor loadings for each item. One can note the amount of total variance of the group of data which is accounted for by the common factors. Finally, by working with the factors after they have been named or conceptualized, one can deal with or communicate the information contained in the original correlation matrix in terms of far fewer measures.

REFERENCES

1. Abel, Theodora M. The influence of social facilitation on motor performance at different levels of intelligence. *Amer. J. Psychol.*, 1938, *51*, 379-389.

2. Adams, S. Status congruency as a variable in small group performance. *Soc. Forces*, 1953, *32*, 16-22. *P.A.*, 28:4111; *S.A.*, 80.

3. Adams, S. Social climate and productivity in small military groups. *Amer. sociol. Rev.*, 1954, *19*, 421-425. *P.A.*, 30:2618.

4. Adorno, T. W., Frenkel-Brunswick, Else, Levinson, D., & Sanford, R. N., *The authoritarian personality*. New York: Harper, 1950. (See No. 826, pp. 636-646.) *P.A.*, 24:5796.

5. Albert, R. S. Comments on the scientific function of the concept of cohesiveness. *Amer. J. Sociol.*, 1953, 59, 231-234. *P.A.*, 28:4112.

6. Alfert, Elizabeth. Two components of assumed similarity. *J. abnorm. soc. Psychol.*, 1958, *56*, 135-138.

7. Allport, F. H. The influence of the group upon association and thought. *J. exp. Psychol.*, 1920, 3, 159-182. (See No. 559.)

8. Allport, F. H. *Social psychology*. Boston: Houghton Mifflin, 1924.

Although no attempt was made to locate all of the books and articles in the bibliography in the *Psychological Abstracts* (*P.A.*) or the *Sociological Abstracts* (*S.A.*), the abstract numbers have been included with many of the items as an aid to the reader who may wish further details.

9. Allport, G. W. The historical background of modern social psychology. In G. Lindzey (Ed.), *Handbook of social psychology.* Reading, Mass.: Addison-Wesley, 1954. Pp. 3-56. *P.A.*, 29:3774.

10. Alpert, B., & Smith, Patricia A. How participation works. *J. soc. Issues,* 1949, 5 (1), 3-13. *P.A.*, 23:6123.

11. Ames, R. Leaderless group discussion and experience in group leadership. *Calif. J. educ. Res.*, 1955, 6, 166-169. *P.A.*, 30:5841.

12. Anderson, C. A. An experimental study of "social facilitation" as affected by intelligence. *Amer. J. Sociol.*, 1929, 34, 874-881.

13. Anderson, H. H. An experimental study of dominative and integrative behavior in children of pre-school age. *J. soc. Psychol.*, 1937a, 8, 335-345. *P.A.*, 12:560.

14. Anderson, H. H. Domination and integration in the social behavior of young children in an experimental play situation. *Genet. Psychol. Monogr.*, 1937b, 19, 341-408. *P.A.*, 12:559.

15. Anderson, H. H. Domination and social integration in the behavior of kindergarten children and teachers. *Genet. Psychol. Monogr.*, 1939, 21, 287-385. (See No. 66.) *P.A.*, 14:514.

16. Andrews, R. E. *Leadership and supervision.* U.S. Civil Service Comm., Personel Mgmt Ser. No. 9. Washington, D.C.: Govt Printing Office, 1955.

17. Anikeeff, A. M. Sociometric empathy. *J. soc. Psychol.*, 1957, 45, 283-287.

18. Ansbacher, H. L. The history of the leaderless group discussion technique. *Psychol. Bull.*, 1951, 48, 383-391. *P.A.*, 26:5116.

19. Argyle, M. Methods of studying small social groups. *Brit. J. Psychol.*, 1952a, 43, 269-279. *P.A.*, 27:5793.

20. Argyle, M. The concepts of role and status. *Sociol. Rev.*, 1952b, 44 (3). *P.A.*, 29:649.

21. Argyle, M. The study of social behavior. In B.A. Farrell (Ed.), *Experimental psychology.* New York: Philosophical Library, 1955. *P.A.*, 30:2620.

22. Argyle, M. Social pressure in public and private situations. *J. abnorm. soc. Psychol.*, 1957a, 54, 172-175.

23. Argyle, M. *The scientific study of social behavior.* London: Methuen, 1957b. *P.A.*, 32:2743.

24. Aronson, E., & Mills, J. The effect of severity of initiation on liking for a group. *J. abnorm. soc. Psychol.*, 1959, 59 177-181. (See No. 249, 1960, pp. 95-103.)

25. Arrington, Ruth E. Time-sampling studies of child behavior. *Psychol. Monogr.*, 1939, 51, No. 2. *P.A.*, 13:6524.

26. Arrington, Ruth E. Time-sampling in studies of social behavior: A critical review of techniques and results with research suggestions. *Psychol. Bull.*, 1943, 40, 81-124. *P.A.*, 17:1630.

27. Arsenian, Jean M. Young children in an insecure situation. *J. abnorm. soc. Psychol.*, 1943, *38*, 225-249.

28. Asch, S. E. Forming impressions of personality. *J. abnorm. soc. Psychol.*, 1946, *41*, 258-290. *P.A.*, 20:4654.

29. Asch, S. E. Effects of group pressure upon the modification and distortion of judgments. In H. Guetzkow (Ed.), *Groups, leadership, and men.* Pittsburgh: Carnegie Press, 1951. Pp. 177-190. (See No. 1214, pp. 2-11; No. 826, pp. 174-183; No. 249, pp. 189-200.)

30. Asch, S. E. *Social psychology.* Englewood Cliffs, N. J.: Prentice-Hall, 1952. *P.A.*, 27:3409.

31. Asch, S. E. Opinions and social pressure. *Sci. Amer.*, 1955, *193* (5), 31-35. *P.A.*, 30:8022.

32. Asch, S. E. Studies of independence and conformity: I. A minority of one against a unanimous majority. *Psychol. Monogr.*, 1956, *70* (9), No. 416. *P.A.*, 31:5875.

33. Avery, R., & Bachelis, W. Reliability of scoring in interaction process analysis. Paper presented at Amer. Sociol. Soc., Detroit, 1956.

34. Azrin, N. H. & Lindsley, O. R. The reinforcement of cooperation between children. *J. abnorm. soc. Psychol.*, 1956, *52*, 100-102. *P.A.*, 31:2394.

35. Babchuk, N., & Goode, W. F. Work incentives in a self-determined group. *Amer. social. Rev.*, 1951, *16*, 679-687. *P.A.*, 27:1491.

36. Back, K. W. Interpersonal relations in a discussion group. *J. soc. Issues,* 1948, *4*, 61-65. *P.A.*, 23:674.

37. Back, K. W. Influence through social communication. *J. abnorm. soc. Psychol.*, 1951, *46*, 9-23. (See No. 1214, pp. 445-459; No. 826, pp. 183-197.) *P.A.*, 25:7362

38. Back, K. W., Festinger, L., Hymovitch, B., Kelley, H. H., Schachter, S., & Thibaut, J. W. The methodology of studying rumor transmission. *Hum. Relat.*, 1950, *3*, 307-312. *P.A.*, 25:2416.

39. Baier, D. E. Note on "A review of leadership studies with particular reference to military problems." *Psychol. Bull.*, 1947, *44*, 466-467. *P.A.*, 22:1145.

40. Baker, Bela O., & Sarbin, T. R. Differential mediation of social perception as a correlate of social adjustment. *Sociometry*, 1956, *19*, 69-83. *P.A.*, 31:6363; *S.A.*, 4284.

41. Baldwin, A., Kallhorn, J., & Breese, F. Patterns of parent behavior. *Psychol. Monogr.*, 1945, *58*, No. 268. *P.A.*, 19:3415.

42. Bales, R. F. Social therapy for a social disorder—compulsive drinking. *J. soc. Issues*, 1945, *1* (3), 14-22. *P.A.*, 20:1507.

43. Bales, R. F. A set of categories for the analysis of small group interaction. *Amer. sociol. Rev.*, 1950a, *15*, 257-263. *P.A.*, 26:4733.

44. Bales, R. F. *Interaction process analysis: A method for the study of*

small groups. Reading, Mass.: Addison-Wesley, 1950b. (See No. 249, 1953.) *P.A.*, 24:4553.

45. Bales, R. F. Some statistical problems in small group research. *J. Amer. Statist. Ass.*, 1951a, *46*, 311-322. *P.A.*, 26:1863.

46. Bales, R. F. Reply to Keller's comment. *Amer. sociol. Rev.*, 1951b, *16*, 843.

47. Bales, R. F. Some uniformities of behavior in small social systems. In G. E. Swanson, T. H. Newcomb, & E. L. Hartley (Eds.), *Readings in social psychology.* New York: Holt, 1952. Pp. 146-159. Also in P. F. Lazarsfeld & M. Rosenberg (Eds.), *The language of social research.* New York: Free Press, 1955. Pp. 345-358.

48. Bales, R. F. The equilibrium problem in small groups. In T. Parsons, R. F. Bales, & E. A. Shils, *Working papers in the theory of action.* New York: Free Press, 1953. Pp. 111-161. (See No. 559.)

49. Bales, R. F. In conference. *Harv. Bus. Rev.* 1954, 32, 44-50.

50. Bales, R. F. How people interact in conferences. *Sci. Amer.*, 1955, *192* (3), 31-35. *P.A.*, 29:7061.

51. Bales, R. F. Task status and likeability as a function of talking and listening in decision-making groups. In L. D. White (Ed.), *The state of the social sciences.* Chicago: Univer. Chicago Press, 1956. Pp. 148-161.

52. Bales, R. F. Small group theory and research. In R. K. Merton, L. Broom, & L. S. Cottrell, Jr. (Eds.), *Sociology today: problems and prospects.* New York: Basic Books, 1958. Pp. 293-305.

53. Bales, R. F. Task roles and social roles in problem solving groups. In Eleanor E. Maccoby, T. M. Newcomb, & E. L. Hartley (Eds.), *Readings in social psychology.* (3rd ed.) New York: Holt, 1958. Pp. 437-447.

54. Bales, R. F., & Borgatta, E. F. Size of group as a factor in the interaction profile. In A. P. Hare, E. F. Borgatta, & R. F. Bales (Eds.), *Small groups: studies in social interaction.* New York: Knopf, 1955. Pp. 396-413.

55. Bales, R. F., & Flanders, N. A. Planning an observation room and group laboratory. *Amer. sociol. Rev.*, 1954, *19*, 771-781. *P.A.*, 30:2686.

56. Bales, R. F., & Gerbrands, H. The "Interaction Recorder": an apparatus and check list for sequential content analysis of social interaction. *Hum. Relat.*, 1948, *1*, 456-463. *P.A.*, 23:2012.

57. Bales, R. F., Hare, A. P., & Borgatta, E. F. Structure and dynamics of small groups: a review of four variables. In J. B. Gittler (Ed.), *Review of sociology: analysis of a decade.* New York: Wiley, 1957. Pp. 391-422.

58. Bales, R. F., & Slater, P. E. Role differentiation in small decision-making groups. In T. Parson, R. F. Bales, et al. *The family, socialization,*

and interaction process. New York: Free Press, 1955. Pp. 259-306.

59. Bales, R. F., & Slater, P. E. Notes on "Role differentiation in small decision-making groups": reply to Dr. Wheeler. *Sociometry,* 1957, *20,* 152-155.

60. Bales, R. F., & Strodtbeck, F. L. Phases in group problem solving. *J. abnorm. soc. Psychol.,* 1951, *46,* 485-495. (See No. 249.) *P.A.,* 26:3911.

61. Bales, R. F., Strodtbeck, F. L., Mills, T. M., & Roseborough, Mary E. Channels of communication in small groups. *Amer. sociol. Rev.,* 1951, *16,* 461-468. Also: Bales, R. F. Reply to Keller's comment. *Amer. sociol. Rev.,* 1951, *16,* 843. *P.A.,* 27:1035.

62. Banks, E. P. Methodological problems in the study of psychiatric wards. *Soc. Forces,* 1956, *34,* 277-280. *P.A.,* 31:4812.

63. Barker, R. G. The social inter-relations of strangers and acquaintances. *Sociometry,* 1942, *5,* 169-179. *P.A.,* 16:4446.

64. Barker, R. G. *One boy's day; a specimen record of behavior.* New York: Harper, 1951. *P.A.,* 25:7962.

65. Barker, R. G., Dembo, Tamara, & Lewin, K. Frustration and regression: an experiment with young children. *Univer. of Iowa Stud. Child Welf.,* 1941, *18,* No. 1.

66. Barker, R. G., Kounin, J. S., & Wright, H. F. (Eds.), *Child behavior and development.* New York: McGraw-Hill, 1943. *P.A.,* 18:1929.

67. Barker, R. G., & Wright, H. F. Psychological ecology and the problem of psychosocial development. *Child Developm.,* 1949, *20* (3), 131-143. *P.A.,* 24:4509.

68. Barnard, C. I. *The functions of the executive.* Cambridge, Mass.: Harvard Univer. Press, 1938.

69. Barnlund, D. C. Experiments in leadership training for decision-making groups. *Speech Monogr.,* 1955, *22,* 1-14. *P.A.,* 30:768.

70. Barr, J. A. A multi-question sociometric procedure. *Personn. Guid. J.,* 1955, *33,* 527-530. *P.A.,* 30:2687.

71. Barron, F. Some personality correlates of independence of judgment. *J. Pers.,* 1952, *21,* 287-297.

72. Barton, W. A., Jr. The effect of group activity and individual effort in developing ability to solve problems in first-year algebra. *Educ. Adm. Superv.,* 1926, *12,* 512-518.

73. Bass, B. M. An analysis of the leaderless group discussion. *J. appl. Psychol.,* 1949, *33,* 527-533. *P.A.,* 24:4043.

74. Bass, B. M. Situational tests: II. Leaderless group discussion variables. *Educ. psychol. Measmt,* 1951, *11,* 196-207. *P.A.,* 26:3041.

75. Bass, B. M. The leaderless group discussion. *Psychol. Bull.,* 1954a, *51,* 465-492. *P.A.,* 29:3777.

76. Bass, B. M. The leaderless group discussion as a leadership evaluation

instrument. *Personn. Psychol.*, 1954b, *7*, 470-477. *P.A.*, 29:7062.

77. Bass, B. M. Authoritarianism or acquiescence. *J. abnorm. soc. Psychol.*, 1955, *51*, 616-623. *P.A.*, 31:2534.

78. Bass, B. M. Reply to Messick and Jackson's comments on authoritarianism or acquiescence. *J. abnorm. soc. Psychol.*, 1957, *54*, 426-427.

79. Bass, B. M., & Coates, C. H. Forecasting officer potential using the leaderless group discussion. *J. abnorm. soc. Psychol.*, 1952, *47*, 321-325. *P.A.*, 27:2607.

80. Bass, B. M., Gaier, E. L., Farese, F. J., & Flint, A. W. An objective method for studying behavior in groups. *Psychol. Reports*, 1957, *3*, 265-280. *P.A.*, 32:4059.

81. Bass, B. M., & Klubeck, S. Effects of seating arrangement on leaderless group discussions. *J. abnorm. soc. Psychol.*, 1952, *47*, 724-727. *P.A.*, 27:3410.

82. Bass, B. M., Klubeck, S., & Wurster, C. R. Factors influencing reliability and validity of leaderless group discussion assessment. *J. appl. Psychol.*, 1953, *37*, 26-30, *P.A.*, 28:671.

83. Bass, B. M., McGehee, C. R., Hawkins, W. C., Young, P. C., & Gebel, A. S. Personality variables related to leaderless group discussion behavior. *J. abnorm. soc. Psychol.*, 1953, *48*, 120-128. *P.A.*, 28:925.

84. Bass, B. M., & Norton, Fay-Tyler M. Group size and leaderless discussions. *J. appl. Psychol.*, 1951, *35*, 397-400. *P.A.*, 26:6175.

85. Bass, B. M., Pryer, Margaret W., Gaier, E. L., & Flint, A. W. Interacting effects of control, motivation, group practice, and problem difficulty on attempted leadership. *J. abnorm. soc. Psychol.*, 1958, *56*, 352-358.

86. Bass, B. M., & White, O. L., Jr. Situational tests: III. Observers' rating of leaderless group discussion participants as indicators of external leadership status. *Educ. psychol. Measmt*, 1951, *11*, 355-361. *P.A.*, 27:5779.

87. Bass, B. M., & Wurster, C. R. Effects of company rank on LGD performance of oil refinery supervisors. *J. appl. Psychol.*, 1953a, *37*, 100-104.

88. Bass, B. M., & Wurster, C. R. Effects of the nature of the problem on LGD performance. *J. appl. Psychol.* 1953b, *37*, 96-99. *P.A.* 28:1595.

89. Bassett, R. E. Cliques in a student body of stable membership. *Sociometry*, 1944, *7*, 290-302. *P.A.*, 19:457.

90. Bates, A. P. Some sociometric aspects of social ranking in a small, face-to-face group. *Sociometry*, 1952, *15*, 330-341. *P.A.*, 27:7105.

91. Bates, A. P., & Cloyd, J. S. Toward the development of operations for

defining group norms and members' roles. *Sociometry*, 1956, *19*, 26-39. *P.A.*, 31:2736; *S.A.*, 3946.

92. Bates, F. L. Position, role, and status: a reformulation of concepts. *Soc. Forces*, 1956, *34*, 313-321. *P.A.*, 31:4469.

93. Bates, F. L. A conceptual analysis of group structure. *Soc. Forces*, 1957, *36*, 103-111.

94. Bavelas, A. Morale and the training of leaders. In G. Watson (Ed.), *Civilian Morale*. New York: Reynal & Hitchcock, 1942. Pp. 143-165.

95. Bavelas, A. A mathematical model for group structures. *Appl. Anthrop.*, 1948, *7*, 16-30. *P.A.*, 23:1731.

96. Bavelas, A. Communication patterns in task oriented groups. *J. Accoustical Soc. Amer.*, 1950, *22*, 725-730. (See No. 249.) *P.A.*, 27:384.

97. Bavelas, A. Communication patterns in problem-solving groups. In H. von Foerster, et al. (Eds.), *Cybernetics: circular casual and feedback mechanisms in biological and social systems*. New York: Josiah Macy Jr. Foundation, 1952. *S.A.*, 1751.

98. Beaver, Alma P. A preliminary report on a study of a preschool "gang." In Dorothy S. Thomas (Ed.), *Some new techniques for studying social behavior*. New York: Teacher's Coll., Columbia Univer., 1929. Pp. 99-117.

99. Beaver, Alma P. The initiation of social contacts by pre-school children. *Child Develpm. Monogr.*, 1932, No. 7.

100. Bechterev, W., & Lange, M. Die ergebnisse des experiments auf dem gebiete der kollektiven reflexologie. (The results of the experiments in the field of collective reflexology.) *Zsch. F. angewand Psychol.*, 1924, *24*, 305-344.

101. Becker, H., & Useem, Ruth H. Sociological analysis of the dyad. *Amer. sociol. Rev.*, 1942, *7*, 13-26. *P.A.*, 16:3661.

102. Beer, M., Buckhout, R., Horowitz, M. W., & Levy, S. Some perceived properties of the difference between leaders and non-leaders. *J. Psychol.*, 1959, *47*, 49-56.

103. Bell, G. B., & French, R. L. Consistency of individual leadership position in small groups of varying membership. *J. abnorm. soc. Psychol.*, 1950, *45*, 764-767. (See No. 559.) *P.A.*, 25:2353.

104. Bell, G. B., & Hall, H. E. The relationship between leadership and empathy. *J. abnorm. soc. Psychol.*, 1954, *49*, 156-157. *P.A.*, 28:7326.

105. Bell, G. B., & Stolper, Rhoda. An attempt at validation of the Empathy Test. *J. appl. Psychol.*, 1955, *39*, 442-443. *P.A.*, 30:7186.

106. Beloff, Halla. Two forms of social conformity: acquiescence and conventionality. *J. abnorm. soc. Psychol.*, 1958, *56*, 99-104.

107. Belyaeff, B. V. The problem of the collective and of its experimental-psychological study. *Psychologica*, 1929, *2*, 179-214; 1930, *3*, 488-549.

108. Bender, I. E., & Hastorf, A. H. The perception of persons: forecasting another person's responses in three personality scales. *J. abnorm. soc. Psychol.*, 1950, *45*, 556-561. *P.A.*, 25:988.

109. Benne, K. D., & Levit, Grace. The nature of groups and helping groups improve their operation. *Rev. educ. Res.*, 1953, *23*, 289-308. *P.A.*, 28:7327.

110. Benne, K. D., & Muntyan, B. *Human relations in curriculum change.* New York: Dryden, 1951.

111. Benne, K. D., & Sheats, P. Functional roles of group members. *J. soc. Issues*, 1948, *4* (2), 41-49. *P.A.*, 23:677.

112. Bennett, Edith B. Discussion, decision, commitment, and consensus in "group decision." *Hum. Relat.*, 1955, *8*, 251-274. (See #826, pp. 212-219.) *P.A.*, 30:5842; *S.A.*, 3140.

113. Bennis, W. G., & Shepard, H. A. A theory of group development. *Hum. Relat.*, 1956, *9*, 415-437.

114. Berelson, B. *Content analysis in communication research.* New York: Free Press, 1952. *P.A.*, 27:7730.

115. Berelson, B. Content analysis. In G. Lindzey (Ed.), *Handbook of social psychology.* Reading, Mass.: Addison-Wesley, 1954. Pp. 488-522. *P.A.*, 29:3956.

116. Berenda, Ruth W. *The influence of the group on the judgments of children.* New York: King's Crown Press, 1950. *P.A.*, 24:5133.

117. Berg, J. Cooperation without communication and observation. *J. soc. Psychol.*, 1955, *41*, 287-296. *P.A.*, 30:5843.

118. Berkowitz, L. Sharing leadership in small, decision-making groups. *J. abnorm. soc. Psychol.*, 1953, *48*, 231-238. (See No. 559.) *P.A.*, 28:2390.

119. Berkowitz, L. Group standards, cohesiveness, and productivity. *Hum. Relat.*, 1954a, *7*, 509-519. *P.A.*, 29:5443; *S.A.*, 1484.

120. Berkowitz, L. Studies in group norms: the perception of group attitudes as related to criteria of group effectiveness. *USAF Personn. Train. Res. Cent. Res Bull.*, 1954b, No. AFPTRC-TR-54-62. *P.A.*, 29:8500.

121. Berkowitz, L. Group norms among bomber crews: patterns of perceived crew attitudes, "actual" crew attitudes, and crew liking related to aircrew effectiveness in Far Eastern combat. *Sociometry*, 1956a, *19*, 141-153.

122. Berkowitz, L. Personality and group position. *Sociometry*, 1956b, *19*, 210-222.

123. Berkowitz, L. Social desirability and frequency of influence attempts

as factors in leadership choice. *J. Pers.*, 1956c, *24*, 424-435. *P.A.*, 31:722.

124. Berkowitz, L. Effects of perceived dependency relationships upon conformity to group expectations. *J. abnorm. soc. Psychol.*, 1957a, *55*, 350-354.

125. Berkowitz, L. Liking for the group and the perceived merit of the group's behavior. *J. abnorm. soc. Psychol.* 1957b, *54*, 353-357.

126. Berkowitz, L., & Levy, B. I. Pride in group performance and group-task motivation. *J. abnorm. soc. Psychol.*, 1956, *53*, 300-306. *P.A.*, 32:4028.

127. Berkowitz, L., Levy, B. I., & Harvey, A. R. Effects of performance evaluations on group integration and motivation. *Hum. Relat.* 1957, *10*, 195-208.

128. Berkowitz, L., & Lundy, R. M. Personality characteristics related to susceptibility to influence by peers or authority figures. *J. Pers.*, 1957, *25*, 306-316. *P.A.*, 32:2660.

129. Berkun, M., & Meeland, T. Sociometric effects of race and of combat performance. *Sociometry*, 1958, *21*, 145-149.

130. Bernhardt, K. S., Millichamp, Dorothy A., Charles, Marion W., & McFarland, Mary P. An analysis of the social contacts of pre-school children with the aid of motion pictures. *Univer. Toronto Stud. Child Develpm.*, 1937, No. 10. *P.A.*, 12:2672.

131. Beum, C. O., Jr., & Brundage, E. G. A method for analyzing the sociomatrix. *Sociometry*, 1950, *13*, 141-145. *P.A.*, 27:2634.

132. Bevan, W., Albert, R. S., Loiseaux, P. R., Mayfield, P. N., & Wright, G. Jury behavior as a function of the prestige of the foreman and the nature of his leadership. *J. Publ. Law*, 1958, 7, 419-449.

133. Biber, Barbara, Murphy, Lois B., Woodcock, Louise P., & Black, Irma S. *Life and ways of the seven-to-eight year old.* New York: Basic Books, 1952. (2nd ed.) *P.A.*, 27:6443.

134. Bieri, J. Changes in interpersonal perceptions following social inter-action. *J. abnorm. soc. Psychol.*, 1953, *48*, 61-66. *P.A.*, 28:673.

135. Bion, W. R. Experiences in groups: I. *Hum. Relat.*, 1948a, *1*, 314-320. *P.A.*, 23:1217.

136. Bion, W. R. Experiences in groups: II. *Hum. Relat.*, 1948b, *1*, 487-496. *P.A.*, 23:2175.

137. Bion, W. R. Experiences in groups: III. *Hum. Relat.*, 1949a, *2*, 13-22. *P.A.*, 23:3678.

138. Bion, W. R. Experiences in groups: IV. *Hum. Relat.*, 1949b, *2*, 295-303.

139. Bion, W. R. Experiences in groups: V. *Hum. Relat.*, 1950a, *3*, 3-14. *P.A.*, 25:2354.

140. Bion, W. R. Experiences in groups: VI. *Hum. Relat.*, 1950b, *3*, 395-402. *P.A.*, 25:6224.

141. Bion, W. R. Experiences in groups: VII. *Hum. Relat.*, 1951, *4*, 221-227. *P.A.*, 26:6176.

142. Bion, W. R. Group dynamics: a review. *Int. J. Psychoanal.*, 1952, *33*, 235-247. *P.A.*, 27:319.

143. Bishop, Barbara M. Mother-child interaction and the social behavior of children. *Psychol. Monogr.*, 1951, *65*, No. 11 (Whole No. 328). *P.A.*, 26:6854.

144. Bjerstedt, A. A "chess-board sociogram" for sociographic representation of choice directions and for the analysis of "sociometric locomotions." *Sociometry*, 1952, *15*, 244-262. *P.A.*, 27:7129.

145. Bjerstedt, A. *Interpretations of sociometric choice status.* Lund, Sweden: Gleerup, 1956a.

146. Bjerstedt, A. The interpretation of sociometric status scores in the classroom. *Acta psychol.*, 1956b, *12*, 1-14. *P.A.*, 31:3670.

147. Bjerstedt, A. The methodology of preferential sociometry. *Sociometry Monogr.*, 1956c, No. 37.

148. Bjerstedt, A. Three types of square sociograms and some auxiliary micro-devices. *Educ. Psychol.*, 1957, *3*, 175-191.

149. Bjerstedt, A. A field-force model as a basis for predictions of social behavior. *Hum. Relat.*, 1958, *11*, 331-340.

150. Blake, R. R. The interaction-feeling hypothesis applied to psychotherapy groups. *Sociometry*, 1953, *16*, 253-265. *P.A.*, 28:4413.

151. Blake, R. R., & Brehm, J. W. The use of tape recording to simulate a group atmosphere. *J. abnorm. soc. Psychol.*, 1954, *49*, 311-313. (See No. 559.) *P.A.*, 29:721.

152. Blake, R. R., Helson, H., & Mouton, Jane S. The generality of conformity behavior as a function of factual anchorage, difficulty of task, and amount of social pressure. *J. Pers.*, 1957, *25*, 294-305. *P.A.*, 32:2745.

153. Blake, R. R., Mouton, Jane S., & Fruchter, B. The consistency of interpersonal behavior judgments made on the basis of short-term interaction in three-man groups. *J. abnorm. soc. Psychol.*, 1954, *49*, 573-578. *P.A.*, 29:5444.

154. Blake, R. R., Rhead, C. C., Wedge, B. W., & Mouton, Jane S. Housing architecture and social interaction. *Sociometry*, 1956, *19*, 133-139. *P.A.*, 31:5957.

155. Blau, P. M. Co-operation and competition in a bureacracy. *Amer. J. Sociol.*, 1954a, *59*, 530-535. *P.A.*, 29:8501.

156. Blau, P. M. Patterns of interaction among a group of officials in a government agency. *Hum. Relat.*, 1954b, *7*, 337-348. *P.A.*, 29:3778.

157. Blau, P. M. Formal organization: dimensions of analysis. *Amer. J. Sociol.*, 1957, *63*, 58-69.

158. Block, J. The assessment of communication: role variations as a func-

tion of interactional context. *J. Pers.*, 1952, *21*, 272-286. *P.A.*, 27:7731.

159. Block, J., & Bennett, Lillian F. The assessment of communication. *Hum. Relat.*, 1955, *8*, 317-325. *P.A.*, 30:5927.

160. Block, J., & Block, Jeanne. An interpersonal experiment on reactions to authority. *Hum. Relat.*, 1952, *5*, 91-98. *P.A.*, 27:178.

161. Blumer, H. Psychological import of the human group. In M. Sherif & M. O. Wilson (Eds.), *Group relations at the crossroads.* New York: Harper, 1953. Pp. 185-202. *P.A.*, 28:7328.

162. Bogardus, E. S. Group behavior and groupality. *Sociol. soc. Res.*, 1954, *38*, 401-403. *S.A.*, 2727.

163. Bonner, H. *Group dynamics: principles and applications.* New York: Ronald Press, 1959.

164. Bonney, M. E. A sociometric study of the relationship of some factors to mutual friendships on the elementary, secondary, and college levels. *Sociometry*, 1946, *9*, 21-47. *P.A.*, 20:2802.

165. Bonney, M. E., Hoblit, R. E., & Dreyer, A. H. A study of some factors related to sociometric status in a men's dormitory. *Sociometry*, 1953, *16*, 287-301. *S.A.*, 478.

166. Bonney, M. E., & Powell, J. Differences in social behavior between sociometrically high and sociometrically low children. *J. educ. Res.*, 1953, *46*, 481-495. *P.A.*, 28:2310.

167. Borg, W. R. The behavior of emergent and designated leaders in situational tests. *Sociometry*, 1957, *20*, 95-104.

168. Borgatta, E. F. A diagnostic note on the construction of sociograms and action diagrams. *Group Psychother.*, 1951a, *3*, 300-308. *P.A.*, 26:224.

169. Borgatta, E. F. An analysis of three levels of response: an approach to some relationships among dimensions of personality. *Sociometry*, 1951b, *14*, 267-316.

170. Borgatta, E. F. Analysis of social interaction and sociometric perception. *Sociometry*, 1954, *17*, 7-31. *P.A.*, 29:722.

171. Borgatta, E. F. Analysis of social interaction: actual, role playing, and projective. *J. abnorm. soc. Psychol.*, 1955, *51*, 394-405. *P.A.*, 31:2682.

172. Borgatta, E. F., & Bales, R. F. Task and accumulation of experience as factors in the interaction of small groups. *Sociometry*, 1953a, *16*, 239-252. *P.A.*, 28:4118.

173. Borgatta, E. F., & Bales, R. F. Interaction of individuals in reconstituted groups. *Sociometry*, 1953b, *16*, 302-320. (See No. 559.) *S.A.*, 479.

174. Borgatta, E. F., & Bales, R. F. The consistency of subject behavior and the reliability of scoring in interaction process analysis. *Amer. sociol. Rev.*, 1953c, *18*, 566-569. (See No. 559.) *P.A.*, 28:5846.

175. Borgatta, E. F., & Bales, R. F. Sociometric status patterns and characteristics of interaction. *J. soc. Psychol.*, 1956, *43*, 289-297.

176. Borgatta, E. F., & Cottrell, L. S. Jr. On the classification of groups. *Sociometry*, 1955, *18*, 665-678. *P.A.*, 32:1471; *S.A.*, 3438.

177. Borgatta, E. F., Cottrell, L. S., Jr. Directions for research in group behavior. *Amer. J. Sociol.*, 1957, *63*, 42-48. *P.A.*, 32:5294.

178. Borgatta, E. F., Cottrell, L. S., Jr., & Mann, J. H. The spectrum of individual characteristics: an inter-dimensional analysis. *Psychol. Rep.*, 1958, *4*, 279-319.

179. Borgatta, E. F., Cottrell, L. S., Jr., & Meyer, H. J. On the dimensions of group behavior. *Sociometry*, 1956, *19*, 223-240.

180. Borgatta, E. F., Couch, A. S., & Bales, R. F. Some findings relevant to the great man theory of leadership. *Amer. sociol. Rev.*, 1954, *19*, 755-759. (See No. 559.) *P.A.*, 30:2623.

181. Borgatta, E. F., & Eschenbach, A. E. Factor analysis of Rorschach variables and behavior observation. *Psychol. Rep.*, 1955, *3*, 129-136. *P.A.*, 30:5976.

182. Borgatta, Marie L. The concept of the group: a brief consideration. *Sociol. soc. Res.*, 1958, *43*, 83-89.

183. Bos, Maria C. Experimental study of productive collaboration. *Acta psychol.*, 1937, *3*, 315-426.

184. Bossard, J. H. S. Law of family interaction. *Amer. J. Sociol.*, 1945, *50*, 292-294. *P.A.*, 19:1519.

185. Bott, Elizabeth. Urban families: conjugal roles and social networks. *Hum. Relat.*, 1955, *8*, 345-384. *P.A.*, 31:879.

186. Bott, Elizabeth. Urban families: the norms of conjugal roles. *Hum. Relat.*, 1956, *9*, 325-341.

187. Bott, Helen McM. *Method in social studies of young children.* Toronto: Univer. of Toronto Press, 1933.

188. Bourricaud, F. La "Democratie" dans les petites groupes. ("Democracy" in small groups.) *Cah. internat. Soc.*, 1955, *19*, 104-113. *S.A.*, 2487.

189. Bovard, E. W., Jr. Group structure and perception. *J. abnorm. soc. Psychol.*, 1951a, *46*, 398-405. (See No. 249.) *P.A.*, 26:2085.

190. Bovard, E. W., Jr. The experimental production of interpersonal affect. *J. abnorm. soc. Psychol.*, 1951b, *46*, 521-528. *P.A.*, 26:3912.

191. Bovard, E. W., Jr. Clinical insight as a function of group process. *J. abnorm. soc. Psychol.*, 1952, *47*, 534-539. *P.A.*, 27:2688.

192. Bovard, E. W., Jr. Conformity to social norms and attraction to the group. *Science*, 1953, *118*, 598-599. *P.A.*, 28:5793.

193. Bovard, E. W., Jr. Grouping error and interpersonal affect: a correction. *J. abnorm. soc. Psychol.*, 1956a, *52*, 283-284. *P.A.*, 31:2683.

194. Bovard, E. W., Jr. Interaction and attraction to the group. *Hum. Relat.*, 1956b, *9*, 481-489.

195. Bowerman, C. E., & Day, Barbara R. A test of the theory of complementary needs as applied to couples during courtship. *Amer. sociol. Rev.*, 1956, *21*, 602-605.

196. Boyd, R. W., & DiMascio, A. Social behavior and autonomic physiology: a sociophysiologic study. *J. nerv. ment. Dis.*, 1954, *120*, 207-212. *P.A.*, 29:7443.

197. Bradford, L. P., & French, J. R. P., Jr. (Eds.) The dynamics of the discussion group. *J. soc. Issues*, 1948, *4* (2).

198. Brandenburg, E. Problems in measuring the results of discussion. *J. Communication*, 1953, *3*, 28-33. *P.A.*, 28:7329.

199. Brandenburg, E., & Neal, P. A. Graphic techniques for evaluating discussion and conference procedures. *Quart. J. Speech.*, 1953, *39*, 201-208. *P.A.*, 28:2394.

200. Breer, P. E. Predicting interpersonal behavior from personality and role. Unpublished doctoral dissertation, Harvard Univer., 1960.

201. Brehm, J., & Festinger, L. Pressures toward uniformity of performance in groups. *Hum. Relat.*, 1957, *10*, 85-91. *P.A.*, 32:144.

202. Briskin, G. J. Identification in group therapy. *J. abnorm. soc. Psychol.*, 1958, *56*, 195-198.

203. Brodbeck, May. The role of small groups in mediating the effects of propaganda. *J. abnorm. soc. Psychol.*, 1956, *52*, 166-170. *P.A.*, 31:2870; *S.A.*, 5384.

204. Bronfenbrenner, U. A constant frame of reference for sociometric research. *Sociometry*, 1943, *6*, 363-397. *P.A.*, 18:2851.

205. Bronfenbrenner, U. A constant frame of reference for sociometric research: II. Experiment and inference. *Sociometry*, 1944, *7*, 40-75. *P.A.*, 18:2852.

206. Bronfenbrenner, U., & Newcomb, T. M. Improvisations—an application of psychodrama in personality diagnosis. *Sociatry*, 1948, *1*, 367-382. *P.A.*, 22:3935.

207. Brown, J. C. An experiment in role-taking. *Amer. sociol. Rev.*, 1952, *17*, 587-597. *P.A.*, 28:791.

208. Brown, Paula, & Brown, R. A note on hypotheses in Homans' *The human group. Amer. sociol. Rev.*, 1955, *20*, 83-85. Homans, G. C. Reply by G. C. Homans. *Amer. sociol. Rev.*, 1955, *20*, 85-86.

209. Bruner, J. S. Social psychology and group processes. *Annu. Rev. Psychol.*, 1950, *1*, 119-150.

210. Bruner, J. S., Goodnow, Jacqueline J., & Austin, G. A. *A study of thinking.* New York: Wiley, 1956. *P.A.*, 31:582.

211. Bruner, J. S., & Tagiuri, R. The perception of people. In G. Lindzey (Ed.), *Handbook of social psychology.* Reading, Mass.: Addison-Wesley, 1954. Pp. 634-654.

212. Buck, R. C. Acquaintance positions in the group. *Sociol. soc. Res.*, 1952, *37*, 33-36. *P.A.*, 27:7385.

213. Bugental, Daphne E., & Lehner, G. F. J. Accuracy of self-perception and group-perception as related to two leadership roles. *J abnorm. soc. Psychol.*, 1958, *56*, 396-398.

214. Buhler, Charlotte. *The child and his family.* New York: Harper, 1939.

215. Burchard, E. M. L., Michaels, J., & Kotkov, B. Criteria for the evaluation of group therapy. *Psychosom. Med.*, 1948, *10*, 257-274.

216. Burchinal, L. G., Hawkes, G. R., & Gardner, B. Personality characteristics and marital satisfaction. *Soc. Forces,* 1957, *35,* 218-222.

217. Burgess, E. W., & Cottrell, L. S., Jr. *Predicting success or failure in marriage.* Englewood Cliffs, N. J.: Prentice-Hall, 1939. *P.A.,* 14:404.

218. Burnham, W. H. The hygiene of home study. *Pedag. Sem.,* 1905, *12,* 213-230.

219. Burnham, W. H. The group as a stimulus to mental activity. *Science,* 1910, *31,* 761-767.

220. Burns, T. The reference of conduct in small groups: cliques and cabals in occupational milieux. *Hum. Relat.,* 1955, *8,* 467-486. *P.A.,* 31:882.

221. Burrow, T. The group method of analysis. *Psychoanal. Rev.,* 1927, *14,* 268-280. *P.A.,* 2:947.

222. Burton, A. The influence of social factors upon the persistence of satiation in pre-school children. *Child Develpm.,* 1941, *12,* 121-129.

223. Burtt, H. E. Sex differences in the effect of discussion. *J. exp. Psychol.,* 1920, 3, 390-395.

224. Butler, J. M. The interaction of client and therapist. *J. abnorm. soc. Psychol.,* 1952, *47,* 366-378. *P.A.,* 27:2773.

225. Byrd, E. A study of validity and constancy of choices in a sociometric test. *Sociometry,* 1951, *14,* 175-181. (See No. 559.) *P.A.,* 27:4162.

226. Byrne, D., & Buehler, J. A. A note on the influence of propinquity upon acquaintanceships. *J. abnorm. soc. Psychol.,* 1955, *51,* 147-148. *P.A.,* 30:5184.

227. Calvin, A. D., Hoffmann, F. K., & Harden, E. L. The effect of intelligence and social atmosphere on group problem solving behavior. *J. soc. Psychol.,* 1957, *45,* 61-74.

228. Campbell, D. T. *A study of leadership among submarine officers.* Columbus, Ohio: Ohio State Univer. Res. Found., 1953. *P.A.,* 29:8020.

229. Campbell, D. T. An error in some demonstrations of the superior social perceptiveness of leaders. *J. abnorm. soc. Psychol.,* 1955, *51,* 694-695. *P.A.,* 31:2738.

230. Campbell, D. T., & Mehra, K. Individual differences in evaluations of group discussions as a projective measure of attitudes toward leadership. *J. soc. Psychol.,* 1958, *47,* 101-106.

231. Campbell, D. T., & Tyler, Bonnie B. The construct validity of work-group morale measures. *J. appl. Psychol.*, 1957, *41*, 91-92.

232. Caplow, T. A theory of coalitions in the triad. *Amer. sociol. Rev.*, 1956, *21*, 489-493.

233. Carey, Gloria L. Sex differences in problem-solving performance as a function of attitude differences. *J. abnorm. soc. Psychol.*, 1958, *56*, 256-260.

234. Carr, L. J. Experimental sociology: a preliminary note on theory and method. *Soc. Forces*, 1929, *8*, 63-74.

235. Carr, L. J. Experimentation in face-to-face interaction. *Amer. sociol. Soc. Papers*, 1930, *24*, 174-176.

236. Carter, L. F. Some research on leadership in small groups. In H. Guetzkow (Ed.), *Groups, leadership, and men: research in human relations*. Pittsburgh: Carnegie Press, 1951. Pp. 146-157. P.A., 26:792.

237. Carter, L. F. Leadership and small-group behavior. In M. Sherif & M. O. Wilson (Eds.), *Group relations at the crossroads*. New York: Harper, 1953. Pp. 257-284. P.A., 28:7330.

238. Carter, L. F. Recording and evaluating the performance of individuals as members of small groups. *Personnel Psychol.*, 1954, *7*, 477-484. (See No. 559.) P.A., 29:7065.

239. Carter, L. F., Haythorn, W., & Howell, Margaret. A further investigation of the criteria of leadership. *J. abnorm. soc. Psychol.*, 1950, *45*, 350-358. (See No. 559.) P.A., 24:5765.

240. Carter, L. F., Haythorn, W., Meirowitz, Beatrice, & Lanzetta, J. A note on a new technique of interaction recording. *J. abnorm. soc. Psychol.*, 1951a, *46*, 258-260. P.A., 25:7773.

241. Carter, L. F., Haythorn, W., Meirowitz, Beatrice, & Lanzetta, J. The relation of categorizations and ratings in the observation of group behavior. *Hum. Relat.*, 1951b, *4*, 239-254. P.A., 26:6190.

242. Carter, L. F., Haythorn, W., Shriver, E., & Lanzetta, J. The behavior of leaders and other group members. *J. abnorm. soc. Psychol.*, 1951, *46*, 589-595. (See No. 249.) P.A., 26:3913.

243. Carter, L. F., & Nixon, Mary. An investigation of the relationship between four criteria of leadership ability for three different tasks. *J. Psychol.*, 1949a, *27*, 245-261. P.A., 23:2640.

244. Carter, L. F., & Nixon, Mary. Ability, perceptual, personality, and interest factors associated with different criteria of leadership. *J. Psychol.*, 1949b, *27*, 377-388. P.A., 23:4183.

245. Cartwright, D. Achieving change in people: some applications of group dynamics theory. *Hum. Relat.*, 1951, *4*, 381-392. P.A., 26:5472.

246. Cartwright, D. Emotional dimensions of group life. In M. L. Reymert

(Ed.), *Feelings and emotions.* New York: McGraw-Hill, 1952. Pp. 439-447. *P.A.*, 26:2087.

247. Cartwright, D. Social psychology. *Annu. Rev. Psychol.*, 1957, *8*, 211-236. *P.A.*, 32:344.

248. Cartwright, D., & Harary, F. Structural balance: A generalization of Heider's theory. *Psychol. Rev.*, 1956, *63*, 277-293. (See No. 249, 1960, pp. 705-726.)

249. Cartwright, D., & Zander, A. (Eds.) Group dynamics: research and *theory.* Evanston, Ill.: Row, Peterson, 1953. (2nd ed.: 1960). *P.A.*, 28:2395.

250. Cattell, R. B. Concepts and methods in the measurement of group syntality. *Psychol. Rev.*, 1948, *55*, 48-63. (See No. 559.) *P.A.*, 22:2577.

251. Cattell, R. B. Determining syntality dimension as a basis for morale and leadership measurement. In H. Guetzkow (Ed.), *Groups, leadership and men: research in human relations.* Pittsburgh: Carnegie Press, 1951a. Pp. 16-27. *P.A.*, 26:829.

252. Cattell, R. B. New concepts for measuring leadership, in terms of group syntality. *Hum. Relat.*, 1951b, *4*, 161-184. (See No. 249, 1960.)

253. Cattell, R. B. *Factor analysis: an introduction and manual for the psychologist and social scientist.* New York: Harper, 1952. *P.A.*, 26:6649.

254. Cattell, R. B. On the theory of group learning. *J. soc. Psychol.*, 1953, *37*, 27-52. *P.A.*, 28:722

255. Cattell, R. B. Second order personality factors in the questionnaire realm. *J. consult. Psychol.*, 1956, *20*, 411-418.

256. Cattell, R. B., Saunders, D. R., & Stice, G. F. The dimensions of syntality in small groups: I. The neonate group. *Hum. Relat.*, 1953, *6*, 331-356. (See No. 559.) *S.A.*, 240.

257. Cattell, R. B., & Stice, G. F. Four formulae for selecting leaders on the basis of personality. *Hum. Relat.*, 1954, *7*, 493-507. *P.A.*, 29:5450.

258. Cattell, R. B., & Wispe, L. G. The dimensions of syntality in small groups. *J. soc. Psychol.*, 1948, *28*, 57-78. *P.A.*, 23:1720.

259. Cervin, V. Experimental investigation of behavior in social situations: I. Behavior under opposition. *Canad. J. Psychol.*, 1955a, *9*, 107-116. *P.A.*, 30:2624.

260. Cervin, V. Experimental investigation of behavior in social situations: II. Individual behavioral effects of change in group attitude from opposition to cooperation. *Canad. J. Psychol.*, 1955b, *9*, 155-160. *P.A.*, 30:4336.

261. Cervin, V. Individual behavior in social situations: its relation to

anxiety, neuroticism, and group solidarity. *J. exp. Psychol.*, 1956, *51*, 161-168. *P.A.*, 31:2686.

262. Cervin, V. Relationship of ascendant-submissive behavior in dyadic groups of human subjects to their emotional responsiveness. *J. abnorm. soc. Psychol.*, 1957, *54*, 241-249.

263. Champney, H. The variables of parent behavior. *J. abnorm. soc. Psychol.*, 1941, *36*, 525-542. *P.A.*, 16:797.

264. Chance, Erika. Methodological problems in the study of parent child relationships from treatment interviews. *Merrill-Palmer Quart.*, 1957, *3*, 272-283.

265. Chance, June E. Adjustment and prediction of others' behavior. *J. consult. Psychol.*, 1958, *22*, 191-194.

266. Chapman, L. J., & Bock, R. D. Components of variance due to acquiescence and content in the F Scale measure of authoritarianism. *Psychol. Bull.*, 1958, *55*, 328-333.

267. Chapman, L. J., & Campbell, D. T. An attempt to predict the performance of three-man groups from attitude measures. *J. soc. Psychol.*, 1957a, *46*, 277-286.

268. Chapman, L. J., & Campbell, D. T. Response set in the F scale. *J. abnorm. soc. Psychol.*, 1957b, *54*, 129-132.

269. Chapple, E. D. Measuring human relations: an introduction to the study of interaction of individuals. *Genet. Psychol. Monogr.*, 1940, *22*, 3-147.

270. Chapple, E. D. The measurement of interpersonal behavior. *Trans. N. Y. Acad. Sci.*, 1942, *4*, 222-233. *P.A.*, 17:223.

271. Chapple, E. D. The standard experimental (stress) interview as used in interaction chronograph investigations. *Hum. Organization*, 1953, *12* (2), 23-32. *P.A.*, 29:5503.

272. Chapple, E. D., & Coon, C. S. *Principles of anthropology.* New York: Holt, 1942. *P.A.*, 16:1989.

273. Chapple, E. D., & Lindemann, E. Clinical implications of measurements on interaction rates in psychiatric interviews. *Appl. Anthrop.*, 1942, *1*, 1-11. *P.A.*, 17:1982.

274. Chesler, D. J., Van Steenberg, N. J., & Brueckel, Joyce E. Effect on morale of infantry team replaceemnt and individual replacement systems. *Sociometry*, 1955, *18*, 587-597. *S.A.*, 3439.

275. Chevaleva-Ianovskaia, E., & Sylla, D. Essai d'une étude sur les enfants meneurs. (A study of leaders among children.) *J. de Psychol.*, 1929, *26*, 604-612. *P.A.*, 4:1293.

276. Chittenden, Gertrude E. An experimental study in measuring and modifying assertive behavior in young children. *Soc. Res. Child Develpm. Monogr.*, 1942, 7, No. 1. *P.A.*, 17:992.

277. Chowdhry, Kamla, & Newcomb, T. M. The relative abilities of leaders

and non-leaders to estimate opinions of their own groups. *J. abnorm. soc. Psychol.*, 1952, *47*, 51-57. (See No. 559.) *P.A.*, 26:6177.

278. Christie, L. S., Luce, R. D., & Macy, J., Jr. *Communications and learning in task oriented groups.* Cambridge, Mass.: Res. Lab. Electronics, 1952.

279. Christie, R., & Cook, Peggy. A guide to published literature relating to the authoritarian personality through 1956. *J. Psychol.*, 1958, *45*, 171-199.

280. Christner, Charlotte A., & Hemphill, J. K. Leader behavior of B-29 commanders and changes in crew members' attitudes toward the crew. *Sociometry*, 1955, *18*, 82-87. *S.A.*, 1488.

281. Clampitt, R. R., & Charles, D. C. Sociometric status and supervisory evaluation of institutionalized mentally deficient children. *J. soc. Psychol.*, 1956, *44*, 223-231.

282. Clark, R. A., & McGuire, C. Sociographic analysis of sociometric valuations. *Child Develpm.*, 1952, *23*, 129-140. *P.A.*, 27:7134.

283. Cleveland, S. E., & Fisher, S. Prediction of small group behavior from a body image schema. *Hum. Relat.*, 1957, *10*, 223-233.

284. Coch, L., & French, J. R. P., Jr. Overcoming resistance to change. *Hum. Relat.*, 1948, *1*, 512-532. (See No. 249, No. 826, pp. 233-250.) *P.A.*, 23:2436.

285. Cocherell, D. L. A study of the play of children of pre-school age by an unobserved observer. *Genet. Psychol. Monogr.*, 1935, *17*, 377-469.

286. Coffey, H. S. Socio and psyche group process: integrative concepts. *J. soc. Issues*, 1952, *8* (2), 65-74. *P.A.*, 28:2712.

287. Coffey, H. S., Freedman, M. B., Leary, T. F., & Ossorio, A. G. (Eds.) Community service and social research: group psychotherapy in a church program. *J. soc. Issues*, 1950, *6* (1), 1-65. *P.A.*, 25:1050, 1117, 1118, 1119.

288. Cohen, A. R. Experimental effects of ego-defense preference on interpersonal relations. *J. abnorm. soc. Psychol.*, 1956, *52*, 19-27. *P.A.*, 31:2539.

289. Cohen, A. R. Upward communication in experimentally created hierarchies. *Hum. Relat.*, 1958, *11*, 41-53.

290. Cohen, B. P. A probability model for conformity. *Sociometry*, 1958, *21*, 69-81.

291. Cohen, E. Stimulus conditions as factors in social change. *Sociometry*, 1957a, *20*, 135-144.

292. Cohen, E. The effect of members' use of a formal group as a reference group upon group effectiveness. *J. soc. Psychol.*, 1957b, *46*, 307-309.

293. Cohen, J. Social thinking. *Acta psychol.*, 1953, 9, 146-158. *P.A.*, 28:2397.

294. Cole, D. "Rational argument" and "prestige-suggestion" as factors influencing judgment. *Sociometry*, 1954, 17, 350-354. *P.A.*, 30:5731.

295. Coleman, Janet F., Blake, R. R., & Mouton, Jane S. Task difficulty and conformity pressures. *J. abnorm. soc. Psychol.*, 1958, 57, 120-122.

296. Comrey, A. L. Group performance in a manual dexterity task. *J. appl. Psychol.*, 1953, 37, 207-210. *P.A.*, 28:3345.

297. Comrey, A. L., & Deskin, G. Further results on group manual dexterity in men. *J. appl. Psychol.*, 1954a, 38, 116-118. *P.A.*, 29:2053.

298. Comrey, A. L., & Deskin, G. Group manual dexterity in women. *J. appl. Psychol.*, 1954b, 38, 178-180. *P.A.*, 29:3529.

299. Comrey, A. L., & Staats, Carolyn K. Group performance in a cognative task. *J. appl. Psychol.*, 1955, 39, 354-356. *P.A.*, 30:6887.

300. Conrad, Dorothy C., & Conrad, R. The use of personal pronouns as categories for studying small group interaction. *J. abnorm. soc. Psychol.*, 1956, 52, 277-279. *P.A.*, 31:2689.

301. Cooley, C. H. *Human nature and the social order.* New York: Scribner, 1902.

302. Cooley, C. H. *Social organization.* New York: Scribner, 1909.

303. Coombs, A. W. & Taylor, C. The effect of the perception of mild degrees of threat on performance. *J. abnorm. soc. Psychol.*, 1952, 47, 420-424.

304. Corsini, R. J. Understanding and similarity in marriage. *J. abnorm. soc. Psychol.*, 1956, 52, 327-332. *P.A.*, 31:4536.

305. Corsini, R. J., & Putzey, L. J. Bibliography of group psychotherapy 1906-1956. *Psychodrama group psychother. Monogr.*, 1957, No. 29.

306. Coser, L. A. The functions of small-group research. *Soc. Probl.*, 1955, 3, 1-6. *P.A.*, 30:4338; *S.A.*, 2221.

307. Cottrell, L. S., Jr. The analysis of situational fields in social psychology. *Amer. sociol. Rev.*, 1942, 7, 370-382. (See No. 559.) *P.A.*, 16:3671.

308. Cottrell, L. S., Jr., & Gallagher, Ruth. Developments in social psychology, 1930-1940. *Sociometry Monogr.*, 1941, No. 1. *PA.*, 15:4736; *P.A.*, 16:1060, 1061.

309. Couch, A. S. Psychological determinants of interpersonal behavior. Unpublished doctoral dissertation, Harvard Univer., 1960.

310. Couch, A. [S.], & Carter, L. F. A factorial study of the rated behavior of group members. Paper read at East. Psychol. Ass., March, 1952.

311. Couch, A. [S.], & Keniston, K. [H.] Yeasayers and naysayers: agreeing

response set as a personality variable. *J. abnorm. soc. Psychol.,* 1960, *60,* 151-174.

312. Coyle, Grace L. *Social process in organized groups.* New York: R. R. Smith, 1930.

313. Coyle, Grace L. (Ed.) *Studies in group behavior.* New York: Harper, 1937. *P.A.,* 11:2824.

314. Cristie, R., Havel, Joan, & Seidenberg, B. Is the F Scale irreversible? *J. abnorm. soc. Psychol.,* 1958, *56,* 143-159.

315. Criswell, Joan H. Social structure revealed in a sociometric retest. *Sociometry,* 1939, *2,* 69-75. *P.A.,* 14:1473.

316. Criswell, Joan H. Sociometric methods of measuring group preferences. *Sociometry,* 1943, *6,* 398-408. *P.A.,* 18:2488.

317. Criswell, Joan H. Sociometric concepts in personnel administration. *Sociometry,* 1949, *12,* 287-300.

318. Criswell, Joan H., & Petrullo, L. Bibliography of unclassified research reports in group psychology. ONR Rep. ACR-22. Washington, D. C.: Office Naval Res., Dept. Navy, 1957.

319. Crockett, W. H. Emergent leadership in small, decision-making groups. *J. abnorm. soc. Psychol.,* 1955, *51,* 378-383. *P.A.,* 31:2690; *S.A.,* 3440.

320. Crockett, W. H., & Meidinger, T. Authoritarianism and interpersonal perception. *J. abnorm. soc. Psychol.,* 1956, *53,* 378-382. *P.A.,* 32:4030.

321. Croft, I. J., & Grygier, T. G. Social relationships of truants and juvenile delinquents. *Hum. Relat.,* 1956, *9,* 439-465.

322. Cronbach, L. J., Response sets and test validity. *Educ. psychol. Measmt.,* 1946, *6,* 475-494. *P.A.,* 21:2489.

323. Cronbach, L. J. Further evidence on response sets and test design. *Educ. psychol. Measmt.,* 1950, *10,* 3-31. *P.A.,* 25:681.

324. Cronbach, L. J. Processes affecting scores on "understanding of others" and "assumed similarity." *Psychol. Bull.,* 1955, *52,* 177-193. *P.A.,* 30:2865.

325. Cronbach, L. J. Proposals leading to analytic treatment of social perception scores. In R. Tagiuri & L. Petrullo (Eds.), *Person perception and interpersonal behavior.* Stanford, Calif.: Stanford Univer. Press, 1958. Pp. 353-379.

326. Crow, W. J. The effect of training upon accuracy and variability in interpersonal perception. *J. abnorm. soc. Psychol.,* 1957, *55,* 355-359.

327. Crow, W. J., & Hammond, K. R. The generality of accuracy and response sets in interpersonal perception. *J. abnorm. soc. Psychol.,* 1957, *54,* 384-390.

328. Crowell, Laura, Problems in measuring participation in discussion. *J. Communication,* 1953, *3,* 17-20. *P.A.,* 28:7331.

329. Crowell, Laura, Katcher, A., & Miyamoto, S. F. Self-concepts of communication skill and performance in small group discussions. *Speech Monogr.*, 1955, *22*, 20-27. *P.A.*, 30:770.

330. Crutchfield, R. S. Assessment of persons through a quasi group-interaction technique. *J. abnorm. soc. Psychol.*, 1951, *46*, 577-588. *P.A.*, 26:3929.

331. Crutchfield, R. S. Social psychology and group processes. *Annu. Rev. Psychol.*, 1954, *5*, 171-202.

332. Crutchfield, R. S. Conformity and character. *Amer. Psychologist*, 1955, *10*, 191-198. *S.A.*, 1972.

333. Cunningham, Ruth, et al., *Understanding group behavior of boys and girls*. New York: Teachers Coll., Columbia Univer., Bureau Publ., 1951. *P.A.*, 25:7069.

334. Curran, C. A. *Personality factors in counseling*. New York: Grune & Stratton, 1945.

335. Dahlke, H. O. Determinants of sociometric relations among children in the elementary school. *Sociometry*, 1953, *16*, 327-338. *P.A.*, 29:1487.

336. Danielsson, B. Some attraction and repulsion patterns among Jibaro Indians. *Sociometry*, 1949, *12*, 83-105.

337. Danzig, E. R., & Galanter, E. H. The dynamics and structure of small industrial work groups. Inst. Rep. No. 7, Inst. res. hum. relat., Philadelphia, 1955.

338. Darley, J. G., Gross, N., & Martin, W. E. Studies of group behavior: the stability, change, and interrelations of psychometric and sociometric variables. *J. abnorm. soc. Psychol.*, 1951, *46*, 565-576. *P.A.*, 26:3915.

339. Darley, J. G., Gross, N., & Martin, W. E. Studies of group behavior: factors associated with the productivity of groups. *J. appl. Psychol.*, 1952, *36*, 396-403. *P.A.*, 27:6472.

340. Dashiell, J. F. An experimental analysis of some group effects. *J. abnorm. soc. Psychol.*, 1930, *25*, 190-199.

341. Dashiell, J. F. Experimental studies of the influence of social situations on the behavior of individual human adults. In C. Murchison (Ed.), *A handbook of social psychology*. Worcester, Mass.: Clark Univer. Press, 1935, 1097-1158.

342. Davie, J. S., & Hare, A. P. Button-down collar culture: a study of undergraduate life at a men's college. *Hum. Organization*, 1956, *14* (4), 13-20. *P.A.*, 31:5091.

343. Davis, F. J. Conceptions of official leader roles in the air force. *Soc. Forces*, 1954, *32*, 253-258. *P.A.*, 29:3786.

344. Davis, J. A., & Warnath, C. F. Reliability, validity, and stability of a sociometric rating scale. *J. soc. Psychol.*, 1957, *45*, 111-121.

345. Davis, R. L. Structures of dominance relations. *Bull. math. Biophysics*, 1954, *16*, 131-140.

346. Davitz, J. R. Social perception and sociometric choice. *J. abnorm. soc. Psychol.*, 1955, *50,* 173-176. *P.A.,* 30:685; *S.A.,* 1973.

347. Dawe, Helen C. The influence of the size of kindergarten group upon performance. *Child Develpm.,* 1934, *5,* 295-303.

348. Dean, J. P., & Rosen, A. *A manual of intergroup relations.* Chicago: Univer. Chicago Press, 1955. *P.A.,* 30:2707.

349. de Charms, R. Affiliation motivation and productivity in small groups. *J. abnorm. soc. Psychol.,* 1957, *55,* 222-226.

350. De Monchaux, Cecily, & Shimmin, Sylvia. Some problems in experimental group psychology: considerations arising from cross-cultural experiments on threat and rejection. *Hum. Relat.,* 1955, *8,* 53-60. *P.A.,* 30:822; *S.A.,* 1756.

351. de Montmollin, Germaine. Effects de groupe sur la structuration perceptive. *Année psychol.,* 1955a, *55,* 1-25. *P.A.,* 31:737.

352. de Montmollin, Germaine. Effects de groupe sur la structuration perceptive, II. *Année psychol.,* 1955b, *55,* 329-348. *P.A.,* 31:738.

353. Deutsch, M. A theory of cooperation and competition. *Hum. Relat.,* 1949a, *2,* 129-152. *P.A.,* 24:137.

354. Deutsch, M. An experimental study of the effects of cooperation and competition upon group process. *Hum. Relat.,* 1949b, *2,* 199-231. (See No. 249.) *P.A.,* 24:4051.

355. Deutsch, M. Field theory in social psychology. In G. Lindzey (Ed.), *Handbook of social psychology.* Reading, Mass.: Addison-Wesley, 1954. Pp. 181-222.

356. Deutsch, M. Some factors affecting membership motivation and achievement motivation in a group. *Hum. Relat.,* 1959, *12,* 81-95.

357. Deutsch, M., & Gerard, H. B. A study of normative and informational social influences upon individual judgment. *J. abnorm. soc. Psychol.,* 1955, *51,* 629-636. (See No. 249, 1960.) *P.A.,* 31:2366.

358. Deutschberger, P. The *tele*-factor: horizon and awareness. *Sociometry,* 1947, *10,* 242-249. *P.A.,* 23:1223.

359. Deutscher, Verda, & Deutscher, I. Cohesion in a small group: a case study. *Soc. Forces,* 1955, *33,* 336-341. *S.A.,* 2488.

360. Dickens, M. A statistical formula to quantify the "spread of participation" in group discussion. *Speech Monogr.,* 1955, *22,* 28-30. *P.A.,* 30:772.

361. Dicks, H. V. *Psychological foundations of the Wehrmacht.* London: War Offices, 1944.

362. Dittes, J. E., & Kelley, H. H. Effects of different conditions of acceptance upon conformity to group norms. *J. abnorm. soc. Psychol.,* 1956, *53,* 100-107. *P.A.,* 32:1443.

363. Dittman, A. T. The interpersonal process in psychotherapy: development of a research method. *J. abnorm. soc. Psychol.,* 1952, *47,* 236-244. *P.A.,* 27:2778.

364. Di Vesta, F. J. Instructor-centered and student-centered approaches

in teaching a human relations course. *J. appl. Psychol.*, 1954, *38*, 329-335. P.A., 29:6161.

365. Di Vesta, F. J., Roach, J. H. L., & Beasley, W. Rating conference participation in a human relations training program. *J. appl. Psychol.*, 1951, *35*, 386-391.

366. Dodd, S. C. A social distance test in the Near East. *Amer. J. Sociol.*, 1935, *41*, 194-204.

367. Dodd, S. C. The interrelation matrix. *Sociometry*, 1940, *3*, 91-101. P.A., 14:3308.

368. Dodd, S. C. The transact model. *Sociometry*, 1955, *18*, 688-703. P.A., 32:1444.

369. Dowing, J. Cohesiveness, perception, and values. *Hum. Relat.*, 1958, *11*, 157-166.

370. Dymond, Rosalind F. A scale for the measurement of empathic ability. *J. consult. Psychol.*, 1949, *13*, 127-133. (See No. 559.) P.A., 23:4497.

371. Dymond, Rosalind F. Personality and empathy. *J. consult. Psychol.*, 1950, *14*, 343-350. P.A., 25:4352.

372. Dymond, Rosalind F., Hughes, Anne S., & Raabe, Virginia L. Measurable changes in empathy with age. *J. consult. Psychol.*, 1952, *16*, 202-206. P.A., 27:5021.

373. Dymond, Rosalind F., Seeman, J., & Grummon, D. L. Patterns of perceived interpersonal relations. *Sociometry*, 1956, *19*, 166-177.

374. Edwards, A. L. Experiments: their planning and execution. In G. Lindzey (Ed.), *Handbook of social psychology*. Reading, Mass.: Addison-Wesley, 1954. Pp. 259-288. P.A., 29:3840.

375. Eister, A. W. Basic continuities in the study of small groups. In H. Becker & A. Boskoff (Eds.), *Modern Sociological Theory*. New York: Dryden, 1957. Pp. 305-339.

376. Ekman, Gosta. The four effects of cooperation. *J. soc. Psychol.*, 1955, *41*, 149-162. P.A., 30:580.

377. Elkine, D. De l'influence du groupe sur les fonctions de la memoire. (The influence of the group on memory functions.) *J. Psychol.*, 1927, *24*, 827-830. P.A., 3:92.

378. Elliott, H. S. *The process of group thinking*. New York: Association Press, 1928.

379. Emerson, R. M. Deviation and rejection: an experimental replication. *Amer. sociol. Rev.*, 1954, *19*, 688-693. P.A., 30:2631.

380. Eng, E. W. An approach to the prediction of sociometric choice. *Sociometry*, 1954, *17*, 329-339. P.A., 30:5875.

381. Exline, R. V. Group climate as a factor in the relevance and accuracy of social perception. *J. abnorm. soc. Psychol.*, 1957, *55*, 382-388.

382. Eysenck, H. J. *The pyschology of politics*. London: Routledge & Keegan Paul, 1954. P.A., 30:909.

383. Faris, R. E. L. Development of small-group research movement. In

M. Sherif & M. O. Wilson (Eds.), *Group relations at the cross-roads*. New York: Harper, 1953. Pp. 155-184. *P.A.*, 28:7335.

384. Farnsworth, P. R., & Behner, Alice. A note on the attitude of social conformity. *J. soc. Psychol.*, 1931, *2*, 126-128.

385. Farnsworth, P. R., & Williams, M. F. The accuracy of the median and mean of a group of judgments. *J. soc. Psychol.*, 1936, *7*, 237-239.

386. Faunce, D., & Beegle, J. A. Cleavages in a relatively homogeneous group of rural youth: an experiment in the use of sociometry in attaining and measuring integration. *Sociometry*, 1948, *11*, 207-216. *P.A.*, 24:611.

387. Feofanov, M. P. Kvoprosu ob izuchenii strukturnykh osobennostei kollektivov. (The question of investigating the structural characteristics of a group.) *Zh. psikhol. pedol. i psikhotekh.*, 1928, *1*, 107-120. *P.A.*, 3:4117.

388. Fessenden, S. A. An index of cohesiveness-morale based on the analysis of sociometric choice distribution. *Sociometry*, 1953, *16*, 321-326. *P.A.*, 29:667.

389. Festinger, L. The role of group belongingness in a voting situation. *Hum. Relat.*, 1947, *1*, 154-180. *P.A.*, 22:2609.

390. Festinger, L. The analysis of sociograms using matrix algebra. *Hum. Relat.*, 1949, *2*, 153-158. *P.A.*, 24:20.

391. Festinger, L. Informal social communication. *Psychol. Rev.*, 1950a, *57*, 271-292. (See No. 249.) *P.A.*, 25:4528.

392. Festinger, L. Laboratory experiments: the role of group belongingness. In J. G. Miller (Ed.), *Experiments in social process*. New York: McGraw-Hill, 1950b. Pp. 31-46. *P.A.*, 25:1715.

393. Festinger, L. Architecture and group membership. *J. soc. Issues*, 1951a, *7* (2), 152-163. (See No. 249, 1953.)

394. Festinger, L. Informal communications in small groups. In H. Guetzkow (Ed.), *Groups, leadership and men: research in human relations*. Pittsburgh: Carnegie Press, 1951b. Pp. 28-43. *P.A.*, 26:797.

395. Festinger, L. An analysis of compliant behavior. In M. Sherif & M. O. Wilson (Eds.), *Group relations at the crossroads*. New York: Harper, 1953a. Pp. 232-256. *P.A.*, 28:7336.

396. Festinger, L. Laboratory experiments. In L. Festinger & D. Katz (Eds.), *Research methods in the behavioral sciences*. New York: Dryden, 1953b. Pp. 136-172. *P.A.*, 28:3542.

397. Festinger, L. Theory of social comparsion processes. *Hum. Relat.*, 1954, *7*, 117-140. (See No. 559.) *P.A.*, 29:2305.

398. Festinger, L. Social psychology and group processes. *Annu. Rev. Psychol.*, 1955, *6*, 187-216.

399. Festinger, L. *A theory of cognitive dissonance*. Evanston, Ill.: Row, Peterson, 1957. *P.A.*, 32:347.

400. Festinger, L., & Aronson, E. The arousal and reduction of dissonance in social contexts. In D. Cartwright & A. Zander (Eds.), *Group dynamics: research and theory*. Evanston, Ill.: Row, Peterson, 1960. Pp. 214-231.

401. Festinger, L., Cartwright, D., Barber, Kathleen, Fleischl, Juliet, Gottsdanker, Josephine, Keysen, Annette, & Leavitt, Gloria. A study of rumor: its origin and spread. *Hum. Relat.*, 1948, *1*, 464-486. *P.A.*, 23:2201.

402. Festinger, L., Gerard, H. B., Hymovitch, B., Kelley, H. H., & Raven, B. The influence process in the presence of extreme deviates. *Hum. Relat.*, 1952, *5*, 327-346. *P.A.*, 27:7114; *S.A.*, 123.

403. Festinger, L., & Hutte, H. A. An experimental investigation of the effect of unstable interpersonal relations in a group. *J. abnorm. soc. Psychol.*, 1954, *49*, 513-522. *P.A.*, 29:5454.

404. Festinger, L., & Katz, D. (Eds.) *Research methods in the behavioral sciences*. New York: Dryden, 1953. *P.A.*, 28:3542.

405. Festinger, L., Pepitone, A., & Newcomb, T. Some consequences of de-individuation in a group. *J. abnorm. soc. Psychol.*, 1952, *47*, 382-389. (See No. 559.) *P.A.*, 27:2609.

406. Festinger, L., Schachter, S., & Back, K. *Social pressures in informal groups: a study of human factors in housing*. New York: Harper, 1950. (See No. 249.) *P.A.*, 25:2994.

407. Festinger, L., & Thibaut, J. Interpersonal communication in small groups. *J. abnorm. soc. Psychol.*, 1951, *46*, 92-99. *P.A.*, 25:7370.

408. Festinger, L., Torrey, Jane, & Willerman, B. Self-evaluation as a function of attraction to the group. *Hum. Relat.*, 1954, *7*, 161-174. *S.A.*, 763.

409. Fiedler, F. E. Assumed similarity measures as predictors of team effectiveness in surveying. *Univer. of Ill., Coll. of Educ., Tech. Rep.*, 1953a, No. 6, pp. 1-20. *P.A.*, 28:4127.

410. Fiedler, F. E. The psychological-distance dimension in interpersonal relations. *J. Pers.*, 1953b, *22*, 142-150. *P.A.*, 28:4128.

411. Fiedler, F. E. Assumed similarity measures as predictors of team effectiveness. *J. abnorm. soc. Psychol.*, 1954a. *49*, 381-388. (See No. 559.) *P.A.*, 28:4127.

412. Fiedler, F. E. The influence of leader-keyman relations on combat crew effectiveness. Urbana, Ill.: Group Effectiveness Res. Lab., Univer. of Ill., 1954b. *P.A.*, 29:3790.

413. Fiedler, F. E. The influence of leader-keyman relations on combat crew effectiveness. *J. abnorm. soc. Psychol.*, 1955, *51*, 227-235. *P.A.*, 30:5346.

414. Fiedler, F. E. A note on leadership theory: the effect of social barriers between leaders and followers. *Sociometry*, 1957, *20*, 87-94.

415. Fiedler, F. E. *Leader attitudes and group effectiveness*. Urbana, Ill.: Univer. Ill. Press, 1958. *P.A.*, 32:1446.

416. Fiedler, F. E. The leader's psychological distance and group effectiveness. In D. Cartwright & A. Zander (Eds.), *Group dynamics: research and theory.* Evanston, Ill.: Row, Peterson, 1960. Pp. 586-606.

417. Fiedler, F. E., Hartmann, W., & Rudin, S. A. The relationship of interpersonal perception to effectiveness in basketball teams. *Univ. of Ill., Coll. of Educ., Tech. Rep.,* 1952, No. 3. *P.A.,* 27:339.

418. Fiedler, F. E., Warrington, W. G., & Blaisdell, F. J. Unconscious attitudes as correlates of sociometric choice in a social group. *J. abnorm. soc. Psychol.,* 1952, 47, 790-796. *S.A.,* 124.

419. Findley, W. G. A statistical index of participation in discussion. *J. educ. Psychol.,* 1948, 39, 47-51. *P.A.,* 22:3414.

420. Fischer, P. H. An analysis of the primary group. *Sociometry,* 1953, 16, 272-276. *P.A.,* 28:4129.

421. Fisher, S., & Lubin, A. Distance as a determinant of influence in a two-person serial interaction situation. *J. abnorm. soc. Psychol.,* 1958, 56, 230-238.

422. Flanders, N. A. Personal-social anxiety as a factor in experimental learning situations. *J. educ. Res.,* 1951, 45, 100-110. *P.A.,* 26:5096.

423. Fleishman, E. A. The leadership role of the foreman in industry. *Engng Expt. Sta. News,* Ohio State Univer., 1952, 24, 27-35.

424. Foa, U. G. Empathy or behavioral transparency? *J. abnorm. soc. Psychol.,* 1958a, 56, 62-66.

425. Foa, U. G. The contiguity principle in the structure of interpersonal relations. *Hum. Relat.,* 1958b, 11, 229-238.

426. Forsyth, Elaine, & Katz, L. A matrix approach to the analysis of sociometric data: preliminary report. *Sociometry,* 1946, 9, 340-347. *P.A.,* 21:2362.

427. Foulkes, S. H. Group therapy: a short survey and orientation with particular reference to group analysis. *Brit. J. med. Psychol.,* 1950, 25, 199-205.

428. Fouriezos, N. T., Hutt, M. L., & Guetzkow, H. Measurement of self-oriented needs in discussion groups. *J. abnorm. soc. Psychol.,* 1950, 45, 682-690. (See No. 249, 1953.) *P.A.,* 25:2359.

429. Fox, J .B., & Scott, J. F. *Absenteeism: management's problem.* Boston: Grad. Sch. Bus. Adm., Harvard Univer., 1943. *P.A.,* 18:1832.

430. Fox, W. F. Group reaction to two types of conference leadership. *Hum. Relat.,* 1957, 10, 279-289.

431. Frank, J. D. Experimental studies of personal pressure and resistance: I. Experimental production of resistance. *J. gen. Psychol.,* 1944, 30, 23-64. *P.A.,* 18:2473, 2474, 2475.

432. Frank, J. D., Margolin, J., Nash, Helen T., Stone, A. R., Varon, E., & Ascher, E. Two behavior patterns in therapeutic groups and their

apparent motivation. *Hum. Relat.*, 1952, *5*, 289-317. *P.A.*, 27:3577.

433. Freedman, M. B., Leary, T. F., Ossorio, A. B., & Coffey, H. S. The interpersonal dimension of personality. *J. Pers.*, 1951, *20*, 143-161. *P.A.*, 27:993.

434. French, Elizabeth G. Motivation as a variable in work-partner selection. *J. abnorm. soc. Psychol.*, 1956, *53*, 96-99.

435. French, Elizabeth G., & Chadwick, Irene. Some characteristics of affiliation motivation. *J. abnorm. soc. Psychol.*, 1956, *52*, 296-300. *P.A.*, 31:5093.

436. French, J. R. P., Jr. The disruption and cohesion of groups. *J. abnorm. soc. Psychol.*, 1941, *36*, 361-377. (See No. 249, 1953.) *P.A.*, 15:5253.

437. French, J. R. P., Jr. Organized and unorganized groups under fear and frustration. In *Univer. of Iowa Stud. Child Welf.*, 1944, *20*, No. 409, 231-308. *P.A.*, 19:3427.

438. French, J. R. P., Jr. Field experiments: changing group productivity. In J. G. Miller (Ed.), *Experiments in social process: a symposium on social psychology.* New York: McGraw-Hill, 1950. Pp. 79-96. *P.A.*, 25:1716.

439. French, J. R. P., Jr. Group productivity. In H. Guetzkov, *Groups, leadership and men: research in human relations.* Pittsburgh: Carnegie Press, 1951. Pp. 44-54. *P.A.*, 26:798.

410. French, J. R. P., Jr. Experiments in field settings. In L. Festinger & D. Katz, *Research methods in the behavioral sciences.* New York: Dryden, 1953. Pp. 98-135. *P.A.*, 28:3542.

441. French, J. R. P., Jr. A formal theory of social power. *Psychol. Rev.*, 1956, *63*, 181-194. (See No. 249, 1960.) *P.A.*, 31:4473.

442. French, J. R. P., Jr., & Raven, B. The bases of social power. In D. Cartwright & A. Zander (Eds.), *Group dynamics: research and theory.* Evanston, Ill.: Row, Peterson, 1960. P.p 607-623.

443. French, J. R. P., Jr., & Zander, A. The group dynamics approach. In A. Kornhauser (Ed.), *Psychology of labor management relations.* New York: American Book, 1949. Pp. 71-80. *P.A.*, 24:3440.

444. French, R. L. Social psychology and group processes. *Annu. Rev. Psychol.*, 1955, *7*, 63-94. *P.A.*, 30:5849.

445. French, R. L., & Mensh, I. N. Some relationships between interpersonal judgments and sociometric status in a college group. *Sociometry*, 1948, *11*, 335-345.

446. Freud, S. *Group psychology and the analysis of the ego.* New York: Liveright Publ. Corp. 1949. (1st Ed., London: Hogarth, 1922.)

447. Freud, S. Libidinal types. In *Collected papers Vol. V.* London: Hogarth, 1950. Pp. 247-251.

448. Fromm, E. *Man for himself.* New York: Holt, 1947. *P.A.*, 22:1441.

449. Fruchter, B. *Introduction to factor analysis.* New York: Van Nostrand, 1954. *P.A.*, 28:8313.

450. Furfey, P. H. Some factors influencing the selection of boys' chums. *J. appl. Psychol.*, 1927, *11*, 47-51. *P.A.*, 1:2062.

451. Gage, N. L. Accuracy of social perception and effectiveness in interpersonal relationships. *J. Pers.*, 1953, *22*, 128-141.

452. Gage, N. L., & Cronbach, L. Conceptual and methodological problems in interpersonal perception. *Psychol. Rev.*, 1955, *62*, 411-422. *P.A.*, 30:5876.

453. Gage, N. L., & Exline, R. V. Social perception and effectiveness in discussion groups. *Hum. Relat.*, 1953, *6*, 381-396. *S.A.*, 242.

454. Gage, N. L., Leavitt, G. S., & Stone, G. C. The intermediary key in the analysis of interpersonal perception. *Psychol. Bull.*, 1956, *53*, 258-266.

455. Gage, N. L., Leavitt, G. S., & Stone, G. C. The psychological meaning of acquiescence set for authoritarianism. *J. abnorm. soc. Psychol.*, 1957, *55*, 98-103.

456. Gardner, E. F., & Thompson, G. G. *Social relations and morale in small groups.* New York: Appleton-Century-Crofts, 1956. *P.A.*, 30:8184.

457. Gardner, G. Functional leadership and popularity in small groups. *Hum. Relat.*, 1956, *9*, 491-509.

458. Gates, Georgina S. The effect of an audience upon performance. *J. abnorm. soc. Psychol.*, 1924, *18*, 334-342.

459. Gebel, A. S. Self-perception and leaderless group discussion status. *J. soc. Psychol.*, 1954, *40*, 309-318. *P.A.*, 29:7070.

460. Gekoski, N. Predicting group productivity. *Personn. Psychol.*, 1952, *5*, 281-292. *P.A.*, 27:6817.

461. Gerard, H. B. The effect of different dimensions of disagreement on the communication process in small groups. *Hum. Relat.*, 1953, *6*, 249-271. *P.A.*, 27:4210; *P.A.*, 28:2404.

462. Gerard, H. B. The anchorage of opinions in face-to-face groups. *Hum. Relat.*, 1954, *7*, 313-325. *P.A.*, 29:3792.

463. Gerard, H. B. Some factors affecting an individual's estimate of his probable success in a group situation. *J. abnorm. soc. Psychol.*, 1956, *52*, 235-239. *P.A.*, 31:2696; *S.A.*, 5290.

464. Gerard, H. B. Some effects of status, role clarity, and group goal clarity upon the individual's relations to group process. *J. Pers.*, 1957, *25*, 475-488.

465. Getzels, J. W., & Guba, E. G. Role conflict and personality. *J. Pers.*, 1955, *24*, 74-85. *P.A.*, 30:5758.

466. Ghiselli, E. E., & Lodahl, T. M. Patterns of managerial traits and group effectiveness. *J. abnorm. soc. Psychol.*, 1958, *57*, 61-66.

467. Gibb, C. A. The principles and traits of leadership. *J. abnorm. soc. Psychol.*, 1947, *42*, 267-284. (See No. 559.) *P.A.*, 22:1149.

468. Gibb, C. A. The sociometry of leadership in temporary groups. *Sociometry*, 1950, *13*, 226-243. (See No. 559.)

469. Gibb, C. A. An experimental approach to the study of leadership. *Occup. Psychol.*, 1951, *25*, 233-248. P.A., 26:5475.

470. Gibb, C. A. Leadership. In G. Lindzey (Ed.), *Handbook of social psychology*. Reading, Mass.: Addison-Wesley, 1954. Pp. 877-920. P.A., 29:3793.

471. Gibb, J. R. The effects of group size and of threat reduction upon creativity in a problem-solving situation. *Amer. Psychol.*, 1951, *6*, 324.

472. Giedt, F. H. Factor analysis of roles patients take in therapy groups. *J. soc. Psychol.*, 1956, *44*, 165-171.

473. Gilchrist, J. C. The formation of social groups under conditions of success and failure. *J. abnorm. soc. Psychol.*, 1952, *47*, 174-187. P.A., 27:2613.

474. Gilchrist, J. C. Social psychology and group processes. *Annu. Rev. Psychol.*, 1959, *10*, 233-264.

475. Gilchrist, J. C., Shaw, M. E., & Walker, L. C. Some effects of unequal distribution of information in a wheel group structure. *J. abnorm. soc. Psychol.*, 1954, *49*, 554-556. P.A., 29:5621.

476. Gittler, J. B. (Ed.), *Review of sociology: analysis of a decade*. New York: Wiley, 1957. PA., 32:348.

477. Gleason, W. J. Predicting army leadership ability by modified leaderless group discussion. *J. appl. Psychol.*, 1957, *41*, 231-235.

478. Goffman, I. Alienation from interaction. *Hum. Relat.*, 1957, *10*, 47-60.

479. Gold, M. Power in the classroom. *Sociometry*, 1958, *21*, 50-60.

480. Goldberg, S. C. Three situational determinants of conformity to social norms. *J. abnorm. soc. Psychol.*, 1954, *49*, 325-329. P.A., 29:3796.

481. Goldberg, S. C. Influence and leadership as a function of group structure. *J. abnorm. soc. Psychol.*, 1955, *51*, 119-122. P.A., 30:4345; S.A., 2489.

482. Goldberg, S. C., & Lubin, A. Influence as a function of perceived judgment error. *Hum. Relat.*, 1958, *11*, 275-281.

483. Goldman-Eisler, Frieda. The measurement of time sequences in conversational behavior. *Brit. J. Psychol.*, Gen. Section, 1951, *42*, 355-362. P.A., 26:5548.

484. Goodacre, D. M. The use of a sociometric test as a predictor of combat unit effectiveness. *Sociometry*, 1951, *14*, 148-152. P.A., 27:4618.

485. Goodacre, D. M. Group characteristics of good and poor performing combat units. *Sociometry*, 1953, *16*, 168-178. P.A., 28:5026.

486. Goodenough, Florence L. Measuring behavior traits by means of repeated short samples. *J. juv. Res.*, 1928, *12*, 230-235.

487. Goodenough, Florence L. Interrelationships in the behavior of young children. *Child Develpm.*, 1930, *1*, 29-48.

488. Goodenough, Florence L., & Anderson, J. E. *Experimental child study.* New York: Appleton-Century-Crofts, 1931.

489. Goodnow, R. E., & Tagiuri, R. Religious ethnocentricism and its recognition among adolescent boys. *J. abnorm. soc. Psychol.,* 1952, *47,* 316-320. *P.A.,* 27:2582.

490. Gorden, R. L. Interaction between attitude and the definition of the situation in the expression of opinion. *Amer. soc. Rev.,* 1952, *17,* 50-58. (See No. 249, 1953.) *P.A.,* 27:3419.

491. Gordon, Kate. Group judgments in the field of lifted weights. *J. exp. Psychol.,* 1924, *7,* 398-400.

492. Gordon, T. *Group-centered leadership: a way of releasing the creative power of groups.* Boston: Houghton Mifflin, 1955. *P.A.,* 30:2644.

493. Gorlow, L., Hoch, E. L., & Telschow, E. F. *The nature of nondirective group psychotherapy.* New York: Teach. Coll., Columbia Univer., 1952.

494. Gottheil, E. Changes in social perceptions contingent upon competing or cooperating. *Sociometry,* 1955, *18,* 132-137. *P.A.,* 30:4346.

495. Gouldner, A. W. (Ed.), *Studies in leadership.* New York: Harper, 1950. *P.A.,* 25:2997.

496. Grace, H. A. The effects of different degrees of knowledge about an audience on the content of communication. *J. soc. Psychol.,* 1951, *34,* 31-40. *P.A.,* 27:3510.

497. Grace, H. A. The effects of different degrees of knowledge about an audience on the content of communication: the male audience. *J. soc. Psychol.,* 1952a, *36,* 83-88.

498. Grace, H. A. The effects of different degrees of knowledge about an audience on the content of communication: the comparison of male and female audiences. *J. soc. Psychol.,* 1952b, *36,* 89-96.

499. Grace, H. A. Conformance and performance. *J. soc. Psychol.,* 1954, *40,* 333-335. *P.A.,* 29:7073.

500. Green, Elise H. Friendship and quarrels among pre-school children. children. *Child Develpm.,* 1933a, *4,* 237-252.

501. Green, Elise H. Group play and quarreling among pre-school children. *Child Develpm.,* 1933b, *4,* 302-307. *P.A.,* 8:2828.

502. Green, G. H. Insight and group adjustment. *J. abnorm. soc. Psychol.,* 1948, *43,* 49-61. *P.A.,* 22:3416.

503. Green, N. E. Verbal intelligence and effectiveness of participation in group discussion. *J. educ. Psychol.,* 1950, *41,* 440-445. *P.A.,* 25:5227.

504. Greenberg, Pearl J. Competition in children: an experimental study. *Amer. J. Psychol.,* 1932, *44,* 221-248. *P.A.,* 6:2940.

505. Greer, F. L. Small group effectiveness. Inst. Rep. No. 6, Inst. Res. Hum. Relat., Philadelphia, 1955.

506. Greer, F. L., Galanter, E. H., & Nordlie, P. G. Interpersonal knowledge and individual and group effectiveness. *J. abnorm. soc. Psychol.*, 1954, *49*, 411-414. P.A., 29:3797.

507. Grinker, R. R., & Spiegel, J. P. *Men under stress.* New York: McGraw-Hill, 1945. P.A., 20:2372.

508. Gronlund, N. E. Sociometric status and sociometric perception. *Sociometry*, 1955a, *18*, 122-128. P.A., 30:4348; S.A., 2223.

509. Gronlund, N. E. The relative stability of classroom social status with unweighted and weighted sociometric choices. *J. educ. Psychol.*, 1955b, *46*, 345-354. P.A., 30:7645.

510. Gronlund, N. E. Generality of teachers' sociometric perceptions: relative judgment accuracy on several sociometric criteria. *J. educ. Psychol.*, 1956a, 47, 25-31. P.A., 31:6556.

511. Gronlund, N. E. The general ability to judge sociometric status: elementary student teachers' sociometric perceptions of classmates and pupils. *J. educ. Psychol.*, 1956b, *47*, 147-157.

512. Gross, E. Some functional consequences of primary controls in formal work organizations. *Amer. sociol. Rev.*, 1953, *18*, 368-373. P.A., 28:5028.

513. Gross, E. Primary functions of the small group. *Amer. J. Sociol.*, 1954, *60*, 24-30. P.A., 30:780.

514. Gross, E. Symbiosis and consensus as integrative factors in small groups. *Amer. sociol. Rev.*, 1956, *21*, 174-179. P.A., 31:2698; S.A., 2924.

515. Gross, N., McEachern, A. W., & Mason, W. S. Role conflict and its resolution. In Eleanor E. Maccoby, T. M. Newcomb, & E. L. Hartley (Eds.), *Readings in social psychology.* (3rd ed.) New York: Holt, 1958. Pp. 447-459.

516. Gross, N., & Martin, W. E. On group cohesiveness. *Amer. J. Sociol.*, 1952, *57*, 546-554. Schachter, S. Comment. 554-562. Gross, N., & Martin, W. E. Rejoinder. 562-564. P.A., 27:1883.

517. Gross, N., Martin, W. E., & Darley, J. G. Studies of group behavior: leadership structures in small organized groups. *J. abnorm. soc. Psychol.*, 1953, *48*, 429-432. P.A., 28:2408; S.A., 82.

518. Gross, N., Mason, W. S., & McEachern, A. W. *Explorations in role analysis: studies of the school superintendency role.* New York: Wiley, 1958.

519. Grossack, M. Controlling interaction in small group research. *J. Psychol.*, 1953, *35*, 241-244. P.A., 28:726.

520. Grossack, M. M. Some effects of cooperation and competition upon small group behavior. *J. abnorm. soc. Psychol.*, 1954, *49*, 341-348. P.A., 29:3798.

521. Grosser, D., Polansky, N., & Lippitt, R. A laboratory study of behavioral contagion. *Hum. Relat.*, 1951, *4*, 115-142. Also in

Dorothea F. Sullivan (Ed.), *Readings in group work*. New York: Association Press, 1952. Pp. 284-317. *P.A.*, 26:1418.

522. Grusky, O. A case for the theory of familiar role differentiation in small groups. *Soc. Forces*, 1957, 35, 209-217. *P.A.*, 32:2751; *S.A.*, 4683.

523. Guetzkow, H. (Ed.), *Groups, leadership and men: research in human relations*. Pittsburgh: Carnegie Press, 1951. *P.A.*, 26:803.

524. Guetzkow, H. Building models about small groups. In R. Young (Ed.), *Approaches to the study of political science*. Evanston, Ill.: Northwestern Univer. Press, 1958. Pp. 265-281.

525. Guetzkow, H. Differentiation of roles in task-oriented groups. In D. Cartwright & A. Zander (Eds.), *Group dynamics: research and theory*. Evanston, Ill.: Row, Peterson, 1960. Pp. 683-704.

526. Guetzkow, H., & Dill, W. R. Factors in the organizational development of task-oriented groups. *Sociometry*, 1957, 20, 175-204.

527. Guetzkow, H., & Gyr, J. An analysis of conflict in decision-making groups. *Hum. Relat.*, 1954, 7, 367-382. *P.A.*, 29:3799.

528. Guetzkow, H., & Simon, H. A. The impact of certain communication nets upon organization and performance in task-oriented groups. *Mgmt Sci.*, 1955, 1, 233-250.

529. Gurnee, H. A comparison of collective and individual judgments of facts. *J. exp. Psychol.*, 1937a, 21, 106-112.

530. Gurnee, H. Maze learning in the collective situation. *J. Psychol.*, 1937b, 3, 437-443.

531. Gurvitch, G. Microsociology and sociometry. *Sociometry*, 1949, 12, 1-31. *P.A.*, 26:4720.

532. Guthe, C. E. (Chm.), Manual for the study of food habits: report of the Committee on Food Habits. *Bull. nat. Res. Council*, 1945, No. 111. *P.A.*, 19:3326.

533. Gyr, J. Analysis of committee member behavior in four cultures. *Hum. Relat.*, 1951, 4, 193-202. *P.A.*, 26:1419.

534. Hagman, Elizabeth P. The companionships of preschool children. *Univer. Iowa Stud. Child Welf.*, 1933, 7, No. 4 (New ser. No. 255).

535. Haigh, G. V., & Schmidt, W. The learning of subject matter in teacher-centered and group-centered classes. *J. educ. Psychol.*, 1956, 47, 295-301.

536. Haiman, F. S. *Group leadership and democratic action*. Boston: Houghton Mifflin, 1951. *P.A.*, 27:1043.

537. Haire, M. Industrial social psychology. In G. Lindzey (Ed.), *Handbook of social psychology*. Reading, Mass.: Addison-Wesley, 1954. Pp. 1104-1123.

538. Hall, R. L. Social influence on the aircraft commander's role. *Amer. sociol. Rev.*, 1955, 20, 292-299. *P.A.*, 30:8498.

539. Hall, R. L. Group performance under feedback that confounds responses of group members. *Sociometry*, 1957, *20*, 297-305.

540. Halpern, H. M. Empathy, similarity, and self-satisfaction. *J. consult. Psychol.*, 1955, *19*, 449-452.

541. Halpin, A. W. The leadership behavior and combat performance of airplane commanders. *J. abnorm. soc. Psychol.*, 1954, *49*, 19-22. *P.A.*, 28:8211.

542. Halpin, A. W. The leader behavior and leadership ideology of educational administrators and aircraft commanders. *Harv. educ. Rev.*, 1955a, *25*, 18-22. *P.A.*, 30:2646.

543. Halpin, A. W. The leadership ideology of aircraft commanders. *J. appl. Psychol.*, 1955b, *39*, 82-84. *P.A.*, 30:1740.

544. Hamblin, R. L. Group integration during a crisis. *Hum. Relat.*, 1958a, *11*, 67-76.

545. Hamblin, R. L. Leadership and crisis. *Sociometry*, 1958b, *21*, 322-335. (See No. 249, 1960.)

546. Hanfmann, Eugenia P. Social structure of a group of kindergarten children. *Amer. J. Orthopsychiat.*, 1935, *5*, 407-410.

547. Harary, F., & Ross, I. C. The number of complete cycles in a communication network. *J. soc. Psychol.*, 1954, *40*, 329-332. *P.A.*, 29:7209.

548. Harary, F., & Ross, I. C. A procedure for clique detection using the group matrix. *Sociometry*, 1957, *20*, 205-215.

549. Hardee, Melvene D., & Bernauer, Margaret. A method of evaluating group discussion. *Occupations*, 1948, *27*, 90-94. *P.A.*, 23:4245.

550. Hardy, K. R. Determinants of conformity and attitude change. *J. abnorm. soc. Psychol.*, 1957, *54*, 289-294.

551. Hardy, M. C. Social recognition at the elementary school age. *J. soc. Psychol.*, 1937, *8*, 365-384. *P.A.*, 12:575.

552. Hare, A. P. A study of interaction and consensus in different sized groups. *Amer. sociol. Rev.*, 1952, *17*, 261-267. (See No. 249, 1953.) Also in B. N. Phillips, R. L. Duke, & M. V. DeVault (Eds.), *Psychology at work in the elementary classroom*. New York: Harper, 1960. Pp. 48-60. *P.A.*, 27:4153.

553. Hare, A. P. Small group discussions with participatory and supervisory leadership. *J. abnorm. soc. Psychol.*, 1953, *48*, 273-275. (See No. 559.) Also in B. N. Phillips, R. L. Duke, & M. V. DeVault (Eds.), *Psychology at work in the elementary classroom*. New York: Harper, 1960. Pp. 25-30. *P.A.*, 28:2410.

554. Hare, A. P. Situational differences in leader behavior. *J. abnorm. soc. Psychol.*, 1957, *55*, 132-135.

555. Hare, A. P. Areas for research in small groups. *Sociol. soc. Res.*, 1958, *42*, 430-435.

556. Hare, A. P. Interview responses: personality or conformity? *Publ. Opin. Quart.*, 1960a, 24, 679-685.

557. Hare, A. P. The dimensions of social interaction. *Behav. Sci.*, 1960b, 5, 211-215.

558. Hare, A. P. Computer simulation of interaction in small groups. *Behavioral Science*, 1961, 6, 261-265.

559. Hare, A. P., Borgatta, E. F., & Bales, R. F. (Eds.), *Small groups: studies in social interaction.* New York: Knopf, 1955.

560. Hare, A. P., & Davie, J. S. The group interview: its use in a study of undergraduate culture. *Sociol. soc. Res.*, 1954, 39, 81-87. *P.A.*, 29:6198.

561. Hare, A. P., & Hare, Rachel T. Family friendship within the community. *Sociometry*, 1948, 11, 329-334.

562. Hare, A. P., & Hare, Rachel T. The draw-a-group test. *J. genet. Psychol.*, 1956, 89, 51-59.

563. Hare, A. P., Waxler, Nancy, Saslow, G., & Matarazzo, J. D. Interaction process in a standardized initial psychiatric interview. *J. consult. Psychol.*, 1960, 24, 193.

564. Harnack, R. V. Problems in measuring discussion process. *J. Communication*, 1953, 3, 13-16. *P.A.*, 28:7341.

565. Harnack, R. V. An experimental study of the effects of training in the recognition and formulation of goals upon intra-group cooperation. *Speech Monogr.*, 1955, 22, 31-38. *P.A.*, 30:781.

566. Harris, E. F., & Fleishman, E. A. Human relations training and the stability of leadership patterns. *J. appl. Psychol.*, 1955, 39, 20-25. *P.A.*, 30:1741.

567. Harrocks, J. E., & Buker, Mae E. A study of the friendship fluctuations of pre-adolescents. *J. genet. Psychol.*, 1951, 78, 131-144.

568. Harrocks, J. E., & Thompson, G. G. A study of the friendship fluctuations of rural boys and girls. *J. genet. Psychol.*, 1946, 69, 189-198.

569. Hartley, Ruth E., Frank, L. K., & Goldenson, R. M. *Understanding children's play.* New York: Columbia Univer. Press, 1952. *P.A.*, 27:269.

570. Harvey, O. J. An experimental approach to the study of status reactions in informal groups. *Amer. sociol. Rev.*, 1953, 18, 357-367. *P.A.*, 28:4136; *S.A.*, 83.

571. Harvey, O. J. An experimental investigation of negative and positive relations between small groups through judgmental indices. *Sociometry*, 1956, 19, 201-209. *P.A.*, 32:1451.

572. Harvey, O. J., Kelley, H. H., & Shapiro, M. M. Reactions to unfavorable evaluations of the self made by other persons. *J. Pers.*, 1957, 25, 393-411.

573. Harvey, O. J., & Rutherford, Jeanne. Gradual and absolute approaches to attitude change. *Sociometry*, 1958, *21*, 61-68.

574. Hastorf, A. H., Bender, I. E., & Weintraub, D. J. The influence of response patterns on the "refined empathy score." *J. abnorm. soc. Psychol.*, 1955, *51*, 341-343. *P.A.*, 30:4349.

575. Hays, D. G., & Bush, R. R. A study of group action. *Amer. sociol. Rev.*, 1954, *19*, 693-701. *P.A.*, 30:2647.

576. Haythorn, W. The influence of individual members on the characteristics of small groups. *J. abnorm. soc. Psychol.*, 1953, *48*, 276-284. (See No. 559.) *P.A.*, 28:2412.

577. Haythorn, W., Couch, A. [S.], Haefner, D., Langham, P., & Carter, L. F. The behavior of authoritarian and equalitarian personalities in groups. *Hum. Relat.*, 1956a, *9*, 57-74. *P.A.*, 31:5887; *S.A.*, 3661.

578. Haythorn, W., Couch, A. [S.], Haefner, D., Langham, P., & Carter, L. F. The effects of varying combinations of authoritarian and equalitarian leaders and followers. *J. abnorm. soc. Psychol.*, 1956b *53*, 210-219. (See No. 826, pp. 511-522.) *P.A.*, 32:2752.

579. Hearn, G. Leadership and the spatial factor in small groups. *J. abnorm. soc. Psychol.*, 1957, *54*, 269-272.

580. Heber, R. F., & Heber, Mary E. The effect of group failure and success on social status. *J. educ. Psychol.*, 1957, *48*, 129-134.

581. Heinicke, C., & Bales, R. F. Developmental trends in the structure of small groups. *Sociometry*, 1953, *16*, 7-38. *P.A.*, 28:692.

582. Heise, G. A., & Miller, G. A. Problem solving by small groups using various communication nets. *J. abnorm. soc. Psychol.*, 1951, *46*, 327-336. (See No. 559.) *P.A.*, 26:2148.

583. Helson, H., Blake, R. R., Mouton, Jane S., & Olmstead, J. A. Attitudes as adjustments to stimulus, background, and residual factors. *J. abnorm. soc. Psychol.*, 1956, *52*, 314-322. *P.A.*, 31:4475.

584. Hemphill, J. K. Situational factors in leadership. *Ohio State Univer., Educ. Res. Monogr.*, 1949, No. 32. *P.A.*, 24:5770.

585. Hemphill, J. K. Relations between the size of the group and the behavior of "superior" leaders. *J. soc. Psychol.*, 1950, *32*, 11-22. *P.A.*, 25:3759.

586. Hemphill, J. K. Group dimensions: A manual for their measurement. *Ohio State Univer. Bur. Bus. Res. Monogr.*, 1956, No. 87. *P.A.*, 31:7657.

587. Hemphill, J. K., Pepinsky, Pauline N., Shevitz, R. N., Jaynes, W. E., & Christner, Charlotte, A. The relation between possession of task-relevant information and attempts to lead. *Psychol. Monogr.*, 1956, *70* (7), No. 414. *P.A.*, 31:4467.

588. Hemphill, J. K., & Westie, C. M. The measurement of group dimensions. *J. Psychol.*, 1950, *29*, 325-342. *P.A.*, 24:5789.

589. Henry, J. Family structure and the transmission of neurotic behavior. *Amer. J. Orthopsychiat.*, 1951, *21*, 800-818. *P.A.*, 26:5681.

590. Henry, W. E., & Guetzkow, H. Group projection sketches for the study of small groups. *J. soc. Psychol.*, 1951, *33*, 77-102. *P.A.*, 26:917.

591. Herbert, Eleonore, L., & Trist, E. L. The institution of an absent leader by a students' discussion group. *Hum. Relat.*, 1953, *6*, 215-248. *P.A.*, 28:2415; *S.A.*, 84.

592. Herbst, P. G. The measurement of family relationships. *Hum. Relat.*, 1952, *5*, 3-35. *P.A.*, 27:371.

593. Herbst, P. G. Analysis and measurement of a situation: the child in the family. *Hum. Relat.*, 1953, *6*, 113-140. *P.A.*, 28:2462.

594. Heyns, R. W. Social psychology and group processes. *Annu. Rev. Psychol.*, 1958, *9*, 419-452. *P.A.*, 32:4035.

595. Heyns, R. W., & Lippitt, R. Systematic observational techniques. In G. Lindzey (Ed.), *Handbook of social psychology*. Reading, Mass.: Addison-Wesley, 1954. Pp. 370-404. *P.A.*, 29:3847.

596. Heyns, R. W., & Zander, A. Observation of group behavior. In L. Festinger & D. Katz (Eds.), *Research methods in the behavioral sciences*. New York: Dryden, 1953. Pp. 381-418. *P.A.*, 30:3542.

597. Hilgard, E. R., Sait, E. M., & Margaret, G. Ann. Level of aspiration as affected by relative standing in an experimental social group. *J. exp. Psychol.*, 1940, *27*, 411-421. *P.A.*, 15:143.

598. Hill, R. Review of current research on marriage and the family. *Amer. sociol. Rev.*, 1951, *16*, 694-701. *P.A.*, 27:3491.

599. Hirota, Kimiyoshi. Shudan no kadai kaietsu to communication. (Group problem solving and communication.) *Jap. J. Psychol.*, 1953, *24*, 105-113. *P.A.*, 29:674.

600. Hites, R. W., & Campbell, D. T. A test of the ability of fraternity leaders to estimate group opinion. *J. soc. Psychol.*, 1950, *32*, 95-100. *P.A.*, 25:3971.

601. Hochbaum, G. M. The relation between group members' self-confidence and their reactions to group pressures to uniformity. *Amer. sociol. Rev.*, 1954, *19*, 678-687. *P.A.*, 30:2649.

602. Hoffman, L. R. Similarity of personality: a basis for interpersonal attraction? *Sociometry*, 1958, *21*, 300-308.

603. Hoffman, M. L. Conformity as a defense mechanism and a form of resistance to genuine group influence. *J. Pers.*, 1957, *25*, 412-424.

604. Hoffman, P. J., Festinger, L., & Lawrence, D. Tendencies toward group comparability in competitive bargaining. *Hum. Relat.*, 1954, *7*, 141-159. *P.A.*, 29:2311.

605. Hollander, E. P. Authoritarianism and leadership choice in a military setting. *J. abnorm. soc. Psychol.*, 1954, *49*, 365-370.

606. Hollander, E. P. The friendship factor in peer nominations. *Personn. Psychol.*, 1956, 9, 435-447. P.A., 32:2780.

607. Hollander, E. P. The reliability of peer nominations under various conditions of administration. *J. appl. Psychol.*, 1957, 41, 85-90.

608. Hollander, E. P. Conformity, status, and idiosyncrasy credit. *Psychol. Rev.*, 1958, 65, 117-127.

609. Hollander, E. P., & Webb, W. B. Leadership, followership, and friendship: an analysis of peer nominations. *J. abnorm. soc. Psychol.*, 1955, 50, 163-167. (See No. 826, pp. 489-496.) *P.A.*, 30:782; S.A., 1977.

610. Hollingshead, A. B. *Elmtown's youth.* New York: Wiley, 1949. P.A., 23:4697.

611. Homans, G. C. The Western Electric researches. In *Fatigue of workers: its relation to industrial production.* New York: Reinhold, 1941. See No. 1214; No. 826, pp. 583-595.)

612. Homans, G. C. The Western Electric researches. In S. D. Hoslett (Ed.), *Human factors in management.* Parkville, Mo.: Park Coll. Press, 1946. Pp. 152-185.

613. Homans, G. C. A conceptual scheme for the study of social organization. *Amer. sociol. Rev.*, 1947, 12, 13-26. P.A., 21:2719.

614. Homans, G. C. *The human group.* New York: Harcourt, Brace, 1950. P.A., 25:3002.

615. Homans, G. C. Status among clerical workers. *Hum. Organization*, 1953, 12 (1), 5-10. P.A., 29:6371.

616. Homans, G. C. The cash posters: a study of a group of working girls. *Amer. sociol. Rev.*, 1954, 19, 724-733. P.A., 30:3526.

617. Homans, G. C. Social behavior as exchange. *Amer. J. Sociol.*, 1958, 63, 597-606.

618. Horney, Karen. *Our inner conflicts.* New York: Norton, 1945. P.A., 20:442.

619. Horowitz, M. W., Lyons, J., & Perlmutter, H. V. Induction of forces in discussion groups. *Hum. Relat.*, 1951, 4, 57-76. P.A., 25:8004.

620. Horowitz, M. W., & Perlmutter, H. V. The concept of the social group. *J. soc. Psychol.*, 1953, 37, 69-95. P.A., 28:694.

621. Horowitz, M. W., & Perlmutter, H. V. The discussion group and democratic behavior. *J. soc. Psychol.*, 1955, 41, 231-246. P.A., 30:5852; S.A., 3667.

622. Horsfall, A. B., & Arensberg, C. M. Teamwork and productivity in a shoe factory. *Hum. Organization*, 1949, 8 (1), 13-25. P.A., 23:6500.

623. Horwitz, M. The conceptual status of group dynamics. *Rev. educ. Res.*, 1953, 23, 309-328. P.A., 28:7345.

624. Horwitz, M. The recall of interrupted group tasks: an experimental study of individual motivation in relation to group goals. *Hum. Relat.*, 1954, 7, 3-38. (See No. 249.) S.A., 486.

625. Horwitz, M., & Cartwright, D. A projective method for the diagnosis of group properties. *Hum. Relat.*, 1953, 6, 397-410. *P.A.*, 28:5860.

626. Horwitz, M., Exline, R. V., & Lee, F. J. *Motivational effects of alterative decision-making processes in groups*. Urbana, Ill.: Bureau of Educ. Res., Univer. of Ill., 1953.

627. Horwitz, M., & Lee, F. G. Effects of decision making by group members on recall of finished and unfinished tasks. *J. abnorm. soc. Psychol.*, 1954, 49, 201-210. *P.A.*, 29:676.

628. Hovland, C. I., Janis, I. L., & Kelley, H. H. *Communication and persuasion: psychological studies of opinion change.* New Haven: Yale Univer. Press, 1953. *P.A.*, 28:5952.

629. Hubbard, Ruth M. A method of studying spontaneous group formation. In Dorothy S. Thomas (Ed.), *Some new techniques for studying social behavior.* New York: Teach. Coll., Columbia Univer., 1929. Pp. 76-85.

630. Hughes, E. C. The knitting of racial groups in industry. *Amer. sociol. Rev.*, 1946, 11, 512-519.

631. Hunt, J. McV., & Solomon, R. L. The stability and some correlates of group-status in a summer camp group of young boys. *Amer. J. Psychol.*, 1942, 55, 33-45. *P.A.*, 16:1997.

632. Hurlock, Elizabeth B. The use of group rivalry as an incentive. *J. abnorm. soc. Psychol.*, 1927, 22, 278-290.

633. Hurwitz, J. I., Zander, A., & Hymovitch, B. Some effects of power on the relations among group members. In D. Cartwright & A. Zander (Eds.), *Group dynamics: research and theory.* Evanston, Ill.: Row, Peterson, 1953. Pp. 483-492.

634. Husband, R. W. Cooperative *versus* solitary problem solution. *J. soc. Psychol.*, 1940, 11, 405-409. *P.A.*, 14:4936.

635. Israel, J. *Self-evaluation and rejection in groups.* Stockholm: Almqvist & Wiksell, 1956. *P.A.*, 31:5891.

636. Jackson, D. N., & Messick, S. J. A note on "Ethnocentrism" and acquiescent response sets. *J. abnorm. soc. Psychol.*, 1957, 54, 132-135.

637. Jackson, D. N., Messick, S. J., & Solley, C. M. How "rigid" is the "authoritarian"? *J. abnorm. soc. Psychol.*, 1957, 54, 137-140.

638. Jackson, J. M. The effect of changing the leadership of small work groups. *Hum. Relat.*, 1953, 6, 25-44. *P.A.*, 28:2419.

639. Jackson, J. M. A space for conceptualizing person-group relationships. *Hum. Relat.*, 1959a, 12, 3-15.

640. Jackson, J. M. Reference group processes in a formal organization. *Sociometry*, 1959b, 22, 307-327. (See No. 249, 1960, pp. 120-140.)

641. Jackson, J. M., & Saltzstein, H. D. The effect of person-group relationships on conformity processes. *J. abnorm. soc. Psychol.*, 1958, 57, 17-24.

642. Jackson, W. M. Interaction in a college fraternity. *Appl. Anthrop.*, 1944, *3* (3), 16-21. *P.A.*, 19:2671.

643. Jacobs, J. H. The application of sociometry to industry. *Sociometry*, 1945, *8*, 181-198. *P.A.*, 20:287.

644. Jacobson, E., Charters, W. W., Jr., & Lieberman, S. The use of the role concept in the study of complex organizations. *J. soc. Issues*, 1951, *7* (3), 18-27.

645. Jahoda, Marie, Deutsch, M., & Cook, S. W. (Eds.) *Research methods in social relations.* New York: Dryden, 1951. *P.A.*, 27:2637.

646. James, B. J. Methodological problems in the application of sociometry under "uncontrolled" conditions. *Sociometry*, 1955, *18*, 111-121. *P.A.*, 30:4398.

647. James, J. Some elements in a theory of small groups. *Res. Stud., State Coll., Wash.*, 1950, *18*, 144-152.

648. James, J. A preliminary study of the size determinant in small group interaction. *Amer. sociol. Rev.*, 1951a, *16*, 474-477. *P.A.*, 27:1045.

649. James, J. Clique organization in a small industrial plant. *Res. Stud., State Coll., Wash.*, 1951b, *19*, 125-130.

650. James, J. The distribution of free-forming small group size. *Amer. sociol. Rev.*, 1953, *18*, 569-570.

651. James, J. Verbal behavior in problem-solving small groups without formally designated leaders. *Res. Stud., State Coll., Wash.*, 1956, *24*, 125-133. *S.A.*, 2925.

652. Janis, I. L., & King, B. T. The influence of role playing on opinion change. *J. abnorm. soc. Psychol.*, 1954, *49*, 211-218. (See No. 826, pp. 472-482.) *P.A.*, 29:677.

653. Jansen, L. T. Measuring family solidarity. *Amer. sociol. Rev.*, 1952, *17*, 727-733. *P.A.*, 28:808.

654. Jaques, E. Interpretive group discussion as a method of facilitating social change. *Hum. Relat.*, 1948, *1*, 533-549. *P.A.*, 23:2207.

655. Jenkins, D. H. Feedback and group self-evaluation. *J. soc. Issues*, 1948, *4* (2), 50-60. *P.A.*, 23:686.

656. Jenkins, D. H., & Lippitt, R. *Interpersonal perceptions of teachers, students, and parents.* Washington, D. C.: Nat. Educ. Ass., 1951. *P.A.*, 26:4175.

657. Jenness, A. Social influences in the change of opinion. *J. abnorm. soc. Psychol.*, 1932a, *27*, 29-34.

658. Jenness, A. The role of discussion in changing opinion regarding a matter of fact. *J. abnorm. soc. Psychol.*, 1932b, *27*, 279-296.

659. Jennings, Helen H. Structure of leadership—development and sphere of influence. *Sociometry*, 1937, *1*, 99-143.

660. Jennings, Helen H. Individual differences in the social atom. *Sociometry*, 1941, *4*, 269-277. (See No. 559.) *P.A.*, 16:1080.

661. Jennings, Helen H. Experimental evidence on the social atom at two time points. *Sociometry*, 1942, *5*, 135-145. *P.A.*, 16:4460.

662. Jennings, Helen H. A sociometric study of emotional and social expansiveness. In R. G. Barker, J. S. Kounin, & H. F. Wright (Eds.), *Child behavior and development.* New York: McGraw-Hill, 1943. Pp. 527-543. *P.A.,* 17:2520.

663. Jennings, Helen H. Leadership and sociometric choice. *Sociometry,* 1947a, *10,* 32-49. *P.A.,* 22:254.

664. Jennings, Helen H. Sociometric differentiation of the psychegroup and the sociogroup. *Sociometry,* 1947b, *10,* 71-79. *P.A.,* 22:255.

665. Jennings, Helen H. *Sociometry in group relations: a work guide for teachers.* Washington, D. C.: Amer. Council Educ., 1948.

666. Jennings, Helen H. *Leadership and isolation* (2nd ed.) New York: Longmans, Green, 1950a. (See No. 66; No. 249, 1953; No. 826, pp. 483-489.) *P.A.,* 24:5772.

667. Jennings, Helen H. Sociometric grouping in relation to child development. In Caroline Tryon (Ed.), *Fostering mental health in our schools.* Wash., D. C.: Ass. Supervis. and Curric. Develpm., Nat. Educ. Ass., 1950b.

668. Jennings, Helen H. Sociometric structure in personality and group formation. In M. Sherif & M. O. Wilson (Eds.), *Group relations at the crossroads.* New York: Harper, 1953. Pp. 332-365. *P.A.,* 28:7347.

669. Jensen, E. M., Reese, E. P., & Reese, T. W. The subitizing and counting of visually presented fields of dots. *J. Psychol.,* 1950, *30,* 363-392. *P.A.,* 25:2830.

670. Jersild, A. T., & Fite, Mary D. The influence of nursery school experience on children's social adjustments. *Child Develpm. Monogr.,* 1939, No. 25. *P.A.,* 13:3892.

671. Joel, W., & Shapiro, D. A genotypical approach to the analysis of personal interaction. *J. Psychol.,* 1949, *28,* 9-17. *P.A.,* 24:657.

672. Johannot, H. *L'individu et le groupe; les relations entre humans, le role des leaders, le travail en equipe.* Neuchatel: Delachaux et Niestle, 1953.

673. Johnson, D. M. *The psychology of thought and judgment.* New York: Harper, 1955. *P.A.,* 29:6894.

674. Jones, E. E., & de Charms, R. Changes in social perception as a function of the personal relevance of behavior. *Sociometry,* 1957, *20,* 75-85. (See No. 826, pp. 102-109.) *P.A.,* 32:352.

675. Jones, E. E., Wells, H. H., & Torrey, R. Some effects of feedback from the experimenter on conformity behavior. *J. abnorm. soc. Psychol.,* 1958, *57,* 207-213.

676. Jones, F. D., & Peters, H. N. An experimental evaluation of group psychotherapy. *J. abnorm. soc. Psychol.,* 1952, *47,* 345-353. *P.A.,* 27:2785.

677. Jones, J. A. An index of consensus on rankings in small groups. *Amer. sociol. Rev.,* 1959, *24,* 533-537.

678. Kagan, J., & Mussen, P. H. Dependency themes on the TAT and group conformity. *J. consult. Psychol.*, 1956, *20*, 29-32. P.A., 31:3042.

679. Kahn, R. L., & Katz, D. Leadership practices in relation to productivity and morale. In D. Cartwright & A. Zander (Eds.), *Group dynamics: research and theory.* Evanston, Ill.: Row, Peterson, 1953. Pp. 612-628.

680. Kaiser, R. L., & Blake, R. R. Aspiration and performance in a simulated group atmosphere. *J. soc. Psychol.*, 1955, *42*, 193-202. P.A., 31:759.

681. Kalis, Betty, L., & Bennett, Lillian F. The assessment of communication: the relation of clinical improvement to measured changes in communicative behavior. *J. consult. Psychol.*, 1957, *21*, 10-14.

682. Kaplan, A., Skogstad, A. L., & Girshick, M. A. The prediction of social and technological events. *Publ. Opin. Quart.*, 1950, *14*, 93-110. P.A., 26:5477.

683. Karson, S., & Pool, K. B. Second-order factors in personality measurement. *J. consult. Psychol.*, 1958, *22*, 299-303.

684. Kasl, S. V., and Mahl, G. F. A simple device for obtaining certain verbal activity measures during interviews. *J. abnorm. soc. Psychol.*, 1956, *53*, 388-390.

685. Kassebaum, G. G., Couch, A. S., & Slater, P. E. The factorial dimensions of the MMPI. *J. consult. Psychol.*, 1959, *23*, 226-236.

686. Katz, D. Social psychology and group processes. *Annu. Rev. Psychol.*, 1951, *2*, 137-172. P.A., 25:3760.

687. Katz, E., Blau, P. M., Brown, M. L., & Strodtbeck, F. L. Leadership stability and social change: an experiment with small groups. *Sociometry*, 1957, *20*, 36-50. P.A., 32:376.

688. Katz, I., Goldston, Judith, & Benjamin, L. Behavior and productivity in bi-racial work groups. *Hum. Relat.*, 1958, *11*, 123-141.

689. Katz, L., & Powell, J. H. A proposed index of the conformity of one sociometric measurement to another. *Psychometrika*, 1953, *18*, 249-256. P.A., 28:4174.

690. Katz, L., & Powell, J. H. Measurement of the tendency toward reciprocation of choice. *Sociometry*, 1955, *18*, 659-665.

691. Kaufman, E. L., Lord, M. W., Reese, T. W., & Volkmann, J. The discrimination of visual number. *Amer. J. Psychol.*, 1949, *62*, 498-525. P.A., 24:3658.

692. Keedy, T. C., Jr. Factors in the cohesiveness of small groups. *Sociol. soc. Res.*, 1956, *40*, 329-332. P.A., 31:5893; S.A., 4296.

693. Keet, C. D. Two verbal techniques in a miniature counseling situation. *Psychol. Monogr.*, 1948, *62*, No. 294. P.A., 24:3225.

694. Keller, J. B. Comment on "Channels of communications in small groups." *Amer. sociol. Rev.*, 1951, *16*, 842-843. (See No. 61.)

695. Kelley, H. H. The warm-cold variable in first impressions of persons. *J. Pers.*, 1950, *18*, 431-439. P.A., 25:4486.

696. Kelley, H. H. Communication in experimentally created hierarchies. *Hum. Relat.*, 1951, *4*, 39-56. (See No. 249.) *P.A.*, 25:8302.

697. Kelley, H. H. Salience of membership and resistance to change of group-anchored attitudes. *Hum. Relat.*, 1955, *8*, 275-290. *P.A.*, 30:5858; *S.A.*, 3141.

698. Kelley, H. H., & Lamb, T. W. Certainty of judgment and resistance to social influence. *J. abnorm. soc. Psychol.*, 1957, *55*, 137-139.

699. Kelley, H. H., & Shapiro, M. M. An experiment on conformity to group norms where conformity is detrimental to group achievement. *Amer. sociol. Rev.*, 1954, *19*, 667-678.

700. Kelley, H. H., & Thibaut, J. W. Experimental studies of group problem solving and process. In G. Lindzey, *Handbook of social psychology*. Reading, Mass.: Addison-Wesley, 1954. Pp. 735-785. *P.A.*, 29:3804.

701. Kelley, H. H., & Volkhart, E. H. The resistance to change of group-anchored attitudes. *Amer. sociol. Rev.*, 1952, *17*, 453-465. *P.A.*, 27:6475.

702. Kelley, H. H., & Woodruff, Christine L. Members' reactions to apparent group approval of a counternorm communication. *J. abnorm. soc. Psychol.*, 1956, *52*, 67-74. *S.A.*, 4396.

703. Kelly, G. A. *The psychology of personal constructs*. New York: Norton, 1955. *P.A.*, 30:4524.

704. Kelly, R. W., & Ware, H. F. An experiment in group dynamics. *Advanc. Mgmt*, 1947, *12*, 116-119. *P.A.*, 22:2356.

705. Kelman, H. C. Effects of success and failure on "suggestibility" in the autokinetic situation. *J. abnorm. soc. Psychol.*, 1950, *45*, 267-285. *P.A.*, 24:5702.

706. Kelman, H. C., & Parloff, M. B. Interrelations among three criteria of improvement in group therapy: comfort, effectiveness, and self-awareness. *J. abnorm. soc. Psychol.*, 1957, *54*, 281-288.

707. Kenkel, W. F. Influence differentiation in family decision making. *Sociol. soc. Res.*, 1957, *42*, 18-25.

708. Kephart, W. M. A quantitative analysis of intragroup relationships. *Amer. J. Sociol.*, 1950, *60*, 544-549. *P.A.*, 25:288.

709. Kerlinger, F. N. On authoritarianism and acquiescence: an added note to Bass and Messick and Jackson. *J. abnorm. soc. Psychol.*, 1958, *56*, 141-142.

710. Kidd, J. S. Social influence phenomena in a task-oriented group situation. *J. abnorm. soc. Psychol.*, 1958, *56*, 13-17.

711. Kidd, J. S., & Campbell, D. T. Conformity to groups as a function of group success. *J. abnorm. soc. Psychol.*, 1955, *51*, 390-303. *P.A.*, 31:2703; *S.A.*, 3442.

712. Killian, L. M. The significance of multiple-group membership in disaster. *Amer. J. Sociol.*, 1952, *57*, 309-314. (See No. 249, 1953; No. 826, pp. 459-464.) *P.A.*, 26:5526.

713. Kinney, Elva E. A study of peer group social acceptability at the fifth grade level in a public school. *J. educ. Res.*, 1953, *47*, 57-64. P.A., 28:4884.

714. Kipnis, D. The effects of leadership style and leadership power upon the inducement of an attitude change. *J. abnorm. soc. Psychol.*, 1958, *57*, 173-180.

715. Kipnis, Dorothy M. Interaction between members of bomber crews as a determinant of sociometric choice. *Hum. Relat.*, 1957, *10*, 263-270.

716. Kirkpatrick, C., & Hobart, C. Disagreement, disagreement estimate, and non-empathetic imputations for intimacy groups varying from favorite date to married. *Amer. sociol. Rev.*, 1954, *19*, 10-19. P.A., 29:3915.

717. Kirscht, J. P., Lodahl, T. M., & Haire, M. Some factors in the selection of leaders by members of small groups. *J. abnorm. soc. Psychol.*, 1959, *58*, 406-408. (See No. 249, 1960, pp. 521-526.)

718. Klein, A., & Keill, N. The experiencing of group psychotherapy. *Sociatry*, 1953, *5*, 205-221. P.A., 28:4440.

719. Klein, Josephine. *The study of groups.* London: Routledge & Keegan Paul, 1956.

720. Klubeck, S., & Bass, B. M. Differential effects of training on persons of different leadership status. *Hum. Relat.*, 1954, *7*, 59-72. S.A., 487.

721. Klugman, S. F. Cooperative versus individual efficiency in problem-solving. *J. educ. Psychol.*, 1944, *35*, 91-100. P.A., 18:2859.

722. Klugman, S. F. Group judgments for familiar and unfamiliar materials. *J. gen. Psychol.*, 1945, *32*, 103-110. P.A., 19:1649.

723. Kogan, N., & Tagiuri, R. Interpersonal preference and cognitive organization. *J. abnorm. soc. Psychol.*, 1958a, *56*, 113-116.

724. Kogan, N., & Tagiuri, R. On visibility of choice and awareness of being chosen. *Psychol. Rep.*, 1958b, *4*, 83-86.

725. Kotkov, B. A bibliography for the student of group therapy. *J. clin. Psychol.*, 1950, *6*, 77-91. P.A., 25:377.

726. Kozman, Hilda C. *Group process in physical education.* New York: Harper, 1951.

727. Krebs, A. M. Two determinants of conformity: age of independence training and *n* achievement. *J. abnorm. soc. Psychol.*, 1958, *56*, 130-131.

728. Krech, D., & Crutchfield, R. S. *Theory and problems of social psychology.* New York: McGraw-Hill, 1948. P.A., 23:1723.

729. Kuusela, Ruth. Systematic observation methods in the study of small groups. *Acta Psychol.*, 1956, *12*, 25-46. P.A., 31:2745.

730. La Forge, R., Leary, T. F., Naboisek, H., Coffey, H. S., & Freedman, M. B. The interpersonal dimensions of personality: II. An

objective study of repression. *J. Pers.*, 1954, *23*, 131-153. *P.A.*, 29:5313.

731. LaForge, R,. & Suczek, R. F. The interpersonal dimension of personality: III. An interpersonal check list. *J. Pers.*, 1955, *24*, 94-112. *P.A.*, 30:5990.

732. Laird, D. A. Changes in motor control and individual variations under the influence of "razzing." *J. exp. Psychol.*, 1923, *6*, 236-246.

733. Laird, D. A., & Laird, Eleanor C. *The new psychology of leadership.* New York: McGraw-Hill, 1956.

734. Landis, M. H., & Burtt, H. E. A study of conversations. *J. comp. Psychol.*, 1924, *4*, 81-89.

735. Landsberger, H. A. Interaction process analysis of professional behavior: a study of labor mediators in twelve labor-management disputes. *Amer. sociol. Rev.*, 1955a, *20*, 566-575. *P.A.*, 31:1864.

736. Landsberger, H. A. Interaction process analysis of the mediation of labor-management disputes. *J. abnorm. soc. Psychol.*, 1955b, *51*, 552-558. *P.A.*, 31:3918.

737. Lanzetta, J. T. Group behavior under stress. *Hum. Relat.*, 1955, *8*, 29-52. *P.A.*, 30:783; *S.A.*, 1765.

738. Lanzetta, J. T. Haefner, D., Langham, P., & Axelrod, H. Some effects of situational threat on group behavior. *J. abnorm. soc. Psychol.*, 1954, *49*, 445-453. *P.A.*, 29:3813.

739. Lanzetta, J. T., & Roby, T. B. Effects of work-group structure and certain task variables on group performance. *J. abnorm. soc. Psychol.*, 1956a, *53*, 307-314. *P.A.*, 32:4038.

740. Lanzetta, J. T., & Roby, T. B. Group performance as a function of work-distribution patterns and task load. *Sociometry*, 1956b, *19*, 95-104. *P.A.*, 31:5895; *S.A.*, 4295.

741. Lanzetta, J. T., & Roby, T. B. Group learning and communication as a function of task and structure "demands." *J. abnorm. soc. Psychol.*, 1957, *55*, 121-131.

742. Lanzetta, J. T., Wendt, G. R., Langham, P., & Haefner, D. The effects of an "anxiety-reducing" medication on group behavior under threat. *J. abnorm. soc. Psychol.*, 1956, *52*, 103-108. *P.A.*, 31:2706.

743. Lasker, B. *Democracy through discussion.* New York: Wilson, 1949.

744. Lasswell, H. D. Person, personality, group, culture. *Psychiatry*, 1939, *2*, 533-561. *P.A.*, 14:2514.

745. Lawlor, Monica. An investigation concerned with changes of preference which are observed after group discussion. *J. soc. Psychol.*, 1955, *42*, 323-332. *P.A.*, 31:763.

746. Lawrence, Lois C., & Smith, Patricia C. Group decision and employee participation. *J. appl. Psychol.*, 1955, *39*, 334-337. *P.A.*, 30:7847.

747. Lawson, E. D., & Stagner, R. Group pressure, attitude change, and autonomic involvement. *J. soc. Psychol.*, 1957, *45*, 299-312.

748. Leary, T. The theory and measurement methodology of interpersonal communication. *Psychiatry*, 1955, *18*, 147-161. *P.A.*, 30:2694.

749. Leary, T. *Interpersonal diagnosis of personality.* New York: Ronald Press, 1957. *P.A.*, 31:2556.

750. Leary, T., & Coffey, H. S. Interpersonal diagnosis: some problems of methodology and validation. *J. abnorm. soc. Psychol.*, 1955, *50*, 110-124. *P.A.*, 29:7241.

751. Leavitt, H. J. Some effects of certain communication patterns on group performance. *J. abnorm. soc. Psychol.*, 1951, *46*, 38-50.(See No. 1214, pp. 108-125; No. 826, pp. 546-563.) *P.A.*, 25:7439.

752. Leavitt, H. J., Hax, H., & Roche, J. H. "Authoritarianism" and agreement with things authoritative. *J. Psychol.*, 1955, *40*, 215-221.

753. Leavitt, H. J., & Mueller, R. A. H. Some effects of feedback on communication. *Hum. Relat.*, 1951, *4*, 401-410. (See No. 559.) *P.A.*, 26:5551.

754. Leeman, C. P. Patterns of sociometric choice in small groups: a mathematical model and related experimentation. *Sociometry*, 1952, *15*, 220-243. *P.A.*, 27:7137.

755. Lemann, T. B., & Solomon, R. L. Group characteristics as revealed in sociometric patterns and personality ratings. *Sociometry*, 1952, *15*, 7-90. *P.A.*, 27:7138.

756. Lennard, H., & Bernstein, A. (with Helen C. Hendin & E. B. Palmore). *The anatomy of psychotherapy: systems of communication and expectation.* New York: Columbia Univer. Press, 1960.

757. Lennard, H., Jarvik, M. E., & Abramson, H. A. Lysergic acid diethylamide (LSD-25): XII. A preliminary statement of its effects upon interpersonal communication. *J. Psychol.*, 1956, *41*, 185-198.

758. Leuba, C. J. A preliminary experiment to quantify an incentive and its effects. *J. abnorm. soc. Psychol.*, 1930, *25*, 275-288.

759. Leuba, C. J. An experimental study of rivalry in young children. *J. comp. Psychol.*, 1933, *16*, 367-378.

760. Levi, M., & Higgins, A. C. A comparison of two methods of conducting critiques. *USAF Pers. Train. Res. Cent. Res. Bull.*, 1954, No. AFPTRC-TR-54-108.

761. Levi, M., Torrance, E. P., & Pletts, G. O. Sociometric studies of combat air crews in survival training. *Sociometry*, 1954, *17*, 304-328. *P.A.*, 30:5895; *S.A.*, 1496.

762. Levine, J., & Butler, J. Lecture vs. group decision in changing behavior. *J. appl. Psychol.*, 1952, *36*, 29-33. (See No. 249, 1953.) *P.A.*, 26:6908.

763. Levine, J., Laffal, J., Berkowitz, M., Lindemann, J., & Drevdahl, J. Conforming behavior of psychiatric and medical patients. *J. abnorm. soc. Psychol.*, 1954, *49*, 251-255. *P.A.*, 29:1305.

764. Levinson, D. J. Role, personality, and social structure in the organizational setting. *J. abnorm. soc. Psychol.*, 1959, 58, 170-180.

765. Lewin, K. Forces behind food habits and methods of change. *Bull. Nat. Res. Council*, 1943, 108, 35-65. (See No. 249, 1953.)

766. Lewin, K. Constructs in psychology and psychological ecology. *Univer. of Iowa Stud. in Child Welf.*, 1944, 20, No. 409, 1-49. *P.A.*, 19:3432.

767. Lewin, K. Frontiers in group dynamics: concept, method and reality in social science: social equilibria and social change. *Hum. Relat.*, 1947a, 1, 5-41. (See No. 559.) *P.A.*, 22:256.

768. Lewin, K. Frontiers in group dynamics: II. Channels of group life; social planning and action research. *Hum. Relat.*, 1947b, 1, 143-153. *P.A.*, 22:2610.

769. Lewin, K. Group decision and social change. In T. M. Newcomb & E. L. Hartley (Eds.), *Readings in social psychology.* New York: Holt, 1947c. Pp. 330-344. (See No. 1214; No. 826, pp. 197-211.)

770. Lewin, K. *Resolving social conflicts: selected papers on group dynamics.* New York: Harper, 1948. *P.A.*, 22:4891.

771. Lewin, K., *Field theory in social science.* New York: Harper, 1951. *P.A.*, 25:6769.

772. Lewin, K., & Lippitt, R. An experimental approach to the study of autocracy and democracy: a preliminary note. *Sociometry*, 1938, 1, 292-300. (See No. 559.)

773. Lewin, K., Lippitt, R., & White, R. K. Patterns of aggressive behavior in experimentally created "social climates." *J. soc. Psychol.*, 1939, 10, 271-299. (See No. 495.)

774. Lewis, Helen B. An experimental study of the role of the ego in work: I. The role of the ego in cooperative work. *J. exp. Psychol.*, 1944, 34, 113-126. *P.A.*, 18:2739.

775. Lewis, Helen B., & Franklin, M. An experimental study of the role of the ego in work: II. The significance of task orientation in work. *J. exp. Psychol.*, 1944, 34, 195-215. *P.A.*, 18:3083.

776. Libo, L. M. *Measuring group cohesiveness.* Ann Arbor: Univer. of Michigan, Res. Center for Group Dynamics, Inst. Soc. Res., 1953. *P.A.*, 28: 8654.

777. Lichtenberg, P. Emotional maturity as manifested in ideational interaction. *J. abnorm. soc. Psychol.*, 1955, 51, 298-301. *P.A.*, 30:4353.

778. Lichtenberg, P. Time perspective and the initiation of cooperation. *J. soc. Psychol.*, 1956, 43, 247-260.

779. Lichtenberg, P. Reactions to success and failure during individual and cooperative effort. *J. soc. Psychol.*, 1957, 46, 31-34.

780. Lifton, R. J. "Thought reform" of Western civilians in Chinese communist prisons. *Psychiatry*, 1956, 19, 173-195.

781. Lindeman, E. C. *Social discovery.* New York: Republic, 1924.

782. Lindgren, H. C., & Robinson, Jacqueline. An evaluation of Dymond's

test of insight and empathy. *J. consult. Psychol.*, 1953, *17*, 172-176.
P.A., 28:2650.

783. Lindzey, G. (Ed.) *Handbook of social psychology.* Reading, Mass.:
Addison-Wesley, 1954. P.A., 29:3817.

784. Lindzey, G., & Borgatta, E. F. Sociometric measurement. In G. Lindzey
(Ed.), *Handbook of social psychology.* Reading, Mass.: Addison-
Wesley, 1954. Pp. 405-448. P.A., 29:3850.

785. Lindzey, G., & Riecken, H. W. Inducing frustration in adult subjects.
J. consult. Psychol., 1951, *15*, 18-23. P.A., 26:6388.

786. Lindzey, G., & Urdan, J. A. Personality and social choice. *Sociometry,*
1954, *17*, 47-63. P.A., 29:731.

787. Linton, Harriet B. Autokinetic judgment as a measure of influence.
J. abnorm. soc. Psychol., 1954, *49*, 464-466. P.A., 29:3571.

788. Lippitt, R. Field theory and experiment in social psychology: autocratic and democratic group atmospheres. *Amer. J. Sociol.*, 1939,
45, 26-49.

789. Lippitt, R. An experimental study of the effect of democratic and
authoritarian group atmospheres. *Univer. of Iowa Stud. in Child
Welf.*, 1940, *16*, 43-195. (See No. 66.) P.A., 14:3655.

790. Lippitt, R. A. program of experimentation on group functioning and
group productivity. In W. Dennis, R. Lippitt, et al., *Current
trends in social psychology.* Pittsburgh: Univer. of Pittsburgh
Press, 1948. Pp. 14-49. P.A., 23:5432.

791. Lippitt, R. *Training in community relations: a research exploration
toward new group skills.* New York: Harper, 1949. P.A.,
24:551.

792. Lippitt, R., Polansky, N., & Rosen, S. The dynamics of power: a field
study of social influence in groups of children. *Hum. Relat.*,
1952, *5*, 37-64. (See No. 249, No. 826, pp. 251-264.) P.A.,
27:278.

793. Lippitt, R., Watson, Jeanne, & Westley, B. *The dynamics of planned
change: a comparative study of principles and techniques.* New
York: Harcourt, Brace, 1958.

794. Lippitt, R., & White, R. K. An experimental study of leadership and
group life. In G. E. Swanson, T. M. Newcomb, & E. L. Hartley
(Eds.), *Readings in social psychology.* (Rev. Ed.) New York:
Holt, 1952. Pp. 340-355. (See No. 826, pp. 496-511.)

795. Lippitt, R., & Zander, A. Observation and interview methods for the
leadership training study. New York: Boy Scouts of America,
1943. (Mimeo.)

796. Lippitt, Rosemary. Popularity among preschool children. *Child
Develpm.*, 1941, *12*, 305-332. P.A., 16:1746.

797. Lipsitt, L. P., & Vallance, T. R. The expression of teleonomic trends
in private and in group-related problem situations. *J. Pers.*, 1955,
23, 381-390. P.A., 30:2661.

798. Loomis, C. P. Informal groupings in a Spanish-American village. *Sociometry*, 1941, *4*, 36-51, *P.A.*, 15:3515.

799. Loomis, C. P., & Beegle, J. A. A topological analysis of social systems. *Sociometry*, 1948, *11*, 147-191. *P.A.*, 24:569.

800. Loomis, C. P., & Pepinsky, H. B. Sociometry, 1937-1947; theory and methods. *Sociometry*, 1948, *11*, 262-283. *P.A.*, 24:570.

801. Lorge, I., Fox, D., Davitz, J., & Brenner, M. A survey of studies contrasting the quality of group performance and individual performance, 1920-1957. *Psychol. Bull.*, 1958, *55*, 337-372.

802. Lorge, I., Tuckman, J., Aikman, L., Spiegel, J., & Moss, Gilda. Solutions by teams and by individuals to a field problem at different levels of reality. *J. educ. Psychol.*, 1955a, *46*, 17-24. *P.A.*, 29:8413.

803. Lorge, I., Tuckman, J., Aikman, L., Spiegel, J., & Moss, Gilda. Problem-solving by teams and by individuals in a field setting. *J. educ. Psychol.*, 1955b, *55*, 160-166. *P.A.*, 30:588.

804. Lorge, I., Tuckman, J., Aikman, L. Spiegel, J., & Moss, Gilda. The adequacy of written reports in problem solving by teams and by individuals. *J. soc. Psychol.*, 1956, *43*, 65-74. *P.A.*, 31:2512.

805. Lorr, M., & Jenkins, R. L. Three factors in parent behavior. *J. consult. Psychol.*, 1953, *17*, 306-308. *P.A.*, 28:4087.

806. Luce, R. D., & Perry, A. D. A method of matrix analysis of group structure. *Psychometrika*, 1949, *14*, 95-116. *P.A.*, 24:889.

807. Luchins, A. S. Social influences on perception of complex drawings. *J. soc. Psychol.*, 1945, *21*, 257-273. *P.A.*, 19:2294.

808. Luchins, A. S. Group structures in group psychotherapy. *J. clin. Psychol.*, 1947, *3*, 269-273. *P.A.*, 22:318.

809. Luchins, A. S. A variational approach to social influences on perception. *J. soc. Psychol.*, 1955, *42*, 113-119. *P.A.*, 30:6694.

810. Luchins, A. S., & Luchins, Edith H. On conformity with true and false communications. *J. soc. Psychol.*, 1955a, *42*, 283-303. *P.A.*, 31:974.

811. Luchins, A. S., & Luchins, Edith H. Previous experience with ambiguous and non-ambiguous perceptual stimuli under various social influences. *J. soc. Psychol.*, 1955b, *42*, 249-270. *P.A.*, 31:975.

812. Luchins, A. S., & Luchins, Edith H. Discovering the source of contradictory communications. *J. soc. Psychol.*, 1956, *44*, 49-63.

813. Lundberg, G. A. Some problems of group classification and measurement. *Amer. sociol. Rev.*, 1940, *5*, 351-360.

814. Lundberg, G. A., Hertzler, Virginia B., & Dickson, Lenore. Attraction patterns in a university. *Sociometry*, 1949, *12*, 158-169.

815. Lundberg, G. A., & Steele, Mary. Social attraction patterns in a village. *Sociometry*, 1938, *1*, 375-419.

816. Lundy, R. M. Assimilative projection and accuracy of prediction in interpersonal relations. *J. abnorm. soc. Psychol.*, 1956a, *52*, 33-38. *P.A.*, 31:2560.

817. Lundy, R. M. Self-perceptions and descriptions of opposite sex socio-
     metric choices. *Sociometry*, 1956b, *19*, 272-277. P.A., 32:1367.
818. Lundy, R. M. Self-perceptions regarding masculinity-femininity and
     descriptions of same and opposite sex sociometric choices. *So-
     ciometry*, 1958, *21*, 238-246.
819. Lundy, R. M., Katkovsky, W., Cromwell, R. L., & Shoemaker, D. J.
     Self-acceptability and descriptions of sociometric choices. *J. ab-
     norm. soc. Psychol.*, 1955, *51*, 260-262. P.A., 30:4356.
820. Maas, H. S. Personal and group factors in leaders' social perception.
     J. abnorm. soc. Psychol., 1950, *45*, 54-63. P.A., 24:4547.
821. Maas, H. S. Evaluating the individual member in the group. In Na-
     tional Conference of Social Work, *Group work and community
     organization, 1953-1954.* New York: Columbia Univer. Press,
     1954a. Pp. 36-44. P.A., 29:5464.
822. Maas, H. S. The role of members in clubs of lower-class and middle-
     class adolescents. *Child Develpm.*, 1954b, *25*, 241-251. P.A.,
     29-7013.
823. Maas, H. S., Varon, Edith, & Rosenthal, D. A technique for studying
     the social behavior of schizophrenics. *J. abnorm. soc. Psychol.*,
     1951, *46*, 119-123. P.A., 25:7583.
824. McBurney, J. H., & Hance, K. G. *The principles and methods of dis-
     cussion.* New York: Harper, 1939. P.A., 14:1996.
825. McCandless, B. R. Changing relationships between dominance and
     social acceptability during group democratization. *Amer. J. Ortho-
     psychiat.*, 1942, *12*, 529-535, P.A., 16:4821.
826. Maccoby, Eleanor E., Newcomb, T. M., & Hartley, E. L. (Eds.)
     Readings in social psychology. (3rd ed.) New York: Holt, 1958.
827. McCurdy, H. G., & Eber, H. W. Democratic *versus* authoritarian:
     a further investigation of group problem-solving. *J. Pers.*, 1953,
     22, 258-269. P.A., 28:5820.
828. McCurdy, H. G., & Lambert, W. E. The efficiency of small human
     groups in the solution of problems requiring genuine co-operation.
     J. Pers., 1952, *20*, 478-494. P.A., 27:3430.
829. McGinnies, E. A method for matching anonymous questionnaire
     data with group discussion material. *J. abnorm. soc. Psychol.*,
     1956, *52*, 139-140.
830. McGrath, J. E. A framework for integration of small groups research
     studies. Arlington, Va.: Psychol. Res. Ass., 1957.
831. McKeachie, W. J. Individual conformity to attitudes of classroom
     groups. *J. abnorm. soc. Psychol.*, 1954a, *49*, 282-289. P.A., 29:688.
832. McKeachie, W. J. Student centered *versus* instructor centered
     instruction. *J. educ. Psychol.*, 1954b, *45*, 143-150. P.A., 29:2974.
833. McKeachie, W. J. Students, groups, and teaching methods. *Amer.
     Psychologist*, 1958, *13*, 580-584.

834. McKenna, S. S. J., Sr., Helen V., Hofstaetter, P. R., & O'Connor, J. P. The concepts of the ideal self and of the friend. *J. Pers.*, 1956, *24*, 262-271. *P.A.*, 31:620.

835. McMillan, J. J., & Silverberg, J. Sociometric choice patterns in hospital ward groups with varying degrees of interpersonal disturbances. *J. abnorm. soc. Psychol.*, 1955, *50*, 168-172. *P.A.*, 30:788.

836. Macy, J., Jr., Christie, L. S., & Luce, R. D. Coding noise in a task-oriented group. *J. abnorm. soc. Psychol.*, 1953, *48*, 401-409. *P.A.*, 28:2544.

837. Mahl, G. F. Disturbances and silences in the patient's speech in psychotherapy. *J. abnorm. soc. Psychol.*, 1956, *53*, 1-15.

838. Maier, N. R. F. *Psychology in industry.* Boston: Houghton Mifflin, 1946. *P.A.*, 20:3287.

839. Maier, N. R. F. The quality of group decisions as influenced by the discussion leader. *Hum. Relat.*, 1950, *3*, 155-174. *P.A.*, 25:2364.

840. Maier, N. R. F. An experimental test of the effect of training on discussion leadership. *Hum. Relat.*, 1953, *6*, 161-173. *P.A.*, 28:2426.

841. Maier, N. R. F., & Maier, R. A. An experimental test of the effects of "developmental" vs. "free" discussions on the quality of group decisions. *J. appl. Psychol.*, 1957, *41*, 320-323.

842. Maier, N. R. F., & Solem, A. R. The contribution of a discussion leader to the quality of group thinking: the effective use of minority opinions. *Hum. Relat.*, 1952, *5*, 277-288. (See No. 249, 1953.) *P.A.*, 27:3432.

843. Maisonneuve, J. A contribution to the sociometry of mutual choices. *Sociometry*, 1954, *17*, 33-46. *P.A.*, 29:732.

844. Maisonneuve, J., Palmade, G., & Fourment, Claude. Selective choices and propinquity. *Sociometry*, 1952, *15*, 135-140. *P.A.*, 27:7390.

845. Maller, J. B. Cooperation and competition: an experimental study in motivation. *Teach. Coll., Columbia Univer., Contrib. Educ.*, 1929, No. 384.

846. Maloney, R. M. Group learning through group discussion: a group discussion implementation analysis. *J. soc. Psychol.*, 1956, *43*, 3-9.

847. Mandelbaum, D. G. *Soldier groups and negro soldiers.* Berkeley: Univer. of Calif. Press, 1952, *P.A.*, 27:2647.

848. Manis, M. Social interaction and the self concept. *J. abnorm. soc. Psychol.*, 1955, *51*, 362-370. *P.A.*, 31:2708.

849. Mann, J. H. The influence of racial group composition on sociometric choices and perceptions. *J. soc. Psychol.*, 1958, *48*, 137-146.

850. Mann, J. H., & Mann, Carola H. The importance of group task in producing group-member personality and behavior changes. *Hum. Relat.*, 1959, *12*, 75-80.

851. Mann, R. D. A review of the relationships between personality and

performance in small groups. *Psychol. Bull.*, 1959, *56*, 241-270.

852. March, J. G. Husband-wife interaction over political issues. *Public Opin. Quart.*, 1953, *17*, 461-470.

853. March, J. G. Influence measurement in experimental and semi-experimental groups. *Sociometry*, 1956, *19*, 260-271.

854. Margolin, J. B. The use of an interaction matrix to validate patterns of group behavior. *Hum. Relat.*, 1952, *5*, 407-416. *P.A.*, 27:6880.

855. Marquart, Dorothy I. Group problem solving. *J. soc. Psychol.*, 1955, *41*, 103-113. *P.A.*, 30:589.

856. Marquis, D. G., Guetzkow, H., & Heyns, R. W. A social psychological study of the decision-making conference. In H. Guetzkow (Ed.), *Groups, leadership, and men: research in human relations.* Pittsburgh: Carnegie Press, 1951, Pp. 55-67. *P.A.*, 26:814.

857. Marriott, R. Size of working group and output. *Occup. Psychol., Lond.*, 1949, *23*, 47-57. *P.A.*, 23:3956.

858. Marston, W. M. Studies in testimony. *J. crim. Law Criminol.*, 1924, *15*, 5-31.

859. Martin, W. E., Darley, J. G., & Gross, N. Studies of group behavior: II. Methodological problems in the study of interrelationships of group members. *Educ. psychol. Measmt*, 1952, *12*, 533-553. *P.A.*, 27:6486.

860. Martin, W. E., Gross, N., & Darley, J. G. Studies of group behavior: leaders, followers, and isolates in small organized groups. *J. abnorm. soc. Psychol.*, 1952, *47*, 838-842. *P.A.*, 27:5065; *S.A.*, 127.

861. Masling, J., Greer, F. L., & Gilmore, R. Status, authoritarianism, and sociometric choice. *J. soc. Psychol.*, 1955, *41*, 297-310. *P.A.*, 30:5914.

862. Mason, D. J. Judgments of leadership based upon physiognomic cues. *J. abnorm. soc. Psychol.*, 1957, *54*, 273-274.

863. Matarazzo, J. D., Saslow, G., & Guze, S. B. Stability of interaction patterns during interviews: a replication. *J. consult. Psychol.*, 1956, *20*, 267-274.

864. Matarazzo, J. D., Saslow, G., & Hare, A. P. Factor analysis of interview interaction behavior. *J. consult. Psychol.*, 1958, *22*, 419-429.

865. Matarazzo, J. D., Saslow, G., & Matarazzo, Ruth G. The interaction chronograph as an instrument for objective measurement of interaction patterns during interviews. *J. Psychol.*, 1956, *41*, 347-367.

866. Matarazzo, J. D., Saslow, G., Matarazzo, Ruth G., & Phillips, Jeanne S. Stability and modifiability of personality patterns during a standardized interview. In P. A. Hoch & J. Zubin (Eds.), *Psychopathology of communication.* New York: Grune & Stratton, 1957.

867. Matarazzo, Ruth G., Matarazzo, J. D., Saslow, G., & Phillips, Jeanne S. Psychological test and organismic correlates of interview interaction patterns. *J. abnorm. soc. Psychol.*, 1958, *56*, 329-338.

868. Matthews, J., & Bendig, A. W. The index of agreement: a possible criterion for measuring the outcome of group discussion. *Speech Monogr.*, 1955, *22*, 39-42. P.A., 30:791.

869. Mausner, B. Studies in social interaction: III. Effect of variation in one partner's prestige on the interaction of observer pairs. *J. appl. Psychol.*, 1953, *37*, 391-393.

870. Mausner, B. The effect of one partner's success in a relevant task on the interaction of observer pairs. *J. abnorm. soc. Psychol.*, 1954a, *49*, 557-560. P.A., 29:5466.

871. Mausner, B. The effect of prior reinforcement on the interaction of observer pairs. *J. abnorm. soc. Psychol.*, 1954b, *49*, 65-68.

872. Mausner, B. Studies in social interaction: I. A conceptual scheme. *J. soc. Psychol.*, 1955, *41*, 259-270. P.A., 30:5861.

873. Mausner, B., & Bloch, Barbara L. A study of the additivity of variables affecting social interaction. *J. abnorm. soc. Psychol.*, 1957, *54*, 250-256.

874. May, M. A., & Doob, L. W. Competition and cooperation. *Soc. Sci. Res. Council Bull.*, 1937, No. 25.

875. Mayer, A. Ueber Einzel- und Gesamtleistung des Schulkindes. (On the school child's work alone and in the group.) *Arch. f. d. ges. Psychol.*, Band I, 1903, 276-416.

876. . Mayo, E. *The human problems of an industrial civilization.* New York: Macmillan, 1933.

877. Mayo, E., & Lombard, G. F. F. *Team work and labor turnover in the aircraft industry of Southern California.* Boston: Grad. Sch. of Bus. Admin., Harvard Univer., 1944. P.A., 19:2036.

878. Mead, G. H. *Mind, self, and society from the standpoint of a social behaviorist.* Chicago: Univer. of Chicago Press, 1950.

879. Medalia, N. Z. Authoritarianism, leader acceptance, and group cohesion. *J. abnorm. soc. Psychol.*, 1955, *51*, 207-213. P.A., 30:4359.

880. Medley, D. M., & Mitzel, H. E. A technique for measuring classroom behavior. *J. educ. Psychol.*, 1958, *49*, 86-92.

881. Mellinger, G. D. Interpersonal trust as a factor in communication. *J. abnorm. soc. Psychol.*, 1956, *52*, 304-309. P.A., 31:5178.

882. Mengert, Ida G. A preliminary study of the reactions of two-year-old children to each other when paired in a semi-controlled situation. *J. genet. Psychol.*, 1931, *39*, 393-398. P.A., 6:463.

883. Merei, F. Group leadership and institutionalization. *Hum. Relat.*, 1949, *2*, 23-39. (See No. 1214, pp. 318-328; No. 826, pp. 522-532.) P.A., 23:3684.

884. Merrill, Barbara. A measurement of mother-child interaction. *J. abnorm. soc. Psychol.*, 1946, *41*, 37-49. *P.A.*, 20:2006.

885. Merton, R. K. The social psychology of housing. In W. Dennis, R. Lippitt, et al., *Current trends in social psychology.* Pittsburgh: Univer. of Pittsburgh Press, 1948. Pp. 163-217. *P.A.*, 23:5482.

886. Messick, S. & Jackson, D. N. Authoritarianism or acquiescence in Bass's data. *J. abnorm. soc. Psychol.*, 1957, *54*, 424-426.

887. Meumann, E. Haus- und schularbeit, experimente an kindern der volkschule. (Home and school work.) *Die Deutsche Schule,* VIII Jahrgang, 1904, 278-303, 337-359, 416-431.

888. Meyer, W. J., & Thompson, G. G. Sex differences in the distribution of teacher approval and disapproval among sixth-grade children. *J. educ. Psychol.*, 1956, *47*, 385-396.

889. Meyers, C. E. The effect of conflicting authority on the child. *Univer. of Iowa Stud. in Child Welf.*, 1944, *20*, 31-98. *P.A.*, 19:3531.

890. Miller, D. C. An experiment in the measurement of social interaction in group discussion. *Amer. sociol. Rev.*, 1939, *4*, 341-351. *P.A.*, 14:455.

891. Miller, J. G. (Ed.) *Experiments in social process.* New York: McGraw-Hill, 1950. *P.A.*, 25:1699.

892. Miller, J. G. Toward a general theory for the behavioral sciences. *Amer. Psychologist,* 1955, *10*, 513-531. *P.A.*, 30:3687.

893. Miller, K. M., & Biggs, J. B. Attitude change through undirected group discussion. *J. educ. Psychol.*, 1958, *49*, 224-228.

894. Mills, T. M. Power relations in three-person groups. *Amer. sociol. Rev.*, 1953, *18*, 351-357. (See No. 249.) *P.A.*, 28:4145; *S.A.*, 89.

895. Mills, T. M. The coalition pattern in three-person groups. *Amer. sociol. Rev.*, 1954, *19*, 657-667. *P.A.*, 30:2668.

896. Mills, T. M. Development process in three-person groups. *Hum. Relat.*, 1956, *9*, 343-354. *P.A.*, 32:2764; *S.A.*, 5022.

897. Mills, T. M., et al. Group structure and the newcomer: an experimental study of group expansion. *Univer. Oslo Inst. Sociol., Stud. in Soc.*, No. 1, 1957. *S.A.*, 4685.

898. Mills, T. M., Lichter, Hope, & Kassebaum, G. G. Frankness and consensus, Cambridge, Mass.: Lab. of Soc. Rel., Harvard Univer., 1957. (Mimeo.)

899. Mintz, A. Non-adaptive group behavior. *J. abnorm. soc. Psychol.*, 1951, *46*, 150-159. (See No. 1214, pp. 190-198; No. 826, pp. 575-582.) *P.A.*, 25:8008.

900. Mitchell, J. V., Jr. The factor analysis of a "Guess-Who" questionnaire designed to identify significant behavior patterns in children. *J. Pers.*, 1956, *24*, 376-386. *P.A.*, 31:1059.

901. Mitnick, L. I., & McGinnies, E. Influencing ethnocentrism in small discussion groups through a film communication. *J. abnorm. soc. Psychol.*, 1958, *56*, 82-90.

902. Miyamoto, S. F., & Dornbush, S. M. A test of interactionist hypotheses of self-conception. *Amer. J. Sociol.*, 1956, *61*, 399-403. *P.A.*, 31:2562; *S.A.*, 3430.

903. Moede, W. Der wetteifer, seine struktur und sein ausmass. *Z. pad. Psychol.*, 1914, *15*, 353-368, 369-393.

904. Moede, W. *Experimentelle massenpsychologie.* (Experimental group psychology.) Leipzig: Hirzel, 1920.

905. Moede, W. Die richtlinien der leitungspsychologie. *Industr. Psychotechn.*, 1927, *4*, 193-209. *P.A.*, 1:431.

906. Moeller, G., & Applezweig, M. H. A motivational factor in conformity. *J. abnorm. soc. Psychol.*, 1957, *55*, 114-120.

907. Moldawsky, S. An empirical validation of a rigidity scale against a criterion of rigidity in an interpersonal situation. *Sociometry*, 1951, *14*, 153-174. *P.A.*, 27:4111.

908. Moore, H. T. The comparative influence of majority and expert opinion. *Amer. J. Psychol.*, 1921, *32*, 16-20.

909. Moore, H. T. Further data concerning sex differences. *J. abnorm. soc. Psychol.*, 1922, *17*, 210-214.

910. Moore, O. K., & Anderson, Scarvia B. Search behavior in individual and group problem solving. *Amer. sociol. Rev.*, 1954, *19*, 702-714. *P.A.*, 30:2436.

911. Moreno, Florence B. Sociometric status of children in a nursery school group. *Sociometry*, 1942, *5*, 395-411. *P.A.*, 17:1760.

912. Moreno, J. L. Foundations of sociometry, an introduction. *Sociometry*, 1941, *4*, 15-35. *P.A.*, 15:3521.

913. Moreno, J. L. Sociometry and the cultural order. *Sociometry*, 1943, *6*, 299-344. *P.A.*, 18:2186.

914. Moreno, J. L. (Ed.) *Group psychotherapy.* Beacon, N. Y.: Beacon House, 1945. *P.A.*, 20:1927.

915. Moreno, J. L. Contributions of sociometry to research methodology in sociology. *Amer. sociol. Rev.*, 1947a, *12*, 287-292. (See No. 559.) *P.A.*, 22:268.

916. Moreno, J. L. *The theatre of spontaneity.* Beacon, N. Y.: Beacon House, 1947b. *P.A.*, 23:186.

917. Moreno, J. L. *Sociometry, experimental method and the science of society.* Beacon, N. Y.: Beacon House, 1951. *P.A.*, 25:8009.

918. Moreno, J. L. *Who shall survive?* (Rev. ed.) Beacon, N. Y.: Beacon House, 1953. *P.A.*, 28:4178.

919. Moreno, J. L. Old and new trends in sociometry: turning points in small group research. *Sociometry*, 1954, *17*, 179-193. *P.A.*, 29:3851.

920. Moreno, J. L., & Jennings, Helen H. Statistics of social configurations. *Sociometry*, 1938, *1*, 342-374.

921. Moreno, J. L., & Jennings, Helen H. Sociometric methods of grouping and regrouping: with reference to authoritative and democratic

methods of grouping. *Sociometry*, 1944, *7*, 397-414. *P.A.*, 19:1748.

922. Moreno, J. L., Jennings, Helen H., & Sargent, J Time as a qualitative index to interpersonal relations. *Sociometry*, 1940, *3*, 62-80. *P.A.*, 14:3663.

923. Motz, Annabelle B. The role conception inventory: a tool for research in social psychology. *Amer. sociol. Rev.*, 1952, *17*, 465-471. *P.A.*, 27:6489.

924. Mouton, Jane S., Blake, R. R., & Fruchter, B. The reliability of sociometric measures. *Sociometry*, 1955a, *18*, 7-48. *P.A.*, 30:5884.

925. Mouton, Jane S., Blake, R. R., & Fruchter, B. The validity of socio-metric responses. *Sociometry*, 1955b, *18*, 181-206. *S.A.*, 3142.

926. Mouton, Jane S., Blake, R. R., & Olmstead, J. A. The relationship between frequency of yielding and the disclosure of personal identity. *J. Pers.*, 1956, *24*, 339-347. *P.A.*, 31:771.

927. Mukerji, N. P. An investigation of ability in work in groups and in isolation. *Brit. J. Psychol.*, 1940, *30*, 352-356. *P.A.*, 14:3781.

928. Mulder, M. Group-structure and group-performance. *Acta Psychol.*, 1959, *16*, 356-402.

929. Munsterberg, H. *Grundzuge der psychotechnik.* (Fundamentals of psychotechnics.) Leipzig: Barth, 1914.

930. Murphy, G., Murphy, Lois B., & Newcomb, T. M. *Experimental social psychology.* New York: Harper, 1937.

931. Murphy, Lois B. *Social behavior and child personality: an exploratory study of some roots of sympathy.* New York: Columbia Univer., 1937.

932. Murphy, Lois B., & Murphy, G. The influence of social situations upon the behavior of children. In C. Murchison (Ed.), *A handbook of social psychology.* Worcester, Mass.: Clark Univer. Press, 1935. Pp. 1034-1096.

933. Murstein, B. I. Some comments on the measurement of projection and empathy. *J. consult. Psychol.*, 1957, *21*, 81-82.

934. Mussen, P. H., & Kagan, J. Group conformity and perceptions of parents. *Child Developm.*, 1958, *29*, 57-60.

935. Nash, D. J., & Wolfe, A. W. The stranger in laboratory culture. *Amer. sociol. Rev.*, 1957, *22*, 400-405. *S.A.*, 4677.

936. Nehnevajsa, J. Chance expectancy and intergroup choice. *Sociometry*, 1955a, *18*, 153-163. *P.A.*, 30:4400.

937. Nehnevajsa, J. Probability in sociometric analysis. *Sociometry*, 1955b, *18*, 678-688.

938. Nehnevajsa, J. Soziometrische analyse von gruppen. (The sociometric analysis of groups. *Köl. Z. Soziol.*, 1955c, *7*, 119-140. *S.A.*, 2493.

939. Nehnevajsa, J. Soziometrische analyse von gruppen. (The sociometric analysis of groups.) *Köl. Z. Soziol.*, 1955d, *7*, 280-302. *S.A.*, 2730.

940. Newcomb, T. M. The consistency of certain extrovert-introvert behavior

patterns in 51 problem boys. *Teach. Coll. Contrib. Educ.*, 1929, No. 382.

941. Newcomb, T. M. *Personality and social change.* New York: Dryden, 1943. *P.A.*, 17:3460.

942. Newcomb, T. M. Role behaviors in the study of individual personality and of groups. *J. Pers.*, 1950, *18*, 273-289. *P.A.*, 25:2912.

943. Newcomb, T. M. An approach to the study of communicative acts. *Psychol. Rev.*, 1953a, *60*, 393-404. (See No. 559.) *P.A.*, 28:5963.

944. Newcomb, T. M. Social psychology and group processes. *Annu. Rev. Psychol.*, 1953b, *4*, 183-214. *P.A.*, 27:6478.

945. Newcomb, T. M. The prediction of interpersonal attraction. *Amer. Psychologist*, 1956, *11*, 575-586. *P.A.*, 31:7607.

946. Newcomb, T. M. Varieties of interpersonal attraction. In D. Cartwright & A. Zander (Eds.), *Group dynamics: research and theory.* Evanston, Ill.: Row, Peterson, 1960. Pp. 104-119. Also in J. Peatman & E. Hartley (Eds.), *Festschrift for Gardner Murphy.* New York: Harper, 1960. Pp. 171-182.

947. Newstetter, W. I. An experiment in the defining and measuring of group adjustment. *Amer. sociol. Rev.*, 1937, *2*, 230-236. *P.A.*, 11:4245.

948. Newstetter, W. I., Feldstein, M. J., & Newcomb, T. M. *Group adjustment: a study in experimental sociology.* Cleveland: School of Applied Soc. Sci., Western Reserve Univer., 1938.

949. Norfleet, Bobbie. Interpersonal relations and group productivity. *J. soc. Issues*, 1948, *4* (2), 66-69. *P.A.*, 23:690.

950. Northway, Mary L. *A primer of sociometry.* Toronto, Canada: Univer. of Toronto Press, 1952. *P.A.*, 27:5083.

951. Olmstead, J. A., & Blake, R. R. The use of simulated groups to produce modifications in judgment. *J. Pers.*, 1955, *23*, 335-345. *P.A.*, 30:840.

952. Olmsted, D. W. Inter-group similarities of role correlates. *Sociometry*, 1957, *20*, 8-20.

953. Olmsted, M. S. Orientation and role in the small group. *Amer. sociol. Rev.*, 1954, *19*, 741-751. *S.A.*, 1505.

954. Olmsted, M. S. *The small group.* New York: Random House, 1959.

955. Oppenheim, A. N. Social status and clique formation among grammar school boys. *Brit. J. Sociol.*, 1955, *6*, 228-245.

956. Ort, R. S. A study of role-conflicts as related to happiness in marriage. *J. abnorm. soc. Psychol.*, 1950, *45*, 691-699. *P.A.*, 25:2409.

957. O. S. S. Assessment Staff. *Assessment of men.* New York: Holt, 1948. *P.A.*, 22:3668.

958. Ostlund, L. A. Group integration in a case discussion course. *J. educ. Psychol.*, 1953, *44*, 463-474.

959. Owens, W. A. Item form and "false-positive" responses on a neurotic inventory. *J. clin. Psychol.*, 1947, *3*, 264-269. *P.A.*, 22:306.

960. Park, R. E., & Burgess, E. W. *Introduction to the science of sociology.* (2nd ed.) Chicago: Univer. of Chicago Press, 1924.

961. Parker, S. Leadership patterns in a psychiatric ward. *Hum. Relat.,* 1958, *11,* 287-301.

962. Parsons, T., Bales, R. F., et al. *Family, socialization, and interaction process.* New York: Free Press, 1955.

963. Parten, Mildred B. Social participation among preschool children. *J. abnorm. soc. Psychol.,* 1932, *27,* 243-269.

964. Parten, Mildred B. Leadership among preschool children. *J. abnorm. soc. Psychol.,* 1933a, *27,* 430-440.

965. Parten, Mildred B. Social play among preschool children. *J. abnorm. soc. Psychol.,* 1933b, *28,* 136-147. (See No. 66.)

966. Partridge, E. D. Leadership among adolescent boys. *Teach. Coll., Columbia Univer. Contrib. Educ.,* 1934, No. 608.

967. Pellegrin, R. J. The achievement of high status and leadership in the small group. *Soc. Forces,* 1953, *32,* 10-16. P.A., 28:4147; S.A., 90.

968. Pepinsky, H. B., Siegel, L., & Van Atta, E. L. The criterion in counseling: a group participation scale. *J. abnorm. soc. Psychol.,* 1952, *47,* 415-419. P.A., 27:2791.

969. Pepinsky, Pauline N., Hemphill, J. K., & Shevitz, R. N. Attempts to lead, group productivity, and morale under conditions of acceptance and rejection. *J. abnorm. soc. Psychol.,* 1958, *57,* 47-54.

970. Pepitone, A. Motivational effects in social perception. *Hum. Relat.,* 1950, *3,* 57-76. P.A., 25:2367.

971. Pepitone, A., & Kleiner, R. The effects of threat and frustration on group cohesiveness. *J. abnorm. soc. Psychol.,* 1957, *54,* 192-199.

972. Pepitone, A., & Reichling, G. Group cohesiveness and the expression of hostility. *Hum. Relat.,* 1955, *8,* 327-337. (See No. 249, 1960.) P.A., 30:5868; S.A., 3143.

973. Pepitone, A., & Sherberg, Janet. Intentionality, responsibility, and interpersonal attraction. *J. Pers.,* 1957, *25,* 757-766.

974. Perkins, H. V., Jr. The effects of climate and curriculum on group learning. *J. educ. Res.,* 1950, *44,* 269-286. P.A., 25:7655.

975. Perkins, H. V., Jr. Climate influences group learning. *J. educ. Res.,* 1951, *45,* 115-119. P.A., 26:5076.

976. Perlmutter, H. V. Group memory of meaningful material. *J. Psychol.,* 1953, *35,* 361-370. P.A., 28:511.

977. Perlmutter, H. V. Impressions of influential members of discussion groups. *J. Psychol.,* 1954, *38,* 223-234. P.A., 29:3821.

978. Perlmutter, H. V., & de Montmollin, Germaine. Group learning of nonsense syllables. *J. abnorm. soc. Psychol.,* 1952, *47,* 762-769. (See No. 559.) P.A., 27:4966.

979. Pessin, J. The comparative effects of social and mechanical stimulation on memorizing. *Amer. J. Psychol.,* 1933, *45,* 263-270.

980. Pessin, J., & Husband, R. W. Effects of social stimulation on human maze learning. *J. abnorm. soc. Psychol.*, 1933, *28*, 148-154.

981. Peters, H. N., & Jones, F. D. Evaluation of group psychotherapy by means of performance tests. *J. consul. Psychol.*, 1951, *15*, 363-367. *P.A.*, 26:7149.

982. Peterson, O. F. Leadership and group behavior. *USAF ATC Instructors J.*, 1955, *6*, 48-54. *P.A.*, 30:2670.

983. Philips, E. L., Shenker, Shirley, & Revitz, Paula. The assimilation of the new child into the group. *Psychiatry*, 1951, *14*, 319-325. *P.A.*, 26:2067.

984. Phillips, B. N., & D'Amico, L. A. Effects of cooperation and competition on the cohesiveness of small face-to-face groups. *J. educ. Psychol.*, 1956, *47*, 65-70. *P.A.*, 31:7613.

985. Phillips, Jeanne S., Matarazzo, J. D., Matarazzo, Ruth G., & Saslow, G. Observer reliability of interaction patterns during interviews. *J. consult. Psychol.*, 1957, *21*, 269-275.

986. Philp, Alice J. Strangers and friends as competitors and co-operators. *J. genet. Psychol.*, 1940, *57*, 249-258. *P.A.*, 15:2423.

987. Piaget, J. *The language and thought of the child.* New York: Harcourt, Brace, 1926.

988. Piaget, J. *The moral judgment of the child.* New York: Harcourt, Brace, 1932.

989. Pigors, P. *Leadership or domination.* Boston: Houghton-Mifflin, 1935.

990. Pintner, R., Forlano, G., & Freedman, H. Personality and attitudinal similarity among classroom friends. *J. appl. Psychol.*, 1937, *21*, 48-65.

991. Plak, H. Problems of objective observation. In L. Festinger & D. Katz (Eds.), *Research methods in the behavioral sciences.* New York: Dryden, 1953. Pp. 243-299. *P.A.*, 28:3542.

992. Plank, R. An analysis of a group therapy experiment. *Hum. Organization*, 1951, *10* (3), 5-21, (4), 26-36. *P.A.*, 26:7037.

993. Polansky, N., Lippitt, R., & Redl, F. An investigation of behavioral contagion in groups. *Hum. Relat.*, 1950a, *3*, 319-348. *P.A.*, 25:6121.

994. Polansky, N., Lippitt, R., & Redl, F. The use of near-sociometric data in research on group treatment processes. *Sociometry*, 1950b, *13*, 39-62.

995. Porter, E. H., Jr. The development and evaluation of a measure of counseling interview procedures. *Educ. psychol. Measmt*, 1943, *3*, 105-126, 215-238. *P. A.*, 18:1901, 2599.

996. Potashin, Reva. A sociometric study of children's friendships. *Sociometry*, 1946, *9*, 48-70. *P.A.*, 20:2953.

997. Powell, R. M., et al. An experimental study of role taking, group status, and group formation. *Sociol. soc. Res.*, 1956, *40*, 159-165. *P.A.*, 31:2714; *S.A.*, 3146.

998. Powell, R. M., & LaFave, L. Some determinants of role-taking accuracy. *Sociol. soc. Res.*, 1958, *42*, 319-326.

999. Precker, J. A. Similarity of valuings as a factor in selection of peers and near-authority figures. *J. abnorm. soc. Psychol.*, 1952, *47*, 406-414. *P.A.*, 27:2626.

1000. Precker J. A. The automorphic process in the attribution of values. *J. Pers.*, 1953, *21*, 356-363. *P.A.*, 28:2434.

1001. Preston, M. G. Note on the reliability and the validity of the group judgment. *J. exp. Psychol.*, 1938, *22*, 462-471.

1002. Preston, M. G., & Heintz, R. K. Effects of participatory *versus* supervisory leadership on group judgment. *J. abnorm. soc. Psychol.*, 1949, *44*, 345-355. (See No. 249, 1953.) *P.A.*, 24:1129.

1003. Proctor, C. H., & Loomis, C. P. Analysis of sociometric data. In Marie Jahoda, M. Deutsch, & S. E. Cook (Eds.), *Research methods in social relations: with especial reference to prejudice*. New York: Dryden, 1951, Pp. 561-585.

1004. Puffer, J. A. Boys' gangs. *Pedag. Sem.*, 1905, *12*, 175-212.

1005. Puffer, J. A. *The boy and his gang*. Boston: Houghton Mifflin, 1912.

1006. Queen, S. A. Social interaction in the interview: an experiment. *Soc. Forces*, 1928, *6*, 545-558.

1007. Rabinowitz, W. A note on the social perceptions of authoritarians and non authoritarians. *J. abnorm. soc. Psychol.*, 1956, *53*, 384-386. *P.A.*, 32:4045.

1008. Rabinowitz, W. Anality, aggression, and acquiescence. *J. abnorm. soc. Psychol.*, 1957, *54*, 140-142.

1009. Radke, Marian, J., & Klisurich, P. Experiments in changing food habits. *J. Amer. Dietetics Ass.*, 1947, *23*, 403-409.

1010. Rapaport, A. Mathematical theory of motivation interactions of two individuals. *Bull. Math. Biophys.*, 1947, *9*, 17-28, 41-61. *P.A.*, 22:4353, 4354.

1011. Rapoport, Rhona, & Rosow, I. An approach to family relationships and role performance. *Hum. Relat.*, 1957, *10*, 209-221.

1012. Rasmussen, G. R. An evaluation of a student-centered and instructor-centered method of conducting a graduate course in education. *J. educ. Psychol.*, 1956, *47*, 449-461.

1013. Rasmussen, G., & Zander, A. Group membership and self-evaluation. *Hum. Relat.*, 1954, *7*, 239-251. *S.A.*, 774.

1014. Raven, B. H., & French, J. R. P., Jr. Group support, legitimate power, and social influence. *J. Pers.*, 1958a, *26*, 400-409.

1015. Raven, B. H., & French, J. R. P., Jr. Legitimate power, coercive power, and observability in social influence. *Sociometry*, 1958b, *21*, 83-97.

1016. Raven, B. H., & Rietsema, J. The effects of varied clarity of group goal and group path upon the individual and his relation to his group. *Hum. Relat.*, 1957, *10*, 29-45. (See No. 249, 1960.) *P.A.*, 32:1461.

1017. Ray, W. S. *A laboratory manual for social psychology.* New York: American Book, 1951. *P.A.*, 27:1053.

1018. Ray, W. S. Complex tasks for use in human problem-solving research. *Psychol. Bull.*, 1955, *52*, 134-149. *P.A.*, 30:2437.

1019. Reckless, W. C. Case studies built around observations of individual foster-children in the playroom of a receiving home. *Amer. sociol. Soc. Papers*, 1930, *24*, 170-173. *P.A.*, 4:1663.

1020. Redl, F. Group emotion and leadership. *Psychiatry*, 1942, *5*, 573-596. Also in Dorothea F. Sullivan (Ed.), *Readings in group work.* New York: Association Press, 1952. Pp. 318-356. (See No. 559.) *P.A.*, 17:2085.

1021. Redl, F. Resistance in therapy groups. *Hum. Relat.*, 1948, *1*, 307-313. *P.A.*, 23:1313.

1022. Rice, A. K. The use of unrecognized cultural mechanisms in an expanding machine shop; with a contribution to the theory of leadership. *Hum. Relat.*, 1951, *4*, 143-160. *P.A.*, 26:1744.

1023. Rich, J. M. Measuring supervisory training: the sociometric approach. *Personnel*, 1952, *29*, 78-84. *P.A.*, 27:3066.

1024. Richardson, Helen M. Studies of mental resemblance between husbands and wives and between friends. *Psychol. Bull.*, 1939, *36*, 104-120.

1025. Richardson, Helen M. Community of values as a factor in friendships of college and adult women. *J. soc. Psychol.*, 1940, *11*, 302-312. *P.A.*, 14:5132.

1026. Riddle, Ethel M. Aggressive behavior in a small social group. *Arch. Psychol.*, 1925, *12*, No. 78.

1027. Riecken, H. W. Some problems of consensus development. *Rural Sociol.*, 1952, *17*, 245-252.

1028. Riecken, H. W. The effect of talkativeness on ability to influence group solutions to problems. *Sociometry*, 1958, *21*, 309-321.

1029. Riecken, H. W., & Homans, G. C. Psychological aspects of social structure. In G. Lindzey (Ed.), *Handbook of social psychology.* Reading, Mass.: Addison-Wesley, 1954. Pp. 786-832. *P.A.*, 29:3824.

1030. Riley, Matilda W., & Cohn, R. Control networks in informal groups. *Sociometry*, 1958, *21*, 30-49.

1031. Riley, Matilda W., Cohn, R., Toby, J., & Riley, J. W., Jr., Interpersonal orientations in small groups: a consideration of the questionnaire approach. *Amer. sociol. Rev.*, 1954, *19*, 715-724. S.A., 1609.

1032. Roberts, B. H., & Strodtbeck, F. L. Interaction process differences between groups of paranoid schizophrenic and depressed patients. *Int. J. group Psychother.*, 1953, *3*, 29-41. *P.A.*, 28:4670.

1033. Roberts, J. M. *Three Navaho households: a comparative study in small group culture.* Cambridge, Mass.: Peabody Museum of Amer. Archeol. and Ethnol., 1951, *P.A.*, 27:1101.

1034. Robinson, K. F. An experimental study of the effects of group discussion upon the social attitudes of college students. *Speech Monogr.*, 1941, *8*, 34-57. *P.A.*, 16:1611.

1035. Roby, T. B., & Lanzetta, J. T. Work group structure, communication, and group performance. *Sociometry*, 1956, *19*, 105-113. *P.A.*, 31:5903; *S.A.*, 4297.

1036. Roby, T. B., & Lanzetta, J. T. Considerations in the analysis of group tasks. *Psychol. Bull.*, 1958, *55*, 88-101.

1037. Rock, M. L., & Hay, E. N. Investigation of the use of tests as a predictor of leadership and group effectiveness in a job evaluation situation. *J. soc. Psychol.*, 1953, *38*, 109-119. *P.A.*, 28:5831.

1038. Roethlisberger, F. J., & Dickson, W. J. *Management and the worker.* Cambridge, Mass.: Harvard Univer. Press, 1939. *P.A.*, 14:509.

1039. Roff, M. A factorial study of the Fels parent behavior scales. *Child Develpm.*, 1949, *20*, 29-44.

1040. Roff, M. A study of combat leadership in the air force by means of a rating scale: group differences. *J. Psychol.*, 1950, *30*, 229-239. *P.A.*, 25:1303.

1041. Rogers, C. R. *Counselling and psychotherapy.* Boston: Houghton-Mifflin, 1941. *P.A.*, 17:2749.

1042. Rohrer, J. H., Baron, S. H., Hoffman, E. L., & Swander, D. V. The stability of autokinetic judgments. *J. abnorm. soc. Psychol.*, 1954, *49*, 595-597. *P.A.*, 29:5480.

1043. Rohrer, J. H., & Sherif, M. *Social psychology at the crossroads: the University of Oklahoma lectures in social psychology.* New York: Harper, 1951. *P.A.*, 26:817.

1044. Roseborough, Mary E. Experimental studies of small groups. *Psychol. Bull.*, 1953, *50*, 275-303. *P.A.*, 28:2438.

1045. Rosen, B. C. Conflicting group membership: a study of parent-peer group cross pressures. *Amer. sociol. Rev.*, 1955a, *20*, 155-161. *S.A.*, 1769.

1046. Rosen, B. C. The reference group approach to the parental factor in attitude and behavior formation. *Soc. Forces*, 1955b, *34*, 137-144. *P.A.*, 31:781.

1047. Rosenbaum, M., & Blake, R. R. Volunteering as a function of field structure. *J. abnorm. soc. Psychol.*, 1955, *50*, 193-196. *P.A.*, 30:799; *S.A.*, 1981.

1048. Rosenbaum, M. E. The effects of stimulus and background factors on the volunteering response. *J. abnorm. soc. Psychol.*, 1956, *53*, 118-121. *P.A.*, 32:1463.

1049. Rosenberg, S., Erlick, D. E., & Berkowitz, L. Some effects of varying combinations of group members on group performance measures and leadership behaviors. *J. abnorm. soc. Psychol.*, 1955, *51*, 195-203. *P.A.*, 30:4372; *S.A.*, 2731.

1050. Rosenthal, D., & Cofer, C. N. The effect on group performance of an indifferent and neglectful attitude shown by one group member. *J. exp. Psychol.*, 1948, *38*, 568-577. *P.A.*, 23:1728.

1051. Rosner, S. Consistency in response to group pressures. *J. abnorm. soc. Psychol.*, 1957, *55*, 145-146.

1052. Rosow, I. Issues in the concept of need-complementarity. *Sociometry*, 1957, *20*, 216-233.

1053. Ross, I. C., & Harary, F. On the determination of redundancies in sociometric chains. *Psychometrika*, 1952, *17*, 195-208. *P.A.*, 29:4749.

1054. Rowland, H. Interaction processes in the State Mental Hospital. *Psychiatry*, 1938, *1*, 323-337.

1055. Rowland, H. Friendship patterns in a mental hospital. *Psychiatry*, 1939, *2*, 363-373.

1056. Rubenstein, A. H. Problems in the measurement of interpersonal communication in an ongoing situation. *Sociometry*, 1953, *16*, 78-100. *P.A.*, 28:870.

1057. Ruesch, J., Block, J., & Bennett, Lillian. The assessment of communication: I. A method for the analysis of social interaction. *J. Psychol.*, 1953, *35*, 59-80. *P.A.*, 27:6491.

1058. Ruesch, J., & Prestwood, A. R. Interaction processes and personal codification. *J. Pers.*, 1950, *18*, 391-430. *P.A.*, 25:4631.

1059. Runkel, P. J. Cognitive similarity in facilitating communication. *Sociometry*, 1956, *19*, 178-191.

1060. Sacks, Elinor, L. Intelligence scores as a function of experimentally established social relationships between child and examiner. *J. abnorm. soc. Psychol.*, 1952, *47*, 354-358. *P.A.*, 27:2761.

1061. Sagi, P. C., Olmsted, D. W., & Atelsek, F. Predicting maintenance of membership in small groups. *J. abnorm. soc. Psychol.*, 1955, *51*, 308-311. *P.A.*, 30:4373; *S.A.*, 2732.

1062. Sakoda, J. M. Factor analysis of OSS situational tests. *J. abnorm. soc. Psychol.*, 1952, *47*, 843-852. *P.A.*, 27:5160.

1063. Salusky, A. S. Collective behavior of children at a preschool age. *J. soc. Psychol.*, 1930, *1*, 367-378.

1064. Samelson, F. Conforming behavior under two conditions of conflict in the cognitive field. *J. abnorm. soc. Psychol.*, 1957, *55*, 181-187.

1065. Sanderson, D. Group description. *Soc. Forces*, 1938, *16*, 309-319.

1066. Sanford, F. H. *Authoritarianism and leadership.* Philadelphia: Inst. Res. in Hum. Relat., 1950. (See No. 1214.) *P.A.*, 26:818.

1067. Sarbin, T. R. Role theory. In G. Lindzey (Ed.), *Handbook of social psychology.* Reading, Mass.: Addison-Wesley, 1954. Pp. 223-258.

1068. Sarbin, T. R., & Jones, D. S. An experimental analysis of role behavior.

J. abnorm. soc. Psychol., 1955, *51*, 236-241. (See No. 826, pp. 465-472.) *P.A.*, 30:4374.

1069. Saslow, G., Goodrich, D. W., & Stein, M. Study of therapist behavior in diagnostic interviews by means of the interaction chronograph. *J. clin. Psychol.*, 1956, *12*, 133-139. *P.A.*, 31:4665.

1070. Saslow, G. Matarazzo, J. D., & Guze, S. B. The stability of interaction chronograph patterns in psychiatric interviews. *J. consult. Psychol.*, 1955, *19*, 417-430. *P.A.*, 30:7176.

1071. Saslow, G., Matarazzo, J. D., Phillips, Jeanne S., & Matarazzo, Ruth G. Test-retest stability of interaction patterns during interviews conducted one week apart. *J. abnorm. soc. Psychol.*, 1957, *54*, 295-302.

1072. Schachter, S. Deviation, rejection, and communication. *J. abnorm. soc. Psychol.*, 1951, *46*, 190-207. (See No. 249.) *P.A.*, 25:8043.

1073. Schachter, S. Comment on "On group cohesiveness." *Amer. J. Sociol.*, 1952, *57*, 554-562.

1074. Schachter, S. Ellertson, N., McBride, Dorothy, & Gregory, Doris. An experimental study of cohesiveness and productivity. *Hum. Relat.*, 1951, *4*, 229-238. (See No. 249.) *P.A.*, 26:6188.

1075. Schachter, S., & Hall, R. Group-derived restraints and audience persuasion. *Hum. Relat.*, 1952, *5*, 397-406. *P.A.*, 27:7178.

1076. Schachter, S., Nuttin, J., De Monchaux, Cecily, Maucorps, P. H., Osmer, D., Duijker, H., Rommetveit, R., & Israel, J. Cross-cultural experiments on threat and rejection. *Hum. Relat.*, 1954, *7*, 403-439. *S.A.*, 1511.

1077. Schanck, R. L. A study of a community and its groups and institutions conceived of as behavior of individuals. *Psychol. Monogr.*, 1932, *43*, No. 2.

1078. Scheidlinger, S. *Psychoanalysis and group behavior: a study in Freudian group psychology.* New York: Norton, 1952. (See No. 249, 1953.) *P.A.*, 27:1887.

1079. Schein, E. H. The Chinese indoctrination program for prisoners of war: a study of attempted "brainwashing." *Psychiatry*, 1956, *19*, 149-172. (See No. 826, pp. 311-334.)

1080. Schiff, H. Judgmental response sets in the perception of sociometric status. *Sociometry*, 1954, *17*, 207-227. *P.A.*, 29:5482; *S.A.*, 1962.

1081. Schmidt, F. Experimentelle üntersuchungen uber die hausaufgaben des schulkindes. (Experimental studies of the school child's home-work.) *Arch. f. d. ges. Psychol.*, 1904, Band III, 33-152.

1082. Schneider, L. I. A proposed conceptual integration of group dynamics and group therapy, *J. soc. Psychol.*, 1955, *42*, 173-191. *P.A.*, 31:1151.

1083. Schonbar, Rosalea A. The interaction of observer-pairs in judging visual extent and movement: the formation of social norms in "structured" situations. *Arch. Psychol.*, 1945, No. 299. *P.A.*, 20:1017.

1084. Schroder, H. M., & Hunt, D. E. Dispositional effects upon conformity at different levels of discrepancy. *J. Pers.*, 1958, *26*, 243-258.

1085. Schutz, W. C. Reliability, continuity, and content analysis. *Psychol. Rev.*, 1952a, *59*, 119-127.

1086. Schutz, W. C. Some theoretical considerations for group behavior. In *Symposium on techniques for the measurement of group performance*, Washington, D. C.: U. S. Govt., Res. and Developm. Board, 1952b. Pp. 27-36.

1087. Schutz, W. C. What makes groups productive? *Hum. Relat.*, 1955, *8*, 429-465. *P.A.*, 31:786; *S.A.*, 3145.

1088. Schutz, W. C. *FIRO: a three-dimensional theory of interpersonal behavior.* New York: Holt, 1958a.

1089. Schutz, W. C. The interpersonal underworld. *Harvard Bus. Rev.*, 1958b, *36* (4), 123-135.

1090. Scodel, A., & Freedman, Maria L. Additional observations on the social perceptions of authoritarians and non-authoritarians. *J. abnorm. soc. Psychol.*, 1956, *52*, 92-95. *P.A.*, 31:2571; *S.A.*, 4288.

1091. Scodel, A., & Mussen, P. Social perceptions of authoritarians and non-authoritarians. *J. abnorm. soc. Psychol.*, 1953, *48*, 181-184. *P.A.*, 28:2443.

1092. Seashore, S. E. Group cohesiveness in the industrial work group. Ann Arbor: Univer. of Michigan, 1954. *S.A.*, 3150.

1093. Seeman, M. Role conflict and ambivalence in leadership. *Amer. sociol. Rev.*, 1953, *18*, 373-380. *P.A.*, 28:4151; *S.A.*, 92.

1094. Seidman, D., Bensen, S. B., Miller, I., & Meeland, T. Influence of a partner on tolerance for a self-administered electric shock. *J. abnorm. soc. Psychol.*, 1957, *54*, 210-212.

1095. Selltiz, Claire, Jahoda, Marie, Deutsch, M., & Cook, S. W. *Research methods in social relations.* (Rev. one-vol. ed.) New York: Holt, 1959.

1096. Sengupta, N. N., & Sinha, C. P. N. Mental work in isolation and in group. *Indian J. Psychol.*, 1926, *1*, 106-110.

1097. Sewell, W., Mussen, P., & Harris, C. Relationships among child training practices. *Amer. sociol. Rev.*, 1955, *20*, 137-148. *P.A.*, 31:691.

1098. Shaw, M. E. Group structure and the behavior of individuals in small groups. *J. Psychol.*, 1954a, *38*, 139-149. *P.A.*, 29:3829.

1099. Shaw, M. E. Some effects of problem complexity upon problem solution efficiency in different communication nets. *J. exp. Psychol.*, 1954b, *48*, 211-217. *P.A.*, 29:5645.

1100. Shaw, M. E. Some effects of unequal distribution of information upon group performance in various communication nets. *J. abnorm. soc. Psychol.*, 1954c, *49*, 547-553. P.A., 29:5646.

1101. Shaw, M. E. A comparison of two types of leadership in various communication nets. *J. abnorm. soc. Psychol.*, 1955, *50*, 127-134. P.A., 29:7098.

1102. Shaw, M. E. Random versus systematic distribution of information in communication nets. *J. Pers.*, 1956, *25*, 59-69.

1103. Shaw, M. E. Some effects of irrelevant information upon problem-solving by small groups. *J. soc. Psychol.*, 1958a, *47*, 33-37.

1104. Shaw, M. E. Some motivational factors in cooperation and competition. *J. Pers.*, 1958b, *26*, 155-169.

1105. Shaw, M. E., & Gilchrist, J. C. Repetitive task failure and sociometric choice. *J. abnorm. soc. Psychol.*, 1955, *50*, 29-32. P.A., 29:7099; S.A., 1983.

1106. Shaw, M. E., & Gilchrist, J. C. Intra-group communication and leader choice. *J. soc. Psychol.*, 1956, *43*, 133-138. P.A., 31:2721.

1107. Shaw, M. E., & Rothschild, G. H. Some effects of prolonged experience in communication nets. *J. appl. Psychol.*, 1956, *40*, 281-286.

1108. Shaw, M. E., Rothschild, G. H., & Strickland, J. F. Decision process in communication nets. *J. abnorm. soc. Psychol.*, 1957, *54*, 323-330.

1109. Shaw, Marjorie E. A comparison of individuals and small groups in the rational solution of complex problems. *Amer. J. Psychol.*, 1932, *44*, 491-504. (See No. 1214, pp. 135-146; No. 826, pp. 564-575.)

1110. Sheffield, A. D. *Joining in public discussion.* New York: Doran, 1922.

1111. Sheffield, A. D. *Training for group experience.* New York: Inquiry, 1929.

1112. Sheffield, A. D., & Sheffield, Ada E. *The mind of a "member."* New York: Exposition Press, 1951.

1113. Shelley, H. P. Level of aspiration phenomena in small groups. *J. soc. Psychol.*, 1954, *40*, 149-164. P.A., 29:5484.

1114. Shelley, H. P. Response set and the California attitude scales. *Educ. psychol. Measmt*, 1956, *16*, 63-67. P.A., 31:5919.

1115. Shelly, M. W., & Gilchrist, J. C. Some effects of communication requirements in group structures. *J. soc. Psychol.*, 1958, *48*, 37-44.

1116. Shepard, H. A., & Bennis, W. G. A theory of training by group methods. *Hum. Relat.*, 1956, *9*, 403-413.

1117. Shepherd, C., & Weschler, I. R. The relation between three interpersonal variables and communication effectiveness: a pilot study. *Sociometry*, 1955, *18*, 103-110. P.A., 30:4376.

1118. Sherif, M. A study of some social factors in perception. *Arch. Psychol.*, 1935, *27*, No. 187.

1119. Sherif, M. *The psychology of social norms.* New York: Harper, 1936. (See No. 1214, pp. 249-262; No. 826, pp. 219-232.)

1120. Sherif, M. A preliminary study of inter-group relations. In J. H. Rohrer & M. Sherif (Eds.), *Social psychology at the crossroads: the University of Oklahoma lectures in social psychology.* New York: Harper, 1951. Pp. 388-424. *P.A.,* 26:834.

1121. Sherif, M. Integrating field work and laboratory in small group research. *Amer. sociol. Rev.,* 1954a, *19,* 759-771. *P.A.,* 30:2699.

1122. Sherif, M. Sociocultural influences in small group research. *Sociol. soc. Res.,* 1954b, *39,* 1-10. *S.A.,* 2733.

1123. Sherif, M. Experiments in group conflict. *Sci. Amer.,* 1956, *195* (5), 54-58.

1124. Sherif, M. Towards integrating psychological and sociological approaches in small group research. In M. Sherif & M. O. Wilson (Eds.), *Emerging problems in social psychology.* Norman, Okla.: Univer. Okla. Book Exch. Dupl. Serv., 1957.

1125. Sherif, M. Superordinate goals in the reduction of intergroup conflict. *Amer. J. Sociol.,* 1958, *63,* 349-356.

1126. Sherif, M., & Cantril, H. *The psychology of ego-involvements.* New York: Wiley, 1947. *P.A.,* 21:3335.

1127. Sherif, M., & Harvey, O. J. A study in ego functioning: elimination of stable anchorages in individual and group situations. *Sociometry,* 1952, *15,* 272-305. *P.A.,* 27:7125.

1128. Sherif, M., & Sherif, Carolyn W. *Groups in harmony and tension.* New York: Harper, 1953. *P.A.,* 28:2446.

1129. Sherif, M., & Sherif, Carolyn W. *An outline of social psychology.* (Rev. ed.) New York: Harper, 1956. Ch. 9. *P.A.,* 31:2722.

1130. Sherif, M., White, B. J., & Harvey, O. J. Status in experimentally produced groups. *Amer. J. Sociol.,* 1955, *60,* 370-379. *P.A.,* 30:800; *S.A.,* 1512.

1131. Shevaleva, E., & Ergolska, O. (Children's collectives in the light of experimental reflexology.) Sbornik, posvyashennyi V. M. Bekhterevu k 40-letnyu professorskoi dyatelnosti. (Bekhterev 40th anniversary commemorative volume.) 1926, 147-182. *P.A.,* 1:2486.

1132. Shils, E. A. The present situation in American sociology. *Pilot Papers,* 1947, *2* (2), 8-36.

1133. Shils, E. A. *The present situation in American sociology.* New York: Free Press, 1948. *P.A.,* 23:1729.

1134. Shils, E. A. Primary groups in the American army. In R. K. Merton & P. F. Lazarsfeld (Eds.), *Continuities in social research: studies in the scope and method of "The American Soldier."* New York: Free Press, 1950. Pp. 16-39.

1135. Shils, E. A. The study of the primary group. In D. Lerner & H. D. Laswell (Eds.), *The policy sciences*. Stanford, Calif.: Stanford Univer. Press, 1951. Pp. 44-69.

1136. Shils, E. A., & Janowitz, M. Cohesion and disintegration of the Wehrmacht in World War II. *Publ. Opin. Quart.*, 1948, *12*, 280-315. *P.A.*, 23:136.

1137. Siegel, Alberta E., & Siegel, S. Reference groups, membership groups, and attitude change. *J. abnorm. soc. Psychol.*, 1957, *55*, 360-364. (See No. 249, 1960, pp. 232-240.)

1138. Simmel, G. The number of members as determining the sociological form of the group. *Amer. J. Sociol.*, 1902-03, *8*, 1-46, 158-196.

1139. Simmel, G. *Conflict*. Trans. by K. H. Wolff. *The web of group-affiliations*. Trans. by R. Bendix. New York: Free Press, 1955. *P.A.*, 29:5485.

1140. Simon, H. A. A formal theory of interaction of social groups. *Amer. sociol. Rev.*, 1952, *17*, 202-211. (See No. 559.) *P.A.*, 27:5084.

1141. Simon, H. A., & Guetzkow, H. A model of short- and long-run mechanisms involved in pressures toward uniformity in groups. *Psychol. Rev.*, 1955a, *62*, 56-68. *P.A.*, 29:8523.

1142. Simon, H. A., & Guetzkow, H. Mechanisms involved in group pressures on deviate-members. *Brit. J. statist. Psychol.*, 1955b, *8*, 93-100. *P.A.*, 31:834.

1143. Simpson, R. H. A study of those who influence and of those who are influenced in discussion. *Teach. Coll., Columbia Univer. Contrib. Educ.*, 1938, No. 748.

1144. Sims, V. M. The relative influence of two types of motivation on improvement. *J. educ. Psychol.*, 1928, *19*, 480-484.

1145. Singer, J. L., & Goldman, G. D. Experimentally contrasted social atmospheres in group psychotherapy with chronic schizophrenics. *J. soc. Psychol.*, 1954, *40*, 23-37.

1146. Slater, P. E. Role differentiation in small groups. *Amer. sociol. Rev.*, 1955, *20*, 300-310. (See No. 559.) *P.A.*, 30:8179.

1147. Slater, P. E. Contrasting correlates of group size. *Sociometry*, 1958, *21*, 129-139.

1148. Slavson, S. R. *Creative group education*. New York: Ass. Press, 1938.

1149. Slavson, S. R. (Ed.) *The practice of group therapy*. New York: Int. Univer. Press, 1947.

1150. Smith, A. J., Jaffe, J., & Livingston, D. G. Consonance of interpersonal perception and individual effectiveness. *Hum. Relat.*, 1955, *8*, 385-397. *P.A.*, 31:790; *S.A.*, 3144.

1151. Smith, A. J., Madden, H. E., & Sobol, R. Productivity and recall in cooperative and competitive discussion groups. *J. Psychol.*, 1957, *43*, 193-204.

1152. Smith, C. E. A study of autonomic excitation resulting from the inter-action of individual and group opinion. *J. abnorm. soc. Psychol.*, 1936, *31*, 138-164.

1153. Smith, E. E. The effects of clear and unclear role expectations on group productivity and defensiveness. *J. abnorm. soc. Psychol.*, 1957, *55*, 213-217.

1154. Smith, H. C. Teamwork in the college class. *J. educ. Psychol.*, 1955, *46*, 274-286. P.A., 30:6282.

1155. Smith, M. A method of analyzing the interaction of children. *J. juv. Res.*, 1933, *17*, 78-88. P.A., 7:4786.

1156. Smith, M. Some factors in the friendship selections of high school students. *Sociometry*, 1944, *7*, 303-310. P.A., 19:494.

1157. Smith, M. B. Social psychology and group processes. *Annu. Rev. Psychol.*, 1952, *3*, 175-204.

1158. Smith, S. L. Communication pattern and the adaptability of task-oriented groups: an experimental study. Cited in A. Bavelas, Communication patterns in task-oriented groups. In D. Lerner & H. Lasswell (Eds.), *The policy sciences: recent developments in scope and method.* Stanford, Calif.: Stanford Univer. Press, 1951. Pp. 193-203.

1159. Smucker, O. Near-sociometric analysis as a basis for guidance. *Sociometry*, 1949, *12*, 326-340.

1160. Snyder, Eloise C. The Supreme Court as a small group. *Soc. Forces*, 1958, *36*, 232-238.

1161. Snyder, W. U. An investigation of the nature of non-directive psychotherapy. *J. gen. Psychol.*, 1945, *33*, 193-223.

1162. Sorokin, P. A., Tanquist, Mamie, Parten, Mildred, & Zimmerman, Mrs. C. C. An experimental study of efficiency of work under various specified conditions. *Amer. J. Sociol.*, 1930, *35*, 765-782.

1163. South, E. B. Some psychological aspects of committee work. *J. appl. Psychol.*, 1927, *11*, 348-368, 437-464. P.A., 2:2885.

1164. Southall, A. An operational theory of role. *Hum. Relat.*, 1959, *12*, 17-34.

1165. Speroff, B. J. Job satisfaction and interpersonal desirability values. *Sociometry*, 1955, *18*, 69-72. P.A., 30:6392.

1166. Spiegel, J. P. The resolution of role conflict within the family, *Psychiatry*, 1957, *20*, 1-16.

1167. Stanton, A. H., & Schwartz, M. S. *The mental hospital.* New York: Basic Books, 1954. P.A., 29:4248.

1168. Starkweather, J. A. Content-free speech as a source of information about the speaker. *J. abnorm. soc. Psychol.*, 1956, *52*, 394-402. P.A., 31:4629.

1169. Steiner, I. D. Interpersonal behavior as influenced by accuracy of social perception. *Psychol. Rev.*, 1955, *62*, 268-274. *P.A.*, 30:2673.

1170. Steiner, I. D., & Dodge, Joan S. Interpersonal perception and role structure as determinants of group and individual efficiency. *Hum. Relat.*, 1956, *9*, 467-480.

1171. Steiner, I. D., & Dodge, Joan S. A comparison of two techniques employed in the study of interpersonal perception. *Sociometry*, 1957, *20*, 1-7. *P.A.*, 32-381.

1172 Steiner, I. D., & McDiarmid, C. G. Two kinds of assumed similarity between opposites. *J. abnorm. soc. Psychol.*, 1957, *55*, 140-142.

1173. Steiner, I. D., & Peters, S. C. Conformity and the A-B-X model. *J. Pers.*, 1958, *26*, 229-242.

1174. Steinzor, B. The development and evaluation of a measure of social interaction. *Hum. Relat.*, 1949a, *2*, 103-121. *P.A.*, 24:152.

1175. Steinzor, B. The development and evaluation of a measure of social interaction: Part II. *Hum. Relat.*, 1949b, *2*, 319-347.

1176. Steinzor, B. The spatial factor in face to face discussion groups. *J. abnorm. soc. Psychol.*, 1950, *45*, 552-555. (See No. 559.) *P.A.*, 25:1007.

1177. Stendler, Celia, Damrin, Dora, & Haines, Aleyne C. Studies in cooperation and competition: I. The effects of working for group and individual rewards on the social climate of children's groups. *J. genet. Psychol.*, 1951, *79*, 173-197. *P.A.*, 26:5454.

1178. Stephan, F. F. The relative rate of communication between members of small groups. *Amer. sociol. Rev.*, 1952, *17*, 482-486. *P.A.*, 27:6519.

1179. Stephan, F. F., & Mishler, E. G. The distribution of participation in small groups: an exponential approximation. *Amer. sociol. Rev.*, 1952, *17*, 598-608. (See No. 559.) *P.A.*, 28:711.

1180. Stevens, S. R. Social begavning som funktion av rollforvantan. (Social intelligence as a function of role expectancy.) *Nord. Psykol.*, 1953, *5*, 203-207. *P.A.*, 29:5488.

1181. Stirn, H. Die "kleine gruppe" in der deutschen soziologie. (The "small group" in German sociology.) *Köl Z. Soziol.*, 1955, *7*, 532-557. *S.A.*, 2927.

1182. Stock, Dorothy, & Thelen, H. A. *Emotional dynamics and group culture: experimental studies of individual and group behavior.* New York: New York Univer. Press, 1958.

1183. Stock, Dorothy, & Whitman, R. M. Patient's and therapist's apperceptions of an episode in group therapy. *Hum. Relat.*, 1957, *10*, 367-383.

1184. Stock, Dorothy, Whitman, R. M., & Lieberman, M. A. The deviant member in therapy groups. *Hum. Relat.*, 1958, *11*, 341-372.

1185. Stogdill, R. M. Personal factors associated with leadership: a survey of the literature. *J. Psychol.*, 1948, *25*, 35-71. *P.A.*, 22:3001.

1186. Stogdill, R. M. Leadership, membership and organization. *Psychol. Bull.*, 1950, *47*, 1-14. (See No. 249, 1953.) *P.A.*, 24:4552.

1187. Stogdill, R. M. *Individual behavior and group achievement: a theory: the experimental evidence.* New York: Oxford Univer. Press, 1959.

1188. Stogdill, R. M., & Coons, A. E. (Eds.) Leader behavior: its description and measurement. *Res. Monogr., Bureau Bus. Res., Ohio State Univer.*, 1957, No. 88. *P.A.*, 32:1466.

1189. Stone, G. C., Gage, N. L., & Leavitt, G. S. Two kinds of accuracy in predicting another's responses. *J. soc. Psychol.*, 1957, *45*, 245-254.

1190. Stone, P., & Kamiya, J. Judgment of consensus during group discussion. *J. abnorm. soc. Psychol.*, 1957, *55*, 171-175.

1191. Stotland, E. Determinants of attraction to groups. *J. soc. Psychol.*, 1959, *49*, 71-80.

1192. Stotland, E., Thorley, S., Thomas, E., Cohen, A. R., & Zander, A. The effects of group expectations and self-esteem upon self-evaluation. *J. abnorm. soc. Psychol.*, 1957, *54*, 55-63.

1193. Stouffer, S. A., et al. *The American soldier.* Princeton: Princeton Univer. Press, 1949.

1194. Strauss, B., & Strauss, Frances. *New ways to better meetings.* New York: Viking Press, 1951. *P.A.*, 26:219.

1195. Strodtbeck, F. L. Husband-wife interaction over revealed differences. *Amer. sociol. Rev.*, 1951, *16*, 468-473. (See No. 559.) *P.A.*, 27:1142.

1196. Strodtbeck, F. L. The family as a three-person group. *Amer. sociol. Rev.*, 1954a, *19*, 23-29. (See No. 559.) *P.A.*, 29:3949.

1197. Strodtbeck, F. L. A case for the study of small groups. *Amer. sociol. Rev.*, 1954b, *19*, 651-657. *P.A.*, 30:2701.

1198. Strodtbeck, F. L. Sociology of small groups, 1945-55. In H. L. Zetterberg (Ed.), *Sociology in the United States of America: a trend report.* Paris: UNESCO, 1956.

1199. Strodtbeck, F. L., & Hare, A. P. Bibliography of small group research: from 1900 through 1953. *Sociometry*, 1954, *17*, 107-178. *P.A.*, 29:3831.

1200. Strodtbeck, F. L., & Hook, L. H. The social dimensions of a 12-man jury table. Univer. of Chicago Law Sch., 1956. (Mimeo.)

1201. Strodtbeck, F. L., James, Rita M., & Hawkins, C. Social status in jury deliberations. *Amer. sociol. Rev.*, 1957, *22*, 713-719. (See No. 826, pp. 379-388.) *S.A.*, 5302.

1202. Strodtbeck, F. L., & Mann, R. D. Sex role differentiation in jury deliberations. *Sociometry*, 1956, *19*, 3-11. *S.A.*, 3950.

1203. Stroop, J. R. Is the judgment of the group better than that of the average member of the group? *J. exp. Psychol.*, 1932, *15*, 550-562.

1204. Strupp, H. H. An objective comparison of Rogerian and psycho-analytic techniques. *J. consult. Psychol.*, 1955a, *19*, 1-7.

1205. Strupp, H. H. Psychotherapeutic technique, professional affiliation, and experience level. *J. consult. Psychol.*, 1955b, *19*, 97-102.

1206. Strupp, H. H. The effect of the psychotherapist's personal analysis upon his own techniques. *J. consult. Psychol.*, 1955c, *19*, 197-204. *P.A.*, 30:2994.

1207. Strupp, H. H. The performance of psychoanalytic and client-centered therapists in an initial interview. *J. consult. Psychol.*, 1958, *22*, 265-274.

1208. Suchman, J. R. Social sensitivity in the small task-oriented group. *J. abnorm. soc. Psychol.*, 1956, *52*, 75-83. *P.A.*, 31:2724.

1209. Sullivan, H. S. Psychiatry: introduction to the study of interpersonal relations. *Psychiatry*, 1938, *1*, 121-134.

1210. Sullivan, H. S. *The interpersonal theory of psychiatry.* New York: Norton, 1954.

1211. Swanson, G. E. The development of an instrument for rating child-parent relationships. *Soc. Forces*, 1950, *29*, 84-90. *P.A.*, 25:4991.

1212. Swanson, G. E. Some problems of laboratory experiments with small populations. *Amer. sociol. Rev.*, 1951a, *16*, 349-358. *P.A.*, 27:1077.

1213. Swanson, G. E. Some effects of member object-relationships on small groups. *Hum. Relat.*, 1951b, *4*, 355-380. *P.A.*, 26:5486.

1214. Swanson, G. E., Newcomb, T. M., & Hartley, E. L. (Eds.) *Readings in social psychology.* (Rev. ed.) New York: Holt, 1952. *P.A.*, 27:4160.

1215. Symonds, P. M. Role playing as a diagnostic procedure in the selection of leaders. *Sociatry*, 1947, *1*, 43-50. *P.A.*, 21:3720.

1216. Taft, R. The ability to judge people. *Psychol. Bull.*, 1955, *52*, 1-23.

1217. Tagiuri, R. Relational analysis: an extension of sociometric method with emphasis upon sociometric perception. *Sociometry*, 1952, *15*, 91-104. (See No. 559.) *P.A.*, 27:7144.

1218. Tagiuri, R. The perception of feelings among members of small groups. *J. soc. Psychol.*, 1957, *46*, 219-227.

1219. Tagiuri, R., Blake, R. R., & Bruner, J. S. Some determinants of the perception of positive and negative feelings in others. *J. abnorm. soc. Psychol.*, 1953, *48*, 585-592. *P.A.*, 28:5838; *S.A.*, 249.

1220. Tagiuri, R., Bruner, J. S., & Blake, R. R. On the relations between feelings and perception of feelings among members of small groups. In Eleanor E. Maccoby, T. M. Newcomb, & E. L. Hartley (Eds.), *Readings in social psychology.* (3rd ed.) New York: Holt, 1958. Pp. 110-116.

1221. Tagiuri, R., Bruner, J. S., & Kogan, N. Estimating the chance expectancies of dyadic relationships within a group. *Psychol. Bull.*, 1955, *52*, 122-131. *P.A.*, 30:2702.

1222. Tagiuri, R., & Kogan, N. The visibility of interpersonal preferences. *Hum. Relat.*, 1957, *10*, 385-390.

1223. Tagiuri, R., Kogan, N., & Bruner, J. S. The transparency of interpersonal choice. *Sociometry*, 1955, *18*, 624-635. *P.A.*, 32:1497; *S.A.*, 3435.

1224. Tagiuri, R., & Petrullo, L. (Eds.) *Person perception and interpersonal behavior*. Stanford, Cal.: Stanford Univer. Press, 1958.

1225. Talland, G. A. The assessment of group opinion by leaders, and their influence on its formation. *J. abnorm. soc. Psychol.*, 1954, *89*, 431-434. *P.A.*, 29:3832.

1226. Talland, G. A. Task and interaction process: some characteristics of therapeutic group discussion. *J. abnorm. soc. Psychol.*, 1955, *50*, 105-109. (See No. 559.) *P.A.*, 29:7396.

1227. Talland, G. A. Rate of speaking as a group norm. *Hum. Organization*, 1957a, *15*(4), 8-10.

1228. Talland, G. A. Role and status structure in therapy groups. *J. clin. Psychol.*, 1957b, *13*, 27-33.

1229. Talland, G. A. Sex differences in self-assessment. *J. soc. Psychol.*, 1958, *48*, 25-35.

1230. Talland, G. A., & Clark, D. H. Evaluation of topics in therapy group discussion. *J. clin. Psychol.*, 1954, *10*, 131-137. *P.A.*, 29:1015.

1231. Taves, E. H. Two mechanisms for the perception of visual numerousness. *Arch. Psychol.*, 1941, *37*, No. 265. *P.A.*, 16:2594.

1232. .Taylor, D. W., & Faust, W. L. Twenty questions: efficiency in problem solving as a function of size of group. *J. exp. Psychol.*, 1952, *44*, 360-368. (See No. 559.) *P.A.*, 27:4994.

1233. Taylor, D. W., & McNemar, Olga W. Problem solving and thinking. *Annu. Rev. Psychol.*, 1955, *6*, 455-482. *P.A.*, 29:5286.

1234. Taylor, F. K. The three-dimensional basis of emotional interactions in small groups. I. *Hum. Relat.*, 1954, *7*, 441-471. *P.A.*, 29:5489; *S.A.*, 1514.

1235. Taylor, F. K. The three-dimensional basis of emotional interactions in small groups. II. *Hum. Relat.*, 1955, *8*, 3-28. *P.A.*, 30:806; *S.A.*, 1774.

1236. Taylor, F. K. Display of dyadic emotions. *Hum. Relat.*, 1957, *10*, 257-262.

1237. Taylor, F. W. Group management. *Trans. Soc. Mech. Engr.*, 1903, *24*.

1238. Taylor, F. W. *The principles of scientific management*. New York: Harper, 1911.

1239. Taylor, J. H., Thompson, C. E., & Spassoff, D. The effect of conditions of work and various suggested attitudes on production and reported feelings of tiredness and boredness. *J. appl. Psychol.*, 1937, *21*, 431-450.

1240. Taylor, M., & Mitzel, H. E. Research tools: observing and recording group behavior. *Rev. educ. Res.*, 1957, *27*, 476-486.

1241. Tear, D. G., & Guthrie, G. M. The relationship of cooperation to the sharpening-leveling continuum. *J. soc. Psychol.*, 1955, *42*, 203-208. *P. A.*, 31:794.

1242. Terman, L. M. A preliminary study of the psychology and pedagogy of leadership. *Pedag. Sem.*, 1904, *11*, 413-451. (See No. 559.)

1243. Thelen, H. A. Engineering research in curriculum building. *J. educ. Res.*, 1948, *41*, 579-596. (See No. 110.)

1244. Thelen, H. A. Group dynamics in instruction: principle of least group size. *Sch. Rev.*, 1949, *57*, 139-148.

1245. Thelen, H. A. Educational dynamics: Theory and research. *J. soc. Issues*, 1950, *6* (2), *P.A.*, 25:3376.

1246. Thelen, H. A. *Dynamics of groups at work.* Chicago: Univer. Chicago Press, 1954.

1247. Thelen, H. A. Emotionality and work in groups. In L. D. White (Ed.), *The state of the social sciences.* Chicago: Univer. Chicago Press, 1956. Pp. 184-200.

1248. Thelen, H. A., Stock, Dorothy, et al. *Methods for studying work and emotionality in group operation.* Chicago: Hum. Dynamics Lab., Univer. of Chicago, 1954.

1249. Thelen, H. A., & Withall, J. Three frames of reference: the description of climate. *Hum. Relat.*, 1949, *2*, 159-176. *P.A.*, 24:148.

1250. Theodorson, G. A. Elements in the progressive development of small groups. *Soc. Forces*, 1953, *31*, 311-320. *S.A.*, 250.

1251. Theodorson, G. A. The relationship between leadership and popularity roles in small groups. *Amer. sociol. Rev.*, 1957, *22*, 58-67. *P.A.*, 32:366; *S.A.*, 3951.

1252. Thibaut, J. W. An experimental study of the cohesiveness of underprivileged groups. *Hum. Relat.*, 1950, *3*, 251-278. (See No. 249, 1953.) *P.A.*, 25:2369.

1253. Thibaut, J. W., & Coules, J. The role of communication in the reduction of interpersonal hostility. *J. abnorm. soc. Psychol.*, 1952, *47*, 770-777. *P.A.*, 27:5076.

1254. Thibaut, J. W., & Kelley, H. H. *The social psychology of groups.* New York: Wiley, 1959.

1255. Thibaut, J. W., & Riecken, H. W. Authoritarianism, status, and the communication of aggression. *Hum. Relat.*, 1955a, *8*, 95-120. *P.A.*, 30:4380.

1256. Thibaut, J. W., & Riecken, H. W. Some determinants and consequences of the perception of social causality. *J. Pers.*, 1955b, *24*, 113-133. (See No. 826, pp. 117-130.) *P.A.*, 30: 7025.

1257. Thibaut, J. W., & Strickland, L. H. Psychological set and social conformity. *J Pers.*, 1956, *25*, 115-129.

1258. Thomas, Dorothy S. (Ed.) *Some new techniques for studying social behavior.* New York: Teach. Coll., Columbia Univer., 1929. Also in *Child Develpm. Monogr.*, 1929, No. 1.

1259. Thomas, Dorothy S. A symposium on the observability of social phenomena with respect to statistical analysis. I. An attempt to develop precise measurements in the social behavior field. *Sociologus*, 1932, *8*, 436-456. II. *Sociologus*, 1933, 9, 1-24.

1260. Thomas, Dorothy S., Loomis, Alice M., & Arrington, Ruth E. *Observational studies of social behavior.* Volume I: *Social behavior patterns.* New Haven: Inst. of Hum. Relat., Yale Univer., 1933.

1261. Thomas, E. J. Effects of facilitative role interdependence on group functioning. *Hum. Relat.*, 1957, *10*, 347-366. (See No. 249, 1960.)

1262. Thomas, W. I., & Thomas, Dorothy S. *The child in America: behavior problems and programs.* New York: Knopf, 1928.

1263. Thompson, W. R., & Nishimura, Rhoda. Some determinants of friendship. *J. Pers.*, 1952, *20*, 305-314. *P.A.*, 27:2630.

1264. Thorndike, R. L. On what type of task will a group do well? *J. abnorm. soc. Psychol.*, 1938a, *33*, 409-413.

1265. Thorndike, R. L. The effect of discussion upon the correctness of group decisions, when the factor of majority influence is allowed for. *J. soc. Psychol.*, 1938b, 9, 343-362.

1266. Thorpe, J. G. A study of some factors in friendship formation. *Sociometry*, 1955, *18*, 207-214. *P.A.*, 30:7026.

1267. Thrasher, F. *The gang.* Chicago: Univer. Chicago Press, 1927.

1268. Thrasher, J. D. Interpersonal relations and gradations of stimulus structure as factors in judgmental variation: an experimental approach. *Sociometry*, 1954, *17*, 228-241. *S.A.*, 1986.

1269. Thurstone, L. L. *Multiple-factor analysis.* Chicago: Univer. Chicago Press, 1947. *P.A.*, 21:2833.

1270. Timmons, W. M. Decisions and attitudes as outcomes of the discussion of a social problem. *Teach. Coll., Columbia Univer. Contrib. Educ.*, 1939, No. 777. *P.A.*, 14:479.

1271. Timmons, W. M. Can the product superiority of discussors be attributed to averaging or majority influences? *J. soc. Psychol.*, 1942, *15*, 23-32. *P.A.*, 16:3225.

1272. Titus, H. E., & Hollander, E. P. The California F scale in psychological research: 1950-1955. *Psychol. Bull.*, 1957, *54*, 47-64. *P.A.*, 32:2688.

1273. Toeman, Zerka. Role analysis and audience structure: with special emphasis on problems of military adjustment. *Sociometry*, 1944, 7, 205-221. Also in *Psychodrama Monogr.*, 1945, No. 12. *P.A.*, 19:499.

1274. Torrance, E. P. Crew performance in a test situation as a predictor of field and combat performance. HFORL Report No. 33, ARDC. Bolling A.F.B., Washington 25, D. C., 1953a.

1275. Torrance, E. P. Methods of conducting critiques of group problem-solving performance. *J. appl. Psychol.*, 1953b, 37, 394-398. (See No. 559.) *P.A.*, 29:708.

1276. Torrance, E. P. Perception of group functioning as a predictor of group performance. *Res. Stud., Wash. State Coll.*, 1953c, 21, 262-265.

1277. Torrance, E. P. Some consequences of power differences on decision making in permanent and temporary three-man groups. *Res. Stud., Wash. State Coll.*, 1954a, 22, 130-140. (See No. 559.) *P.A.*, 30:2676.

1278. Torrance, E. P. The behavior of small groups under the stress of conditions of "survival." *Amer. sociol. Rev.*, 1954b, 19, 751-755. *P.A.*, 30:2675.

1279. Torrance, E. P. Perception of group functioning as a predictor of group performance. *J. soc. Psychol.*, 1955a, 42, 271-282. *P.A.*, 31:799.

1280. Torrance, E. P. Sociometric techniques for diagnosing group ills. *Sociometry*, 1955b, 18, 597-612. *P.A.*, 32:1498; *S.A.*, 3445.

1281. Torrance, E. P. Group decision-making and disagreement. *Soc. Forces*, 1957, 35, 314-318. *P.A.*, 32:5328; *S.A.*, 5024.

1282. Torrance, E. P., & Mason, R. The indigenous leader in changing attitudes and behavior. *Int. J. Sociometry*, 1956, 1, 23-28. *P.A.*, 31:7632.

1283. Trapp, E. P. Leadership and popularity as a function of behavioral predictions. *J. abnorm. soc. Psychol.*, 1955, 51, 452-457. *P.A.*, 31:2726.

1284. Travers, R. M. W. A study in judging the opinions of groups. *Arch. Psychol.*, 1941, 47, No. 266. *P.A.*, 16:2787.

1285. Travers, R. M. W. A study of the ability to judge group-knowledge. *Amer. J. Psychol.*, 1943a, 56, 54-65. *P.A.*, 17:2091.

1286. Travers, R. M. W. The general ability to judge group-knowledge. *Amer. J. Psychol.*, 1943b, 56, 95-99. *P.A.*, 17:2092.

1287. Travis, L. E. The effect of a small audience upon eye-hand coordination. *J. abnorm. soc. Psychol.*, 1925, 20, 142-146.

1288. Travis, L. E. The influence of the group upon the stutterer's speed in free association. *J. abnorm. soc. Psychol.*, 1928, 23, 45-51. *P.A.*, 2:3572.

1289. Triplett, N. The dynamogenic factors in pace-making and competition. *Amer. J. Psychol.*, 1898, 9, 507-533.
1290. Trist, E. L., & Bamforth, K. W. Some social and psychological consequences of the longwall method of coal-getting. *Hum. Relat.*, 1951, 4, 3-38. *P.A.*, 25:8304.
1291. Trow, D. B. Autonomy and job satisfaction in task-oriented groups. *J. abnorm. soc. Psychol.*, 1957, 54, 204-209.
1292. Trow, W. C., Zander, A., Morse, W. C., & Jenkins, D. H. Psychology of group behavior: the class as a group. *J. educ. Psychol.*, 1950, 41, 322-338. *P.A.*, 25:3377.
1293. Tuddenham, R. D. The influence of a distorted group norm upon individual judgment. *J. Psychol.*, 1958, 46, 227-241.
1294. Tuddenham, R. D., MacBride, P., & Zahn, V. The influence of sex composition of the group upon yielding to a distorted norm. *J. Psychol.*, 1958, 48, 243-251.
1295. Tupes, E. C., Carp, A., & Borg, W. R. Performance in role-playing situations as related to leadership and personality measures. *Sociometry*, 1958, 21, 165-179.
1296. Turner, C. E. Test room studies in employee effectiveness. *Amer. J. publ. Hlth*, 1933, 23, 577-584. (See No. 559.)
1297. Turner, R. H. Role-taking, role standpoint, and reference-group behavior. *Amer. J. Sociol.*, 1956, 61, 316-328.
1298. Tyler, F. T. A factor analysis of fifteen MMPI scales. *J. consult. Psychol.*, 1951, 15, 451-456. *P.A.*, 26:7015.
1299. Updegraff, Ruth, & Herbst, Edithe K. An experimental study of the social behavior stimulated in young children by certain play materials. *J. genet. Psychol.*, 1933, 42, 372-390.
1300. Van Dusen, A. C. Measuring leadership ability. *Personn. Psychol.*, 1948, 1, 67-79. *P.A.*, 22:3919.
1301. Van Zelst, R. H. An interpersonal relations technique for industry. *Personnel*, 1952, 29, 68-76. *P.A.*, 27:3069.
1302. Vaughan, W., & McGinnies, E. Some biographical determiners of participation in group discussion. *J. appl. Psychol.*, 1957, 41, 179-185.
1303. Vernon, G. M., & Stewart, R. L. Empathy as a process in the dating situation. *Amer. sociol. Rev.*, 1957, 22, 48-52.
1304. Verplanck, W. S. The control of the content of conversation: reinforcement of statements of opinion. *J. abnorm. soc. Psychol.*, 1955, 51, 668-676. *P.A.*, 31:2940.
1305. Verplanck, W. S. The operant conditioning of human motor behavior. *Psychol. Bull.*, 1956, 53, 70-83.
1306. Vinacke, W. E. Some variables in buzz sessions. *J. soc. Psychol.*, 1957, 45, 25-33.

1307. Vinacke, W. E., & Arkoff, A. An experimental study of coalitions in the triad. *Amer. sociol. Rev.*, 1957, *22*, 406-414.

1308. Von Wiese, L., & Becker, H. *Systematic sociology: on the basis of the Beziehungslehre and Gebildelehre.* New York: Wiley, 1932.

1309. Vreeland, F. M. Social relations in the college fraternity. *Sociometry*, 1942, *5*, 151-162. *P.A.*, 16:4481.

1310. Wallen, R. Individuals' estimates of group opinion. *J. soc. Psychol.*, 1943, *17*, 269-274. *P.A.*, 17:3896.

1311. Wapner, S., & Alper, Thelma G. The effect of an audience on behavior in a choice situation. *J. abnorm. soc. Psychol.*, 1952, *47*, 222-229. *P.A.*, 27:2633.

1312. Warriner, C. K. Leadership in the small group. *Amer. J. Sociol.*, 1955, *60*, 361-369. *P.A.*, 30:809; *S.A.*, 1519.

1313. Washburn, Ruth W. A scheme for grading the reactions of children in a new social situation. *J. genet. Psychol.*, 1932, *40*, 84-99.

1314. Watson, G. B. Do groups think more efficiently than individuals? *J. abnorm. soc. Psychol.*, 1928, *23*, 328-336.

1315. Watson, G. B. An evaluation of small group work in a large class. *J. educ. Psychol.*, 1953, *44*, 385-408.

1316. Watson, Jeanne. A formal analysis of sociable interaction. *Sociometry*, 1958, *21*, 269-280.

1317. Weber, L. C. A study of peer acceptance among delinquent girls. *Sociometry*, 1950, *13*, 363-381.

1318. Wells, W. D., Weinert, G. & Rubel, Marilyn. Conformity pressure and authoritarian personality. *J. Psychol.*, 1956, *42*, 133-136.

1319. Weschler, I. R., Tannenbaum, R., & Talbot, E. A new management tool: the multi-relational sociometric survey. *Personnel*, 1952, *29*, 85-94. *P.A.*, 27:3073.

1320. Wheeler, D., & Jordan, H. Change of individual opinion to accord with group opinion. *J. abnorm. soc. Psychol.*, 1929, *24*, 203-206.

1321. Wheeler, D. K. Notes on "Role differentiation in small decision groups." *Sociometry*, 1957, *20*, 145-151.

1322. Wheeler, W. M., Little, K. B., & Lehner, G. F. J. The internal structure of the MMPI. *J. consult. Psychol.*, 1951, *15*, 134-141. *P.A.*, 26:6307.

1323. Whitehead, T. N. *The industrial worker.* Cambridge, Mass.: Harvard Univer. Press, 1938.

1324. Whittemore, I. C. The influence of competition on performance: an experimental study. *J. abnorm. soc. Psychol.*, 1924, *19*, 236-253.

1325. Whyte, W. F. *Street corner society: the social structure of an Italian slum.* Chicago: Univer. Chicago Press, 1943. *P.A.*, 18:2198.

1326. Whyte, W. F. The social structure of the restaurant. *Amer. J. Sociol.*, 1949, *54*, 302-310. *P.A.*, 23:2457.

1327. Whyte, W. F. Observational field-work methods. In Marie Jahoda, M.

Deutsch, & S. W. Cook (Eds.), *Research methods in social relations: with especial reference to prejudice.* New York: Dryden, 1951a. Pp. 493-513.

1328. Whyte, W. F. Small groups and large organizations. In J. H. Rohrer & M. Sherif, *Social psychology at the crossroads: the University of Oklahoma lectures in social psychology.* New York: Harper, 1951b. Pp. 297-312. *P.A.,* 26:838.

1329. Whyte, W. F. Leadership and group participation. *Bull. 24, New York State Sch. of Industr. and Labor Relat.,* Cornell Univer., 1953.

1330. Wiener, M. The effects of two experimental counseling techniques on performances impaired by induced stress. *J. abnorm. soc. Psychol.,* 1955, *51,* 565-572. *P.A.,* 31:2996.

1331. Wiener, M., Carpenter, Janeth T., & Carpenter, B. Some determinants of conformity behavior. *J. soc. Psychol.,* 1957, *45,* 289-297.

1332. Willerman, B. Group decision and request as means of changing food habits. In K. Lewin (Ed.), *Forces behind food habits and methods of change. Bull. Nat. Res. Council,* 1943, *108,* 35-65.

1333. Willerman, B. The relation of motivation and skill to active and passive participation in the group. *J. appl. Psychol.,* 1953, *37,* 387-390. *P.A.,* 29:715.

1334. Willerman, B., & Swanson, L. An ecological determinant of differential amounts of sociometric choices within college sororities. *Sociometry,* 1952, *15,* 326-329. *P.A.,* 27:7394.

1335. Williams, H. W., & Lawrence, J. F. Comparison of the Rorschach and MMPI by means of factor analysis. *J. consult. Psychol.,* 1954, *18,* 193-197. *P.A.,* 29:2484.

1336. Williams, R. M., Jr. *The reduction of intergroup tensions.* New York: Soc. Sci. Res. Coun. Bull., 1947, No. 57. *P.A.,* 22:688.

1337. Williams, Ruth M., & Mattson, Marion L. The effect of social groupings upon the language of pre-school children. *Child Develpm.,* 1942, *13,* 233-245. *P.A.,* 17:2539.

1338. Williams, S. B., & Leavitt, H. J. Group opinion as a predictor of military leadership. *J. consult. Psychol.,* 1947, *11,* 283-291. *P.A.,* 22:2347.

1339. Williamson, E. C. Allport's experiments in "social facilitation." *Psychol. Monogr.,* 1926, *35,* No. 163, 138-143.

1340. Wilner, D. M., Walkley, Rosabelle, P., & Cook, S. W. Residential proximity and intergroup relations in public housing projects. *J. soc. Issues,* 1952, *8* (1), 45-69.

1341. Wilson, L. Sociography of groups. In G. Gurvitch & W. E. Moore (Eds.), *Twentieth century sociology.* New York: Phil. Libr., 1945. Pp. 139-171.

1342. Wilson, R. C., High, W. S., Beem, Helen P., & Comrey, A. L. A factor-analytic study of supervisory and group behavior. *J. appl. Psychol.*, 1954, *38*, 89-92. *P.A.*, 29:3180.

1343. Wilson, R. C., High, W. S., & Comrey, A. L. An iterative analysis of supervisory and group dimensions. *J. appl. Psychol.*, 1955, *39*, 85-91. *P.A.*, 30:1756.

1344. Winch, R. F. The theory of complementary needs in mate-selection: final results on the test of the general hypothesis. *Amer. sociol. Rev.*, 1955, *20*, 552-554. *P.A.*, 31:937.

1345. Winch, R. F. Comment on "A test of the theory of complementary needs as applied to couples during courtship," by Bowerman and Day. *Amer. sociol. Rev.*, 1957, *22*, 336.

1346. Winch, R. F., Ktsanes, T., & Ktsanes, Virginia. The theory of complementary needs in mate selection: an analytic and descriptive study. *Amer. sociol. Rev.*, 1954, *19*, 241-249. *P.A.*, 30:2795.

1347. Winch, R. F., Ktsanes, T., & Ktsanes, Virginia. Empirical elaboration of the theory of complementary needs in mate selection. *J. abnorm. soc. Psychol.*, 1955, *51*, 508-513. *P.A.*, 31:2863.

1348. Winslow, C. N. A study of the extent of agreement between friends' opinions and their ability to estimate the opinions of each other. *J. soc. Psychol.*, 1937, *8*, 433-442.

1349. Wirth, L. Social interaction: The problem of the individual and the group. *Amer. J. Sociol.*, 1939, *44*, 965-979. *P.A.*, 13:4795.

1350. Wischmeier, R. R. Group-centered and leader-centered leaderships: an experimental study. *Speech Monogr.*, 1955, *22*, 43-48. *P.A.*, 30:811.

1351. Wispe, L. G. Evaluating section teaching methods in the introductory course. *J. educ. Res.*, 1951, *45*, 161-186. *P.A.*, 26:6521.

1352. Wispe, L. G. Teaching methods research. *Amer. Psychologist*, 1953, *8*, 147-149. *P.A.*, 28:1503.

1353. Wispe, L. G. A sociometric analysis of conflicting role-expectations. *Amer. J. Sociol.*, 1955, *61*, 134-137. *P.A.*, 31:806.

1354. Withall, J. The development of a technique for the measurement of social-emotional climate in classrooms. *J. exp. Educ.*, 1949, *17*, 347-361. *P.A.*, 24:1456.

1355. Withall, J. The development of the climate index. *J. educ. Res.*, 1951, *45*, 93-100. *P.A.*, 26:5084.

1356. Withall, J. An objective measurement of a teacher's classroom interaction. *J. educ. Psychol.*, 1956, *47*, 203-212.

1357. Wolff, K. H. *The sociology of Georg Simmel.* New York: Free Press, 1950.

1358. Wolman, B. Leadership and group dynamics. *J. soc. Psychol.*, 1956, *43*, 11-25. *P.A.*, 31:2731.

1359. Wright, M. E. The influence of frustration upon the social relations of young children. *Charact. & Pers.*, 1943, *12*, 111-122. P.A., 18:1952.

1360. Wrightstone, J. W. An instrument for measuring group discussion and planning. *J. educ. Res.*, 1934, *27*, 641-650. P.A., 8:4309.

1361. Wrightstone, J. W. Measuring the social climate of a classroom. *J. educ. Res.*, 1951, *44*, 341-351. P.A., 25:8287.

1362. Wurster, C. R., & Bass, B. M. Situational tests: IV. Validity of leaderless group discussions among strangers. *Educ. psychol. Measmt*, 1953, *13*, 122-132. P.A., 28:717.

1363. Wyatt, S., Frost, L., & Stock, F. G. L. *Incentives in repetitive work.* Med. Res. Council, Industr. Hlth. Res. Bd, Rep. No. 69. London: H. M. Stationery Office, 1934.

1364. Yablonsky, L. An operational theory of roles. *Sociometry*, 1953, *16*, 349-354. P.A., 29:718.

1365. Yuker, H. E. Group atmosphere and memory. *J. abnorm. soc. Psychol.*, 1955, *51*, 17-23. S.A., 2495.

1366. Zander, A. The WP club: an objective case study of a group. *Hum. Relat.*, 1948, *1*, 321-332. P.A., 23:1258.

1367. Zander, A. Systematic observation of small face-to-face groups. In Marie Jahoda, M. Deutsch, & S. W. Cook (Eds.), *Research methods in social relations: with especial reference to prejudice.* New York: Dryden, 1951. Pp. 515-538.

1368. Zander, A. Group membership and individual security. *Hum. Relat.*, 1958, *11*, 99-111.

1369. Zander, A., & Cohen, A. R. Attributed social power and group acceptance: a classroom experimental demonstration. *J. abnorm. soc. Psychol.*, 1955, *51*, 490-492. P.A., 31:2733; S.A., 3446.

1370. Zeleny, L. D. Characteristics of group leaders. *Sociol. soc. Res.*, 1939a, *24*, 140-149. P.A., 14:1518.

1371. Zeleny, L. D. Sociometry of morale. *Amer. sociol. Rev.*, 1939b, *4*, 799-808. P.A., 14:2026.

1372. Zeleny, L. D. Experimental appraisal of a group learning plan. *J. educ. Res.*, 1940a, *34*, 37-42. P.A., 14:6242.

1373. Zeleny, L. D. Measurement of social status. *Amer. J. Sociol.*, 1940b, *45*, 576-582.

1374. Zeleny, L. D. Measurement of sociation. *Amer. sociol. Rev.*, 1941, *6*, 173-188. P.A., 15:3085.

1375. Zeleny, L. D. Selection of compatible flying partners. *Amer. J. Sociol.*, 1947, *52*, 424-431. P.A., 21:2447.

1376. Zentner, H. Primary group affiliation and institutional group morale. *Sociol. soc. Res.*, 1955, *40*, 31-34. S.A., 2928.

1377. Ziller, R. C. Scales of judgment: a determinant of the accuracy of group decisions. *Hum. Relat.*, 1955, *8*, 153-164. S.A., 1987.

1378. Ziller, R. C. Four techniques of group decision making under uncertainty. *J. appl. Psychol.*, 1957a, *41*, 384-388.

1379. Ziller, R. C. Group size: a determinant of the quality and stability of group decisions. *Sociometry*, 1957b, *20*, 165-173.

1380. Ziller, R. C. Communication restraints, group flexibility, and group confidence. *J. appl. Psychol.*, 1958, *42*, 346-352.

1381. Ziller, R. C. Leader acceptance of responsibility for group action under conditions of uncertainty and risk. *J. Psychol.*, 1959, *47*, 57-66.

1382. Ziller, R. C., & Exline, R. V. Some consequences of age heterogeneity in decision-making groups. *Sociometry*, 1958, *21*, 198-211.

1383. Zimet, C. N., & Fine, H. J. Personality changes with a group therapeutic experience in a human relations seminar. *J. abnorm. soc.*

1384. Zimmer, H. Motivational factors in dyadic interaction. *J. Pers.*, 1956, *24*, 251-261.

      Psychol., 1955, *51*, 68-73. P.A., 30:4715.

1385. Znaniecki, F. Social groups as products of participating individuals. *Amer. J. Sociol.*, 1939, *44*, 799-812. P.A., 13:4798.

SUBJECT INDEX

AUTHOR INDEX

Babchuk, N., 377
Bachelis, W., 400
Back, K. W., 36, 130, 155, 217, 294, 397
Baier D. E., 145
Baker, Bela, 88, 99
Baldwin, A., 198
Bales, R. F., vii, 2, 3, 10, 13, 14, 18, 46, 59, 64, 68, 71, 72, 73, 75, 76, 78, 93, 107, 111, 115, 116, 124, 129, 142, 169, 170, 175, 177, 180, 231, 240, 243, 249, 251, 253, 269, 273, 274, 292, 320, 341, 342, 375, 378, 397, 398, 399, 400, 406
Bamforth, K. W., 227
Banks, E. P., 397
Barber, Kathleen, 216
Barker, R. G., 131, 397, 407
Barnard, C. I., 341
Barnlund, D. C., 309, 330
Baron, S. H., 26
Barr, J. A., 128
Barron, F., 33
Barton, W. A., Jr., 340, 354
Bass, B. M., 33, 107, 177, 179, 228, 252, 273, 292, 299, 300, 309, 328, 399
Bassett, R. E., 130
Bates, A. P., 24, 101, 141, 214
Bates, F. L., 101, 104
Bavelas, A., 72, 274, 279, 288, 308, 309, 328, 412
Beasley W., 406
Beaver, Alma P., 207, 407
Bechterev, W., 340, 362, 371
Becker, H., 240, 241, 242
Beegle, J. A., 3, 140, 159
Beem, Helen P., 390
Beer, M., 292
Behner, Alice, 352
Bell, G. B., 86, 89, 308
Beloff, Halla, 33
Belyaeff, B. V., 292, 340
Bender, I. E., 82
Benjamin, L., 213
Benne, K. D., 3, 115
Bennett, Edith B., 35, 37, 51
Bennett, Lillian F., 83, 87, 411
Bennis, W. G., 75
Bensen, S. B., 39
Berelson, B., 400
Berenda, Ruth W., 31, 40
Berg, J., 285
Berkowitz, L., 33, 36, 116, 269, 276, 289, 300, 318, 376, 378, 379, 387, 388
Berkowitz, M., 32

Berkun, M., 140
Bernauer, Margaret, 406
Bernhardt, K. S., 207
Bernstein, A., 77
Beum, C. O., Jr., 409
Bevan, W., 361
Biber, Barbara, 407
Bieri, J., 85, 86
Biggs, J. B., 46
Bion, W. R., 65, 115, 171, 289, 295
Bishop, Barbara M., 180
Bjerstedt, A., 127, 129, 139, 408, 409
Black, Irma S., 407
Blaisdell, F. J., 85, 95
Blake, R. R., 26, 31, 33, 35, 39, 51, 64, 71, 84, 139, 146, 252, 269, 308, 410
Blau, P. M., 105, 145, 215, 255, 308
Bloch, Barbara L., 34
Block, J., 33, 37, 411
Block, Jeanne, 33
Blumer, H., 79
Bock, R. D., 33, 179
Bogardus, E. S., 3
Bonner, H., 3
Bonney, M. E., 140, 158, 214, 222, 223
Borg, W. R., 300, 308
Borgatta E. F., vii, 3, 18, 72, 127, 128, 129, 142, 169, 177, 180, 205, 240, 241, 269, 292, 300, 390, 396, 400, 406, 407, 409, 410
Borgatta, Marie L., 3
Bos, Maria C., 216, 360
Bossard, J. H. S., 228, 410
Bott, Elizabeth, 116
Bott, Helen McM., 407
Bourricaud, F., 293
Bovard, E. W., Jr., 35, 36, 72, 279, 317, 332, 333
Bowerman, C. E., 141, 164
Boyd, R. W., 399
Bradford, L. P., 46
Brandenburg, E., 389, 406
Breer, P. E., 181
Breese, F., 198
Brehm, J. W., 26, 36
Brenner, M., 355
Briskin, G. J., 46
Brodbeck, May, 39
Bronfenbrenner, U., 131, 150, 301
Brown, J. C., 210
Brown, M. L., 308
Brown, Paula, 3
Brown, R., 3
Brueckel, Joyce E., 227

DATE DUE

GAYLORD			PRINTED IN U.S.A.